Cultural GEOGRAPHY

FOURTH EDITION

Dennis Bollinger

bju press®

Greenville, South Carolina

NOTE: The fact that materials produced by other publishers may be referred to in this volume does not constitute an endorsement of the content or theological position of materials produced by such publishers. Any references and ancillary materials are listed as an aid to the student or the teacher and in an attempt to maintain the accepted academic standards of the publishing industry.

Cultural Geography
Fourth Edition

Dennis Bollinger, PhD

Contributing Authors
Brian Collins, PhD
Lauren Kowalk
Nathan Lentfer, MA
Dennis Peterson, MS
Rachel Santopietro

Editor
Manda Kalagayan, MEd

Project Manager
Dan Berger

Cover Design
Drew Fields

Book Design
Drew Fields
Dan Van Leeuwen

Page Layout
Jessica Johnson

Page Design
Dan Van Leeuwen

Bible Integration
Brian Collins, PhD
Bryan Smith, PhD

Photo Permissions
Ashley Hobbs
Carrie Walker

Text Permissions
Sylvia Gass

Illustration
Preston Gravely, Jr.
Kathy Pflug
Dave Schuppert

Consultant
Elijah Wilcott, MDiv

Photograph credits are listed on pages 632–34.

Front cover: Paternoster Square seen from St. Paul's Cathedral (51.514525° N, 0.099261° W)

Back cover: St. Angelo Bridge in Rome (41.901577° N, 12.466482° W)

© 2015 BJU Press
Greenville, South Carolina 29609

First Edition © 1987
Second Edition © 1998
Third Edition © 2008

Printed in the United States of America
All rights reserved

ISBN 978-1-60682-499-3

15   14   13   12   11   10   9   8   7   6   5   4   3   2

CONTENTS

CONTENTS

Unit 7: THE MIDDLE EAST

Unit 8: AFRICA

Unit 9: THE AUSTRALIAN AND PACIFIC REALMS

PRONUNCIATION GUIDE

Vowels			
symbol	example	symbol	example
a	cat = KAT	aw	all = AWL
a-e	cape = KAPE	o	potion = PO shun
ay	paint = PAYNT	oa	don't = DOANT
e	jet = JET	o-e	groan = GRONE
eh	spend = SPEHND	oh	own = OHN
ee	fiend = FEEND	u	some = SUM
i	swim = SWIM	uh	abet = uh BET
ih	pity = PIH tee	oo	crew = CROO
eye	icy = EYE see	*oo*	push = P*OO*SH
i-e	might = MITE	ou	loud = LOUD
ah	cot = KAHT	oy	toil = TOYL
ar	car = KAR		

Consonants			
symbol	example	symbol	example
k	cat = KAT	th	thin = THIN
g	get = GET	*th*	then = *TH*EN
j	gentle = JEN tul	zh	fusion = FYOO zhun

The pronunciation key used in this text is designed to give the reader a self-evident, acceptable pronunciation for a word as he reads it from the page. For more accurate pronunciations, the reader should consult a good dictionary.

Stress: Syllables with primary stress appear in LARGE CAPITAL letters. Syllables with secondary stress and one-syllable words appear in SMALL CAPITAL letters. Unstressed syllables appear in lowercase letters. Where two or more words appear together, hyphens separate the syllables within each word. For example, the pronunciation of Omar Khayyam appears as (OH-mar kie-YAHM).

READY REFERENCE TO MAPS

Physical and Political Maps

Miscellaneous Maps

FEATURES OF THE BOOK

Amazing color photographs throughout help the students "see" the sites and people around the world.

Fast Facts present a wealth of information about each country/region discussed in the chapter.

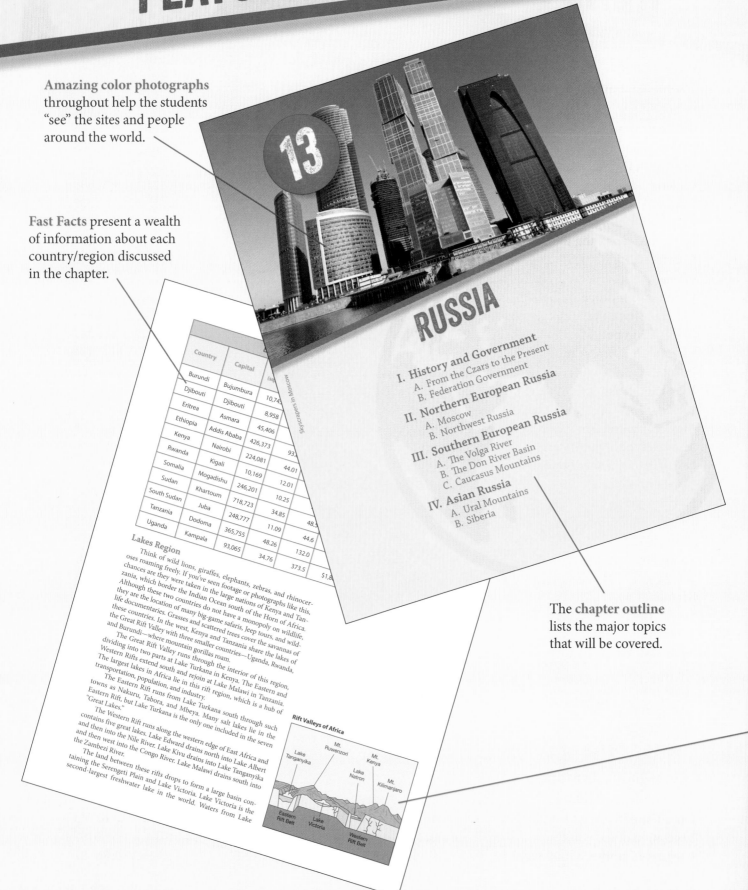

Skyscrapers in Moscow

13

RUSSIA

I. History and Government
  A. From the Czars to the Present
  B. Federation Government

II. Northern European Russia
  A. Moscow
  B. Northwest Russia

III. Southern European Russia
  A. The Volga River
  B. The Don River Basin
  C. Caucasus Mountains

IV. Asian Russia
  A. Ural Mountains
  B. Siberia

The **chapter outline** lists the major topics that will be covered.

Country	Capital	(sq
Burundi	Bujumbura	10,745
Djibouti	Djibouti	8,958
Eritrea	Asmara	45,406
Ethiopia	Addis Ababa	426,373
Kenya	Nairobi	224,081
Rwanda	Kigali	10,169
Somalia	Mogadishu	246,201
Sudan	Khartoum	718,723
South Sudan	Juba	248,777
Tanzania	Dodoma	365,755
Uganda	Kampala	93,065

Lakes Region

Think of wild lions, giraffes, elephants, zebras, and rhinoceroses roaming freely. If you've seen footage or photographs like this, chances are they were taken in the large nations of Kenya and Tanzania, which border the Indian Ocean south of the Horn of Africa. Although these two countries do not have a monopoly on wildlife, they are the location of many big-game safaris, Jeep tours, and wildlife documentaries. Grasses and scattered trees cover the savannas of these countries. In the west, Kenya and Tanzania share the lakes of the Great Rift Valley with three smaller countries—Uganda, Rwanda, and Burundi—where mountain gorillas roam.

The Great Rift Valley runs through the interior of this region, dividing into two parts at Lake Turkana in Kenya. The Eastern and Western Rifts extend south and rejoin at Lake Malawi in Tanzania.

The largest lakes in Africa lie in this rift region, which is a hub of transportation, population, and industry.

The Eastern Rift runs from Lake Turkana south through such towns as Nakuru, Tabora, and Mbeya. Many salt lakes lie in the Eastern Rift, but Lake Turkana is the only one included in the seven "Great Lakes."

The Western Rift runs along the western edge of East Africa and contains five great lakes. Lake Edward drains north into Lake Albert and then into the Nile River. Lake Kivu drains into Lake Tanganyika and then west into the Congo River. Lake Malawi drains south into the Zambezi River.

The land between these rifts drops to form a large basin containing the Serengeti Plain and Lake Victoria. Lake Victoria is the second-largest freshwater lake in the world. Waters from Lake

Rift Valleys of Africa

Terms in bold type draw attention to important facts, ideas, people, or definitions.

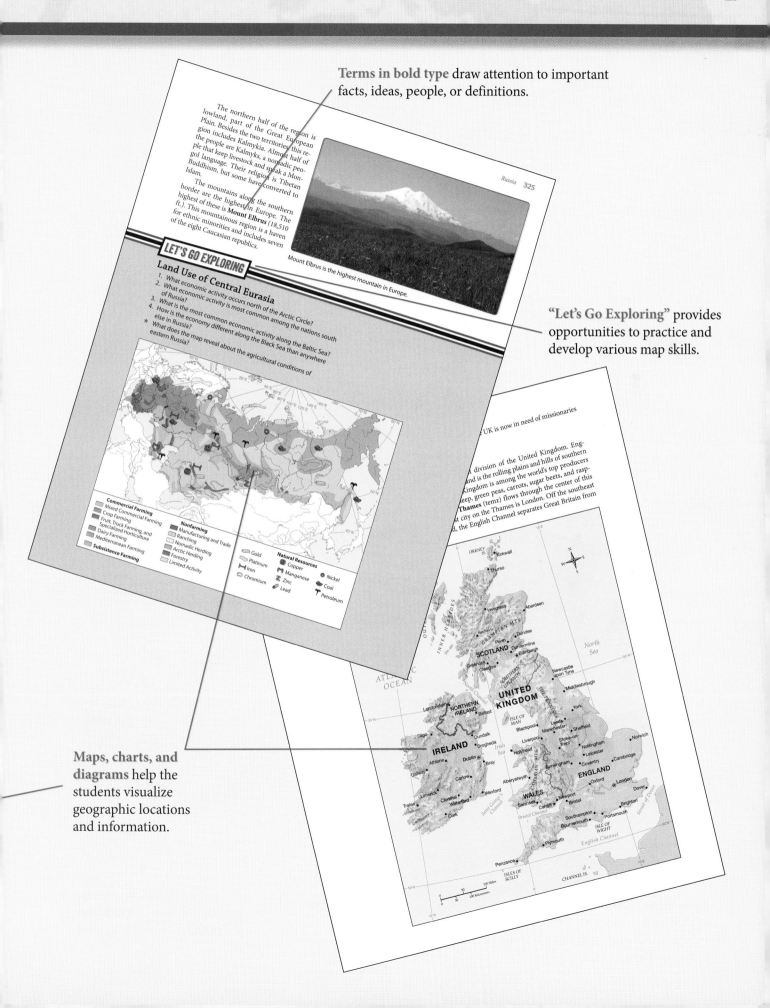

The northern half of the region is lowland, part of the Great European Plain. Besides the two territories this region includes Kalmykia. Almost half of the people are Kalmyks, a nomadic people that keep livestock and speak a Mongol language. Their religion is Tibetan Buddhism, but some have converted to Islam.

The mountains along the southern border are the highest in Europe. The highest of these is **Mount Elbrus** (18,510 ft.). This mountainous region is a haven for ethnic minorities and includes seven of the eight Caucasian republics.

Russia 325

Mount Elbrus is the highest mountain in Europe.

LET'S GO EXPLORING

Land Use of Central Eurasia

1. What economic activity occurs north of the Arctic Circle?
2. What economic activity is most common among the nations south of Russia?
3. What is the most common economic activity along the Baltic Sea?
4. How is the economy different along the Black Sea than anywhere else in Russia?
★ What does the map reveal about the agricultural conditions of eastern Russia?

Commercial Farming
Mixed Commercial Farming
Crop Farming
Fruit, Truck Farming, and Specialized Horticulture
Dairy Farming
Mediterranean Farming
Subsistence Farming

Nonfarming
Manufacturing and Trade
Ranching
Nomadic Herding
Arctic Herding
Forestry
Limited Activity

Gold
Platinum
Iron
Chromium

Natural Resources
Copper
Manganese
Zinc
Lead
Nickel
Coal
Petroleum

"Let's Go Exploring" provides opportunities to practice and develop various map skills.

UK is now in need of missionaries

...t division of the United Kingdom. England is the rolling plains and hills of southern ...ingdom is among the world's top producers ...eep, green peas, carrots, sugar beets, and rasp-... **Thames** (temz) flows through the center of this ...t city on the Thames is London. Off the southeast ...d, the English Channel separates Great Britain from

Maps, charts, and diagrams help the students visualize geographic locations and information.

FEATURES OF THE BOOK

General feature boxes provide a deeper look at a person, event, or concept mentioned in the text.

World's Leading Coffee-Producing Countries (2010)

1. Brazil
2. Vietnam
3. Colombia
4. Indonesia
5. India
6. Ethiopia
7. Honduras
8. Peru
9. Guatemala
10. Mexico

the nation. As in other Latin American cities, however, rural workers live in large slums, or *turgurios* (toor GOO ree ohs).

The four other Colombian cities with populations of more than a million lie along the two river valleys between Colombia's three Andes ranges. Cartagena (cahr tah HAY nah) are near the Caribbean coast on the deepest river, the Magdalena, "the lifeline of Colombia." Oceangoing ships can travel up the river far into the interior. Major oil wells operate in the Magdalena near Panama, and Cali (CAH lee) is in the west central area near the Pacific coast. Both cities are on the Cauca (COW cah) River. Bogotá, Medellín, and Cali form Colombia's "industrial triangle."

The Andes provide Colombia with several important products. Colombia is one of the world's largest coffee-producing countries, harvesting most of the beans used to make Arabica coffee. Colombia is also rich in natural resources. It has the largest coal reserves in Latin America and the only platinum mines in South America. It is a leading producer of gold and also mines about half of

Who Grows the Best Coffee Bean?

Coffee has become the world's most popular hot beverage, and the United States leads the world in coffee consumption. The ten-minute coffee break is a common ritual. But not all coffees are the same. Even the closest of friends argue over which coffee bean is best.

According to legend, a goat herder in Ethiopia discovered coffee in the fourteenth century when his goats stayed awake all night after munching on the beans. Arab traders were the first to popularize brewed coffee. From the Arabian Peninsula, coffee plants have been transported around the world. The world's leading coffee-producing countries are located in or very near the tropics.

Two species of coffee plants are grown on plantations. The Arabs cultivated *Coffea arabica*, exporting beans from the famous coffee port of Mocha.

Arabica is now grown throughout Latin America and much of Asia. The other species is *Coffea robusta*. This hardy plant thrives in the hot, rainy tropics of Africa. A robusta coffee plant produces about four pounds of beans, twice th...

So why doe...
robusta, if it i...
tive? The key...
or smell. Afri...
a cereal-like...
drinkers pre...
two popula...
off a fruity a...
of flowers;...
aroma with...

Although...
coffee pro...
sidered in...
Brazil's m...
tor. The A...

much better for flavor than the soil of Brazil. Perhaps surprisingly, Vietnam is the second-leading coffee producer, and Colombia is third. Excellent coffees are also grown on the Indonesian island of Java, and sometimes coffee is even called java.

...for coffee's popu-

The Monongahela...
the Allegheny River...
developed on the Golden Triangle (Ground) Pittsburgh two rivers meet, forming the Ohio River.

Earth Matters: Fracking

Hydrologic fracturing, or fracking, has recently become a popular way of accessing natural gas that was previously too expensive to extract. The spread of hydrologic fracturing in states like Pennsylvania has created thousands of jobs and has resulted in lower natural gas prices. But people in some communities are concerned that fracking will pollute their water and endanger their communities.

A machine used for fracking in Wyoming

"Earth Matters" feature boxes in each unit, beginning in Unit III, demonstrate the challenges of carrying out the Dominion Mandate recorded in Genesis 1:28.

---

exports. The nomadic people who live in this region are called Moors. They account for over two-thirds of all the people in Mauritania. The Moors continue to engage in the prosperous slave trade, even though the government outlawed slavery in 1981 and made it a crime in 2007. Estimates of the percentages of slaves vary from 10 to 20 percent of the Mauritanian population.

The southern border, which is in the Sahel, is more hospitable. Black tribes farm the country's only fertile plain along the Sénégal River. However, recent drought, overgrazing, and deforestation have contributed to desertification. Many rural farmers and nomads have migrated to the capital, Nouakchott, located on the coast, living in makeshift camps and relying on foreign aid for survival.

Mauritania was not always so poor. The **Ghana Empire**, which may have risen to power as early as the fourth century, was centered in Kumbi Saleh, a city at the southeast corner of Mauritania. The empire controlled all the western trade routes across the Sahel into the thirteenth century, keeping all the gold nuggets and allowing the gold dust to continue north. The ancient capital now lies in ruins.

Mauritania's recent political history has been one of short-lived democracies followed by military coups. The Arab Spring of 2011 (when Arabs in many countries protested political and economic inequality) spread into this country, and future political stability remains uncertain.

WORLD RELIGIONS

Folk Islam

Religion as presented in a textbook and religion as practiced by people are often two different things. This is especially true of Islam in Africa. Officially, Islam centers on submission to the one god who controls all things. The Qur'an and the Hadith are the basis for Muslim teaching. Rites of prayer, cleansing, fasting, almsgiving, and pilgrimage are at the heart of the religion. Folk Islam maintains all of the teachings of official Islam, but it has other concerns, such as how to deal with sickness or famine or other negative events. Folk Islam is more concerned with spirits and ancestors. Often, folk Islam draws on the traditional religious practices of a region.

The Jinn play a large role in folk Islam. Jinn are believed to be spirits that stand between men and angels. They can be good or bad, but most are viewed as bad. For instance, in Egypt many Muslims believe there is a Jinn who will cause miscarriages. To be freed from a Jinn who has possessed a person or who is interfering with a person, a powerful person who can provide charms or curses is needed.

In Morocco one might go to the "old woman" who can make a magical drink to ward off or cure sickness. In West Africa one might go to a medicine man for a charm or amulet that can ward off evil powers. Often these amulets are made with verses from the Qur'an to give them power. Or a Muslim might go to a saint. In Asia, saints are often living and can intercede or bless a person. In Africa, the saints are typically dead. A pilgrimage is often made to the shrines of the saints. The saints and their shrines are believed to possess great power. Many Muslims believe they can heal people, make the future known, or provide protection.

Place and time are also important to Muslims. Even with a talisman, a Muslim might avoid going to a place where he thinks a Jinn might be present. Or he will take special precautions before going. In Egypt the Jinn are thought to inhabit toilets, so a person will call out for Allah's protection. In Morocco, the Jinn are thought to inhabit wells or rivers. On the other hand, the shrine of a saint is believed

to be an especially good place. Certain times can be good or bad. In some places the Jinn are thought to interfere with people more on Tuesday, Wednesday, and Saturday nights. Thursdays and Fridays are good days, though on Friday there is a bad hour in which misfortune may strike. The second month in the Muslim calendar is considered a bad month, but Ramadan is the best month since the Jinn are said to be bound that month.

African Muslims will often practice divination to help them make right decisions. For instance, they may open a Qur'an at random to see if the words on the page give them some direction. Or they might go to a fortune-teller to learn something of their future.

Many Muslims practice both official Islam and folk Islam without seeing any inconsistency. However, some Muslims see folk Islam as a corruption. They think shrines to saints promote idolatry. They reject the idea that saints can intercede with their god for people.

"World Religions" feature boxes provide a thorough examination of a number of world religions.

Cultural margin boxes offer short verbal snapshots that emphasize unusual cultural information about the region(s) covered in the chapter.

The **Chapter Review** asks students about terms, people, places, and concepts to help them prepare for the test and develop critical thinking skills.

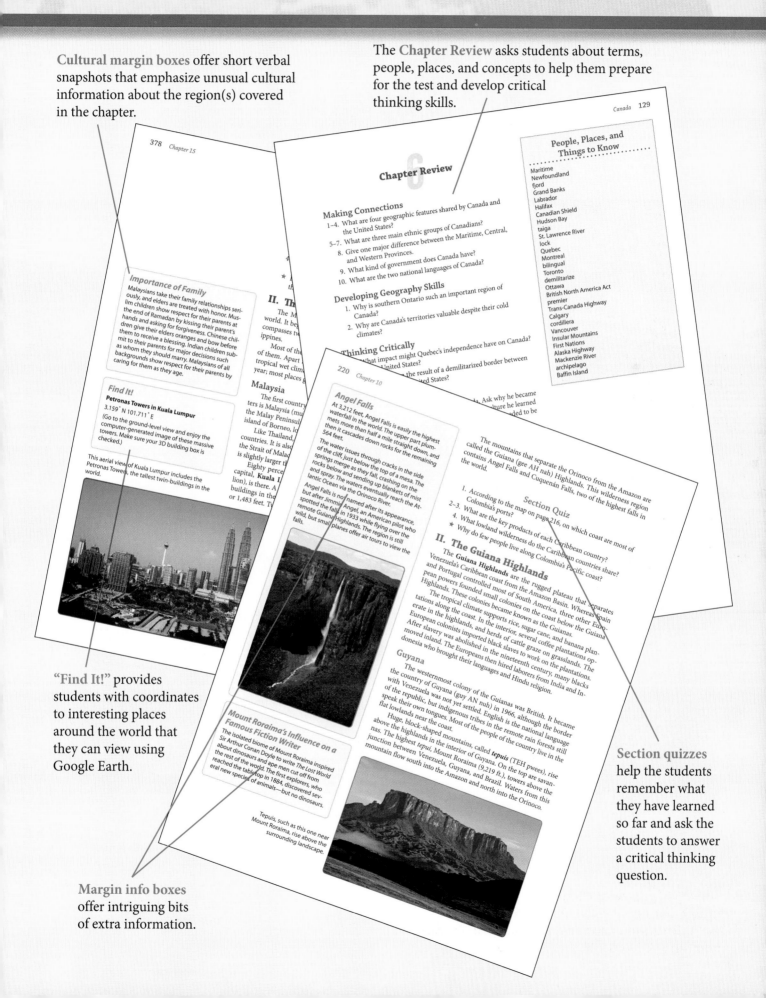

378   Chapter 15

Importance of Family

Malaysians take their family relationships seriously, and elders are treated with honor. Muslim children show respect for their parents at the end of Ramadan by kissing their parents' hands and asking for forgiveness. Chinese children give their elders oranges and bow before them to receive a blessing. Indian children submit to their parents for major decisions such as whom they should marry. Malaysians of all backgrounds show respect for their parents by caring for them as they age.

Find It!

Petronas Towers in Kuala Lumpur

3.159˚ N 101.711˚ E

(Go to the ground-level view and enjoy the computer-generated image of these massive towers. Make sure your 3D building box is checked.)

This aerial view of Kuala Lumpur includes the Petronas Towers, the tallest twin-buildings in the world.

"Find It!" provides students with coordinates to interesting places around the world that they can view using Google Earth.

Canada   129

People, Places, and Things to Know

Maritime
Newfoundland
fjord
Grand Banks
Labrador
Halifax
Canadian Shield
Hudson Bay
taiga
St. Lawrence River
lock
Quebec
Montreal
bilingual
Toronto
demilitarize
Ottawa
British North America Act
premier
Trans-Canada Highway
Calgary
cordillera
Vancouver
Insular Mountains
First Nations
Alaska Highway
Mackenzie River
archipelago
Baffin Island

Chapter Review

Making Connections

1–4. What are four geographic features shared by Canada and the United States?

5–7. What are three main ethnic groups of Canadians?

8. Give one major difference between the Maritime, Central, and Western Provinces.

9. What kind of government does Canada have?

10. What are the two national languages of Canada?

Developing Geography Skills

1. Why is southern Ontario such an important region of Canada?

2. Why are Canada's territories valuable despite their cold climates?

Thinking Critically

1. What impact might Quebec's independence have on Canada?
   United States?

2. ... the result of a demilitarized border between ... ted States?

II. Th...

The M... world. It be... compasses tw... ippines.

Most of the... of them. Apart... tropical wet clim... year; most places ...

Malaysia

The first country... ters is Malaysia (mu... the Malay Peninsul... island of Borneo, lo...

Like Thailand,... countries. It is also... the Strait of Malac... is slightly larger th...

Eighty perce... capital, **Kuala L...** lion), is there. A... buildings in the... or 1,483 feet. Tv...

220   Chapter 10

Angel Falls

At 3,212 feet, Angel Falls is easily the highest waterfall in the world. The upper part plummets more than half a mile straight down, and then it cascades down rocks for the remaining 564 feet.

The water issues through cracks in the side of the cliff, just below the top of a mesa. The springs merge as they fall, crashing on the rocks below and sending up blankets of mist and spray. The waters eventually reach the Atlantic Ocean via the Orinoco River. Angel Falls is not named after its appearance, but after Jimmie Angel, an American pilot who spotted the falls in 1933 while flying over the remote Guiana Highlands. The region is still wild, but small planes offer air tours to view the falls.

Mount Roraima's Influence on a Famous Fiction Writer

The isolated biome of Mount Roraima inspired Sir Arthur Conan Doyle to write *The Lost World* about dinosaurs and ape men cut off from the rest of the world. The first explorers, who reached the tabletop in 1884, discovered several new species of animals—but no dinosaurs.

Tepuis, such as this one near Mount Roraima, rise above the surrounding landscape.

...a. Ask why he became ...ture he learned ...ded to be

The mountains that separate the Orinoco from the Amazon are called the Guiana (gee AH nah) Highlands. This wilderness region contains Angel Falls and Cuquenán Falls, two of the highest falls in the world.

Section Quiz

1. According to the map on page 216, on which coast are most of Colombia's ports?

2–3. What are the key products of each Caribbean country?

4. What lowland wilderness do the Caribbean countries share?

★ Why do few people live along Colombia's Pacific coast?

II. The Guiana Highlands

The **Guiana Highlands** are the rugged plateau that separates Venezuela's Caribbean coast from the Amazon Basin. Whereas Spain and Portugal controlled most of South America, three other European powers founded small colonies on the coast below the Guiana Highlands. These colonies became known as the Guianas.

The tropical climate supports rice, sugar cane, and banana plantations along the coast. In the interior, several coffee plantations operate in the highlands, and herds of cattle graze on grasslands. The European colonists imported black slaves to work on the plantations. After slavery was abolished in the nineteenth century, many blacks moved inland. The Europeans then hired laborers from India and Indonesia who brought their languages and Hindu religion.

Guyana

The westernmost colony of the Guianas was British. It became the country of Guyana (guy AN nuh) in 1966, although the border with Venezuela was not yet settled. English is the national language of the republic, but indigenous tribes in the remote rain forests still speak their own tongues. Most of the people of the country live in the flat lowlands near the coast.

Huge, block-shaped mountains, called **tepuis** (TEH pwees) rise above the highlands in the interior of Guyana. On the top are savannas. The highest *tepui*, Mount Roraima (9,219 ft.), towers above the junction between Venezuela, Guyana, and Brazil. Waters from this mountain flow south into the Amazon and north into the Orinoco.

Section quizzes help the students remember what they have learned so far and ask the students to answer a critical thinking question.

Margin info boxes offer intriguing bits of extra information.

Unit One
THE WORLD AS GOD MADE IT

"In the beginning, God created the heaven and the earth" (Gen. 1:1). God changed the original geography of the earth by the Flood (Gen. 6) and gave us the current surface and climates that we will study in this book. The Tower of Babel (Gen. 9) resulted in the beginning of cultures we will find as we visit each part of the earth.

Ruins of a Buddhist temple in Thailand

FOUNDATIONS

I. Geography and Culture in the Bible
Geography and Culture in Genesis 1-2

*T*he Bible begins with a playwright, an actor, and a stage. God writes the script. He creates a man—in His own image—to be the lead actor. And He places that actor on a stage—the earth He has created. Geography is, then, the stage on which the human drama is acted out.

The earth, however, is not just a painted backdrop you stop noticing once the actors come out. God's very first words to humanity include a commission about their role on the earth: "Be fruitful, and multiply, and replenish the earth, and subdue it: and have dominion over the fish of the sea, and over the fowl of the air, and over every living thing that moveth upon the earth" (Gen. 1:28). These words of God are often called the **Creation Mandate**. When the actors in God's drama obey or live out that mandate, they start changing the very stage they were placed on. They do this literally: they form the earth into clay bricks that bake in the sun. They use these bricks to build houses and cities. They cut down reeds and form them so that beautiful music comes out. Or they dig metals such as copper, tin, and iron from the earth. And we—like they—do this largely so we can turn around and mold and shape the earth even more easily; we make plows and backhoes and cranes and all sorts of other tools.

But we do not do this work alone. To accomplish the tasks of mining, crafting, farming, and city-building—to obey the Creation Mandate—humans must work together. And whenever humans get together to create and build, they generally create something else almost by accident: culture.

A **culture** is the system of customs and traditions and habits that a group of people uses to make something of their world. Culture includes the knowledge of how to survive in the world. It includes the technological knowledge necessary for this survival. It also includes social structures that enable people to live and work together in harmony. Finally, because humans were created as thinking beings designed to worship God, culture includes religion and philosophy.

From the very beginning geography and culture have played key roles in God's purposes for mankind. The stage and the groups of actors on it are always interacting.

Notice, for example, that the author of Genesis is very specific about the location of the garden in which God places Adam. After creating the man, the Lord God plants a garden in the eastern part of a region with the name of Eden. A single river flows from the region of Eden into the garden. Within the garden the river divides into four rivers: the Pishon, Gihon, Tigris, and Euphrates. The author also mentions a few of the lands that the rivers flow into and some of the natural resources there: gold, precious stones, and resins. It is as though a brief geography lesson appears in the middle of Genesis 2.

But why the geography lesson? It's included for an important reason. This passage links the Creation Mandate of chapter 1 to the more specific task given to Adam in Genesis 2: keeping and tending the garden. Think about what it means to tend a garden. As one writer pointed out, "The gardener makes nothing, but rather gathers what God has made and shapes it into new and pleasing forms.

Garden of the Pieskowa State Castle in Poland

Thorns, a consequence of the Fall

The well-designed garden shows nature more clearly and beautifully than nature can show itself." A garden is, simply put, a plot of earth over which someone has exercised dominion. But God told Adam not only to take care of the Garden of Eden but also to "fill the earth." Human dominion is supposed to move outward until that filling is done. The geography lesson about the rivers around Eden reveals that the building blocks of society are already close at hand. The four rivers are highways into the world. They lead to other lands where important natural resources can be found. They facilitate the spread of the cultures and civilizations that God intends to populate the world stage.

The Fall, Geography, and Culture

Genesis 1 and 2 begin with great prospects for mankind, but history takes a disastrous turn in chapter 3. The Fall of mankind touches every aspect of God's good creation. Genesis 4 records some of mankind's first cultural achievements: city-building, animal husbandry, and the fabrication of musical instruments and tools of bronze and iron. But this account also begins with Cain's exile for murder, continues with the record of the first polygamous marriage, and concludes with violent poetry spoken by Lamech. Humans quickly corrupted their God-given capacities for dominion.

Genesis 4 does not teach that every cultural advance is bad. Revelation ends with a vision of a coming heavenly city. The book of Psalms is a book of inspired poetry, and it notes some of the instruments that originally accompanied the singing of psalms. It is not an accident that the Bible begins with a garden (Eden) and ends with a city (the New Jerusalem). Mankind is supposed to make progress in filling the earth and subduing it. But from the moment the Fall occurred, that good cultural progress has been mixed up with sinful perversions.

This is true in part because the very building blocks of our cultural work are affected by sin. It is worth pausing a moment to remember what God did to the ground itself when His creatures rebelled against Him: He cursed it. The ground would no longer produce food quite so easily. The apostle Paul put it this way: the creation is *in bondage to corruption*. It is, he said, groaning and longing to be set free (Rom. 8:20–22).

God also exiled Adam and Eve from the garden to the wider world. Exile remains a punishment for sin throughout much of the Old Testament. Cain was exiled for his sin (Gen. 4:14), and when people refused to fill the earth after the Flood but instead gathered to build the tower of Babel, God confused their language to scatter them across the earth. Sin often affects people and cultures geographically. The Flood demonstrates this more than any other event in the Bible. In

Artist's conception of Noah's ark during the early stages of the Flood

the Flood, God judged the world by washing it clean and dramatically changing its surface. This kind of physical judgment could have been a repeated event in the earth's history. Because the human heart is wicked from its youth, God could have sent one flood after another in order to judge succeeding generations of sinful people. However, God graciously made a covenant with Noah, his descendants, and all creatures on earth that He would never again send a worldwide flood. This ensures that the earth will remain a habitable stage on which God can work out His plan of redemption.

Abraham, Israel, and Land

The first big step God takes toward fixing His broken world includes three promises to a man named Abraham—and one of them is about geography. Along with a huge number of descendants and a promise to bless the whole earth through him, Abraham gets a special promise that his descendants will inherit a particularly nice portion of the earth. They would be a nation. And as a nation they would have their own unique land: Canaan (today known as Israel).

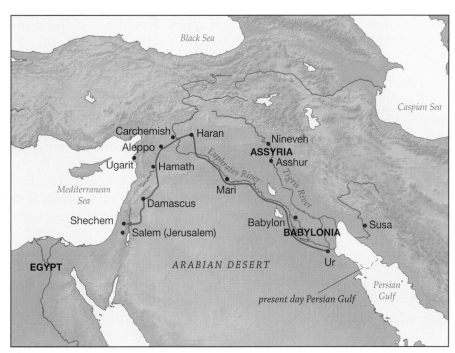

Abraham's journey to Canaan

And do not forget culture: the laws and customs given to Israel were supposed to create a unique system of life that would attract other nations to the Lord. God's chosen people, Abraham's descendants, were not supposed to be different from the other nations in literally everything. But parts of their culture were supposed to make them stand out as a "holy nation." The clothes they wore, the way they cut their hair and their beards, the food they ate or did not eat—all these practices set them apart, culturally speaking. If the people of Israel lived out God's law, the other nations would marvel at a society that worked as God intended it to. The peoples of the nations would then be drawn to seek the true God (Deut. 4:5–8).

But God's people had to live according to God's law or they would be exiled from the land. Ominously, after allotting the Promised Land among the tribes, Joshua warned the people that keeping the law was not in their power (Josh. 24:19). And soon he was proved right. The book of Judges reveals that far from becoming a redemptive, culturally distinct people, Israel became increasingly like the Canaanites who remained in the land. Eventually, as recorded in the opening chapters of 1 Samuel, the people asked for a king so that they could be "like all the nations" (8:20). But their determination to be like other nations had geographic consequences. Foreign nations repeatedly invaded the land of Israel and subjugated the Israelites. Finally, the Israelites were exiled from the land for their sins.

The New Testament, Geography, and Culture

It might seem as if the themes of land and culture become less important in the New Testament than in the Old Testament. God's people are no longer confined to a particular land. And early on, the church recognizes that God does not require Gentile people to adopt Jewish cultural practices. So Christianity is geographically and culturally much more diverse than Old Testament Israel.

But it is a mistake to think that geography and culture have become any less significant. The book of Acts is structured by geography. The outline is provided in Jesus' last words to the apostles: "Ye shall be witnesses unto me both in Jerusalem, and in all Judea, and in Samaria, and unto the uttermost part of the earth" (1:8). The narrative of the early church in Acts begins in Jerusalem and ends with the gospel spreading throughout the known world. Acts is structured this way to demonstrate the fulfillment of the **Great Commission**. This is the command that Christ gave to all of His followers to evangelize and disciple all the people groups of the earth (Matt. 28:18–20). The nations no longer have to come watch Israel to learn about the one true God. Now God's people are to take the gospel to the nations. And no longer are God's people restricted to a particular ethnic group; now all the nations are invited to become the people of God. Geography remains important in the New Testament because world missions is important.

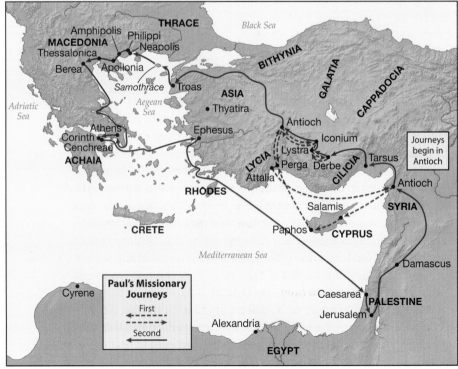

Paul's first two missionary journeys as recorded in the book of Acts

Paul's third missionary journey as recorded in the book of Acts

Culture also remains important in the New Testament. Christians are not under the Mosaic code, which regulated the details of diet and dress. But Christians remain a distinctive people in the world (1 Pet. 2:9). God identifies Christians as sojourners in the present evil age (1 Pet. 1:1, 17; Gal. 1:4; 1 Cor. 7:29–31). A sojourner is not a monk who has withdrawn from society into a cloister. Nor is a sojourner a pilgrim in the sense of someone who wanders through a land. A sojourner is someone who makes his home in a foreign place but who remains, to some degree, a foreigner there.

Christians are to be both at home and at odds with their surrounding cultures. We can be at home in our cultures because we do conform to those cultures in many ways. A Christian banker in New York City wears a suit and tie just like his non-Christian counterparts. And a Christian coffee grower in Colombia uses the same cultivation methods as non-Christian coffee growers. There's no special form of Christian architecture for suburban houses, nor do Christians drive oddly shaped cars. And yet a Christian in this fallen world will often be at odds with his culture. A Christian banker will not build professional relationships by taking clients to popular entertainments that are characterized by sensuality, violence, or oppression. A Christian farmer in a developing country will not participate in a culture of corruption to move his product to market. In some cultures, Christians may need to dress somewhat differently from the norm. Certain vocations may not be open to Christians in certain cultures. The Christian way of life will sometimes seem laughable to others within the culture (1 Pet. 4:4).

The Christian's sojourning, being both at home in and distinct from the surrounding world, remains a significant part of his mission. By sojourning within the cultures of the world, Christians live attractively different lifestyles that will draw people to Christ (1 Pet. 2:12).

Culture and geography will never go away, not even in eternity. The land God promised to Abraham four thousand years ago will one day belong to a redeemed Israel. In fact, the whole earth will be ruled by God's people, Jew and Gentile, under Christ. And yet, somehow, these people will still be divided into nations. The very last chapters of the Bible make this clear. The "glory and honour" of the nations will enter God's city, the New Jerusalem (Rev. 21:24). The trajectory of history does not run from an untamed garden back to a wild state. No, God's intent is that humans will exercise dominion over this world's geography within multiple God-honoring cultures.

Section Quiz

1. Define *culture*.
2. Why does Genesis 2 include a geography lesson?
3–4. How does the Bible reveal that the Fall corrupted human culture? How does it reveal that culture is not inherently bad?
5. How did God intend for Israel to draw the nations to the one true God?
✴ Why are Christians to be both conformed to and distinct from their various cultures?

II. Biblical Foundations for Studying Geography and Culture

The survey of the biblical storyline demonstrates that culture and geography remain important themes from the Bible's first chapter to its last. The priorities set by the biblical storyline will govern the priorities of this textbook.

Dominion over and Care for the Creation

The Bible is clear that the earth is important to God. The false teachers that emerged shortly after the church was founded taught that the god who created the world was evil. They promised salvation from everything material. But in Scripture exile is always a judgment for sin. God does not plan to exile His people from creation in the future. Rather He intends to restore creation so that it can be our eternal dwelling place.

This means that Christians, of all people, should seek to take care of God's creation. They should be concerned when water becomes undrinkable or when smog chokes the people of the world's great cities. God gave Adam the responsibility to tend and care for a garden, and though not everyone is given this particular task, we should all delight in and seek to conserve the beauty of creation.

With responsibility comes blessing. Mankind is permitted and encouraged to use the earth's resources for God-honoring dominion. This biblical view stands at odds with much of modern **environmentalism**, which is motivated by a concern to protect the natural environment, especially from harmful human activity. A Christian desires to protect the creation, but contemporary environmentalists often suggest that mankind is an unnatural and dangerous blight on the earth. The best world in their minds is one on which humans make the least impact. This is not the biblical view. God designed the world for mankind, and He designed its resources for man's good and

---

A Glimpse into Environmentalist Thinking

"The enemy is not only 'us' but virtually all human activities. . . . What is called for, then, is a strategy for transforming society so that the present rapid acceleration of extinction becomes a deceleration. The transformation must be universal because it is the everyday activities of human beings that most threaten other organisms. . . . Halting the growth of the human population as rapidly as is humanely possible and starting a gradual decline to a permanently sustainable level are obviously essential if the populations of most other organisms are to have a chance of persisting."

Paul and Anne Erlich, *Extinction: The Causes and Consequences of the Disappearance of Species* (New York: Random House, 1981), 242–43.

Solar panels, an example of making wise use of God's resources

man's progress. The emergence of human civilizations that make use of earth's resources is a good thing.

The Christian student of geography will, therefore, have a different motivation from the non-Christian student. A Christian will be interested in using his geographical knowledge to wisely manage the earth's resources for the betterment of other people—and for the good of the rest of the creation as well. This is one way geographical knowledge can be put to God-glorifying use.

Christianity and Cultures

Just as the physical world is important to God, so are human cultures. The many global varieties of architecture, dress, speech, music, and even table manners all point to one source: people's abilities as image-bearers of God. As Christians study the cultures of other people, they should learn to see the good in what other cultures have made of our world.

This respect for others is not something to be taken for granted. In the latter half of the twentieth century, Westerners became aware that they were often arrogant toward other cultures. However, the pendulum has swung in the opposite direction. Now many proclaim that all cultures are equally good and that each culture has its own truths and values that those in other cultures must always accept as valid. This view is called **multiculturalism**.

But the Christian knows that every culture, including his own, has been infected by the Fall. God has made certain that no culture is as bad as it could possibly be—but no culture is as good as it could be, either. Every culture combines creational goodness and human fallenness. Because God has given us divine standards of right and wrong, it is possible and necessary to compare cultures. Some will look better than others when God's light shines on them.

But that doesn't mean cultural evaluation is easy. Christian missionaries know this. Their daily work is to learn another culture and discern how to translate the gospel—and the Christian life that flows from it—into that culture without distorting the gospel message.

A Glimpse into Multiculturalism

The following quotation provides a synopsis of the thinking of adherents of multiculturalism. Those who embrace this philosophy essentially declare that all religions are of equal worth and all lead to the same destination.

"Around the different ways of conceiving, experiencing and responding to the Real there have grown up various religious traditions of the world with their myths and symbols, their philosophies and theologies, their liturgies and arts, their ethics and life-styles. Within all of them basically the same salvific process is taking place, namely the transformation of human existence from self-centeredness to Reality-centeredness. Each of the great traditions thus constitutes a valid context of salvation/liberation; each may be able to gain a larger understanding of the Real by attending to the reports of conceptualism of the others."

John Hick, *Problems of Religious Pluralism* (New York: Macmillan, 1985), 102.

Harmony Day celebration in Australia

One of the purposes of this book is to help you realize something very important: you, if you are a Christian, are a missionary in contact with foreign cultures. This is true in at least two respects:

(1) Human dominion over this world has now extended to the skies and the airwaves, and this means easy travel and lightning-fast communication. That, in turn, means that the whole world appears to be smaller. Cultures are often pushed together and shaken up. This is why America used to be called a "melting pot," and it means you will have neighbors who are culturally very different from you.

(2) Western culture itself is more and more foreign to Bible-believing Christianity. Believers are sojourners no matter where they live. But in America, Canada, and Western Europe there was a time when we sojourners had a signficant influence. This has changed. Cultural forces such as secularization have pushed Christianity to the margins in the West. And it does little good to complain about it. Instead, a study of cultural geography can help you seize the opportunity to learn about the very different cultures even of people who look like you, speak your language, and live in the same country.

Studying cultural geography is a great opportunity to learn about the world God made and the people He created to fill and subdue it. For the Christian it provides tools for moving God's plan of redemption forward as the gospel of Christ is proclaimed among the nations.

Section Quiz

1. What distinguishes Christian concern for the creation from modern environmentalism?
2. Why should Christians respect cultures that are foreign to their own?
3. Why must Christians not give blanket approval to any culture, including their own?
★ Why do Christians need to be skilled at cultural evaluation, even if they never become involved in foreign missions?

Chapter 1 Review

Making Connections

1. How does culture emerge as humans live out the Creation Mandate?
2. What geographical punishment for sin reoccurs in the Old Testament?
3. How was Israel to evangelize the nations around it?
4–5. In what two ways does geography remain important in the New Testament?

Developing Geography Skills

1. Sketch a map of Eden and the surrounding land based on the information provided in Genesis 2. Compare your map with maps of the Middle East. Is it possible to identify where Eden was located?
2. Find a map that shows the dominant religions in the various regions of the world. How might such a map shape a missions strategy? How might such a map be misleading?

Thinking Critically

1. Consider the governments or family structures in various societies. In some cases the government or family structure in a culture is flawed in many ways, yet even a totalitarian government or a flawed family is better than anarchy or the dissolution of the family unit. How does the goodness of the creation itself help cultural institutions such as government and the family retain some measure of goodness?
2. Essayist Alan Jacobs notes that gardens glorify God by shaping nature and thus "showing nature more clearly and beautifully" than before it was shaped. What does this truth about gardening teach about the Creation Mandate as a whole?

Living in God's World

1. Respond to the claim that Christian missions is culturally destructive because it seeks to turn people away from their cultural practices and beliefs.
2. Write a brief paragraph that responds to those environmentalists who claim that technology, economic growth, and a growing human population threaten the earth.

GEOGRAPHY: FINDING OUR PLACE IN THE WORLD

*T*he earth is important to God. He created it, He preserves it, and one day He will renew and perfect it into a new earth. God's first words to man, the Creation Mandate, were about the earth: fill it and subdue it. But the earth is a vast place, and humans cannot fulfill God's command without tools. Geography is a study that helps people make sense of the world and make use of it. Humans cannot exercise wise dominion without knowing about the earth's physical features, its climates, and the ways in which humans interact on it. This use of geography may be as simple as checking an online map for the best place to meet a friend for lunch. Or it may be as significant as a missionary investigating the demography of a particular region so he can be most effective in bringing the gospel to the peoples who live there.

I. What Is Geography?

History and geography are both necessary to help us understand the world around us. History is the study of events in *time* (what happened and *when*); geography is the study of *space* and *place* (*where* things happen). The basic tool of history is a timeline; the basic tool of geography is a map. One could compare history and geography to a play. History would be the actors and the plot; geography would be the stage on which those actions are played out.

It is not enough, however, just to memorize a list of dates and names of people and places. Beyond *when* and *where*, we want to know *how* and *why*. Geography helps us learn not only where places are but also how they differ and why.

Branches of Geography

The word **geography** comes from two roots meaning "earth" (*geo-*) and "written description" (*-graphy*). In other words, geography is a description of humanity's God-given abode—and everything and everyone on it—and how people interact with it and on it in fulfilling their God-given role as stewards of God's creation.

Geography has two main branches: *physical geography* (the study of the earth and its resources) and *human geography* (the study of man as he lives on the earth and uses its resources). This distinction is revealed by the titles of the first two units of this book: "The World as God Made It" (physical geography) and "The World as Man Subdues It" (human geography). These two branches are divided into dozens of smaller branches, such as climatology, oceanography, meteorology, and demographics.

One can study the main branches of geography in two ways. *Systematic geography* examines one branch of geography at a time, tying together examples from every region of the world. For example, a chapter titled "Urban Geography" might discuss New York City, London, and Tokyo. *Regional geography*, on the other hand, examines only one region of the world at a time, tying together all of the branches of geography simultaneously. For example, a chapter titled "The Far East" would cover not only the major cities there but also the climate, mountains, resources, and much more about the whole area.

This book combines both approaches. Chapters 2–5 are a general, systematic study of geography concepts, with two chapters on physical geography and two chapters on human geography. These

This is an example of human geography in the midst of physical geography.

chapters present the big picture, including the basic terms and concepts of geography that are used in the rest of the book to examine the unique features of individual regions and the countries within each region.

Themes of Geography

The study of geography has five fundamental themes:

1. *Location*—either specific (absolute) or relative to the surrounding environment
2. *Place*—physical characteristics (mountains, rivers, soils, plant and animal life, etc.) and human characteristics (roads, buildings, agriculture, industry, culture, etc.)
3. *Interaction*—both among people and between people and their environment
4. *Movement*—of people, goods, ideas, diseases, etc.
5. *Region*—defined by formal boundaries or functions

As you study geography, continually remind yourself of these five themes. They will recur many times throughout this book and are critical to a proper understanding of geography.

History of Geography

Ancient Views of the Earth

Humans probably began exploring their world soon after the Fall, but any written records of those explorations were lost in the Flood. After the Flood, the Lord commanded Noah to replenish the earth (Gen. 9:1); the work of geography began again. Early mapmakers supplied kings with maps for many reasons, including the planning of wars, the opening of new trade routes, and the building of new cities. The earliest surviving map is a clay tablet from around 2300 BC, discovered near the ancient city of Babylon, that depicts rivers and mountains.

The Greeks were the first known ancient people to study the earth extensively. Early seafarers wanted to learn all about their trade routes and the people they traded with or might trade with in the future. Alexander the Great, who rose to power in 336 BC, dreamed of conquering the world. After defeating Persia, he hired surveyors to accompany his army on a four-year journey "to the ends of the earth." His march into unexplored central Asia and India greatly expanded the Greeks' knowledge of world geography.

The first great geographer was a Greek mathematician named **Eratosthenes** (ER uh TAHS thuh neez), who lived about two centuries before Christ's birth. He summarized Greek understanding of the world in a book titled *Geography* and was the first writer to use the word *geography*. He believed that the world was a sphere and even calculated its circumference as about 25,000 miles, which is very

This is how ancient geographers thought the world must look.

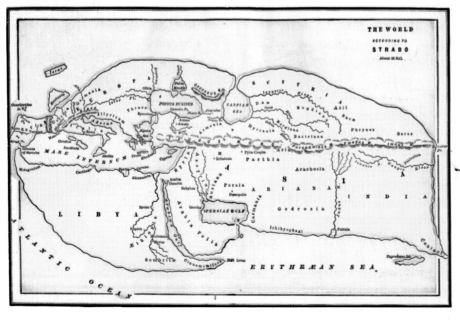

close to its actual 24,860-mile circumference. A century later, another Greek philosopher, **Hipparchus** (hih PAHR kus), made it easier to locate places on maps by perfecting Eratosthenes's idea of using a **grid** (a regular pattern of intersecting vertical and horizontal lines).

The Romans borrowed their mapmaking techniques from the Greeks. They used maps of their vast empire to help them build roads and rule efficiently. The most famous Roman geographer was **Ptolemy** (TAHL uh mee), who lived in the second century after Christ. Although he promoted a **geocentric** (earth-centered) **theory**, which states that the sun, stars, and planets revolve around the earth, Ptolemy's amazingly accurate map of the world represented islands, continents, and bodies of water from Britain to China. Both his map and his theory remained unchallenged for almost fourteen centuries.

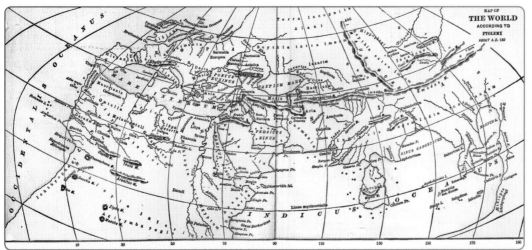

Map based on the descriptions that Ptolemy included in his book (second century AD)

The Age of Exploration

The translation of Ptolemy's works in the early fifteenth century revived Europe's interest in maps and helped to spark the Age of Exploration. Sea captains mapped the stars and charted the winds to help them plot new sea routes to reach the spices, gold, and jewels of the Orient. After studying Ptolemy's map (which greatly exaggerated the size of Asia), an ambitious young man named Christopher Columbus decided to try a shortcut to the Orient by sailing westward. Instead, he discovered a new, uncharted world—the Americas. In 1543, **Nicolaus Copernicus** (koh PUR nuh kus) published a lengthy argument for a **heliocentric** (sun-centered) **theory** of the universe.

Along with these advances in science, the art of **cartography** (mapmaking) reached new heights. **Gerhardus Mercator** (mer KAY tuhr) of Flanders published a map in 1569 that became the standard of his day. His well-designed grid enabled seafarers to plot their courses in a straight line. The maps of that period were beautifully illustrated with sea creatures, ships, and other designs to fill in the large areas about which geographers had no information. Mercator's system is still used today.

The Modern Age

As European kings began to colonize and conquer the newfound lands, they demanded maps with increasingly more detail and accuracy. They also commissioned extensive surveys of their own lands. The new maps included symbols for **topography** (detailed

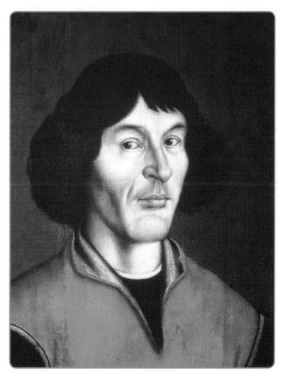

Copernicus concluded that the earth revolved around the sun, not the sun around the earth.

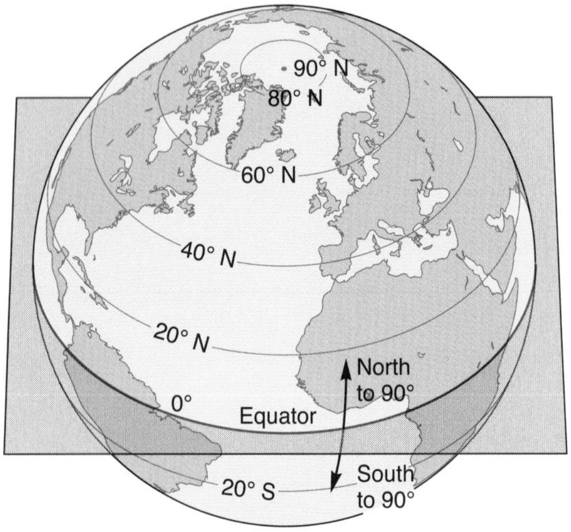

Lines of latitude

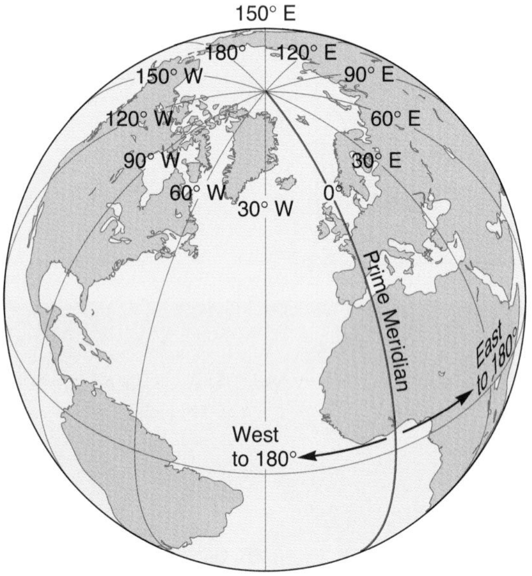

Lines of longitude

land features, including their elevations) to help generals move their armies more quickly. When England became the world's leading sea power in the eighteenth century, it also became the world's leading mapmaker.

As modern states began gathering more information about their climates, populations, and resources, they produced *thematic maps* (maps designed to communicate information on particular topics) to display their abstract findings. The United States was late in joining the map race but quickly caught up. World War II especially spurred U.S. mapmaking efforts. Today, the United States produces hundreds of maps for its troops stationed around the world. The development of airplanes and satellites made it possible to create better, more detailed maps. The U.S. Geological Survey (USGS), founded in 1879, has created a wealth of detailed maps. Radar and infrared satellites have now mapped the ocean floors and the frigid poles.

The most recent innovation is the global positioning system (GPS), which is financed and operated by the U.S. Department of Defense. Although GPS was designed specifically for military use, the government also allows many civilian uses. While the number of satellites varies, around thirty GPS satellites transmit coded signals to a receiver and calculate position, velocity, and time. GPS remains the most precise indicator of location available today. Although civilian use is accurate to within ten meters, military applications are accurate to within ten centimeters.

Although cartographers have produced very detailed and accurate maps of the earth as a result of such innovations, exploration continues. The jungles teem with myriad plant species that have never been cataloged. Millions—even billions—of undiscovered animal communities dot the ocean floor. Despite many famous expeditions, many mountain peaks still have not been climbed. Immense caves remain hidden and beg to be explored.

Section Quiz

1–2. Define *geography* and distinguish its two main branches.
3–4. Who were three great ancient geographers, and what did each contribute to geography?
5. What contributions from Copernicus and Mercator are still used today?
✯ List three different ways that maps can be used to manage God's earth for the benefit of others.

II. The Geographic Grid

Suppose a ship becomes disabled while far from land. How would potential rescue crews locate it? If the ship's crew could communicate their exact position, such a rescue would be much easier. Their exact location could be calculated using the imaginary lines of the *geographic grid* that divide the globe into small sections.

Hemispheres

Since the earliest times, geographers have divided the earth's sphere into two halves, calling each half a **hemisphere**. The line that divides the earth into the Northern and Southern Hemispheres is the **equator**.

Let us suppose the ship in our illustration is located in the Northern Hemisphere. If the earth were flat, officials could locate it north of the equator using feet and miles. But the earth is not flat; it is round. It is easier to locate points on a sphere using *degrees* (°). Authorities would need only two measurements to pinpoint the stranded ship's location: degrees of latitude and longitude.

Latitude and Longitude

The first measurement that rescuers would need is degrees of **latitude**. Imaginary lines run east and west around the earth. They form circles that are parallel to the equator and are therefore called **parallels** of latitude. They are numbered from 0° at the equator to 90° at the North and South Poles. Those numbers are determined by measuring the angle of these circles from the equator. The number of the parallel is followed by an N or an S to designate whether it is north or south of the equator.

The distance from one degree of latitude to the next is about sixty-nine miles. But that still is not precise enough to find a disabled ship floating in the middle of a huge ocean. Therefore, each degree of latitude is further divided into sixty *minutes* (′), with the minutes being a little more than a mile apart. Furthermore, each minute is subdivided into sixty *seconds* (″), with seconds being about one hundred feet apart.

Even if authorities determined the latitude of the disabled ship, they would need to know the point on that parallel where it was located. To find that point, they would need to know the **longitude**. Imaginary lines called **meridians** run north and south, stretching from pole to pole. Because no equator runs north and south, one meridian is designated as the **prime meridian** from which all other meridians are numbered. That prime meridian extends through Greenwich, England, just outside of London. Scientists at the Royal Observatory there made the original calculations for modern meridians, and their meridian became the basis of all other measurements of longitude.

Like parallels of latitude, meridians are measured in degrees, minutes, and seconds but with one major difference: the highest degree for meridians is 180, not 90. Why? The farthest point from the prime meridian is halfway around the world. Since a full circle is 360°, halfway is 180°. All other points are closer to the prime meridian and must be less than that.

The 180° meridian lies directly opposite the prime meridian and is actually a continuation of the same line. Together, these lines form a **great circle** and cut the earth into two equal parts (hemispheres). Every meridian except 0° and 180° is labeled as east (E) or west (W), depending on the hemisphere in which it lies. With the help of such exact readings, rescuers could easily find the stranded ship.

Locating places on a map using latitude and longitude uses basically the same principles used to play the game Battleship. The game uses a grid with columns that are designated by letters of the alphabet and rows that are numbered. You try to locate your opponent's

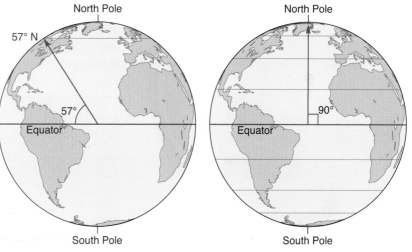

The number for a line of latitude is determined by measuring the angle of its circle from the equator.

hidden ships by designating a spot on the game board where a lettered column and a numbered row intersect, such as E-6. To locate a place using latitude and longitude, you simply substitute degrees of latitude and longitude for the letters and numbers.

Section Quiz

1. What is the term for each half of the earth?
2. What is another name for the lines of latitude?
3. What is the 0° line of latitude called?
4. What is another name for the lines of longitude?
5. What is the 0° line of longitude called?
★ Why is the meridian that extends through Greenwich, England, referred to as the prime meridian?

III. Map Projections

Globes show information about the earth's surface with almost perfect accuracy. Both globes and the earth are spheres, and both can be divided easily with lines of latitude and longitude. Although globes are useful, they are difficult to carry in a briefcase or fit into a textbook.

Flat maps are much more useful than globes and can show much greater detail. Any method used to show the earth's round surface on a flat map is called a **map projection**.

The Problem of Distortion

When a globe is transferred onto a flat map, a serious problem known as **distortion** occurs. The earth's surface is not a flat rectangle like a sheet of paper; it does not "flatten" without distorting the image. When mapmakers are making a flat map, they try to avoid or reduce the distortion of four features of a globe:

- area
- shape
- distance
- direction

Usually, a flat map will distort two or three of these features while minimizing or eliminating the other distortion(s). No flat map of the world can be accurate in all four ways. Manufacturers of globes must print the outer layer on a flat surface and then glue it to the globe. A typical globe is covered by twelve paper strips called **gores**. If you were to take the gores and lay them flat, you would have a gore map.

How accurate is such a map? *Areas* of land and water are accurate, and compass *directions* are fairly accurate. *Distances* also seem to be accurate—an inch equals the same number of miles on every gore. But measuring distances *between* gores is awkward. The *shapes* have the most obvious distortions because of all the gaps. Although the gore map is fairly accurate in three respects, it is obviously not very useful as a flat map.

Solutions to the Problem

In an effort to solve the problem of distortion, cartographers developed three basic types of map projections: cylindrical, planar

A globe is a model of the earth.

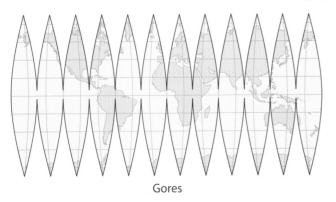

Gores

(azimuthal), and conic. Each type of projection tries to address weaknesses inherent in other types of projections, but each also has its own problems. These projections get their names from the geometric surface onto which the globe is projected.

Although maps are drawn using mathematical equations, we can picture what takes place with the help of an imaginary globe made from wire. The wires represent lines of latitude and longitude. An imaginary light shines from the center of the globe onto the map surface.

Cylindrical Projections

Most world maps use a variation of the **cylindrical projection**. First, the mapmaker rolls a sheet of paper into the shape of a cylinder around the wire globe. Next, he traces the shadows cast by the light, and then he unrolls the paper to get a flat map.

Mercator's Projection—The first important cylindrical projection was published by Mercator in 1569. Not until the second half of the twentieth century was it replaced.

On a Mercator projection, all lines of latitude and longitude look straight. This feature means that compass *directions* are always constant. *Shapes* are also accurate. *Areas* and *distances*, however, are increasingly distorted the farther one moves north or south from the equator. Greenland, for example, looks larger than the entire continent of South America although it is really only one-eighth its size.

Goode's Interrupted Projection—The cylindrical projection has several popular variations, including a map that cuts and flattens the earth like an orange peel. It is called an **interrupted projection**. (The map made from gores before they are glued to a globe is an example.) It remains in one piece, but the image is "interrupted" with gaps or cuts. The most popular of these maps is Goode's interrupted projection. It is useful because the *areas* remain fairly accurate and the *shapes* of continents are less distorted than shapes on the gore map. Unfortunately, Goode's projection distorts *distances* and all north-south *directions*.

Cylindrical projection

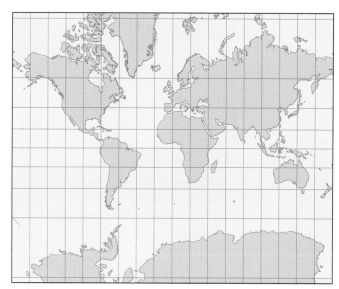

Mercator projection

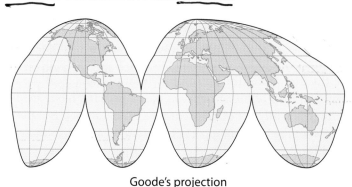

Goode's projection

Robinson's Projection—Popular for textbooks is Robinson's projection, which combines the best elements from the other projections. Its greatest advantage is that it minimizes (but does not eliminate) all four types of distortions. Everything is distorted but only a little. Almost every world map in this textbook uses Robinson's projection.

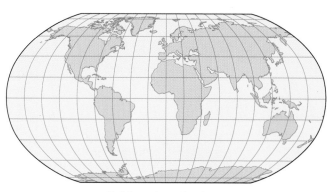

Robinson's projection

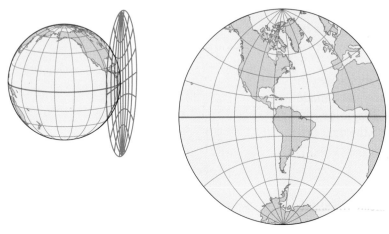

Azimuthal projection

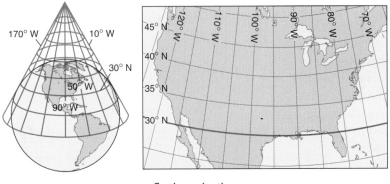

Conic projection

Azimuthal Projections

Cylindrical projections such as Mercator's, Goode's, and Robinson's are all good for world maps. But planar and conic projections work better on smaller-scale maps.

The planar projection, also called an **azimuthal** (AZ uh MUTH uhl) **projection**, uses a flat plane instead of a cylinder. To make the projection, one places a flat sheet of paper on an imaginary wire globe, touching only one point. The shadows traced on this paper form an azimuthal map. The map is most accurate in the center but becomes increasingly distorted near the edges. Therefore, it is useful for compact areas, such as South America and Antarctica, where land is surrounded by water.

Conic Projections

To make a **conic projection**, the mapmaker places a cone-shaped piece of paper on an imaginary wire globe and traces the shadow onto the cone. Then he opens and flattens the cone to make a conic projection. Unlike the planar projection, which touches a single point, the cone touches an entire line of latitude. The conic map is most accurate where the cone touches the line. Away from that line the features become gradually distorted. Thus, it is most useful for showing wide regions, such as the United States.

Choosing a projection is very important when one wants to display the whole world or a large region of the world. However, cartographers do not worry much about projections of small areas, such as cities, because distortions of such small areas are virtually undetectable.

Types of Maps

Whenever someone asks you for directions for getting somewhere (perhaps from your school or church to your home), you consult a **mental map** to communicate the directions to the person. As you give the directions, the person to whom you are speaking is forming a mental map of his or her own based on what he or she is hearing. It might or might not be accurate. A mental map is a person's perception of the world or a part of it based on available knowledge. In addition to boundaries and major physical features (e.g., major rivers, mountains, towns), mental maps involve one's cultural perceptions, including any biases (a preference for one thing over another) or prejudices (a judgment about something or someone before you have examined all of the facts) toward the geographic region in question. One usually views his home area positively but might view "foreign" areas—rightly or wrongly—with a degree of negativity. These perceptions are influenced by a person's home life, the news and entertainment media, and his or her educational experiences. One purpose of studying geography is to expand and improve the accuracy of one's mental map of the world.

A map is a flat representation of the world or a specific portion of it. Many types of maps exist, each communicating a different type of information. The ability to read and interpret maps is essential, not only in the study of geography but also in everyday living—for example, in using a road map effectively. Some of the most common map types are the following.

1. *Political maps* indicate state or national boundaries, capitals, and major cities.

2. *Physical maps* show mountains, rivers, lakes, elevation, and other natural features. Color is often used extensively to indicate bodies of water, various elevations, etc.

3. *Topographic (relief) maps* use special lines to indicate the shape and elevation of the landforms shown.

4. *Roadmaps* are used extensively by travelers, whether they are military commanders, professional truckers, or families on vacation. They show primary and secondary transportation routes.

5. *Climate maps* provide information about weather patterns in an area.

6. *Economic or resource maps* show the natural resources or economic activities of a place. Such maps might show where various industries are located, where specific types of crops are grown, or other such data.

Other specialized maps are also available, including geological, vegetation, soil, and meteorological (weather) maps. Hydrological maps give information about the water in an area, such as groundwater, runoff, and water levels in reservoirs. Ecological maps deal with the environment. Plat maps show boundaries between landowners. (If your parents own your home, they received a copy of the plat map of their property at the time of purchase, and the original is on file at the county courthouse.) Nautical maps represent the waterways and bodies of water of an area and are invaluable to boaters, shippers, and engineers who design and build bridges and other structures in, over, or under the water. Military maps are essential to a nation's self-defense. There are even celestial maps for astronomers, scientists who study the stars and planets.

Regardless of the type, most maps include symbols that represent various features in an abbreviated form. Those symbols are of three basic types. *Point symbols* are used to indicate such things as cities or even such specific objects as buildings, wells, or monuments. *Line symbols* represent such things as roads, railroads, rivers, and water or power lines. *Area symbols* indicate bodies of water, swamps or marshes, glaciers, or other such physical features.

The meanings of the symbols are shown in a **legend**, which is usually located in a corner of the map that does not contain critical information. Often located near the legend are two other helpful features, a **compass rose** and a **scale**. The compass rose shows the orientation of the map, that is, whether the top of the map is north, south,

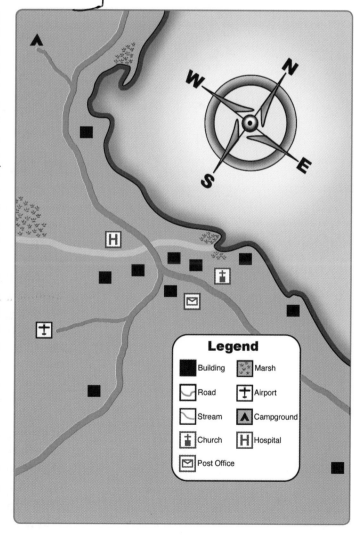

Legend

■ Building	✿ Marsh
✉ Road	✝ Airport
⌇ Stream	▲ Campground
⛪ Church	H Hospital
✉ Post Office	

east, or west. (Although north is generally the top of most maps, that is not always the case, which makes the compass rose very important.) The scale is a calibrated (marked) line that indicates distance. For maps of large areas, the scale might read, "1 in. = 200 mi." On smaller-scale maps, it might read, "1 in. = 100 ft."

GIS

Modern maps, including those accessible via the Internet, are the result of **GIS** or geographic information system technology. These maps are produced using computerized map data.

Using this data, information highlighted in modern versions of the six previously mentioned map types remains relatively current and easily accessible. GIS data is collected by engineers who physically survey the land using modern equipment, including GPS (global positioning satellites) and laser transits. Additional information is gathered by remote sensing using aircraft or satellites. Remote sensing utilizes photographs, laser sensors, and height-measuring radar. Some GIS software even provides a virtual tour of streets in many cities. This is made possible by high-speed photographs taken by cameras mounted on vehicles that physically traverse these streets. The possibilities of planning a trip or viewing locations via the Internet are seemingly endless thanks to this burgeoning technology.

Section Quiz

1. What are the four types of distortion on flat maps?
2. What is an interrupted projection? Give an example of one.
3. In what two ways is Goode's interruped projection distorted?
4. What projection minimizes all four distortions?
5. What type of projection is good for compact areas?
✯ How might a person who is considering a visit to a mission field use GIS?

IV. Relief Maps

Map projections show the general outlines of the earth. But these two-dimensional maps are not very helpful in describing surface features, such as mountains and valleys. Soldiers, road crews, and backpackers all need detailed information about the third dimension: altitude, or elevation.

Any type of map that shows surface features is a physical map because it shows physical things. Physical maps that show specific changes in elevation are called relief maps. **Relief** refers to the height and depth of land features in relation to surrounding land. Many relief maps include not only water features, such as rivers, but also man-made features, such as dams.

Showing the Three-Dimensional Earth

Relief maps can show the third dimension of the earth's surface in many ways. Early maps included ink drawings of hills and mountains to show upper elevations. "Raised relief" maps, such as plaster models, are literally three-dimensional. Recent advances in technology, such as computers, satellite imagery, and aerial photography, make possible the use of color to indicate different altitudes. On most color relief maps, green represents land near sea level. Yellow or light

Benchmarks

In describing elevation, a surveyor refers to distance above sea level. But what does he do when he cannot see the ocean? He relies on special monuments or markers called "benchmarks" that have been placed in key spots around the world to give the exact altitude of the location. If you have ever hiked to the peak of a mountain, you might have seen a benchmark. It looks like the head of a giant nail and has writing on it.

How did surveyors measure the original benchmarks? Although the details are complex, the theory is simple. A surveyor stands in a place where he can see the ocean with a telescope (on his theodolite). By measuring angles, he can calculate the altitude of his position and nail a marker. Then he moves farther inland and looks back at his first marker. On and on he goes. The surveyor carries an *altimeter*, too, to check his altitude. The altimeter measures air pressure, which becomes lower as one moves up in elevation.

In the past, government surveyors sometimes had to hack through dense woods to get a clear line of sight. The work was difficult and time consuming. Today, surveyors use satellites as reference points, making their work easier and more precise.

Benchmarks indicate a location's elevation.

brown represents a slight rise in land. Dark brown, gray, or white indicates mountains.

The lines that separate colors on a relief map are called **contour lines**. Each line shows all points on the map that have the same altitude. For this reason, the line is also known as an isoline (*iso-* means equal). The difference in elevation between two contour lines is called the contour interval.

Reading Relief Maps

Look at the first of the three views of a landscape (diagram A). It illustrates what one region might look like to a camera, but it is not a map. It cannot show distances, directions, or the shapes and areas of the land. The second view, diagram B, shows the comparative elevations of the cross section of the same landscape. It does not, however, give any information about the other dimensions.

The relief map (diagram C), however, gives accurate information about all three dimensions. It helps us visualize the landforms and compare the elevations of those landforms. Relief maps also show us the general shapes, areas, distances, and directions of landforms.

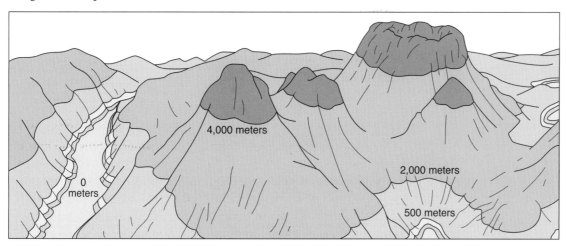

Diagram A

Diagram B

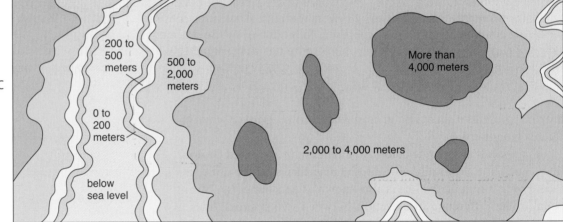

Diagram C

Section Quiz

1. What is the term for a map that shows the altitude of land features?

2–3. Explain the difference between a contour line and a contour interval.

4. What color is used in diagram B to indicate altitude between 0 and 200 meters?

★ What advantage does diagram C have over diagrams A and B?

Chapter 2 Review

Making Connections

1. What would the US Navy need to know in order to locate a stranded ship at sea?

2–4. What is the difference between geography, cartography, and topography?

5. Why do all flat maps of the earth contain distortions?

6. What is the purpose of a compass rose on a map?

Developing Geography Skills

1. Draw a map of your city (or one near you) and include the location of your church, post office(s), hospital(s), airport, and other local points of interest. (Include a legend and compass rose.) For an additional challenge, try doing this from memory to increase your mental mapping skills.

2. With your parents' permission, download Google Earth (free software) and enter your home address in the search box. Zoom in or out to find churches, hospitals, and businesses listed on the map. Practice with the controls and find out how to set the map to point north.

Thinking Critically

1. Why were cartographers able to define the equator long before they devised the prime meridian?

2. Why do most relief maps employ a common color scheme?

Living in God's World

1. Chart out your mental map of the world by recording your thoughts and impressions about the various regions of the world. Note if you have positive, negative, or mixed views about different regions. Document what these views are and the reasons you hold them. As you progress through the course, evaluate your mental map to see how well it conforms to a Christian understanding of these various regions.

2. Maps can play an important role in local church ministry. What are some ways that maps could enhance your church's ministry? Formulate a plan. Consider taking it to one of your church leaders to see if it would truly be profitable to implement.

People, Places, and Things to Know

- geography
- Eratosthenes
- Hipparchus
- grid
- Ptolemy
- geocentric theory
- Nicolaus Copernicus
- heliocentric theory
- cartography
- Gerhardus Mercator
- topography
- hemisphere
- equator
- latitude
- parallels
- longitude
- meridians
- prime meridian
- great circle
- map projection
- distortion
- gores
- cylindrical projection
- interrupted projection
- azimuthal projection
- conic projection
- mental map
- legend
- compass rose
- scale
- GIS
- relief
- contour lines

3

A waterway in Croatia

THE EARTH'S SURFACE AND CLIMATE

The psalmist reminds us that God created the earth and all that it contains: He stretched out the heavens like a curtain and He laid the foundations of the earth so that it will remain forever (Ps. 104:1–5). The psalmist also teaches that God rules over the climate. Frost and snow come as His gifts, and it is His words which melt them (Ps. 147:15–18). The earth is not unimportant to God. The earth is God's great masterpiece. Whether you are looking at marvels such as the Grand Canyon and the savannah of Africa or standing amazed at the power of volcanoes and the beauty of freshly fallen snow, you are seeing God's handiwork. In a fallen world, that handiwork is marred. The creation groans, awaiting its redemption (Rom. 8:21–22). But even this marred creation testifies to the Creator (Rom. 1:20).

Grand Canyon

I. The Earth's History

God's work on the earth can be divided into four phases: the Creation, the Flood, the current world, and the future world. We cannot understand the present world without understanding its past and its future. What we see today is the result of what happened in the past. According to the apostle Peter, however, mankind is "willingly" ignorant of God's intervention in the earth's history (2 Pet. 3:5–7).

The Creation

Earth's history begins with Creation. Genesis 1 describes how God gave the earth light, atmosphere, land, and seas. A fully functioning world appeared within six days, filled with soil, tall trees, and all of the creatures—not bare rocks, seeds, and primitive life forms.

God takes delight in what He made (Ps. 104:31). The creation is "very good" (Gen. 1:31). This is so not only because God is the Creator, but also because God has a very special purpose for His creation. He designed the creation to declare His glory to all the peoples of the world (Ps. 19:1–4). God's great goal in all He does is the glory of His name, and God says that His glory is proclaimed by the

Earth Developing over Billions of years=uniformitarism

physical world (Rom. 1:19–20). Consider how the creation reflects God's wisdom, power, creativity, and love.

The Flood

Other than Creation, the Flood was the most significant physical event in history. Genesis 7–8 provides a glimpse of the process leading to the enormous changes the Flood brought to the earth's surface. The Flood also provided a clear demarcation between God's original creation and life after the Flood. One example is the marked decrease in lifespans recorded after the Flood when compared to those preceding it.

Evidence for a **cataclysm** (a violent upheaval or change in the earth's crust) caused by a flood can be found around the world. How that evidence is interpreted is determined by one's worldview. Up until the late 1700s, most people who studied the earth in the early days of geological science interpreted the geological evidence based on a biblical view of a global flood. Since that time, those who embraced a secular worldview have ignored the evidence of a worldwide flood and have rejected the biblical record that clearly describes a universal flood. Any who dared to accept the biblical account were denounced as catastrophists. Those who believed in an old earth developing over billions of years tried to explain that the surface of the earth was gradually shaped by observable natural processes over vast spans of time. This position became known as **uniformitarianism** because geologic processes were believed to be relatively uniform in activity and rate. Given the amount of geologic evidence for past catastrophic events and processes that have contributed to shaping

Above: A cataclysmic universal flood would explain the existence of the natural wonders along the Colorado River.

Below: Rock layers are displayed on a butte near Sedona, Arizona.

the earth's surface, most professional geologists today call themselves **neocatastrophists**. These scientists continue to reject the biblical account but admit that the current condition of the earth's surface cannot be explained by gradual, uniform processes alone.

The same evidence studied through the lens of a Christian worldview provides strong support for the biblical account of a universal flood. From widespread fossil remains, including those deposited on high mountaintops, to miles-thick sedimentary rock units, to deep, sculpted canyons, only a universal flood provides an adequate explanation for the many geologic features of the surface of the world we see today.

The impact of the Flood was greater than anything we have ever witnessed. Its waters sprang from the ground, probably accompanied by massive explosions of magma, when the "fountains of the great deep" were broken up. There is much evidence for tremendous volcanic activity that accompanied the erosion and sedimentation of rock strata seen today. Torrential rain fell from the atmosphere for forty days. Creationary scientists believe the ejected superheated subterranean water and the volcanic steam condensed to provide most of the rain that fell upon the earth. When the geologic activity subsided, the heavy rain abated; the water covered the earth to a height of fifteen cubits (about twenty-two feet) above the "high hills" (Gen. 7:19). The high mountains that we see today were probably formed during or after the Flood as tectonic plates collided. The supercontinent broke up, and new continents formed.

The Flood fractured the earth's surface, and the swirling waters churned soil, vegetation, and animal carcasses together in layer upon layer of sediment. Under the weight of tons of water, thick sediments quickly solidified. The tectonic forces easily folded and buckled sedimentary strata into unique formations even as they were hardening into rock.

Following the Flood, the global climate likely cooled for centuries afterward due to the large amount of water vapor and volcanic dust in the atmosphere. The resulting clouds would have blocked a significant portion of the sun's incoming heat and light, cooling the continents. The accumulation of snow and ice produced a single ice age that lasted for several centuries. Evidence for such a glacial period includes not only the remaining ice caps in the polar regions and glaciers in high mountains, but widespread glacial erosional and depositional features in northern Europe, Siberia, and North America. Similar evidence exists in the Southern Hemisphere. Viewing the Ice Age as a product of the biblical Flood suggests that the current global warming trend may be simply the earth returning to a more temperate global climate.

> ### The Future
>
> For centuries people have been tempted to think that the material world is unimportant and transitory. The early Christians struggled against heretics who denied the resurrection because they thought matter was evil. These heretics preached a salvation message of escape from this world. But the Bible's vision of salvation is quite different. God does not intend to throw His good creation away. He promises to restore creation. This is why the New Testament proclaims a bodily resurrection and a new earth. This world does not go away when God brings to completion the salvation that He has in store for those who trust Him. Instead, the world is released from its bondage and obtains even greater freedom and glory.

Section Quiz

1–2. What are the four main phases of God's work on earth, and what does the Bible say about each phase in 2 Peter 3:5–7?

3–4. What is uniformitarianism? What biblical view better explains the changes in the world's land formations?

5. Why did the earth become unstable after the Flood?

★ How is mixing cement a useful way to explain the softness of the earth after the Flood but its hardness today?

II. The Earth's Surface

In their study of the earth's surface, scientists have developed models that divide the earth into three parts. The covering of air that surrounds our planet is the **atmosphere**, the solid part of the earth is the **lithosphere** (LITH uh sfeer), and the water on the earth's surface is the **hydrosphere** (HYE druh sfeer).

The Land

The earth can be described as a *lithosphere* (literally, "rock ball") that is nearly eight thousand miles in diameter. We think of the earth's surface as very rough. But when astronauts view it from space, it seems to them as smooth as the surface of an apple.

The Earth's Layers

The earth seems to be divided into several layers. The thin (4.5 to 31 miles deep) outer "skin" is called the **crust** and consists mainly of two layers. The bottom layer of basaltic rock spreads over the whole earth. Above that are the oceans and slabs of granitic rock, which are many miles thick. Where these slabs rise above the level of the ocean, they form our continents.

Earthquakes give tantalizing hints about the secrets that lie below the earth's crust. In 1909, scientists noticed that earthquake waves decelerated abruptly and then accelerated again below the crust. They proposed that the waves were entering a layer of hot, plastic (capable of being shaped) material called the **mantle**. Earthquake waves move faster through the hot, dense mantle than through the crust.

Waves from earthquakes indicate that beneath the mantle is a core divided into a liquid outer core and a solid inner core. After studying the magnetism of the earth and its powerful gravity as it interacts with the moon, many scientists conclude that the core might be made of two heavy metals, iron and nickel.

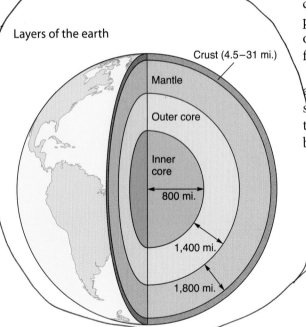

Layers of the earth

Crust (4.5–31 mi.)

Mantle

Outer core

Inner core

800 mi.

1,400 mi.

1,800 mi.

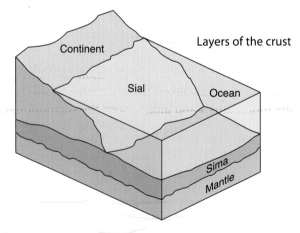

Continent

Layers of the crust

Sial

Ocean

Sima

Mantle

Islands

If the oceans were a little lower, the largest islands of the world would all become part of the nearby continents. We call these areas **continental islands** (for example, the British Isles). In contrast, **oceanic islands** rise from the ocean floor. If the ocean were lower, they would still be islands but slightly larger (for example, most of the islands of Micronesia in the Pacific).

The Continents

The total surface area of the earth is 197 million square miles. Of that total, 29 percent, or 57 million square miles, is land; the rest is ocean. All of the surface is divided between **continents**, the main landmasses of the earth, and **islands**, landmasses surrounded by water. The earth has six continental landmasses and seven continents: North America, South America, Africa, Australia, Antarctica, and Eurasia (Europe and Asia), which is divided by the Ural Mountains.

Fast Facts About the Earth's Continents				
Continent	Area (sq. mi.)	Percent of World's Land	High Point (ft.)	Low Point (ft.)
Asia	17,129,000	29.7	Mt. Everest 29,035 (Nepal)	Dead Sea -1,339 (Israel)
Africa	11,707,000	20.0	Mt. Kilimanjaro 19,340 (Tanzania)	Lake Assal -510 (Djibouti)
North America	9,363,000	16.5	Mt. McKinley 20,320 (Alaska)	Death Valley -282 (California)
South America	6,886,000	12.0	Mt. Aconcagua 22,834 (Argentina)	Laguna del Carbón -344 (Argentina)
Antarctica	5,500,000	9.0	Vinson Massif 16,067	Sea Level
Europe	4,057,000	7.0	Mt. Elbrus 18,510 (Russia)	Caspian Sea -92 (Russia)
Australia	2,942,000	5.7	Mt. Kosciusko 7,310 (New South Wales)	Lake Eyre -52 (South Australia)

The Major Landforms

God's world is filled with a beautiful variety of land formations. Every variation in the landscape is called a **landform**. Geographers have classified three major landforms—mountains, plains, and plateaus—each of which has played a unique role in human civilization.

Mountains

Mountains stand high above the surrounding landscape. Geographers distinguish them from hills in that hills are generally smaller than mountains, although no set elevation distinguishes the two. Rather, local usage of the terms is the deciding factor.

Many mountains stand alone above the surrounding landscape. When several mountains appear together, however, such as the Rocky Mountains, the formation is called a **mountain range**. (The Rocky Mountain range is a system so large that it actually contains ranges within ranges, which are then called mountain systems.)

Mount Elbert, Colorado, is the highest peak in the Rocky Mountains.

The highest mountain range in the world is the Himalayas (him uh LAY uhz), meaning "abode of snow." The highest peak is Mount Everest, or Chomolungma in Tibetan. Farmers many miles away depend on the rivers that flow from the melting snows of Mount Everest and other Himalayan peaks.

In addition to influencing weather, climate, and vegetation, mountains have influenced the pattern of human settlement. Many cities arose near mines, which burrow deep into the belly of mountains. Other cities lie in the fertile valleys of mountain ranges, where they are protected from extreme weather. But in most cases, mountains are too cold, rugged, or infertile for extensive human settlement.

Mountain ranges also hinder travel and contact between people. Populations living in the mountains can easily hide from attack, and social changes are slow to reach them. As you study geography, you will see how cultures, languages, dialects, and national borders are often defined by mountain ranges.

Plains

In contrast to mountains, **plains** are wide areas of level land. Some plains that lie in coastal areas, such as land along the Gulf of Mexico, are called *coastal plains*. But low elevation does not define plains; plains can be found at high elevation, too. For example, nestled among the Andes Mountains of South America is the Altiplano, which averages twelve thousand feet above sea level. Plains are not totally flat, either. For instance, the Great Plains region of North America has many rolling hills.

Plains are generally thought of as being flat, as this one is, but some have rolling hills.

Plains are the most valuable landform for farmers. Rivers bring water and sediments down from the mountains, and deposits called **alluvium** settle in the flat plains. Alluvium is often rich in nutrients that enable farms to produce large quantities of food. Therefore, such *alluvial plains* are the "breadbaskets" of many nations. They are often named after the river that flows through them. For example, the Congo Basin (an area drained by a river system) is an alluvial plain named for the mighty Congo River.

Plateaus

Plateaus (pla TOHS), a third landform, are wide areas of relatively flat land, like plains, but they rise abruptly above surrounding lands. They are what was left after erosion of soft sedimentary material by the massive movement of the Flood waters. Steep cliffs or slopes mark at least one edge of a plateau. Indeed, plateaus are often called *tablelands* because their surface is sometimes elevated like a tabletop.

A plateau rises abruptly from the plain.

The surfaces of plateaus are much more varied than plains, often including hills, mountains, and deep canyons. For example, the Grand Canyon cuts through one of North America's largest plateaus. The most rugged plateaus of the world are often called *highlands*. Plateaus can occur at almost any elevation. The highest is the Tibetan Plateau, which lies on the northern border of the Himalayan range in Asia.

Plateaus generally have poor soils and few resources, except for grass for grazing animals. Many of the world's deserts are located on plateaus.

Section Quiz

1. What are three basic landforms on the earth?

2–3. Which of the basic landforms includes ranges? Which include basins?

4–5. What is the main similarity between plains and plateaus? What is the main difference?

✶ What are the advantages to living on a plain? What are the disadvantages?

III. The Earth's Waters

Like landforms, bodies of water play a major role in human life. The three main bodies of water—oceans or seas, lakes, and rivers—are at the heart of a great deal of human activity.

The Importance of Water

Without a ready supply of fresh water, we would quickly die; therefore, human settlements develop near sources of fresh water. Less than 3 percent of the earth's water is fresh, and more than two-thirds of that water is in polar ice caps and glaciers or is underground. The remaining water, in lakes and rivers, is a precious resource, essential to our growth and survival.

Large bodies of water often provide means for travel and trade. When settlers first arrived in America, they clustered along the coast and rivers rather than moving into the mountains. It was much cheaper to ship foods by water than to transport them overland. Ships could carry ten wagonloads of goods for the same price as one cart pulled over the mountains. Food on ships arrived at the marketplace much sooner; the food cost less and was fresher. Even today, water transportation is by far the least expensive way for most nations to ship products to each other, especially if they do not share a land border.

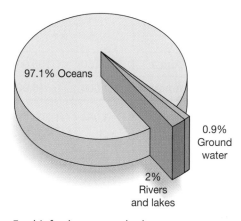

Earth's fresh water and salt water

The Major Bodies of Water

Oceans

The earth is unique in the solar system. Scientists have not found evidence of liquid water on any other planet or moon, yet water covers 71 percent of the earth's surface, amounting to more than three hundred million cubic miles. Although 97 percent of the water is in the oceans, traces of water can be found on almost every square inch of land.

There are four principal ocean basins in the world: the Pacific, the Atlantic, the Indian, and the Arctic Oceans. (Some scientists suggest that the waters around Antarctica should be classified as a fifth ocean. More will be said about this in Chapter 24.) All of the world's seas, gulfs, and bays belong to one of these oceans. Continents generally mark the borders of each ocean. If you look at the world map, however, you will see that the divisions are not always clear. The oceans flow into each other. For this reason, the whole system is sometimes called the **world ocean**.

The oceans provide humans with many blessings—distributing thermal energy from the sun, providing water for rain clouds, and guarding nations from foreign invasion.

The Principal Oceans of the World			
Ocean	Area (sq. mi.)	Percent of World Ocean	Lowest Point (ft.)
Pacific	70,000,000	50.0	Mariana Trench 35,840
Atlantic	36,000,000	25.5	Puerto Rico Trench 28,232
Indian	29,000,000	20.5	Java Trench 23,376
Arctic	5,400,000	4.0	Eurasian Basin 17,881

Ocean waters teem with tasty fish and pearl-producing clams. The most obvious but often overlooked bounty of the sea, however, is its salt. Salt has many uses, including a seasoning for and preservative of food, a cleaning agent, a means of destroying moths and driving away ants, and an antiseptic.

If we could drink ocean water and pump it into our parched fields, it would solve many of our worst problems. But the high concentration of salt—about 3.5 percent of the total mass of seawater—is harmful to crops and land animals. Swallowing too much salt water leads to a quick, painful death from dehydration. Irrigating farmland with ocean water stunts the growth of plants and quickly makes the land unproductive. (We will discuss the oceans more in Chapter 24.)

The Longest Rivers in the World

River	Location	Length (mi.*)	Discharge (cu. ft./sec.)	Drainage Area (sq. mi.)
Nile	Africa	4,160	100,000	1,293,000
Amazon	S. America	4,000	6,350,000	2,722,000
Chang (Yangtze)	Asia	3,964	1,200,000	756,000
Huang He (Yellow)	Asia	3,395	52,900	288,000
Congo	Africa	2,718	1,458,000	1,314,000
Amur	Asia	2,744	438,000	716,000
Lena	Asia	2,734	547,000	961,000
Mackenzie	N. America	2,635	400,000	711,000
Mekong	Asia	2,600	500,000	307,000
Niger	Africa	2,590	215,000	730,000

* Estimates of length vary depending on the reference consulted and the location chosen as the river's source.

The Amazon River discharges an average of 6.3 million cubic feet of water every second.

Rivers

Water is in constant motion. Unless something gets in its way, water will eventually flow to the ocean. Small streams flow into rivers, which, in turn, flow into even larger rivers. Rivers that "feed" other rivers are called **tributaries.** The main river and all of its tributaries are called a **river system.** Many of the world's great river systems flow more than two thousand miles from their *headwaters* (source) to their mouth. The "greatest" river systems are determined by comparing various features, including the following.

Length—The most obvious comparison is length. The Nile is considered the longest river, an impressive 4,160 miles. But depending on which tributary one designates as the headwaters, the Amazon might be longer.

The longest river in the United States—the Missouri River (2,540 miles)—and the Mississippi (2,340 miles), which it flows into, are not among the top ten longest rivers shown on the chart. But considered as a river system, the Mississippi-Missouri River (including tributaries of the Missouri) measures 3,735 miles long, giving it a rank of fourth place in the world.

Discharge—Another feature of comparison is the amount of water flowing out into the ocean—the discharge. It would take about sixty-three rivers the size of the Nile to match the volume of water that flows from the Amazon. The volume is so large that the water from the Amazon remains fresh and drinkable two hundred miles out into the Atlantic Ocean.

Drainage Area—A third feature for comparison is the size of the **drainage basin**, the total land area drained by the main river and its tributaries. The Nile's drainage basin is small and mostly dry and has few tributaries. In contrast, the Amazon River drains a rain forest that covers 40 percent of the continent of South America. The Missouri River has the fifth largest drainage basin (1,244,000 sq. mi.).

Navigability—A fourth feature of comparison is depth, how far up a river ocean-going vessels can travel. Steamboats used to ply the Missouri River more than one thousand miles from the ocean. Barges rely on

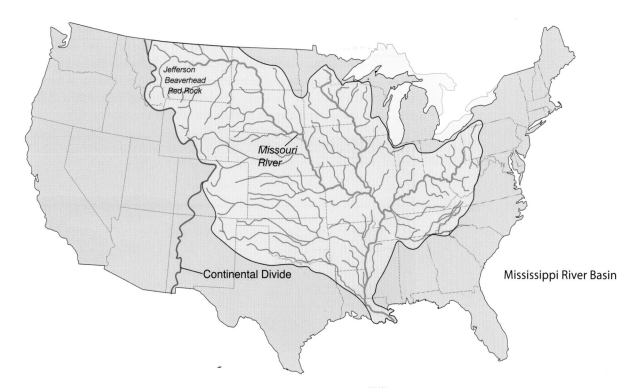

Jefferson
Beaverhead
Red Rock

Missouri
River

Continental Divide

Mississippi River Basin

deep, navigable rivers for carrying goods from their distant sources to coastal cities. The Mississippi River and its tributaries include more than fifteen thousand miles of navigable water, making it the second largest inland water route in the world. The Amazon is the only river system that has more navigable miles than the Mississippi.

Rivers have played a central role in the history of almost every nation. Historically, explorers have used these waters as roads to the interior. Many pioneers who came after the explorers settled near these rivers, and most cities were founded beside rivers. For example, St. Louis sprang up at the point where boats floating down the Missouri entered the Mississippi River. Even where rivers are too shallow for travel, they provide drinking water, irrigation, fish, game, power generation, and recreation. The birthplace of almost every great civilization, such as ancient Egypt, was somewhere along a river.

Lakes

Bodies of water fully enclosed by land are called lakes and are remnants of the Flood and the Ice Age. Many cities are located on the shores of lakes because lakes provide fish, drinking water, transportation, and recreation. Lakes make it possible for some cities to be built deep in the interior of continents.

The Great Lakes of North America are the largest system of freshwater lakes in the world. This system includes the world's largest freshwater lake (by area)—Lake Superior. The Great Lakes support many large cities, including Chicago and Detroit.

Barges ply the Mississippi River as far inland as Minneapolis, eighteen hundred miles from the ocean.

The World's Largest Lakes				
Lake	Location	Area (sq. mi.)	Depth (ft.)	Volume (cu. mi.)
Caspian Sea	Asia	143,200	3,363	18,900
Superior	N. America	31,700	1,330	2,916
Victoria	Africa	26,828	270	637
Huron	N. America	23,000	220	827
Michigan	N. America	22,300	750	1,161
Tanganyika	Africa	12,700	4,823	4,659
Baikal	Asia	12,162	5,315	5,520
Great Bear	N. America	12,096	1,463	529
Nyasa	Africa	11,150	2,280	2,009

Other continents also have important freshwater lakes. Lake Titicaca, high in the Andes Mountains, is the largest lake in South America (by volume) and the highest navigable lake in the world. Africa's Lake Chad has been the heart of great empires in central Africa. In east Africa is Lake Victoria, the largest lake on the continent (by area) and the second largest freshwater lake in the world.

Lake Baikal

Lake Baikal, located in Asia, is both the deepest lake and the largest freshwater lake (by volume). More than a mile deep, it holds almost as much fresh water as all of the Great Lakes combined, although its surface area is relatively small.

The Caspian Sea, also in Asia, is the world's largest lake (by both area and volume). Unlike Lake Superior, however, its water is salty. While the water in freshwater lakes is kept clean by rivers or other outlets that carry dissolved minerals downstream, a few drainage basins of the world have no outlet to the ocean. Water collects at the lowest spot, called a depression. The Caspian Sea is actually below sea level. As the water evaporates, minerals are left behind. Though rare, such salt lakes are often large and famous. For example, the Dead Sea, which is nearly 37 percent salt, is the saltiest lake in the world. (Utah's Great Salt Lake is 10–25 percent salt, and ocean water is typically 3 percent salt.)

Seas

Seas are arms of the ocean partially enclosed by land. Seas can vary greatly in size, and some even have seas within seas. For example, a map of the Mediterranean Sea reveals seven arms in the north that ancient peoples called the "seven seas." The Greek and Roman civilizations arose along their shores. Sailors prefer carrying people and goods on the smaller seas because they normally have smaller waves. The shores blunt the blows of the violent storms that batter ships on the "open" seas, such as the Mediterranean.

Ships need safe places to anchor while they load and unload their cargo. A sheltered body of deep water next to the shore is called a harbor. Good harbors are rare. The water must be deep enough that the ships do not run aground. The shore must encircle enough of the sea to shelter ships from winds and waves that might otherwise drive them into the rocks or sand. A key to the success of America's original colonies was their harbors. Boston, New York, Philadelphia, and Charleston quickly became major port cities because of their great harbors.

The World's Largest Seas		
Sea	**Location**	**Area (sq. mi.)**
Philippine Sea	Pacific Ocean	2,700,000
Coral Sea	Pacific Ocean	1,850,000
Arabian Sea	Indian Ocean	1,492,000
South China Sea	Pacific Ocean	1,148,000
Weddell Sea	Atlantic Ocean	1,080,000
Caribbean Sea	Atlantic Ocean	971,000
Mediterranean Sea	Atlantic Ocean	969,100
Tasman Sea	Pacific Ocean	900,000
Bering Sea	Pacific Ocean	873,000
Bay of Bengal	Indian Ocean	839,000

Charleston Harbor is one of the many good harbors along the U.S. east coast.

Wetlands

Areas of stagnant water—often referred to as bogs, swamps, moors, fens, muskegs, or marshes—are collectively known as *wetlands*. They are not actually bodies of water, but neither are they dry land. Wetlands most often form in lowland areas near coasts, rivers, and lakes, where water cannot drain away. Water saturates the ground of these areas and often collects to form murky pools a few inches deep. Wetlands are often at sea level.

Wetlands are categorized into three basic divisions according to their appearance and vegetation. Bogs are spongy areas that look dry but are covered with wet organic materials.

These soggy lands may have formed on top of old lakes, and a layer of water may remain below the surface. Mosses commonly grow in bogs, but few other plants survive. The mosses may collect and form a thick layer of dead organic matter called peat, which in some areas of the world is cut, dried, and burned for fuel.

A marsh has visible standing water, and the main kinds of vegetation growing there are grasses and small water plants that survive with their roots submerged. The Florida Everglades is a very large marsh.

Like marshes, swamps are covered by standing water. The basic difference is that swamps are dominated by large trees whereas marshes are not. Cypress, mangrove, and willow trees grow in swamps with their roots

reaching down through the mire. Alligators, snakes, and other wild animals make swamps and marshes mysterious and somewhat scary places.

Unusual forms of plant life thrive in wetlands, as do insects and water animals. Mosquitoes, which reproduce abundantly in standing water, have been such a menace, because of the diseases they carry, that people have tried to drain many wetland areas. (Malaria and West Nile disease are but two such diseases.)

In recent years, however, governments have been declaring many of the remaining wetlands protected areas because of their scenic beauty and endangered plant and animal species. Wetlands aid in flood control and water storage. They also are believed to serve as the nursery for much of the world's food chain, and they filter pollution from the water.

Section Quiz

1. What are the two main reasons that water is important to human activity?

2–3. What four factors must one consider when comparing rivers?

4. Why are some large lakes salty?

5–6. Define *sea* and *harbor* and explain why they are important to trade.

★ Why did many major cities develop along rivers?

Pangaea

By putting the pieces of the earth together like a jigsaw puzzle, especially when the continental shelf is included, it is easy to see how all of the continents could have originally been one huge landmass when God created the earth. The name *Pangaea* ("entire earth") is often used to describe this landmass. Some old-earth scientists speculate that the continents must have drifted over millions of years to their present positions. However, there is no evidence for millions of years. There is ample evidence for the Flood. The violent upheaval resulting in the shift of tectonic plates during the Flood would have been powerful enough to break apart the supercontinent and to set the continents in their present positions. This would have occurred over weeks and months rather than millions of years.

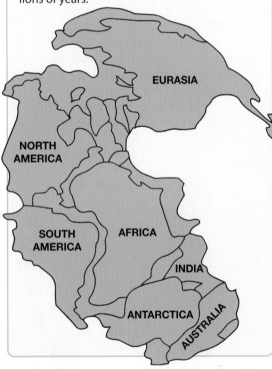

Evidence of the destructive power of the earth's internal forces was seen in an earthquake in New Zealand.

IV. The Earth's Surface-Changing Forces

The earth's surface is constantly changing. Since the Flood, two basic processes continue to shape the earth. Internal forces (earthquakes and volcanoes) push rocks up, and external forces (wind and water) break rocks down. Both forces help to shape the mountains and other landforms we see today.

Internal Forces

Earthquakes and volcanoes are evidences of powerful forces at work deep within the earth. These internal forces are not perfectly understood, but scientists have some clues. They have known for a long time that volcanoes and earthquakes are clustered along distinct lines on the earth's surface. Using sonar (a method of using underwater sound waves, or "echoes," to detect objects or waves), scientists discovered that these lines continue under the oceans. The ocean floor is scarred by lines of deep trenches and high ridges.

Plate Tectonics

Basing their conclusions on this evidence, scientists proposed that the crust is broken into pieces called plates. According to the **plate tectonics** (tek TAHN iks) **theory**, the plates crash into and pull apart from one another, releasing energy from the earth's interior and causing earthquakes and volcanoes. As previously discussed, this may, in part, explain how God brought about the Flood. Those plates continue to move today, resulting in earth tremors and earthquakes.

One of the most noticeable evidences of tectonic activity is faulting. **Faults** are deep cracks in the earth's surface where two pieces of land have moved in different directions. Although the movement is rarely more than a few inches, it can devastate life and property. The greatest land displacement ever recorded—nearly fifty feet—took place during the Alaska earthquake of 1964. Faulting is of two types: *strike-slip* and *normal*, both of which are illustrated here.

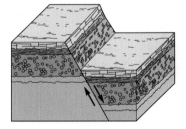

Strike-slip   Normal

The other notable evidence of tectonic activity is folding. Just as a piece of paper will bend when you push the edges toward the center, so unconsolidated sediment can bend upward into a fold when it is pushed from both sides.

Many mountains seem to have been formed by faulting

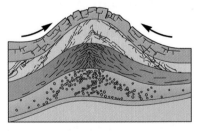

Fold

and folding during or soon after the Flood. The Sierra Nevada of the western United States offers a classic example of *fault mountains*.

Folding is evident in the Himalayas, the Rockies, and the Alps, but some of the best examples of *fold mountains* are in the Appalachians. Both fault mountains and fold mountains are called *deformational mountains* because tectonic forces seem to have "deformed" the rocks that were already on the surface.

Volcanic Forces

Another mountain-building force still active today is volcanoes. Volcanoes deposit new lava on the earth's surface, and it hardens into *depositional mountains*. In Mexico in 1943, the fourteen-hundred-foot volcano Paricutín (pah REE koo TEEN) formed in a farmer's cornfield. Similarly, in 1963, a mountain rose from the sea near Iceland, creating the island of Surtsey. It now stands five hundred feet above sea level and is a mile long. The world's largest active volcano is Mauna Loa, on the island of Hawaii. The island is the tip of a massive volcano that rises 33,476 feet from the sea floor—higher than Mount Everest!

External Forces

Landforms do not remain the same. External forces called weathering and erosion wear away the landforms that internal forces have pushed up.

Weathering

Although rock might seem solid and unmoving, it is constantly weakened by the action of **weathering**, the breakdown of rocks by water, plant roots, temperature changes, and the formation of ice and mineral crystals.

Some kinds of rocks break down more easily than others. Rocks with layers are easily separated. Others shatter under extreme temperature changes. When water collects in pores and freezes, it expands, and the rock breaks. When plants take root and grow, the roots exert tremendous pressure, causing more disintegration. Natural acids (from rain, plants, and decaying matter) can dissolve some rocks.

Weathering is crucial to life on the earth because it enriches the soil, the thin layer of the earth's surface where plants grow. Weathering produces particles of sand, silt, and clay (called sediment) that mix with **humus** (decayed formerly living matter) to form soil. Farmers carefully study their soils to find out which of them, combined with fertilizers, will be most productive.

Erosion

After weathering breaks down rock into small pieces, those materials are removed by the following forms of **erosion**.

Wind erosion is strongest in dry areas, particularly deserts. The abrasive action of tiny particles of sand blown by the wind can, over time, do great damage to landforms. The loss of soil through winds can also be destructive to farmers. For example, windstorms ruined American farmers throughout the Great Plains during the Dust Bowl of the 1930s. "Black blizzards" of choking dust darkened the skies as far away as New York.

Thor's Hammer at Bryce Canyon, Utah, is an example of a weathered pillar.

Tides eroded this sea stack.

Wave erosion alters the seashore, creating sea caves, sea stacks, and sea arches. Waves also deposit sand offshore, making sandbars or whole islands. That is how many of the popular barrier islands along the North American coast were formed.

Briksdal glacier in Norway

Glacial erosion occurs when **glaciers**, large masses of moving ice and snow, flow downhill under the pull of gravity. Like gigantic bulldozers, glaciers push and scrape the earth in their paths. When glaciers receded to their current locations, they left behind hills of debris known as *terminal moraines*. Two famous moraines extend across the entire length of Long Island, New York.

Running water, however, is the most powerful force of erosion. It quickly flows through soil and soft rocks, carrying away materials as it goes. During floods, water can carve deep gullies very quickly. But water's slow action over years can be just as devastating. Farmers are constantly battling to keep water from eroding their *topsoil* through normal runoff.

Running water can erode vast amounts of fertile soil, depriving an area of valuable nutrients and leaving ugly ditches.

Section Quiz

1. What evidence supports the plate tectonics theory?
2. What are the two most notable types of tectonic activity?
3. What is the difference between weathering and erosion?
4. List four forces that cause erosion.
5. What does weathering produce that is essential for life on earth?
★ How can people reduce or control harmful weathering and erosion?

V. The Earth's Climate

Before God created the sea and dry land, He created light and the atmosphere, both of which are essential to life on earth. Light is the "fuel" that drives the earth's "engine." It supplies energy for plants to grow and warms the sea and the land. The atmosphere is a blanket of air around the earth. It is part of the earth's "heating and ventilation system" that distributes thermal energy to the remote corners of the globe and draws ocean water back up to the mountaintops.

Thermal Energy in Motion

Without the constant movement of thermal energy and water, the continents would become dust, the equator would be an inferno, and the polar oceans would be ice. Thankfully, God has designed three main systems to distribute thermal energy over the earth: seasons, winds, and ocean currents. They enable the earth to avoid such extremes.

Seasons

The sun is the source of nearly all of the thermal energy that warms the earth. The most obvious evidence of the sun's influence is in the seasons. The United States has four seasons, but some places have other kinds of seasons. Near the equator, where the air is always warm, for example, two seasons are evident: rainy and dry. Near the poles, where the air is always cold, the major seasonal change is six months of constant darkness, followed by six months of a "midnight sun." All of these changes can be considered seasons.

Seasons are caused by the slant of sunlight and the tilt of the earth's axis. These factors explain why different latitudes have different seasons. There are three distinct *latitude zones*. The **low latitudes** lie between the equator (0°) and the Tropic of Cancer (in the Northern Hemisphere) and the Tropic of Capricorn (in the Southern Hemisphere). Because the sunlight is always direct, or nearly so, this zone consistently has very warm temperatures. It is usually called the **tropics**.

In the **middle latitudes** (between the Tropic of Cancer and the Arctic Ocean in the Northern Hemisphere and between the Tropic of Capricorn and the Antarctic Circle in the Southern Hemisphere), the sunlight is nearly direct half of each year, creating seasonal changes from warm summers to cool winters. Because these regions have neither the constant warmth of the tropics nor the extreme cold of the poles, they are called the **Temperate Zone**.

During the long winter nights in the **high latitudes** (between the Arctic Circle and the North Pole in the Northern Hemisphere and between the Antarctic Circle and the South Pole in the Southern Hemisphere), sunlight is always either very slanted or nonexistent. These **polar regions** receive only a small amount of sunlight in winter.

Climate Change

Various theories of global warming are popular today. Some predict dire consequences if certain emissions are not drastically reduced. Others look to "green" technology to minimize humankind's damage to the earth caused by burning fossil fuels. Christians should be concerned about responsibly exercising dominion over the earth. However, this is a complex issue, and good people will differ as to what should be done. When evaluating the concerns expressed about climate change, you should consider several questions. Is global warming caused by humans? If gradual warming of the earth is a reality, is that a bad thing, or are there positive aspects to such warming? What groups are behind the calls for increased government regulation, carbon credits, and other actions designed to mitigate climate change? What are their motives? Christians should seek wisdom from God and His Word when answering these questions and drawing conclusions about possible climate change.

Latitude Zones

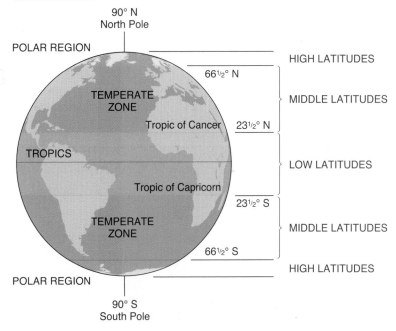

**North Pole in Winter
December 21**

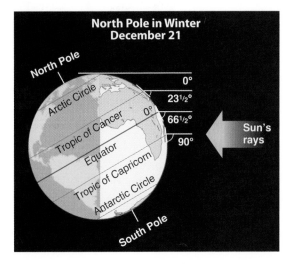

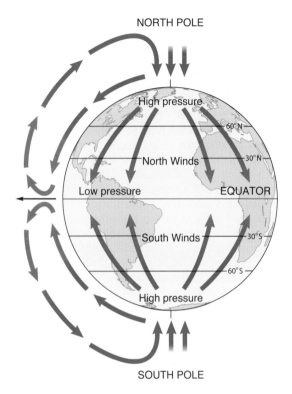

NORTH POLE

High pressure

60° N

North Winds   30° N

Low pressure   **EQUATOR**

South Winds   30° S

60° S

High pressure

SOUTH POLE

Warm and cold air masses

Winds

The sun's energy is always in motion, even after it reaches the earth's atmosphere. The air carries thermal energy between and within latitude zones. What we call *wind* is basically the movement of air caused by the heating and cooling of air masses.

Warm and Cold Air Masses—A large area of moving air with a similar temperature is called an air mass. Warm air masses are warmer than the surface of the earth over which they move; cold air masses are cooler than the surface.

Warm and cold air masses move over the earth in regular patterns. A permanent warm air mass sits over the tropics, where the rays of the sun are direct. At the same time, a cold air mass sits over the polar regions. Warm air is constantly rising at the equator and moving toward the cold polar regions. As the air cools over the poles, it falls and moves back toward the equator. If the sun were the only factor affecting the circulation of air, surface winds in the United States would always blow to the south, and winds in South America would blow to the north.

In reality, however, a large portion of the tropical air mass loses its thermal energy and falls *before* it reaches the poles. The air drops in the middle latitudes near 30°. Some of the air moves back toward the poles. As the air travels along the surface, it hits frigid air from the poles at about 60° latitude and rises again. Some of this air continues its journey until it finally reaches the frigid poles, where the air drops a second time. The polar air begins moving back toward the equator. As a result of this cycle, the earth has *three* moving cells of air from the equator to the poles.

Hurricanes are caused by rapid heating and cooling of air in the tropics.

Coriolis Effect—Few winds blow strictly north or south. The rotation of the earth greatly influences wind direction in something known as the **Coriolis effect**. This phenomenon is somewhat difficult to visualize. You do not feel the earth rotating, but it is moving quite rapidly (about one thousand miles per hour at the equator and five hundred miles per hour at 30° latitude). The rotation yanks the land out from under the wind. The wind continues to flow straight, but the land beneath it veers away.

Jet Streams

Jet streams occur where temperate air meets air of more extreme temperature—either cold polar air or warm tropical air. Meteorologists use the jet streams in predicting weather, and scientists are trying to better understand the effect that jet streams have on weather. For example, winter jet streams looping down from Canada pull Arctic air as far south as Texas.

Jet streams were discovered during World War II when B-29 Superfortress pilots discovered that they were reaching—and overshooting—their bomb targets earlier than they had calculated. When possible, modern-day pilots flying from west to east take advantage of the jet stream to increase speeds by up to three hundred miles per hour, thereby saving both fuel and time. Because the jet stream does not flow in a straight line, however, they cannot use it for any great distance. Also, pilots flying from east to west must avoid the jet stream or it will slow them down.

Wind Belts—The movement of warm and cold air masses, combined with the Coriolis effect, explains the basic movement of thermal energy around the earth. Winds flow in three belts that circle the globe. These belts influence the world's climate and have also influenced the exploration and conquest of the world.

The hot tropics have the most powerful prevailing winds. Tropical islands are famous for the constant warm winds, called trade winds, that blow over the beaches. (The word *trade* once meant "a regular path.") Columbus used these steady winds to carry his ships west to the New World. European sailors called them the "northeast trades." (They named winds after the direction *from which they came*, not the direction they were going.)

The prevailing winds that blow over the middle latitudes are called the **westerlies**. They are important because they bring warm air from the tropics to lands far to the north, such as Europe. Less powerful than the trade winds, westerlies still helped Columbus and other explorers sail back east to Europe from the New World.

Ocean Currents

Like the atmosphere, the ocean absorbs thermal energy from the sun. Because water holds thermal energy much longer than air does, the oceans are even more predictable than the wind in distributing thermal energy. Temperature differences create warm and cold ocean currents that circle the globe, following a pattern similar to the prevailing winds. Water is heated near the equator and moves toward the poles. Cold water from the poles sinks and returns to the equator. The presence of continents causes the most obvious variations between these ocean currents.

The prevailing winds help to propel surface currents. But ocean currents move more slowly than winds. The normal speed is less than ten miles per hour. The slowest currents are called *drifts*. In some cases, however, currents may move very fast. For example, the Gulf Stream, which begins in the Gulf of Mexico, flows beyond Florida, up the U.S. Atlantic coast, and to the northeast of the British Isles near the polar region, where it finally weakens and becomes the North Atlantic Drift.

The currents flow in circular patterns. That constant circulation of thermal energy in the oceans keeps tropical water from becoming too warm for sea life, and it keeps polar water from freezing solid.

Ocean currents also influence the amount of rain that enters the air and falls on the continents. Cold air contains less moisture than warm air does. Therefore, the coast of Chile is a barren desert because the cold Peru Current flows nearby, but Brazil's coast is a tropical rain forest, supplied by the warm Brazil Current.

Section Quiz

1. What causes wind?
2. How does the Coriolis effect change the direction of wind?
3. Where do jet streams occur?
* Contrast the role of wind and ocean currents in distributing thermal energy.

Water in Motion

Mount Waialeale in Hawaii receives almost *forty feet* of rain annually. In contrast, no record of rain exists for the Empty Quarter (Rub Al Khali) of the Arabian Peninsula. Few places ever see anything near these extremes because the same systems that distribute thermal energy over the land also help to distribute life-giving water.

The Hydrologic Cycle

Water appears in three forms: solid (ice), liquid, and gas (water vapor). Ocean water must change form before it reaches plants and animals on land. This change begins as ocean water absorbs thermal energy. When the liquid water absorbs enough thermal energy, it changes into water vapor in a process called evaporation. When water vapor loses thermal energy, it changes back to a liquid, suspended in clouds as water droplets, in a process called condensation.

Warm winds carry water vapor into the interior of the continents. Warm air can hold a lot of water vapor, or **humidity**, because the molecules are very active. This humidity is not useful, however, until it returns to the earth's surface. The point at which water vapor begins condensation is called the **dew point**. When the temperature

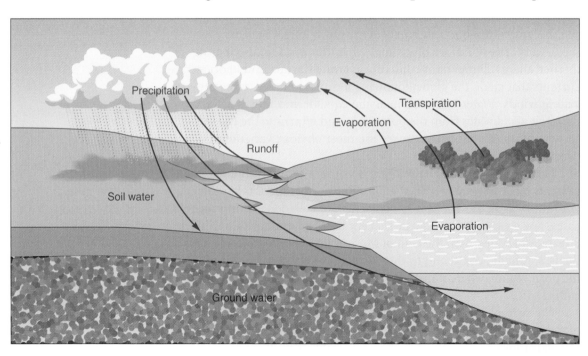

Hydrologic cycle

drops, the water vapor loses energy, condensation occurs, and water falls to the earth in a process called **precipitation.**

Most precipitation is in the form of rain, but water also can fall in solid form. A sudden drop in temperature causes water vapor to freeze, lose energy, and fall to the earth as snow, sleet, or hail. The process of evaporation, condensation, and precipitation is called the **hydrologic cycle**. The Lord designed it to replenish the soil, lakes, and rivers with water.

About 80 percent of precipitation occurs over the oceans, but the rest falls on land. The water stays on the earth's surface, however, for only a brief time. Some runs off into rivers or lakes. Some seeps through the soil to become **ground water**. (Ground water is like a slow-moving river under the ground.) Eventually, however, all water returns to the oceans or evaporates, completing the cycle.

Causes of Precipitation

Three situations cause a humid air mass to cool and produce precipitation. One of them is the presence of mountains. When a warm mass of humid air passes over a mountainous area, the air moves upward and cools rapidly. Water vapor condenses into droplets, clouds form, and precipitation quickly follows. Because mountains are often bitterly cold, snow and sleet are common. This precipitation is said to be **orographic** (*oros*, "mountain," and *–graph*, "description").

Orographic precipitation is common in mountain ranges close to the ocean or big lakes. Large amounts of water enter the air, and prevailing winds drive the water vapor over the mountains. The land beyond the mountains, an area called the **rainshadow**, is usually very dry because little water vapor survives passage over the mountains.

Another important cause of precipitation is the meeting of cold and warm air masses. The warmer air is lighter, so it rises above the cooler, denser air as if it were moving over a mountain range. Rain or snow falls along the line where the two air masses meet. The line is called a **front**. For precipitation to occur, the warm air mass must have water vapor that it picked up over an ocean or large lake. Frontal precipitation is common in the eastern United States, where warm air masses move in over the Gulf of Mexico and the Great Lakes.

A third cause of precipitation is **convection**, the rise of warm air over a hot surface. In the heart of continents, the land cools at night and then heats up rapidly under the summer sun. The hot air is sometimes trapped beneath a cool air mass. When the warm, light air breaks through the cool air above, it rushes upward and cools quickly. Precipitation falls immediately and often violently. Lightning and hail may accompany such storms.

Situations that create precipitation

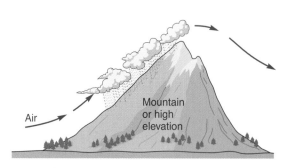

Orographic Precipitation

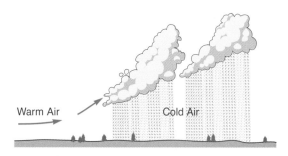

Frontal Precipitation

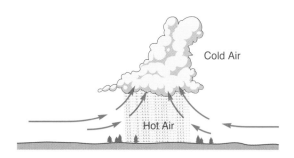

Convection Precipitation

Section Quiz

1. What is the difference between condensation and precipitation?
2. Explain how the dew point is related to precipitation.
3. Describe the hydrologic cycle.
4. What are the three main situations that contribute to precipitation? Which is most obvious on a map?
☆ Both sides of mountains on the East Coast of the United States are wet, but the mountains in California are wet on the west side and dry on the east side. Why?

LET'S GO EXPLORING

Climates of the World

1. For each type of climate, give the continent where it appears most.
2. What is the most common climate at the equator?
3. What is the most common climate at the Arctic Circle?
4. Where is a humid subtropical climate most common, on the east coast or on the west coast of continents?
★ Why do deserts almost never occur on the equator?

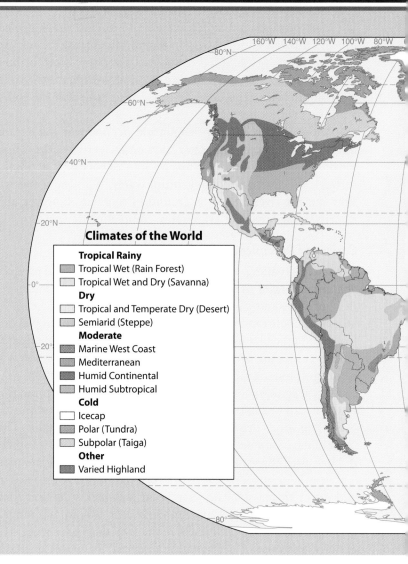

Climates of the World

Tropical Rainy
- Tropical Wet (Rain Forest)
- Tropical Wet and Dry (Savanna)

Dry
- Tropical and Temperate Dry (Desert)
- Semiarid (Steppe)

Moderate
- Marine West Coast
- Mediterranean
- Humid Continental
- Humid Subtropical

Cold
- Icecap
- Polar (Tundra)
- Subpolar (Taiga)

Other
- Varied Highland

Climates

The amount of thermal energy and water that reaches each region of the world determines its basic **climate**—the typical weather in a region over a long period of time. **Weather**, on the other hand, is the atmospheric conditions of a location at a specific moment in time. Weather often changes, but climate, with only slight occasional variations, remains generally the same.

Daily changes in weather seldom determine what lives in a region or whether it is a good place for humans. Even a year of record lows or highs in temperature or rainfall does not make much of a difference. There are five broad categories of world climate. This classification system will be used on the climate maps and in the text throughout the rest of your textbook.

Tropical Rainy

Two climates occur in the warm tropics, where the rainfall is extremely heavy. Trees grow in the *tropical wet* areas, where rain falls all year (averaging ten inches per month). Grasses predominate in the *tropical wet and dry* areas. With only about half an inch of rain during the winter months, few trees can survive the dry season.

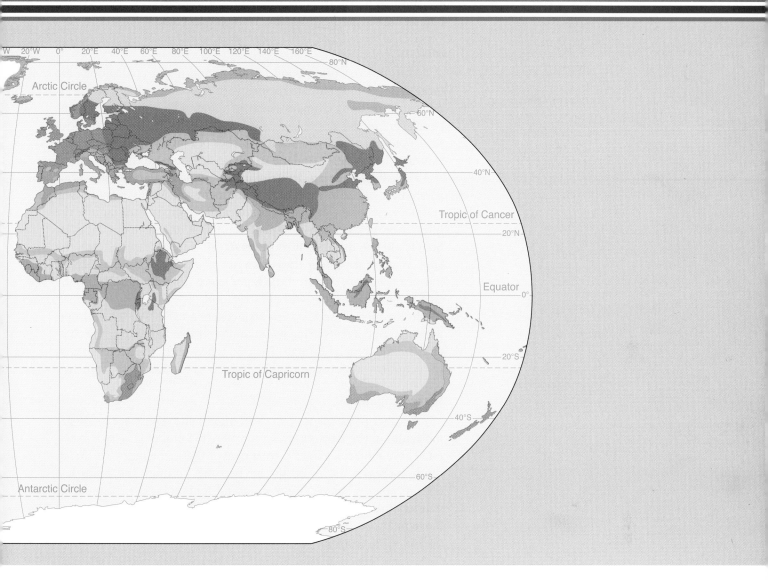

Dry

In *deserts*, annual precipitation is ten inches or less. Lack of water, not high temperatures, creates deserts. Deserts are often called **arid**, which means "lacking moisture." Deserts can occur at any latitude, cold or hot. The ice-covered interior of Greenland is technically a desert!

Semiarid regions receive a few more inches of rainfall than deserts and therefore can support grasses. Pioneers once called the Great Plains of the United States the "Great American Desert," but large parts of it are actually semiarid grassland, where wheat and other grains now grow.

Cold

Some regions receive sufficient rainfall but are too cold to support many kinds of plants. For example, nothing grows on the world's two *ice caps* in Antarctica and Greenland, which have a thick layer of ice that never melts. Although *polar regions* are cold year-round, plants grow for a brief period in the middle of the summer, when some of the snow cover melts. *Subpolar regions* are not as severe in the summer, permitting hardy evergreen trees to grow. Winters are bitterly cold in all three regions, averaging less than 0°F (−18°C).

Moderate

Most of the world's good farmland and major civilizations are located in the four climate regions with moderate rainfall and temperatures. All four climates occur in the middle latitudes, or Temperate (moderate) Zone. *Humid subtropical* refers to lands just above the tropics that receive about fifty inches of rain a year, mostly in the summer. The richest farmland in the world is located there.

The other three moderate climates are named after the regions where they occur in Europe: the continent, the Mediterranean Sea, and the west coast. The *humid continental* region extends far into the interior of the Eurasian continent. Rainfall is adequate but irregular because of the distance it must travel from the ocean to reach the land. Winters are colder there than in any other moderate region. In the *mediterranean* climate, little water falls during the summer, so the land supports few crops without irrigation.

In the *marine west coast*, which covers most of Western Europe, warm ocean currents bring warm, moist air that blows over the coast and provides regular rainfall. The rain is heavier in the winter than in the summer—about six inches per month in contrast to three inches.

Varied Highland

Another principle is at work in mountains. There are many gas molecules in the air near sea level, where the pull of gravity is greatest. These molecules hold a great deal of thermal energy. As the altitude increases, however, the air becomes thinner and holds less thermal energy. For every one-thousand-foot increase in altitude, the temperature drops about 3½°F. This drop is called the **lapse rate**. If the temperature at sea level is 65°F, one can expect it to be 30°F at the peak of a ten-thousand-foot mountain.

Mt. McKinley, in the Denali National Park in Alaska, rises more than 20,000 feet and is the highest mountain peak in North America.

VI. The Earth's Vegetation

The type of plants, or **vegetation**, that grows in each region depends on the climate. If you compare the vegetation and climate maps, you will see that the regions are similar. Differences between the two maps are caused by local variations in soil, mountains, and rivers.

A vegetation map also indicates the types of animals that live in a region because animals in a region depend on certain types of plants for food. For example, one would expect to find koalas only in areas where there are eucalyptus trees—the koalas' only food. A **biome** is any large region where distinct populations of plants and animals are found living together. Biomes influence how people make a living, what they eat, and even what their homes look like. The unique characteristics of each biome help to explain why human cultures are so different.

Three basic biomes exist—forests, grasslands, and wastelands—and within each are many variations.

Caribbean Rainforest in Basse Terre, Guadeloupe; French Antilles

Forests

Wherever trees are the predominant plants, the region is called a *forest*. Because trees require a large amount of water, most forests are found in rainy climates.

Tropical Rain Forest

Tropical rain forests are found in the tropics, where many kinds of trees and animals proliferate. Teak, mahogany, and ebony are a few of the giant trees found there. The branches and leaves spread out to form a large canopy more than one hundred feet above the forest floor. The trees protect the thin soil from being washed away by the heavy rains. The forests are good for logging but not for farms. Native people who live in rain forests often build tree houses or temporary leaf huts.

Shrub Forest

Shrub forests occur in the mild mediterranean climate, where the dry summers do not provide enough rain for trees to reach great

Thick brush is typical of shrub forests or chaparral.

LET'S GO EXPLORING

Vegetation of the World

1. Compare the coniferous forests on this map with the climate map (pp. 46–47). In which climate are they most common?
2. Compare the deciduous forests on this map with the climate map. In which climates are they common?
* Compare the rain forests on this map with the rainy wet climate on the climate map. Explain the differences.

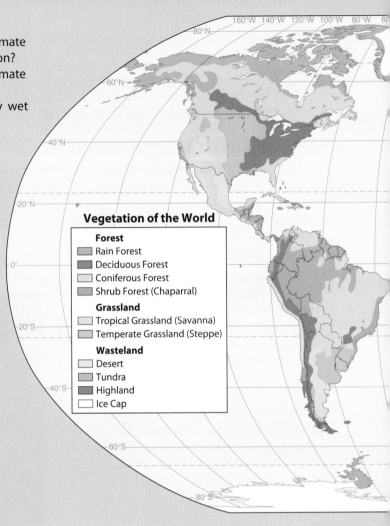

Vegetation of the World

Forest
- Rain Forest
- Deciduous Forest
- Coniferous Forest
- Shrub Forest (Chaparral)

Grassland
- Tropical Grassland (Savanna)
- Temperate Grassland (Steppe)

Wasteland
- Desert
- Tundra
- Highland
- Ice Cap

Coniferous forest in Colorado

heights. Gnarled trees are widely scattered. Dense bushes, or shrubs, are common. This biome is sometimes called *woodlands* or *chaparral* (Spanish, "dense thicket").

Coniferous Forest

Conifers (KAHN uh furz) are trees that produce their seeds in a cone. Coniferous forests grow in the cold, harsh subpolar climates where most other trees cannot survive. Water does not evaporate as quickly from their needle leaves as it does from broad leaves. Nearly all needle-leaf trees stay green throughout the year and are known as evergreens. Pines and firs are among the best known evergreens.

Wood from conifers is useful for pulp in paper and for construction, but it contains too much resin to be good firewood. Limited coniferous forests are found in warm, rainy climates near the coast where the soil is poor. Examples

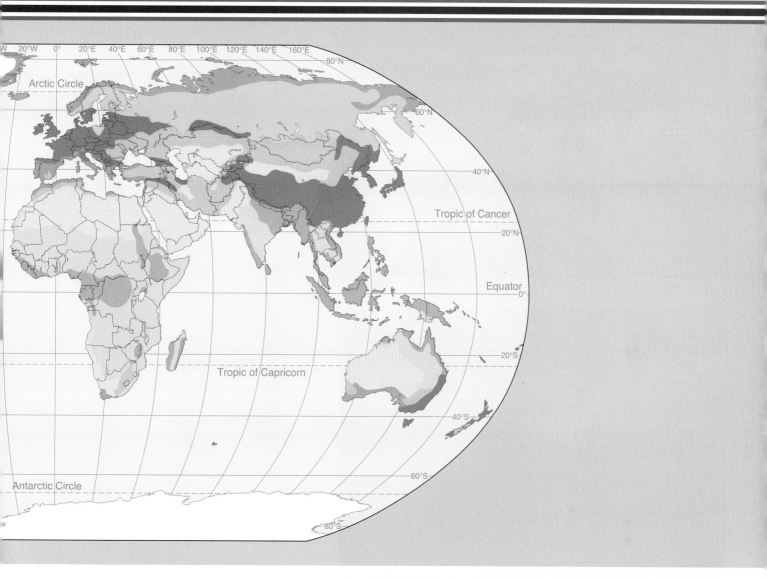

include the giant redwoods of California and the pine forests in Florida.

Deciduous Forest

Some trees, called **deciduous** (dih SIJ oo us), lose their leaves during a particular season of the year. Most deciduous trees have flat, broad leaves and require a great deal of water and a growing season of at least four months. (The growing season is the time between the last killing frost of spring and the first killing frost of fall.) Common broadleaf, deciduous trees include maple, oak, and elm. These, too, are used to make wood pulp for paper, and they are also good for heating and the making of furniture.

Many great civilizations developed near deciduous forests. The people there used the hardwoods to build houses, furniture, forts, and ships. Once settlers cleared the forest, the soil proved very fertile. Many areas that were once

Deciduous forest

Savanna in Kenya

These steppes in Inner Mongolia are similar to the high plains of South Dakota.

Saguaro cacti near Tuscon, Arizona

marked "deciduous forests" on maps are now farms or cities.

Grasslands

Many tropical and temperate regions lack sufficient rainfall to support forests. They might have a substantial rainy season, but a prolonged dry season follows. Although trees can grow under such conditions, they are scattered, mostly near creeks and rivers. Grasses, on the other hand, grow quickly and produce seeds before the dry season comes. Because grasses are so common in these regions, they are called **grasslands**. With little wood available, people in the grasslands often build grass huts, sod houses, or animal-skin tents.

Tropical Grassland

Tropical grasslands, or **savannas**, are natural "parks" with open areas and only a few scattered trees. Some grasses grow ten feet high in the rainy season, but the scorching sun soon withers the grass and makes it highly susceptible to fire. African savannas teem with wildebeests, elephants, giraffes, and lions.

Temperate Grassland

Temperate grasslands, often called **steppes**, are found in temperate regions where rainfall is between ten and thirty inches per year. The soil is extremely fertile, but farmers need steel plows to cut the hard ground, and their crops sometimes need to be irrigated. In North America the fertile grasslands are called prairies.

Wastelands

Some areas, called **wastelands**, are barren most of the year because of low amounts of precipitation. Whenever rain does fall or snow melts, however, the wastelands become a colorful sea of blooming life. The two types of wastelands are deserts and tundra. The people who live there, such as Aborigines (Australia) and Eskimos (Alaska), developed special survival skills as hunters and herders.

Desert

Two kinds of plants grow in deserts. Cacti conserve water efficiently and are the most common of the succulent plants that store water in their stems and leaves. Other kinds of plants come to life quickly, produce seeds, and die in the brief period following each rain shower. A surprising variety of animals, such as the Gila monster and the kangaroo rat, can survive in this extreme biome. With wise management and sufficient irrigation, even deserts can be transformed into productive land, as was the case in many parts of Israel in the last century.

Tundra

The cold regions near the poles are called **tundra** and support only limited vegetation. Precipitation, mainly as snow, is minimal, but it covers the ground most of the year. During the short summer, only the top three feet of the soil thaws, and shallow-rooted plants (mosses, lichens, and grasses) grow in the soggy soil. Melting snow does not evaporate quickly but collects in mosquito-infested bogs and lakes. When winter comes, the water freezes, and a white blanket of snow returns. The rest of the soil is **permafrost**, which remains frozen year-round. Not even coniferous trees can grow in the tundra.

Herds of caribou and reindeer migrate to the tundra during the summer. Only a few hardy animals—such as musk oxen, hares, and wolves—remain year-round.

Alpine tundra in the Rocky Mountains, during the fall season when the bushes turn bright red

Highland Vegetation

Many kinds of vegetation grow on mountains. In fact, it is possible to see all of the major biomes on one mountain because higher altitudes have lower temperatures (the lapse rate) and because air masses passing over the mountain drop their moisture (orographic precipitation).

Our Place in the World's Biomes

God created the world's biomes to supply man's need for food, clothing, and shelter. After the Flood, Noah's descendants encountered completely new biomes, which emerged as the animals on the ark replenished the earth. Those biomes apparently went through many changes during an ice age. Some animals adapted to the cold climate, while others migrated to warmer regions.

Mankind altered biomes, too, as he attempted to fulfill the Creation Mandate and make the earth more productive by irrigating fields, domesticating animals, draining swamps, terracing steep hillsides, and constructing dams. Unfortunately, fallen humanity has not always been a good steward of God's creation and has often had a severe impact on the environment. When merchants transport seeds to other lands, for instance, they run the risk of introducing new weeds, diseases, and harmful insects. As native plants and animals compete with foreign "invaders," only the hardiest species survive. By the end of the twentieth century, the world's vegetation had become increasingly uniform, or *homogenized*.

Modern nations have debated the effects of human activity on the world's climate and vegetation. In 1992 the United Nations held a historic Earth Summit in Rio de Janeiro, Brazil, to discuss the global environment. The key term in the UN's discussions was *sustainable development*, the ability to meet present needs without depleting the resources to support future generations. In 2012 the UN sponsored a

Commuter train in Stuttgart, Germany

second summit in Rio de Janeiro and continued to focus on sustainable development.

Christians recognize that as stewards of God's world, humans are responsible for using the world's resources wisely. But Christians also need to be wise about the solutions they pursue. Sometimes zealously pursued solutions do more damage to the creation, including God's image-bearers, than the problem they were meant to fix. Nevertheless, Christians should not simply dismiss concerns scientists raise about the effects that human development has on the earth. Christians with gifts and callings in the area of environmental science should pursue viable solutions to the problems of our groaning creation.

Section Quiz

1. What are the three basic biomes?
2. Contrast coniferous and deciduous forests.
3. What are the two types of grasslands?
4. Why is tundra considered a wasteland?
* Should Christians strive for sustainable development? Why or why not?

Chapter Review

Making Connections

1. What two formative events in the earth's history occurred only once and will never occur again? How do those events contradict uniformitarianism?
2. What is tectonic activity, and what are its two most notable types?
3. How do weathering and erosion work together to shape the earth's surface?
4. What causes air masses to rise or fall?
5. What is the basic cause of all precipitation? Under what three conditions does precipitation usually occur?

Developing Geography Skills

1. What evidence contradicts the theory of neocatastrophism?
2. What major landforms are in your area?
3. What kind of natural vegetation is most common near your home and why?

Thinking Critically

1. What was the impact of the Flood on the surface of the earth? Illustrate your answer with examples.
2. Develop a position on climate change and support your position.

Living in God's World

1. What would you say to a friend who says that Christians should not be concerned about the environment because only spiritual things really matter and God is going to burn up the earth one day anyway? Be sure to use Scripture in your answer.
2. How would you respond to a friend who claimed that working to save the environment is just as much a part of the Christian mission as seeking to save souls because God intends to save both in the end? Use Scripture in your answer.

People, Places, and Things to Know

cataclysm
uniformitarianism
neocatastrophists
atmosphere
lithosphere
hydrosphere
crust
mantle
continents
islands
continental islands
oceanic islands
landform
mountain range
plains
alluvium
plateaus
world ocean
tributaries
river system
drainage basin
seas
plate tectonics theory
faults
weathering
humus
erosion
glaciers
low latitudes
tropics
middle latitudes
Temperate Zone
high latitudes
polar regions
Coriolis effect
westerlies
humidity
dew point
precipitation
hydrologic cycle
ground water
orographic
rainshadow
front
convection
climate
weather
arid
lapse rate
vegetation
biome
conifers
deciduous
grasslands
savannas
steppes
wastelands
tundra
permafrost

Unit Two
THE WORLD AS MAN SUBDUES IT

4 Industry: Man's Use of God's Resources

5 Society: Human Interactions

God commanded humans to make full use of the earth as stewards of the great material wealth found in His good creation. God placed raw materials on the earth from which people have produced energy and precious as well as common goods. Mankind has yet to fully develop all of the resources that God has provided.

Steel wire being manufactured

4

INDUSTRY: MAN'S USE OF GOD'S RESOURCES

omputers get smaller and faster, farmers are able to grow more food and feed more people than ever before, and new techniques enable companies to mine natural resources that were previously inaccessible. As never before, people living today see the world transformed around them. This progress is what we should expect in a world in which God has given humans the abilities to subdue and make use of the creation. And yet there is much wrong with creation as well. Nations fight wars over natural resources, some countries promote or require abortions because of fears of overpopulation, and the personal computer combined with the Internet has unleashed a flood of pornography. One author says the world is like a child who contracts a serious illness. The child continues to grow and develop into an adult while at the same time the sickness continues to eat away at his body. Growth and decay occur together. The Christian looks forward to the day when Christ will return to fully and finally deal with the disease of sin. In the meantime, the believer can rejoice in the growth. It is an evidence of God's goodness despite human sin.

The word ***industry*** is often used to describe people's "hard work" to make a living. Although there are many types of jobs, or industries, the basic categories have been around since God made man to exercise dominion over His earth. The U.S. government has developed a system for classifying jobs. Every job can be classified under one of the categories in the chart titled "U.S. Employment by Industry." This chapter examines each category in turn and shows how industry contributes to the wealth of nations.

I. Primary Industries

All industries are primary, secondary, or tertiary. **Primary industries** are the most basic industries. They take from the earth materials that are needed for food, clothes, and shelter. Primary industries include agriculture, fishing, forestry, and mining.

One part of God's Creation Mandate to Adam was control over every animal and plant in the world. God intended for Adam to be His steward, or caretaker, of the environment that He had created. The Lord Himself planted the first garden, filling it with plants and foods for Adam and Eve's use. In addition to using the earth to meet basic needs, we should endeavor to make the earth both more productive and more beautiful. This requires us to be careful about how we treat the earth.

Agriculture

Contrary to an evolutionary view of human history, mankind did not take millions of years to figure out how to plant seeds and domesticate animals. God taught Adam to be a gardener, and his two sons specialized in the two major branches of agriculture: farming and animal husbandry. (Cain tilled the ground, and Abel kept sheep.)

Look closely at the world land-use map (pages 62–63). By comparing this map with the climate map in Chapter 3 (pages 46–47), you will see a clear correlation. First, notice that crops are raised in the moderate climates. Second, herds of

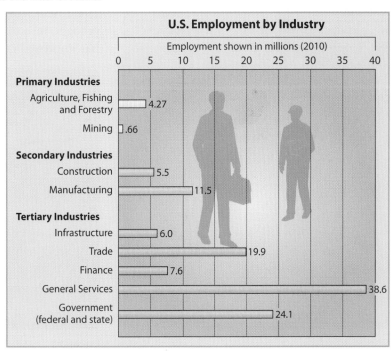

U.S. Employment by Industry

Employment shown in millions (2010)

Primary Industries	
Agriculture, Fishing and Forestry	4.27
Mining	.66
Secondary Industries	
Construction	5.5
Manufacturing	11.5
Tertiary Industries	
Infrastructure	6.0
Trade	19.9
Finance	7.6
General Services	38.6
Government (federal and state)	24.1

animals are raised in the semiarid climates. Third, little or no agriculture takes place in the two most extreme climates—the tropics and the Arctic—where widely scattered bands of people pursue *basic* activities, such as hunting, fishing, and gathering various foods. They must make good use of their marginal resources to eke out a meager living.

Farming

The first main branch of agriculture is farming. Throughout the ages, farming has supplied most of the earth's food. Planting seeds provides a much more reliable food supply than hunting wild animals and gathering wild fruits.

Subsistence farming

In the past, most farmers produced only enough food to meet the needs of their own households. They made their own clothes, furniture, and homes. Such farmers were **subsistence farmers**. Some of them raised a **cash crop**, such as rice or corn, to sell. But the money was barely enough to keep food on the table, and the household still made most of its own belongings. Billions of people in the world still live by subsistence farming.

At the end of the eighteenth century, an agricultural revolution took place in Great Britain and then spread to the United States. Farmers began applying science and machinery to increase their yields, enabling **commercial farmers** to raise large cash crops for profit and thereby freeing other people to pursue other types of work, such as manufacturing, and even cultural work, such as teaching, painting, and sculpting. Modern cities depend on the steady supply of food from commercial farms.

All farms, whether subsistence or commercial, face the same challenges; they differ only in scale. Drought, disease, and insect plagues can wipe out crops. Windstorms, hail, and floods can devastate fields. In many places, irrigation has reduced the threat of drought, insecticides have limited the threat of insects, and breeding has improved crop yields and resistance to disease. But one major

Commercial farming

Irrigation

problem remains: loss of soil. Wind and water can wash away soil and nutrients, and certain crops can deplete the soil's nutrients. As you study geography, notice how farmers in the various regions are dealing with these challenges.

Animal Husbandry

The second main form of agriculture is animal husbandry, which also can be subdivided into subsistence and commercial types. Subsistence husbandry, known as **nomadic herding**, is common in rugged mountains and dry areas where regular farming is difficult. Jabal, a descendant of Cain, became the "father of such as dwell in tents, and of such as have cattle" (Gen. 4:20). Because large herds of animals quickly consume the vegetation in an area, nomads must move frequently in search of fresh pastures.

Many nomads also became raiders and conquerors, famous for their toughness and skill with horses. Examples include the Huns of Central Asia, the Sioux of North America, and the Masai of East Africa. They often built their homes of animal skins stretched over wooden poles because these homes were portable and the raw materials were more readily available in the grasslands.

World's Largest Beef Producing Countries (2010)	
Country	**% of World's Beef**
1. United States	25
2. Brazil	20
3. European Union	17
4. China	12
5. Argentina	6
6. India	6
7. Australia	4
8. Mexico	4
9. Russia	3
10. Pakistan	3

Shepherd in the Hantes-Alps of southeastern France

During the eighteenth century, Europeans developed a second method of animal husbandry called *ranching*. Wealthy landowners let their herds and flocks graze on enclosed tracts of land. In the American West, ranchers let their cattle run free on the "open range" (government land to which no one had claim). Ranchers periodically rounded up their cattle to be branded or shipped to market. Sheep owners rounded up their sheep to shear them of their wool.

Section Quiz

1–2. What are the two major divisions of agriculture?

3. Define *subsistence farming*.

4. Explain the difference between ranching and nomadic herding.

★ What type of agriculture did Abraham, Isaac, and Jacob practice?

LET'S GO EXPLORING

Land Use of the World

1. Which continent is used almost entirely for commercial farming and manufacturing?
2. Which continent has the largest proportion of subsistence farming?
3. What type of activity is most common along the equator?
4. On which continent is ranching predominant?
5. Which hemisphere, north or south, has most of the world's forestry?
6. What three continents have most of the world's manufacturing and trade?
★ What type of activity is always found beside every manufacturing area? Why?

Land Use of the World

- Commercial Farming
- Subsistence Farming
- Manufacturing and Trade
- Ranching
- Nomadic Herding
- Forestry
- Subpolar Primitive Activity
- Tropical Primitive Activity
- Limited Activity

Fishing and Forestry

Agriculture is not the only primary industry, although it is very important. Fishing, forestry, and mining have also been around for a long time. Each of these industries extracts **natural resources** (useful substances found in the earth). *Fishing* is an important source of food in many countries. *Forestry* provides wood for homes, furniture, and paper.

Commercial fishing is an essential food industry that demands good stewardship.

Fishing

Seafood is the world's second largest export commodity, trailing only oil. Demand has outpaced supply, so the industry is expanding worldwide.

The seafood industry includes essentially two varieties—fish and seaweed—and uses two methods to obtain the products: capture (products gathered in the wild, natural state) and **aquaculture** (cultivation or farming in a controlled artificial environment). The latter

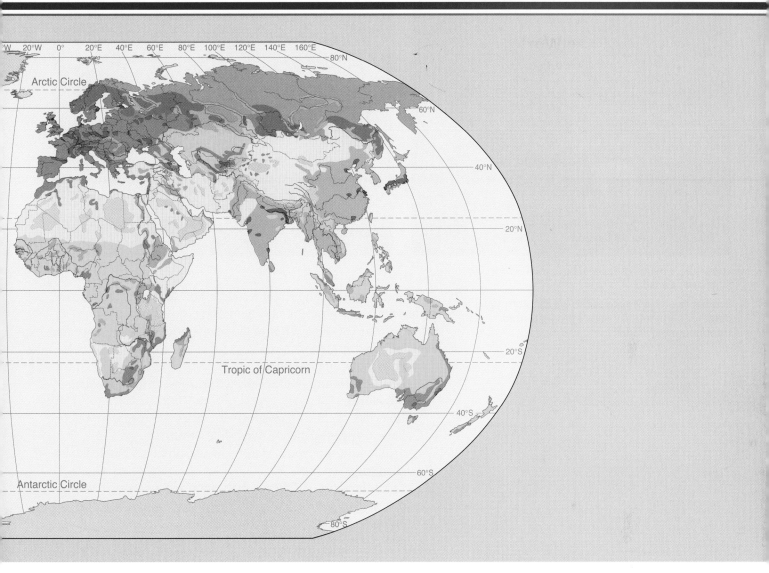

method still generates only a fraction of total production, but it is a fast-growing part of the industry. China leads the nations by producing around two-thirds of the world's cultivated fish.

Another important aspect of the fishing industry is seaweed production, which has grown to become a six-billion-dollar-a-year industry. About 80% of that seaweed is produced as food; the rest is used to obtain extracts used in making fertilizers, cosmetics, animal food additives, fuels, and wastewater treatments.

A growing number of countries harvest seaweed, but China, Japan, and South Korea are among the largest producers. They are also some of the largest consumers, although the emigration of those nationalities to other countries is increasing demand in those areas.

Seafood-producing countries are coming under increasing pressure both from conservationists and from within the industry to emphasize sustainability and care of the environment to ensure continuation of the industry. This pressure is leading to a united effort by scientists, conservationists, and the fishing industry. Such efforts to meet human needs while protecting the environment and endangered species are an important part of fulfilling God's expectations of responsible stewardship.

Woman carrying seaweed she has harvested

Logging is a major industry in both the United States and Canada.

Lumber operations such as this are the starting point for numerous consumer products used throughout the world.

Forestry

Wood is another important resource, and the size of the forestry products industry proves it. How important is the wood products industry to you? Consider a few of the many products made from the following parts of a tree.

Fruit, nuts: food products

Leaves: furniture polish, car wax, crayons, lipstick, medicines, fragrances

Branches: chemicals, plastics, various types of paper products

Bark: medicines, mulch, dyes, shoe polish

Trunk: furniture, musical instruments, plywood, baseball bats, charcoal

Sap: adhesives, ice cream, hair spray, soaps, cough syrups/drops, shampoo

Stumps: wood resin, turpentine, pine cleaners, laundry detergent, sports drinks

Mining

As important as agriculture, fishing, and forestry are, *mining* has far surpassed them in economic importance. Modern countries spend great sums of money mining three types of resources: metals, nonmetal minerals, and fossil fuels.

Metals

The earth's crust is composed mainly of rock that contains a variety of **minerals** (solid crystals that occur naturally and have a definite chemical composition). Scientists have identified about three thousand different minerals, but only about one hundred are common.

Metals are the most important type of mineral because of four useful properties: they are shiny, malleable (able to be hammered into sheets), ductile (able to be drawn into wire), and conductive (able to conduct electricity). Metal tools and utensils last longer and work better than tools made from stone or wood. The first metalworker was Tubal-cain, a descendant of Cain, who became "an instructor of every artificer in brass and iron" (Gen. 4:22).

Metals are of three types: precious metals, common metals, and alloys. The modern production of gold, silver, and platinum is small if measured in tons, but those *precious metals* are far more valuable

Gold nugget

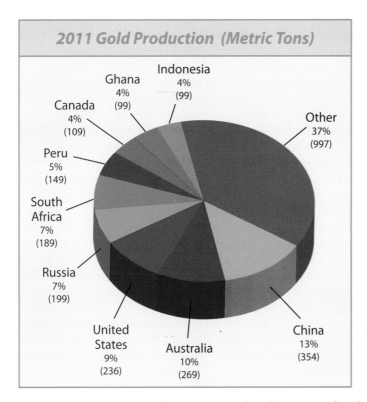

2011 Gold Production (Metric Tons)

Ghana 4% (99)

Indonesia 4% (99)

Canada 4% (109)

Peru 5% (149)

South Africa 7% (189)

Russia 7% (199)

United States 9% (236)

Australia 10% (269)

China 13% (354)

Other 37% (997)

<table>
<tr><td colspan="2">**World's Leading Silver Producers (2011)**</td></tr>
<tr><td>**Country**</td><td>**Millions of ounces**</td></tr>
<tr><td>1. Mexico</td><td>152.8</td></tr>
<tr><td>2. Peru</td><td>109.8</td></tr>
<tr><td>3. China</td><td>103.9</td></tr>
<tr><td>4. Australia</td><td>55.2</td></tr>
<tr><td>5. Chile</td><td>42.1</td></tr>
<tr><td>6. Poland</td><td>40.8</td></tr>
<tr><td>7. Russia</td><td>40.0</td></tr>
<tr><td colspan="2">(U.S. is 9th with 36.0)</td></tr>
</table>

Nuggets of copper

than other metal products. They are considered precious for their beauty, durability, scarcity, and trade value.

Common metals get their name because they are mined in great quantities from the earth's surface and are therefore common. Three such metals have been used extensively since ancient times: copper, lead, and iron.

Copper, a "native metal" like silver and gold, can be found in pure nuggets in the earth's crust. Copper was once used to make weapons, but it is relatively soft. Sixty percent of the copper mined today is used in the electrical industry because it is the least expensive conductor of electricity.

Lead does not occur in pure form in nature. Like most metals, it must be extracted from an *ore* (a mineral composed of several different elements). Lead is combined with sulfur in an ore called galena. A wood fire is hot enough to melt lead. Because it is such a soft metal, artists originally used lead to cast statues. Lead is now the main ingredient in car batteries.

Lead is extracted from galena.

More _iron_ is mined each year than all other metals combined. People in the ancient world extracted iron too, but the process was difficult and expensive. The temperature had to be high (2,795°F), and the refined ore often contained many impurities (traces of other elements). In 1784, Britain developed a process of "puddling"

Iron ore

<table>
<tr><td colspan="2">**Leading Iron Ore Producers (2010)**</td></tr>
<tr><td>**Country**</td><td>**% of world total**</td></tr>
<tr><td>1. China</td><td>37.5</td></tr>
<tr><td>2. Australia</td><td>17.5</td></tr>
<tr><td>3. Brazil</td><td>15.4</td></tr>
<tr><td>4. India</td><td>10.8</td></tr>
<tr><td>5. Russia</td><td>4.0</td></tr>
<tr><td>6. Ukraine</td><td>3.0</td></tr>
<tr><td>7. South Africa</td><td>2.0</td></tr>
<tr><td>8. United States</td><td>2.0</td></tr>
</table>

Precious Gems

On every continent, precious gems are popular adornments and symbols of wealth. Because of their small size and great value, gems were once a form of currency, especially when long caravans journeyed to distant lands.

Asians value gems mostly for their weight, so they polish the large stones and keep them in their original irregular shape. Westerners, on the other hand, cut the gems to enhance their color and symmetry. Lapidaries (gem cutters) chip slivers from the stone to leave flat surfaces called facets. The facets reflect light, making the gem sparkle. The largest diamond ever discovered originally weighed 3,024.75 carats (1 carat = 200 mg, or 0.007 oz.). The queen of England had it cut into nine large diamonds for inclusion in the British crown jewels.

Different countries have become famous for certain gems. Turquoise, prized for its sky-blue color, is popular in the western United States. The Chinese have carved jade for almost three thousand years. Australia is the largest producer of rainbow-like opals. Emeralds, second only to rubies in value, are mined primarily in Colombia. Rubies and sapphires come from the mines of Burma. Most diamonds, the most popular of all gems, are excavated in South Africa, where in 1867 a salesman discovered them when he noticed some children playing with "pretty stones." Diamonds are also excavated in Canada, India, Russia, Brazil, and Australia.

The two kinds of gems are organic (products of plants and animals) and inorganic (minerals). The organic gems include pearls (from oysters), amber (from fossilized tree resin), jet (from fossilized driftwood), and coral (from the skeletons of tiny sea animals). Most inorganic gems apparently formed as volcanic lava forced its way upward through small cracks in the earth and superheated the minerals nearby. Rubies and sapphires came from aluminum oxide, and diamonds came from carbon. People have tried to produce artificial gems by simulating the heat and pressure of volcanoes, but the value of such stones is not as high as that of natural gems.

The Bible includes many references to gems. The twelve stones on Aaron's breastplate (Exod. 39) may have led to the sixteenth-century tradition of birthstones for each month. Revelation 21 tells us that God will build the foundation of the New Jerusalem with twelve layers of different gems.

Aluminum is extracted from bauxite.

(stirring) iron ore to remove the impurities. This strong, versatile metal became useful for making cannons, bridges, trains, and other modern machines.

The second most common metal on earth is *aluminum.* It was once considered a precious stone because it was so difficult to extract from its ore, **bauxite**. The bond holding the elements together in bauxite (hydrogen, oxygen, and aluminum) is so powerful that a process of separating them was not discovered until 1886. This process, using electrical currents, is still used today. Aluminum's light weight and resistance to corrosion make it ideal for cars, aircraft, and other machines.

The four metals just mentioned—copper, lead, iron, and aluminum—are useful not only by themselves but also in combination with other metals. Early in history, people learned that they could combine such metals to form **alloys**. The other six common metals—chromium, manganese, zinc, nickel, tin, and tungsten—are not usually used by themselves but are combined with one or more of the first four metals.

The first useful alloys were made with copper. Copper and tin form *bronze*, from which we get the term *Bronze Age*. A pliable metal, bronze could be made into beautiful statues, weapons, and tools that were stronger than copper. The Romans learned to make *brass* by combining copper and zinc. It is useful in making objects with intricate designs, such as musical instruments. Bronze and brass are often confused with one another because they both have the yellow color common to all copper alloys.

Steel is the world's most important alloy. It is formed by combining iron with the carbon in coal. Early civilizations knew how to produce this metal, but the process was even more difficult and unreliable than iron-making. In 1856, Henry Bessemer devised a better process. First, he shot a jet of air into molten iron to rid it of impurities. Then, when he added coal and manganese, the iron turned into a tough steel. Nearly all of the world's iron ore is now turned into steel. In a sense, the Iron Age has become "the Steel Age."

Nonmetal Minerals

Metals are not the only useful minerals that God has provided. Many other kinds of minerals play an important role in industry.

Limestone is formed mainly from calcite (calcium, carbon, and oxygen). When crushed and mixed with clay, it makes a powder called cement. Adding sand to cement produces mortar. Adding crushed rock to cement makes concrete, the most widely used building material in the world.

Sulfur is another versatile mineral known since ancient times. It has many modern uses. Combined with charcoal and potassium nitrate, it makes gunpowder. It is also used to process petroleum and steel, to produce fertilizer, to vulcanize (improve the strength and texture of) rubber, and even to make matches.

Other minerals that have been used since early history include clay (for bricks, plates, pitchers, cups, and bowls); sand (for making glass for windows and bottles); granite, marble, slate, and sandstone (for monuments and decorative buildings); salt (for seasoning and preserving food); and graphite (for the "lead" in pencils). From phosphates, nitrates, and potassium we get fertilizers for enriching the soil. Look at bags of fertilizer at your local home and garden store, and you will see three numbers on the bag, perhaps 5–10–10. They indicate the percentage of those three nutrients in the bag: 5 percent nitrogen, 10 percent phosphorus, and 10 percent potassium.

A few minerals contain *uranium*, a mineral that was used in the first atomic bombs in 1945 and was later used in nuclear reactors. Its high radioactivity makes it very harmful to the human body.

Fossil and Hydrocarbon Fuels

For centuries, people used wind, water, and wood to power their equipment for transportation and manufacture. Gradually, mankind realized the potential of other energy resources—**fossil fuel and hydrocarbon fuels**. Coal is technically not a mineral but the remains of living things. The Flood waters trapped plants and animals beneath layers of sedimentary rock. The pressure changed this *organic matter* into its present form. This fossil fuel and other fuels such as petroleum and natural gas have dramatically changed our way of life.

Coal is a solid rock that occurs in various grades, or levels of quality, depending on the amount of heat produced per pound. The Chinese burned coal for heat more than a thousand years before Christ. In the late eighteenth century, Europeans began using coal to power steam engines. Later, it was used to make *coke*, a necessary ingredient in steel. Coal is now used to generate most of the world's electricity. Most of the coal produced is used by the producing countries. The remaining coal is exported.

Leading Steel Producers (2012)

Country	Million tons
1. China	1,547.8
2. Japan	107.2
3. United States	88.6
4. India	(est.) 76.7
5. Russia	70.6
6. S. Korea	69.4
7. Germany	42.7

Alternative Sources of Energy

Coal extractor for surface mining

Fossil and Hydrocarbon fuels.

One of the most remarkable events in the history of energy was the harnessing of steam in the eighteenth century. Early steam engines used coal, but most engines now use petroleum. In 1884 scientists learned how to turn steam into a new type of energy—electricity. Coal, petroleum, or natural gas heats water to make steam; the steam turns wheels, called turbines, to generate electricity. Fossil and hydrocarbon fuels still provide around 80 percent of the energy in the United States.

Nuclear fuel.

World War II spawned the next great innovation in energy—nuclear fuel. Splitting atoms can create enough heat to drive steam turbines to make electricity. This resource promised to solve all of the world's energy needs because atoms are everywhere. In practice, nuclear power has serious drawbacks. However, properly employed and wisely built and operated, nuclear reactors hold great promise for safe energy production.

Renewable resources.

Renewable resources include such things as wind, rain, and sunlight. Renewable fuels have a virtually unlimited supply because they are constantly replenished and produce relatively little pollution. Modern technology is making great strides in reducing the cost of developing renewable energy.

Hydroelectricity.

The most important source of renewable energy is moving water. The Romans invented the first water wheel two thousand years ago. When scientists learned to make electricity from steam, they also learned to turn turbines with dammed water. The United States has now dammed most of its major rivers to take full advantage of the country's potential for hydroelectricity.

Biofuel.

Plants have been used for fuel since Adam first built a fire. Recently, America has begun experimenting with waste products from farms and city garbage. Many electric power plants are fueled with municipal wastes, nearly half of which is paper and its derivatives. In addition, a large number of power facilities in the Northeast and Northwest burn wood to generate electricity.

Geothermal.

In some places, geothermal energy (heat from the earth) can produce enough steam to drive turbines or to heat houses. The United States accounts for most of the world's geothermal power, and much of that is produced at one installation located about sixty miles north of San Francisco. One negative side effect of commercially produced geothermal energy is that the process releases polluting gases and corrosive chemicals.

Geothermal plant near San Francisco

Solar.

The sun is the greatest source of energy in our solar system. But scientists have not yet found an economical way to harness that energy. The cost of generating electricity or heating water directly by the sun is still higher than the cost of conventional sources. However, great progress has been made to increase the efficiency of solar panels. In isolated areas, a combination of solar panels with diesel-powered generators is sometimes the best choice, given the cost of gaining access to distant power lines.

Wind.

Experts estimate that as much as 20 percent of U.S. electrical needs could be supplied by wind. But in most cases wind generators would take up too much area to be practical. In addition, wind does not supply a constant supply of energy, and wind turbines have a relatively low lifespan when compared with conventional energy-producing equipment.

Wind turbines

At the present, renewable sources of energy are more expensive and often less reliable than fossil fuels. But costs of most nonrenewable resources are climbing, and these resources will not last forever.

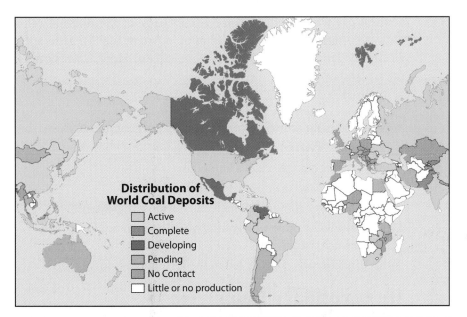

Distribution of World Coal Deposits
- ☐ Active
- ▨ Complete
- ▨ Developing
- ▨ Pending
- ▨ No Contact
- ☐ Little or no production

Leading Coal Producers (2011)

Country	Million tons/ year (est.)
1. China	3471
2. United States	1004
3. India	585
4. Australia	414
5. Indonesia	376
6. Russia	334
7. South Africa	253

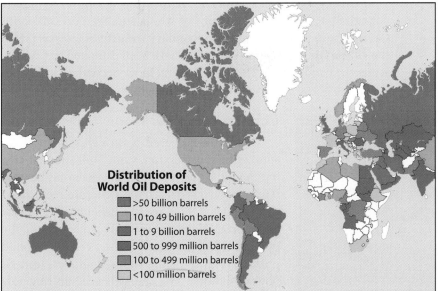

Distribution of World Oil Deposits
- ▨ >50 billion barrels
- ☐ 10 to 49 billion barrels
- ▨ 1 to 9 billion barrels
- ▨ 500 to 999 million barrels
- ▨ 100 to 499 million barrels
- ☐ <100 million barrels

Leading Oil-Producing Countries (2011)

Country	Billion barrels/ day (est.)
1. Russia	10.21
2. Saudi Arabia	10.00
3. United States	9.02
4. Iran	4.23
5. China	4.07
6. Canada	3.59
7. Iraq	3.30

Petroleum is a liquid hydrocarbon fuel. The ancient Chinese used petroleum that had seeped into pools on the earth's surface; however, the first commercial oil well was not drilled until 1859. At first, Americans extracted kerosene for lamps and discarded the rest of the oil. But scientists soon realized that petroleum produces much more energy than coal. The invention of gasoline engines turned petroleum into the most important mining product in the world.

Located in many underground oil pools is a hydrocarbon fuel in gaseous form called natural gas. Many scientists believe it is a by-product of the process that formed petroleum.

Offshore drilling rig

Leading Natural Gas-Producing Countries (2010/2011)	
Country	**Trillion cu. ft./year**
1. Russia	2197
2. United States	2137
3. European Union	550
4. Canada	525
5. Iran	479
6. Qatar	383
7. Norway	338

Natural gas was initially burned off as waste at the first oil wells. However, natural gas is now used as an efficient fuel for generating electricity. Its many residential uses include furnaces, water heaters, dryers, and ovens.

Section Quiz

1. What is the world's second largest export commodity?
2. Define *mineral*.
3. List four characteristics of metals.
4. Which metal is mined more than any other?
5. What is an alloy, and which alloy is most important?
6. What is the most widely used building material today, and how is it made?
* What event in history led to the formation of fossil fuels?

II. Secondary Industries

Primary industries do not change the form of natural resources. For example, they produce grains of wheat and live beef cattle, not sacks of flour and hamburgers. **Secondary industries**, however, take **raw materials** (natural resources that have been extracted by primary industries) and change them into a useful form. Secondary industries are of two types: construction and manufacturing.

Construction of infrastructure, such as this elevated multiple-lane highway, is essential in order to handle a nation's transportation needs.

Construction

Mankind has used a variety of natural resources in construction. Cain built the first city, but the Bible does not say what materials he used (Gen. 4:17). The first large structure mentioned in Scripture is the Tower of Babel, made of brick and mortar. Egyptians used cut stone to build the pyramids, and the Romans used cement to build great coliseums. In the 1850s, engineers learned how to reinforce concrete with steel, making possible modern dams, bridges, and skyscrapers. You will see examples of these in later chapters.

Manufacturing

For most of human history, people made their clothes, bowls, and tools at home. The word *manufacture* originally meant "to make by hand" (*manus-*, "hand"; *factus*, "to make"). As cities grew, some individuals specialized in making certain products. Cities had bakers, cobblers, tailors, potters, and other specialists. In the past two centuries, however, "cottage industries" have been overshadowed by large factories. **Manufacturing** now refers to big businesses and machines that turn raw materials into new products on a large scale.

Industrial Revolution

Discoveries and inventions between 1750 and 1850 made modern industries possible. That period of radical change, known as the **Industrial Revolution**, began in the textile industry of Britain. Prior to this time, individuals raised sheep for wool and grew flax and turned these products into clothes by hand with simple tools. Many hours of work went into the production of just a few yards of finished cloth. Gradually, inventors developed machines that simplified and quickened production. When the steam engine came along to power the machines, the revolution took off, spreading to other countries.

Industry experienced a "second revolution" in the second half of the nineteenth century. Exciting discoveries in chemistry, physics, and biology made that revolution possible. The application of science to industry is called **technology**. The harnessing of electricity became one of the key technological breakthroughs of the nineteenth century. During this period, gasoline engines, telegraphs, and telephones were also invented. During the early twentieth century, modern technology spawned whole new industries, such as the automobile and airplane industries.

Modern textile machines

Computer technology has revolutionized manufacturing.

In the second half of the twentieth century, manufacturing entered a third period of revolution called variously the Computer Age, the Electronics Age, or the Information Age. New high-tech industries, such as computer-chip manufacturing, used the most advanced discoveries of science and engineering. Robotics and computers made industries so efficient that fewer people were needed to work in factories producing basic manufactured goods. Many people were freed from manual labor to find jobs outside the farm and factory in our *postindustrial society*.

Durable and Nondurable Manufacturing

Manufacturing industries are subdivided into two types, according to the lifespan of their products. **Nondurable manufacturing** makes products that generally last less than a year. Such products include food, chemicals, fossil fuels (petrochemicals), tobacco products, wood pulp (paper), and many other consumable products.

Durable manufacturing makes products that last more than a year, including most of the products needed for building homes, furniture, machines, and other equipment. Most durable products come from five sources: lumber, stone, clay, glass, and metals. Many

These cups are an example of nondurable goods.

A Christian Perspective

Workers in secondary industries fulfill God's intent, as expressed in the Creation Mandate, for humans to take the resources of the world and make something of them. Advances in technology and industry have produced many goods for mankind. And yet the Christian should also be aware of the dangers. A society with ever-improving technology may be tempted to think that all of its problems can be solved through technology. Moral reasoning is left to the side. At its most pernicious, the thought that because we *can* do it we *should* do it becomes culturally engrained. Morality is dismissed as an obstacle to progress. The Christian must insist that progress be measured not only by technological advancement, but also, and especially, by greater conformity to God's will.

This car is an example of durable goods.

of these industries take the products of other secondary industries and further improve them. For example, automobile manufacturers shape steel from steel industries and combine it with textiles, plastic, and rubber.

Section Quiz

1–2. What are the two types of secondary industries? How are they similar?

3. Explain the difference between raw materials and natural resources.

4. What do we call the changes in industry from 1750 to 1850? What industry was the first to experience these changes?

5. What is technology? Give an example of a high-tech industry.

✶ What was accomplished during the the Industrial Revolution, the "second revolution," and the Information Age, and how did these developments change daily life?

III. Tertiary Industries

As countries develop, they move from mainly primary industries (meeting basic needs) to secondary industries (construction and manufacturing). The more developed a country becomes, the greater the percentage of its workers move into a third type of industry. For example, in 1870 between 70 and 80 percent of Americans worked in agriculture. Today that figure has dropped to 0.7 percent. In addition, the number of people employed in manufacturing continues to decrease. Because of advances in technology, workers in these primary and secondary industries are able to provide all of the country's needs for food, construction materials, and manufactured products. The majority of America's workers are employed in what are called **tertiary industries**, also known as *service* industries. *Services* are generally intangible, meaning that they cannot be seen or touched. Such jobs as teaching, advertising, repairing products, cleaning offices, and driving trucks are service jobs. In contrast, primary and secondary industries produce goods (products that can be seen and touched). All industries either produce goods or provide services.

Service industries are the vital link between goods and the people who need them. Goods would be useless if they just sat in the fields, at the mines, or at the factories. Service workers are involved at every step of human activity. The U.S. Department of Labor recognizes five categories of service jobs: infrastructure, trade, finance, general services, and government.

Infrastructure

Infrastructure refers to the basic energy and equipment needs of all industries and is divided into three types: utilities, transportation, and communication.

Utilities

Utilities provide electricity, gas, water, sewage-disposal, and trash collection services. Governments own most utilities, or they control the prices that utilities can charge.

Electric and gas utilities produce the energy that runs modern industries and heats and cools homes. Nearly 90 percent of the world's energy comes from fossil fuels, followed by water (hydroelectricity), uranium (nuclear fuel), and wind. Most energy is converted into electricity. The United States remains the world's leading producer and consumer of electricity.

Transportation

Industries have three basic choices when transporting products and people: water, land, and air. These modes of transportation have undergone major changes in the last two centuries.

Water Transportation—People have used water for cheap transportation throughout history. Noah's descendants built the first great civilizations along the mighty rivers of the world. But river routes have some obvious limitations. Shallow water limits the distance boats can travel, and rivers are often far from mineral resources. In the nineteenth century, industrial nations attempted to overcome these limitations by building a vast network of canals. Railroads eventually became more important, but flat-bottomed barges are still common on U.S. waterways and are used to carry freight, particularly coal and metal ores.

Commercial crude oil supertanker

The ocean is another vital means of world transportation. Petroleum-powered ships transport everything from avocados to zinc. Some ships have large holds (open cargo areas below deck) to carry bulky materials, such as grain, coal, and ores. Other ships carry manufactured goods in twenty-foot-long containers, which can be loaded and unloaded quickly and pulled as trailers by trucks when on land. A new class of thousand-foot-long superfreighters is transforming the shipping industry. A small crew of fifteen can handle up to six thousand containers on a superfreighter.

Land Transportation—Merchants need ways to carry goods across land. Trade by caravan has a long history because it is relatively easy to travel across flat plains. The invention of the steam engine revolutionized land transportation. In the last half of the nineteenth century, steam locomotives began carrying large quantities of goods across continents. Railroads provide reliable, year-round

Although railroads have lost their status as the prime movers of freight in the United States, they are still a critical part of U.S. transportation, especially intermodal trains such as the one shown here.

Common Transportation Statistics			
Country	Railroad Miles	Roadway Miles	Airports (2012)
Australia	23,888	511,523	467
Bangladesh	1,629	13,215	18
Brazil	17,732	982,365	4105
Canada	28,926	647,655	1453
China	53,437	2,551,590	497
Egypt	3,158	4,0420	84
France	18,417	591,048	473
Germany	26,085	400,461	541
India	39,751	2,063,207	352
Israel	605	11,364	47
Japan	16,890	752,015	175
Mexico	10,666	227,480	1724
Russia	54,157	610,186	1218
S. Africa	12,546	224,997	567
United States	139,679	4,042,767	15,079

transportation and still account for a significant amount of inland freight tonnage.

The invention of gasoline and diesel engines introduced a new mode of transportation. After World War II, cars and trucks outpaced railroads in importance. Approximately two-thirds of U.S. freight tonnage travels on trucks and other commercial vehicles. In many instances today, imports arrive in the country in containers by ocean freighter, are unloaded in an intermodal (more than one form of transportation) terminal, and then loaded onto either tractor-trailer trucks or intermodal freight trains for transportation across the country.

More dramatic is the almost complete reliance on cars for human transportation. Americans own more passenger cars than any other nation. They also have the lowest ratio of persons per car. This fact has led to problems of increased demand for petroleum-based fuels, overcrowding on highways, increased wear on those highways, and higher numbers of accidents and traffic deaths.

The United States has more paved roads than any other country, and new roads are being paved every day. However, paved roads are also becoming more common in small, densely populated countries such as the Netherlands.

Air Transportation—Airplanes are the fastest form of transportation on earth, and they are the least limited by geographic features. The fastest passenger plane in the world was the *Concorde*, a supersonic transport (SST) built by England and France. It could fly 1,550 miles per hour, or twice the speed of sound. Such aircraft made once-popular ocean liners obsolete, but their use was discontinued in 2004, just thirty-five years after the first flight in 1969, because of low (10 percent of capacity) ridership.

Because of its great expense, air travel is practical only for transporting people and small cargo, such as mail. The industry is highly susceptible to fluctuations in fuel prices. The United States, however, leads the world in commercial aviation. Its passenger planes fly nearly ten times more passenger-miles than those of any other country. (One passenger-mile represents one passenger transported one mile.) The United States also has more airports than any other country.

Communication

Communication is a form of transportation, not of goods or people, but of ideas and information. Communication industries can be divided into two broad categories, based on the medium used to pass on information: print media and electronic media.

Print Media—Written language has been around for a long time, perhaps since Adam's day. Until two hundred years ago, private couriers carried most of the world's *personal communication*, such as letters and packages. Since then, national governments have taken over most of the world's postal services. The Universal Postal Union, established in 1875, regulates international mail to ensure that it is delivered. The United Nations now operates this agency.

In the early days, the primary means of **mass communication** were speeches and lectures given in one place to a large audience. The invention of the printing press in the 1450s enabled individuals to share ideas and discoveries with the masses. The **publishing industry** prints three major forms of publications: books, newspapers, and magazines.

European monarchs feared the power of publishers and strictly controlled what they could write. After gaining independence in 1783, the United States became one of the first countries to guarantee freedom of the press. Steam engines made it possible to print "penny papers" quickly and cheaply in the early nineteenth century, making daily information available to even the poorest citizen.

Electronic Media—In earlier times, people devised some clever methods of rapid, long-distance communication, including flags and smoke signals. In the 1830s, Samuel Morse discovered a new medium for communicating ideas—electricity. Sending messages through electronic impulses is called **telecommunications**, which includes the telephone, radio, television, and Internet industries.

The telephone was patented in 1876 by the American inventor Alexander Graham Bell. It allowed people to talk directly rather than in Morse code. In 1920, the Radio Corporation of America (RCA) began the first commercial radio broadcasts. Regularly scheduled television broadcasts began in London sixteen years later. Radio and television became the dominant mass media of the world. Unlike print media, they transmit information (sound and pictures) that even illiterate adults and young children can enjoy. The United States has more radios and televisions than any other country.

The "space age" brought radical changes to personal and mass communications. Since Russia launched the first satellite in 1957, more than 8,000 satellites have been positioned in space. Signals can be transmitted instantly around the world without cable connections. Computer modems allow people at any corner of the globe to exchange any form of media—text, sound, and pictures—with a keystroke. E-mail, instant messaging, and the Internet have dramatically reduced the time needed for communicating messages, news, and ideas. Cell phones have further reduced the relative size of the world in terms of communication ability.

Common Communication Statistics		
Country	Internet Users (in millions)	Telephones (Mainline/Cell) (in millions)
Australia	15.81	10.6/24.5
Bangladesh	0.62	.98/84.4
Brazil	75.98	43.0/244.4
Canada	26.96	18.2/27.4
China	389.00	285.1/986.3
Egypt	20.14	8.7/83.4
France	45.62	39.9/59.8
Germany	65.13	51.8/108.7
India	61.34	32.7/893.9
Italy	29.24	22.1/96.0
Japan	99.18	64.7/132.8
Mexico	31.02	19.7/94.6
Russia	40.85	44.2/236.7
United Kingdom	51.44	33.2/81.6
United States	245.00	146.0/290.3

Communications satellite

Trade

Someone needs to sell the products of primary and secondary industries. This is the function of trade industries. They buy and sell natural resources and manufactured goods. **Wholesale businesses** buy goods from producers in large quantities to sell in smaller quantities to **retail businesses**, which sell goods directly to consumers. A notable exception is Wal-Mart, which is so large and which controls so much of the world consumer market that it can buy goods directly from the producers in huge quantities and therefore at very low prices. Wal-Mart then sells directly to consumers through its Wal-Mart and Sam's Club chains. Eliminating the middleman (the wholesalers) allows Wal-Mart to charge lower prices.

Finance

Modern industry would have been impossible without the rise of modern banking. Bankers, insurance companies, real estate agents, and investment firms help people to buy property, goods, and services. Finance industries make money available to help start and fuel the growth of other industries.

General Services

Many other tertiary industries sell "support" services. They repair machines and also keep people healthy and happy while they do their work. They include maids, mechanics, nurses, teachers, zookeepers, engineers, lawyers, researchers, computer programmers and repair technicians, and amusement park attendants.

Government

The fifth form of tertiary industry is government. Most government employees, such as police officers, work for cities and states. The national government employs soldiers, lawmakers, judges, and bureaucrats (officials or clerks who carry out the daily functions of government).

Section Quiz

1. What is another name for tertiary industries?
2–3. List three of the five kinds of tertiary industries.
4–5. What are three of the four types of telecommunications industries?
   ✶ How should principles found in Ephesians 5:1–16 govern the Christian's use of modern communications technology?

IV. The Wealth of Nations

The earth's resources are neither unlimited nor evenly divided among the nations. Each country must make difficult choices about the best way to develop and distribute its resources, goods, and services. The study of the process by which people and countries make such choices is called *economics*.

Who Makes the Choices

The Creator owns all of the earth's resources (Ps. 24:1; 50:10). Humans are merely stewards, placed in charge of the creation to use and develop its resources for His glory (see Gen. 1:28). Every system for making economic choices should be evaluated in light of that fact. The governments of the world generally have economic systems that can be classified as capitalist, socialist, or mixed economies.

Capitalism

The money and equipment (buildings, tools, computers, vehicles, etc.) necessary to build industries are called **capital**. Most Western countries follow a system of **capitalism**. Private individuals or corporations build most industries, risking their own capital by making investments in hopes of making a profit.

Anyone can start a business and attempt to profit financially. Another name for such an economy (in its ideal form) is a **free market** because businesses freely compete in the marketplace for buyers with little interference from the government. People who take risks to start businesses are called *entrepreneurs*.

The free market system performs well in the economic realm. Its very success, however, contains some dangers. Christian businessmen must ensure that biblical moral teaching, rather than market expediency, guides their business practices. They must recognize that some business actions may be economically profitable but morally wrong.

Factory where goods are mass produced

Socialism

During the nineteenth century, opponents of capitalism developed an alternative system called **socialism**. Under socialism, the government owns the major industries and promises to make production decisions for the welfare of society. In such a *command economy*, the government determines which industries are developed, where they are built, and what they produce. In socialist economies, few businessmen are willing to take risks with capital because much of the profit goes to the government in the form of high taxes. The most extreme form of socialism is called **communism**, under which the government owns everything.

More than just an economic system, socialism is a worldview with particular ideas about what is wrong with the world and how to set it right. Inequality is the chief problem that socialism seeks to solve. Common ownership of all property is the proposed solution. Socialists have tended to think that people will do right when everyone is equal and no one is competing for possessions.

Christians do recognize that when people amass wealth and power they often oppress other people (cf. Amos 1:6–7; 4:1; Isa. 5:8). But the Bible never holds out absolute equality as the ideal. It seems that even in eternity some nations will enjoy more privilege than others (Jer. 31:7), some people more responsibility than others (Rev. 21:24), and some individuals more rewards than others (Luke 19:16–19; 1 Cor. 3:12–15). Private property also seems to persist through the millennial period (Mic. 4:3–4; Zech. 3:10). Because socialism runs contrary to the way God designed his world to work, it has led to economic hardship and tyranny in the nations that have attempted most strenuously to put it into practice.

Mixed Economies

Most of those countries whose socialist economies collapsed adopted a *mixed economy* that attempted to combine elements of capitalism and socialism. In a mixed economy, private citizens can own property and businesses, but the government closely regulates their choices. In spite of socialism's poor record, even some leaders in capitalist countries have sought to move toward mixed economies.

How Countries Measure Wealth

Most people think of wealth as the ownership of things, such as cattle, land, and money. But real **wealth** is the ability to *produce* new things. Consider the biblical example of Jacob. His wealth was not in the size of his flocks and herds but in the plentiful offspring his animals produced each year to feed and clothe his growing family. The more a country produces each year, the more things its people can eat and enjoy that year, and the better prepared they can be to face the next year.

The most common measurement of a country's wealth is the **gross domestic product (GDP)**. The GDP is the monetary value of all the goods and services produced for sale within a country's borders over the course of a year. Economists total the value of the products produced by all of the primary, secondary, and tertiary industries. Look at the definition of GDP again. It is the *gross* (total) value of all *products* (goods and services) made by *domestic* (home, or inside the country) workers in one year.

The total GDP means very little, however, until it is compared to the number of workers who produced those products. A more meaningful measurement is **per capita GDP** (the average value of products produced by each person in the country). This measurement shows how much each person is producing each year. In other words, it shows the average worker's *productivity*.

A high per capita GDP does not always mean that a country has a lot of industry or that the average worker makes a lot of money. Several rich countries, such as the United Arab Emirates and Qatar, have a high per capita GDP because primary industries ship valuable exports (oil, in their case), but a few rich sheiks and bureaucrats pocket the money. The average citizen receives little benefit.

Countries with the Highest GDPs in 2011 *(in billions)*	
Country	**GDP**
1. United States	15,480
2. China	11,300
3. Japan	4,444
4. India	4,421
5. Germany	3,114
6. Russia	2,383
7. Brazil	2,294
8. United Kingdom	2,288

How Countries Distribute Wealth Among Themselves

Socialist countries view the world as a pie with a limited supply of wealth that must be cut into equal pieces to feed everyone. In theory, they imitate Robin Hood, who stole from the rich and gave to the poor. In reality, however, the world's supply of wealth is unlimited. Industrial countries do not steal to become rich; they make new wealth that did not exist before. For example, they turn iron ore into automobiles and silicon into computer chips. Their industries just keep making bigger pies and more of them.

Developed and Developing Countries

The effective use of raw materials, labor, and capital is called **development**. Economists measure the value that manufacturers add to raw materials. If the original metals in a sports car are worth $1,500 and the final car is worth $30,500, then the **value added** is $29,000.

Development translates into power. Countries with productive economies can afford to buy weapons and influence neighbors with their money. Eight countries produce more than three-fourths of all value added by manufacture. The leaders of this **Group of 8** (G-8) meet in a different country each year to resolve economic and political disputes.

G-8 members are **developed countries**, which have a wide range of industries that take full advantage of their people's skills. Most citizens enjoy the financial benefits of such development as reflected in a high per capita GDP.

China and several other big nations are not included in the G-8. They have high national GDPs and many factories, but they are considered **developing countries**. Their GDPs are high because of their large population, but their per capita GDPs are very low. Developing countries have not yet taken full advantage of their people's skills.

Division of Labor

The best evidence of a nation's development is its *division of labor*, which is highly sophisticated in developed nations. Rather than everyone working on subsistence farms, workers can choose from among hundreds of different occupations. Most jobs are in tertiary, or service, industries. Developing nations, on the other hand, have relatively few jobs available in service industries.

The distiction between developed and developing countries is not always so clear-cut. Brazil, which has a growing number of industrial and service industries, does not really belong in the same category as poor, agricultural Bangladesh. The world's poorest countries—with a per capita GDP of $3,000 or less—belong in a separate category of "underdeveloped" or "least developed" countries. Many of those countries are not underdeveloped because they lack resources but because they have unstable governments or cultural habits that discourage initiative and progress.

The Hope of Prosperity

What makes some countries rich and others poor? This is not an easy question to answer. Possessing natural resources is not essential for having wealth. Japan's industries have thrived even though

Sample of Per Capita GDP (2012 est.) of Various Countries

Country	Per Capita GDP
1. Qatar	$98,900
3. Luxembourg	$80,600
5. Singapore	$59,700
10. Hong Kong	$50.700
12. United States	$49,800
33. United Kingdom	$36,700
118. China	$9,100

G-8 Countries

🍁	Canada
	France
	Germany
	Italy
	Japan
	Russia
	United Kingdom
	United States of America

its islands lack natural resources. On the other hand, the Democratic Republic of Congo's mines are rich in resources, but its per capita GDP is among the lowest in the world.

Factors that are far more important in developing wealth include labor and government. People are a resource, not a drain on the economy. The more hard workers a country has, the more possibilities it has for creating new wealth. Hard work includes a willingness to study, to learn, and to try new things, even if it means taking risks. The Bible clearly states that stealing, cheating, and mistreating others diminish wealth, but God blesses hard work (Prov. 13:11).

Proverbs also states that the Lord blesses righteous living (Prov. 14:34). The word *righteousness* means "following a rule or standard." The main factor in wealth is God, who blesses those who live according to the standard of His Word and judges those who do not. The question of the wealth of nations, which has puzzled economists for centuries, is best answered this way.

However, it is important to note that righteousness does not automatically lead to wealth. In fact, for a period of time the wicked do sometimes prosper. The account of Lazarus and the rich man in Luke 16 reminds us that Lazarus was a righteous man who endured extreme poverty, while the wicked man prospered in this life. However, God will ultimately settle all accounts by rewarding the righteous and punishing the wicked.

It is also important to realize that wickedness undermines national prosperity. God designed the world to work in certain ways and not work in others. When sin becomes common and accepted in a culture, there are social and economic consequences. In history, God has often sent judgment on wicked nations and stripped them of their prosperity.

National progress and wealth are also dependent on a stable government. People are more willing to work hard, take risks, and invest in business if they are free and have a government that encourages such efforts and works to protect them from exploitation or external attacks.

For a government to be fair and stable, it must be good. Repeatedly in Proverbs, God states that rulers who obey His law will enjoy stability and peace (Prov. 16:12; 20:28; 25:5; 28:2; 29:4, 14). So why do wicked people and countries sometimes seem to prosper? The Lord temporarily exalts whom He will. Babylon was "a golden cup in the Lord's hand" (Jer. 51:7), destroying Jerusalem in 586 BC and carrying the Jews away as captives. But the ill-gotten wealth of the wicked Babylonians was fleeting. God eventually judged that empire for its sin. No nation that rejects God's Word will ultimately escape divine judgment.

Although "the love of money is the root of all [kinds of] evil" (1 Tim. 6:10), money itself is not evil. Wealth—and the ability to enjoy it—is a gift of God (Eccles. 5:18–20). God gave mankind resources to serve Him and people, and through that service to find joy and fulfillment. True wealth is found in heaven, not on earth (Matt. 6:19–20).

How Countries Wage Trade Wars

Some countries have tried to achieve **economic self-sufficiency**, the ability to produce everything they need without buying or selling from other countries. In 1961, the Communist leader in Albania isolated his country in every way possible. As a result, Albania became the poorest country in Europe. In contrast, the world's wealthiest nations are also the biggest trading nations.

God meant for people to trade. For example, Israel under Solomon enjoyed extensive trade with the surrounding nations (1 Kings 10). Throughout history, nations have depended on trade to acquire from others the raw materials that they lack. The United States, though rich in resources, must import 100 percent of its bauxite, manganese, and graphite. It also must import most of its industrial diamonds, platinum, tungsten, chromium, tin, and nickel. Without these resources, assembly lines for many critical industries would come to a halt. Efforts to ensure trade promote peace among nations.

Ship being loaded for export

Trade is essential for more than exchanging raw materials. Every industry needs a **market**—people or businesses to buy its products. **Exports** are the primary and secondary goods that a country ships to other countries. **Imports** are all of the goods that a country receives from other countries. Countries measure international trade in terms of the monetary value of exports and imports. The difference between these two values is called the *balance of trade*.

Occasionally, countries have disputes over trade. Sometimes those conflicts lead to war, but countries have other weapons at their disposal. **Tariffs** are taxes on imports and exports. In theory, if the United States places a high tariff on Japanese automobiles, sales of Japanese cars will drop and domestic sales will increase. (In reality, sometimes consumers are willing to pay the higher prices for the foreign-made products, so domestic sales continue to languish.) Another weapon is an **embargo** (ban on importing or exporting certain products or trading with a particular country). Arab nations used an oil embargo in the 1970s to drive up the price of oil and to hurt the U.S. economy. (Oil prices affect practically all other prices because fuel is used in the production and distribution processes.)

Free Trade vs. Fair Trade

Suppose that your father has just lost his job making jackets because of foreign competition. Meanwhile, your friends are rushing to the mall because a retail store is having a fabulous sale on jackets, the labels of which read "Made in China." How do you resolve this tension? There are two possibilities. **Protectionism** is the belief that the government should restrict foreign imports because they take away jobs. The main way of achieving this goal is to place high tariffs (import taxes) on the foreign goods, making them more expensive than similar domestic goods. On the other hand, free trade (imposing no or only low tariffs) allows retailers the freedom to sell any products their customers want.

The United States government has taken different sides on this heated issue at different times in its history. When the British Parliament began restricting **free trade**, colonial leaders staged the Boston Tea Party. But after the colonies won independence, trade wars between the states hindered trade and threatened economic disaster. So the authors of the Constitution dropped all barriers to trade between states (called domestic trade). Since then, protectionist debates have raged in Congress over foreign trade. This issue created regional strife, with the North favoring high restrictive tariffs and the South supporting free trade.

Protectionism reached its height in the 1920s. The United States imposed high tariffs to protect its industries from European industries, which were rebuilding after the ravages of World War I. The tariffs seriously curtailed international trade and hurt the economies of both European countries and the United States. Since World War II, free trade has become popular among capitalist nations. These nations held several rounds of talks to draw up rules for trade, which became known as the **General Agreement on Tariffs and Trade (GATT)**. Tariffs fell from 40 percent to 5 percent, and the volume of worldwide trade ballooned.

Countries with common interests have been negotiating *regional free trade agreements*, which drop trade restrictions within a region but keep a wall of protective tariffs against outsiders. The earliest and most far-reaching regional agreement was the European Union (EU), whose roots go back to 1951. Its members have torn down trade barriers within Western Europe while maintaining barriers to Eastern Europe and Asia. The Association of Southeast Asian Nations (ASEAN) was formed in 1967. In 1993, Mexico joined Canada and the United States in the North American Free Trade Agreement (NAFTA).

But Americans became increasingly disillusioned with low tariffs. Most businessmen were willing to compete in a free market—but not if foreign businesses had unfair advantages. Supporters of *fair trade* argued that the United States was losing jobs and exports because of the following practices.

1. Unfair labor practices: Some countries allow cheap labor, child labor, and prison or slave labor.

2. Unfair government policies: Governments of some developed nations gave businesses tax breaks and subsidies (financial assistance). Governments of less developed nations imposed few costly regulations.

3. Unfair pricing: Businesses in some developed countries sometimes flooded American markets with products sold at below-cost prices to drive American companies out of business.

4. Piracy: This includes the theft of ideas and products, copies of designer clothes with false labels, and unlicensed copies of music, computer programs, and books.

In 1987, the United States and 117 other countries entered a new round of GATT negotiations to find a way to stop such practices. Seven years later, they established the **World Trade Organization (WTO)**, a permanent body with one representative for every nation. The WTO replaced GATT. Individual countries no longer had the final say in their trade policies. In essence, free trade turned into "managed free trade" under the direction of international bureaucrats.

In 2005, the U.S. Senate approved the Central American Free Trade Agreement (CAFTA) with five Central American countries (Guatemala, El Salvador, Honduras, Costa Rica, and Nicaragua) and the Dominican Republic.

Section Quiz

1. What measurement shows the value of all the goods and services produced within a country in one year?
2. What is the main difference between capitalism and socialism?
3. What is another name for the least developed countries?
4. What term is used for the people who want to buy a product?
5. What are import and export taxes called?
★ In what sense is every nation a "developing country"?

Chapter Review

Making Connections

1–5. Identify each of the following as primary, secondary, or tertiary industry.

    a. a local drug store

    b. a peach orchard

    c. a petroleum refinery

    d. a copper mine

    e. a local fire department

6–8. What are the fossil and hydrocarbon fuels, and in what form is each found?

9–10. What are two products derived from petroleum?

Developing Geography Skills

1. What is the most common industry in your area?

2. Why are some countries poor even though they have valuable raw materials?

3. List the occupations of five adult friends or relatives and label their jobs as primary, secondary, or tertiary.

Thinking Critically

1. Why does China have a high GDP but a low per capita GDP?

2. Read Exodus 34:21. Explain why this command was difficult to obey. What was God teaching about man's first priority in life?

Living in God's World

1. What new technological gadget do you wish you possessed? Make a list of both the advantages and disadvantages of this item. In light of both lists, determine if the item is worth acquiring or not.

2. Socialism is a worldview that identifies inequality as the world's chief problem and common ownership as the solution. According to the Christian worldview, what is the major problem in the world and its solution?

People, Places, and Things to Know

industry
primary industry
subsistence farmer
cash crop
commercial farmer
nomadic herding
natural resource
aquaculture
mineral
metal
bauxite
alloy
fossil fuel
hydrocarbon fuels
coal
petroleum
secondary industry
raw material
manufacturing
Industrial Revolution
technology
nondurable manufacturing
durable manufacturing
tertiary industy
infrastructure
mass communication
publishing industry
telecommunications
wholesale business
retail business
capital
capitalism
free market
socialism
communism
wealth
gross domestic product (GDP)
per capita GDP
development
value added
Group of 8
developed country
developing country
economic self-sufficiency
market
export
import
tariff
embargo
protectionism
free trade
General Agreement on Tariffs and Trade (GATT)
World Trade Organization (WTO)

Tokyo

5

SOCIETY: HUMAN INTERACTIONS

*I*n all earthly relationships, people are to reflect the image of their Creator. As part of His image, humans have the God-given ability to do things with His creation. The giving of this ability is often called the Creation Mandate. God made his image bearers male and female because God intended for humans to work with His creation in the contexts of relationships with other humans. These relationships began with family relationships and then spread to the community and nation.

Geography includes the study of **society**, the relationships among human beings. When societies work together to do things with God's creation, they create cultures.

I. Culture: The Ways of Society

When people hear the word *culture*, they usually think of daily life—clothing, food, sports, customs, music, literature, art, and crafts. But culture involves much more. It is society's total way of life, including all of its traditions and institutions. *Traditions* are the customs or usages that society passes down from one generation to the next. *Institutions* are the formal organizations by which society transmits traditions.

Because a culture represents a society's total way of life, Christians must study world cultures with discernment. Much good may be found in every culture since culture emerges as God's image bearers work with His good creation. But much evil will also be found in every culture because sin has affected every part of man and every aspect of the creation. Christians must learn how to celebrate the good aspects of culture while resisting its evils.

Language—The Foundation of Culture

No one is born with culture. It is taught, and language is the primary instrument for transmitting culture. The ability to speak and reason distinguishes humans from the animal world. Man's speech imitates his Maker, who communicates through both His written Word, the Bible, and His living Word, Jesus Christ (Heb. 1:1–2).

After the Flood, the descendants of Noah had one language and one culture. God commanded them to spread all over the earth, but

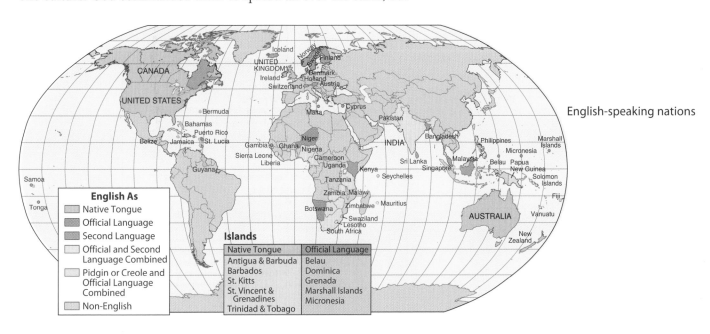

English-speaking nations

English As
- Native Tongue
- Official Language
- Second Language
- Official and Second Language Combined
- Pidgin or Creole and Official Language Combined
- Non-English

Islands

Native Tongue	Official Language
Antigua & Barbuda	Belau
Barbados	Dominica
St. Kitts	Grenada
St. Vincent & Grenadines	Marshall Islands
Trinidad & Tobago	Micronesia

they wanted to stay together in a single society. So they moved down from the mountains of Ararat to build a city on the fertile plain of the Euphrates River (Gen. 11:1–4). The people began building a worship center to promote their wicked, man-centered culture.

God's response ("nothing will be restrained from them"; Gen. 11:6) reveals that the abilities He has given to humans are very powerful. When humans work together, they can accomplish a great deal. In the hands of sinful people, this power was dangerous, so God disrupted human language so that the people could not understand each other's speech. This forced people into language groups. The end result was that humanity obeyed the divine command to scatter (Gen. 1:28; 9:1, 7; 11:4, 7-8). Different cultures sprang up around the world. The confusing of language at Babel was a judgment, but it was also a blessing. By limiting the power of a united humanity and scattering the human race across the globe, God was placing the peoples of the earth into situations that should have prompted them to seek Him (Acts 17:26-27).

Furthermore, God did not scatter people randomly. The descendants of Ham, Shem, and Japheth spread abroad "after their families, after their tongues, in their lands, after their nations" (Gen. 10:5, 20, 31). Each family spoke a common language and traveled as a unit.

LET'S GO EXPLORING

Language Families of the World

1. What language family appears on every inhabited continent?

2. List all the language families that appear on the continent of Africa.

3. Which continent has the largest number of language families? How many?

4. Look at the eight culture regions on the map (Africa, Asia, Central Eurasia, Europe, Latin America, the Middle East, Northern America, and Oceania). List what appears to be the main language family in each region.

✶ Look at the climate map on pp. 46–47 and the vegetation map on pp. 50–51. What climates and land features are most often associated with "other" languages? Why?

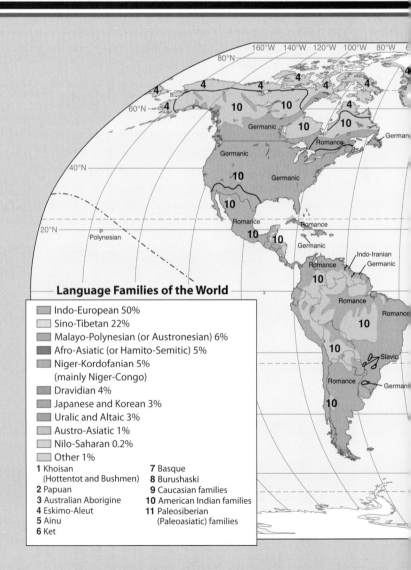

Language Families of the World

- Indo-European 50%
- Sino-Tibetan 22%
- Malayo-Polynesian (or Austronesian) 6%
- Afro-Asiatic (or Hamito-Semitic) 5%
- Niger-Kordofanian 5% (mainly Niger-Congo)
- Dravidian 4%
- Japanese and Korean 3%
- Uralic and Altaic 3%
- Austro-Asiatic 1%
- Nilo-Saharan 0.2%
- Other 1%

1 Khoisan (Hottentot and Bushmen)	7 Basque
2 Papuan	8 Burushaski
3 Australian Aborigine	9 Caucasian families
4 Eskimo-Aleut	10 American Indian families
5 Ainu	11 Paleosiberian (Paleoasiatic) families
6 Ket	

Those families became the founders of the ancient culture regions. (Genesis 10 is a catalog of these regions.)

Spoken Languages

What God did at Babel was not the end of the confusing of human language. Ever since Babel, wherever mountains, oceans, and deserts have prevented people from talking to one another, new languages and cultures have developed. Approximately sixty-six hundred languages are spoken in the world today. Agreeing on a total is difficult, however. Speech patterns within a single language often vary considerably, in which case each speech pattern is called a **dialect**. But sometimes different languages are so similar that they are mutually understandable. For example, speakers of Portuguese can understand Spanish with little difficulty.

While opinions differ, many linguists recognize at least ten major **language families**, groups of languages that share many common characteristics. Ninety-nine percent of all people speak a language that belongs to one of the ten major families, the most prominent of which is the Indo-European family. Indo-Europeans account for nearly half of the world's total population. Many linguists believe that the Indo-European family originated in a region somewhere between

Most-Spoken Languages (2009)	
Language	**Percent of World Population**
Mandarin Chinese	12.40
Spanish	4.85
English	4.83
Arabic	3.25
Hindi	2.68
Bengali	2.66
Portuguese	2.62
Russian	2.12
Japanese	1.80
German	1.30

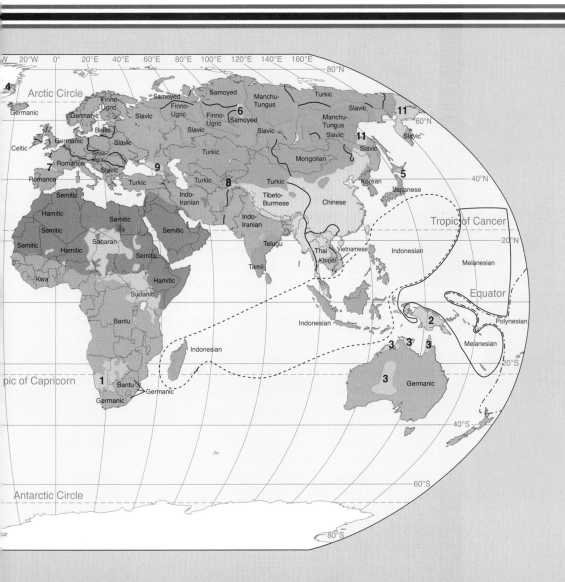

India and Europe. The modern boundaries of this and other language families reflect mankind's fascinating history of exploration, wars, and migration.

Language families are divided into language subfamilies. For example, Germanic is a major subfamily of the Indo-European family. It includes German, English, Swedish, and Norwegian. Another major subfamily is the Romance languages, which descended from Latin, the language of the ancient Romans. This subfamily includes Spanish, French, and Italian.

Written Languages

Primitive societies rely on word of mouth to transmit culture. But advanced societies use written languages to keep more accurate and complete records. Writing allows the rapid spread of culture. Before 1900, less than 10 percent of the world's population was literate. Now approximately 84 percent of the world's people are literate. Most developed countries have a literacy rate of around 95 percent.

Regions—The Locations of Culture

As descendants of Noah spread over the earth after the Tower of Babel, they developed many different cultures. The term *culture* refers to not only human society as a whole but also the distinctive ways of doing things that are easily recognizable and associated with definable regions or groups of people. A **culture region** is a human society that shares the same basic culture.

Maps make it easier to study complex information about people, just as they make it easier to study physical relief. The world is divided into eight main culture regions: Africa, Asia, Central Eurasia, Europe, Latin America, the Middle East, Northern America, and Oceania.

Although individual countries change names, grow, shrink, or cease to exist, the world culture regions remain fairly constant. If you learn the characteristics of these regions, you will be well equipped to understand events in your lifetime, no matter what happens to individual countries.

The boundaries of the world regions are similar to those of the continents but are not necessarily the same. The main exception is Eurasia, which is divided into four distinct culture regions, two of which, Central Eurasia and the Middle East, sit at the crossroads of the world. Both regions have been the focus of conflict throughout history.

Although sin has marred God's image in man, every culture reflects some of His attributes, including an appreciation of beauty, concern for order, a moral sense, and creative genius. Look for these characteristics as you study the cultures of the world.

Within each world region are many **subregions** that display increasingly similar characteristics. Northern America, for example, consists of two large subregions, the United States and Canada. Subregions are further divided into even smaller subregions within the chapters.

Scottish man

Brazilian woman

Filipino girl

Section Quiz

1. Why is language the foundation of culture?
2. What is a language family?
3–6. Name the eight culture regions of the world.
   ✷ Why did God divide mankind by multiplying languages?

Institutions—The Transmission of Culture

Every society has many institutions that transmit culture. The proper goal of all institutions is to help people glorify God, but Adam's sin separated man from God and marred every human relationship. Ever since, society has struggled to subdue not only the earth but also the evil in human hearts.

We can determine how well society is accomplishing God's purposes by studying cultural institutions. Because God has put in every heart a knowledge of both the spiritual world and of human obligations to the Creator (Rom. 1:19–20; 2:14–15), all are without excuse.

But human institutions have diverged from their purpose of glorifying God to two extremes: glorifying the group or glorifying the individual. Although there are many exceptions, Eastern institutions generally value the group, and Western institutions generally value the individual.

Students can learn their nation's culture by learning to read and write.

The Family

The foundation of society is the family. The Lord instituted the home in the Garden of Eden before sin ever entered the world. He created Eve to be Adam's helper in the work of dominion (Gen. 2:18). At their marriage, the Lord gave them the pattern of a godly home (Gen. 2:24).

Family life teaches traits that both parents and children need—how to obey, how to serve, how to lead, and how to love. Parents also pass on wisdom to their children. The apostle Paul instructed fathers to bring up their children "in the nurture and admonition of the Lord" (Eph. 6:4).

Every society honors the central role of the family. Western societies often focus on the **nuclear family**—a man, his wife, and their children. Eastern societies typically focus on the **extended family**—the nuclear family plus grandparents, uncles, aunts, and cousins. Every

Extended families are typical in the Orient.

balanced society honors elders, nurtures children, and emphasizes the central role of the parents.

Fallen societies, however, have taken family responsibilities to extremes. Eastern cultures often worship ancestors, and some husbands seek more than one wife (*polygamy*). In contrast, Western cultures tend to overemphasize the rights of individuals, leading to broken families—aborted and illegitimate children in the name of women's rights, and divorce in the name of human rights.

Religion

Religion includes a people's worldview or beliefs about every aspect of life and the practices that are considered important for a meaningful life. In most cases these worldviews include beliefs about a supernatural realm that includes a god or gods. The practices of a religion often include worshiping the god or gods. Because religion is all encompassing, some peoples do not distinguish between their religion and their culture.

Practically, religion is what gives a people its sense of purpose in life. It provides a culture with both a set of beliefs as well as a formal code of conduct that regulates how people should live and worship. Religion—or the rejection of religion—guides all other expressions of culture, including holidays, dress, and even food preparation.

The world's cultures have fallen from the worship of the one true God into different forms of idolatry. Eastern cultures tend to worship the state or the group. You might remember the story of Nebuchadnezzar, who built a golden idol and demanded that all of his subjects worship him. Many Eastern cultures, such as Islamic nations, still have an "official religion" that their society expects its members to follow. Communist nations developed "cults of personality" that elevated the ruler as the savior of the people. For example, North Koreans exalt the founder of communism there, Kim Il Sung, in a religion called Juche (also known as Kimilsungism-kimjongilism).

Protestant church

Hindu temple

Muslim mosque

The Great Commission

Some young Christians ask themselves, "Does God want me to be a missionary?" In one sense every Christian is supposed to be a missionary. Every Christian has the responsibility to fulfill the Great Commission (Matt. 28:18-20) and to live a life of good works that glorifies God (Matt. 5:13-16). But the term *missionary* is often used to designate a person who takes the gospel to another nation or another culture.

Knowledge of geography is essential to missions work. Mission boards use geographic knowledge in determining where to locate their missionaries. Most of the unevangelized populations of the world live in what is known as the "10/40 window." That term designates the area between West Africa and East Asia and between 10 degrees north latitude and 40 degrees south latitude. Keep the 10/40 window in mind as you study the various countries of the world.

Knowledge of culture is also essential to missions work. The gospel is not just for Americans; it is for all peoples of the world. Therefore, people do not need to become like Americans to receive the gospel. The missionary has the difficult task of understanding how to express the gospel and church life in terms of a new culture rather than his own culture. He has to be able to discern the good in a foreign culture and the bad. Understanding culture also helps the missionary avoid misunderstandings about the gospel.

Western cultures, on the other hand, tend more toward religious liberty. (For example, the ancient Greeks chastised Alexander the Great when he made himself a god to solidify his rule over the conquered Persians.) Western societies allow freedom of worship as long as each religion obeys general public laws. Unfortunately, Western governments also tend toward radical individualism, which leads to a failure to govern the conduct of their people by moral standards of right and wrong. Too often such governments allow individuals to do as they choose.

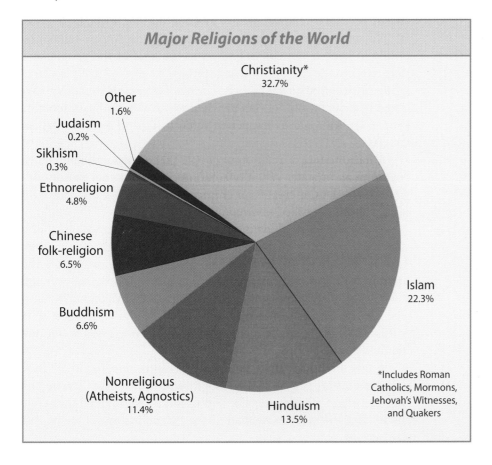

Major Religions of the World

- Christianity* 32.7%
- Islam 22.3%
- Hinduism 13.5%
- Nonreligious (Atheists, Agnostics) 11.4%
- Buddhism 6.6%
- Chinese folk-religion 6.5%
- Ethnoreligion 4.8%
- Sikhism 0.3%
- Judaism 0.2%
- Other 1.6%

*Includes Roman Catholics, Mormons, Jehovah's Witnesses, and Quakers

Seven Largest Countries (Area)	
Country	**Square miles**
1. Russia	6.60M
2. Canada	3.82M
3. United States	3.79M
4. China	3.70M
5. Brazil	3.29M
6. Australia	2.98M
7. India	1.26M

With so many religions in the world, many people wonder how they can know what is true. Biblical Christianity alone offers satisfying and consistent answers to mankind's most troubling problems. Almost everyone recognizes that this world is broken—and that people are as well. Most religions provide a list of works or a set of ideals that people must live up to in order to have any hope of salvation. These religions leave their followers uncertain of having done enough to gain salvation. The Christian faith teaches that salvation is acceptance of Jesus' work on the cross to pay for sins followed by Spirit-empowered service to God in loving obedience. Some religions locate the problems of the world in God's good creation itself. Thus they promise a release from the body and absorption into some universal force. Christianity promises the believer an eternal glorified body with individual existence and unending fellowship with God and fellow believers on a new earth.

The Nation

After God divided the languages at Babel and scattered the people, nations arose to transmit culture. A **nation** is a large group of people with a common history and language who have developed a strong sense of identity. Even after a nation loses control of its homeland, it often retains its identity. For example, Israel remained a nation even after foreigners drove the Hebrews out of the Promised Land. Today, we often call the Kurdish people of the Middle East a "nation" although they are divided among five separate countries.

Definition of Terms—According to Acts 17:26, God has directed the settling of all the ethnic groups, or nations, of the world. The Greek word translated "nation" is *ethnos*, from which we get the word *ethnic*. The English word *nation* comes from a Latin root meaning "born." Both of these words share the idea of a "common birth."

Nation is often confused with related words. *Nation* refers primarily to people, but *country* refers to the land of the people, and *state* refers to the institution that governs the people. A *tribe* is a large group of people who share a common ancestor and is usually governed by elders. Conflicts occur when political boundaries separate peoples of a nation, as happened often to Poland and the Balkan nations.

A **nation-state** is a nation of people that has established its own government, or state. When one nation conquers other nations beyond its borders, it creates an **empire**. Governments that rule over many nations are called *multinational states*.

Political Maps—A *political map* shows the boundaries that a state has drawn around its people regardless of differences in culture. The world is divided into 196 states. Each state has *sovereignty*, the unlimited authority to run affairs within its own borders. Sovereign states come in all shapes and sizes. The smallest is Vatican City, situated on 108.7 acres inside the city of Rome, Italy. The largest state is Russia, which spans two continents and encompasses about one hundred ethnic groups.

A few territories that claim independence and run their own governments are not officially recognized by most other states. The Chinese island of Taiwan is the best example. Although Taiwan has run its own affairs for more than fifty years and has one of the biggest economies in the world, members of the United Nations refuse to recognize its status and allow it a seat in the United Nations.

Political boundaries are a fundamental feature of culture maps because they mark the limit of a state's authority over the lives of people. People in two neighboring countries may share many culture traits but follow completely different laws. Some political boundaries follow the twists and turns of **natural boundaries**, such as rivers and mountains. **Geometric boundaries** connect geometric points or follow lines of latitude or longitude. Most of the U.S. border with Canada is a geometric boundary drawn along the forty-ninth parallel (49° N). On the other hand, the border of Texas and Mexico follows primarily the Rio Grande.

As you study nations, look for the political boundaries that are unstable. Many boundaries cut across natural features, languages, religions, ethnic groups, or climates. To keep its borders intact, each state must win both the loyalty of its own people and the respect of its neighbors.

Disagreements over the limits of state authority breed the worst kind of violence in the drama of human history—war. At any time, as many as thirty or forty states are at war. When people within a state's borders fight their own government, it is called a **civil war**. The most common goal of a civil war is to replace the ruler. *International* wars occur when independent states fight each other.

Mass Media

Given the apparent prosperity of Western nations, poorer countries often borrow extensively from Western culture. Thanks to mass media, people around the world have adopted such American icons as blue jeans and athletic shoes. In addition, businessmen on every continent wear suits and ties. The rapid rise of cities and mass communication has aided this **cultural convergence**, a growing similarity between cultures.

More subtly, mass media undermines traditional institutions such as the family and the church. Sometimes this undermining is part of the content of the programming, but often it is simply a matter of mass media's existence as a competing authority that claims to represent what is popular, what the masses like. The emphasis on popularity or trendiness often results in media of the lowest common denominator. The news must be entertaining rather than informative. The music must reflect popular trends rather than be rooted in a rich tradition. None of this is to say that mass media is inherently bad. However, it does mean that Christians should carefully consider how they consume mass media lest it undermine biblical authorities or values in their lives.

Seven Largest Countries (Population) (est. 2012)	
Country	*Population*
1. China	1,343,240,000
2. India	1,205,074,000
3. United States	313,847,000
4. Indonesia	248,645,000
5. Brazil	199,321,000
6. Pakistan	190,291,000
7. Nigeria	170,124,000

Section Quiz

1. What is a basic difference between Eastern and Western institutions?
2. What is a nuclear family?
3. What is an extended family?

4–5. Name two common types of political boundaries.

★ Why do political boundaries often lead to conflict?

II. Demography: The Statistics of Society

The study of human populations and their characteristics is called **demography**. Societies use three basic methods to gather demographic information: vital statistics, censuses, and surveys. **Vital statistics** are official records of births, marriages, divorces, and deaths. **Censuses** are official government counts of the entire population within the nation's boundaries. **Surveys** are counts of small samples of the total population. Surveyors and census takers collect information about age, marriage, family size, education, and so on.

Vital Statistics

The word *vital* means "related to life." Vital statistics are the "life signs" of a society. Like a doctor taking a pulse, nations seek statistics about the life and health of their people. The two basic vital statistics are (1) the rate of natural increase and (2) life expectancy.

Natural Increase

Countries measure population increase by comparing the number of births to the number of deaths each year. The number of children born per 1,000 people is called the **crude birthrate**. In 2012 the United States had a crude birthrate of 13.7 (13.7 live births for every 1,000 people). If new babies were the only factor in population growth, the population would increase by 1.4 percent each year. But demographers must also calculate the number of people who die each year per 1,000 people, called the **crude death rate**. In 2012 the U.S. crude death rate was 8.4. Subtracting the number of deaths from the number of births (13.7 – 8.4) gives the **rate of natural increase**. It is 5.3 per 1,000 or 0.5 percent.

Christians and non-Christians alike are discouraged by high death rates. However, some move further by opposing high growth rates. They want to decrease the world's growth rate, which is now about 1.1 percent, to match the low rate in Western societies. But the Bible gives a different perspective on birth and death. Suffering and death are the inevitable consequence of sin in this fallen world (Rom. 8:22), and having children is a sign of God's blessing as families obey God's Creation Mandate. In the midst of sorrow and death, children offer hope of new life (Ps. 127:3–5).

Life Expectancy

Before the Flood, people lived long lives; Methuselah, for example, lived a record 969 years. But after the Flood, **life expectancy** (the number of years a person is expected to live) declined rapidly. By Moses' day, life expectancy had fallen to seventy years (Ps. 90:10). Over the next several centuries life expectancy fluctuated depending on several factors, including war, disease, and food supply. For example, Europe experienced population stagnation during the Middle Ages.

Around 1650, however, the growth in world population began to increase. Over the next two hundred years, the world's population doubled (from five hundred million to one billion). Eighty years later, the population had doubled again. By 1975 the world population had reached four billion and was adding nearly one billion people every decade. By 2012 the world population had passed seven billion.

One measure of national development is increasing life expectancy, which includes lower infant mortality and a longer average life span.

Advances in technology and medicine have done much to increase world population. Better crops and new vaccinations have practically eliminated the effects of malnutrition and some common diseases that once took countless lives. Life expectancy in the United States in 1901 was forty-nine years; by the turn of the next century it was seventy-seven years. As of 2012 it was approximately 78.5 years. The statistics are even better for women, who usually outlive men by about 5.4 years, although this gap is shrinking.

Health improvements are most apparent in the declining death rate among children, called **infant mortality**. Infant mortality is measured by comparing the number of live births to the number of infants who die in their first year. Before the Industrial Revolution, nearly half of all babies died before they reached their first birthday. In 2012 the world infant mortality rate was 39.48 (a little more than 39 infants per 1,000 live births die before their first birthday). Infant mortality in the United States is only 6. Singapore has the lowest rate at 2.65. This achievement is the result of numerous factors, including better nutrition, better prenatal care, improved medicines, and advances in technology that allow earlier detection and treatment of formerly fatal health problems.

Despite modern advances, however, science still faces many obstacles in the quest to increase human life expectancy. About thirty-four hundred years ago, Moses lived to the age of 120. The only post-Flood person known to have surpassed that age to date is Madame Jeanne Calment of Arles, France, who died in 1997 at age 122.

Section Quiz

1. What do we call the study of human populations and their characteristics?
2. What two statistics are used to compute the rate of natural increase of a population?
3. What are the main reasons for recent increases in life expectancy?
★ What role has America played in the decline of the infant mortality rate?

Community Statistics

Vital statistics help us to understand the life of a typical family in each nation. Nations are also interested in communities—groups of families who live and work together. The growing population of communities indicates a healthy society.

Urbanization

No hard and fast rule distinguishes among the different types of communities. Usage varies regarding what constitutes a city, town, or village. For simplicity, demographers have divided populated areas into two broad categories: *urban areas*, which have a large number of buildings and people in a small area, and *rural areas*, which have few buildings and people in a large area. According to the arbitrary definitions of the U.S. Census Bureau, rural communities have a population of less than five thousand, and cities have a population of more than five thousand.

The size and number of communities have increased throughout most of history. Since the Industrial Revolution, however, the move to urban areas has become a virtual stampede, as people have left their farms and small villages to seek opportunities in big cities. Two hundred years ago, 95 percent of Americans lived on farms, but now fewer than 5 percent do. The growth of urban areas at the expense of rural areas is called **urbanization**. More than 80 percent of Americans (and 51 percent of the world population) live in an urban area.

Vancouver, Canada, presents an orderly, inviting urban atmosphere.

The rise of large cities during the twentieth century was amazing. In 1900, only twelve cities had a population of more than one million. Today, over four hundred cities fit that category, and more are added almost every year. Another trend affecting urbanization is the tendency of many Americans to prefer living in the **suburbs**, an area between urban and rural areas that offers proximity to urban benefits but without the attending problems.

Cities in developing countries are growing rapidly and will soon overtake older, established cities in developed countries. In 2013, nine of the world's top ten fastest-growing cities were in Asia.

Population Density

Crowding has been a serious problem since early in history. Abraham and Lot were forced to separate because their herds had become so large that "the land was not able to bear them" (Gen. 13:6). Daniel Boone and other pioneers on the American frontier moved steadily westward in search of "elbow room." Even in modern industrial cities, where people can buy their basic needs from afar, crowding is still a concern. City leaders must work hard to provide adequate services such as sanitation, hospitals and emergency medical services, and police and fire protection.

Population density is the average number of people who live on each square mile (or kilometer) of land. For example, the average density in Egypt is about 219 people on every square mile of land. France has about the same population as Egypt, but its density is 303 people per square mile because it has a smaller area than Egypt.

Population density is a fairly good measure of crowding, but people are not spread evenly across the landscape. They generally cluster around good farmland. Nearly all of the Egyptian people, for example, live in a narrow band of land along the banks of the Nile River and in the Nile Delta. Thousands of square miles of that desert country are virtually uninhabited.

Demographers have developed an even more accurate way to measure how dense the population is. They take into account the amount of **arable land** (land that can be used to plant crops). For example, only 2.9 percent of Egypt's 386,660 square miles of land is arable. By comparing the total population to the arable land, demographers find the **physiological density**. Egypt's physiological density is more than six thousand people per square mile. Unlike Egypt, France has 33.53 percent arable land, and its physiological density is less than one thousand. This statistic also indicates that the lower the physiological density, the easier it is for a nation to feed itself.

Many groups are worried about the increasing size of cities, the loss of wilderness, and the decline in rural societies. But the Bible has a different perspective on urbanization and population density. God meant for the earth to be subdued. He provided Israel with walled cities in the Promised Land, and He made provisions to ensure that the land would not return to its wild state (Deut. 7:22). The ultimate

El Salvador has one of the highest population densities in the Western Hemisphere.

Terracing steep land, such as this area in Nepal, makes hilly or mountainous land arable and is an example of good stewardship.

Thomas Malthus on Overpopulation

Many people in the eighteenth century believed that humans could make society perfect. Thomas Malthus (1766–1834) attacked this idealistic view in a new economic theory based on the harsh realities at that time in Britain. In *An Essay of the Principle of Population As It Affects the Future Improvement of Society* (1798), he argued that people will never escape misery and poverty because food supplies cannot keep up with the population increase. Malthus claimed the only checks on population growth were war, famine, disease, and self-restraint.

Embracing Malthus's theory, many people of that day began to believe that if the world population did not stop growing, widespread famine would soon prevail as agriculture failed to provide enough food. People came to view humanity's growth as its own worst enemy. Economists began to discourage charity and to justify subsistence wages for labor as a means of restraining the population growth.

However, the people of Great Britain soon discovered that Malthus's predictions were not accurate. He had not treated the facts scientifically. Neither was he aware of all of the changes that the Industrial Revolution was bringing. Before he died, a new wave of economic optimism swept Britain. But whenever the economy periodically declines, Malthus's theory again becomes popular. Today, many predict the end of humanity unless people take drastic measures to curb the rising world population, especially in India and China. However, proposed "solutions" such as abortion and euthanasia ("mercy killing") are nothing less than murder.

Malthus mistakenly believed that poverty and famine, such as have been widely evident in many parts of Africa, were caused by overpopulation. In reality, people are a country's greatest natural resource.

destination of His people is not a wilderness but the New Jerusalem, a massive city that will cover some two thousand square miles and be filled with people.

The following chapters examine urban areas (why they arose and what they show about human geography) as well as rural areas. You will discover some of the natural limitations that God has placed on human settlement and see some of the natural wonders every nation takes pride in.

Section Quiz

1. Why have rural populations decreased in most developed countries?
2. What term describes the growing trend of populations to migrate to cities?
3. What is population density?
★ Should Christians oppose urbanization and the utilization of wilderness areas? Support your answer.

III. Politics: The Governance of Society

When the waters receded and Noah stepped off the ark, God instituted human *government*, the rule of man over man. He gave rulers the power of life and death for one primary purpose: restraining violence. By executing murderers, the government shows respect for the value of human life and helps deter other murders (Gen. 9:6).

Duties of Government

The Bible defines the duties of government (Rom. 13:1–6). Its basic responsibility is to preserve order and protect its citizens from violence by promoting good and punishing evil. To fulfill these obligations, governments provide justice and defense. *Justice* entails a system of laws and courts to settle disputes between citizens. *Defense* entails a police force to protect law-abiding citizens from domestic criminals and military forces to protect citizens from foreign attack. When no form of governing authority exists and people are doing whatever they want, a state of **anarchy** exists.

Types of Government

Governments can be classified many ways. The most basic way, however, is according to the ruler's source of power. Romans 13:1 teaches that all governments, whether secular or religious, receive their ultimate authority from God.

Authoritarian Government

Authoritarian governments hold power by claiming an authority higher than the people they govern. Monarchies are an authoritarian form of government. Monarchs, usually kings or queens, receive their authority by birth. An **absolute monarch** rules as he pleases. Although monarchies were far more common in the past than they are now, a few absolute monarchies still exist (e.g., Saudi Arabia and Jordan).

Government's primary purpose—at local, state or provincial, and national levels—is to ensure justice.

A few countries' governments are headed by absolute monarchs, such as Saudi Arabia's King Abdullah.

Another type of authoritarian government is a **dictatorship**. A dictator is a person who rules by the authority of the military. Often, as in the case of Napoleon, he rises to power with public support. Some dictatorships, however, are ruled by a small group that has forced itself on the people. Dictators usually establish their own political party and allow no opposition to their actions. Dictatorships are common in undeveloped and developing countries.

The most extreme form of authoritarian government is a **totalitarian government**. Such governments tend to make decisions about almost every detail of their people's lives. Citizens must get permission before they can perform most activities that we take for granted. China is the largest country ruled by a totalitarian government. The leaders of the Chinese Communist Party also have behind them tremendous military power to back their rule. Although the people must vote, the only candidates are members of the Communist Party, and they face no opposing candidates. North Korea is perhaps the most repressive totalitarian government today.

Government

It is important to note that not all monarchies are bad and not all elected governments are good. Any form of government can be corrupted. Some Christian political philosophers have noted that what is needed is government that mixes monarchy, aristocracy, and democracy. Democracy gives people a voice, but if it has no moral underpinning or if it is swayed by a demagogue, it needs to be checked by an aristocracy, rule by men known for their wisdom. While a nation benefits from the decisive leadership of a single person, he or she needs to be accountable to the people and other officials to avoid being corrupted by power.

Elected Government

In contrast to authoritarian governments, elected governments rely on the consent of the people to remain in power. The word *democracy* is often used to describe elected governments. **Democracy** originally described a government in which the whole population ruled. The first *direct* or *pure democracies* arose in Athens and some other ancient Greek city-states. Adult male citizens could vote on laws and other issues that came before the government. However, given the size of many modern nations, most democracies today are *indirect* or *representative democracies* in which the people elect representatives who vote on laws for them. The people have an opportunity to voice their opinions and even to run for office if they wish.

Another form of modern democracy is a limited or **constitutional monarchy**, in which the people have limited the power of the monarch by law. The monarch functions more as a figurehead;

Iraqi women were finally allowed to vote in their country's first free elections in 2005.

Representative democracies permit the greatest degree of personal freedom of any form of government.

the real power belongs to an elected legislature. The most powerful leader of the elected assembly supervises the writing of laws and heads the bureaucracy that executes the laws. Great Britain is an example of such a government.

The other major type of representative democracy is a **republic**. Unlike constitutional monarchies, republics elect their national leader, generally known as the president, who supervises the bureaucracy while the legislature writes laws.

Section Quiz

1. What is government's basic responsibility?
2. What is anarchy?
3. Where does an absolute monarch obtain his authority? a dictator? a president?
4. What is the main difference between a pure democracy and a representative democracy?
✶ Is it possible for a dictatorship to retain a democratic form of government? Why or why not?

Relations Among Governments

Every nation is concerned about its relations with other countries. The set of principles that guides a government's international relations is called its **foreign policy**. Governments have two alternatives to resolve disputes: negotiation or war.

The Threat of War

Nations can influence their neighbors through foreign trade and *foreign aid* (gifts of money, goods, or technology to foreign nations). But the most obvious (although not necessarily the best) way to influence neighbors is the threat of military attack.

Nations frequently evaluate their military strength and that of their potential enemies to ensure that they can defend themselves against attack. Military strength can be measured in many ways. *Active troop strength* (the number of full-time soldiers in uniform) is the most common measurement, but it can be misleading; the largest army is not necessarily the most effective army. For example, with fewer than fifty thousand men, Alexander the Great defeated a Persian army of more than a quarter of a million men by relying on high discipline and superior tactics. The best measurement of modern military strength is national *annual defense spending* on military technology. As of 2012 the United States remained the only superpower in the world. However, Russia and China have greatly increased their military expenditures.

Powerful nations tend to vie for cultural and political leadership (hegemony) over their weaker neighbors. The powerful nations consider the weaker neighbors they try to influence to be their *sphere of influence*. One cannot understand events in any of the world's culture regions without appreciating who the "big dogs" are and who the underdogs are.

Because the United States is currently the world's only superpower, its sphere of influence circles the globe. The U.S. has built military bases and stationed troops in many regions to help it "project power" for the benefit of its allies. As a capitalist nation that thrives

Greatest Military Expenditures as Percentage of GDP (2012)

Country	% of GDP
1. Saudi Arabia	8.7
2. United States	4.7
3. Russia	3.9
4. South Korea	2.7
5. United Kingdom	2.6
6. India	2.6
7. France	2.3
8. Turkey	2.3
9. China	2.0

Greatest Military Expenditures (2012)

Country	Amount ($B)
1. United States	711.0
2. China	143.0
3. Russia	71.9
4. United Kingdom	62.7
5. France	62.5
6. Japan	59.3
7. India	48.9

on trade, the United States believes the spread of freedom and capitalism is a vital *national interest* that should guide its foreign policy.

The first concern of U.S. foreign policy is the seven leading world powers that have the most influence on world politics. They are, by region, Russia in Central Eurasia; France, the United Kingdom, Germany, and Italy in Western Europe; and China and Japan in East Asia. Almost every other nation consults them when making foreign policy decisions.

The United States is also concerned about *militarized states*, nations that have a large number of soldiers and spend a large percentage of their GDP on weapons. Militarized states might be poor, but they are very dangerous. War could break out on their borders at any moment. Examples include North Korea, India, and Pakistan. (You will be studying more about militarized states as you study each cultural subregion.)

A third area of concern is the nations that oppose the role of the United States as a superpower and that reject democracy and capitalism. The most dangerous of these nations are **rogue nations** that ignore some of the most fundamental principles of international relations. They willingly use chemical weapons, terrorism, or any other means they deem necessary—even against their own people—to get their way or increase their power. The two most common types of rogue nations are Communist countries, such as North Korea, and radical Muslim nations, such as Iran. The free nations are especially concerned that such rogue nations might provide terrorists with weapons of mass destruction, whether chemical, biological, or nuclear.

Negotiating Peace

Diplomacy is the art of negotiating agreements between nations. Formal agreements between nations are called **treaties**. To avoid war, nations can negotiate two kinds of treaties. They can either talk to their enemies and sign a *peace treaty* or make strong *military alliances* with their friends, agreeing to help each other in case of attack.

For most of its history, the United States followed Thomas Jefferson's advice to pursue "peace, commerce, and honest friendship with all nations—entangling alliances with none." But the tragedy of two world wars and the successive threats of communism and terrorism to world peace have forced it to change its foreign policy. The United States has made military alliances with more than forty countries. In the 1940s it led the world in creating two significant *international organizations*: the North Atlantic Treaty Organization (NATO) and the United Nations (UN).

In 1947 the United States joined Canada and most of the free nations of Western Europe in establishing **NATO** to protect Western Europe from the threat of the Soviet Union. NATO's arsenal of nuclear weapons, tanks, and soldiers prevented the Soviet Union from invading Western Europe and avoided open war.

The **UN** was also formed in the wake of World War II. From past experience, most member nations knew that the UN would

Diplomacy and treaties, such as this one being signed by the Russian and American leaders, often prevent wars.

Flags representing the member nations fly on the grounds of the United Nations Building in New York City.

not stop war, but they wanted a neutral place where they could negotiate peaceful solutions to disputes. Representatives of the UN member nations meet in the General Assembly to vote on agreements. But the five major Allies of World War II—the United States, the United Kingdom, France, China, and Russia—hold the reins of power. They are the five permanent members of the **Security Council**. Any one of them can veto (reject) decisions of the General Assembly. Therefore, the UN cannot make important policies without support from these major members.

The UN has proved to be much less successful than NATO. Because of the Soviet Union's veto power, the UN was helpless to intervene in dozens of bloody wars that the Soviets supported around the world. America's military alliances and resolve, not the UN, helped contain communism and bring about the final collapse of the Soviet Empire. The UN has also proven itself weak in acting against rogue nations.

When the elder George Bush was president of the United States, he hoped that a "new world order" would emerge from the ruins of communism. But his vision did not materialize. In 1991 civil war engulfed the multinational state of Yugoslavia on Europe's southern border. The bloodshed between 1991 and 1995 was the worst in Europe since World War II. It seemed that every action taken by NATO, the UN, or the United States only worsened the situation. Eventually, however, peace was restored, and Yugoslavia was divided into smaller states.

Yugoslavia's civil war revealed some of the serious flaws in the Enlightenment concept of the nation-state. One flaw was the two competing principles that were working against each other. According to the principle of **self-determination**, all peoples have a right to vote for the type of government they will have. However, if self-determination were taken too far, almost every sovereign country would be in danger. Few countries are true nation-states, consisting wholly of only one kind of people. If every minority voted to become independent, most nations would lose their **territorial integrity** (defensible borders).

When four ethnic minorities in Yugoslavia voted to become independent in 1990 and 1991, the Western nations recognized their independence, in spite of protests from the Serbs, the most powerful

Red Cross

The Red Cross is one of the most widely recognized volunteer organizations in the world. This organization demonstrates people's willingness to make sacrifices to relieve the sufferings of others in times of war or natural disaster.

Red Cross headquarters in Geneva

The Red Cross headquarters is in Geneva, Switzerland. Its universally recognized symbol—a red cross on a white field—is based on the flag of Switzerland. Each nation organizes its own society, which agrees to follow the general guidelines of the headquarters. Muslim countries also have a relief agency called the Red Crescent.

Swiss businessman Jean Henri Dunant (doo-NAHN) founded the Red Cross in 1863 after he witnessed the carnage of the Battle of Solferino in 1859. At a Red Cross meeting in 1864, various nations drew up the **Geneva Convention**, a treaty establishing basic rules for how nations should treat wounded soldiers and prisoners of war. The Red Cross monitors adherence to the Geneva Convention and delivers aid packages to prisoners. Although the original focus of the Red Cross was assisting victims of war, it has expanded its activities to include collecting blood, reuniting families, assisting during natural disasters, and distributing medicine and relief goods to needy nations.

ethnic group in Yugoslavia. But when minorities in the new republics voted to break away and rejoin the Serbs, Europe refused to recognize their right to self-determination, revealing a major inconsistency.

Another flaw was that the Enlightenment failed to recognize that God in His sovereignty has established each government. People need to learn to live together despite their differences. It is foolish to believe that self-determination will bring peace. The root problem is the sinful human heart, which does not change based on where people live or how they govern. The only solution to world strife is a miraculous change of heart, which is the realm of Christ, not human kings.

Section Quiz

1. What is the best measurement of the military strength of a nation?
2. What is a rogue nation?
3. Name the alliance between the U.S., Canada, and many free nations of Western Europe.
4. How can the five permanent members of the Security Council control the policies of the UN?
★ Why do you think the UN is weak in opposing the actions of rogue nations?

Chapter 5 Review

Making Connections

1. What is the most widespread language family in the world?
2. How is the rate of natural increase derived for a country?
3. Why has the world's population increased dramatically since 1650?
4. What is the value of calculating physiological density?
5. Using terms from this chapter, describe the government of the United States.

Developing Geography Skills

1. Use a map of your state to find and list all of its natural and geometric boundaries.
2. Consider your own city or a city near you. What advantages might attract rural people, and what problems might they find?

Thinking Critically

1. Why are death rates relatively high in some developed countries?
2. Why do most rogue nations have authoritarian governments?

Living in God's World

1. Missionaries find demographic information helpful as they plan to reach the nations for Christ. Pick a country to research. Use the CIA Factbook or Operation World websites to gather demographic information about that country, and write a brief paragraph explaining how that information could be useful to a missionary.
2. Make a list of the mass media that you use in a given week (websites, news magazines, TV programs, recorded music, etc.). Evaluate this media in light of both its explicitly stated content and its implicit values. Describe how your evaluation should adjust your consumption of mass media.

People, Places, and Things to Know

society
dialect
language family
culture region
subregion
nuclear family
extended family
nation
nation-state
empire
political boundary
natural boundary
geometric boundary
civil war
cultural convergence
demography
vital statistics
census
survey
crude birthrate
crude death rate
rate of natural increase
life expectancy
infant mortality
urbanization
suburb
population density
arable land
physiological density
anarchy
absolute monarch
dictatorship
totalitarian government
democracy
constitutional monarchy
republic
foreign policy
rogue nation
diplomacy
treaty
NATO
UN
Security Council
self-determination
territorial integrity
Geneva Convention

Unit Three
NORTH AMERICA

𝒩orth America offers a great variety of scenes, from large cities to mountains and long stretches of plains. People settled on this continent a few centuries after the Flood, and many civilizations have developed here. Rivers continue to play an important role in many cities, including the Allegheny River that flows beside Pittsburgh.

CANADA

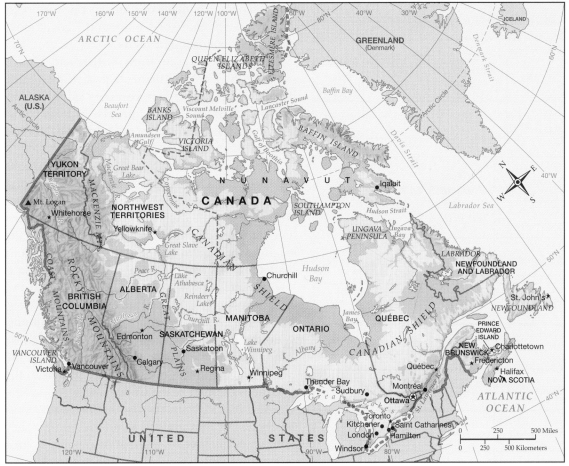

The North American continent can be divided into three sections: Canada, the United States, and Middle America. Because of the vast cultural differences between Middle America and the other two countries, however, we include our study of that region in Latin America and focus in this unit on Canada and the United States.

Canada has the second-largest land area in the world (3,855,174 square miles). It also has the longest coastline (151,485 miles), including the coastlines of its 52,455 islands. Yet it has a relatively small population (34,300,083 as of 2012). This unusual combination offers Canada great benefits. Canadians are able to make a comfortable living, enjoy the blessings of both rural and urban environments, and export large quantities of raw materials.

Canada has much in common with the United States, and the two nations are almost like siblings in many ways. Canada shares its only international border with the United States—3,987 miles along the lower forty-eight states and another 1,538 miles with Alaska. In fact, the U.S.–Canadian border is the longest unfortified border in the world. The two nations have been at peace for more than 150 years. Tourists, workers, and goods cross the borders with relative ease, although security has been tightened since the 2001 terrorist attacks on the United States. Around 90 percent of Canadians live within a hundred miles of the U.S.–Canada border.

Canada and the United States are the richest and most industrialized nations in the Western Hemisphere. They trade more goods with each other than with any other nation in the world. The United

Canada Fast Facts					
Capital	Area (sq. mi.)	Pop. (M)	Pop. Density (per sq. mi.)	Per Capita GDP ($US)	Life Span
Ottawa	3,855,106	34.3	8.9	$40,500	81.48

Province/ *Territory	Capital	Date of Entry to Confederation	Area (sq. mi.)	Pop. (2011) (K)
Newfoundland and Labrador	St. John's	1949	143,050	515
Nova Scotia	Halifax	1867	20,440	922
Prince Edward Island	Charlottetown	1873	2,195	140
New Brunswick	Fredericton	1867	27,559	751
Quebec	Quebec City	1867	523,775	7,903
Ontario	Toronto	1867	350,825	12,852
Manitoba	Winnipeg	1870	213,265	1,208
Saskatchewan	Regina	1905	227,125	1,033
Alberta	Edmonton	1905	247,145	3,645
British Columbia	Victoria	1871	356,185	4,400
*Yukon Territory	Whitehorse	1898	183,295	34
*Northwest Territories	Yellowknife	1870	441,625	41
*Nunavut	Iqaluit	1999	725,025	32

States depends on many of Canada's raw materials, such as nickel and wood pulp; and Canada buys many U.S. manufactured goods.

Both nations grew from British and French roots. Both cleared settlements in a wild frontier. Both worship primarily in churches led by Protestant preachers or Catholic priests. In both countries, significant numbers of native peoples still live in the West and the cold North.

Canada also shares many geographic regions with the United States. The Canadian Atlantic coast is similar to the coast of New England. A few miles inland are the Appalachian Highlands, the northern tip of the same Appalachian Mountains that run the length of the eastern United States. The two nations share the St. Lawrence Seaway and the Great Lakes.

The interior lowlands and the Great Plains of Canada resemble the heartland of the United States. The Rocky Mountains run through both nations, as do the Pacific mountain ranges. Between those mountains are the intermountain basins. And the Northwest Territories of Canada are similar to the Alaskan wilderness of the United States.

Also like siblings, the two nations sometimes squabble, but they are still a cultural family. They sometimes disagree on international policies, such as environmental regulations and trade. But the common geographic and cultural bonds that link Canada and the United States have only deepened with the passage of time.

I. The Maritime Provinces

Canada has ten provinces and three territories. The four smallest provinces, located in the eastern corner along the Atlantic coast, are known as the Maritime Provinces. **Maritime** means "bordering the sea." For centuries, sailors have lived in scattered villages along the coasts, depending on the sea for their livelihood, just as many of their neighbors do in New England.

Newfoundland

The rocky island of **Newfoundland** (NOO fun lund) along with a large strip of land on the mainland form the province known as Newfoundland. In 1964, however, the province officially adopted the name "Newfoundland and Labrador" to give both parts of the province equal honor.

The island is actually the northeastern edge of the Appalachian Mountain system, part of which lies underwater. Its rocky coasts and rolling hills are covered by stunted forests. Beautiful **fjords** (FYORDZ)—long, narrow bays carved by glaciers and filled with sea water—attract many tourists to the western coast, while bird sanctuaries attract puffins and hosts of other nesting birds.

The Grand Banks

Most Newfoundlanders live on the island. Although the climate is cool, the Gulf Stream keeps the climate from becoming too harsh. The capital, St. John's, sits beside the world-famous **Grand Banks** fishing grounds, where the cod-fishing industry reigned as king for almost five hundred years. John Cabot discovered the Grand Banks in 1497 and reported to the king of England that enough fish were there to feed his kingdom "till the end of time."

In just a few years, fishing boats from many parts of Western Europe were braving the icebergs, fogs, and storms to harvest fish. Cod became the most important commercial fish, but haddock, flounder, and herring were also abundant. The continental shelf off the southeast coast of Newfoundland extends far out into the Atlantic Ocean, providing a perfect fish "nursery." The comparatively shallow (averaging six hundred feet) waters receive plenty of sunlight, and the warm Gulf Stream mixes with the icy, oxygen-rich Labrador Current, encouraging explosive growth of plankton and other fish food. Sadly, this thriving industry was not to last. After World War II, the number of European trawlers (large commercial fishing ships) operating on the Grand Banks increased dramatically. By 1992, fish stocks had dwindled to the point of collapse, prompting the Canadian government to impose a moratorium on cod fishing there. One of the responsibilities humans have under the Creation Mandate is the wise management of natural resources. Due to the Fall, however, greed and misuse can greatly damage the creation.

Europeans built their first settlement in the New World in Newfoundland—a Viking outpost dating back to AD 1000. The British claimed the island in 1583, but they opposed settlement, fearing that local fishermen might become rivals to British companies. Fishermen, however, secretly built winter camps in the coves (small sheltered bays) around the island. Fishing villages sprang up long before the first official settlements in the nineteenth century. The prosperous and independent-minded residents of Newfoundland did not join Canada until 1949. It was the last province to join the Confederation.

Labrador

The peninsula of **Labrador** on the mainland is cold year-round. The frigid Labrador Current carries Arctic water and icebergs past the coast. As air temperatures dip below -50°F in the winter, the surface of the coastal waters freezes, and freshly caught fish freeze almost instantly. Clarence Birdseye saw how this freezing kept fish edible for months and in 1915 conceived the idea of preparing frozen foods.

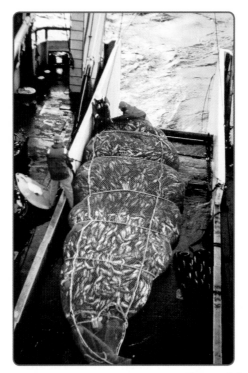 

The catch from a commercial trawler (left) is as large as the entire boat holding the pre-industrial fishing catch (right), leading to overfishing.

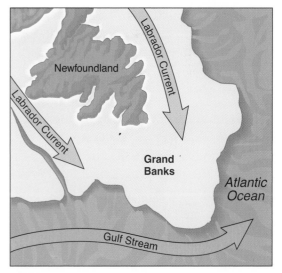

Mixing of ocean currents at the Grand Banks

In spite of the cold, Labrador has stark beauty. Rocky tundra covers the north, and thick forests of spruce and pine blanket the south. During the summer, lumberjacks fell the evergreen trees and ship the logs to mills at the island city of Corner Brook. Several mountain ranges have alpine summits. Mount Caubvick, the highest peak in Canada east of the Canadian Rockies, dominates the Torngat Range in the far north. One of the largest herds of caribou in the world migrates to Labrador each spring to calve.

Under Labrador's rugged mountains lie zinc and one of the largest iron ore deposits in Canada. Mines near Labrador City, in what is known as the Labrador Trough, extract more iron ore than any other province.

Nova Scotia

The French settled the three southernmost Maritime Provinces, and called the region Acadia. They established the first French settlement in the New World, Port Royal, in 1604 on the Bay of Fundy in Nova Scotia.

Henry Wadsworth Longfellow's poem *Evangeline* helped make Acadia famous. It tells about the tragic conflict between British and French settlers. The trouble started in 1621 when Scottish colonists arrived and began claiming land that the French wanted. They fought numerous wars before the Treaty of Utrecht (1713) awarded the area to Britain. But disputes continued. In 1755, the British decided to resolve the problem by forcing thousands of French Acadians from their homes and shipping them south. Some of the Acadians settled in New Orleans, where they became known as Cajuns. A few others escaped expulsion and later returned to Acadia. Their descendants continue to speak French and follow French ways.

Today, most Nova Scotians have a British heritage. Scottish settlers named the province Nova Scotia ("New Scotland") because of the striking geographic similarities to Scotland.

Nova Scotia is a long, narrow peninsula connected to the mainland by a twenty-mile-wide strip. Residents are never far from one of the many sandy beaches. The Canso Causeway connects the peninsula to Cape Breton Island, off the northeast corner of the peninsula. Canso Strait is some of the deepest water ever bridged. Nova Scotia leads the nation in its lobster and scallop catch.

The Atlantic Upland dominates the landscape. Coastal lowlands permit fruit growing and dairy farming. The Annapolis Valley is extensive and is the third most important fruit-growing area in Canada. Forests provide many of the Christmas trees sold each year in Canada and around the world. In 1996, the capital, **Halifax**, merged with several suburbs and became the Halifax Regional Municipality (HRM). In 2012, *MoneySense* magazine rated Halifax the fourth best place to live in Canada.

The Canso Causeway links Cape Breton Island to mainland Nova Scotia.

Bay of Fundy — *Highest tide*

Situated between Nova Scotia and New Brunswick, the Bay of Fundy is the most famous bay of the Atlantic Ocean. It has the highest tides in the world, rising and falling an average of forty-seven feet every twelve hours.

Irregularities in the shapes of the coast cause the height of tides to vary. Because the Bay of Fundy gradually narrows and gets shallower as it extends north, the bay creates a natural funnel. The tides rush farther inland here than anywhere else in the world. Visitors at Moncton, New Brunswick, at the north end of the bay, can watch a two-foot-high bore (tidal wave) flow in from many miles away.

The tides have other interesting effects along the Bay of Fundy. The tide climbs thirteen feet up over the rapids of the St. John River, making the rapids flow backwards. Visitors come from around the world to watch the St. John Reversing Falls. Another popular destination is "the Rocks." At low tide, people walk safely onto a dry beach at the foot of towering rock formations; but at high tide the ocean surrounds the rocks, which become islands. Visitors must quickly climb ladders to stay above the water.

High tide (left) and low tide (right) in the Bay of Fundy are dramatically different.

New Brunswick

French Acadians make up about 40 percent of New Brunswick's population and represent the second-largest French population of any province (after Quebec). The rest of New Brunswick's citizens are mainly of British or Loyalist ancestry. During the American War for Independence, approximately thirty thousand Americans who remained loyal to King George III fled to New Brunswick, the only Maritime Province that shares a border with the United States.

Most of New Brunswick is coastal lowland. Farmers in the south grow potatoes, as do their neighbors in Maine. The southwestern part of the province is Atlantic Upland, a continuation of Maine's New England Upland. The Appalachian Mountains, which extend into the northern parts of New Brunswick, are mined for lead, copper, and zinc. The forests also provide lumber.

The Swallowtail Lighthouse in New Brunswick shines from an island at the entrance to the Bay of Fundy.

Prince Edward Island

Prince Edward Island is a tiny island in the Gulf of St. Lawrence. P.E.I., as it is affectionately called, is the smallest Canadian province,

This house at Cavendish, Prince Edward Island, inspired the novel *Anne of Green Gables*.

only slightly larger than the state of Delaware. Its farmland supports the highest population density of any Canadian province—about sixty-two people per square mile. Yet, because the people are so spread out, this "crowded" island is mostly rural.

Because the entire island is arable lowland, it is sometimes called Canada's Million-Acre Farm. The fertile soil has a distinct red color from rusted oxides. Leading the provinces in potato production, P.E.I. has earned the nickname "Spud Island." Beef and dairy cattle also enjoy good pastureland.

The quaint villages and sandy beaches make the scenery picturesque and inviting to tourists. Many foreigners visit the Victorian-style Green Gables House, made famous by L. M. Montgomery's novel *Anne of Green Gables*. Many residents opposed the construction of a bridge to the mainland because it threatened the island's quaint lifestyle and their individualism. Nevertheless, the bridge was completed in 1996.

A majority of the islanders have a Scottish heritage. In fact, more than half of their last names begin with "Mac." Weekend festivals feature Scottish traditions such as bagpipes and kilts.

Section Quiz

1–2. What two European countries competed for control of Canada?
 3. Who is Canada's major trading partner?
 4. Contrast Newfoundland with the provinces of Acadia.
 5. Where are the highest tides in Canada?
 ★ Which of the Maritime Provinces would you like to visit? Why?

II. The Central Provinces

Canada lies far north of the equator, where the rays of the sun provide less warmth. Furthermore, huge inland areas lack the moderating effect of the oceans. As a result, most Canadian cities are on the southern strip of the nation, where the temperatures are less severe.

The area along the Great Lakes and the St. Lawrence River is a band of humid continental climate that escapes the frigid extremes found farther north. Summer temperatures along that band rise into the eighties, and farmland remains frost-free for about six months. The two biggest and most populous provinces—Quebec and Ontario—are in this climate on the rich southern plains and valleys. Pioneers cleared forests of pine, hemlock, sugar maple, and beech to plant their farms and to found their greatest cities.

Few people live in the harsh "northland." A solid mass of hard rock, called the **Canadian Shield**, covers most of eastern Canada. The Canadian Shield (or *Laurentian Plateau*) rims **Hudson Bay** like a giant horseshoe. The soil is thin and very poor. Either during the Flood or the Ice Age that followed, the top soil was removed and the bedrock was exposed. The glaciers that formed during the Ice Age also might have carved out the thousands of lakes and marshes in the shield. Although it is poor in soil, the northland has been a blessing to miners, who exploit rich deposits of iron, copper, nickel, gold, lead, zinc, and cobalt.

A subpolar climate dominates the Canadian Shield. Needle-leaf evergreen trees, such as spruce, fir, and pine, are about the only trees that grow, and they become increasingly stunted as one travels north. These coniferous forests, called **taiga** (TYE gah), cover most of the Central Provinces. Moose, beaver, and black bear live in the cool forests, and plenty of insects appear during the warm months. In the northernmost extremes, trees cannot grow at all and give way to tundra.

Quebec

Canada's earliest European explorers came from France. Jacques Cartier, Samuel de Champlain, and Robert de La Salle mapped the St. Lawrence and Great Lakes regions, which they called New France.

The discovery of valuable furs of beaver, mink, otter, and muskrat lured many hardy Frenchmen during the early seventeenth century. These pioneers became part of Canada's folklore, much like the free-spirited frontiersmen in the United States. They crisscrossed the interior lakes and frigid rivers, often carrying their canoes for miles on their backs.

While the French trapped furs and traded with the Huron Indians, the English explored the Hudson Bay farther north. The Hudson Bay Company, chartered in 1670, opened a thriving trade with the Algonquian Indians. As the British increased their holdings near Hudson Bay, and as the thirteen American colonies expanded, the French felt squeezed from both sides. The French and the British fought sporadically until Britain won a decisive victory in the Seven Years' War (1757–63). Tensions between the British and the French still exist in Canada today.

Unlike America, which is often called a "melting pot" of peoples, Canada takes pride in its cultural "mosaic." The varied peoples who settled Canada have retained more of the distinct and colorful attributes of their Old World cultures. This mosaic is most apparent in Quebec, Canada's largest province. Eighty percent of the population of Quebec are French speaking and call themselves

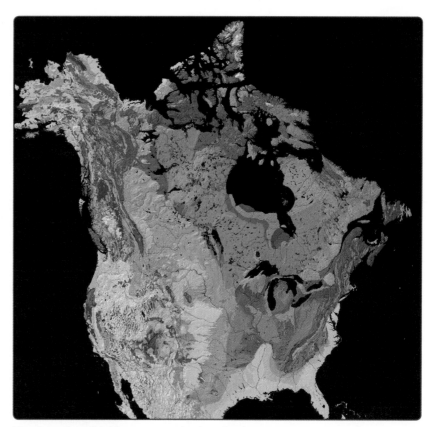

The Canadian Shield appears in shades of red.

Great variety in vegetation is evident in North America.

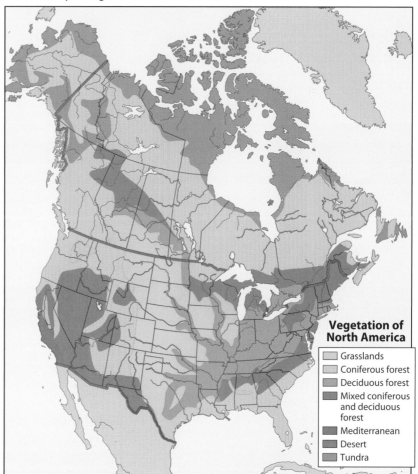

Vegetation of North America

- Grasslands
- Coniferous forest
- Deciduous forest
- Mixed coniferous and deciduous forest
- Mediterranean
- Desert
- Tundra

Saint Lawrence Seaway

The **St. Lawrence River** is one of the largest rivers in Canada. The French explorer Jacques Cartier, who sailed up the river in 1535, called it the River of Canada. Others have called it the Mother of Canada because it conveyed Canada's early explorers, traders, and colonists. The Saint Lawrence is a vital water route for both Canada and the United States, linking the Atlantic Ocean to the Great Lakes and the interior of the continent.

Early in Canada's history, Indians and trappers brought furs from lake areas in the north to forts on Lake Superior. The main forts were at Thunder Bay, Duluth, and Grand Portage (now a national monument in Minnesota). Large ships could sail most of the twenty-three hundred miles from Duluth to the mouth of the St. Lawrence River, but rapids and shallow water closed several stretches to ships. To make the entire seaway navigable, Canada built several canals and **locks** (a section of water with gates on both sides). Ships enter one gate, the water level is changed to match the other side, and then the ships exit the other gate.

Canadians first built canals in the most difficult spots near Montreal. They completed the Welland Canal in 1829, using several locks to bypass Niagara Falls. The last important canal, completed in 1895 at Sault Ste. Marie (SOO saint muh-REE), permitted ships to enter Lake Superior.

By the mid-1900s, when the size of ships exceeded the size of the canals, Canada and the United States joined forces on the Saint Lawrence Seaway project. They built new canals and enlarged existing ones. By 1959, oceangoing ships could again reach industrial centers on the Great

An American lock on the St. Lawrence Seaway

Lakes. The increased shipping of grain, wood, cars, and machinery boosted the regional economy.

The seaway does have limitations. Ice packs close much of the waterway during the winter, and many of the newest cargo ships are too large to pass through the new locks. Despite these setbacks, the Saint Lawrence Seaway has dramatically helped both Canada and the United States.

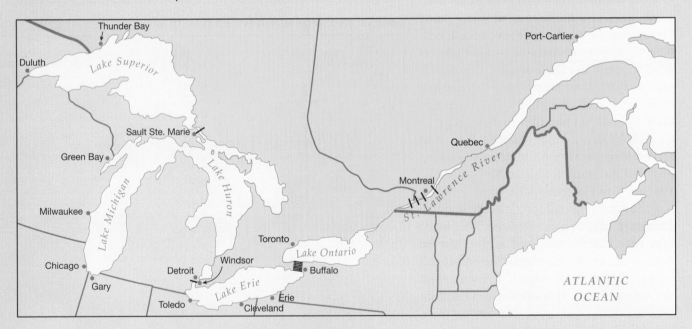

Quebecois (kay beh KWAH). In 1974, Quebec made French the province's sole official language (the language used in government records and road signs).

Cities of the St. Lawrence Valley

Quebec's most productive land lies in the St. Lawrence Valley, on the southern edge of the province. The growing season is just long enough for fruits, vegetables, and some grains. Quebec leads the nation in dairy products and in maple syrup production. Most people in Quebec have chosen to live in this productive valley.

Quebec (Quebec City) is the capital and second largest city of the province. Founded in 1608 on a rocky bluff overlooking the St. Lawrence River, Quebec City became the cradle of French civilization in North America. There the French built the only walled city north of Mexico. By capturing Quebec in 1759, Great Britain effectively ended French rule in Canada. Today, the winding streets and beautiful old buildings give the city an old-Europe charm.

The heights of Old Quebec made it a good fortress for defending the St. Lawrence River.

Upstream from Quebec City is **Montreal**, the largest city in the province. It sits on an island in the middle of the river. The explorer Jacques Cartier named the island Mont Réal (French for "Mount Royal") after he climbed its highest point, a 770-foot-high royal "mountain."

Located at the farthest navigable point on the St. Lawrence River, Montreal became the commercial center of the province. With more than one million inhabitants, the population of Montreal proper surpasses that of any other city in the nation. Indeed, it is the second-largest French-speaking city in the world, after Paris.

Unlike Quebec City, Montreal has a large minority of English speakers. The city has French newspapers and English newspapers, French-speaking schools and English-speaking schools, and radio and television broadcasts in both languages. To get ahead in business and politics, many Canadians are **bilingual** (able to speak two languages).

Modern Montreal

In an effort to escape the cold winters, Montreal has built a vast underground mall with stores, restaurants, businesses, and hotels. A subway, called the Métro, carries people throughout the city.

Hockey is the national sport. In fact, some people believe that hockey originated in Montreal. During the winter, fans fill the stadium to cheer the Montreal Canadiens, a National Hockey League team with many winning seasons.

Land's End

Most of Quebec's mines are located north and west of the St. Lawrence River on the Canadian Shield. Some mining, however, takes place on a peninsula east of the St. Lawrence. The Gaspé (gas PAY) Peninsula derives its name from a Micmac Indian word, *Gespeg*, meaning "land's end." The mineral-rich Appalachian Mountains cover this region. It includes the highest Appalachian peak north of Maine, Mount Jacques Cartier (4,190 ft.).

Section Quiz

1–2. What two conditions keep temperatures cool throughout most of Canada?

3. What important water routes serve the two provinces of central Canada?

4. What is the Canadian Shield?

5. Which province has the largest French-speaking population?

✯ Why are the Central Provinces more populous than the Maritime Provinces?

Declining Christianity in Canada

The following table shows how the number of Canadians claiming to be Christians is continuing to decline.

Year	Percentage of professing Protestants or Catholics	Percentage professing other (or no) religion
1901	98	2
1981	90	10
1991	83	17
2011	72	28

Ontario

Although the province of Ontario ranks second in size, it is first in population. Canadians sometimes refer to it as the Heartland of Canada. In sharp contrast to Quebec's French heritage, Ontario's people have a strong British heritage.

Northern Ontario

Few people live in Ontario's cold north. A narrow strip of swampy lowlands and coastal plains runs along the Hudson Bay. Although the Hudson Bay lowlands are not part of the Canadian Shield, they are just as stark and uninhabitable. A large portion of the lowlands is set aside as the Polar Bear Provincial Park. Some shipping takes place on Hudson Bay during the ice-free months, but little activity takes place during the long winter.

The Canadian Shield covers about half of Ontario. Though sparsely populated, this region has magnificent forests and 250,000 lakes. The word *Ontario* comes from an Iroquois word meaning "shining waters." The lakes support large numbers of animals, and under the shield lie important mineral resources, making Ontario the nation's leader in gold and nickel mining.

Canada's Population Centers

About 90 percent of Ontario's people live south of the Canadian Shield on a tiny finger of land between Lake Huron and Lake Ontario. It is the southernmost region in Canada. In fact, the city of Windsor lies farther south than Boston, Massachusetts. Part of Windsor actually lies south of the closest American city, Detroit. The

Missions and National Pride

How do you feel when an American swimmer wins a gold medal in the Olympics? People in other countries feel just as proud when their athletes are honored and when their national anthem is played.

Although Canada is similar to the United States in some ways, missionaries there must make many adjustments, just as they would on any other mission field. For example, for whom should they cheer for in a close race between American and Canadian Olympic swimmers? How should they respond to a hockey contest between Canadian and American teams? Their responses could greatly help—or hinder—their testimony.

When an American missionary couple finally obtain their visas and reach Canada, they must be careful not to offend nationals with their American political attitudes. They must show proper respect for the queen and

become knowledgeable about Parliament. They must show an interest in Canada's national symbols: the CN Tower, not the Statue of Liberty; Butchart Gardens, not the Golden Gate Bridge; Banff National Park, not Yellowstone; the maple leaf, not the bald eagle. The missionaries must also adapt their vocabulary and greetings and be prepared to use the metric system without complaining.

In these ways, missionaries can de-emphasize (without totally surrendering) their heritage to minister to foreign peoples. They seek to understand the people's beliefs and to overcome their own national pride to share the gospel. As the apostle Paul reminded the Corinthians, "I am made all things to all men, that I might by all means save some" (1 Cor. 9:22).

Roman Catholicism is the largest religious group in Canada, claiming about 40 percent of the population.

The next largest group (19 percent) is made up of people who claim no religion at all. Most other Canadians claim to be Protestants. Yet few Canadians rank religion highly in importance, few believe that the Bible is God's Word, and many have never read the Bible. As in America, most Protestants in Canada belong to mainline denominations. The largest denomination is the United Church of Canada, formed in 1925 by the union of several denominations. However, all Protestant denominations continue to experience a decline in attendance.

In spite of opposition from national church leaders and the apparent indifference of many Canadians to religion, missionaries play a crucial role in the work of Christ's kingdom in Canada.

Toronto

Toronto is arguably the most culturally diverse city in Canada. More than one hundred languages are spoken there, and more than one-third of its residents speak a language other than English. Almost half of the population was born outside of Canada. The 1990s witnessed the biggest increase in immigration into the city, and each immigrant brought his or her unique culture to the Toronto metropolitan area.

The city of Toronto was founded and established by serious-minded and conservative Canadians, and their logical planning and organization of the city is evident in its well laid out and easily navigated streets. The downtown area is filled with towering modern skyscrapers, parks, and museums that reflect not only the city's illustrious past but also its modernity.

The CN Tower in Toronto rises 1,821 feet into the sky.

Among its notable features, Toronto boasts one of the world's tallest free-standing structures (the CN Tower), the first retractable-roofed stadium (the Sky-Dome), Canada's largest museum (the Royal Ontario Museum), and Canada's largest university (the University of Toronto).

relatively warm climate, fertile soil, and shipping advantages of the Great Lakes Plain make this region the center of Canada's industry and population.

Dairy farms, orchards, vegetable gardens, and grain fields dot the countryside. Industries dominate the western shore of Lake Ontario, sometimes called the Golden Horseshoe. Its proximity to iron mines and ports enabled factories to thrive in the late nineteenth century. Ontario quickly became Canada's leading automobile manufacturer, just as Michigan became the leader in the United States. With the coming of the information age, computer industries have sprouted along the Golden Horseshoe.

Half of Canada's twenty largest cities lie in the Great Lakes Plain. At the hub is **Toronto**, the capital of Ontario and the largest metropolitan area in the nation. Toronto is the nation's commercial center. Its stock exchange and banks handle more business than those in any other Canadian city. Five of Toronto's suburbs rank among the nation's twenty largest cities. Outside the Toronto metropolitan area lie the busy industrial cities of Hamilton, London, and Windsor. Ontario shares Niagara Falls with the state of New York.

The Great Lakes Plain was the last place in Canada invaded by foreign troops. During the War of 1812, the United States invaded Canada, capturing Detroit and Fort Dearborn (modern Chicago). After that war ended, Britain and the United States agreed to demilitarize the Great Lakes. (**Demilitarize** means to remove all forts and soldiers from a common border.) Both sides also accepted a border of 49° N, from Lake of the Woods westward to the Rockies.

Ottawa

The national capital, **Ottawa**, is not in the Great Lakes Plain. It lies farther east, sharing the St. Lawrence River valley with Montreal

A busy intersection in Ottawa

and Quebec City. The Ottawa River, which flows by the city and drains into the St. Lawrence, marks the border between the provinces of Ontario and Quebec.

In 1837, colonists in Upper Canada (Quebec) and Lower Canada (Ontario) rebelled against Great Britain, demanding more democracy. After putting down the rebellions, Britain combined the two colonies into one and called it Canada. Because the British government wanted to avoid another prolonged and violent war for independence, it granted the new Province of Canada the right to govern its internal affairs. This union lasted until the **British North America Act** (1867) established a confederation of four provinces—Ontario, New Brunswick, Quebec, and Nova Scotia. Since then, six other provinces have joined the confederation. July 1 is celebrated as Canada Day.

The Dominion of Canada is modeled after the British parliamentary system. Canadians elect representatives to the House of Commons, a law-making body similar to the U.S. House of Representatives. The leader of the Commons becomes the prime minister. Like the president of the United States, the prime minister runs the executive branch of government. The Canadian Parliament also has a senate. Unlike the U.S. president, the prime minister chooses all 104 senators. Their job is to protect the interests of the various provinces and territories.

Under the parliamentary system, the Canadian prime minister is both the speaker in the House of Commons and the chief executive. Canada has voluntarily chosen to remain a member of the British Commonwealth and retains the British monarch as head of state. The monarch is represented in Parliament by the governor general, who is appointed at the recommendation of the prime minister. Today, Parliament makes most national decisions while the roles of monarch and governor general are primarily ceremonial.

Canada has a federal system of government. Ottawa shares power with the provinces, each of which has its own unicameral (one-house) legislature and a governor called the **premier**. Like the prime minister, the premier is chosen by the legislature.

Canada has never had a civil war, but the union historically has been fragile. Because some French Canadians want a constitutional right to veto any laws that might threaten their distinctive French culture, Quebec refused to ratify the 1982 Charter of Rights and Freedoms, Canada's equivalent of the Bill of Rights. The charter made both French and English official languages, but French Canadians did not get the veto power. In 1995, Quebec almost passed a referendum to become a sovereign country. The vote failed, 49.4 percent to 50.6 percent.

A Missionary Gains Cultural Awareness

Catherine McQuaid, missionary to Canada.

Equipped with the misconception that "Canada is just like the States," we made one of our first forays into Canadian culture by phoning a local hardware store. Being good, inquisitive Americans, we began questioning the clerk about one of the products. After he answered a few questions (and he would have immediately noticed our "accent" as well), his responses became shorter and terser, until he finally said, "Why don't you just come down to the store and look for yourself."

How does that translate into church planting? Every small church loves a visitor. However, Canadians do not appreciate seeing someone sprint toward them, scrambling over chairs while waving a pen and visitor card. They prefer, rather, to slip in unobtrusively and to leave unaccosted. If they want to return, they will—even without a follow-up call or visit the following week. Prodding and questioning may even impede church growth if the visitor feels coerced—especially if it is by an American.

Section Quiz

1. Which province has the largest population?
2. To what church do most Canadians belong?
3. How many provinces are in Canada's confederation?
4. Who becomes the prime minister of Canada?
5. Who is the head of state in Canada?
★ How might you effectively witness to a Canadian teenager?

III. The Western Provinces

The common traits shared by the United States and Canada continue into the West. In the four Western Provinces, which were settled much later than those in the East, the frontier spirit lives on.

The 4,860-mile **Trans-Canada Highway** links the East and the West. A network of railroads also crosses the continent. Canada has over 30,000 miles of track, and rail transportation is provided through a combination of privately owned companies and government operated corporations. Isolated people in the far north, however, depend on airplanes for transportation.

The Trans-Canada Highway stretches from the Atlantic coast of Canada to the Pacific coast.

The Central Plains of the United States extend northward into Canada's heartland, between the Canadian Shield and the Rocky Mountains. Temperatures in southern Canada are comfortable in the summer. Even so, the continental heating and cooling makes the Canadian climate somewhat harsh. Summer temperatures can climb to 100°F, whereas winter nights often drop below 0°F. Because the plains lie in the rainshadow of the Rocky Mountains, rainfall is scarce, with most areas receiving only about fifteen inches of precipitation per year. Grasses characterize the plains' vegetation.

Because of the colder climate, Canada's frontier remained open long after the American frontier had closed. Immigrants from Germany, Poland, Russia, and eastern Canada moved in during the late nineteenth and early twentieth centuries. Early farmers struggled each year to glean crops from the rich soil before drought, insects, and untimely frosts destroyed them. "Wait until next year" became a popular saying. During the 1930s, farmers shared the misery of the Dust Bowl with America's midwestern states; Canadians call this bleak period the Dirty Thirties. Nowadays better seed and irrigation equipment have greatly improved the lot of the prairie farmer.

The Prairie Provinces have become the breadbasket of Canada. Tall grain elevators that rise from the flat landscape are a frequent sight. These "skyscrapers of the prairie" hold mounds of wheat and barley. Canada is the world's fourth largest exporter of wheat. Canada's barley harvest is second only to Russia's, and its flax harvest ranks first in the world.

A few people eke out a living in the northern Canadian Shield. Scattered bands of Indians struggle to survive on isolated reserves. Lakes and streams help make the taiga and tundra beautiful in the summer, but it becomes a lonely, white wilderness in winter.

Winnipeg, Manitoba, is Canada's "Gateway to the West," much like St. Louis is the gateway to the western United States.

Manitoba

Two strings of lakes straddle the center of Manitoba. The larger, Lake Winnipeg, sits in the east, and Lakes Manitoba and Winnipegosis sit in the west. Winnipeg, the province's capital and main city, is on the Red River, which flows into Lake Winnipeg from its source in Minnesota.

Métis (may-TEES), descendants of French men and Indian women, once lived by hunting the bison that dotted the plains. When Irish and Scottish settlers established a farming community on the Red River in 1812, the *métis* attacked them and killed their colonial

leader. After the creation of the Dominion of Canada in 1867, the *métis* rebelled again. They feared that a rush of farmers would take over their land, for which they had no title. The Red River Rebellion forced Canada to grant the local people a bill of rights in 1870 and to create Canada's fifth province.

Only the southwest portion of Manitoba, the easternmost prairie province, is a prairie. Its farms lead Canada in the production of flax, buckwheat, sunflowers, and peas. But not all of the grassland is tilled. At Riding Mountain National Park, wolves, bison, and lynx continue to roam the meadows and scattered forests.

Most of Manitoba is covered by the unproductive Canadian Shield. The far northeast consists of swampy lowlands along the Hudson Bay, which it shares with Ontario. Churchill, the largest town in this desolate region, claims the title of "Polar Bear Capital of the World."

Saskatchewan

The other two Prairie Provinces, Saskatchewan and Alberta, were settled later than Manitoba. The *métis* were the first to settle there, moving out of Manitoba and establishing farms along the North and South Saskatchewan Rivers.

In the southern half of the province is the Saskatchewan Plain, a productive extension of the interior plains of the United States. Modern wheat farms make Saskatchewan the Northern Hemisphere's leading wheat producer. The wheat is processed in either the capital, Regina, or Saskatoon, a city farther north. From there, it is transported across the nation.

The prairies of Saskatchewan show why the province is called Canada's breadbasket.

A few low hills bring variety to the flat plain. The Cypress Hills, which straddle the southwest border with Alberta, have the highest point between Labrador and the Canadian Rockies. Buffalo roam the wilderness of Prince Albert National Park, a few miles north of Saskatoon.

Northern Saskatchewan is known for its wilderness and for its uranium. Taiga and tundra cover that part of the Canadian Shield, and rich deposits of uranium lie under the surface. Canada is one of the world's leading producers of uranium.

Alberta

West of Saskatchewan is Alberta. The Great Plains extend north over the entire province, except for the southwestern mountains and

Calgary Stampede

Rodeos in Canada? Yes, rodeos are as popular in Canada as they are in the American West. In fact, the biggest rodeo in the world is the Calgary Stampede in Calgary, Alberta, Canada. Guy Weadick organized the first Calgary Stampede in 1912. Although it is not the oldest rodeo, it has been an annual event since 1919.

Most rodeos feature the popular rough stock events, which require riders to sit on the backs of either untamed bucking broncos (horses) or Brahma bulls. Cowboys must hold on with only one hand while spurring the animal. These events, which are also called roughriding, include bull riding,

bronco riding, and saddled bronco riding.

The other events are timed. Cowboys compete, both individually and in teams, in calf roping, steer wrestling, and steer roping. Cowgirls enjoy barrel racing, riding horses in tight curves around barrels. A few rodeos add milking contests, trick riding, fancy roping, and other events. The Calgary Stampede is famous for its chuck wagon races. Another favorite event is open to young people in the audience—catching a greased pig.

The Calgary Stampede is a world-renowned rodeo.

---

the northeastern shield. Alberta is a leading producer of barley and has the most beef cattle of any province. Edmonton is the capital and agricultural center of Alberta.

The northeastern tip of Alberta is notable for valuable oil reserves said to exceed those of Saudi Arabia. Also noteworthy is Wood Buffalo National Park, established in 1922. It features sand dunes, salt plains, boreal forests, gypsum karst formations, and river deltas at the mouth of the Peace and Athabasca Rivers. Its wild herd of three thousand wood buffalo is the largest in the world.

Calgary is the gateway to the Canadian Rockies. Its growth is due partly to tourism and partly to the discovery of a major petroleum field nearby. Calgary is famous for its annual rodeo, the Calgary Stampede, held in July. Skiers flock to the nearby ski resorts in the winter. The city has also hosted the Winter Olympics.

The southwestern border of Alberta follows the Continental Divide through a succession of spectacular parks in the Canadian Rockies. The southernmost national park is Waterton Lakes, which adjoins Montana's Glacier National Park. Next is Banff, and beyond that is Jasper. Another interesting place in Alberta is Head-Smashed-In Buffalo Jump near Fort MacLeod. Visitors can see where the Plains Indians stampeded bison herds over the cliffs to their deaths. At a campsite below the cliffs, the Indians would then butcher the carcasses for meat.

British Columbia

British Columbia is the third-largest and third most populous province. The only province on the Pacific Ocean, it is closely tied to America's Pacific Northwest.

The Rockies and the Pacific ranges cut the Pacific Northwest off from the rest of the continent. British sailors did not sight its shores

Moraine Lake is one of the most famous lakes in Banff National Park near Calgary. Banff was the first national park in Canada.

Mount Robson is the second highest peak that is entirely in British Columbia.

The flowers in the forty-nine-acre Butchart Gardens thrive in the marine-west-coast climate of Victoria, British Columbia.

until 1778, but fur trade with coastal Indians quickly prospered. Americans arrived a decade later to explore the Columbia River. However, the two nations could not agree on ownership. They almost went to war in the early 1840s after American settlers began pouring into the Oregon country. Americans demanded all lands south of latitude 54°40' N; Britain claimed the lands north of the Columbia River. The two countries eventually agreed on a compromise boundary at 49° N.

Western Cordillera

The chain of mountains that stretches from Alaska to the southern tip of South America is called the Western Cordillera. **Cordillera** (kor dil YARE uh) means "a chain of mountains." The cordillera covers most of British Columbia, except for the northeastern corner, where the Peace River valley provides some agriculture on the Great Plains.

The map of North America reveals some important differences between the mountains in Canada and those in the United States. America's portion of the cordillera encompasses a one-thousand-mile-wide band of three mountain systems—the Rockies, the Sierra Nevada and Cascades, and the Coastal Ranges. In Canada, the cordillera forms a five-hundred-mile-wide band of two systems—the Rockies and the Coastal Mountains. The third U.S. system—the Coastal Ranges—disappears under the ocean off Canada's west coast.

Although logging and lead mining occur in the Canadian Rockies, and although more copper is mined there than in any other province, the biggest industry of British Columbia is tourism. Four national parks there—Yoho, Kootenay, Glacier, and Mount Revelstoke—display pristine mountain beauty. Several peaks exceed ten thousand feet. A plateau separates the Canadian Rockies from the Coast Mountains, which have the highest peaks in all of Canada.

Pacific Coast

The warm Japan Current gives the coast of British Columbia a marine-west-coast climate. The coast enjoys the most pleasant climate in Canada. Although winters are wet, temperatures generally stay above freezing. In the summer they rarely climb above 80°F. Orchards grace the valleys, and salmon fill the rivers. The tall, dense forests of Douglas fir, red cedar, and hemlock that cover the mountains make British Columbia the producer of the most lumber and other forest products in the Northern Hemisphere.

Vancouver, the largest city in British Columbia and the third-largest metropolitan area in Canada, is ideally located at the mouth of the Fraser River, which empties into the Pacific Ocean north of Puget Sound. The soil of the Fraser River valley is the most fertile in the province. The city of Vancouver began growing rapidly in 1885, after the completion of the nation's first transcontinental railroad—the Canadian Pacific Railway (now called the Canadian Pacific Railway Limited). Vancouver's deep port is one of the busiest in the nation. Lumber, salmon, minerals, and prairie wheat pass through Vancouver to America, Japan, and the rest of the Pacific rim.

Off the west coast of British Columbia is a chain of islands that are the tops of the Coastal Range, which continues northward from Washington's Olympic Peninsula. Because the ocean has flooded this range, it is sometimes called the **Insular Mountains**. Vancouver Island is the largest insular mountain. In fact, it is the largest island off the west coast of the Americas.

British Columbia's capital, Victoria, sits on the southern edge of Vancouver Island, across from the city of Vancouver. Victoria is one of the few Canadian cities where British Canadians have been careful to keep British traditions intact. The streets and houses look much like those of British cities, and many of the people speak with a distinctly British accent. Evidence of British influence is everywhere, from the double-decker buses to the formal arrangements of world-famous Butchart Gardens. Flowered walks and ivy-covered buildings add to Victoria's charm.

Section Quiz

1. What province borders the Pacific?
2–3. Define *cordillera*. Which two provinces contain part of the Western Cordillera?
4. Where is Canada's mildest climate? Why is it so mild?
* What type of boundary divides Canada from the United States? (You might need to refer to Chapter 5.)

IV. The Canadian Territories

More than 40 percent of Canada's land is located in its northern territories, but their combined population is less than that of tiny Prince Edward Island. The obvious reason is the cold climate. Only a few Eskimos, Indians, and European Canadians brave the cold to work at reservations, trading posts, mines, and military installations.

Eskimos and Indians are the two native peoples of Canada. Indians settled south of the Arctic Circle. The Eskimos lived north of the Arctic Circle, hunting seals, walruses, and whales on the coast and caribou in the interior. Europeans called them Eskimos (possibly from a Montagnais word *ayashkinew,* a term referring to the manner of lacing a snowshoe.)

When the Europeans arrived, they traded blankets, knives, guns, and other goods for animal fur and skins, helping them establish friendly relations. The trickle of French trappers did not upset the native peoples, as the rush of immigrants in America did the native peoples there. The large country had more than enough room for everyone.

The modern Indian population exceeds nine hundred thousand. The Canadian government has given the Indians large tracts of land as reserves, and many Indians remain on these reserves. Unfortunately, government subsidies and little opportunity for real work have encouraged alcoholism and other evils. Some Indians move to Canadian cities, but this drastic step can be a great shock to individuals from a tribal culture.

In 2006 (latest survey available), Canada's Eskimos numbered over fifty thousand and had increased by 26 percent since the previous survey ten years earlier. Most of the Eskimos live in

First Nations

The Indian tribes in Canada are referred to as the First Nations. They have diverse religious beliefs with common traits in the main regions of Canada. The nations in Eastern Canada tend to believe in a supreme god along with their worship of nature and ancestral spirits. The religious beliefs of nations in Northwestern Canada tend to follow a totem or caste system. These nations in the Northwest also place great faith in the power of shamans to interact with and influence the spiritual realm.

Christian missionaries face a great challenge in reaching out to the members of the First Nations. They must overcome real and perceived concerns that past efforts stripped away too much of Indian culture and that current missionary efforts will continue this trend. Missionaries must acknowledge that past wrongs committed against the First Nations were contrary to Scripture. They should value aspects of Indian culture that reflect wise use of God's good creation. Successful missionaries will develop deep and long-term relationships with the Indians. They will help the Indians recognize that the gospel challenges all cultures—the sins of Western cultures as well as the sins of Indian cultures.

Some Eskimos in the Arctic region live in igloos, especially when they are on hunting trips.

northern military and mining settlements, where they hold regular jobs. A few continue to hunt and fish, mostly with the aid of modern weapons and equipment. Rifles have replaced most harpoons, and snowmobiles are as common as dogsleds.

Yukon Territory

The cold Yukon Territory, north of British Columbia and bordering Alaska, is slightly larger than California. Gold brought thousands of miners to the Klondike region in the 1890s, and mining continues to be the major activity. Today, however, lead and zinc mining have surpassed gold. The Yukon leads Canada in lead production, and it helps to make Canada a major supplier of zinc.

The **Alaska Highway** (also called the Alaska-Canada Highway, or Alcan) winds through the mountains of the Yukon to connect

The Alcan Highway

When the Japanese attacked Pearl Harbor, pulling the United States into World War II, the only access to Alaska from the mainland was by airplane. The U.S. government needed a land route to get supplies and equipment to its airfields and military bases in greater quantities. They persuaded Canada to donate the right of way for a road to be built by the U.S. Army Corp of Engineers at U.S. expense. After the war, ownership of the road would revert to Canada.

Construction on the road began at Dawson Creek, British Columbia, in March 1942. The 93rd, 95th, 97th, and 388th Engineer Regiments—10,607 men, including 3,695 blacks—were assigned the arduous task. The 1,522-mile-long road would follow old Indian paths through rugged, unmapped regions to link existing airfields. Critics said it could not be done and complained that black men did not have the mentality to operate heavy equipment.

But the men proved the critics wrong. They worked seven days a week, sometimes putting in twenty-hour days. In the spring and summer, they fought mosquitoes, flies, and gnats. They overcame the marshy thawed areas by building a "corduroy" road of logs laid side by side. In the winter, the men endured temperatures of -40°F for weeks at a time and struggled to move the rock-solid frozen ground. (One day the temperature was a record low of -79°.)

In June 1942, the Japanese invaded Attu and Kiska, two Alaskan islands in the Aleutians, increasing the urgency of the task. By October 25, 1942—barely eight months from the time they began—the engineers had achieved what critics said was impossible. They reached the city of Fairbanks, Alaska, completing the Alaska-Canada Highway. Supplies began pouring into U.S. military bases in Alaska. The Alcan is still the only land route from the lower forty-eight American states to Alaska, and it is a monument to the soldiers' courage, stamina, and ingenuity.

Once the Alcan Highway was completed, military supplies and equipment poured into Alaskan bases.

(top) Soldiers worked under extreme conditions to complete the Alcan Highway.

(bottom) Black soldiers proved the skeptics wrong and made a valuable contribution during construction of the Alcan Highway.

Dawson Creek, British Columbia, with Anchorage, Alaska. The U.S. Army blazed the first rough highway as an overland route for military supplies during World War II. A narrow central valley lies along the Yukon River. Here miners established the capital, Whitehorse, the only real city between Dawson and Anchorage. The Coast Mountains include Canada's highest mountain, Mount Logan (19,524 ft.).

Northwest Territories

This vast territory covers one-third of Canada, but less than fifty thousand people live there. Nearly one-fifth of the population lives in the capital, Yellowknife. It stands beside Great Slave Lake, the deepest lake in North America. Great Bear Lake is the only lake in Canada that covers more area than the Great Slave Lake.

The **Mackenzie River**, one of the longest river systems in North America, winds northward from the Great Slave Lake through the western part of the territory to the Arctic Ocean. The river is named after Sir Alexander Mackenzie, a trapper who first explored the length of the river in 1789. Most settlements in the Northwest Territory are scattered along the Mackenzie River valley. Oil companies have found petroleum in the ice-choked Mackenzie delta.

A few forests of small evergreens grow near the Mackenzie River and the southern part of the territory, but most of the land lies above the timberline. Trapping, fishing, and the mining of lead and zinc are the major industries. The discovery of diamonds in 1991 northeast of Yellowknife sparked the biggest mineral rush in Canada's history, exceeding even the Klondike gold rush. More than two hundred companies have staked claims around Lac de Gras.

North of the continent is one of the earth's great **archipelagos**, or island groups. Nine of these islands exceed ten thousand square miles in area. The southern islands are flat, but the northern islands are mountainous. Barbeau Peak on Ellesmere Island is the highest peak in the archipelago (8,582 ft.). Most of the Arctic islands sit above the Arctic Circle. With few exceptions, these rocky, barren islands are uninhabited and covered by snow and ice throughout the year.

The Arctic islands and northern parts of the Canadian Shield have a polar or tundra climate. Winter temperatures often fall to −30°F or lower. Summer temperatures rarely climb above 50°F, and they stay above freezing for only about two months. Permafrost keeps large plants from growing, but small lichens and some other tiny plants and bushes grow in colorful profusion during summer's brief thaw.

Nunavut

On May 4, 1992, the Northwest Territories approved a plan to split the territory in April 1999 and to allow native self-government. The new territory, *Nunavut* (Inuit for "our land"), includes most of the old territory, except for the westernmost Arctic islands and the Mackenzie River valley. Only twenty-eight small villages exist in this wide wilderness. The most populous town, Iqaluit (under 4,000), is the capital.

The Alcan Highway can be beautiful in the winter.

From Sea to Sea

As in the United States, many of Canada's government buildings reflect the biblical heritage of the nation. For example, the western portal to the Peace Tower of the Parliament Buildings exhibits the inscribed words of Proverbs 29:18: "Where there is no vision, the people perish." Elsewhere are two inscriptions: "He shall have dominion also from sea to sea" (Ps. 72:8) and "Give the king thy judgments, O God, and thy righteousness unto the king's son" (Ps. 72:1).

Many other artifacts attest to that heritage. Canada's national motto, adopted in 1921, *A mari usque ad mare* ("From sea to sea"), is taken from Psalm 72:8. Consequently, Canada's national holiday was originally known as Dominion Day. *Desiderantes meliorem patriam* (taken from Hebrews 11:16, "They desire a better country") is displayed on Canada's official coat of arms. Even the provincial saying of Newfoundland and Labrador, taken from Matthew 5:33, bears testament to Canada's Christian heritage: "Seek ye first the kingdom of God."

One of the most powerful reminders today of Canada's Christian heritage is its national anthem. The English version sung today was written in 1908 by R. Stanley Weir in honor of the three hundredth anniversary of the founding of Quebec City. The last verse reads,

> Ruler supreme, who hearest humble prayer,
> Hold our dominion within thy loving care;
> Help us to find, O God, in thee
> A lasting, rich reward,
> As waiting for the Better Day,
> We ever stand on guard.
> God, keep our land glorious and free!
> O Canada, we stand on guard for thee.
> O Canada, we stand on guard for thee.

It is important to remember that a godly history is not what makes a country right and pleasing before God. Each generation must be taught to love and fear the Lord and to live accordingly. If one generation neglects its obligation, the link is broken and so is the chain. Nevertheless, the age-old promise in Psalm 2:10–12 remains unchanged to all countries: "Be wise now therefore, O ye kings. . . . Serve the Lord with fear. . . . Blessed are all they that put their trust in him."

©2007 The Heritage Canada Foundation, www.heritagecanada.org, Reproduced with the permission of the Minister of Public Works and Government Services, 2007.

Nunavut includes **Baffin Island**, the largest island in the Canadian archipelago and the fifth largest island in the world. Ten thousand glaciers creep down its sides to the sea. Iqaluit is located on Baffin Island's southernmost bay, facing the Atlantic Ocean.

Section Quiz

1–2. Distinguish the two native peoples of Canada.

3. The Europeans traded blankets, knives, and other goods for what items supplied by the Indians?

4. Where are most settlements in the Northwest Territory?

★ How did the builders of the Alcan Highway manage to prove their critics wrong?

Chapter Review

Making Connections

1–4. What are four geographic features shared by Canada and the United States?

5–7. What are three main ethnic groups of Canadians?

8. Give one major difference between the Maritime, Central, and Western Provinces.

9. What kind of government does Canada have?

10. What are the two national languages of Canada?

Developing Geography Skills

1. Why is southern Ontario such an important region of Canada?

2. Why are Canada's territories valuable despite their cold climates?

Thinking Critically

1. What impact might Quebec's independence have on Canada? on the United States?

2. What has been the result of a demilitarized border between Canada and the United States?

Living in God's World

1. Write a letter to a missionary in Canada. Ask why he became a missionary to Canada, what parts of the culture he learned to adopt, and what aspects of Canadian culture needed to be challenged by the gospel.

2. Canada has a Christian heritage but an increasingly secular population. Write a paragraph that explores ways to overcome the evangelistic challenges.

People, Places, and Things to Know

Maritime
Newfoundland
fjord
Grand Banks
Labrador
Halifax
Canadian Shield
Hudson Bay
taiga
St. Lawrence River
lock
Quebec
Montreal
bilingual
Toronto
demilitarize
Ottawa
British North America Act
premier
Trans-Canada Highway
Calgary
cordillera
Vancouver
Insular Mountains
First Nations
Alaska Highway
Mackenzie River
archipelago
Baffin Island

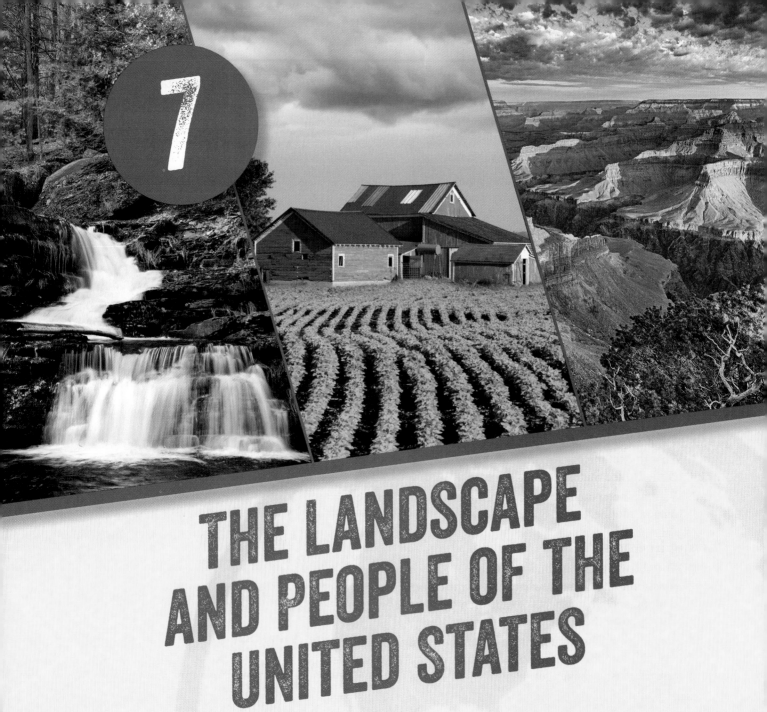

THE LANDSCAPE AND PEOPLE OF THE UNITED STATES

I. The American Landscape
- A. Boundaries
- B. Topography
- C. Climate
- D. Resources

II. The American People
- A. Core Values
- B. Demographics
- C. Government
- D. Economy

*I*n many ways, the United States of America is unique among the countries of the world. Its topography and climate are widely varied. It is blessed with enormous amounts and varieties of natural resources and fertile croplands. Its population is an amalgam (mixture) of practically every people and culture on earth, each of which has made valuable

United States Fast Facts					
Capital	Area (sq. mi.)	Pop. (M)	Pop. Density (per sq. mi.)	Per Capita GDP ($US)	Life Span
Washington, D.C.	3,794,100	314 (2012 est.)	82.76	$49,800	78.49

contributions to the cultural landscape, yet the nation has developed its own distinct culture. It has a proud history and the freest, most stable government in existence. Its economy is the strongest on earth. And it has unequaled power and influence among the nations.

At the same time, however, the United States does not have every resource its people need and must therefore trade with other nations to obtain what it lacks. It faces problems unique to the diverse cultures in its midst. Its great economy presents both challenges and opportunities. Its government faces its own problems even as it attempts to spread freedom to the undemocratic nations of the world. And it must continually deal with devastating natural disasters and an ongoing war against Islamic terrorism.

The United States ranks third among the nations of the earth in physical size (behind only Russia and Canada). It is third in population (behind China and India). Its wealth and prosperity are attributable in part to its rich farmland, abundant resources, good climate, and hard-working people. Perhaps its greatest blessing, however, is the Christian heritage that extends from the Pilgrims through several spiritual awakenings to the present. True freedom and economic prosperity are ultimately gifts from the Lord. God wants Christians to use their liberty not selfishly but for the good of all, and we are to be good stewards of not only our personal finances and resources but also our national wealth. As long as the United States fears and honors the one true God and uses its God-given gifts wisely, it will continue to prosper among the nations (Ps. 33:12).

The American population is an amalgam of multiple religions, nationalities, and ethnicities.

I. The American Landscape

The land of the United States stretches from the Atlantic Ocean in the east to the Pacific Ocean in the west through the middle of the North American continent. It also includes the large peninsula of Alaska to the northwest, the islands of Hawaii farther west in the Pacific, and several territories in the Pacific and the Caribbean.

Boundaries

The United States is bounded on the north and the south by generally peaceful neighboring countries. On the north, Canada and the United States share the longest nonmilitarized border in the world. The lower forty-eight U.S. states share a 3,987-mile border with Canada. Alaska adds an additional 1,538-mile border. The main border essentially follows the St. Lawrence River from New England to Quebec and divides four of the Great Lakes. (Only Lake Michigan is completely within the United States.) It then follows the 49th parallel from Lake of the Woods in Ontario/Minnesota to the Strait of Juan de Fuca on the west coast.

Border crossing from Canada to the United States

The Complicated Issue of Immigration

Since the 1990s, illegal immigration from Mexico and other Latin American countries has increased dramatically. In 2006, an estimated 9–11 million undocumented immigrants resided in the United States. Of those, about 60-70 percent were from Mexico. This situation presents great problems for the U.S. government. Health care and education costs for undocumented immigrants and their families are high. In addition, millions of tax dollars that are owed to the government by undocumented immigrants go uncollected.

It is important, however, for Americans to realize that these undocumented immigrants do not come to the U.S. to steal, cheat, or abuse others. For the most part, Mexicans and other Latin Americans are happy to work very hard in the United States in order to send money back home each week and then join their families again after a few years. The opportunity for higher paying jobs is greater in America since the dollar is much stronger than the peso. By working in the United States, they can earn more money in a shorter amount of time. Many come from impoverished conditions and seek to raise the standard of living here and back home.

Stopping illegal immigration is a daunting task, one that few politicians desire to undertake because of the emotionally charged issues involved. The issues are complicated, and there are no easy answers. First, Mexico is the second-largest trade partner of the United States, and an aggressive policy against illegal immigration could slow the flow of trade between Mexico and the United States. Second, immigrants, both legal and illegal, often provide a needed source of labor for many service-sector jobs in the United States. Dramatically reducing immigration could harm productivity in those parts of the U.S. economy. Third, the cost of constructing and maintaining a continuous, gated border would be very high.

Finally, Latin Americans and Hispanics already legally living in the United States—many of whom are now voting citizens—could see such policies as a racist attack on their people and culture. Thus, the political consequences of trying to stop illegal immigration could be very costly.

President George W. Bush proposed a program that would employ new technology at border crossings while still allowing current illegal immigrants to continue working for a limited time. Congress rejected this plan. President Obama used executive orders to bypass Congress and granted a virtual path to citizenship for many young Hispanics.

Members of Congress continue to wrestle with this thorny issue. Some recognize the need to develop a balanced approach while others make sweeping promises to gain the Hispanic vote.

Customs officials do check traffic crossing the border on major roads. Although it has been relatively easy to pass between the two countries in the past (the time required for a typical crossing is ten to twenty minutes), the terrorist attacks on the United States on September 11, 2001, forced both countries to tighten security dramatically. Nonetheless, the border remains a friendly boundary between cooperative nations and many crossings remain unmanned.

An average of 300,000 people cross the border each day. Fifteen percent of the crossings are commercial. The United States and Canada are great trading partners. Thousands of trucks cross the border each day carrying imports or exports. In 2012 the United States exported $292 billion worth of goods to Canada and imported $324 billion worth of goods from Canada for a total annual trade of $616 billion.

On the south, the United States is bounded by the **Rio Grande** (Spanish, "big river"); the Mexican border in California, Arizona, and southwestern New Mexico; and the Gulf of Mexico. Mexico is the second-largest trading partner of the United States, with the value of trade running $494 billion a year in 2012. The U.S.–Mexico border is also unfortified,

Unlike the U.S.–Canadian border, the U.S.–Mexican border presents the challenges of illegal aliens and the infusion of illegal drugs into the United States.

but law enforcement is much more obvious than on the U.S.–Canada border because of the heavy traffic of illegal drugs, illegal immigrants, and possible terrorists across the border. Securing the border using a variety of devices, including fences, barricades, and electronic surveillance, has slowed the rate of crossings in some areas. However, border states continue their struggle to restrict the flow of illegal immigrants and the increasing violence along the border.

Section Quiz

1. What is the world rank of the United States in physical size?
2. What is the U.S. rank in population?
3. Which of the five Great Lakes is totally within the United States?
* Why do many people cross into the United States illegally?

Topography

The lower forty-eight states of the United States can be divided into eight distinct topographical regions, each of which has played an important role in the historical and cultural development of the country. We discuss each of these areas in the following sections of the text, moving from east to west across the map. We then deal briefly with Alaska and Hawaii, each of which has its own unique topographical characteristics.

The Coastal Plains

The sandy plains along the coasts of the Atlantic Ocean and the Gulf of Mexico are called the **Coastal Plains**. They are three hundred feet or less in elevation and extend from Maine to Texas. The plain is very narrow in the Northeast and expands gradually as one goes south until it extends inland one hundred miles or more in the South. Some areas—such as the Everglades in Florida, the Okeefenokee Swamp in Georgia, and the Dismal Swamp in Virginia and North Carolina—have poor drainage. Other areas have fertile soil and provide numerous kinds of products, including rice, indigo, peanuts, and fruits.

Inlets that cut into the **Atlantic Coastal Plain** provide fine harbors, especially in the north. New York, Boston, and Philadelphia are famous seaports of the Atlantic coast. Good harbors are less plentiful farther south but include Wilmington, North Carolina; Charleston, South Carolina; and Savannah, Georgia. Tampa, Florida; Mobile, Alabama; New Orleans, Louisiana; and Houston and Galveston, Texas, are some of the major port cities of the **Gulf Coastal Plain**. That plain also extends inland up the Mississippi River Valley into the Midwest.

Much of the Coastal Plains region is flat and wet, like this portion of the Gulf Coastal Plain in Louisiana.

The Piedmont

Farther inland from the Atlantic Ocean and beyond the Coastal Plains is an area known as the **Piedmont**. The word *piedmont* ("foothills") is appropriate because the area is the foothills of the Appalachian Mountains. The Piedmont extends from Maine to

Waterfalls such as the Great Falls of the Potomac in Montgomery County, Maryland, are common along the fall line, where the Piedmont and the Coastal Plain meet.

The Great Smoky Mountains are one range in the Appalachian chain.

Pioneers called the Great Plains the "Great American Desert," but they soon discovered that, with proper care, the plains could be a rich and fertile farmland.

Alabama, with elevations ranging from three hundred to fifteen hundred feet. Many rivers run from the mountains through the Piedmont and the Coastal Plain and into the ocean. Where the rivers drop from the Piedmont to the Coastal Plain, there are many waterfalls, which explains why that area is called the **fall line**. Westward-moving settlers founded many towns along the fall line, where they later took advantage of the powerful waterfalls to build mills and factories. The fertile ground of the Piedmont was also conducive to growing great quantities of cotton.

The Appalachian Mountains

West of the Piedmont, the **Appalachian Mountains** extend from eastern Canada southward into northern Alabama. Several mountain groups—for example, the Smoky, Blue Ridge, Allegheny, Pocono, Catskills, Berkshire Hills, White, and Green Mountains—form the Appalachian chain. The highest peak in the chain is Mount Mitchell (6,684 feet) in North Carolina. The Appalachians form the **Eastern Continental Divide**, meaning that waters that flow down the eastern side of the mountains eventually empty into the Atlantic Ocean, and waters that flow down the western side flow into either the Great Lakes or the Mississippi River and then down to the Gulf of Mexico.

For the most part, the Appalachians are relatively low, rounded, tree-covered mountains, but they were a significant obstacle to settlement during the colonial era. After explorers discovered the Cumberland Gap—a mountain pass on the borders of what today are Virginia, Tennessee, and Kentucky—large numbers of settlers poured west of the Appalachians.

The Central Plains

West of the Appalachians, settlers discovered the fertile rolling hills, forests, and prairies of the **Central Plains** stretching about a thousand miles across the heart of the country. The **Mississippi River** and its tributaries and the Great Lakes provide numerous water transportation routes. The rich soils produce abundant opportunities for raising livestock and growing corn, soybeans, wheat, and other crops.

The Great Plains

West of the Central Plains lies another plains region called the **Great Plains**, which begins about the ninety-eighth meridian and stretches to the base of the Rocky Mountains. The altitude rises gradually from about one thousand feet above sea level in the east to about five thousand feet against the mountains in the west. The Great Plains are characterized by flat grasslands and a dry climate. Although the soil is rich, the dry prairie sod was long thought to be useless for farming. Irrigation, however, has brought the Great American Desert to life with fields of grain and herds of cattle.

Geographic Regions of the United States

Legend:
- Mountain
- Plateau
- Plain
- Basin

The Rocky Mountains

The mountains that mark the western boundary of the Great Plains are the **Rocky Mountains**, the peaks of which exceed ten thousand feet. The tallest, Mount Elbert, is 14,433 feet in elevation. The Rockies presented a formidable obstacle to extensive westward settlement until the completion of the transcontinental railroad in 1869. Today, the Rockies provide mineral resources and scenic beauty. National parks and ski resorts make the region a popular vacation area.

Just as the Appalachian Mountains form the Eastern Continental Divide, the Rockies form the **Western Continental Divide**. Waters that flow down the eastern side of the mountains run into the Mississippi River and to the Gulf of Mexico, whereas waters that flow down the western side run into the Pacific Ocean.

The Great Basin

Between the Rocky Mountains and the mountains along the Pacific coast is a lowland area called the **Great Basin** that includes most of Nevada and a large part of Utah. Although altitudes in this intermountain region are generally five thousand feet or more, compared to the mountain ranges on either side the area

> **Find It!**
> **Mount Elbert**
> 39.117° N, 106.445° W

Mount Moran is located in the Grand Teton National Park in Western Wyoming.

El Capitan in the Yosemite Valley is part of the central Sierra Nevada range.

Mount St. Helens literally "blew its top" in 1980, and periodic seismic activity is still detected there.

Find It!

Mount St. Helens

46.191° N, 122.194° W

(Use this exercise to answer the Critical Thinking question on page 137.)

Five Largest States by Area

State	Area (sq. mi.)
1. Alaska	570,641
2. Texas	261,232
3. California	155,779
4. Montana	145,546
5. New Mexico	121,298

is a lowland. On the north is the Columbia Plateau. To the south is the Colorado Plateau. Rivers have cut deep canyons through this region, and winds have carved unusual rock formations there.

The Pacific Mountain Ranges

Along the Pacific coast of the United States is a series of mountain ranges interspersed with low valleys. The mountains are part of a system called the **Pacific Mountain Ranges** and include the Sierra Nevada along the eastern side of California, the Cascade Mountains in Oregon and Washington, and the Coastal Ranges along the Pacific shore.

The Central Valley of California and the Willamette Valley of Oregon are two of the many fertile valleys in the area. The Pacific mountains are much narrower than the Rockies, but they contain some high peaks. For example, Mount Whitney in the Sierra Nevada is the highest point in the forty-eight contiguous (adjacent or touching) states.

The Pacific mountains also contain some active volcanoes, including **Mount St. Helens** in Washington's Cascades. The largest major eruption of that volcano was in 1980, but seismic activity in the area intensified dramatically in 2004, and the volcano has had several minor eruptions since.

The fertile valleys with their mild climates and mountain streams bearing gold brought a rush of settlers to the Pacific Mountain Ranges in the 1840s and 1850s. The climate and thriving businesses continue to make the Pacific area an attractive place to settle.

Alaska

The United States is what is known as a "fragmented" state, meaning that part of its land area is separated from the rest by water or another country. Such is the case with Alaska, which is separated from the "lower forty-eight" by Canada, and Hawaii, which is separated from the mainland by the Pacific Ocean. Although Alaska is

Mount McKinley in Alaska is the highest mountain in North America.

far to the north of the northwestern states, its geographic regions are a continuation of those we have mentioned in the lower forty-eight states. Coastal mountains rim the Gulf of Alaska, reaching their highest elevations in the Alaska Range. At 20,237 feet, **Mount McKinley** is the highest point in North America. In northern Alaska, the Brooks Range is the northern end of the Rocky Mountain chain. Between those two mountain groups lies an area of hills and plains drained mainly by the Yukon River.

Like the northernmost regions of Canada, Alaska has a cold climate most of the year. It is, however, an area that is rich in resources, especially oil.

Hawaii

Finally, the southernmost state of the United States is Hawaii, a chain of volcanic islands near the center of the Pacific Ocean. The remaining active volcanoes are at the southeast end of the chain on the largest island (also called Hawaii).

Rich soil covers much of these islands, and their tropical climate helps make them valuable spots for pineapple and sugar-cane plantations. Some of the islands' beaches have made Hawaii a famous tourist destination. The U.S. military also uses Hawaii as its headquarters for the Pacific region.

Although Hawaii is known as a tourist destination, its rich soils make it an important agricultural state as well.

Section Quiz

1. Into what two parts are the Coastal Plains divided?
2. What does the term *piedmont* mean?
3. In what mountain chain is the Eastern Continental Divide?
4. By what other name were the Great Plains once known?
5. What mountain is the highest in North America, and in which state is it located?
* What is the current shape of the peak of Mount St. Helens? What caused it to develop this shape?

Climate

Prevailing wind patterns in North America are generally from west to east across the central section of the continent. The warm **Japanese Current** flows across the northwest coast, bringing plentiful rains to that region. A cool ocean current blows by the coast of California, giving that area a mild mediterranean climate with dry, sunny summers and mild, wet winters.

These westerly winds have an important influence on the climate patterns of the United States. As they flow over the Pacific coastal mountains, they lose much of their moisture. Therefore, on the eastern side of the mountains, the winds are cooler, milder, and drier, producing arid conditions for this rainshadow area, which includes the Great Basin and the desert Southwest. Although such areas are very hot during the daytime, they lose their heat quickly at night.

After the winds pass the Great Basin, they must climb over the Rocky Mountains, losing on the western slopes of the Rockies any moisture they might have picked up. On the eastern side, the rainshadow effect once again prevails. The area of the Great Plains

In March 1966, North Dakota experienced a blizzard that resulted in more than normal accumulation for even that cold state, nearly burying the telephone poles.

Hurricane Sandy in 2012

immediately east of the Rockies typically receives only ten to twenty inches of precipitation a year.

The temperatures of the Great Plains are affected greatly by the warming and cooling of the great landmass of the heart of the North American continent. In temperate regions, this continental effect results in wide temperature extremes, hot in summer and cold in winter. For example, temperatures might average in the 80s and 90s in summer but dip to below 0° in winter. A place at the same latitude on the west coast might have temperatures that rarely exceed 80° or go below 30°.

In the eastern United States, two basic climates predominate. The northern half is influenced by not only the westerly flow of air across the plains but also the cold winds that sometimes dip down from Canada. The East has a generally cool, humid climate. The winters are cold, and the summers are hot. Precipitation totals range from twenty to more than forty inches a year. States around the Great Lakes also get "lake-effect snows" since the air picks up moisture as it crosses the Great Lakes. States of the Northeast are sometimes subjected to terrific storms known as "**nor'easters**," which, as their name indicates, move in from the northeast over the North Atlantic.

The South is influenced by not only the westerly flow of air across the continent and occasionally the cold Canadian air but also the warm, moist breezes from the Gulf of Mexico. Average temperatures are much milder in the South than in the North. Temperatures along the Gulf coast rarely dip below freezing. When the warm, moist air from the Gulf moves northeast and meets the cooler air moving southwest, violent thunderstorms and tornadoes occur in the summer and snowstorms in the winter, especially in the border states that divide the North from the South.

Between June and November, the southern Atlantic and Gulf coasts are susceptible to hurricanes and tropical storms that develop in the Atlantic Ocean off Africa and move across the Atlantic and through the Caribbean. The 2004 and 2005 hurricane seasons proved to be especially destructive in southwest Florida and from eastern Texas to Mississippi. Florida was hit by three major hurricanes in 2004, including Category 4 Charley; and New Orleans was hit by Category 5 (the highest level) Hurricane Katrina in 2005. In October 2012, Hurricane Sandy swept across the eastern seaboard as a Category 3 storm with winds spanning 1,100 miles. Wind damage and resulting floods killed 147 in the United States and a total of 285 in the seven countries affected.

Resources

God has graciously blessed the United States with an abundance of natural resources. Although the United States does not lead the world in the production of many of the common and necessary natural resources, it is generally among the top producers of the resources it does possess. Whatever resources it lacks, it is able to obtain through trade with other countries. Of the resources that it does possess, the United States has more than enough for its own needs and trades the excess to other nations that need them.

The key to the economic success of the United States or any other country, however, is not how many resources it has but rather how well its government creates an environment that encourages

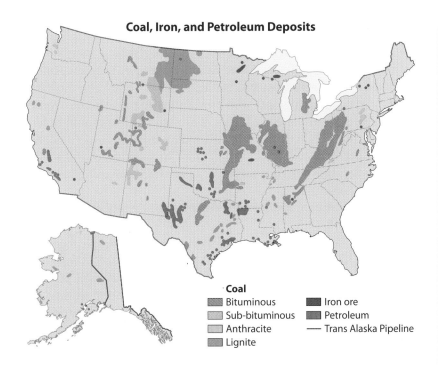

Coal, Iron, and Petroleum Deposits

Coal
- ▨ Bituminous
- ▨ Sub-bituminous
- ▨ Anthracite
- ▨ Lignite
- ▨ Iron ore
- ▨ Petroleum
- — Trans Alaska Pipeline

domestic production of the available resources. Other countries have more of certain resources than the United States has, but they often have governments and economies that hinder the proper use and development of those resources. God has blessed the United States with a heritage of free government and broad economic freedoms that have encouraged individual and corporate initiative and genius, and those gifts have led to generally wise stewardship of natural resources.

The greatest and most valuable natural resource a country can have, however, is its people. Countries that value human life and provide governments and economies that encourage individual initiative tend to succeed economically. Conversely, societies that denigrate their people, unduly restrict or regulate their economic activities, or punitively tax their efforts to improve themselves tend to be proportionately less successful in the use of their resources.

Another measure of a country's stewardship involves the use of its plant and animal life to produce foods and other products necessary for not only subsistence but also trading with other countries and improving the quality of life for its citizens. The United States has been very successful in doing this; its agricultural industries have been able to produce more than enough to meet U.S. needs and to "feed the world" with the surplus—and yet that production represents less than 1 percent of the U.S. GDP.

Leading Milk Producing States (2012)

State	Million Lb.
1. California	41,801
2. Wisconsin	27,224
3. Idaho	13,558
4. New York	13,196
5. Pennsylvania	10,493
6. Texas	9,596
7. Minnesota	9,071
All other states combined	73,385

Section Quiz

1. From which direction do prevailing winds in the United States come?
2. What current brings a lot of rain to the Northwest?
3. To what type of weather feature are the U.S. Atlantic and Gulf coasts susceptible between June and November?
4. What hurricane struck the eastern seaboard in 2012?
✶ How should a Christian respond to the suffering of others during a natural disaster?

Religious Affiliations of Americans

As of 2011, about 64% of Americans claimed affiliation with an organized religious group; those 201 million Americans represented a wide variety of religious bodies.

Protestants	28%
Roman Catholics	21%
Other (unspecified)	7.8%
Mormons	1.7%
Jews	1.7%
Other (Christian)	1.6%
Muslims	1.6%
Buddhists	0.7%

II. The American People

Just as the word *diverse* describes the geographic variety of the United States, it also describes the American people. Very few Americans can trace their ancestry to Native American ethnicity; most are descended from immigrants who brought to their new home diverse languages, customs, and traditions. Through hard work and determination, the early settlers eventually built a strong, prosperous, and united country. They shared a respect for Christian values and a willingness to endure personal sacrifice. They were also unified by certain core values.

Core Values

Core values forge a common culture and bind a people together. For Americans from the colonial period to the present, those ideals have been freedom, equality, individualism, and growth. American Christians must evaluate these values from a biblical worldview. These values can all be lived out in ways that reflect God's purposes for His people. But they can also be understood and lived out in ways that are contrary to God's Word and will.

Freedom

Abraham Lincoln declared in the Gettysburg Address that the United States was "conceived in Liberty." This statement echoes Patrick Henry's cry on the eve of the American Revolution, "Give me liberty or give me death!" The Preamble of the Constitution declares that one purpose for the new nation was to "secure the Blessings of Liberty to ourselves and our Posterity." The idea of liberty has persisted into recent American history. Franklin Roosevelt set forth the ideal of the "Four Freedoms," which included freedoms of speech and religion, as well as freedom from want and freedom from fear. Ronald Reagan spoke in Normandy, France, in 1984 for the observance of the fortieth anniversary of D-day: "We're here to mark that day in history when the Allied armies joined in battle to reclaim this continent to liberty."

Americans have always valued freedom, but they have not always agreed on what it means. For many Americans liberty is primarily about freedom from authorities or laws. Liberty is the freedom to do whatever one wants. This was not the view of the Pilgrim or Puritan

The landing of the Pilgrims at Plymouth, Massachusetts, was the beginning of America's religious heritage.

forefathers, however. The Pilgrims and Puritans had a great deal to say about liberty, but the liberty they valued was the freedom to submit to Christ their King and His law.

This view of liberty maintained a long heritage in the United States. On the eve of the War for Independence, Baptist pastor Isaac Backus argued that religious liberty should be given to Christians to worship according to their own consciences. But he insisted that this religious liberty did not undermine the government's authority to protect the Christian religion and public morality. Backus wanted laws against vices such as blasphemy and gambling. He said, "The true liberty of man is, to know, obey and enjoy his Creator, and to do all the good unto, and enjoy all the happiness with and in his fellow-creatures that he is capable of."

Alongside the liberty to do right came the Enlightenment ideal of political liberty. The English philosopher John Locke, along with others, focused on a person's right to life, liberty, and property, rights that came from the "state of nature." Thomas Jefferson in the Declaration of Independence altered it to read "Life, Liberty, and the pursuit of Happiness." Their ideas, which were radical in an age of kings and nobles, centered on the right of the people to govern themselves. Political liberty has taken firm root in the United States. It is an essential part of the American political system.

While political liberty and the liberty to live a life pleasing to God often work hand in hand, sometimes they conflict. For instance, Abraham Lincoln opposed settling the slavery question in the territories by popular sovereignty because he did not believe political liberty should enable Americans to violate the rights of others.

More recently Christians have opposed a woman's "right" to choose to kill her unborn children. Christians must agree with the early Americans that true liberty is freedom from sin and the ability to serve God. James spoke of Scripture as the "law of liberty" (James 1:25). Modern Americans might find it strange to find law and liberty so closely related, but Americans such as Winthrop and Backus would have understood that without law there can be no liberty.

Equality

Another core American ideal is that of equality. In the same Declaration of Independence where he highlighted liberty, Jefferson also stated, "We hold these truths to be self-evident, that all men are created equal." Equality is a powerful concept, and it can be applied in many different ways. For instance, one can speak of all humans as equal by virtue of their humanness. This is probably what Jefferson was highlighting in the Declaration. Or one can speak of equality of opportunity, equality of income, equality of outcomes, or equality of authority.

Americans differ about which kinds of equality are good or bad. Political liberals often work toward equality of outcomes. Political conservatives often object that in a society that permits freedom, some citizens will achieve more than others and inequality will result. Efforts on the part of the government to ensure equality of outcome will result in a curtailment of some liberty.

Christians recognize that liberty is not an absolute good, so they must evaluate precisely what is being gained and lost in particular situations. Nor is every kind of equality an absolute good. The equality

John Winthrop on Liberty

"There is a liberty of corrupt nature, which is affected both by men and beasts, to do what they list [want]; and this liberty is inconsistent with authority, impatient of all restraint; by this liberty, *sunuis omnes deteriores* [we are all the worse for it]; 'tis the grand enemy of truth and peace, and all the ordinances of God are bent against it. But there is a civil, a moral, a federal liberty, which is the proper end and object of authority; it is a liberty for that only which is just and good; for this liberty you are to stand with the hazard of your very lives; and whatsoever crosses it is not authority, but a distemper [disease] thereof. This liberty is maintained in a way of subjection to authority; and the authority set over you will in all administrations for your good be quietly submitted unto, by all but such as have no disposition to shake off the yoke, and lose their true liberty, by their murmuring at the honour and power of authority."

From a 1645 speech that was published in Cotton Mather's *The Life of John Winthrop* (1702) *Nehemias Americanus*. www.matherproject.org/node/33

Lincoln and Liberty

"Most of all, Lincoln condemned popular sovereignty because it tried to dodge the moral issue of slavery. . . . Liberty was not an end in itself, as popular sovereignty seemed to claim; it was a means, and it was intended to serve the interests of the natural rights that Jefferson had identified in the Declaration of Independence—life, liberty, the pursuit of happiness. Otherwise liberty would itself be transformed into power, the power of a mob to do whatever it took a fancy to."

Allen C. Guelzo, *Fateful Lightning: A New History of the Civil War and Reconstruction* (New York: Oxford University Press, 2012), 89.

Evangelicalism

Originally the term *evangelical* referred to Protestants as distinguished from Roman Catholics. Evangelicals believed in justification by faith alone, salvation through Christ alone, and the final authority of Scripture. Until the eighteenth century the words *protestant* and *evangelical* were synonymous.

By the eighteenth century many Protestant churches had compromised the truth, and followers of rational religion in the United States rejected the Bible as God's Word and the deity of Jesus. Some Americans thought that evangelicalism would die out. Instead, spiritual awakenings swept the nation and millions became Christians.

The nineteenth century was the evangelical century for the United States. Churches grew as people came to Christ. Evangelicals played key roles in higher education. They also worked together to form societies that promoted reading, Bible distribution, and many other issues.

The twentieth century began with a struggle to prevent liberalism from gaining access to and eventually seizing control of many evangelical institutions. The evangelicals lost most of these battles and started new organizations such as schools and mission boards to replace those lost to liberalism. During the second half of the twentieth century, evangelicalism split between those who stressed the fundamentals of the faith and separation and those who sought broader acceptance by working with ecumenical groups. The first group became known as Fundamentalists and the second group called themselves New Evangelicals.

At the present, conservative evangelicals remain vigilant lest liberalism works its way into their institutions. Others are concerned that worship has become infected by the culture of American entertainment. Despite these and other concerns, many churches are still being planted, missionaries are still going abroad, and mature Christians are still resisting the pull of the world. American Christians do not know if the future holds another awakening or a season of persecution. They do know, however, that God is faithful and will continue to build His church.

of all people as humans is biblical because all humans are created in the image of God. It is for this reason that slavery in any form and abortion are wrong. But not all inequality is bad. All the persons of the Trinity are equally God, yet within the Trinity there is an order of authority (John 8:29; 16:13). Likewise even in eternity some believers will receive more than other believers (Matt. 19:28; Luke 19:17–19). Ultimate equality of outcome does not seem to be God's purpose even in eternity. Nevertheless, Christians should object when people use their power or wealth to take advantage of the poor and to keep them in that condition (Deut. 15:1–11; Isa. 5:8).

Individualism

Americans celebrate the ideal of the self-reliant individual, often at the expense of the group or society. American myths recount the adventures of individual explorers and frontiersmen. The independent American spirit contributed to a work ethic that encouraged capitalism and economic success for many. The roots of this spirit run deep in Western civilization, beginning with the ancient Greeks and Romans and reinforced in the Renaissance and the Enlightenment, when philosophers declared that individuals had natural rights.

Once again the Christian recognizes that individualism is not an unqualified good. On the one hand, the Bible stresses the individual and his or her need of salvation. Luther, in the Reformation, dramatically shifted the focus to the individual's access to God, not through the priest or church but through Christ alone. On the other hand, the Bible teaches that all Christians are to gather together into a community, the church. Christian worship each week is a communal event. Paul told Christians that they should look out for the interests of others (Phil. 2:4), and Jesus said the second greatest commandment is to love one's neighbor as oneself (Matt. 22:39). The Bible also teaches that we are to help those in need, the poor, especially widows and orphans. Not every person can afford to take care of himself. A French observer of American society in the 1830s, Alexis de Tocqueville, observed in *Democracy in America* that the Christian religion in this country countered some of the selfishness that resulted from individualism.

Growth

Americans also value growth. From the beginning Americans pressed westward, expanding the borders of their territory. As the nation grew, so did the roads, canals, and railroads that connected its growing towns and cities. Factories sprang up beside rivers, and crops filled fertile valleys. American inventors developed new ways to communicate, travel, and work. In time the United States emerged as an industrial leader and then as a world power.

From a Christian perspective, much of this growth is good. God blessed humans in the beginning with the abilities needed to rule over His creation. When the Pilgrims established a colony on the edge of a wilderness, when Slater brought the factory system to the United States, and when Morse developed the telegraph, they were living out the Creation Mandate that God gave to mankind. And when the Pilgrims thanked God for preserving their lives, when Slater used his factories to introduce the Sunday school to America, and when Morse praised God for the ability to invent, God received the glory He is due.

But like the other American core values, growth is not an unadulterated good. When Andrew Jackson removed the Cherokee Indians from their lands or Polk seized land belonging to Mexico, growth ceased to be good because growth was being valued for itself rather than as a means for glorifying God and loving others.

Summary

The combination of these core values sets the United States apart as a distinct culture. Americans have celebrated this culture and even sought to spread it around the world. While it is normal for any nation to feel proud of its way of life, Americans must recognize that their core values can be lived out in ways that are pleasing to God or ways that are displeasing to Him. American Christians must realize that they have often fallen short of God's expectations for a God-fearing nation. Nonetheless, God has graciously blessed the United States with many citizens throughout its history who have honored Him in their lives. For this, American Christians can be truly grateful.

Section Quiz

1–4. What are the four core values that traditionally bind Americans together as a united people?

5. How do many Americans define freedom or liberty? How does that view differ from the Puritan concept of liberty?

★ Does equality of opportunity guarantee that all Americans will have an equal amount of the nation's wealth or an equality of outcome? Why or why not?

Demographics

A big part of studying geography is understanding **demographics**, the study of the characteristics of people in a particular place or a segment of that population. The goal of such study is to understand better who the people are, why they live as they do, and what makes them "tick." It includes the population count, of course, but it also includes much more.

In 2012 the United States had an estimated population of 314 million. Of those, 80.7 percent lived in **urban areas**, places with a population of 50,000 or more. This number also includes those who lived in suburbs, areas between cities and **rural** (country) settings.

The 2010 census showed that forty-nine states increased in population, although the greatest growth has been in the southern third of the nation from the Carolinas to California, an area known as the **Sun Belt**. The increased growth there might be the result of increased numbers of retirees who move from the cooler north to the warmer climates of southern states.

The census also noted that total U.S. growth was 9.7 percent. The growth of individual states ranged from a low of -0.6 percent (Michigan) to an impressive 35.1 percent (Nevada). Five states had a growth rate above 20 percent; six states had a population increase ranging from 1.3 to 4.3 million. Most of the U.S. growth occurred in the West and the South. The most heavily populated areas continue to be the Northeast and the West Coast, although other metropolitan areas are also growing.

The growth of minority groups continued, especially among the Hispanic population. Many minority populations tend to cluster in

Countries of Birth of Foreign-Born U.S. Population

Rank	1880	1930	1960	1990	2000	2010
1	Germany 1,967,000	Italy 1,790,000	Italy 1,257,000	Mexico 4,298,000	Mexico 7,841,000	Mexico 11,700,000
2	Ireland 1,855,000	Germany 1,609,000	Germany 990,000	China 921,000	China 1,391,000	China 2,200,000
3	Great Britain 918,000	United Kingdom 1,403,000	Canada 953,000	Philippines 913,000	Philippines 1,222,000	Philippines 1,800,000
4	Canada 717,000	Canada 1,310,000	United Kingdom 833,000	Canada 745,000	India 1,007,000	India 1,800,000
5	Sweden 194,000	Poland 1,269,000	Poland 748,000	Cuba 737,000	Cuba 952,000	Vietnam 1,220,000
6	Norway 182,000	Soviet Union 1,154,000	Soviet Union 691,000	Germany 712,000	Vietnam 863,000	El Salvador 1,200,000
7	France 107,000	Ireland 745,000	Mexico 576,000	United Kingdom 640,000	El Salvador 765,000	Cuba 1,110,000
8	China 104,000	Mexico 641,000	Ireland 339,000	Italy 581,000	Korea 701,000	Korea 1,100,000
9	Switzerland 89,000	Sweden 595,000	Austria 305,000	Korea 568,000	Dominican Republic 692,000	Dominican Republic 900,000
10	Bohemia 85,000	Czechoslovakia 492,000	Hungary 245,000	Vietnam 543,000	Canada 678,000	Guatemala 800,000

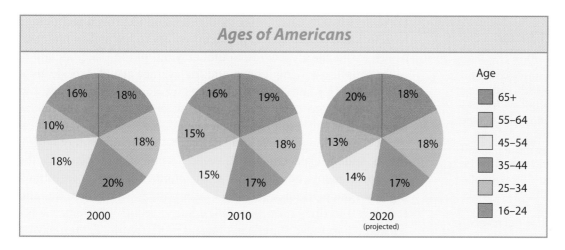

Ages of Americans

| | | 2000 | 2010 | 2020 (projected) |

2000: 16%, 18%, 10%, 18%, 18%, 20%

2010: 16%, 19%, 15%, 18%, 15%, 17%

2020 (projected): 20%, 18%, 13%, 18%, 14%, 17%

Age
- 65+
- 55–64
- 45–54
- 35–44
- 25–34
- 16–24

certain regions—Hispanics and Native Americans in the West and Southwest, black Americans along the southeastern seaboard and in the Deep South, and Asian Americans in the West.

The non-Anglo population is growing in all fifty states. For example, the non-white population of Texas was 57 percent of all Texans, the largest group of which was Hispanics. The statistics are similar for California and New Mexico. A similar situation exists in Hawaii, where the largest minority group is Asians. Five states (Maryland, Mississippi, Georgia, New York, and Arizona) have about 40 percent minority populations. It is estimated that more than half of the nation's population will be minorities by 2050.

In 2012 the birth rate of the United States was approximately 13.7 (13.7 live births per 1,000 people in the general population). The average life span of an American is 78.49 years. (This is in stark contrast to both the world average of 67.59 years and that of the lowest in the world, Chad, at 48.69 years. Monaco has the highest average life span at 89.68 years.) Advances in

Since fewer people are needed to work on farms, populations have moved from rural to urban and suburban locations.

Demographics and Church Planting

Some areas of the United States have been blessed with strong churches and vibrant outreach ministries. However, other areas of the country have few churches, and the churches that do exist are far apart and small. To address this issue, churches and mission boards sometimes use demographics to find the best places to plant new churches. They look at an area's population and growth rate as well as the number and size of existing churches. An area with a growing population but no gospel-preaching church would be a much more promising prospect for a church plant than an area with a shrinking population or with many good churches.

Another factor influencing church planting is the growth of immigrant communities. Growing numbers of immigrants from Latin America, China, and other countries have settled in various places, drawn perhaps by an international company or simply by educational or economic opportunities. Churches have a variety of options when seeking to reach out to these groups. Some churches have added a pastor who speaks the language of one of these ethnic groups to the staff as a means of outreach. Others choose to support a separate church pastored by a qualified person from that ethnic group who understands the culture and can minister effectively.

In response to this growing opportunity, some missionaries who have served on foreign fields have returned to the United States in order to minister to immigrant communities here. As people from all over the world come to this country, there are abundant opportunities to win the lost from many cultures right here in our own backyard.

Though demographics can be a useful tool, it can be misused. For instance, a church planter might be tempted to focus on upper-middle class suburbs if statistics seemed to indicate that growth is faster there. And how should a church respond if research shows that reaching out to lower-income groups slows the rate of upper-middle-class growth? The Bible commands that Christians reach out to all people, and it specifically warns against partiality (James 2:1–7). These clear teachings from Scripture should ultimately overrule demographic considerations.

preventive health care, better medicines, and improved technology to detect and treat physical problems earlier in life and to maintain health in old age are leading to the "graying" of the U.S. population. More people are living longer, and the average age of Americans is increasing. The number of Americans who are 65 years of age and older is expected to double by 2050. Another factor is the falling birthrate that will result in a smaller workforce.

Although longer life is good news from the standpoint of health, fitness, and life expectancy, it also presents potential problems for the U.S. government and economy. As the number of retirees withdrawing from the workforce (i.e., no longer paying taxes) increases and they begin to draw money from the Social Security System, the tax burden on younger Americans increases. Currently, 2.9 tax-paying workers support every retiree, but by 2030 that number is projected to have shrunk to two workers per retiree. Unless significant changes are made to this system, drastic measures will have to be taken that will result in either the collapse of the system or crushing taxation on those still working.

Section Quiz

1. What term refers to the study of the characteristics of people in a particular place?
2. In which area—urban or rural—do most Americans live?
3. What is the southern third of the United States called?
4. What is the average life expectancy in the United States?
* How should Christians respond to the growth of various minority groups in the United States?

Government

The United States government functions as a **federal republic**, meaning that supreme power rests in the people and their elected representatives, and that power is shared between the national government and the governments of the fifty states. In addition are the various local governments within each state—counties, townships, boroughs, cities, and so forth. Each state government functions under a constitution, with the U.S. Constitution being the overriding governing document or "law of the land."

The U.S. Capitol houses the Senate and the House of Representatives.

Show Your Colors

The first flag used by General George Washington during the American Revolution was called the Grand Union flag and was hoisted at the siege of Boston, 1776. It had thirteen alternating red and white stripes and the British Union Jack in the upper left-hand corner (where the stars are today).

In 1777 Congress passed the first Flag Act, which specified that "the flag . . . be made of thirteen stripes, alternate red and white; that the union be thirteen stars, white in a blue field, representing a new Constellation."

Between then and 1960, twenty-six laws changed the design of the flag, adding stars and arranging and rearranging those features. The current design is thirteen horizontal stripes, alternating red and white, representing the original thirteen colonies. The stars represent the individual fifty states. The colors are also symbolic. Red represents valor, or courage; white represents purity and innocence; and blue represents vigilance, perseverance, and justice.

The Constitution (specifically the Tenth Amendment) delegates certain powers to the national government and reserves all other powers to the individual states. It includes the principle of **separation of powers**, which divides the national government into three distinct branches: legislative (Congress), executive (the president), and judicial (Supreme Court and other lower courts). Each branch has its own powers, responsibilities, and limitations. State governments are organized similarly. The separation of powers principle prevents any elected official or branch of government from becoming too powerful.

The foundation of American freedom was set forth in the Declaration of Independence and included the "unalienable rights" of "life, liberty, and the pursuit of happiness." These rights were further delineated in the Constitution and subsequent amendments. One important right of Americans is that of participating in their government at all levels by voting, speaking or publishing their opinions, or even running for public office.

Freedom of speech is an important part of American government at local, state, and national levels.

Economy

The United States economy is a system of **free enterprise capitalism** in which private individuals own most of the factors of production and make most of the economic decisions. Those individuals—or groups of individuals formed into corporations—can compete with other individuals or companies to earn money. Tension has always existed, however, between those who want unrestricted economic freedom and those who advocate government control or regulation of various aspects of economic activity, usually to give themselves or their businesses favored treatment. The United States moved dramatically toward government control during the Great Depression of the 1930s and during World War II, and, with few exceptions, that trend has continued ever since. Nonetheless, the United States still has one of the freest economies of any nation in the world. Its phenomenal material success is a direct result of the degree of its freedom.

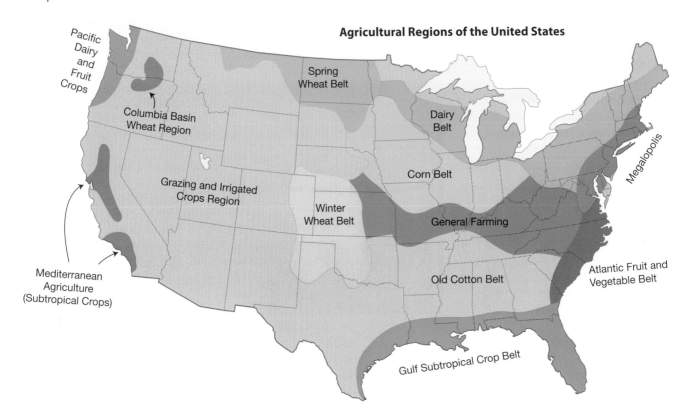

Agricultural Regions of the United States

States with the Greatest Income from Agriculture (2011)

(Amounts shown are $ millions)

1.	California	16.3
2.	Iowa	10.8
3.	Nebraska	7.5
4.	Illinois	6.1
5.	Minnesota	5.8
6.	Texas	5.3
7.	Kansas	5.2

In 2012 the GDP of the United States was estimated to be $15.66 trillion. Of that figure, 1.2 percent came from agriculture. That percentage is deceptive, however, because America's farmers literally feed the world. America's farmers are the most productive in the world. On average, an American farmer produces food and other related products for about 155 people.

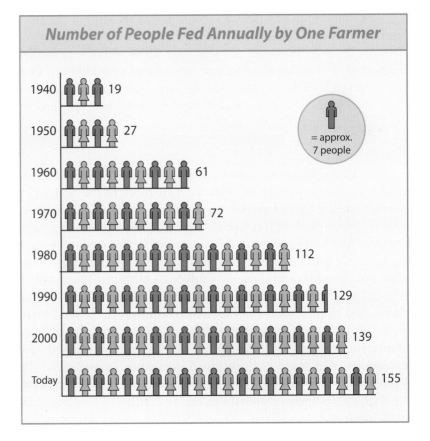

Number of People Fed Annually by One Farmer

= approx. 7 people

Year	People Fed
1940	19
1950	27
1960	61
1970	72
1980	112
1990	129
2000	139
Today	155

Almost 20 percent of the GDP is industry, and an amazing 80 percent is services. The per capita GDP is $49,800. One cause of concern is the national debt, which is 73.6 percent of the GDP and growing. Six percent of government expenditures are payments of interest (not principal) on the national debt, while spending on national defense remains around 19 percent. The combined expenses incurred by the ongoing war on terrorism and relief for victims of an

The floor of the New York Stock Exchange, which is symbolic of the U.S. economy, is the heart of the New York City financial district known as Wall Street.

America's Pastime: Baseball

Baseball has long been called "America's pastime." Alexander Cartwright invented the game in 1845 and founded the Knickerbocker Base Ball Club of New York. The first recorded game was in 1846 between Cartwright's club and the New York Nine. Cartwright's team lost. Baseball was also played by soldiers during the Civil War.

The first salaried team was the Cincinnati Red Stockings in 1869. The first professional baseball league was formed two years later as the National Association of Professional Base Ball Players, and the first formal major league, the National League, began in 1876. A rival American League was formed in 1893. These same two leagues have competed ever since.

At first, the teams played other teams in their own league and then the winners of each league played each other in the World Series. Today, some interleague play is scheduled during each season.

Initially, only white Americans played professional baseball. Blacks had their own league, the Negro League, but they did not get to play in the World Series. In the 1940s, however, Branch Rickey, owner of the Brooklyn Dodgers, hired the black player Jackie Robinson. This breaking of the color barrier opened the door for extensive black participation. Soon, players of still other races and nationalities were allowed into baseball. Today, teams include whites, blacks, Hispanics, and Asians. Baseball is no longer merely a sport; it is big business, with players demanding—and getting—multimillion-dollar contracts.

Although baseball must now compete with other professional sports for both participants and spectators, the names of baseball's legends—such men as Babe Ruth, Lou Gehrig, Ty Cobb, Willie Mays, Hank Aaron, and others—still carry great meaning among Americans today.

Natural Treasures of the United States

The U.S. government has sought to preserve the natural wonders of the nation for the benefit of future generations so that they can experience what the early settlers of the fledgling country saw during their westward migration. Such areas have been preserved in the form of national parks, most of which are west of the Mississippi River. The most visited national park, however, the Great Smoky Mountains National Park, is in eastern Tennessee and western North Carolina. This national park has the largest number of people living within a day's drive. Chapter 8 includes photographs of several national parks. Perhaps you have visited some of them yourself.

Maybe you would like to visit others in the future and enjoy firsthand the natural treasures of the United States of America. Consider conducting an in-depth study of one or more of the parks you find most interesting.

Sunset in the Great Smoky Mountains National Park

States Containing the Most Federally Owned Lands	
Rank/State	% Federally owned
1. Nevada	84.5
2. Alaska	69
3. Utah	57.4
4. Oregon	53.1
5. Idaho	50.1
6. Arizona	48
7. California	45.8

unprecedented number of natural disasters in the last decade only exacerbate the problem, making it harder to pay down the national debt. Many economists say that this situation cannot be allowed to continue without disastrous results to the economy.

Although the United States has a free enterprise economy, the federal government owns and controls nearly one-third of the land in the nation. Only 2.4 percent of government-owned land is used for military purposes. Much of the rest is national parks, forests, wilderness areas, or protected areas.

Section Quiz

1. What type of government does the United States have?
2. What three branches of government guarantee separation of powers?
3. What form of economy does the United States have?
4. What sector of the economy makes up only 1.2 percent of U.S. GDP yet is the most productive such sector in the world?
5. What sector makes up 80 percent of the U.S. GDP?
★ Why does the federal government own nearly one-third of the land in the nation?

Chapter 7 Review

Making Connections

1–2. What countries and geographic features constitute the northern and southern boundaries of the United States?

3–4. What are two problems the United States confronts along its southern border?

5–6. What word best describes both the American landscape and the people who live there? Why?

Developing Geography Skills

1. In which of the eight topographical regions do you live? Where might you also live other than these regions and yet live in the United States?

2. Describe what the culture is like in your region of the United States. What foods are unique to your region? What aspects of your region's culture most honor God? What aspects of your region's culture least honor God?

Thinking Critically

1. What challenges will the United States face as its minority population continues to grow?

2. Why have some countries with just as many resources as the United States been unable to duplicate U.S. economic success?

Living in God's World

1. What core values are in play when a person argues that the federal government should accept same-sex marriage because it is discriminatory against homosexuals to deny them a choice in whom they are allowed to marry?

2. What core values are in play when a person argues that in order to eliminate poverty, a society's property, means of production, and profits should be held in common and equally distributed among the members of that society? Evaluate this perspective based on the core American values.

People, Places, and Things to Know

Rio Grande
Coastal Plains
Atlantic Coastal Plain
Gulf Coastal Plain
Piedmont
fall line
Appalachian Mountains
Eastern Continental Divide
Central Plains
Mississippi River
Great Plains
Rocky Mountains
Western Continental Divide
Great Basin
Pacific Mountain Ranges
Mount St. Helens
Mount McKinley
Japanese Current
nor'easters
demographics
urban areas
rural
Sun Belt
federal republic
separation of powers
free enterprise capitalism

The Statue of Liberty symbolizes the hope and opportunities of the American nation.

THE REGIONS OF THE UNITED STATES

I. The Northeast
   A. New England
   B. The Middle Atlantic

II. The South
   A. The Upper South
   B. The Lower South

III. The Midwest

IV. The Plains

V. The West
   A. Continental West
   B. Outlying States

*I*n the previous chapter, you got a broad picture of the United States. You studied the American landscape, noting its boundaries, topographical regions, and climate. You examined the diverse peoples who make up the American population and the heritage that they share. And you looked briefly at the form of government and the economic system by which the American nation functions. In this chapter, you will take a closer look at the major geographic regions of the United States, noting each region's unique qualities and contributions to the broader American nation and the world, and will take a brief look at each state.

Each region has unique qualities, resources, activities, needs, and cultural distinctions. You will study the various regions as they are divided on the following map of the United States (refer to the map as you read your assignments). Often the importance of natural resources in these regions is determined by the needs which they meet. One of the big needs in the world today is energy that can be produced on a large scale and at affordable prices. Keep an eye out for the different resources in each region, but take special note of the energy resources.

I. The Northeast

The Northeast region can be further divided into two subregions, New England and the Middle Atlantic, which are divided by a series of hills and mountains. Nine of the thirteen original colonies were in the Northeast, so the region played a critical role in the history of the United States, especially in gaining its liberty and independence. The area has abundant monuments and other historical sites that remind visitors of the region's role in history.

The Northeast is one of the most populated coastal regions in the United States, with around one third of the nation's total coastal population living there. In 2010, four of the ten largest metropolitan areas in the nation were located along the northeast coast, where the population density was heaviest: 305 people per square mile.

New England

The six states at the far northeast corner of the United States are very small; all six could fit inside Missouri. Yet they have played a big role in the nation from the beginning. John Cabot, an explorer who claimed the area for England in 1497, called it New England. It became the cradle of capitalism, democracy, and freedom of religion in the New World. The colonists engaged in trans-Atlantic trade early in their history. They divided their settlements politically into townships, and town meetings were the basis of self-government. Because the earliest settlers in this region had come to the New World to escape religious persecution, they emphasized freedom of worship, and Christian principles guided life in the colonies there.

The entire Northeast has a humid continental climate, but New England is not favorable for farming. The winters are cold, and the growing season is short. For these reasons New Englanders have historically relied on commercial and manufacturing industries.

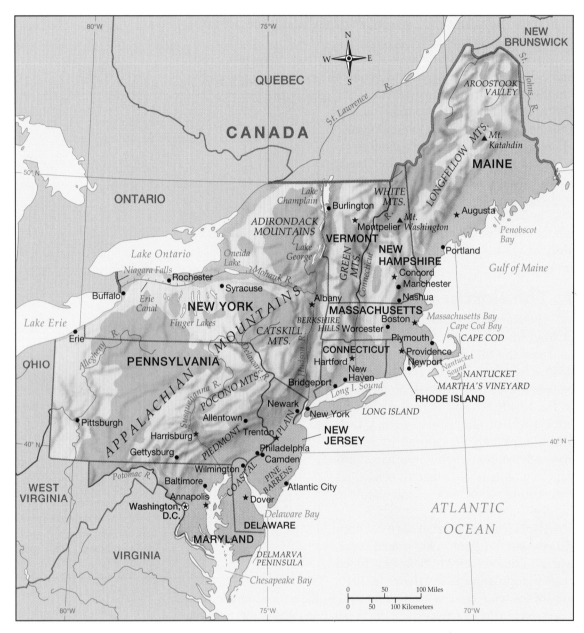

New England is divided into three types of terrain: lowlands, uplands, and mountains. The lowlands are a narrow strip of coastal plains. Deep harbors along the coast allowed large cities to thrive on trade and fishing. This area also produces almost half of the nation's cranberries. The **New England uplands** are a low, rocky plateau that rises above the coast. The soil in the uplands is too rocky for profitable farming, even along the stretches of coastal lowlands. Most of the good farmland is in the river valleys. Farther inland, several mountain ranges, including the Berkshire Hills, rise within the Appalachian Mountain chain.

Northeastern Fast Facts						
State	PO Code	Capital	Date of Statehood	Nickname	Area (sq. mi.)	Population (2012 est.)
Connecticut	CT	Hartford	1788	Constitution State	5,543	3,590,347
Delaware	DE	Dover	1787	First State	2,489	917,092
Maine	ME	Augusta	1820	Pine Tree State	35,387	1,329,192
Maryland	MD	Annapolis	1788	Old Line State	12,407	5,884,563
Massachusetts	MA	Boston	1788	Bay State	10,555	6,646,144
New Hampshire	NH	Concord	1788	Granite State	9,351	1,320,718
New Jersey	NJ	Trenton	1787	Garden State	8,722	8,864,590
New York	NY	Albany	1788	Empire State	54,475	19,570,261
Pennsylvania	PA	Harrisburg	1787	Keystone State	46,058	12,763,536
Rhode Island	RI	Providence	1790	Ocean State	1,545	1,050,292
Vermont	VT	Montpelier	1791	Green Mountain State	9,615	626,011

Lower New England

The first New England colony was established in 1620 by the Pilgrims in what is today Massachusetts. The Mayflower Compact (a contract or agreement) laid the foundation for self-government in the colony and set precedents for the future nation. The main port that developed along the coast of Massachusetts was Boston, which became the capital and largest city of the Bay State.

Massachusetts was a focal point of the American War for Independence, the home of famous writers such as Henry David Thoreau, and at one time the whaling capital of the world. It is also famous for a number of leading political families, including the Adamses and the Kennedys.

The rocky New England coast made lighthouses, such as this one in Massachusetts, necessary for the safety of merchant ships.

Rhode Island, sandwiched between Massachusetts and Connecticut, was founded by Roger Williams, who named the capital Providence in recognition of the way God had provided for the colony. It was the smallest colony, but its contributions to the development of the new nation far surpassed its size. It is considered the birthplace of the Industrial Revolution in the New World because Slater's Mill in Pawtucket was the first major industry in the nation. Its owner, Samuel Slater, built a growing textile industry on the Blackstone River, and New England at one point produced more cloth than any other place in the world.

Connecticut was the first colony to write a constitution to describe and limit its government; hence, its nickname, "The

The construction of Slater's Mill on the Blackstone River marked the beginning of the Industrial Revolution in New England.

The First Sunday School in the U.S.

In addition to ushering in the Industrial Revolution to the nation, Samuel Slater also introduced the Sunday school to the U.S. His goal was to provide an education to the families of his employees in the areas of reading, writing, and the basics of the Christian faith.

Constitution State." The people have a high standard of living in spite of the lack of natural resources. Some famous Connecticut inventors include Samuel Colt (revolver) and Eli Whitney (cotton gin and mass production of musket parts). Connecticut was also home to Jonathan Edwards, a famous preacher of the Great Awakening. Hartford, the capital, is known as the insurance capital of the world because of the large number of insurance companies that are headquartered there. Connecticut is also the home of both Yale University and the submarine-building port of Groton.

Upper New England

Although the three states in the northern part of New England are also small, they are nonetheless larger than the lower three states. Settlement in Upper New England was hindered by the high mountains and rocky soil, which made farming and transportation difficult. Each of the states has mountains that reach above the **timber line**, the altitude at which the climate is too cold for trees. Above the timber line is the **alpine zone**, which is much like the Alps of Europe.

New Hampshire is the only Upper New England state that was one of the original colonies. The northern part of the state is dominated by the **White Mountains**, which are known for their snowy peaks and Christmas tree farms. In the Presidential Range of the White Mountains, the highest peaks (most of which exceed 5,000 feet in elevation) are named for presidents: Mt. Washington (the highest at 6,288 feet), Mt. Adams, Mt. Quincy Adams, Mt. Jefferson, Mt. Madison, Mt. Monroe, Mt. Pierce, and Mt. Eisenhower. Highways pass through low places in the mountains that New Englanders call **notches**. (People in other regions call them passes or gaps.)

The White Mountains in New Hampshire

Most people live in the southern part of the state; the industrial centers are also there, including Nashua, Manchester, and the capital, Concord. The state has only eighteen miles of coastline, and its only port, Portsmouth, is located there.

Vermont was once divided between New York and New Hampshire, but the settlers there declared their independence and set up their own government before the American Revolution. It is the only landlocked New England state and has the lowest population. Because the state lacks a seaport and good soil for farming, it must make the most of its natural resources, which include granite, slate, and marble. It is also famous for its maple syrup.

The **Green Mountains** run the length of the state, and river valleys form its eastern and western borders: the Connecticut River on the east and Lake Champlain on the west. Most of the state's people live in these two valleys.

Maine, the largest New England state, was once part of Massachusetts. Most of its cities are small, and most of its coastline is rocky. Although its Cadillac Mountain is only 1,500 feet in elevation, it is

Inner-City Ministries

The city holds a unique place in society. It is home to business and industry as well as to a variety of cultures, ethnicities, and economic classes. Cities are also the source of "high" culture in society, as seen by the many concert halls, museums, and exhibition centers. More importantly, cities serve as the nerve center for culture in general. Those who influence the life of the city will bring significant change to the surrounding area as well. Paul realized the importance of reaching the city and thus gave much effort to evangelizing in Ephesus, Corinth, and Rome—some of the largest, most influential cities in the world at the time.

Inner-city ministries, however, face inherent challenges. There is often more crime in the heart of a city than in the suburbs. There is a greater number of homes without fathers. This leads to poverty, which can lead to crime. Another problem is the perception that many Christians have of the city. Some people view the city as unredeemable.

Christians should not avoid the city out of fear but rather should focus on working for change. The spiritual power available through the Holy Spirit is greater than any opposing force—human or supernatural.

The inner city presents a myriad of opportunities to minister and proclaim Christ's love, whether through politics, relief work, or personal relationships. Believers have the opportunity to minister to a great diversity of ethnicities and cultures (Rev. 5:9). The church can help people navigate changing cultures. It can help young Christians evaluate and improve their culture. It can also function as a family for those who have been cut off from their families through immigration, relocation, or sin. Financial needs should not be ignored but should be viewed as opportunities for showing the love of Christ. Programs could incorporate meeting basic physical needs as well as allowing people to learn developmental skills so they can provide for themselves. Such care for the poor not only expresses love for God but also builds relationships that allow for ministering the gospel to people's eternal needs (Matt. 25:34–40).

Cities have always played a major role in the plan of God. When God gave His people the land of Canaan, He gave them a land full of cities (Deut. 6:10). When He chose the place for His glory to dwell, He chose a city, Jerusalem (1 Kings 8:1; 9:3). When He commanded Jonah to preach repentance to Assyria, He sent him to its chief city, Nineveh (Jonah 1:2). When Jesus sent His disciples to preach the gospel, He sent them first to Jerusalem (Luke 24:46–47; Acts 1:8). And when the fullness of redemption is accomplished, the center of human life on earth will be a city, the new Jerusalem (Rev. 21:1–3). God's heart is in the city, and Christians should be willing to have their hearts in the city as well.

---

the highest point along the North Atlantic seaboard. Maine also includes the only national park in the Northeast.

Maine is famous for its lobsters, the most valuable seafood catch in the world. Tourists also enjoy seeing whales and puffins around the islands of Penobscot Bay. The northernmost of the Appalachian Mountains, the Longfellow and White Mountains, are in Maine. Trees from these mountains provide most of the nation's toothpicks. The Aroostook Valley is a productive source of potatoes.

The Middle Atlantic

The lower portion of the Northeast is composed of five states: New York, Pennsylvania, New Jersey, Maryland, and Delaware. They were settled by a diversity of nationalities, including Swedish, Finnish, Dutch, German, Irish, and Italian.

New York is the northernmost Middle Atlantic state and the most populous. Its largest city, New York City, is also the largest city in the nation. It is a megacity, or **megalopolis** (literally "great city"), an urban area made up of many different cities that are close enough together to be considered a single urban area. New York City has suburbs in four other states! In fact, New York is the heart of a larger megalopolis that runs from Boston to Washington, D.C.

The Statue of Liberty

"Give me your tired, your poor, your huddled masses yearning to breathe free. . . ."

These words are inscribed on the Statue of Liberty, which has become a symbol of the freedoms and opportunities that the United States affords to immigrants from all over the world. She is dressed in a long, flowing robe; chains of bondage lie broken at her feet; she holds a law tablet in one hand and is raising the torch of freedom in the other hand. From her crown radiate seven rays to light the way to freedom for the other nations of the world.

The statue was a gift from the people of France to commemorate America's first one hundred years of independence, which France had helped her win. It was built in France, disassembled for transport to America, and then reassembled upon arrival in New York.

Lady Liberty is the tallest statue in the United States, standing 111 feet tall from toe to crown. The arm with the torch adds another 40 feet to the statue. Her nose alone is the size of a person. The statue is made of an iron framework and is covered with copper sheets, which have now turned green because of oxidation. The statue weighs 225 tons.

Niagara Falls is on the border between the United States and Canada.

Find It!

Niagara Falls
43.083° N, 79.070° W

The Monongahela River (foreground) and the Allegheny River (background). Pittsburgh developed on the Golden Triangle where these two rivers meet, forming the Ohio River.

The Upstate of New York is the vast area outside the megalopolis of New York City. The area runs from the Hudson and Mohawk River valleys, which slice through the Catskills and the Adirondacks in the east, to Lake Erie and Lake Ontario in the west. The Allegheny Plateau extends westward into the interior of the state. The middle area is called the **Finger Lakes** area, where long, narrow, glacier-made lakes extend from north to south. West of the plateau is a narrow plain along the eastern coast of the two **Great Lakes** that border New York. The moderate climate makes New York a productive farming state. It ranks third in the nation in both dairy products and grape production.

The Delaware River begins in New York and forms the eastern border of Pennsylvania, a Middle Atlantic state. Pennsylvania figured prominently in the nation's early history and boasts such landmarks as Independence Hall and the Liberty Bell in Philadelphia, the largest city in the state. Planned from its earliest days by Quaker William Penn, Philadelphia quickly developed into a major port city and is the fifth-largest city in the nation. Nearby are such important sites as the Gettysburg battlefield, where the bloodiest battle of the Civil War occurred, and Hershey, home of the largest chocolate factory in the world.

Northeastern Pennsylvania is rich in **anthracite**, a clean-burning form of coal. Much of that coal is used on the other end of the state in the steel mills of Pittsburgh, Pennsylvania's second-largest city. Pittsburgh is located at the confluence of the Monongahela and Allegheny Rivers. Between Philadelphia and Pittsburgh is some of the richest farmland in the country. Pennsylvania ranks fourth in the nation in dairy products, fifth in grapes, and sixth in chicken eggs. The capital, Harrisburg, is situated on the Susquehanna River in the south central part of the state.

Pennsylvania is also rich in natural gas deposits. However, until recently, these deposits were difficult and expensive to extract. With improved methods of fracturing shale rock deep below the surface, using hydrologic fracturing, vast amounts of natural gas are being captured and used to meet many of the nation's energy needs. This industry has created many jobs and generated tax revenue that has revitalized many cities in Pennsylvania. Other states are also tapping into this immense and financially rewarding natural resource.

Pennsylvania's neighbor to the east is New Jersey. Most of its citizens live in the northeastern part of the state near New York City.

Earth Matters: Fracking

Hydrologic fracturing, or fracking, has recently become a popular way of accessing natural gas that was previously too expensive to extract. The spread of hydrologic fracturing in states like Pennsylvania has created thousands of jobs and has resulted in lower natural gas prices. But people in some communities are concerned that fracking will pollute their water and endanger their communities.

What if you were serving on a state or local committee tasked with deciding whether or not to allow fracking in your state? You will get the opportunity to think through this in Activity 2 in the Student Activity Manual.

A machine used for fracking in Wyoming

The District of Columbia

Washington, D.C., the U.S. capital, is not a part of any state. Rather, it is a district run by Congress; therefore it is called the *District of Columbia* (D.C.). The city is built on and around Capitol Hill overlooking the Potomac River. Streets of the city radiate outward, like the spokes of a bicycle wheel, from a central hub called the National Mall, which is surrounded by beautiful government buildings. The six most important such buildings are the White House, where the President lives; the Capitol, where Congress meets; the Supreme Court building; the Bureau of Engraving and Printing, which makes the nation's paper money; the Federal Bureau of Investigation (FBI) Building, which houses the government's crime-fighting bureau; and the Pentagon, which is the headquarters of the U.S. armed forces.

Washington also is home to the Smithsonian Institution, the largest museum in the nation. It includes fourteen buildings and the National Zoo. The most famous monument in the city is the Washington Monument, which honors the first president of the United States. Other memorials to presidents include the Lincoln and the Jefferson Memorials and the eternal flame in Arlington National Cemetery, marking John Kennedy's grave.

Numerous other memorials honor military personnel who have given their lives for the country, including the Tomb of the Unknown Soldier, the World War II Memorial, the Iwo Jima Memorial, and the Vietnam Memorial. The Holocaust Memorial Museum is also in Washington, D.C.

The Christian who visits Washington will doubtless be struck with the many references, both subtle and overt, to the influence of God and His Word on the nation's history. This testifies to the great blessing of a Christian heritage. But it also stands as a warning of two dangers: the danger of forgetting God (Deut. 8:11, 17) and the danger of civil religion, in which politics hijacks biblical religion to use it for its own purposes.

Washington, D.C., is a well-organized, well-structured city.

A string of cities stretches from that area southwest to Trenton, the capital, on the Delaware River. Most of New Jersey is composed of coastal plains, including the **Pine Barrens** region, a wooded, boggy wilderness.

The moist air from the Gulf Stream gives much of New Jersey a humid, subtropical climate, and its soil is very fertile. Consequently, the state has developed many small farms, called **truck farms**, on which beans, tomatoes, peppers, and melons are grown, giving the state its nickname, the Garden State. It is fourth in the nation in lettuce production and tenth in greenhouse/nursery products.

Maryland and Delaware form the border between the Northeast and the South. Although they once had much in common with the Old South (i.e., before the Civil War), they remained in the Union and have been associated with the Middle Atlantic states ever since. They share with Virginia the **Delmarva Peninsula**, the largest peninsula in the Northeast. (The name of the peninsula comes from the names of the three states that share it: *Del*aware, *Mary*land, and Virginia [*Va.*].) The rivers of the peninsula flow into the Delaware Bay and the **Chesapeake Bay**. The Delmarva Peninsula is connected to the mainland in Virginia by the nearly eighteen-mile-long Chesapeake Bay Bridge-Tunnel.

Delaware, on the Delaware Bay, is the nation's second-smallest state (behind Rhode Island). Its largest city, Wilmington, is famous

An aircraft carrier navigates through a section of the Chesapeake Bay Bridge-Tunnel between Cape Charles and Virginia Beach, Va.

for the large number of chemical plants, including DuPont, and is known as the Chemical Capital of the World.

Maryland has several large cities, all located on the Chesapeake Bay, the largest bay in the nation, which cuts the state in two. The capital, Annapolis, is the home of the U.S. Naval Academy. Baltimore, the largest city, was the first railroad center and was one end of the first telegraph line. It is also the site of Fort McHenry, which survived British attack in 1812, inspiring Francis Scott Key's poem "The Star-Spangled Banner," which became the U.S. national anthem. Maryland's **panhandle**, the narrow strip of the state that extends deep into the continent, is only two miles wide at its narrowest point but stretches beyond the Appalachian Mountains into the Allegheny Plateau.

Section Quiz

1. Into what two subregions can the Northeast be divided?
2. What served as the basis of self-government in New England?
3. What is the largest of the New England states?
4. Which city is known as the Chemical Capital of the World?
* What role will fracking play in enabling the U.S. to become energy independent?

II. The South

The southeastern quadrant of the United States is collectively called the South and is generally thought of as being those states south of Maryland and those from the Atlantic coast westward to Texas. The South often refers to the states that made up the Confederacy plus two border states (Kentucky and West Virginia).

Historian W. J. Cash viewed the South as essentially a nation within a nation, not quite separate but still different enough from the

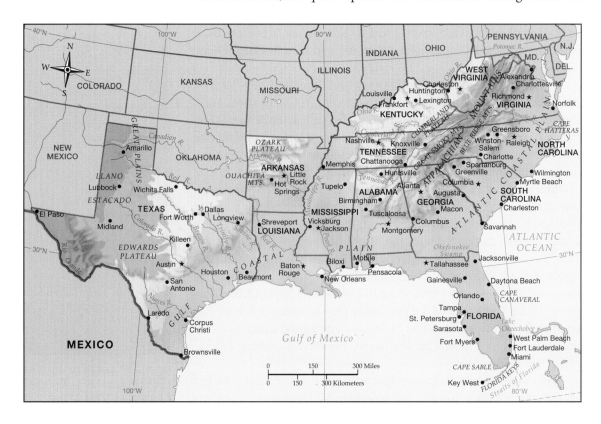

Southern Fast Facts						
State	PO Code	Capital	Date of Statehood	Nickname	Area (sq. mi.)	Population (2012 est.)
Alabama	AL	Montgomery	1819	Heart of Dixie	52,423	4,822,023
Arkansas	AR	Little Rock	1836	Natural State	53,182	2,949,131
Florida	FL	Tallahassee	1845	Sunshine State	65,758	19,317,568
Georgia	GA	Atlanta	1788	Peach State	59,441	9,919,945
Kentucky	KY	Frankfort	1792	Bluegrass State	40,411	4,380,415
Louisiana	LA	Baton Rouge	1812	Pelican State	51,843	4,601,893
Mississippi	MS	Jackson	1817	Magnolia State	48,434	2,984,926
North Carolina	NC	Raleigh	1789	Tar Heel State	53,821	9,752,073
South Carolina	SC	Columbia	1788	Palmetto State	32,008	4,723,723
Tennessee	TN	Nashville	1796	Volunteer State	42,146	6,456,243
Texas	TX	Austin	1845	Lone Star State	268,601	26,059,203
Virginia	VA	Richmond	1788	Old Dominion	42,769	8,185,867
West Virginia	WV	Charleston	1863	Mountain State	24,231	1,855,413

rest of the country to be considered in its own right. Although his view was more true then than it is today, the South still has unique traits that set it apart from the rest of the nation. Southerners are especially noted for their unique accent, which tends to vary widely even within the South, and their general friendliness and hospitality.

The South, which is sometimes called "Dixie," can be subdivided by several geographic features, including the Appalachian Mountains and the Mississippi River. Like the Northeast, the South also can be divided into upper and lower sections for convenience of study. Although the South has traditionally been predominantly agricultural, its diverse soils and natural resources have enabled it to become diversified industrially as well. Many tertiary industries have developed, and Southern urban areas are growing rapidly. As a result, the South is one of the most rapidly growing parts of the country.

The Upper South

The Upper South includes Virginia, North Carolina, West Virginia, Kentucky, Tennessee, and Arkansas. The first two states are separated from the other four by the Appalachian Mountains.

Virginia

Many rivers from the mountains flow through the coastal region of Virginia and into the Chesapeake Bay. Because the ocean tides

The Shenandoah Valley has been the breadbasket of Virginia throughout its history.

flow into and out of these rivers' mouths, the region is called the **Tidewater**. Many historically significant places, including Jamestown and the sites of numerous Civil War battles, are in the Tidewater. Virginia's largest metropolitan area is Norfolk, where the James River empties into the Chesapeake and where the busiest naval base in the nation guards water access to Washington, D.C. Between the Tidewater and the Appalachian Mountains is the Piedmont, and west of the mountains is the **Shenandoah Valley**, which has been called the "breadbasket" of Virginia. The western part of the state is marked by the Appalachian Mountains. Virginia's economy is diverse. As in many other Southern states, agriculture, which was once the leading income-producing activity, has now fallen behind other industries. Virginia still produces large amounts of tobacco, corn, soybeans, peanuts, cotton, apples, and other farm products. It is also high in poultry production. The Shenandoah Valley is known for cattle and dairy products. The people living along the coastal areas are especially effective in harvesting shellfish, mainly crabs and oysters.

Virginia's mineral wealth includes coal, stone, sand, and gravel. Roanoke is a major manufacturing center for railroad equipment, and several shipyards are located at Hampton Roads, Newport News, and Portsmouth. Chemicals and tourism are other major industries. Thousands of Virginians work for the national government in Washington and live in the surrounding suburbs.

West Virginia

When Virginia seceded from the Union in 1861, the mountainous westernmost counties of Virginia did not want to secede. Instead, they held their own election, voided the Virginia vote for secession, and petitioned the U.S. Congress for admission to the Union as a separate state called Kanawha. Although the Constitution forbade the formation of a new state from an existing state, Congress agreed to admit the petitioning counties as the state of West Virginia in 1863. The area was hotly contested during the war; the town of Romney changed hands fifty-six times!

The Appalachian Mountains and rugged Allegheny Plateau cover the entire state. Most of the population and industries are in the valleys of the Ohio and Kanawha Rivers, Wheeling and Parkersburg being in the Ohio Valley. The state is best known for its production of low-grade **bituminous coal**; it is second only to Wyoming in coal production. West Virginia continues to diversify its economy.

North Carolina

The terrain of North Carolina ranges from the **barrier islands** of the **Outer Banks** in the east to the Appalachian Mountains in the west. In between is the Piedmont.

North Carolina's economy was once dominated by agriculture, but other industries have grown dramatically. North Carolina is a leading turkey, sweet potato, and tobacco producer, but it is also a leader in the wholesale textile trade. The **Research Triangle**, in the Raleigh-Durham area, is a world-leading center for research and

The Cape Hatteras Lighthouse has been guiding sailors along the North Carolina coast since the mid-nineteenth century.

development in biotechnology, pharmaceuticals, computers, and other high-tech applications.

The mountains of North Carolina include the highest mountains in the eastern United States, such as Grandfather Mountain and Mount Mitchell. Asheville is the highest major city in the eastern United States. The mountain forests provide hardwood for the nation-leading North Carolina furniture industry.

Also located in the North Carolina mountains is the Cherokee Indian Reservation, one of the South's "Five Civilized Tribes" of Native Americans. The Cherokee developed a system for writing their own language in the early 1800s. When the U.S. government forced the Indians to leave the Southeast for lands west of the Mississippi, some Cherokees fled to the mountains. Eventually, the government agreed to let them remain on a reservation established for that purpose. Each summer they present an outdoor drama, *Unto These Hills*, that tells the story of the tribe's forced removal.

Kentucky

Like many other southern states, Kentucky has a variety of geographic terrains. It has mountains in the east, where it borders West Virginia, flat and fertile areas in the **Bluegrass region**, and a low plain in the far western part of the state. It is heavily coal oriented in the mountainous east (third in the nation in coal production). The edge of the rugged **Cumberland Plateau** runs down into Tennessee, dividing the eastern and central parts of that state. North of that area, however, the Bluegrass region of north-central Kentucky has the best soil in the state, and the area produces large numbers of thoroughbred horses. The northwest part of the state is known as the Western Coal Field. The far west is called the Purchase and is characterized by swamps, lakes, and flood plains.

About half of the state is classified as woodlands, and the state is third in hardwood production. The majority of Kentucky's exports are manufactured goods, including transportation equipment, chemicals, machinery, and computer and electronic products. Agricultural products make up about 2 percent of exports. Less than 2 percent of its exports are mineral resources.

Tennessee

Literature on Tennessee invariably mentions its "three great states," referring to the state's three distinct geographic regions: mountainous East Tennessee, the Cumberland Plateau of Middle Tennessee, and flat West Tennessee. These three regions also have their own unique political and cultural traits that make the "three states" designation even more profound. These "grand

The seventy-foot-high Cumberland Falls in Kentucky near the Tennessee border is on the edge of the Cumberland Plateau.

Mammoth Cave

Mammoth Cave in Kentucky is reputedly the largest cave in the world. The portion of the cave that has been mapped totals more than 325 miles. Many of its long, winding passages are bare, but others have amazing formations called stalactites (forming from the ceiling downward) and stalagmites (forming from the ground upward). They often meet to form tall columns, the largest of which is 192 feet tall.

The cave became a national park in 1933, but people knew of and explored it long before that. Indians used it for hiding, protection from the elements, and as a meeting hall. Settlers mined saltpeter from it to make gunpowder.

Knoxville is on the Tennessee River, just below the confluence of the Holston and French Broad Rivers.

divisions" are represented by the three stars in the state flag.

The state is roughly a parallelogram that is divided twice by the **Tennessee River**. The river begins in the east in Knoxville, at the confluence of the Holston and French Broad Rivers, and flows southwest past Chattanooga and into Alabama before curving and flowing due north up to Kentucky between Middle and West Tennessee. Nashville, the capital, is on the Cumberland River. Memphis, the largest city, is on the **Mississippi River** in the southwest corner of the state.

The state motto, "Agriculture and Commerce," reflects Tennessee's diverse economy. Major agricultural products include cotton, soybeans, tobacco, cattle, dairy products, and hogs. It ranks second in the production of zinc. Aluminum is such an important product that the Aluminum Corporation of America built an entire city (Alcoa) in East Tennessee to house its workers. Other important industries include chemicals, textiles, and electrical machinery. Tourism is also a big income producer for the state. Research, especially related to nuclear power and its uses, is an important focus of the U.S. Department of Energy facilities in Oak Ridge, where the first atomic bomb was developed.

Arkansas

Tennessee's neighbor across the Mississippi River is Arkansas. Mountains and forests cover half of the state. It has a smaller population than any other southern state except West Virginia.

Arkansas has two major geographic regions. The Lowlands in the southeastern half of the state consist of the Gulf Coastal Plain and the Mississippi Flood Plain. The Ozark Plateau in the northwestern half includes the low **Ozark Mountains**. Flowing between the two regions from northwest to southeast into the Mississippi River is the Arkansas River.

Like other Southern states, Arkansas has diversified its economy. It is a major producer of chicken eggs and broilers, cotton, and soybeans. Its natural resources include oil and natural gas, bromine, bauxite, and lumber products. It is also a major chemical producer as well as the headquarters of the retail giant Walmart, founded by Sam Walton.

The Lower South

The area designated the Lower South (sometimes called the Deep South) includes South Carolina, Georgia, Florida, Alabama, Mississippi, Louisiana, and Texas. All of those states are at least partially in the Atlantic or Gulf Coastal Plain, and that fact is reflected in the types of crops and industries that predominate there. Across the central portions of many of these states is a region called the **Black Belt** because of its dark, rich soil. Cotton once ruled the economies of the Deep South states, but they are all diversified today. Just as diverse as their economies are their demographics. The largest percentage of minorities, especially black people, is located in the Deep South, and it was the home of the civil rights movement of the 1960s.

South Carolina

Like other Atlantic coastal states, South Carolina has several narrow geographic regions (coastal plains, piedmont, etc.), but it can essentially be divided into the Low Country and the Upstate. The heart of the Low Country is Charleston, a major port city through which millions of dollars' worth of imports and exports pass. The entire coastal region is bordered by numerous barrier islands. The Upstate region ranges from the fall line (see page 134 in Chapter 7) near the capital, Columbia, to the Appalachian Mountains in the northwest corner of the state. The cities of Greenville and Spartanburg are the largest cities in the Upstate.

Despite the loss of many jobs resulting from companies moving overseas, South Carolina remains a major producer of textiles. Its orchards also produce more peaches than the self-styled "Peach State" of Georgia, its neighbor to the southwest. Chemical products, machinery, tires, and automobiles (BMW) are major industries in the state. Tourism, however, remains the state's leading source of income.

Georgia

Like South Carolina, Georgia's geography ranges from swampy wetlands along the coast in the southeast to mountains in the north. Though nicknamed "The Peach State," Georgia leads the nation in the production of peanuts and pecans, both lucrative alternatives to the soil-depleting cotton that was once a staple of Georgia agriculture. Atlanta, the state capital, lies in the Piedmont and boasts one of the South's highest skyscrapers. It is also the headquarters of Coca-Cola, which features an interesting museum of the company's history.

Agriculture continues to make an important contribution to Georgia's economy. In addition to the other crops named, Georgia is a leader in livestock, poultry, and grape production. Although cotton is no longer the staple that it once was, Georgia remains a leading cotton producer. It also produces lumber and pulpwood, and its fine marble is world famous. It is also a major auto-producing state.

Florida

Florida is the only state with coasts on both the Atlantic Ocean and the **Gulf of Mexico**. It can be divided into three regions: the panhandle, along the northwest Gulf coast; the peninsula; and the mainly marshy area south of Lake Okeechobee, including the **Everglades** and the Florida Keys. Topography in all three areas is flat, the highest elevation in the state being only 345 feet above sea level.

The panhandle stretches 225 miles west from the peninsula, more than halfway to the Mississippi River.

Middleton Place in Charleston, South Carolina, reveals the natural beauty cultivated by colonial planters in the Low Country.

Atlanta, Georgia, demonstrates the development of major cities throughout the South.

The Florida Everglades is a beautiful, but forbidding, alligator- and mosquito-infested wetland.

Tallahassee, the capital, and several tourist cities are on the panhandle. Most of the population, however, is on the peninsula. Both the largest city (Jacksonville) and the oldest city (St. Augustine) are in the northern part of the peninsula.

Both the second-largest metropolitan area—Tampa-St. Petersburg-Clearwater on the Gulf coast—and the Disney-oriented city of Orlando are located in the central area of the peninsula. Plant City, near Orlando, is famous for its vegetable and strawberry production. The Kennedy Space Center at Cape Canaveral is on the east central coast. The southern Atlantic coast from West Palm Beach to Miami is heavily populated. The southernmost point of Florida—and the United States—is Key West, the last of a chain of small islands (keys) connected by the 113-mile Overseas Highway.

Although Florida is famous for its tourist industry (it is a major world travel destination), it also has a thriving agricultural and industrial economy. Its major agricultural products are citrus fruits (oranges and grapefruit). Nonfarm industries include electronics, space-related products, fishing, and mining (it produces a quarter of the world's phosphates).

Alabama

More than half of this state, which is called "the Heart of Dixie," is **Gulf Coastal Plain**, and the rest is subdivided into River, Metropolitan, and Mountain areas. The northeastern portion is hill country that includes the trailing end of the Appalachian Mountain chain. The Metropolitan area includes Birmingham, called the "Pittsburgh of the South" for its heavy steel industry, and Tuscaloosa, home to the University of Alabama. The River region is fertile cropland and is part of the Black Belt. On the Gulf at the mouth of the Alabama River is Mobile, a major port city.

Long associated with the growth of cotton, Alabama now has a diversified economy, including high-tech industries in the city of Huntsville that are associated with the National Aeronautics and Space Administration. Although cotton is still its chief crop, poultry products, cattle, lumber, and pulpwood are important contributors to the state's economy.

Mississippi

Almost the entire state of Mississippi is coastal plain. The Mississippi River and its tributaries dominate the area. Floodwaters from these rivers have deposited rich soil across the vast flood plain, making the growth of cotton very profitable. As a result, Mississippi continues to be a major cotton producer.

However, the state is also working hard to diversify its economy, increasing other viable industries, both agricultural and industrial, to supplement its cotton empire. Included among its farm products are rice, soybeans, wood products, and poultry. The chemical, plastics, petroleum, and natural gas industries are also important to the overall economy.

Louisiana

This state, located at the mouth of the Mississippi River, is important to both the South and the nation for many reasons, not the least of which is its port cities. Three of the nation's ten largest ports

For years, cotton was the number one crop of the Deep South, and it remains an important crop in the Deep South today.

The Mississippi Delta is a maze of waterways through which the river reaches the Gulf of Mexico southeast of New Orleans.

are located there. Also, Louisiana has been influenced by more cultures than any other Southern state.

The entire state is coastal plain. Slow-moving, meandering streams and rivers crisscross the state as they seek an outlet into the Gulf through the **Mississippi Delta**. Swampy areas in this region are called bayous and are home to nearly half a million people known as **Cajuns**. Their ancestors were French refugees from an area of Maine and Canada known as Acadia. (In fact, part of Louisiana is called Acadia.) The Cajuns speak an interesting form of French and are famous for their unique spicy foods, including gumbo and jambalaya. Another ethnic group prominent in Louisiana is the **Creoles**, people of mixed black and European (French or Spanish) ancestry.

Key ingredients of the Louisiana economy are agriculture, fishing, and processing of natural resources. Agricultural products include sweet potatoes, rice, sugar cane, soybeans, and cotton. Fishing, especially shrimp and oysters, is very important, as are muskrat and mink trapping. Louisiana is also a leading producer of salt. Crude oil production at off-shore rigs in the Gulf and oil refining are important industries that benefit the state and the nation.

Texas

The final state included in the South is also its largest. In fact, it is the second-largest state (by area) in the nation, trailing only Alaska, and it has more large cities that any other Southern state.

Texas is located on the U.S.–Mexico border and is so big that it shares characteristics with not only the Hispanic culture of Mexico and the American Southern culture but also the cultures of the Midwest and the Southwest. East Texas is much like other nearby Southern states, having large forests and cotton farms. On its Gulf Coastal Plain are several important port cities, including Houston and Beaumont. The **Central Plains** are much like the flat, grassy plains in the states north of Texas, and the arid western part of the state resembles the neighboring states of the Southwest. The lower portion of the Rocky Mountains extends through that part of Texas. Four of the nation's ten busiest ports are in Texas. (Recalling that Louisiana has three of the ten largest ports, one can readily see the importance to the nation of the South's Gulf region.) Texas is first in the nation in cattle and cotton production and second in hay. Its other agricultural products include poultry, wheat, and dairy products. Texas boasts three of the ten largest cities in the nation—Houston, Dallas, and San Antonio—and the industries of these and other urban areas add greatly to the Texas economy. This state is the leading producer of oil and natural gas and a major producer of chemicals, machinery, and salt.

Oil pump jacks are a familiar sight in Texas.

Section Quiz

1. What is the coastal region of Virginia called?
2. Which region has been called the breadbasket of Virginia?
3. What is the southernmost location in the United States?
4. What is the largest state in the South and the second-largest in the nation?
★ Which southern state actually produces the most peaches?

III. The Midwest

The north central portion of the United States—generally encompassing the states surrounding the Great Lakes—is called the Midwest. It was referred to as "the West" when explorers first began crossing the Appalachian Mountains. After the United States gained territories on the Pacific coast, the north central states were somewhat in the middle of the country; hence, the area became known as the Midwest.

This region is of great importance to the nation for several reasons. It is a transportation hub. It is called the "breadbasket of the nation." And the states in the region were among the first to grant universal manhood suffrage, the right of every adult male to vote.

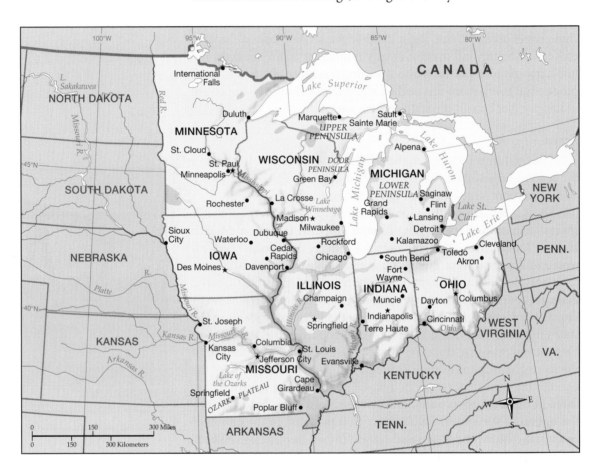

Ohio

West of Pennsylvania is Ohio. The **Ohio River** forms the state's southern border with West Virginia and Kentucky. The good farmland of the **till plains** (soil left by ancient glaciers) covers the western part of the state. The hills of the Appalachian Plateau run along the border with Pennsylvania and West Virginia and yield coal but little good farmland. Lake Erie on the northeast and the state of Michigan on the northwest form Ohio's northern extent, and most of the population lives in the northern part of the state.

Ohio is recovering from its reputation as the heart of the "rust belt," a region of declining steel industries. Its ports on Lake Erie—Toledo and Cleveland—remain busy transporting iron and copper. The state is also the center of the glass and ceramics industry, and Akron is famous for its tires and other rubber products.

Midwestern Fast Facts						
State	**PO Code**	**Capital**	**Date of Statehood**	**Nickname**	**Area (sq. mi.)**	**Population (2012 est.)**
Illinois	IL	Springfield	1818	Prairie State	57,918	12,875,255
Indiana	IN	Indianapolis	1816	Hoosier State	36,420	6,537,334
Michigan	MI	Lansing	1837	Great Lakes State	96,810	9,883,360
Minnesota	MN	St. Paul	1858	North Star State	86,943	5,379,139
Ohio	OH	Columbus	1803	Buckeye State	44,828	11,544,225
Wisconsin	WI	Madison	1848	Badger State	65,503	5,726,398
Iowa	IA	Des Moines	1846	Hawkeye State	56,276	3,074,186
Missouri	MO	Jefferson City	1821	Show Me State	69,709	6,021,988

Indiana

West of Ohio is Indiana, the smallest in area of the Midwestern states. Till plains cover most of the state. Southern Indiana is a hilly plateau that extends up from Kentucky. The Ohio River makes the state's southern border, and Michigan and Lake Michigan make its northern border. Evansville, the largest city in southern Indiana, is a major port on the Ohio River.

Indiana has several large industrial cities, including Gary, a port on Lake Michigan; Fort Wayne, an automotive city; and Elkhart, which is a leading manufacturer of brass musical instruments. Indianapolis, another major city and the state's capital, is perhaps best known for its annual auto race, the Indianapolis 500.

Indianapolis, Indiana, is the home of the annual Indy 500.

Illinois

Farther west is Illinois, the northern part of which is a great **prairie**, rolling plains with high grasses that spread across the western half of the Midwest. The prairie does not receive enough rainfall to support forests, but the soil is rich and productive of corn, soybeans, and wheat. Associated with the farmland is the city of Moline, considered the "farm-equipment capital" of the nation. Peoria is the headquarters of Caterpillar, Inc., which makes earthmoving machines. On Lake Michigan is Chicago, the largest city in the Midwest and the transportation capital of the nation. Six major interstate highways converge there, and it is a rail and airline hub.

Southern Illinois is hilly and rocky, resembling some of the southern states. The southernmost tip of the state, where the Ohio River meets the Mississippi River, is part of the Gulf Coastal Plain.

Michigan

North of Ohio and Indiana is Michigan, the largest Midwestern state and the only state with shoreline on four of the five Great Lakes. It is split in two by Lake Michigan. The lower portion, called the Lower Peninsula, is shaped like a mitten and contains most of

The Mackinac Bridge joins the upper and lower peninsulas of Michigan.

the land and population of the state. The entire area is covered by the Great Lakes Plain, but the best soil is in the south. The "thumb" of the mitten in the east includes the largest city of the state and the fourth-largest in the Midwest, Detroit. Detroit is known as the Motor City because it is the headquarters of the "Big Three" American auto makers: Ford, Chrysler (now owned by Fiat), and General Motors.

The capital, Lansing, is near the center of the "palm" of the mitten. Farther west is Battle Creek, the "cereal capital of the world." On Lake Michigan in the west is Grand Rapids, home of four of the largest Christian book publishers: Baker, Kregel, Eerdmans, and Zondervan.

The Upper Peninsula is much less densely populated and includes more wilderness area. The eastern part of the peninsula is part of the Great Lakes Plain, and the western half rises into the Superior Uplands, a plateau that continues westward into Minnesota. At the western edge of the uplands are the rugged peaks and wilderness of the Porcupine Mountains.

Wisconsin

Wisconsin is known as "America's Dairyland" because it produces one-fourth of all the cheese produced in the United States. It also is a major producer of milk, ice cream, and butter.

Most of the state's dairy farms and cities are in the fertile Great Lakes Plain in the eastern half of the state. Milwaukee, the state's largest city, is on Lake Michigan and is famous for its breweries. The western half of the state is divided between the Superior Uplands in the north and the Driftless Area in the south. (**Drift** is deep soil deposited by glaciers. Southern Wisconsin has no drift; hence, it is "driftless.") Forestry and paper manufacturing are important industries in the northwest. Wisconsin has more than eight thousand lakes in that area. However, the poor soil there can support few farms.

Minnesota

The northeastern half of Minnesota is composed of the North Woods. Although the state is called the "Land of Ten Thousand Lakes," it actually has closer to fifteen thousand lakes.

Duluth is the major port on the Great Lakes. It was used originally for furs and later for lumber and iron ore from the **Mesabi Range**, the site of the richest iron ore-producing mines in the nation.

The Central Plains cover the rest of the state. Nearly 60 percent of the state's population lives in the Twin Cities of Minneapolis and St. Paul, which are divided by the Mississippi River. St. Paul is the capital. Minneapolis is the home of the massive Mall of America,

Wisconsin's huge farms give the state the nickname "America's Dairyland."

The Mesabi Range in Minnesota produces iron ore (taconite) in abundance.

Minneapolis can boast of having one of the world's largest malls, the Mall of America.

which includes over five hundred stores, several theaters, and the largest indoor amusement park in the United States. Minneapolis is also the headquarters of the 3M Company (Minnesota Mining and Manufacturing).

Iowa

Iowa is covered by the Central Plains but has three distinct parts. The southern and western edges are till plains. The north central region has some of the most fertile soil in the world in the Drift Prairie. The third area is the hilly Driftless Area along the northeastern border, which has no drift and poor soil. **Bluffs**, steep riverbanks, overlook the Mississippi River and are the primary nesting place for bald eagles.

Iowa produces about 7 percent of the nation's food supply. It is a leading producer of corn in the nation, growing about one-fifth of the total. It also raises more hogs than any other state.

Iowa enjoys commercial access to two major rivers. Sioux City is its main port on the Missouri River, and Davenport is the chief port on the Mississippi River. The capital, Des Moines, is on the Des Moines River in the middle of the state.

Missouri

Missouri is called the "Gateway to the West" because it was the "jumping off" point for many settlers who were heading west. St. Louis, the first major city, developed at the confluence of the Mississippi and Missouri Rivers. The Gateway Arch, the largest monument in the nation, marks the spot where thousands of pioneers launched their trek into the western frontier.

Kansas City arose farther up the Missouri River at its confluence with the Kansas River. The metropolitan area includes Independence, where the Oregon Trail began. Farther north is St. Joseph, where the Pony Express route began.

Most people live in the eastern part, which is in the Central Plains. The southern half of the state, the Ozark Plateau, is sparsely populated but has the most productive lead mines in the nation. The southeastern corner of the state, called the "boot heel," is in the Gulf Coastal Plain and has soil well suited to growing cotton.

Section Quiz

1. What name is given to the fertile type of soil found in western Ohio?
2. What word means rolling plains covered with high grasses?
3. What is the only state with shoreline on four of the five Great Lakes?
4. What is the name of the iron ore-rich area in Minnesota?
★ Why is Wisconsin known as "America's Dairyland"?

IV. The Plains

The Central Plains of the Midwest are essentially flat. Farther west, however, the **Great Plains** slope gradually upward as one moves west so that the western end at the foot of the Rockies is four thousand feet higher than the eastern end. The Great Plains are drier than the Central Plains and do not get enough rainfall to support

The Gateway Arch is a monument to the opening of the western frontier.

more than grasses and short bushes. Early pioneers called the area the "Great American Desert," but the grasslands proved to be very fertile, requiring only steel plows and irrigation to grow wheat, which requires much less rain than corn. Consequently, this area became America's wheat belt. Most of the major cities in the area arose on the banks of the Missouri River and its tributaries.

Four of the states on the Great Plains border the Midwest: Kansas, Nebraska, South Dakota, and North Dakota. They tend, especially in their eastern portions, to resemble typical Midwestern towns and farms.

North Dakota

The name of this state comes from the name that the Sioux Indians gave themselves, meaning "friends." Many tribes roamed both this state and its neighbor South Dakota.

North Dakota shares its northern border with Saskatchewan, Canada. The eastern half of North Dakota is part of the Central Plains and produces the second-largest spring wheat crop in the nation (behind only Kansas). It has the largest barley production and vies, again with Kansas, for growing the most sunflowers. It also has productive dairy farms. Agriculture remains the state's greatest source of income.

The Great Plains cover the western half of the state. That dry area includes three Indian reservations, the Theodore Roosevelt National Park, and numerous cattle ranches. Honey is produced in the central region of the state. Oil in the northwestern part of the state is the second-largest source of income.

Major cities in North Dakota include Fargo and Grand Forks on the Red River and Bismarck, the capital, on the Missouri River. Tourism is the third-greatest source of income for the state.

South Dakota

South Dakota is geographically much like the neighboring states. The southeast corner is till plain and is the location of the largest city, Sioux Falls. The Great Plains stretch across the west of the state, and the capital, Pierre, is located there. Also on the state's Great Plains are nine Indian reservations, including the site of the last battle between whites and Native Americans, Wounded Knee. The southwest corner is a remote, rugged area of knobs, spires, rock pinnacles, isolated buttes, and windswept ridges called the Badlands. The area became a hideout for outlaws and renegade Indians.

The Black Hills rise in the far western part of the state. This pocket of mountains towering above the Midwestern grasslands includes the highest peaks east of the Rockies. The most popular (but by no means the highest) peak is Mount Rushmore, on which the likenesses of four presidents have been carved. Deadwood is an Old West town to which prospectors came during the 1874 gold rush, sparking a war with the local Indians.

Sources of income include raising cattle and sheep and growing corn, soybeans, oats, and wheat. Meatpacking and food processing are the major industries in the state. Gold is the state's most important mineral. Tourism and gambling are also sources of income.

Mount Rushmore

Mount Rushmore in the Black Hills of South Dakota is famous for the four sixty-foot-high heads that gaze from its side. It is the work of sculptor Gutzon Borglum, who began the carving in 1927 when he was sixty and spent the rest of his life creating his masterpiece. The mountain, which has become a "shrine to democracy," features the likenesses of presidents George Washington, Thomas Jefferson, Theodore Roosevelt, and Abraham Lincoln.

The sculpted heads of the presidents on Mount Rushmore took ten years to complete.

The South Dakota Badlands

Plains Fast Facts						
State	PO Code	Capital	Date of Statehood	Nickname	Area (sq. mi.)	Population (2012 est.)
Kansas	KS	Topeka	1861	Sunflower State	82,282	2,885,905
Nebraska	NE	Lincoln	1867	Cornhusker State	77,358	1,855,525
North Dakota	ND	Bismarck	1889	Peace Garden State	70,704	699,628
Oklahoma	OK	Oklahoma City	1907	Sooner State	69,903	3,814,820
South Dakota	SD	Pierre	1889	Mount Rushmore State	77,121	833,354

Nebraska

Farms cover 93 percent of Nebraska's land, a higher proportion than in any other state. The end of the corn belt is in the eastern part of the state, which produces enough to make Nebraska the second-leading corn producer. The wheat belt slices through the southern part of the state, and Nebraska is among the top ten producers of wheat. Other major agricultural products include soybeans and hogs.

Nebraska is the only state that has a **unicameral** (one-house) legislature. All other states have **bicameral** (two-house) legislatures. The capital is Lincoln in the southeast corner of the state. Lincoln and Omaha, which is northeast of Lincoln on the Missouri River, are major insurance company headquarters.

Kansas

Kansas is known as the "Sunflower State" for a good reason—it leads the nation in the production of sunflower seeds. Its most important crop, however, is winter wheat, and it leads the nation in that crop as well. The till plains in the northeast have the most fertile soil in the state. Major cities there include Topeka and Kansas City, which are on the Kansas River. The other major city, Wichita, is in the Osage Plains on the Arkansas River. Kansas trails only Texas and Montana in total agricultural production.

Although Kansas is known as a leading agricultural state, the manufacturing and services industries are larger income producers. Big industries include transportation equipment and computer machinery. Wichita's aircraft industry primarily produces private planes. Major natural resources include oil, natural gas, and helium.

Oklahoma

The name of this state means "red man" (*okla*, "red"; *homa*, "man") and derives from the Five Civilized Tribes (Cherokee, Chickasaw, Choctaw, Creek, and Seminole) of the Southeast who were forcibly relocated there in the early 1800s. Oklahoma has a larger Native American population than any other state.

In the east, Oklahoma is made up of small portions of the Gulf Coastal Plain and the Ozark Plateau, but the rest of the state is covered by the Central Plains, where the capital, Oklahoma City, is located. The elevation in that flat, treeless area is higher than even the mountains in the eastern part of the state.

Kansas is in the heart of a region called "Tornado Alley" due to frequent tornadoes.

Oklahoma is a great producer of wheat, hay, cattle, and hogs. The most important nonagricultural products of the state are oil and helium.

Section Quiz

1. What did early pioneers mistakenly call the Great Plains?
2. In what area of South Dakota did outlaws and renegade Indians hide?
3. What percentage of the land in Nebraska is farmland?
4. What does the name *Oklahoma* mean?
* What is unique about the government of Nebraska?

V. The West

The American West is a land of extremes. It includes the highest and the lowest, the wettest and the driest, the biggest and one of the smallest, and the most and the least populated places in the nation. It also has riches beyond the early settlers' wildest dreams.

Continental West

The continental West includes the Rocky Mountains, the Great Basin (a bowl-shaped area in central Nevada), the **Sierra Nevada**, and the various mountain ranges along the Pacific coast. The Rockies, however, are the largest single geographic feature of the West.

Montana

The eastern two-thirds of Montana is the treeless Great Plains, and the state's two largest cities, Great Falls and Billings, are in that region. Montana is also almost double the size of other Rocky Mountain states. The size and openness of the state explain one of its nicknames, "Big Sky Country." The western third of the state is mountainous, and the capital, Helena, lies in the Lewis Range.

Montana leads the nation in production of talc, vermiculite, and gem sapphires. It has the only platinum mine in the country and also produces gold, silver, copper, zinc, and lead. Agriculture, however, is the main income producer, and Montana is the fourth-largest wheat-producing state. Tourism is also a big industry, especially in Glacier National Park.

Wyoming

The eastern quarter of Wyoming is made up of the Great Plains and part of the Black Hills. The largest cities of the state—Cheyenne, Laramie, Casper, and Sheridan—are on the plains. The Rocky Mountains cover the western three-quarters of the state and include Yellowstone National Park, the first such park in the nation. The park includes such attractions as the geyser Old Faithful. The state also features Grand Tetons National Park, where peaks soar as high as 13,770 feet above sea level.

Most residents of Wyoming are employed directly or indirectly in farming, with cattle, hay, sugar beets, and wheat being the largest cash crops. Wyoming has larger ranches than any other state except Arizona. The largest sector of the economy, however, is mining, which makes up one-fourth of the gross state product (GSP). The most important resource is oil. The state also mines large amounts of

Four Corners

In only one place in the United States can you be in four states simultaneously. In the middle of the Navajo Indian Reservation is a place called the Four Corners, where the borders of Utah, Colorado, Arizona, and New Mexico meet.

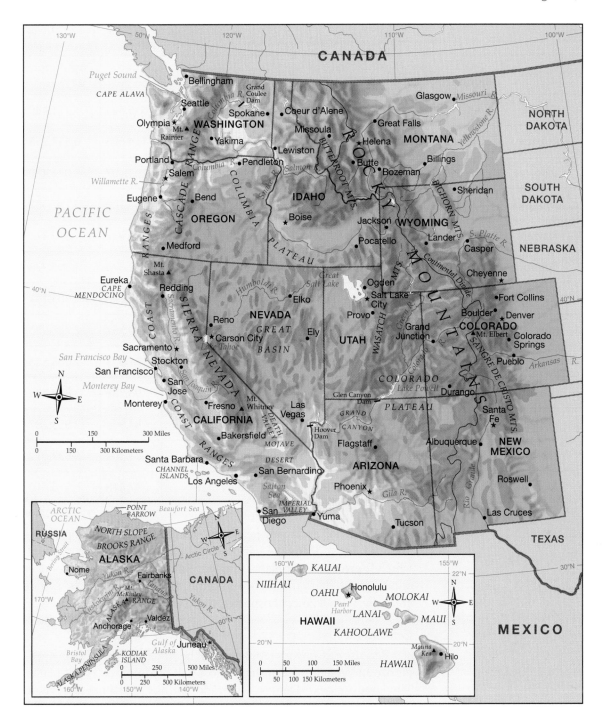

gold, coal, and uranium. Tourism dollars flow into the state's national parks and numerous dude ranches.

Idaho

The northern half and eastern border of Idaho are the remote mountains of the Bitterroot Range. West of the Idaho Rockies is the Columbia Plateau, which extends into neighboring Washington and Oregon. The Snake River slithers its way across the plateau, cascading 212 feet at Shoshone Falls, which is thirty feet higher than Niagara Falls. The first white residents in Idaho were missionaries to the Nez Perce Indians, Henry and Eliza Spalding, who settled along the Snake River at what is now Lewiston. Most of Idaho's other major cities are also located on or near the Snake River.

Western Fast Facts						
State	PO Code	Capital	Date of Statehood	Nickname	Area (sq. mi.)	Population (2012 est.)
Alaska	AK	Juneau	1959	The Last Frontier	656,424	731,449
Arizona	AZ	Phoenix	1912	Grand Canyon State	114,006	6,553,255
California	CA	Sacramento	1850	Golden State	163,707	38,041,430
Colorado	CO	Denver	1876	Centennial State	104,100	5,187,582
Hawaii	HI	Honolulu	1959	Aloha State	10,932	1,392,313
Idaho	ID	Boise	1890	Gem State	83,574	1,595,728
Montana	MT	Helena	1889	Treasure State	147,046	1,005,141
Nevada	NV	Carson City	1864	Silver State	110,567	2,758,931
New Mexico	NM	Santa Fe	1912	Land of Enchantment	121,593	2,085,538
Oregon	OR	Salem	1859	Beaver State	98,386	3,899,353
Utah	UT	Salt Lake City	1896	Beehive State	84,904	2,855,287
Washington	WA	Olympia	1889	Evergreen State	71,302	6,897,012
Wyoming	WY	Cheyenne	1890	Equality State	97,818	576,412

Say "Idaho," and many people think immediately of its top crop—potatoes. Idaho leads the nation in the production of that product, which is grown in the plateau region. But it is also a great producer of hay, wheat, dairy products, and cattle. Its natural resources include gold, silver, lead, zinc, phosphates, molybdenum, and antimony.

Colorado

Because of Denver's reputation as the "mile-high city," many people are surprised to learn that almost half of Colorado is flat plains. The largest cities—Denver, Colorado Springs, and Pueblo—are on the plains at the foot of the Rockies. The plains are very fertile there, making Colorado a large producer of lettuce, cattle, and potatoes.

Denver is a gateway to even higher elevations. It is the largest city in the four-state Rocky Mountain region. The federal mint at Denver produces coins and stores gold worth more than two billion dollars. The dome of the capitol there is covered with 24-carat gold leaf.

The centerpiece of Colorado, however, is the Rockies. The state has the highest mountains of the entire range, including fifty-four peaks over fourteen thousand feet. Tourism in the state, much of it on its many ski slopes, is a major part of Colorado's economy. The state is also a big producer of lumber, chemicals, and computer equipment and is home to several Christian ministries and printing and publishing businesses. Although the state does not produce as much gold as it once did, it produces oil and mines large quantities of silver, lead, uranium, and coal.

Utah

The area immediately west of the Rockies is a bowl of low, rugged land called the Great Basin. It is surrounded by higher elevations, so water there cannot drain to any ocean. The western half of Utah is in the Great Basin. The Rockies intrude into the extreme northeastern corner of the state. The rest of the east and southeast is in the **Colorado Plateau**. Utah has five national parks and seven national monuments, so tourism is a major part of its economy.

Delicate Arch in Arches National Park, Utah, shows the results of massive erosion.

Utah is very dry and has very little land that is fit to farm, but it does produce hay, corn, and barley. The bulk of its agricultural income comes from cattle and poultry. It is rich in copper, gold, molybdenum, and magnesium. The state is also a key player in the aerospace and computer hardware and software industries. Provo is a steel center. Salt Lake City is also a major industrial center, although it is more famous as the headquarters of Mormonism.

New Mexico

New Mexico includes five different geographic regions. The eastern third is part of the Great Plains. The southern two-thirds of the

Great Salt Lake

Great Salt Lake is the largest lake west of the Mississippi River, with dimensions of 75 miles long, 28 miles wide, and an average of 30 feet deep (max. 35 ft.). It is the fourth-largest terminal (having no outlet) lake in the world. High temperatures and infrequent rains cause rapid evaporation. It was once much larger, but parts of the lake have dried up, leaving behind dried salt flats. With a salt content from 10 to 25 percent, the lake's water is three to five times saltier than normal ocean water, which is about 3.5 percent salt, and only slightly less salty than the Dead Sea (26–35 percent). The water in the Great Salt Lake is so salty that nothing more than brine shrimp will grow in it.

Early explorers avoided the Great Salt Lake because of its desert climate, but later settlers soon learned that it offered the flattest, easiest route to California. The first transcontinental railroad was completed at Promontory Summit, Utah, north of Great Salt Lake in 1869. The Bonneville Salt Flats also became a testing ground for fast cars, and many land speed records were set there.

Salt-covered boulders rim the edge of Great Salt Lake.

Starting Churches in the West

There is a great need for Bible-teaching churches in many of the western states. Often people have to travel for many miles to find a good church. In many areas, there is no gospel-preaching church to be found. Compounding the problem, many churches are reluctant to provide the long-term support needed to sustain these struggling church plants. To address this need, some mission boards are sending men to areas in the West that have no Christian witness, and supporting them as they start a mission work. One family, the Duponts, has taken over a church that grew out of a Bible study in 1983. They have patiently labored for ten years at the First Baptist Church in Beaver, Utah. In addition to regular church responsibilities, the Duponts have a Frontline Club and hold a summer VBS to reach children in the community. Mark also has developed a relationship with a local prison and holds Bible studies with inmates. The Duponts use the Internet to broadcast a radio ministry, KEZB-FM. This station is accessible to anyone with Internet access and has great potential. Mark also helps with the local food bank, serving as its treasurer, and uses this activity to demonstrate the love of Christ to the community. He serves as the hospice chaplain at a local hospital. Mark uses this opportunity to give the gospel to those who are closest to death. The ministry grows slowly but steadily as the Duponts faithfully serve in this difficult region.

Carlsbad Caverns in New Mexico contains some fascinating natural sculptures formed by mineral deposits.

The Pacific Coastal Mountains run down to the ocean at some places.

middle portion is the **Rio Grande Basin,** whereas the northern third of the middle is part of the Rocky Mountains. The western third is primarily part of the Colorado Basin, with the extreme southwestern corner being part of the **Sonoran Desert**. The heart of New Mexico, however, is the Rio Grande Valley, in which the river provides water for irrigation of crops and where the three largest cities—Santa Fe, Albuquerque, and Las Cruces—are located.

Because the state is so dry, it is not a major agricultural state, but it does produce some dairy products, hay, piñon nuts, chili peppers, and pinewood. Most of the arable land is used for grazing, and the state has many large ranches. It is rich in minerals and is a leading producer of uranium, manganese, potash, salt, perlite, and other minerals. It also produces large amounts of turquoise. Albuquerque is a leading industrial center.

The federal government is the largest employer, accounting for one-fourth of all jobs in the state. The Sandia and Los Alamos National Laboratories engage in many types of scientific research, including top-secret military projects. Tourism at Carlsbad Caverns, White Sands, the Gila Cliff Dwellings, and other attractions also produces income for the state.

Arizona

Arizona can be divided into three regions. The southern third of Arizona is the Sonoran Desert, the only American desert where saguaro (sah WHAR oh) cacti grow. Two-thirds of the nation's copper is mined in Arizona, mostly from mines in the Sonoran Desert. The northern two-thirds is part of the Colorado Plateau. The eastern half of that area is the Navajo and Hopi Indian reservations. Other reservations are located in the east central and south central portions of the state. On the Colorado Plateau are the Painted Desert, the Petrified Forest, and the Meteor Crater, all of which draw many tourists. The centerpiece of the plateau, however, is the Grand Canyon.

Arizona is a large producer of lettuce and cotton. But its most valuable agricultural products are cattle and dairy goods. Arizona is a major player in the electronics and aerospace industries. The state also has forested regions. However, logging is limited because the federal government has set aside several million acres of this land as national forests.

Arizona is fast becoming a major retirement destination. Its sunny, dry climate appeals to both retirees and those who suffer from allergies elsewhere. Phoenix is the largest city in the eight interior western states. The second-largest city in the state is Tucson.

California

If California were a separate country, it would rank tenth in area, thirty-fifth in population, and among the top ten economies in the world. Among the fifty states, it is third in size and first in population. Geographically, it is divided into the coastal mountains, the Central Valley, the High Sierra, and the southern deserts. One desert, the Sonoran, is at the southeastern end of California. Moist winds blowing inland from the Pacific lose their moisture while crossing the coastal mountains in the rainshadow effect. The Imperial Valley is in this area, but irrigation from the Colorado River has turned the desert into productive farmland. Just north of the Sonoran Desert is

WORLD RELIGIONS

Mormonism

The first people to settle Utah were the Mormons. **Mormonism** is a made-in-America religion. Joseph Smith founded the Mormons in New York in 1830, a time in which the democratization of the United States led numbers of Americans to abandon orthodox churches and develop new variations of the Christian religion. Smith claimed to have been visited by an angel named Moroni, who revealed that all churches of the time were false and showed Smith writings on golden plates, which he was to translate and share with others. The result was the Book of Mormon. The book tells about the lost tribes of Israel, who allegedly migrated to America about 600 BC during the Babylonian Captivity. Smith called the new church that arose from these teachings the Church of Jesus Christ of Latter-Day Saints. Those who followed Smith were persecuted and driven from New York, first to Ohio, then Missouri, and finally Illinois, where Smith was jailed and later killed by a mob. Brigham Young assumed leadership and led the group to what is now Utah.

Though Joseph Smith taught that all other churches were false, today Mormons seek to be accepted as a legitimate Christian denomination (though the claim that Mormonism restored a gospel lost by all other churches is still Mormon teaching). Many Americans accept this Mormon claim to be a Christian denomination. Mormons say they love Jesus, they raise model families, and they are often good citizens who contribute to their communities. Nevertheless, Mormonism differs from the fundamental doctrines of Christianity.

Mormonism has four sacred books: the King James Version of the Bible, the Book of Mormon, *Doctrine and Covenants*, and *Pearl of Great Price*. Unlike evangelical Christians, however, Mormons do not believe that all of their sacred books are without error. For instance, Mormons claim that the Bible has been corrupted, has errors in it, and is missing some passages.

The Book of Mormon, however, is considered to be without error. It primarily tells the story of alleged Israelite groups that made their way to America. *Doctrine and Covenants* is the book that teaches Mormon doctrine. This book has been revised several times. In Mormon thought, the President and Prophet (a man elected by Mormon leaders) can receive new revelation that can alter older revelation. For instance, in 1890 a revelation was said to be received that called for the end of polygamy, and in 1978 a revelation was said to be received which allowed black men into the Mormon priesthood.

The Mormon Temple in Salt Lake City

In Mormon teaching, there are several levels of salvation. The lowest level is universal salvation. This salvation is by grace alone and is received by everybody. It consists of resurrection from the dead and an unending life, but it does not mean that the person will spend eternity with the Father god or escape eternal suffering. Hell is reserved for Satan, demons, and Mormon apostates. Above Hell are three kingdoms: the Telestial kingdom, the Terrestrial kingdom, and the Celestial kingdom. Those in the Telestial kingdom are wicked people who must suffer for their sins. Unworthy Mormons and non-Mormons who accepted Mormonism after death inhabit the Terrestrial kingdom. They will suffer regret for not having reached the Celestial kingdom. The Celestial kingdom has two levels. In the lower level are Mormons who remained unmarried and never had a temple wedding and Christians who did not hear of Mormonism, but would have accepted it had they heard. Those in the lower level of the Celestial kingdom will be angelic servants for those in the higher level. Those in the higher level of the Celestial kingdom must have undergone a temple marriage and obeyed the Celestial laws faithfully. These may become gods with their own spirit children, just as all humans are the spirit children of the Father god. In Mormon teaching Jesus was a spirit child of the Father god who became a god himself—just as faithful Mormons may do themselves.

The Celestial commandments that good Mormons must keep include faith, repentance, baptism by immersion, confirmation by the Holy Ghost (given by the laying on of hands of LDS priests), and various temple ceremonies. Mormons believe that spirits in spirit-prison can receive Mormonism after death, but they cannot leave the spirit-prison until someone has been baptized for them. For this reason Mormons have compiled a huge database of genealogical information about millions of people.

For the Christian, Mormonism serves as a reminder that upholding good moral values, raising upstanding children, and being responsible citizens are not sufficient in God's eyes. The greatest responsibility people have before God is to know Him truly and to love Him fully.

Yosemite National Park offers a variety of natural wonders.

the south end of the Great Basin, which includes Death Valley and the Mojave Desert. Death Valley is the lowest spot on the continent—282 feet below sea level.

Running from southern California to Washington State are the Coastal Mountains. Within this region are California's largest metropolitan areas—San Diego, Los Angeles, San Francisco, Oakland, and other large and important cities.

The Central Valley includes the San Joaquin Valley in the south and the Sacramento Valley in the north, which make up the best farming region in the West. Because of the good soil and long growing season in these valleys, California is a leading producer of dairy products, greenhouse/nursery products, hay, grapes, and lettuce. It is also a great producer of cotton, poultry, potatoes, and wine.

The Sierra Nevada ("snow-clad mountains") are in the western section of the state and include Mount Whitney, the highest U.S. mountain outside Alaska. The Cascade Mountain range extends from Oregon into northern California. The range includes a series of volcanic peaks with numerous waterfalls.

California is the home of "Silicon Valley," an area that concentrates on the development and production of computer technology. Of course, Hollywood has long been the center of the motion picture industry. Tourism is also a major source of income for California as people visit its many natural and man-made wonders.

Nevada

Nevada is the heart of the dry Great Basin. It is the driest of all states, receiving less than ten inches of rain a year. Its only major river, the Colorado, runs along its southern border. Hoover Dam was built on the Colorado River, creating Lake Mead, which now supplies water for drinking and irrigation. Nonetheless, very little agricultural development has occurred. Several parallel mountain ranges run down the Great Basin like a giant washboard. The highest of them are in the west along the California border.

Although Nevada is called the Silver State, it leads the nation in the production of not only that metal but also gold and mercury. More than 90 percent of Nevada is owned by the federal government, including test sites for the U.S. defense industry.

Half of Nevada's employment is in the services sector. Many of those jobs are related to the state's legalized gambling, which occurs mainly in Las Vegas (the largest city), Reno, and Lake Tahoe.

Oregon

Oregon is divided into five regions. The western fifth of Oregon is coastal mountains. Moving eastward, the **Cascade Mountains** cover another fifth of the state. Sandwiched between the two mountain ranges in the northwestern part of the state is the Willamette Valley. The south central region is part of the Great Basin. The rest of the state northward and eastward is part of the Columbia Plateau.

All of the major cities of Oregon are in the Willamette Valley, which has fertile soil and mild weather all year. This was the region about which early missionaries spoke so highly, luring settlers to travel west on the Oregon Trail in the 1840s and 1850s. The valley is a great producer of grapes, greenhouse/nursery products, hay, potatoes, beans, peppermint, cherries, and various kinds of berries.

Crater Lake, in Oregon, was formed when water collected in an extinct volcano.

Oregon is a leading lumber producer in the nation and has an abundant supply of salmon. Lumber production has made the state a flashpoint between loggers and environmentalists. An associated industry is wood processing. Salmon fishing is also a major income producer.

Washington

The last of the forty-eight contiguous states is Washington. The eastern half of the state is part of the Columbia Plateau. The other half is split about evenly between the Coastal Mountains, which jut out into the Pacific Ocean at Olympic Peninsula, and the Cascade Mountains, with the Puget (PYOO jit) Sound Lowlands sandwiched between those mountains.

The Olympic Peninsula is sparsely populated but has several Pacific Coast Indian reservations. The peninsula gets more rain than any other place in the United States outside of Hawaii. Puget Sound is an arm of the Pacific Ocean. Its deep waters give Washington its best natural harbors. Seattle, the largest port north of San Francisco, is on Puget Sound. Its metropolitan area includes Tacoma and the capital, Olympia.

At the heart of the Cascade Range is **Mount Rainier**, which has twenty-five glaciers, the most outside of Alaska. South of Rainier are two volcanic mountains, Mount Adams (12,276 ft. elev.) and Mount St. Helens (8,365 ft. elev.). Mount St. Helens was 1,312 feet higher before it "blew its top" in a 1980 eruption. It remains active even today, with periodic rumblings being recorded.

The Columbia Plateau includes Spokane, the hub of a region called the Inland Empire. This area's fertile soils make Washington the leading producer of apples, pears, and sweet cherries. The state is second in potato and grape production and third in wheat and hay. Industries include aircraft manufacturing (Boeing), computer technology (Microsoft), chemicals, and aluminum. More than half of Washington is forested, so wood-products industries are also a major income source.

Outlying States

Alaska

Alaska is vast and remote, being more than twice the size of Texas, which is the next largest state. The distance from its southeastern islands to its western islands is greater than that between Maryland and California! It is the northernmost state, touching the Arctic Ocean, and its mountains are the highest in the nation. Some of its national parks are larger than some entire states.

Juneau, the state capital, is in Alaska's southeastern panhandle, a narrow strip of the mainland and a chain of islands that extend down the Pacific coast toward Washington State. The waterway between those islands and the mainland is called the Inside Passage. Most of the state's people live along the Pacific coast, where the warm ocean breezes keep the temperature an average of 60 degrees. Half of the state's population lives in Anchorage.

North of Anchorage is the **Alaska Range**, the northern end of the Pacific Mountain System, which includes the Cascades and the Sierra Nevada. Denali National Park has the highest U.S. peak, Mount McKinley (Denali) (20,237 ft.). The range continues into the Pacific Ocean, where it becomes the chain of **Aleutian** (uh LOO

The heart of the Cascade Range is Mount Rainier in Washington State.

A portion of the 800-mile-long Alaska Pipeline

Molten lava from Hawaii's volcanoes flows right into the sea, creating walls of steam and new land.

shun) **Islands**, which are named for the Aleut (uh LOOT) people. North of the Arctic Circle is the Brooks Range, the northernmost extent of the Rockies. The North Slope, a coastal plain along the Arctic Ocean, slopes down from the Brooks Range to the ocean.

Alaska ranks last in farms and the value of farm products, but it does produce potatoes, dairy products, and greenhouse products. It is first, however, in commercial fishing, primarily salmon, crab, shrimp, halibut, herring, and cod. Anchorage and Dutch Harbor are its major ports. Lumber is also an important product. Mining of gold, which was once done extensively, has greatly diminished. Alaska's most valuable resources are oil and natural gas, which are transported via the Alaska Pipeline from the North Slope to the ice-free port of Valdez. The largest employer is local, state, and federal governments.

Hawaii

Twenty-four hundred miles west of the American mainland is the fiftieth state, Hawaii. The state consists of 132 islands spread across fifteen hundred miles. The eight largest islands are sometimes called the High Islands because their elevations exceed five hundred feet.

The largest of the islands, Hawaii, is logically called the Big Island and makes up almost half of the state's area. It was formed by five volcanoes, two of which—**Mauna Loa** and **Kilauea**—are still active. Average temperatures are about 80 degrees along the beaches, but skiers enjoy snow-clad slopes on Mauna Kea during the winter. Trade winds bring heavy rains to the eastern side of the mountains. Hilo, the second-largest city, gets 138 inches of rain a year. Those rains help make Hawaii the nation's top producer of coffee, orchids, and macadamia nuts.

Lanai is called the Pineapple Island. With Maui, it produces almost all of America's pineapples. Molokai, sometimes called the Forgotten Island, is sparsely populated. Three-fourths of the state's population, however, lives on Oahu ("gathering place"). The capital and largest city, Honolulu, is on this island, which also boasts Diamond Head, a volcanic mountain, as well as Waikiki Beach and the U.S. naval base at Pearl Harbor.

The United States also has territories elsewhere in the Pacific Ocean (American Samoa and Guam) and in the Caribbean Sea (Puerto Rico and the U.S. Virgin Islands). You will study them later when we examine those regions more carefully.

Section Quiz

1. In which state is the geyser Old Faithful?
2. People of which religious group settled in Utah?
3. Which desert covers the southwestern corner of New Mexico, the southern third of Arizona, and the extreme south of California?
4. Which states meet at the Four Corners?
5. What chain of islands in Alaska are a continuation of the Alaska Range?
★ Why do you think the United States maintains a naval base in Hawaii?

Chapter Review

Making Connections

1–2. What two northeastern states were not among the original thirteen colonies?

3. What area became the cradle of capitalism, democracy, and freedom of religion?

4. Contrast anthracite and bituminous coal and list the two states where each is abundant.

5. Why are the Great Plains so arid?

Developing Geography Skills

1. What northeastern state is landlocked and lacks good soil for farming? What resources must this state rely on to support itself?

2. In what major region of the United States do you live? What are the main geographic features of your area?

Thinking Critically

1. Why is it good for a state's economy to diversify?

2. Is regionalism good or bad for a country? Support your answer.

3. Why do some people oppose fracking? What do you think about this practice?

Living in God's World

1. Imagine that you have developed a friendship with a Mormon at work. He says that he is confused and even a little hurt that you do not consider him a Christian since he also loves Jesus. Map out the main points you would like to share with him over a lunch meeting.

2. What must a Christian know about a society's values, goals, and tendencies in order to minister to the people in that society?

People, Places, and Things to Know

New England uplands
timber line
alpine zone
White Mountains
notches
Green Mountains
megalopolis
Finger Lakes
Great Lakes
anthracite
Pine Barrens
truck farms
Delmarva Peninsula
Chesapeake Bay
panhandle
Tidewater
Shenandoah Valley
bituminous coal
barrier islands
Outer Banks
Research Triangle
Bluegrass region
Cumberland Plateau
Tennessee River
Mississippi River
Ozark Mountains
Black Belt
Gulf of Mexico
Everglades
Gulf Coastal Plain
Mississippi Delta
Cajuns
Creoles
Central Plains
Ohio River
till plains
prairie
drift
Mesabi Range
bluffs
Great Plains
unicameral
bicameral
Sierra Nevada
Colorado Plateau
Great Salt Lake
Rio Grande Basin
Sonoran Desert
Mormonism
Cascade Mountains
Mount Rainier
Alaska Range
Aleutian Islands
Mauna Loa
Kilauea

Unit Four
LATIN AMERICA

9 Middle America

10 South America

From ancient Indian civilizations to the invasion by Spanish forces and continued migration by other groups, Latin America is a land rich in history and the mingling of cultures. Latin America has a wealth of potential and a rapidly growing population that presents many challenges.

Pyramid of the Niches in El Tajín, Mexico

MIDDLE AMERICA

I. Mexico
  A. Northern Mexico
  B. Mesa Central
  C. The Southern Tropics
  D. U.S.-Mexican Relations Today

II. Central America
  A. Guatemala
  B. Belize
  C. El Salvador
  D. Honduras
  E. Nicaragua
  F. Costa Rica
  G. Panama

III. The West Indies
  A. The Bahamas
  B. The Greater Antilles
  C. The Lesser Antilles

anada and the United States are the main English-speaking nations of the Western Hemisphere. To the south is a different cultural region called **Latin America**. Latin people speak one of the languages descended from ancient Latin—Spanish, Portuguese, Italian, or French, also known as the Romance languages.

Latin America has two main subregions: Middle America and South America. **Middle America** consists of the nations and islands that lie between the United States and South America. It is what is known as a **land bridge** between North and South America. Several empires clashed for control of that area, which has become a colorful

Middle America Fast Facts						
Country	Capital	Area (sq. mi.)	Pop. (2013 est.) (M)	Pop. Density (per sq. mi.)	Per Capita GDP ($US)	Life Span
Mexico	Mexico City	761,601	116.22	153	$14,700	76.66
Belize	Belmopan	8,866	0.33	37	$8,200	68.28
Costa Rica	San Jose	19,575	4.70	240	$11,900	77.89
El Salvador	San Salvador	8,260	6.11	740	$7,500	73.69
Guatemala	Guatemala City	42,042	14.37	349	$5,100	71.17
Honduras	Tegucigalpa	43,277	8.45	195	$4,400	70.71
Nicaragua	Managua	50,193	5.79	115	$3,200	72.18
Panama	Panama City	29,208	3.56	122	$14,100	77.96
Bahamas	Nassau	5,380	0.32	59	$30,400	71.44
Cuba	Havana	44,218	11.06	250	$9,900	77.87
Dominican Republic	Santo Domingo	18,816	10.22	543	$9,300	77.44
Haiti	Port-au-Prince	10,714	9.90	758	$1,200	62.51
Jamaica	Kingston	4,232	2.91	688	$8,900	73.43
Antigua & Barbuda	St. John's	171	0.09	526	$17,100	75.69
Barbados	Bridgetown	166	0.29	1,746	$25,000	74.52
Dominica	Roseau	290	0.07	241	$14,300	76.18
Grenada	St. George's	133	0.10	752	$13,800	73.3
St. Kitts & Nevis	Basseterre	104	0.05	480	$15,600	74.84
St. Lucia	Castries	238	0.16	672	$13,100	77.04
St. Vincent & the Grenadines	Kingstown	150	0.10	667	$11,500	74.39
Trinidad & Tobago	Port of Spain	1,980	1.23	621	$20,000	71.67

Machismo

The American Heritage College Dictionary defines *machismo* as "a strong sense of masculinity usually entailing aggressiveness, domination of women, virility, and physical courage." The Spanish brought this concept to the Americas in the sixteenth century, and it became popular in Latin American culture. Though masculinity is a biblical concept, the aggressiveness and domination that have become common in some cultures are the result of the Fall. It is important for men of every culture to distinguish physical courage from aggression or abuse of others.

blend of native Indians, Europeans, Africans, and Asians. Local superstition has blended with Roman Catholicism, and local words have blended with Latin languages. Even different ethnicities have mixed, creating a diverse culture.

Such mixing of people groups was not without conflict. Middle America has a violent past, stretching back to the bloody wars and human sacrifices by ancient native empires. The European conquest of the region in the sixteenth century was no less bloody. In the nineteenth century, as revolutionaries cast off their colonial powers, they tried to create prosperous democracies similar to the American republic to the north.

Over the past century and a half, the United States has tried, sometimes not too diplomatically, to use its influence to encourage democracy, peace, and prosperity among its southern neighbors. It wants the region to have governments that respect American property, thereby fostering an environment that makes free trade possible for the benefit of all participants. The nations of Middle America, however, have often interpreted such U.S. attempts as efforts to exert imperialistic control over them, creating suspicion and mistrust that hinders understanding and cooperation.

I. Mexico

Mexico was once the crown jewel of the Spanish Empire. Its borders included much of what today is the American Southwest. In spite of its eventual loss of much of that land to the United States and its recurring internal conflicts, Mexico remains the major force in Middle America. It has the largest Spanish-speaking population and

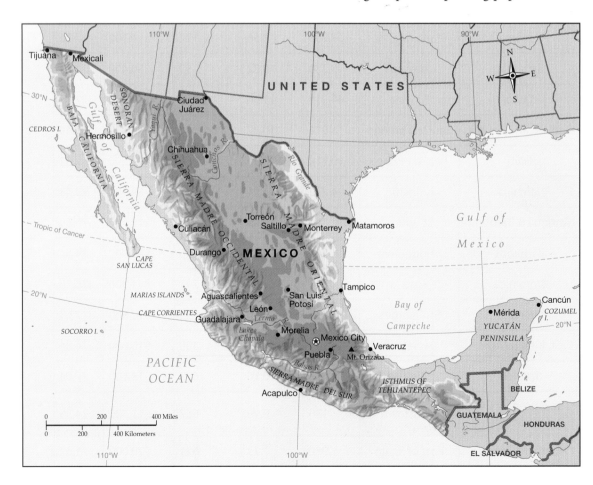

the second-largest city in the Western Hemisphere. Mexico's population exceeds that of all other Middle American countries combined. It epitomizes both the strengths and the weaknesses of Latin American culture.

Mexico is shaped much like a funnel, with the wide part in the north and the "spout" in the extreme south. Its entire northern border is with the United States. Its western shores are washed by the Pacific Ocean. Between the mainland and the long peninsula called **Baja** (bah hah) **California**, south of the U.S. state of California, is the Gulf of California (or, as the Mexicans call it, the Sea of Cortés). Mexico's eastern shores are on the Gulf of Mexico. The southern tip of the "spout" of Mexico curves north and east to form the Yucatán (yoo kah TAHN) Peninsula. Nestled between the Yucatán and the central portion of the mainland is the **Bay of Campeche** (kahm PEH cheh).

Two mountain ranges run the length of Mexico along each coast, the **Sierra Madre** (see-EH-ruh MAH-dray) **Oriental** on the east and the **Sierra Madre Occidental** on the west. The ranges join to form one range near the twentieth parallel at the Valley of Mexico, where Mexico City is located. That range forms the spine of the isthmus and continues into neighboring Guatemala.

The climate of Mexico ranges from desert in the north to subtropical in the south. The major population areas are in the south, although some northern border towns, such as **Tijuana** (tee HWA nah) and **Juárez** (HWA rez), are quite large. **Monterrey** (MAHN tuh RAY), a modern high-tech city, is about 150 miles south of the U.S.-Mexico border. The Mexican government is a federal republic with thirty-one state governments and one central government.

In our study of Mexico, we will begin in the northern and coastal areas and work our way southward through the central area, which is called the *Mesa Central* (MAY-suh cehn-TRAHL), and end with the tropical southern region.

Northern Mexico

The northern part of Mexico has been greatly influenced by its proximity to and contact with the United States. Its geography is much like that of the American Southwest—hot, dry, and generally flat desert. Quite often, wherever a city or town exists on the U.S. side of the border, a corresponding city or town is found on the Mexican side. Prominent examples include San Diego and Tijuana on the west coast, El Paso and Juárez in the central area, and Brownsville and Matamoros on the Gulf Coast. Sometimes such cross-border towns even have the same name, as is the case with Nogales and Laredo.

Mexicans continue to migrate to the border area in a quest for jobs in agriculture and manufacturing that abound in the border towns. Thousands of them keep going, however, and enter the United States illegally.

Importance of the Family

Latin American cultures tend to place a strong emphasis on the extended family. Several generations will live in the same area, and children have the blessing of being influenced by grandparents and aunts and uncles. As a result, family relationships have a strong impact on the life and character of Latinos. This positive aspect of the Latin culture reflects the biblical emphasis on God's building block for society—the family.

A small fence separates densely populated Tijuana, Mexico, right, from the United States in the Border Patrol's San Diego Sector.

Deserts, Mines, and Ranches of the Northern Plateau

The Sierra Madre ("Mother Range") extends from the American Rockies into northern Mexico. In the upper area between the ranges lies the rugged **Northern Plateau**.

The hot, dry winds of the subtropics, which blow across the American Southwest, also blow across northern Mexico, keeping it dry year-round. Westerlies occasionally blow in from the Pacific Ocean, dropping water as they rise over the high Sierra Madre Occidental. Except for these mountains, however, all of northern Mexico is desert and semiarid grassland. The Chihuahuan (chee WAH wan) Desert covers large parts of the Northern Plateau. The state of Chihuahua—the largest state by area in Mexico—takes its name from this desert.

Irrigation permits some farming around the cities of Monterrey, Ciudad Juárez, Chihuahua, Torreón, and Saltillo. Monterrey is the most populous northern city. Chihuahua is a center for silver, lead, and zinc mining. Silver mines there and throughout the country make Mexico the world's leading producer of silver. Durango also has important iron mines.

The Copper Canyon is a rugged area of the Sierra Madre Occidental, much of which is accessible only by train.

Cattle ranching is common outside the cities. American cowboys patterned their clothing, gear, and skills after the Spanish *vaqueros* (vah KAY rohs). For the popular *charrería* (chah ray REE ah), or Mexican rodeo, the participants—called *charros* (CHAH rohs)—dress up in fine clothes as part of the ritual.

On the western edge of the Northern Plateau rises the Sierra Madre Occidental. Few paved roads cross these tree-covered mountains between the U.S. border and Durango, five hundred miles south. Only one railroad, a true feat of human engineering, winds between them. The highlight of the route is **Copper Canyon**, the Grand Canyon of Mexico. Its Basaseachic Falls is the second highest in Mexico.

Oil and Tourism on the Gulf

The Gulf Coastal Plain extends along the Gulf Coast from Texas all the way to the Yucatán Peninsula. Mexico's Gulf states have grown in importance since the discovery of reserves of natural gas and petroleum. A large offshore oil field was discovered under the Bay of Campeche in the 1970s. The sale of gas and oil to the United States is Mexico's most important source of foreign currency.

The biggest port in Mexico, **Veracruz**, lies on the Gulf Coastal Plain at the gateway to Mexico City and the Mesa Central. Most goods shipped from Texas and other American Gulf states pass through Veracruz before reaching the interior. Cortés landed his invasion force there in 1519, establishing the first Spanish settlement in Mexico.

Cancún (can KOON), on the eastern tip of the Yucatán Peninsula, is a major tourist destination. It was named by the native Mayans for its many snakes, but those reptiles are no longer plentiful there. The city was designed to be a resort location and is today Mexico's "showcase resort." Its white, powdery beaches are legendary. With a population in excess of 600,000, it—along with its Pacific Ocean counterpart, **Acapulco** (ah cah POOL coh)—contributes greatly to the nearly $10 billion Mexican tourist industry. Approximately 20 million tourists visit the country each year.

Gulf of California

The Gulf of California juts deep into the rugged, desert lands west of the Sierra Madre Occidental. Mexico's Pacific Northwest is nothing like America's Pacific Northwest. The **Sonoran** (soh NOH rahn) **Desert**, with its **saguaro** (sah WHA roh) **cacti**, covers much of the area.

Four Mexican states border the Gulf of California, two on the mainland and two on Baja California.

Tijuana, across the border from San Diego in Southern California, is a popular stop for American tourists visiting Mexico. Crowds haggle in the markets for good prices on silver jewelry and other souvenirs. To the east, Mexicali sits at the southern end of California's Imperial Valley. Its elevation of thirty-three feet below sea level marks the lowest point in Mexico. As in California, irrigation from the Colorado River permits large-scale agriculture. Wheat, cotton, and sesame seeds are among the most important crops.

Saguaro cacti thrive in the Sonoran Desert of northwest Mexico.

Mesa Central

The vast **Mexican Plateau**, bordered by the two Sierra Madres, dominates the landscape of Mexico. Most of Mexico is too dry for farming. But during the rainy season in the late spring and summer, easterly trade winds from the Caribbean Sea blow over the southern end of the Mexican Plateau, bringing adequate water for crops. This region, where the mountain ranges come together, is called the Mesa Central.

Although the Mesa Central is located in the tropics, the high altitude keeps the temperatures relatively mild. The early Spanish explorers noticed the influence of altitude and gave different names to each **altitude zone**. They called the low tropical coasts the *tierra caliente* (tee-EH-rah kah-lee-EN-tay; "hot land"). The best lands on the plateaus and mountain valleys they called *tierra templada* (tem PLAH dah; "temperate land"). They divided the high mountains into the *tierra fría* (FREE ah; "cold land") of the subalpine zone, the *páramo* (PAH rah moh; "bleak plateau"), and the *tierra helada* (ay LAH dah; "frozen land") of the permanent snow cap.

The peso, available in many denominations of either coins or bills, is the Mexican monetary unit.

Thousands of small farms and villages cover the *bajío* (bah HEE oh), the flat western portion of the Mesa Central. Many subsistence farmers eke out a living on small plots, typically growing corn, beans, squash, and peppers. But more and more young Mexicans are seeking work in the *bajío*'s manufacturing cities. Guadalajara, the third-largest city in Mexico, stands on the western side of the country near Lake Chapala, Mexico's largest lake. Puebla and León also rank among the ten largest cities in Mexico. People who cannot find work in these cities move to the southeastern part of the Mesa Central, where the capital, **Mexico City**, is located.

Find It!

Mexico City

19.433° N, 99.133° W

Conquest of the Aztec Capital

The Mesa Central was the center of a series of civilizations. Ancient ruins may date back to about 2000 BC. Around AD 500, a mysterious early people built the first city in Middle America—Teotihuacán, the ruins of which still stand north of Mexico City. Tourists can climb the Temple of the Sun, which has a longer base than the great pyramids of the Egyptian pharaohs. The **Toltec** (TOHL tek) and later the Aztec empires dominated the Mesa Central. Tourists today can visit the temple to the rain god Quetzalcoatl (a feathered serpent), where fifteen-foot-tall stone warriors still stand guard. The **Aztecs** were especially ingenious in building their empire, including their capital, Tenochtitlán, which they built on an island in Lake Texcoco. In the center of the city was a temple to the sun god where Aztecs offered human sacrifices, cutting out the hearts of their victims.

In 1519 the Spanish *conquistador* (kohn KEEST ah dohr) Hernando Cortés, aided by neighboring tribes who hated the Aztecs, conquered the Aztecs. For the next three hundred years, Spanish viceroys ruled Mexico for the Spanish monarch and called their empire "New Spain." Spanish priests built missions and spread Roman Catholicism among the Indians. Spanish noblemen owned most of the land and built vast ranches, called **haciendas** (hah see EN dahs), which they ran like feudal manors. They forced the Indians whom they called **peones** (pay OH nays; unskilled laborers) to farm the land and to mine gold and copper for them. The Spaniards became wealthy; the native peoples remained poor, and many died under the harsh working conditions. (As a result, the Spanish imported African slaves to replace the Indian workers.) Even after the Mexicans drove the Spaniards from power, Mexico suffered one dictator after another. Recently, however, the nation has become more stable and has begun to recover from the poverty created by centuries of abuse.

Spanish architecture is apparent in the Campeche Public State Library.

Metropolitan Church in Mexico City, Mexico

The Seat of Government

At the center of Mexico City is the country's main public square, the *Zócalo* (ZOH kah lo). The squares of most Spanish colonial cities are surrounded by government buildings and a church, and Mexico City is no exception. City Hall, the Metropolitan Church, and the National Palace surround the square. Nearby is the Senate, the Chamber of Deputies, and the Supreme Court of Justice. Like Washington, D.C., the capital of Mexico is a federal district run by the legislature.

History of Revolt—Mexico's history is an ongoing story of revolution, beginning with the war for independence from Spain (1810–21). From the beginning, however, the nation's leaders disagreed on states' rights and religious freedom. During the next forty years, forty presidents rose and fell. Dissatisfied opponents often took power in a **coup** (koo)—the sudden, illegal overthrow of the government by a military officer or other government official.

Most of the early fighting took place between full-blooded Spaniards. Under the Spanish colonial system, men born in Spain (called *peninsulares*) could own estates, but Spaniards born in the colonies—called *criollos* (kree OH yohs)—were treated as second-class citizens. The inheritors of the large estates wanted to keep everything after the revolution, but the landless people believed that the lands should be broken up. A major goal of the criollos was land reform, the "fair" distribution of land. In a region that depends on agriculture for survival, land reform became a recurring theme of revolt and remains so today.

Finally, the overtaxed, landless **mestizos** (mess TEE zohs), people of mixed Spanish and Indian ancestry, and Indians revolted (1910–20). More than one million Mexicans died during the revolution, but the Liberal faction broke the power of the Conservatives, confiscated church lands, and forbade Catholic priests from entering politics. Since then, Mexico has been the only Latin American country to avoid a coup attempt, but authorities continue to battle revolutionaries in the southernmost state of Chiapas.

The volcano Popocatépetl towers over Mexico City.

Reforms Since the Revolution—The Mexican government began a land-redistribution program, taking land from the wealthy and distributing it among the poor. The land grants, called **ejidos** (ay HEE dohs), were owned in common by the people of the village. No other nation has accomplished such a large transfer of land with relative peace.

The revolutionary constitution of 1917 established a federal government similar to that in the United States. Each of Mexico's thirty-one states has its own governor and legislature. The country also has a bicameral legislature, with a Senate and a Chamber of Deputies.

But Mexico was not always a true republic. From 1929 to 1997, the Revolutionary Institutional Party (PRI) controlled the government and used its money and power to win elections. The party chose the candidate for president and most of the candidates for the legislature. The legislature had little real power to make laws. All power was vested in the president, who ruled much as a dictator for a six-year term. But he could serve for only one term before the party selected another candidate. Perhaps this blend of dictatorship and democracy is one reason Mexicans tolerated the system so long.

Mexican president Enrique Peña Nieto in 2013

Demands for change increased as the PRI became corrupt and wasteful, however, and its programs failed to help the average citizen. In the late 1980s, the president began encouraging more private ownership of land and other economic reforms. But economic freedoms spurred demands for political freedom. In 1989, the opposition National Action Party (PAN) won a governorship for the first time. In 1997, a non-PRI majority was elected to the legislature. Then, in 2000, PAN elected its candidate to the presidency. The fifty-seventh president, Enrique Peña Nieto, was elected in 2012.

Section Quiz

1–2. What two factors make the Mesa Central the most populous part of Mexico?

3–5. Name three empires that have dominated the Mesa Central.

6. What are people of mixed Spanish and Indian ancestry called?

★ Has the Mexican government's redistribution of land resulted in increased prosperity for most Mexicans? Why or why not?

The Sierra Madre del Sur rises behind the tourist town of Acapulco.

A Missionary's Encounter with Death in Mexico

Mike and Faith Goldfuss, Mexico City

Death often strikes without warning in Mexico, and embalming is rare. Instead, the family holds a wake or all-night vigil that very night, followed the next day with the burial or cremation. During the vigil, they bring the body in a casket into the house and set up some candles with lots of flowers. Neighbors and family members come and stay for the whole night. When a family member of someone in my church dies, I am often asked to preach. I make it a point to remind those attending, "This morning, none of us thought we would be here tonight." Given the strong Roman Catholic influence, family members and friends often do rosaries and prayers for the dead person, but I always mention Hebrews 9:27 and the fact that this day is coming for everyone who is in attendance. Then I preach to the people who are there and urge them to think of eternity and their own souls.

During one wake, the widow asked me to preach three times. These were three tremendous opportunities to give the gospel, and between preaching sessions, my wife and I had very good conversations with some of the people at the vigil. Realizing the importance of always being ready to give an answer for the hope that is in us, we have made ministry opportunities, including speaking at wakes, a central part of our work in Mexico.

The Southern Tropics

Southern Mexico has a rainy season and a dry season, rather than the four seasons that the United States has. Savannah covers the coastal areas, although it gives way to mangrove swamps in some parts. In the interior, colorful parrots, chattering monkeys, tapirs, and other exotic animals roam the lush rain forests.

Poverty of the Southern Highlands

The greatest influence in the dry north has been the United States, but the greatest influence in the tropical south has been the Indian culture. Many Indians continue to live in the isolated valleys of the **Sierra Madre Del Sur**, or "Southern" Sierra Madre, which runs parallel to the southern curve of Mexico's Pacific Coast. The map on page 188 shows that the three Sierra Madre ranges join at Mexico's narrowest point, the Isthmus of Tehuantepec (tay WHAN tah pehk). From there, the range continues down the coast into Central America.

The Southern Highlands is the poorest region in the country, and one of its states, Chiapas, is the poorest state in Mexico. Many American tourists see only Acapulco, "the pearl of the Pacific," or Cancún, where tropical beaches remind them of Hawaii. But the posh resorts stand in stark contrast to the poverty of the surrounding rural areas.

The state of Michoacán (mee cho wah KAHN) is known for the Tarascan (tah RAH skan) Indians. Although they are not as famous as the Aztecs, they had a powerful empire throughout the fifteenth century. Many Tarascan Indians still carry on their traditional way of life. They fish, weave nets and baskets, and grow traditional Indian foods—corn, beans, squash, and chili peppers. The majority of the 2 percent of Mexicans who do not speak Spanish are Tarascans.

Chiapas (chee AH pahs) is the southernmost state in Mexico. A third of the people are full-blooded Indians, few of whom speak Spanish. The state broke away from Guatemala and joined the original nineteen states of Mexico in 1824. But Chiapas has become the poorest and most unstable state in Mexico. The passage of the North American Free Trade Agreement (NAFTA) in 1994 sparked a rebellion among Indian farmers, who feared they could not compete with the low prices of American grain.

Although most Indians in Chiapas claim to be Roman Catholics, they have retained many traditions from the times before Columbus. They still hold to many ancient superstitions and celebrations today. Local *caciques* (cah SEE kays, "party bosses") rule as small dictators. The *caciques* make their money by selling alcohol at pagan religious festivals, but Protestants refuse to participate. Although many Protestant church members have been beaten and several pastors murdered, the gospel witness continues.

Mayas in the Yucatán

The ancient Maya Indians built cities and massive pyramids in the southern jungles of Mexico, east of the Isthmus of Tehuantepec. The greatest concentration of Mayan ruins is on the Yucatán Peninsula. Although the great Mayan cities fell into decay long before the arrival of the Spanish, descendants of the Mayas remained on the peninsula. As Spanish dominion increased, the Mayas retreated to jungle hideouts. The Indians resented Mexican rule. Twice since Mexico became independent, the Mayas have declared the Yucatán independent.

The largest city on the peninsula today is Mérida (MEHR ih dah). Its chief product is henequen (HIN uh kwin), a plant whose fibers sailors used to make string, twine, and rope.

A Religious Nation

About 96 percent of the Mexican people affiliate with some religious group, and 95 percent identify with some form of Christianity. The growth of evangelicals has increased from 2 percent in 1960 to 8 percent in 2010, and the pace is accelerating. Local churches in Mexico have matured to the point where they are sending out a growing number of missionaries to other nations. Christian institutions have developed in Mexico to prepare believers for work in local churches and foreign ministries.

U.S.-Mexican Relations

Mexico and the United States, which share a two-thousand-mile-long border, have a long history. The United States has greatly influenced Mexico, especially the northern area. Despite various problems, both countries have benefited greatly from their exchange of cultures and goods. The United States is one of Mexico's main

Sisal fibers from the cactus-like henequen plant are hung out to dry before being processed into ropes.

Chichén Itzá

Of the major Mayan ruins that have been found in the Yucatán jungles, perhaps the most famous is Chichén Itzá. This complex includes more than one hundred structures, including a seventy-five-foot-high pyramid, the Temple of the Warriors, the tomb of a high priest, an observatory, and the largest ball court in Middle America.

The high pyramid called the Castillo ("castle") is an engineering marvel. Each side, aligned along a point on the compass, has eighteen parts for each Mayan month. Each staircase has ninety-one steps: the steps on four sides plus the top platform equal 365 days of the Mayan year. At each equinox, the shadow of a snake appears; the shadow cast by the steps forms the body and a statue provides the head.

An entrance on the north side of the Castillo leads to two often-photographed chambers. One chamber contains an altar in the form of a reclining god, Chac Mool. The other has a huge throne in the shape of a red jaguar with eyes of green jade.

The Mayas performed bloody pagan rituals. During famines, children were thrown into the seventy-five-foot-deep Well of Sacrifice to appease the rain god. Nearby stood Skull Rack and the Platforms of the Jaguars and the Eagles. There Mayas placed human heads on stakes and sacrificed still-throbbing hearts on bloody altars. At ball games, losing contestants were beheaded, as shown in Mayan artwork.

Although some Mayan ruins date to before Christ, Chichen Itza did not flourish until around AD 1000 and declined sometime after 1224. The cause of the decline of the Mayas remains a mystery. Whatever the observable causes were for the decline of the Mayas, Christians should consider the possibility that God destroyed this civilization because of His hatred of child sacrifice (cf. Jer. 19:4–7).

trading partners, and Mexico is the fourth largest importer of American goods. Nevertheless, the relationship has been very strained at times.

Americans fought two wars against Mexico (1835–36 and 1846–48) before their boundary dispute was settled. From those wars, the United States obtained not only Texas down to the Rio Grande but also what later became California, New Mexico, and Arizona. The United States added even more territory by paying Mexico $10 million for a strip of land called the Gadsden Purchase below those southwestern territories.

The United States invaded Mexico during the Mexican revolution of 1910–20. In 1914, U.S. Marines landed on the Gulf Coast to cut off arms shipments to Mexico's dictator and to help the revolutionaries. In 1916, General John Pershing led U.S. soldiers across the Texas border to track down the outlaw leader Pancho Villa (PAHN-choh VEE-yah), who had been making raids in American territory. The army withdrew the following year, as the clouds of World War I turned America's attention to Europe.

The wars, threats of war, and the Mexicans' perception of America as an arrogant bully tainted U.S.-Mexican relations for generations to follow. Signs reading "Yanqui, go home!" have expressed the resentment that many Mexicans feel toward the United States. In turn, however, many Americans are concerned about illegal immigration, and the automatic U.S. citizenship of children born to illegal immigrants in the United States. The parents of these children can then begin to collect welfare and other government financial aid, putting further strains on the U.S. economy. The traffic in illicit drugs across the border and growing gang violence from Mexico are also major points of conflict between the two peoples. In spite of these problems, the two governments have tried to work together to accomplish mutually beneficial goals, such as the enactment of NAFTA.

NAFTA and CAFTA–DR

In 1988, Mexico's main trading partner was the United States. But U.S.-Canadian trade was eighty times greater than U.S.-Mexican trade. Hoping to improve trade, Mexico asked to join a trade agreement with Canada and the United States. The North American Free Trade Agreement (NAFTA), signed in 1993, created the second-largest free-trade zone in the world (after the European Union).

The NAFTA negotiations stirred controversy in all three countries. Canada and the United States are industrial giants, whereas Mexico is a developing nation with one-twentieth the economy of the United States. Mexico had much to offer: a potentially big market, cheap labor, and inexpensive products, such as cement

and farm produce. But some Americans feared "unfair" competition from Mexican companies, which had fewer regulations on working conditions and pollution. Mexican farmers feared competition from America's cheap grain.

A similar agreement has been adopted throughout the rest of Middle America. The Dominican Republic Central American Free Trade Agreement (CAFTA–DR) is a treaty that has been signed by (to date) the United States and six Central American countries: Costa Rica, El Salvador, Guatemala, Honduras, Nicaragua, and the Dominican Republic. The agreement is modeled after NAFTA and is considered a steppingstone toward the development of a broader Free Trade

Area of the Americas (FTAA), which would incorporate thirty-four economies.

It may be several years before we see the full impact of NAFTA, CAFTA–DR, and, if it materializes, FTAA. Factories in the United States send many of their parts across the border to Mexican assembly plants, called *maquiladoras* (mah KEE lah DOR ahs). Although these jobs are not technical, they provide Mexicans with above-average wages. As a result of this change, some U.S. factories have either closed or laid off workers. To resolve this problem, many American workers are being trained for other jobs. In addition, employment in the trade industry has grown in the U.S.

Life in the Mexican Village

Life in the big cities of Mexico is modern, but the rural towns and villages still retain many of the old ways. Villages are built around a *plaza* or public square, which is the center of life in the town. A Catholic church usually stands on one side of the plaza, which is often decorated with walks, flowers, and sometimes even a fountain.

Every week on market day, the plaza bustles with activity. Some people sell their goods from covered stalls; others sit on the pavement with their goods spread around them. Those who sit in the open might wear a *sombrero* (sohm BREH roh), a wide-brimmed hat, as shade from the sun. Indians wear colorful blankets, called *ponchos*, by putting their head through a hole in the center. The different designs tell which Indian group wove them. The people work hard during the week to have items to sell on market day. With the money they earn, they buy corn, blankets, and other items.

The goods do not have price tags, so the people negotiate. One party suggests a certain number of *pesos* (PAY sohs)—the Mexican monetary unit—for an item, and the other makes a counteroffer to his liking. The verbal exchange continues until they agree on a price.

Narrow streets radiate from the plaza and are lined with homes usually made of *adobe* (uh DOH bay; bricks made from clay and straw), many of which have balconies and an interior courtyard called a *patio* (PAH tee oh), which is a place of privacy for the family. Following the Spanish custom, everyone comes home from work in the middle of the day for the main meal. After the meal, many people take a *siesta* (see ESS tah), or nap. They prefer to eat and rest during the hottest part of the day and to work in the cool of the morning and late afternoon. Because they work in late afternoon, their evening meal usually is not served until as late as 9:30 p.m.

This public market in Chiapas is representative of markets found all over Mexico.

Most meals include tortillas. Many Mexican women grind corn into meal on a flat stone, mix it with water to make dough, and roll it into thin cakes. The fried cakes are called tortillas unless they are fried to crispness, in which case they are called *tostadas*. A tortilla folded to hold other food is a taco, a tortilla rolled around grilled meat makes a *fajita*, and a tortilla stuffed and covered with chili sauce makes an *enchilada*. Cornmeal rolled up with meat and hot chili peppers makes *tamales*. When flour is substituted for cornmeal, the stuffed flour tortilla is called a *burrito*. *Frijoles* (free HOH lays), or refried beans, are the most common supplement to the tortillas. The hotness or spiciness of Mexican foods varies throughout the regions of Mexico.

The whole town comes alive on special celebrations called *fiestas* (fee ESS tahs). On Independence Day (September 16), fireworks, special toys and decorations of tissue paper and cardboard, and mariachi music complete the festivities. The unusual fiesta of November 2 is the Day of the Dead (All Soul's Day), a celebration in memory of the dead. Children eat sugar skeletons and play with wind-up toy skeletons, while families picnic in the cemetery. Cinco de Mayo (May 5) is a regional holiday. Nativity scenes, snow scenes, and carols are used to celebrate the Holy Week of Christmas season. Groups representing Mary and Joseph travel from home to home but are refused until they reach a prearranged home. There, the children take turns trying to break the brightly decorated *piñata* (peen YAH tah) while blindfolded. When one succeeds in breaking the papier-mâché or earthenware *piñata*, all of its candy, fruit, and toys spill out for the children.

Section Quiz

1. What three mountain ranges dominate Mexico's geography?
2. In what Mexican state are the ruins of the Tarascan Indian empire located?
3. In addition to Roman Catholicism, what do the Indians in Chiapas hold to?
4. What is a sombrero? Why is it important in Mexico?
★ Why would the northern states of Mexico support NAFTA but the southern states oppose it?

LET'S GO EXPLORING

Climates of Latin America

1. What is the most common climate along Mexico's northern border?
2. What three climates does Mexico share with most nations of Middle America?
3. What is the most common climate west of the highlands in Middle America?
4. What climates appear in South America but not in Middle America?
★ How can Mexico feed so many people even though it lacks a moderate climate?

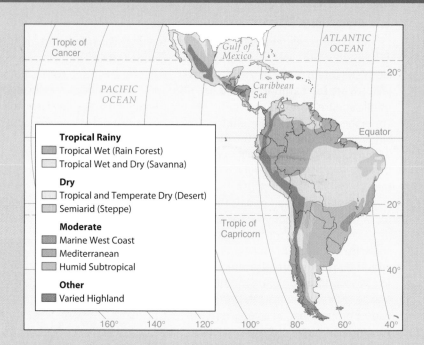

Tropical Rainy
- Tropical Wet (Rain Forest)
- Tropical Wet and Dry (Savanna)

Dry
- Tropical and Temperate Dry (Desert)
- Semiarid (Steppe)

Moderate
- Marine West Coast
- Mediterranean
- Humid Subtropical

Other
- Varied Highland

II. Central America

An **isthmus**, or narrow land bridge, connects Mexico with South America. Seven small countries lie in this region, known as **Central America**. Although they are strung out over one thousand miles, all seven countries would fit into Texas, with enough room left for Georgia.

Central America is very similar to southern Mexico. The mountains of the Western Cordillera continue south along the Pacific shore. The eastern coast receives more than one hundred inches of rain from trade winds blowing over the Caribbean Sea. But the Pacific Coast, which lies in the rainshadow, receives only forty inches of rain. Most people live in the comfortable *tierra templada* of the highlands.

Like southern Mexico, the nations of Central America are relatively poor. The Pacific Ring of Fire poses the constant danger of earthquakes and volcanic eruptions. The fertile volcanic soils are the region's only important resource. Many Central Americans are subsistence farmers, growing just enough corn and vegetables to feed their own families.

The early European settlers introduced a new kind of farming called a **plantation economy**. Plantations require large numbers of workers to raise specialized crops, such as cotton, cacao, coffee, and bananas, all crops that require many hands to tend, gather, and ship to foreign markets. The early Spaniards forced the Indians to clear the forests and work the plantations. Later, they brought slaves from Africa. Today, the owners hire local workers.

Central American countries share several other characteristics with Mexico. All but Belize were Spanish colonies, and their people speak Spanish. The Roman Catholic Church is predominant.

Revolutions and civil strife have wracked these struggling republics, and that political instability causes economic instability.

The United States has had a profound influence in the region. American and British warships helped to keep the region free from foreign invasion during the nineteenth century. At times, the United States has supplied weapons or sent troops to restore peace. Today, although the Central American nations often resent the interference of "the Colossus of the North," they each trade with the United States more than with any other nation, including each other.

Lands of the Mayas

Like southern Mexico, the four nations of northern Central America (Guatemala, Belize, El Salvador, and Honduras) were settled long ago by the **Mayas**. The Mayan civilization dates back to about 1000 BC. Its peak was from AD 300 to 900. It crumbled about 1200.

Of all of the Indian civilizations, the Mayas are the most famous because they left written records. Until recently, their hieroglyphics and number system remained a great mystery, but accurate calendars found on the walls of Chichén Itzá and other cities helped experts decipher many inscriptions that tell of the Mayas' military prowess and their sacrifices to the god Kukulcan.

Up to six million descendants of the Mayas still live in the five nations of the old Mayan Empire. The jungle has reclaimed most of the Mayan cities, but the nations are working to protect Mayan art and architecture and to capitalize on their tourism potential.

Guatemala

On the Yucatán's southern border lies Guatemala (gwah tuh MAHL ah), the center of Mayan civilization, which included Tayasal, the last Mayan city to fall to Spanish forces. The Highland Mayas

Mayas, such as this woman in Guatemala, live throughout Central America today.

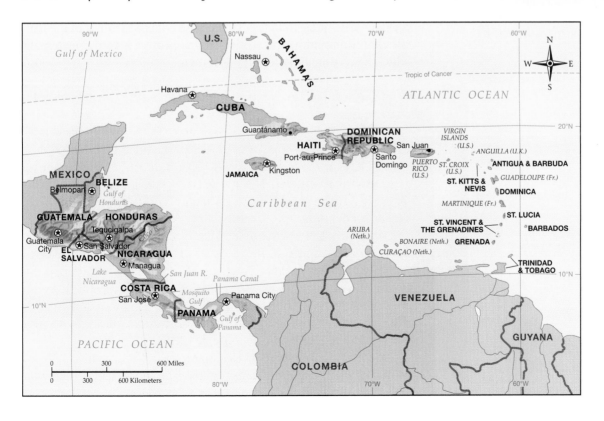

Guatemala is a leading producer of coffee.

Lifestyles in Guatemala

There are two major ways of life in Guatemala. The ladino culture is urban and Western. The Indian culture is rural and traditional. While many Indian women continue to use communal laundry areas along lake shores, the ladinos enjoy many modern conveniences and maintain a higher standard of living. The line between rich and poor generally follows the percentage of the population that is ladino or Indian.

In light of the poverty among the Indian population, many of the men leave home in search of work. This leaves the women to raise their families and carry on the traditions of the Indian culture. These women often continue to speak their tribal language and dress in the customary clothing of their culture. To survive, many Indian women have learned to make Mayan crafts that are in great demand by tourists.

lived in the mountains near the Pacific; the Lowland Mayas lived on the great plain of northern Guatemala, called the Petén. The Mayan capital, Tikal, and most of the population centers were in the lowlands. More than half the people of Guatemala are descendants of the Mayas, many of whom live as their ancestors in the northern plain did. The rest of the people are *mestizos*, called *ladinos*, who follow more Spanish traditions.

Guatemala has more people than any other Central American country and the largest city in Central America: Guatemala City, the capital. Plantations in the highlands produce coffee beans whereas the plantations on the Pacific lowlands produce sugar cane and cotton. The highlands boast the highest mountain in Central America, Volcán Tajumulco (13,845 ft.).

After a devastating earthquake struck Guatemala in 1976, Protestant missionaries found hearts receptive to the gospel. Nearly 30 percent of the people are now Protestant in contrast to an average of 6 percent in the rest of Central America. In 1991, a Guatemalan became the first Protestant elected president in a Latin American country.

Guatemala was the scene of the longest-running civil war in Central America. Some 140,000 people died in thirty-five years of bloodshed before peace was restored in 1996.

Belize

All of Belize (buh LEEZ) was once part of the Mayan Empire. Lowland Mayas lived in the Caribbean lowlands, which extend down from the Yucatán and cover most of Belize.

Unlike the other Central American nations, Belize was settled by the British. Forsaken by the Spanish because it lacked gold, this difficult coastland was first settled by shipwrecked British sailors in 1638. The Spanish, Caribbean pirates, and Indians tried to drive the settlers away, but they did not budge. The country was called British Honduras and remained a colony until independence in 1981, when it changed its name to Belize. Like Canada, it is a member of the British Commonwealth, and British troops protect it from Guatemala, which has claimed the country as its own.

Belize Barrier Reef

Belize has the smallest population in Central America. About 49 percent of the population are mestizos, and 25 percent are Creoles. Only about 10 percent of the people are descended from the Mayas. The rest have African ancestry and are the descendants of slaves brought to work on the plantations. Those with mixed African and European ancestry are called **mulattoes** (moo LAH tohs). Belize has the largest black population in Central America.

Belize has a distinctly British heritage, and the people speak primarily English. About 50 percent of the people are Roman Catholics, and 27 percent are Protestant. Major products of the country include bananas, cacao, citrus, sugar, fish, and garment manufactures. The Mayan ruins and the Belize Barrier Reef, one of the world's longest barrier reefs, make tourism a major industry.

Belize is characterized as a secular nation that allows freedom of religion. Eighty-four percent of the people identify with some form of Christianity, 8 percent are nonreligious, and the remainder follow a variety of eastern or animist religions. Many of those who identify with Christianity also embrace superstitions, black magic, and paganism. The challenge for pastors is great as they teach their people from the Bible and strive to break Satan's hold on those in their congregation who cling to pagan practices. Evangelical Christianity has experienced steady growth from nearly 5 percent in 1960 to 19 percent in 2010.

El Salvador

Although El Salvador has a few Mayan ruins in the mountains, it is most famous for its volcanoes, more than two dozen of which rise above the central plateau—more than in any other Central American nation. Izalco, rising to 6,398 feet and called the "Lighthouse of the Pacific," began to form in 1770 and remained active for almost two hundred years.

Although El Salvador has the smallest area of any Central American country, it is the most densely populated nation on either American continent. Its capital, San Salvador, rivals Guatemala City as the largest metropolitan area in Central America.

Whereas Belize touches only the Caribbean Sea, El Salvador touches only the Pacific Ocean. Most of its people live in the central plateau between the northern mountains and the coast, where they grow coffee, the nation's major crop.

The close-knit "Fourteen Families," descendants of the original Spanish landholders, have owned most of the plantations and controlled the government of El Salvador for most of its history. Bloodshed has been common. Several **juntas** (HOON tahs)—councils of military and civilian leaders—have seized power. A civil war raged from the 1970s to 1992, during which seventy-five thousand people died. Such instability has hindered economic development.

El Salvador's constitution gives special recognition to the Roman Catholic Church but guarantees freedom of religion for other groups. As is true thoughout Central America, a high percentage of the population (95 percent) identifies with some form of Christianity. Evangelical Christians have experienced dramatic growth from 2.3 percent in 1960 to 32 percent in 2010. Since 1990 some nine thousand churches have been planted. Three Christian universities along

Mennonites in Belize

As with most if not all Latin American countries, Belize is culturally diverse and reflects many ethnic groups. In Central America, Belize has—in addition to Creole, Mayan, mestizo, and Indian populations—a group of Mennonites. Mennonite immigrants began to move to Belize after 1958 when the government of Belize granted them exemption from serving in the military and exemption from paying taxes.

Unlike many of the other people groups in Belize, the Mennonites remain isolated, retain their German dialect, and continue to practice their unique culture. While the Mennonites are hard working and skillful in many areas, their contact with other citizens in Belize is limited to commerce.

Although bananas are the major crop of Honduras, it is only one of many countries that produce this fruit.

with eighty Christians schools have been established to train young believers for lay as well as pastoral ministries.

Honduras

The capital and largest city of Honduras, Tegucigalpa (tay goos ih GAHL pah), lies in the mountains that cover most of the country. Most people are peasants, or *campesinos* (kahm pay SEE nohs), who live in one-room bamboo homes called *ranchos* (RAHN chohs). Honduras is 90 percent mestizo. The northeastern region, called the Mosquito Coast, is sparsely populated tropical rain forests and grasslands that extend into Nicaragua.

The major crop of Honduras is bananas, which are grown on the north Caribbean coast. In the early twentieth century, U.S. fruit companies bought large tracts of land and provided much of the nation's income. But the companies used their money to influence politics and to win special privileges. At times, the U.S. government used the threat of military intervention to protect U.S. companies. Because the economy—and governments—rose or fell with the price of one cash crop, Honduras earned the nickname "the banana republic" although it is not even among the top ten banana producers. That term has been used to describe any unstable third world republic, especially one in Latin America.

Honduras has had trouble with both internal coups and its neighbors. In addition to the Nicaraguan Communist insurgency, which the United States sent troops to suppress, Honduras has had border disputes with Nicaragua over the Mosquito Coast and with El Salvador over the removal of squatters. A "Soccer War" in 1969 was precipitated by two highly charged soccer games between Honduras and El Salvador. Fans rioted, the violence spread, and a four-day war resulted.

About 97 percent of the people identify with some form of Christianity. Evangelical churches have experienced steady growth since the 1960s and have grown from 1.7 percent to 23 percent by 2010. Church leaders are struggling to train enough pastors and other Christian workers to meet the rate of growth in the local churches. Several foreign mission agencies are assisting in the area of training and development to meet this need.

Nicaragua

Because highlands cover the central region of Nicaragua, most people live in the fertile Pacific lowlands. Lake Nicaragua, the largest lake in Central America, is famed for its freshwater sharks and three nearby volcanoes. The San Juan River flows east from the lake to the Caribbean Sea. The United States considered building a canal there in the late nineteenth century but built it in Panama instead.

Although Nicaragua is the largest country in Central America, political divisions have stifled its economic progress. The United States has intervened several times to restore order. When Communist rebels (the Sandinista Liberation Front) took over the country in 1979, it marked the second time that a country in the Western Hemisphere was controlled by Communists. (The first was Cuba; see p. 207.) Despite their promises of land reform, the **Sandinistas** (sahn din EES tahs) committed human rights violations and suppressed all opposition. The United States sent large amounts of money and weapons to protect Nicaragua's neighbors and supply the opposition **Contras** (COHN trahs). The Soviet Union supplied arms to the Sandinistas. The collapse of communism in Europe in 1989 left the Sandinistas without financial and military support and forced free elections, which the Sandinistas lost.

Nicaragua continues to struggle to restore and develop its economy. It is primarily an agricultural nation, with almost half of its population employed in agriculture. Its main crops, typical of Central American countries, are sugar, bananas, and coffee.

Ninety-seven percent of the population claim some connection to Christianity, and only 1.7 percent consider themselves nonreligious. In Nicaragua, as in many other Central American countries, Evangelical Christianity has experienced tremendous growth. From 2 percent of the population in 1960, the percentage of Christians has increased to 30 percent in 2010. To support this growth, Christian radio has developed along with distribution of Bibles in Spanish and two other dialects. Christians are also entering the political arena to exercise a stabilizing and moral influence on the unstable political environment.

WORLD RELIGIONS

Roman Catholicism

Roman Catholicism is one of the largest religions in the world with almost a billion members. It is led by the bishop of Rome, who is called the pope. The headquarters of this religion is the country of Vatican City. Catholicism developed in Western Europe during the medieval period, and it now has a worldwide presence.

Roman Catholic religion centers on the seven sacraments of the church, which are believed to bestow saving grace to its members. According to Roman Catholicism, baptism removes original sin from a person. Children of Roman Catholic parents are baptized as infants. At baptism a person is regenerated by the Holy Spirit and is made righteous before God. Baptism, or the desire to be baptized, is necessary for salvation.

Confirmation is a means of receiving strengthening grace from the Holy Spirit. It is usually received when a Catholic child reaches an age of understanding. Even though baptized Catholics are purified and made right with God at baptism, they can still lose this purity by sinning. Mortal sins especially put them in danger of eternal judgment.

Penance is the sacrament that restores a person to a state of grace with God. To receive penance, the person must be truly sorry in his heart for his sin, confess his sin, and make satisfaction for his sin. For a small sin, the satisfaction may be reciting the "Our Father" (the Lord's Prayer) or the "Hail Mary" a set number of times.

The eucharist is the central sacrament in Roman Catholic worship. In the eucharist the bread and wine of the Lord's Supper are believed to become in their essence the actual body and blood of Jesus (though in appearance and taste they remain bread and wine). The eucharist is said to be a sacrifice which makes present Christ's sacrifice on the cross.

Marriage, or matrimony, is also considered a sacrament. Actual grace from God is given to the couple in the wedding to enable their union.

Holy orders is the sacrament given to those who are ordained as deacons, priests, or bishops. At ordination a priest receives the power to absolve sins through the sacrament of penance and to consecrate the bread and wine so that it becomes the body and blood of Christ in the eucharist.

Extreme unction, more commonly called last rites or the anointing of the sick, is the sacrament given to a person who is dying. It provides grace to the dying person so that they do not go to hell because a mortal sin obviated the grace of justification.

Historically, Roman Catholicism has had a strong presence in Latin America. Protestant missionaries were not permitted in Latin American countries until the nineteenth century. However, after liberal governments gained control, many Latin American countries passed laws to limit the influence of the Roman church. It was seen as a supporter of the wealthy oppressors, with some notable exceptions such as Bartolomé de las Casas.

Beginning in the twentieth century, Pentecostalism has proved a significant rival to Catholicism. Nevertheless, Catholicism retains a strong influence on the culture of this region as demonstrated in the various festivals and holidays that are still celebrated. The significance of Latin America to Catholicism may be indicated by the choice of an Argentinian as pope in 2013.

Costa Rica

The area south of Nicaragua's Mosquito Coast has long been known as Costa Rica ("rich coast"), and the name still fits today. Costa Rica has a pleasant climate that has helped the people attain the highest per capita GDP in Central America. The capital, San José, is high in the central plateau and has spring-like temperatures year-round.

Scenic beach in Costa Rica

The main reason for Costa Rica's wealth is its large number of private landowners. About 95 percent of the people are direct descendants of the early Spanish settlers, who developed an efficient system of small, independent farms. In contrast, other Spanish colonies relied on Indian slave labor on large plantations. In Costa Rica, however, most of the Indians fled to the mountains, leaving the Spanish to fend for themselves. Costa Rica was the first Central American country to grow coffee, and that product is its leading export today. Costa Rica was also the first country to raise bananas, its second major crop, for export.

The country is the oldest continuous democracy in Latin America. Except for a dictatorship in 1917–19 and a civil war in 1948–49, the people have freely elected their president since 1889. The country has no army. Its political stability has brought great material prosperity. It has the best education, sanitation, health care, and public services in Central America, and life expectancy is similar to that in North America.

Ninety-four percent of Costa Ricans affiliate with some form of Christianity, and 4 percent identify as nonreligious. Roman Catholicism remains the nation's official religion, and other faiths have religious freedom in theory. However, these groups do not enjoy equality before the law. In spite of this disadvantage, evangelical churches have grown to include 15 percent of the population. Costa Rican Christians also enjoy some of the best training opportunities in Latin America with nearly thirty Bible schools and seminaries.

Panama

Panama is the most developed of all the Central American nations. It has the second-highest per capita GDP in Central America, primarily because of income from the **Panama Canal** and canal-related jobs. Outside the Canal Zone, most people are subsistence farmers. The canal's presence has earned Panama the title "Crossroads of the World."

In 1907–20, the United States built the canal and received control of the zone in perpetuity (essentially forever). In 1979, the United States and Panama signed a treaty whereby Panama would get control of the canal in 1999, which it did.

Panama is considered a secular state that allows religious freedom. Ninety-one percent of the population identifies with some form of Christianity, and 4.3 percent have no religious affiliation. Evangelicals have enjoyed a rapid growth since 1970 and have increased to 20 percent as of 2010. Panama has more than thirty Bible schools and seminaries to train Christians for lay and pastoral positions of leadership. An additional sign of growth is the sending of missionaries from Panamanian churches to other countries.

Panama Canal

The United States keeps separate navy fleets in the Atlantic and Pacific Oceans. During the Spanish-American War, the United States experienced great difficulty in transferring battleships from one ocean to the other. The U.S.S. *Oregon* sailed 12,000 miles around Cape Horn before it finally reached Cuba. Naval officers realized that a canal through Central America would cut the distance by two-thirds, to only 4,600 miles.

French engineers had attempted to build a canal across Panama in 1882 but gave up after seven years and twenty thousand deaths from diseases, such as yellow fever, bubonic plague, and malaria. Before Americans began construction, they drained the mosquito-infested swamps. Construction began in earnest in 1907, with the building of the Gatún Dam that created a 163-square-mile lake. Next came six pairs of locks. Finally, though plagued by landslides, American workers dug the Gaillard Cut, a channel across the continental divide. The S.S. *Ancon* made the first trial crossing in August 1914, and President Woodrow Wilson officially opened the $340 million canal on July 12, 1920.

The Panama Canal Authority has recently invested $1 billion to widen and modernize the canal. In addition, two new flights of locks are being built to allow larger ships to use the canal and handle the expected growth in ship traffic. This construction is anticipated to cost $5.25 billion, with the new locks becoming operational in 2015.

The Gatún Locks are on the Caribbean end of the canal.

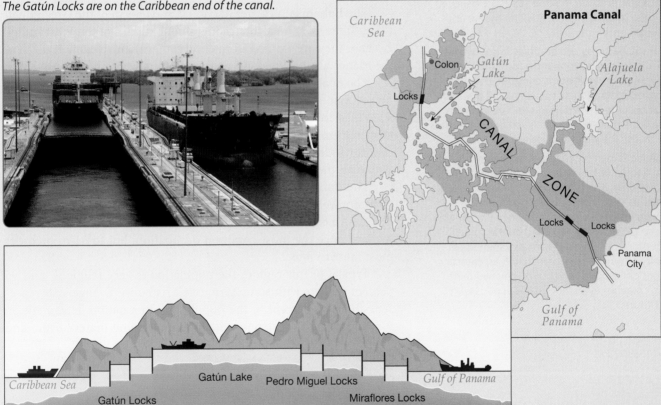

Section Quiz

1–2. What is the most populous nation in Central America? the most densely populated?

3. Which nation was the heart of the Mayan Empire?

4. How is Belize different from the other nations of Central America?

5. What Marxist group once controlled Nicaragua?

★ Why does Costa Rica have the highest per capita GDP in Central America?

Importance of the Spiritual Realm in the Bahamas

The Bahamas is reputed to have the highest ratio of churches per capita in the world. Churches range in size from cathedrals to small single-room buildings. Therefore, it should come as no surprise that most Bahamians practice some form of Christianity. The list includes Anglicans, Baptists, Church of God, Nazarenes, Lutherans, and Roman Catholics. In addition, many have embraced Mormonism and Jehovah's Witness teaching.

However, many Bahamians also embrace superstitions handed down from their African ancestors. There are procedures to ward off malicious spirits and evil influences that include reciting the number 10, reciting the word *Bible*, and spreading guinea grain to keep malicious spirits distracted (the spirits are believed to have to pick up the seeds one by one and count them).

Many Bahamians also embrace forms of magic, including love potions and a form of voodoo. Keeping a dream book is considered a form of good magic. Practitioners record numbers that occur to them during their dreams with the hope that spirits have given these numbers to enable them to win a lottery.

Christians in every culture need to beware of the danger of syncretism—mixing false religious ideas with Christianity. Syncretism seems obvious to cultural outsiders, so American Christians easily recognize it when Bahamians recite the word *Bible* to ward off evil spirits. But American Christians are also sometimes guilty of syncretism. For instance, an entertainment philosophy characterizes many American churches even though it is at odds with Scripture.

III. The West Indies

Between Florida and the northern coast of South America lie about one thousand islands and thousands of tiny *islets* (small, usually uninhabitable islands). Combined, these islands, called the **West Indies**, contain about twice as much land as Pennsylvania. They fall into three main groups: the Bahamas, the Greater Antilles (an TILL ees), and the Lesser Antilles.

Most of the West Indies lie in the tropics, and all have a mild climate. Rainfall averages about thirty inches a year, temperatures are in the 70s or 80s all year, and the vegetation is lush.

Christopher Columbus discovered the West Indies in 1492, landing first in the Bahamas and then on Cuba and Hispaniola. Because he believed the islands to be near India, he called them the Indies and the native peoples Indians. Spanish sailors soon discovered, explored, and claimed most of the other islands of the West Indies.

The Bahamas

The **Bahamas**, a cluster of coral islands north of the Greater Antilles, differ from the other mountainous islands of the West Indies. Because they are formed from coral rather than volcanic lava, all of the islands are low and have neither mountains nor good soils.

The Spanish did not consider the islands of value. The British, however, founded a colony there and, because of their strong navy, soon mastered the whole island chain. Several thousand British Loyalists relocated in the Bahamas with their slaves after the American War for Independence. As more African slaves were brought to the Bahamas, they became a large majority of the population.

The Bahamas are now an independent member of the British Commonwealth. As such, they enjoy the highest standard of living in Middle America. Tax breaks have attracted international banks. Fishing was once the most common occupation, but tourism provides most modern jobs.

Typical of this region, the population is very religious, and 95 percent affiliate with some form of Christianity. Evangelicals represent about 36 percent of the population. In a nation dependent on tourism, there is a strong tendency to become materialistic, and

Nassau, Bahamas

Bahamian Christians struggle with this temptation. A steady decline in moral standards is also adversely affecting the younger generation of believers.

The Greater Antilles

The Antilles islands are the crests of an underwater mountain chain. The western "range" consists of the four largest islands—Cuba, Hispaniola (his pahn YOH lah), Puerto Rico, and Jamaica. Collectively, they are called the **Greater Antilles**.

Spain used these islands as a base for exploring the New World and to protect their shipping routes. They built large sugar plantations and later introduced coffee, tobacco, and fruits. Most islanders in Jamaica and Haiti are descendants of African slaves who worked on the plantations, whereas the people of Cuba, Puerto Rico, and the Dominican Republic are predominantly of Spanish descent.

Cuba

With an area slightly larger than that of Tennessee, **Cuba** is the largest and most populous island in the West Indies. It has more arable land than any other country in Central America or the West Indies. Its fertile soil and central location near both Florida and Mexico made it the most influential island in the Western Hemisphere.

Cuba was once the world's third-largest producer of sugar, but production has fallen significantly because of droughts, declining sugar prices, and excessive government regulation. Most sugar cane is grown on the eastern edge of the island, which receives moist trade winds. Low central mountains block this moisture from reaching the western end. The wet-and-dry climate on the west end of the island is perfect for grazing cattle and growing tobacco. Cuba is also famous for its cigars.

Cuba was one of the last Spanish holdings in Latin America. Spain lost this island, however, in the Spanish-American War in 1898. The victorious United States soon gave up all of Cuba except a naval base at Guantanamo (gwahn TAHN uh moh) Bay, which it still operates. American politicians and businessmen greatly influenced the development of the new Cuba, but the Cubans went through a succession of governments and dictators in trying to establish a strong republican government. The island fell to rebel leader **Fidel Castro** in 1959, and he established the first Communist government in the Western Hemisphere. The Soviet Union became his main ally. As a result, the United States severed diplomatic and trade relations with Cuba.

Thousands of Cubans fled Castro's oppressive rule and came to the United States. Over the years, others have risked their lives on flimsy rafts, including automobiles converted into rafts, trying to

Because of the trade restrictions that have been in place since the Castro revolution, no new cars have been imported, and many Cubans still use 1950s-era cars.

These Cubans modified an old truck into a raft and sought freedom from Castro's regime.

cross the ninety miles to freedom in Florida. Many have succeeded, but many more have been turned back by the U.S. Coast Guard.

Havana, the capital of Cuba, was a thriving tourist and commercial center during the heyday of republican government. It remains the largest city in the West Indies, but it has lost its elegance. While Castro amassed a personal fortune, his people sank into increasing poverty. After the Soviet Union collapsed in 1991, Cuba lost its major trade partner and source of oil. Industries closed, and cities went without power for hours at a time. In the summer of 1994, Havana experienced its worst rioting since Castro took power. Acknowledging economic realities, Castro allowed small-scale private businesses, a few private produce markets, and the foreign ownership of private property. But he failed to achieve his central goal: to reopen trade with the United States. In recent years, Hugo Chavez, leader of Venezuela, has provided Cuba with low cost oil to help improve the Cuban economy. His death in 2013 may lead to the end of this economic assistance. With the impending death of Castro, and the announced retirement of his brother Raúl, observers are speculating on the future of the people and government of Cuba.

Despite five decades of Communist rule, 57 percent of Cubans identify with some form of Christianity. About 9 percent of the population is evangelical, and their numbers continue to increase. While official persecution is not as severe as in the past, Cuban Christians continue to be harrassed and leaders imprisoned. With official opposition to church construction, congregations have resorted to house churches. These churches have proven to be an effective means of growing the church.

Hispaniola: Haiti and the Dominican Republic

Two countries occupy the island of **Hispaniola**. Haiti is on the west side, and the Dominican Republic is on the east side. Although the Spanish were the first settlers on the mountainous island, they gave the western third to France in 1697. France and Spain brought African slaves to both parts of the island.

Haiti—Haiti is the poorest country in the Western Hemisphere but was not always so. Before the slaves on the island revolted against France during the French Revolution, Haiti was the richest colony in the Western Hemisphere, providing most of Europe's tea and sugar cane. When Haiti was declared a republic on January 1, 1804, it became the second republic in the New World.

Unfortunately, revolutionaries had burned the plantations and devastated the countryside. Today, conflicts between rival groups keep the nation in a constant state of turmoil. Another reason for the poverty, especially food deficiency, is linked to land usage. The best land is used for cash crops for export, which limits the amount of good land for food production and produces poorer-quality crops.

Another major cause of Haiti's troubles is its religion. The one characteristic that united the slaves was **voodoo**, a strange mixture of West African spirit worship, black magic, and elements of Roman Catholicism. Many Haitian leaders still rely on voodoo curses and bloodshed to retain power.

Haitians have suffered under a succession of violent dictators, and such instability hinders economic growth. Like most other Latin American countries, Haiti grows such crops as coffee, rice, sugar, mangoes, and corn. What industries it has are primarily associated in some way with those crops, including refining of sugar and milling of flour. Textiles is also one of Haiti's few industries.

The people are divided into two classes: a rich minority (about 5 percent) of mulattoes and a large majority of blacks, most of whom cannot read. Educated Haitians still speak French, but the majority of the people speak a mixture of French and African words called **Creole**.

Ninety-five percent of Haitians identify themselves as Christians and yet around 75 percent of these also practice vodoo. Evangelical Christians represent about 16 percent of the population and are increasing in number. An earthquake in 2010 resulted in 230,000 deaths and 300,000 injuries but also opened the hearts of many Haitians to the truth of the gospel, and many trusted Christ. The need for trained Christian workers and leaders remains great.

Haiti is the poorest and most densely populated Caribbean country.

Dominican Republic—Like Haiti, the Dominican Republic is mountainous. It boasts the highest point in the West Indies: Duarte (DWAHR tay) Peak (10,417 feet). But mountains are the only characteristic the Dominican Republic shares with Haiti. The islanders enjoy a normal life expectancy, high literacy, and a better economy. In the late 1960s, the Dominican Republic, with the help of U.S. military intervention, finally set up a stable republic.

The capital, **Santo Domingo** (SAHN-toh doh-MEEN-goh), founded in 1496 by the brother of Columbus, is the oldest European-established city in the Western Hemisphere. It vies with Havana as the largest city in the West Indies.

Agriculture represents 6 percent of the GDP in the Dominican Republic and produces a variety of crops, including coffee, rice, sugar, cotton, cacao, potatoes, and bananas. Industry is 32 percent of the GDP and includes sugar processing, nickel and gold mining, textiles, cement, and tourism.

Descendants of African slaves intermarried with the Spanish in the Dominican Republic, so today the majority of its people are mulattoes. Spanish is spoken throughout the country, and Catholicism is the major religion. In addition, the people have developed a famous blend of the music and customs of Africa and Spain.

Roman Catholicism is the state religion of the Dominican Republic based on an agreement with the Vatican. While persecution of other faiths is rare, government officials discourage other religious groups. Despite this opposition, Evangelical Christians represent 9 percent of the population.

Jamaica

The island of **Jamaica** was a Spanish colony for 150 years, until the British captured it in 1655. But it took many years for Britain to establish complete control. During the interlude, the Jamaican city of Port Royal became a notorious haven for pirates.

Medical Missions

In Matthew 25:34-46, Jesus gave us an example of how to love the poor and the sick by helping them. Although some Latin American cities are very modern, others are very poor. Haiti remains one of the poorest nations in the world. Without money, the people cannot afford proper medical care. Haiti has only about one doctor per four thousand people, and the infant mortality rate is high at 8.1 per thousand.

The hearts of many missionaries reach out to such needy people. They are willing to forego modern conveniences to bring help. Medical missionaries view their provision of medical care as an opportunity to share the gospel. Christian doctors and nurses work patiently using substandard (by Western expectations) facilities and equipment. Like Paul in 1 Corinthians 9:22, they willingly become weak, even risking tropical diseases, to gain the weak.

Medical missionaries also recognize that the greatest need anyone has is salvation by the work of Jesus Christ. Because of their love for people, medical missionaries take the opportunity to share the gospel of Jesus as they help meet people's medical needs.

Medical missionaries serve God in foreign countries by meeting both the physical and spiritual needs of the people.

Large numbers of African slaves once worked on Jamaica's sugar plantations. Their descendants now make up about 95 percent of the population.

Most Jamaicans speak "Jamaica Talk," a colorful English dialect that mixes many old English words and African pronunciation and grammar. For example, a common greeting is, "Everyt'ing irie?" (Everything all right?)

Some Jamaicans are Roman Catholic, but far more belong to Protestant denominations. Many Jamaicans also follow Rastafarianism (rahs tuh FAHR ee uh niz um), a mixture of African religions and a form of Christianity.

Jamaica became independent in 1962 and has great economic potential. Plantations still produce sugar cane, and Jamaica is a center of the spice trade in the West Indies. It produces some of the world's finest ginger and is a leading producer of allspice. Large deposits of bauxite make the island a major bauxite supplier for the aluminum industry. The stable parliamentary government helps the economy by promoting peace and tourism.

Eighty-four percent of Jamaicans identify with some form of Christianity, and 5 percent have no religious affiliation. Evangelical Christians make up 28 percent of the population, and local churches are beginning to send missionaries to other countries. Much of the recent growth has been under the leadership of Jamaicans rather than foreign missionaries. This has resulted in a strong Jamaican church.

U.S. Commonwealth of Puerto Rico

The Spanish island of **Puerto Rico** came under the control of the United States after the Spanish-American War. The people are mostly of Spanish descent. A few mestizos are the last descendants of the indigenous Arawak (air uh WAHK) people, who intermarried with the Spanish. Puerto Rican farmers produce sugar cane and coffee, but manufacturing has become the island's chief source of income.

In 1951, Puerto Rico voted to become a **commonwealth** of the United States. Puerto Ricans are U.S. citizens with most of the privileges of other American citizens. They have their own constitution and elect a governor, but they cannot vote in presidential elections. They do, however, have a voice in both of the major political parties' presidential nominating conventions. Until recently, the drawback of not having the right to vote in presidential elections was balanced by their having freedom from federal income taxes. An increasing number of Puerto Ricans support becoming the fifty-first state.

Ninety-five percent of the Puerto Rican people affiliate with some form of Christianity, and 4 percent consider themselves nonreligous. Evangelicals represent 25 percent of the population.

The Lesser Antilles

The **Lesser Antilles** are a chain of smaller islands that form the eastern boundary of the Caribbean Sea. The chain curves southward from Puerto Rico to the South American coast. Tourism, fishing, and farming are the main economic activities. Tropical fruits and vegetables are common crops, and some farmers also raise sugar cane, cotton, or coffee.

The Spanish lost interest in the Lesser Antilles when they learned that the islands have no gold and silver, so the islands were left open to settlement by British, French, and Dutch colonists. The people of these islands are mostly black descendants of early slaves. Today, most of the islands remain territories of these three European countries or of the United States. Eight British islands, however, gained independence between 1962 and 1983.

Leeward Islands

The northern islands of the Lesser Antilles, from the Virgin Islands to Dominica (dah mih NEE cuh), are called the **Leeward Islands**. The word *leeward* refers to an island that is sheltered from prevailing winds on the open ocean. The Leeward Islands are sheltered from many tropical storms that rip through the Windward Islands farther south and east.

Just east of Puerto Rico are the most famous Leewards—the Virgin Islands. Three major islands and about a hundred islets belong to the United States, and the rest belong to Great Britain.

Most of the remaining colonies lie southeast of the Virgin Islands. Anguilla (an GWIL uh) and Montserrat (mahnt suh RAHT) are British. The Dutch control Saba (SAY buh), St. Eustatius (yoo STAY shus), and St. Maarten (MAHR tin). Guadeloupe (gwah duh LOOP) is the main French island. Three independent countries lie in the Leeward Islands: St. Kitts and Nevis (NEE vis), Antigua (an TEE guh) and Barbuda (bar BOO duh), and Dominica (doh min NEE cuh). English is the national language of all three countries, each of which has a high literacy rate. Their economies are similar to those of the Central American nations.

Windward Islands

The **Windward Islands** face the prevailing southeasterly winds that blow off the Atlantic Ocean. They suffer the full brunt of hurricanes. The chain runs from Martinique (mahr tih NEEK) to Grenada (greh NAY dah). Martinique is a French territory, but the other islands are former British territories that gained independence in the 1970s. St. Lucia (LOO shuh) is the northernmost of the three nations. Most of the middle islands are owned by St. Vincent and the Grenadines (gren uh DEENZ). The southernmost Windward nation is Grenada.

These Barbadian sailors are taking part in an Independence Day parade.

Outlying Lesser Antilles

The other islands of the Lesser Antilles are not part of the chain of Leeward and Windward Islands. Trinidad, nearly two thousand square miles in area, is the largest of the Lesser Antilles. Trinidad and Tobago (tuh BAY goh) became independent of Great Britain in 1962, making it the first independent nation in the Lesser Antilles. Barbados (bahr BAY dohs) is the only other independent nation in the Lesser Antilles. It has by far the greatest population density in the Western Hemisphere, yet its people vie with Trinidad and Tobago for the highest GDP in Middle America.

Section Quiz

1–3. What three island groups form the West Indies?

4–5. What two nations share the island of Hispaniola?

6–7. What two island chains form the east boundary of the Caribbean Sea?

★ Do you think Puerto Rico should become the fifty-first state? Why or why not?

Chapter Review

Making Connections

1. Contrast the federal governments of Mexico and the United States.
2. Contrast the hacienda and the plantation economy.
3. What is the most productive and populous region of Mexico? Why?
4. What role has land ownership played in Latin America's political unrest?
5. Why is Roman Catholicism prominent throughout Latin America?

Developing Geography Skills

1. What geographic obstacles make securing the border between the U.S. and Mexico difficult?
2. What geographic obstacles in your state would make securing the borders of your state difficult?

Thinking Critically

1. Why have many Latin American countries been plagued by political turmoil? Why have the United States and Canada experienced more political stability?
2. Should the United States try to prevent illegal aliens from entering our country? Why or why not? What is the solution to this problem?

Living in God's World

1. The good aspects of any culture reflect something of the image of God in humanity that is preserved despite the Fall. What aspect or aspects of Mexican or Central American culture could you as a Christian learn from? Write a paragraph describing this aspect of culture and how you could implement aspects of it in your daily life.
2. Compare and contrast Roman Catholic and conservative Protestant teachings regarding baptism, penance/repentance, and the Lord's Supper. Evaluate which position best matches the biblical data.

People, Places, and Things to Know

Latin America
Middle America
land bridge
Baja California
Bay of Campeche
Sierra Madre Oriental
Sierra Madre Occidental
Tijuana
Juarez
Monterrey
Northern Plateau
Copper Canyon
Veracruz
Cancún
Acapulco
Sonoran Desert
saguaro cacti
Mexican Plateau
altitude zone
Mexico City
Toltec
Aztecs
hacienda
peones
coup
mestizos
ejidos
Sierra Madre Del Sur
Chiapas
isthmus
Central America
plantation economy
Mayas
mulattoes
junta
Sandinistas
Contras
Panama Canal
West Indies
Bahamas
Greater Antilles
Cuba
Fidel Castro
Havana
Hispaniola
voodoo
Creole
Santo Domingo
Jamaica
Puerto Rico
commonwealth
Lesser Antilles
Leeward islands
Windward Islands

Children dressed in Incan clothing

SOUTH AMERICA

*S*outh America is a continent that is significant for many reasons, including its cultural diversity and wealth of resources. People all over this continent depend on its resources, ranging from the lush rainforests of the Amazon to the snowy peaks of the highlands.

During the Age of Exploration, the Spanish and Portuguese were the first Europeans to discover this continent and soon came to realize the immense potential for wealth that would benefit their respective nations. In order to prevent conflict between these powers, Pope Alexander VI drew a line on a map to divide the world between Spain and Portugal. A revised line resulted in Brazil being given to Portugal. That is why Brazilians speak Portuguese instead of Spanish, the only nation in South America to do so.

While the geographic features of South America are majestic, they have tended to isolate people groups. Thus, these countries often had more interaction with Europe than with each other. However, increased international trade and management of resources have led to more regional interaction.

Sadly, one of South America's greatest resources, the Amazon, is losing trees. The largest rainforest in the world, it has undergone massive deforestation during the past two decades, and this jungle graveyard has grown to cover an area the size of France. Such extensive deforestation could change the climate of the area and push unique and useful plants and animals to the brink of extinction.

South America Fast Facts						
Country	Capital	Area (sq. mi.)	Pop. (M) (2013 est.)	Pop. Density (per sq. mi.)	Per Capita GDP ($US)	Life Span
Argentina	Buenos Aires	1,068,297	42.61	40	$17,700	77.14
Bolivia	La Paz & Sucre	424,162	10.46	25	$4,800	67.9
Brazil	Brasília	3,286,472	201.00	61	$11,800	72.79
Chile	Santiago	292,257	17.22	59	$17,400	78.1
Colombia	Bogotá	439,735	45.75	104	$10,200	74.79
Ecuador	Quito	109,483	15.44	141	$8,500	75.94
Guiana	Cayenne	32,253	0.24	7	$20,904	77.1
Guyana	Georgetown	83,000	0.74	9	$7,600	67.39
Paraguay	Asunción	157,047	6.62	42	$6,200	76.4
Peru	Lima	496,222	29.85	60	$10,100	72.73
Suriname	Paramaribo	63,037	0.57	9	$11,800	71.12
Uruguay	Montevideo	68,037	3.32	49	$15,100	76.41
Venezuela	Caracas	352,143	28.46	81	$12,600	74.08

I. The Caribbean Countries

Two South American nations—Colombia (coh LOHM bee yah) and Venezuela (vehn uh ZWAY lah)—border the Caribbean Sea. Their peoples are a mixture of descendants from native Indians, Spanish conquerors, and African slaves.

Venezuela and Colombia share many geographic features with Middle America. The Western Cordillera extends into South America, where it is known as the **Andes** (AN dees). Although Colombia and Venezuela are located in the tropics, altitude is the major influence on climate. Most people live in the temperate *tierra templada*.

The Spanish and Portuguese colonial systems created great resentment in the colonies. The ruling *peninsulares* (peh neen soo LAHR ehs) from Spain treated their subjects with contempt. Their subjects included the Spanish criollos (cree OH yohs), or Creoles (CREE ohls), born in America. The Creoles became restive and finally revolted, led by the greatest hero of Latin America, **Simón Bolívar** (see-MOHN boh-LEE-vahr), "the Liberator." He was born in 1783 to a rich Creole family in Caracas, Venezuela. During a trip to Europe, he was inspired by the revolutionary fervor of the French Revolution. After a failed attempt to liberate his homeland, he fled to Haiti. Returning, he defeated the Spanish in 1819 outside the capital of New Granada (Santa Fe de Bogotá). The Battle of Boyacá (boy yah CAH) liberated Colombia but not the other divisions of New Granada. Next, Bolívar turned east and freed Venezuela. Finally, he turned south and liberated Ecuador. Bolívar then became the president and dictator of a united nation he called Gran (grahn, "great") Colombia. But the union broke apart a decade later.

During the sixteenth and seventeenth centuries, Cartagena was part of the Spanish Main, a series of seaports for the Spanish treasure fleet.

Colombia

Like Central America, Colombia is located at the crossroads of the American continents. Its one-hundred-mile border with Panama is South America's only geographic tie to North America. In fact, the lowlands of Panama were once part of Colombia. Colombia also shares South America's two main geographic features—the Andes Mountains and the Amazon Basin.

Ninety-four percent of Colombians identify with some form of Christianity, and 3 percent practice traditional religions. Evangelical Christians make up 8 percent of the population and have grown significantly from about 0.6 percent in 1960. This growth has occurred despite violent opposition by drug cartels and paramilitary groups. More encouraging is the fact that most of the growth has been in indigenous congregations.

Caribbean and Pacific Lowlands

Colombia is unique in South America because it has coasts on both the Caribbean and the Pacific. Although the Caribbean lowlands are hot, about one-fifth of the population lives there, many of the people working on plantations. Few people live on the swampy Pacific coast, where the average annual rainfall is four hundred inches.

The Mountainous Interior

Most Colombians live in the cool valleys of the Andes Mountains. The Andes, which follow the entire west coast of South America, split into three separate ranges in Colombia, part of them stretching northward toward the Caribbean. The western range, or **Cordillera Occidental**, is the lowest of the three. Next is the **Cordillera Central**. The easternmost range, or **Cordillera Oriental**, reaches into Venezuela.

The capital of Colombia, Santa Fe de **Bogotá** (boh guh TAH), lies in the Cordillera Oriental. A teeming city of 7.8 million people (8.5 million in the metropolitan area), Bogotá is the cultural center of

Bogotá is both the capital and the chief economic center of Colombia.

World's Leading Coffee-Producing Countries (2010)

1. Brazil
2. Vietnam
3. Colombia
4. Indonesia
5. India
6. Ethiopia
7. Honduras
8. Peru
9. Guatemala
10. Mexico

the nation. As in other Latin American cities, however, rural workers live in large slums, or *turgurios* (toor GOO ree ohs).

The four other Colombian cities with populations of more than a million lie along the two river valleys between Colombia's three Andes ranges. Cartagena (cahr tah HAY nah) and Barranquilla (bahr rahn KEE yah) are near the Caribbean coast on the deepest river, the Magdalena, "the lifeline of Colombia." Oceangoing ships can travel up the river far into the interior. Major oil wells operate in the Magdalena River valley. Medellín (meh deh YEEN) is in the west central area near Panama, and Cali (CAH lee) is farther to the southwest near the Pacific coast. Both cities are on the Cauca (COW cah) River. Bogotá, Medellín, and Cali form Colombia's "industrial triangle."

The Andes provide Colombia with several important products. Colombia is one of the world's largest coffee-producing countries, harvesting most of the beans used to make Arabica coffee.

Colombia is also rich in natural resources. It has the largest coal reserves in Latin America and the only platinum mines in South America. It is a leading producer of gold and also mines about half of

Who Grows the Best Coffee Bean?

Coffee has become the world's most popular hot beverage, and the United States leads the world in coffee consumption. The ten-minute coffee break is a common ritual. But not all coffees are the same. Even the closest of friends argue over which coffee bean is best.

According to legend, a goat herder in Ethiopia discovered coffee in the fourteenth century when his goats stayed awake all night after munching on the beans. Arab traders were the first to popularize brewed coffee. From the Arabian Peninsula, coffee plants have been transported around the world. The world's leading coffee-producing countries are located in or very near the tropics.

Two species of coffee plants are grown on plantations. The Arabs cultivated *Coffea arabica*, exporting beans from the famous coffee port of Mocha.

Arabica is now grown throughout Latin America and much of Asia. The other species is *Coffea robusta*. This hardy plant thrives in the hot, rainy tropics of Africa. A robusta coffee plant produces about four pounds of beans, twice that of an arabica coffee plant.

So why doesn't everyone grow C. robusta, if it is so hardy and productive? The key to good coffee is *aroma*, or smell. Africa's robusta plant has a cereal-like aroma. Most coffee-drinkers prefer arabica coffee. It has two popular varieties: the Milds give off a fruity aroma mixed with the smell of flowers; the Brazils have an earthy aroma with more neutral flavors.

Although Brazil leads the world in coffee production, its beans are considered inferior to those of Colombia, Brazil's main South American competitor. The Andean soil of Colombia is

much better for flavor than the soil of Brazil. Perhaps surprisingly, Vietnam is the second-leading coffee producer, and Colombia is third. Excellent coffees are also grown on the Indonesian island of Java, and sometimes coffee is even called java.

The major reason for coffee's popularity is not its aroma and flavor but the stimulant caffeine, which explains why so many people drink coffee to "get going" in the morning. Caffeine, however, is highly addictive. Withdrawal symptoms include headaches and nervousness. Mormons and conservative Muslims believe that it is sinful to drink coffee.

Of the two major types of coffee beans, arabica beans (left) are preferred for their flavor. Robusta beans (right) contain almost twice as much caffeine and are often used in cheap instant coffees.

the world's emeralds. Those emeralds set the standard of quality for all other countries' emeralds.

On the east side of the Andes lies a vast wilderness, one of the largest undeveloped areas in the world. These broad grassy plains, called the **Llanos** (YAH nohs), cover 60 percent of Colombia and 30 percent of Venezuela. The northernmost rivers of the Llanos flow into the Caribbean Sea, but the southern rivers flow into the Amazon River. Most of this area had been controlled by guerrillas who drove out at least 500,000 settlers during the 1990s. Recent agreements have led to the disbanding of the guerillas and improved prospects for peace.

Venezuela

In 1802, Venezuela became the first Spanish colony to declare independence. Like the merchants in Boston who reacted against Britain's Stamp Act, merchants in Venezuela resisted Spanish laws restricting trade. **Caracas** (kah RAH kahs), the nation's capital, still honors the man who eventually became their liberator, Simón Bolívar, whose tomb is there.

Venezuela's culture is shaped by a great diversity of people groups. Influences include American Indian, Spanish, African, Portuguese, Arab, and German. While Spanish is the official language, over forty languages are spoken. Venezuela's proximity to the Caribbean is reflected in its architecture and art. While the people enjoy a great variety of music, *joropo* (hoh ROH poh) which is similar to the waltz, is one of the most popular genres.

Ninety-four percent of Venezuelans practice some form of Christianity, and only 0.5 percent claim to be nonreligious. Sadly, many of those claiming to be Christian also practice spiritism (occult, witch doctors, etc.). Evangelical Christians represent about 11 percent of the population and continue to increase numerically and in influence. Members of local congregations are becoming socially and politically involved to help solve problems such as poverty, crime, and political corruption.

Coastal Mountains

In Venezuela, the Andes taper into the Caribbean Sea. The people prefer to live in the mild highlands on the coastal side of the Andes. Although it is short compared to some other summits of the Andes, Bolívar Peak exceeds sixteen thousand feet.

Near the northwest coast of Venezuela is **Lake Maracaibo** (mah rah KYE boh), the largest lake on the continent of South America. This shallow lake connects to the Caribbean Sea by a narrow inlet, but its water is fresh. The discovery of oil fields under the lake made Venezuela the richest country on the continent. Venezuela sells most of its oil to the United States.

The Interior Wilderness

On the far side of the Andes, Venezuela shares the Llanos with Colombia. Waters flowing off the Andes drain into the Llanos's **Orinoco** (oh ree NO koh) **River**, the third-longest river on the continent. In one strange place near the source of the Orinoco, it splits so that some of the water flows into the Amazon River system. Flesh-eating fish called piranha live in these two great river systems.

Missions in Venezuela

While Venezuela's government is described as a federal republic, in reality, it is little more than a dictatorship. Following the death of Hugo Chavez in 2013, the hope for stability and increased representation remains in doubt.

With a totalitarian government as well as high inflation and high unemployment, Venezuela continues to be a very difficult field for missionaries. While the Venezuelan constitution guarantees freedom of worship, in practice, the government sometimes expels missionaries and imprisons national Christians with no regard for their rights.

Given these circumstances, missionaries in Venezuela are concentrating on training national Christians to become pastors and teachers. Since the door of opportunity for foreign missionaries may close at any moment, the need for well-equipped Christian Venezuelan leaders is urgent.

Angel Falls

At 3,212 feet, Angel Falls is easily the highest waterfall in the world. The upper part plummets more than half a mile straight down, and then it cascades down rocks for the remaining 564 feet.

The water issues through cracks in the side of the cliff, just below the top of a mesa. The springs merge as they fall, crashing on the rocks below and sending up blankets of mist and spray. The waters eventually reach the Atlantic Ocean via the Orinoco River.

Angel Falls is not named after its appearance, but after Jimmie Angel, an American pilot who spotted the falls in 1933 while flying over the remote Guiana Highlands. The region is still wild, but small planes offer air tours to view the falls.

Mount Roraima's Influence on a Famous Fiction Writer

The isolated biome of Mount Roraima inspired Sir Arthur Conan Doyle to write *The Lost World* about dinosaurs and ape men cut off from the rest of the world. The first explorers, who reached the tabletop in 1884, discovered several new species of animals—but no dinosaurs.

The mountains that separate the Orinoco from the Amazon are called the Guiana (gee AH nah) Highlands. This wilderness region contains Angel Falls and Cuquenán Falls, two of the highest falls in the world.

Section Quiz

1. According to the map on page 216, on which coast are most of Colombia's ports?
2–3. What are the key products of each Caribbean country?
4. What lowland wilderness do the Caribbean countries share?
⭑ Why do few people live along Colombia's Pacific coast?

II. The Guiana Highlands

The **Guiana Highlands** are the rugged plateau that separates Venezuela's Caribbean coast from the Amazon Basin. Whereas Spain and Portugal controlled most of South America, three other European powers founded small colonies on the coast below the Guiana Highlands. These colonies became known as the Guianas.

The tropical climate supports rice, sugar cane, and banana plantations along the coast. In the interior, several coffee plantations operate in the highlands, and herds of cattle graze on grasslands. The European colonists imported black slaves to work on the plantations. After slavery was abolished in the nineteenth century, many blacks moved inland. The Europeans then hired laborers from India and Indonesia who brought their languages and Hindu religion.

Guyana

The westernmost colony of the Guianas was British. It became the country of Guyana (guy AN nuh) in 1966, although the border with Venezuela was not yet settled. English is the national language of the republic, but indigenous tribes in the remote rain forests still speak their own tongues. Most of the people of the country live in the flat lowlands near the coast.

Huge, block-shaped mountains, called **tepuis** (TEH pwees), rise above the highlands in the interior of Guyana. On the top are savannas. The highest *tepui*, Mount Roraima (9,219 ft.), towers above the junction between Venezuela, Guyana, and Brazil. Waters from this mountain flow south into the Amazon and north into the Orinoco.

Tepuis, such as this one near Mount Roraima, rise above the surrounding landscape.

From 1965 to 1985 this country was ruled by a Marxist regime that promoted atheism. However, 53 percent of the people identify with some form of Christianity, and only 4 percent have no religious affiliation. Evangelical Christians make up 20 percent of the population, and they continue to grow numerically despite a declining population. While not all churches are multiethnic, some are. These multiethnic churches help to bridge the racial division that remains a serious problem in this fragile country.

River taxis are one means of getting around in Paramaribo, the capital of Suriname.

Suriname

East of Guyana is a country formerly named Dutch Guiana but today called Suriname (soo rih NAH muh). It changed its name after receiving its independence in 1975. The Dutch brought the first coffee to South America, but the modern economy depends on bauxite (aluminum ore). Suriname has the fewest people per square mile of any nation on the continent. Its population density is similar to Canada's.

About half of Suriname's population embraces some form of Christianity. Evangelical Christians represent about 14 percent of the population. Many of the Maroon people and the Amerindians have thriving churches. Some local Amerindian congregations have started to send out missionaries to other tribes, villages in Guiana, and other regions of their own country.

Guiana

Formerly known as French Guiana, Guiana is the only part of the continent that is still under European control. It sends a representative to the French legislature in Paris. Although Cayenne (KYE en) is the major town, the most famous place in the territory is Devil's Island, an abandoned prison colony much like Alcatraz in San Francisco Bay.

Guiana is considered a secular state but does allow freedom of religion. Ninety-one percent of the population identifies with some form of Christianity, 3 percent are non-religious, and 2 percent practice traditional religions. Evangelicals represent about 5 percent of the population and are experiencing steady numerical growth. Churches are also being planted among many minority populations, especially Amerindian groups.

Until 1946, Devil's Island was the virtually inescapable maximum security prison that housed some of France's most notorious political and violent criminals.

Section Quiz

1. What word is used for the huge, block-shaped mountains that tower above the highlands of Guyana?
2. Besides Spain and Portugal, what European nations had colonies in South America?
3. What is the highest waterfall in the world?
4. What nation has the lowest population density in South America?
5. What is the only foreign-controlled region in South America?
* Why is the wildlife so unusual on the *tepuis*?

III. The Andean Countries

The Andes Mountains dwarf the mountains of North America. They form the highest mountain range in the Western Hemisphere, making them the highlight of the entire cordillera from Alaska to Chile. More than fifty peaks exceed twenty thousand feet, and at least forty of them are higher than Mount McKinley. These peaks are the highest mountains outside of Asia.

The Andes also form the longest mountain range in the world, stretching about forty-five hundred miles. These mountains divide the continent of South America. Water flowing west runs immediately into the Pacific. Water flowing east runs for many miles before it reaches the Atlantic. The Andes lie so close to the Pacific coast that in some areas the mountains slope directly down to the shore, leaving steep cliffs and jagged rocks at the water's edge. In other areas, a narrow plain lines the shore.

Because the Andean nations lie mostly in the warm and humid tropics, most of the people live high in the *tierra templada*. Isolated Indians there have been able to retain much of their culture. In sharp contrast to the Caribbean nations, four out of five people in Andean nations have some Indian heritage, either mestizo or full-blooded Indian. Unfortunately, the volcanoes of the Pacific Ring of Fire threaten many mountain villages.

Ecuador

Ecuador means "equator," an apt name for the country because the equator cuts across it. Hot coastal lowlands cover about one-quarter of Ecuador, a much greater percentage than other Andean nations. As a result, Ecuador is a major exporter of bananas and cacao (a plant that is used to make chocolate, cocoa, and cocoa butter). The nation's largest city and leading commercial center is Guayaquil (gwy uh KEEL), a port city. It is the center of one of the world's largest shrimp-producing industries.

The Andes cover another one-quarter of Ecuador. Chimborazo (chim boh RAH zoh), Ecuador's tallest peak, is higher than Mount McKinley. More famous is **Cotopaxi** (koh toh PAHK see), one of the highest active volcanoes in the world at 19,347 feet.

Volcanic Mount Cotopaxi looks down on the surrounding landscape of Ecuador.

A Missionary Encounters Cultural Differences

Sid and Susie Messer, Ecuador

The more a missionary understands the culture to which God has called him, the more success he will have in reaching the people of that culture. We encountered a specific cultural difference when we moved into our first home in Ecuador. Several Ecuadorian workers had come to the house to place new tile in one of the rooms. As on any other day in Ecuador, the sun was shining with all its glory and causing the workers to sweat profusely. With our eye fixed on developing a friendship with the visitors in order to share the gospel, we wanted to display the love and kindness of the Lord. So we naturally set out for them a large pitcher of ice water and several cups. To our surprise, at the end of the day, not a single drop of water had been taken, and our relationship with the workers was about as cold as the ice water.

We later found out that many Ecuadorians do not drink ice water because they believe it will give them a cold and make them sick. Obviously, setting something out to drink that they believed would make them sick was not the best way to develop rapport and trust. Once we were aware of that mentality, we set out the same pitcher of water but with no ice. This time at the end of the day, not a single drop of water was left and the gospel was more readily received. Now we know that a pitcher of water at room temperature is the best way to initiate a friendly relationship with visiting Ecuadorians.

Find It!

Cotopaxi

0.680° S, 78.438° W

The Galápagos Islands

The Galápagos (gah LAH pah gohs) Islands, five hundred miles west of Ecuador, were named by the Spanish for the huge five-hundred-pound tortoises that roamed the islands. These giants provided crews with a ready source of fresh meat and could survive in the ship's hold for a year or more without food or water.

Some Spanish sailors first discovered these remote islands when their vessel drifted off course. The sixteen islands are dotted with volcanoes, a handful of which are still active. During the seventeenth and eighteenth centuries, English pirates buried stolen treasures on the islands. In the nineteenth century, whaling ships and seal hunters visited to pick up fresh water and supplies. Their mailbox on Santa Maria Island, where outbound whalers left letters for inbound vessels, is still in use. In 1832, the islands became a part of Ecuador.

Isolation allowed many unusual animals to flourish on the islands. Although the islands straddle the equator, the cold Peru Current keeps the weather mild and dry. Antarctic animals, such as penguins and fur seals, live alongside tropical animals, such as four-foot-long iguanas, flamingoes, and a mockingbird unknown elsewhere. Twenty-eight species of birds and nineteen species of reptiles on the Galápagos are found nowhere else in the world. Charles Darwin used his study of Galápagos finches in 1835 to support his theory of evolution.

Most of the Galápagos Islands are too rocky and dry to support human life. However, in 2006, an estimated 25,000 people lived on the islands of Santa Cruz, Floreana (Santa Maria), Baltra, Isabela, and San Cristobal. The people living close to the coast earn a living by fishing. Although less than 4 percent of the island's land area is suited for agriculture, parts of the moist highlands produce vegetables, tropical fruits, and field crops. Coffee and cattle are among the few products exported to the mainland.

Most Ecuadorians live in the Andes. **Quito** (KEE toh), the capital and second-largest city in the nation, lies on a high and cool mountain plateau. At a monument outside Quito, one can stand with one foot in the Northern Hemisphere and the other foot in the Southern Hemisphere.

To the east of the Andes lies the **Amazon rain forest**, where few people lived until the discovery of oil in 1967. A pipeline across the Andes has turned Ecuador into the second-leading oil producer in South America, and oil now is Ecuador's top export. Oil spills and the resulting pollution have caused problems, however, as the Ecuadorians learn how to be good stewards of their most valuable resource—the land.

After centuries of control by Spain, Ecuador remains 81 percent Roman Catholic. Evangelical Christianity multiplied from 17,000 in 1960 to 1.2 million (11.5 percent of the population) in 2010. Most of this growth occurred in the cities and among the Quichua people.

The mountainous terrain of Quito, the capital of Ecuador, differs sharply from the coastal lowlands.

Peru

South of Ecuador is Peru, the largest Andean nation. The Andes ranges, which narrow to 100 miles near Quito, spread to 250 miles in Peru. Eleven peaks exceed twenty thousand feet. One of the highest railroads in the world crosses these mountains.

The Cordillera Blanca (*White Range*), a mountain range in Peru

The mountains are broken by some of the deepest canyons in the world. Colca Canyon, which slices through the west side of the Andes into the Pacific, is twice the depth of the Grand Canyon. The second-deepest canyon, the Apurimac, cuts through the eastern side of the Andes. Its streams form the headwaters of the mighty Amazon River.

Peru has some of the highest major mines in the world. It is one of the largest gold producers in the world. It is also a major producer of zinc and copper.

Ninety-five percent of the Peruvian people associate with some form of Christianity, and 3 percent have no religious affiliation. Twelve percent of the population are evangelicals, a dramatic increase from 1960 when they represented less than 1 percent of the Peruvian people. In addition to strengthening local churches, evangelicals are addressing social and political issues that negatively impact the people of Peru.

Children of the Sun

A series of Indian civilizations arose along the plateaus and valleys of the Andes. The last and greatest was the civilization of the **Incas**, whose name means "children of the sun." At its height, the Incan Empire controlled most of the Andes. The Incas, far from being the primitive people one might envision, were quite ingenious. They built an amazing two-thousand-mile network of stone roads, some of which are still used today; dug tunnels through mountains; built causeways over swamps; and bridged chasms with rope suspension bridges. The Incan Empire was particularly impressive because, unlike the Egyptian and Mesopotamian Empires, the Incas had no waterways to provide easy transportation.

Although they had no written language, the Incas invented the *quipu* (KEE poo), a code using strings of llama wool knotted together on a rope. The meaning of each message depended on the size and number of knots and the color of the wool. Runners relayed these knot messages to and from the capital. The emperor could send a message two hundred miles in a single day.

Cusco (KOOS koh) was the sacred Inca capital. The streets were laid out in the shape of a puma, with the fortress Sacsayhuaman forming the puma's head. When the Spanish conquistador **Francisco**

The Andes Mountains of Peru include deep canyons and a large concentration of snow peaks.

Machu Picchu

For centuries, the Inca stronghold of Machu Picchu (MAH-choo PEEK-choo) remained hidden from European eyes. Legends spoke of a mountain "city in the clouds," but adventurers were baffled by the rugged terrain and tangled vegetation. Finally, Hiram Bingham of Yale University set out to find Vilcabamba, the last refuge of the Incas who fled from Pizarro. However, the breathtaking ruins he found in 1911 were those of Machu Picchu. Located just sixty miles northwest of Cusco, these ruins continue to amaze visitors.

Machu Picchu rises precariously between two craggy peaks. Somehow Inca craftsmen carried supplies up to the five-acre plateau, 7,875 feet in the clouds. Pure white granite temples, palaces, and dwellings served about

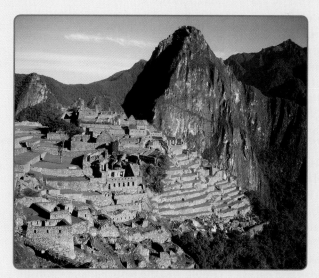

fifteen hundred people. Without mortar or iron tools, the engineers cut stones that fit together perfectly. Even earthquakes of recent centuries have not toppled them. The Incas also hauled dirt from the valley to provide soil for vegetable gardens on the slopes.

No one knows what happened to the Incas who lived there. Perhaps they abandoned the stronghold when their last emperor died. Tradition says that seventy young ladies who served in the Sun Temple at Cusco escaped to Machu Picchu and died there. A later exploration discovered the ruins of Vilcabamba and determined that it was a minor outpost deep in the Amazon rain forest.

Pizarro (frahn-SEES-coh pee-SAHR-oh) arrived in 1531, the empire was torn by feuds, allowing Pizarro to easily capture the Great Inca and hold him for ransom. He promised to let him go if the people filled a royal chamber once with gold and twice with silver. When the deed was done, however, the Spanish did not keep their end of the bargain. They killed the Inca emperor but left the city intact. After plundering the gold and silver, the Spaniards forced the Incas to work in the haciendas and mines. More than a quarter million Indians still live in Cusco, making it the oldest continually inhabited city in the New World.

Old ethnic distinctions remain strong in Peru, partly because social values left over from the Incan Empire help maintain the divide between Indian and Hispanic populations. The so-called upper class consists of descendants of Europeans, who own the coastal plantations and hold most positions of leadership. More than 40 percent of Peruvians are mestizos, who make up the middle class. They own most of the farms in the Andes. Mestizos usually speak an Indian language but learn Spanish to improve their social status.

The so-called lower classes consist of Indians descended from the Incas. Most of them speak the Inca language, **Quechua** (KEH chwa), the most widely spoken native language in South America. Several English words, such as *puma* and *llama*, come from Quechua. Many Indians believe they should keep their place in society. They look down on the *cholos* (CHOH lohs)—Indians who learn Spanish and dress like mestizos.

Desert Coasts

The high mountain barrier of the Andes has a disadvantageous effect on the coastal climate of South America. Easterly winds from

> ### *Converting Quechua to a Written Language*
>
> Quechua, along with many other indigenous languages in South America, was once only spoken; it had no standard written alphabet or grammar. During the last century, Christian missionaries labored to establish spelling and grammar standards. Their work demonstrated the effectiveness of using linguistics to spread the gospel. As Christians help create the means by which a people group is able to communicate in writing, they are able to shape that culture with the Scriptures.

Camels of the Western Hemisphere

The Indians of the New World never had the advantage of large beasts of burden—such as horses, cattle, and camels—that were essential to the Old World. The Indians of North America had only dogs, but the peoples of the Andes made use of four small members of the camel family called lamoids.

The four "camels of the Andes" are the guanaco (gwah NAH koh), vicuña (vi KOO nyah), alpaca (al PAK uh), and llama. The first two are found mainly in the wild, but alpacas and llamas were domesticated and live only in captivity. Generally speaking, lamoids have small heads, long legs and necks, and large pointed ears. Unlike camels,

Alpacas in Northern Chile

they have no hump. The lamoids supplied the ancient Incas with wool, meat, and leather. The most useful lamoid was the large llama, which stands four feet tall at the shoulder and weighs up to three hundred pounds.

The llama is well suited for mountain life. Its lungs are used to the thin air, and like other lamoids, it has a much greater concentration of oxygen-carrying red blood cells than other mammals. Its coarse, woolly hair provides plenty of warmth. It can survive on the sparse grasses and shrubs on the rocky mountain slopes. The llama can go for weeks without a

Guanaco (above) in Chilean Patagonia; vicuña (below) in Northern Chile

drink, drawing both fluid and nourishment from the food alone.

A sure-footed pack animal, the llama easily climbs the steep trails of the high mountains. It is able to travel eighteen miles per day while carrying a load of up to 130 pounds. However, a llama knows its limits. When overburdened or exhausted, a llama will sit down and refuse to move. If forced to get up, it may hiss and spit foul saliva (like its camel cousins do).

Llamas occupied a special place in the Inca religion. An excavation of an ancient Inca city in Peru uncovered a large sacrifice table in the shape of a llama. Because llamas were indispensable for transporting people and their goods, they played a key role in the Incan economy and culture. Today people still find many uses for the llama: the hide for sandals, the hair for rope, the fat for candles, and even the droppings for fuel.

North American llama

the Atlantic Ocean drop their moisture as they cross the Andes, leaving almost no water for the rain shadow on the western side of the Andes. The problem is compounded by the **Peru Current** (also called the Humboldt Current), which flows north from the Antarctic. The cold current keeps the air cold and dry. The Sechura (seh CHOO rah) Desert lies on the north coast of Peru. However, irrigation is possible farther south, where swift rivers descend from the Andes.

Pizarro established his headquarters, **Lima** (LEE mah), on one of these swift rivers, and it became the capital of Peru and the largest city of the Andean countries. The average rainfall there is only two inches per year, but a moist cloud, called garúa, settles on the desert city during the winter. One-quarter of Peru's people live there. It is a city of contrasts; along with beautiful Spanish architecture, it has the largest *barriadas* (bahr ree AH dahs), or slums, on the continent.

Ruins from several ancient Indian empires dot the coastal desert. North near the modern city of Trujillo (troo HEE yoh) lies Chan Chan. Covering six square miles, it is all that remains of the powerful Chimu Empire of the twelfth century. Nearby, archeologists have found ruins of the earlier Moche Empire (AD 100–700), including burial chambers stocked with gold, silver, ceramics, and paintings.

Even more intriguing are the Nazca Lines located south of Lima. These mysterious designs, formed by the people of an unknown civilization digging trenches, include outlines (the size of a football field) of condors and other animals. Among the unsolved mysteries are the depictions of monkeys and insects that lived, not on the Pacific coast, but hundreds of miles east in the Amazon forest. These geoglyphs were possibly formed centuries before the birth of Christ.

Central historic district in Lima, Peru

Section Quiz

1. What Andean nation lies on the equator?
2. What Indians built the biggest civilization in South America?
3. What is the oldest continuously inhabited city in the New World?
4. Why is Peru's coast a desert?
* How can Christian linguists influence and assist cultures with no formal written language?

Bolivia

After Bolívar freed the region known as Upper Peru, it changed its name to Bolivia in his honor. Bolivia was once a large nation, but wars with neighbors deprived it of almost half of its territory, including access to the sea. Bounded by mountains in the west and jungles in the east, modern Bolivia is a **landlocked** nation, which means it is completely surrounded by land, and it is called the "Tibet of South America" for that reason. This isolation has hindered the development of its trade and industry. Chile, however, has offered to help Bolivia by giving it access to the sea.

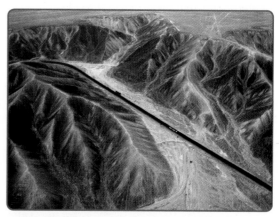

Aerial view of the Pan-American Highway that passes through the Nazca Desert in Peru. This highway stretches about 16,000 miles from Fairbanks, Alaska, to Puerto Montt, Chile.

About 60 percent of Bolivians are full-blooded Indians who live in villages and work on subsistence farms and villages. Another 30 percent of Bolivians are mestizos, and the rest are of European descent. Bolivian mestizos and Bolivians of European descent speak Spanish, whereas most Bolivian Indians speak Quechua, Guaraní, or Aymara, but all four are national languages.

Although city life in Bolivia is very modern, rural Indians continue to live in primitive conditions. An estimated 70 percent of the Bolivian population lives in poverty. Dysentery, measles, tuberculosis, and whooping cough are common because the Indians cannot travel easily to doctors in the city. Consequently, Bolivians have the highest infant mortality rate and the lowest literacy rate in South America.

The nation's only important natural resources are in the mountains. Bolivia ranks fourth among the world's tin producers, but primitive mining methods hinder the mines' profitability. Farmers raise chinchillas for fur and guinea pigs for meat.

The Roman Catholic Church continues to be the state church in Bolivia and represents about 78 percent of the population. In addition, the government has encouraged a revival of indigenous religious traditions. Despite these obstacles, evangelical Christians have enjoyed an exponential increase since 1960 and represent 16 percent of the Bolivian population. The need for trained leaders to keep pace with the numerical growth of churches remains critical, but thirty seminaries and Bible schools are preparing leaders to meet this need.

The Altiplano

Most of the people of Bolivia live on the **Altiplano** (ahl tee PLAH noh, "high plain"), the largest of several plains that lie between the Andes ranges. The cold and windy Altiplano, which Bolivia shares with Peru, is more than two miles above sea level and covers an area almost as large as West Virginia—twenty thousand square miles.

At the heart of the Altiplano, on the border between Peru and Bolivia, is **Lake Titicaca** (tee tee KAH kah), the second-largest lake in South America. The lake helps to moderate the cold temperatures of the Altiplano, permitting agriculture. The shores of Lake Titicaca became the center of the Tiahuanaco (tee ah wah NAH coh) Empire, which preceded the Incas. The Incas believed that the first man and woman were created on an island in the lake.

Lake Titicaca moderates the weather of the surrounding area in what would otherwise be a cold, inhospitable climate.

Titicaca is one of the highest navigable lakes in the world. Many Indian settlements dot the shore. Some Uru (OO roo) Indians actually live on the water itself, building islands from the totora reeds that grow along the water's edge. Indians also use the versatile totora for fuel, animal food, baskets, mats, houses, and boats.

A few miles southeast of Lake Titicaca is the largest city in Bolivia and, at 12,000 feet, the world's highest capital, **La Paz**, which has nearly one million people. Because most government offices are located in La Paz, it is considered Bolivia's administrative capital. The legal capital, however, is Sucre (SOO kray), which is farther south in one of the many valleys of the Andes.

The Yungas and the Eastern Lowlands

As the Andes drop in the east, ridges and valleys abound. Bolivians call this rugged region the **Yungas** (YOON gahs). Farmers have transformed the fertile valleys to meet most of Bolivia's food needs.

At the base of the Yungas is the **Amazon Basin**. These lowlands constitute more than half of Bolivia's land area, but few people live in the swamps and jungles.

Chile

The Andes Mountains form a wall three thousand miles long, dividing Chile from Argentina. Yet Chile is only one hundred miles wide. This peculiar "shoestring" of land divides into three regions:

the northern desert, the Central Valley, and the southern archipelago (ar kuh PEHL uh goh; a large group of islands).

Eighty-seven percent of Chileans associate with some form of Christianity, and 10 percent consider themselves nonreligious. Evangelical Christians represent 18 percent of the population. Several foreign mission agencies continue to operate in this country, and missionaries serve in teaching and leadership development ministries.

The Atacama Desert

The northern twelve hundred miles of Chile is covered by the **Atacama** (ah tuh KAH mah) **Desert**, a continuation of Peru's southern desert. The climate is so dry that some places have no record of any rainfall. The red sands, barren rock, and salt flats bear mute testimony to the Atacama's reputation as the driest desert on earth.

Limited farming is possible with irrigation in the southern portions of the Atacama, where some rains fall. In spite of the harsh conditions, a few cities manage to survive. The Peru Current might hurt the climate, but it supports one of the world's best sardine fishing grounds. The largest city in the desert is the fishing port of Antofagasta (ahn toh fah GAH stah).

People brave the scarred desert to exploit its mineral wealth. Chile has one of the world's few natural deposits of sodium nitrate, which is used to make explosives and fertilizer. Other countries, however, compete for that market by making synthetic sodium nitrate. Chile is third behind China and the United States in the production of molybdenum. Chile's primary resource, however, is copper; it is one of the world leaders in copper production. Near the southwestern border of Bolivia, Chuquicamata (choo kee cah MAH tah) has one of the world's largest open pit copper mines. As of 2011, Chile was also the world's fifth-largest producer of silver.

The Central Valley

The **Aconcagua** (ah cohn CAH gwah) **River** marks the southern edge of the Atacama Desert. Three-fourths of all Chileans live south of that river in the Central Valley. It extends six hundred miles from Valparaíso (vahl pah rah EE soh) to Puerto Montt (PWEHR-toh MAWNT) in the south.

The Central Valley is similar to California's lush Central Valley. Both have a mediterranean climate, with westerlies bringing winter rains from the Pacific Ocean. Mineral deposits in both valleys have attracted miners: southeast of Santiago (sahn tee AH goh) is one of the world's largest underground copper mines, El Teniente (teh NYEHN teh, "the lieutenant or colonel"). East of the valleys are high mountains with ski resorts and spectacular scenery.

Chile's cold mountain valleys are unsuitable for large populations. Unlike other Andean nations, which have large Indian populations, most of Chile's people are Europeans or mestizos who live on the coastal lowlands. One-third of the nation's people live in the capital, **Santiago**, a modern city whose metropolitan area has more than six million inhabitants.

Chile has been one of the most successful nations in South America, both economically and militarily. Chile's victory against Peru and Bolivia in the War of the Pacific (1879–83) won it possession of the mineral-rich Atacama Desert. The wealth derived from nitrates and copper has created a small but growing middle class in the Central Valley.

The poorer classes voted **Salvador Allende** (ah YEHN day), a Marxist, into the office of president in 1970. But his efforts to redistribute land ruined the economy and sparked a coup in 1973. General **Augusto Pinochet** (ow-GOOS-toh peen-oh-SHAY) took power and ruled with an iron fist for nearly two decades. Although Pinochet relied on secret police to keep political power, he also introduced the first free-market reforms in South America. His policies turned Chile into an economic dynamo. In 1989, Pinochet allowed the people to vote on whether or not to continue his military dictatorship. They chose democracy instead. Chile continues to enjoy a stable government and a prosperous economy.

The Archipelago

A rugged archipelago stretches one thousand miles to the southern tip of South America. The archipelago includes some three hundred islands. Most of Chile's full-blooded Indians live there. The fierce Araucanian (ahr uh CAYN ee uhn) Indians resisted Spanish and Chilean armies for centuries but were defeated in 1883. Now the Indians farm or raise sheep or cattle on reservations.

Chile's archipelago is similar to Alaska's Inside Passage. Both have a mild and wet marine-west-coast climate. Forests cover the mountains and islands, but the trees are deciduous, not coniferous. Glaciers have carved deep gorges, and the ocean has flooded them to form fjords. National parks protect spectacular spots, such as pink granite pinnacles called the Torres (Towers) del Paine. A park that protects one hundred miles of fjord country was named for Bernardo O'Higgins, Chile's first president, who freed the slaves.

Below the southern tip of the continental landmass is the perilous Strait of Magellan, which was named for Ferdinand Magellan, whose fleet sailed through the strait in 1520 and ultimately became the first to *circumnavigate* (journey around) the earth. Until the construction of the Panama Canal, the strait was the main shipping route between the Atlantic and Pacific Oceans. Punta Arenas (POON-tah ah-RAY-nahs), a city of 120,000 on the strait, is one of the southernmost cities in the world.

South of the Strait of Magellan is the large island of **Tierra del Fuego** (FWAY goh, "Land of the Fire"). Early explorers called it that because they saw many Indian campfires flickering near the shore. Oil rigs now dot the landscape, giving Chile precious petroleum.

A string of islands continues south from Tierra del Fuego toward Antarctica. The southernmost islet is Cape Horn. Nearby is Puerto Williams, one of the southernmost settlements (not a city) in the world. The six-hundred-mile-wide **Drake Passage** separates Cape Horn from the frozen continent of Antarctica. It was named after Sir Francis Drake, the first Englishman to "round the Horn" and circumnavigate the earth.

The western half of Tierra del Fuego belongs to Chile and the eastern half to Argentina.

Section Quiz

1. How is being landlocked a disadvantage for Bolivia?
2. What nation has two capitals?
3–4. Describe two unusual features of Lake Titicaca.
5. What dictator helped to bring prosperity to Chile?
＊ Why do you think Chile has offered to help Bolivia by giving it access to the sea?

IV. The Río de la Plata

As you learned from reading about Chile, the southern half of South America is quite different from the tropical north. The climate is colder in the mountains and more temperate in the lowlands. Also, few Indians in that region survived the Spanish conquest.

The center of Spanish settlement in the east was the **Río de la Plata**, the widest **estuary**, or ocean inlet, on the Atlantic coast. The mighty Paraná (pah rah NAH) and Uruguay (oo roo GWYE) Rivers flow into the Río de la Plata. These navigable rivers are essential for three nations—Argentina, Paraguay (pah rah GWYE), and Uruguay.

The great liberator of these lands was **José de San Martín** (sahn mahr-TEEN). After winning Argentina's independence from Spain in 1813, he led his army over the Andes into Chile and surprised the Spanish garrison there. After that success, San Martín sailed to Lima and helped Bolívar free Bolivia.

Argentina

With an area of more than one million square miles, Argentina is the eighth-largest country in the world. Although less populous than Mexico, Argentina has the largest number of Spanish speakers in South America. Almost all Argentines (85 percent) are of European descent; half of those are descended from Italian colonists and a third from Spanish colonists. Mestizos make up the remaining 15 percent of the population.

Argentina has the potential to become a leader in world affairs, but political strife has devastated the country from its very beginning. For fifty years after independence, merchants fought ranchers for control of the government.

Argentina enjoyed a brief "Golden Age" between 1880 and 1914 as European immigrants poured into the country. After the Great Depression, however, Argentina was plagued by a series of juntas (HOON tahs). The most famous *caudillo* (cow DEE yoh; "strongman") was **Juan Perón**, who held power 1946–55. Perón and his wife, Evita, promised to help the poor workers, but they led the country into debt and economic ruin. The most recent political couple to wield power in Argentina was Néstor and Christina Fernández Kirchner. He served as president from 2002 to 2006. Néstor then declined to run for another term. Instead, he supported his wife, Christina Fernández, who won the election in 2006 and was reelected in 2011.

Eighty-nine percent of Argentinians identify with some form of Christianity, 9 percent are non-religious, and 0.5 percent are Jews. The Jewish population in this country is one of the world's largest outside of Israel and is largely secular. Evangelical Christians make up 9 percent of the population, and their ranks continue to grow.

Gauchos, Cowboys of the South

The cowboys of Argentina, or **gauchos** (GOW chohs), are national folk heroes. Hordes of them rode the Pampas in the nineteenth century, rounding up wild horses and cattle. Today, the few who remain work on ranches.

In the early days, the gauchos spent most of their time in the saddle. They were distinguished by not only their riding skills but also their clothes, which included a wide silver belt, baggy trousers, and a brightly colored scarf. They were rovers who loved the wide open spaces and the freedom of the plains.

The gaucho holds a position in Argentine history similar to that of the Western cowboy in U.S. history.

One of the most effective outreach ministries has been to prisons. Fifty percent of the inmates in the Olmos high-security prison have converted to Christianity, and other prison ministries have reported similar results. As of 2010, around 250 pastors were serving in prison ministries.

The Pampas

Argentina's low plains around the Río de la Plata are called the **Pampas** (PAHM pahs). Most of the nation's people, industry, and agriculture are there. The plains extend south and west across central Argentina.

The Pampas are similar to the Great Plains in the American West. A semiarid climate supports vast grasslands. The soil, among the most fertile in the world, is ideal for alfalfa, wheat, and corn. In fact, Argentina exports more corn than the United States. Cattle and sheep, which graze on huge ranches called *estancias* (eh STAHN see yahs), provide meat, hides, and wool for industries in the city.

Half of the people of the Pampas live in **Buenos Aires** (BWEH-nohs EYE-rehs), the nation's capital. It is one of the largest cities by area and population on the continent. Buenos Aires is ideally located near the mouth of the Paraná River on the Río de la Plata. The humid subtropical climate provides much more rain than the semiarid areas in the western and southern Pampas. Winter temperatures rarely drop below freezing, even in July, the coldest month in the Southern Hemisphere.

Buenos Aires is the main industrial center of Argentina. Industries process primary products from the Pampas, including meat and leather. The nation has two other industrial cities. Rosario (roh SAHR ee oh), also on the Río de la Plata, is known for oil refineries. Córdoba (COHR doh bah), where the Pampas meet the Andes, manufactures automobiles and railroad cars.

The Andes Border

West of the Pampas lie the Andes. Steady rainfall on the eastern valleys and slopes supports several cities, including Mendoza, Salta, and San Miguel de Tucumán. But most of the Andes are remote and sparsely populated.

Pampas grass, which grows abundantly on the Argentine Pampas, is used as an ornamental lawn decoration in the southeastern United States.

Buenos Aires, which means "fair winds," is a key to South America's international trade.

LET'S GO EXPLORING

Land Use of Latin America

1. What types of land use occur in both Central and South America?
2. Where does mediterranean farming occur?
3. What nation has the largest area of crop farming?
4. What is the most common type of land use in the Amazon Basin?
★ Which nation has the greatest variety of land use?

Commercial Farming

- Mixed Commercial Farming
- Crop Farming
- Fruit, Truck Farming, and Specialized Horticulture
- Dairy Farming
- Plantation Farming
- Mediterranean Farming

Subsistence Farming

Shifting Agriculture

Nonfarming

- Manufacturing and Trade
- Ranching
- Forestry
- Limited Activity

- Gold
- Silver
- Iron
- Aluminum Ore (Bauxite)
- Chromium
- Copper
- Manganese
- Zinc
- Petroleum

The Andes mountain system reaches its highest peaks in Argentina, where nine of the Western Hemisphere's ten highest peaks exist. The tallest of them all is Aconcagua, at 22,834 feet. Only a half dozen roads cross this rugged chain along the two-thousand-mile border with Chile.

San Martín mustered his army at Mendoza before leading them over the Andes into Chile. His history-making route to Santiago went through a pass called Uspallata Pass, or La Cumbre, south of Aconcagua. At the top of the pass stands the massive statue *Christ of the Andes*. Chile and Argentina fought over their border for many years before they finally reached a settlement in 1902. They built the statue in honor of their pledge before Christ to maintain peace. The purpose of the monument is similar to that of the Peace Garden on the border between the United States and Canada.

Patagonia

South of the Pampas is a high plateau called **Patagonia** (pah tah GOHN yah). It rises in step-like cliffs toward the Andes Mountains. Scenic hills and canyons resemble America's Great Basin, complete with a petrified forest. Temperatures are similar to those of Canada's cold Maritime Provinces.

The European explorers named the region Patagonia ("big feet") after the Indians, who stuffed their oversized boots with grass for insulation from the cold. Today, the Indians are gone, and most of the scattered settlers live in small coastal villages. A few inland residents

The Reversal of Seasons in Different Hemispheres

An interesting geographic fact is that the Northern and Southern Hemispheres have opposite seasons at any given time. When it is summer in North America, for example, the people who live south of the equator are experiencing winter. On December 25, when people in the northern United States are longing for a "white Christmas," the people of Paraguay and Uruguay are probably perspiring in summer heat! And when North Americans are raking their autumn leaves, the people of South America are planting their spring crops. This information is very helpful if you plan to travel to another hemisphere and need to know what clothes to pack.

Pentecostalism

Pentecostalism arose in America from a Methodist-Holiness tradition. Christians in this tradition sought a second blessing, or a second gift of the Holy Spirit following conversion. This blessing was believed to be an aid to holy living. In the Pentecostalism that emerged in the U.S. early in the twentieth century, speaking in tongues came to be seen as the sign of this blessing. During this same period, a number of Pentecostal groups began. At first they were looked upon with skepticism even by many in the holiness tradition. However, as Pentecostals moved into the middle class by the middle of the twentieth century, they gained greater respect from other groups. By the 1960s, Pentecostal teachings and practices appeared in some evangelical, mainline, and Roman Catholic churches. Much of the spread of Christianity in Latin America and Africa is due to Pentecostal and Charismatic groups.

Pentecostal and Charismatic churches are diverse. They hold in common the belief in miraculous gifts such as tongues and healing. But many differences also exist. Initially, the gift of tongues was defined as the ability to speak in unknown foreign languages. However, tongues are now described as ecstatic speech rather than human languages. While most Pentecostals and charismatics hold to the biblical doctrine of the Trinity, Oneness Pentecostals teach that God exists as a singular spirit who reveals himself in many ways, including Father, Son, and Holy Spirit. Traditional Pentecostals continue to believe that the baptism of the Holy Spirit is a second blessing following conversion. Charismatics who are not from a holiness background may hold that the baptism of the Holy Spirit occurs at conversion or water baptism. Given this diversity, it is difficult to give a doctrinal description of Pentecostalism beyond noting the emphasis on the Holy Spirit and miraculous gifts.

raise sheep on the sparse grasses and shrubs. Their ranches are built in the canyons to protect them from the constant winds.

Northern Argentina

North of the Pampas, Argentina has two regions: Mesopotamia in the northeast and the Gran Chaco in the northwest.

Mesopotamia is named after the region of the Middle East that lies between two rivers. The western edge of Mesopotamia is the Paraná River; the eastern edge is the Uruguay River, at Argentina's border with Uruguay and Brazil. The climate is hot and humid.

West of the Paraná River is the **Gran Chaco**. Like the Pampas, it is flat and dry, but it is covered by shrubs and forest rather than grass. Part of the Gran Chaco, between Rosario and Tucumán (too cuh MAHN), is desert. The rhea, or South American ostrich, lives on the plains. The main human occupation is harvesting *quebracho* (kay BRAH choh; "ax-breaker"), a hardwood tree used for railroad ties and telephone poles. Tannin, a chemical derived from the quebracho, is used in tanning leather.

Uruguay

The Río de la Plata is the focus of life in the tiny nation of Uruguay. **Montevideo** (mohn teh vee DEH oh), the capital, is on this estuary. About half of the nation's people live in the Montevideo metropolitan area. Another one-quarter million people live in towns along the Uruguay River. Uruguay's population, like that of Argentina, is composed of primarily European descendants (Spanish and Italian) rather than indigenous peoples. The country's location between the two giants of Brazil and Argentina has made life there difficult.

Uruguay is considered the most secular nation in South America. Those associating with some form of Christianity represent 65 percent of the population, and 27 percent claim to have no religious affiliation. Evangelical Christians make up 6 percent of the Uruguayan people, and their growth has been significant during the last two decades. Given the lack of leadership, itinerant church planters from other Latin American countries have played an important role in the growth of the church in Uruguay.

Industry

Spanish is the national language of Uruguay, although Portuguese is common along the Brazil-Uruguay border. The economy is very much like Argentina's, but it has been less stable. Terrorism and foreign and civil wars have plagued the tiny nation throughout its history.

Key industries of Uruguay include textiles, apparel, chemicals, meat processing, and leather production. A software-development industry is growing rapidly. The country is working to increase exports, particularly to the United States. To do so, its government is reducing its previously heavy intervention in the economy and is developing a business-friendly environment.

Paraguay

Spanish explorers first visited Paraguay while searching for an alternate route to the riches of Peru. **Asunción** (ah soon see OHN), founded on the Paraguay River in 1537, became the first capital of Spain's colonies in southeastern South America. But Spain neglected the landlocked, unproductive region. Dissatisfied with Spanish rule, the people of Asunción declared their independence in 1811. Since then, dictators, civil war, and wars with every neighbor have decimated the nation. The nation did not hold its first multiparty elections until 1993. Again, such instability has hampered economic development.

About 95 percent of Paraguayans are mestizos. Most are bilingual. They speak Spanish for education, government, and commerce, but they use their native tongue, **Guaraní** (gwah rah NEE), in daily life. Paraguay might be the most thoroughly bilingual nation in the world.

Like Bolivia, Paraguay is a struggling country with few mineral resources. Its one advantage over Bolivia is the **Paraná River**, the second-longest river system in South America. Steamboats can go up the Paraguay River, a tributary of the Paraná, to Asunción, the capital. Most of the nation's population lives along the river system.

Many Paraguayans are subsistence farmers, who make their living from the rich alluvial soils of the Paraná and Paraguay Rivers. They grow barely enough crops to feed their families, cutting down forests on public lands and moving on when the soil is depleted. Most of them live in one-room ranchos, with dirt floors and no plumbing.

The Gran Chaco, west of the Paraguay River, is largely uninhabited, except for a few Guaraní Indians and Mennonites. Mennonite communities that were founded in the Chaco in 1926 now produce nearly one-half of the nation's dairy products.

In 1992 Paraguay declared the separation of church and state with the promise of equality before the law of any religious body. However, the Roman Catholic Church continues to enjoy a significant political and social advantage over other religious groups. Ninety-six percent of Paraguayans identify with some form of

Christianity, and 3 percent are equally divided between nonreligious and traditional religions. Evangelical Christians represent 6 percent of the population, and many of them are from immigrant backgrounds. However, the Evangelical congregations continue to grow as Christians plant churches among indigenous minority groups in Paraguay. Foreign missionares are still needed and provide effective help in areas such as church planting, leadership training, and education.

Section Quiz

1. What is an estuary?
2. Who liberated Argentina and Chile from Spain?
3–4. In what city do half of the people of the Pampas live? Why is that city so big?
★ Why is Buenos Aires an important component in South America's trade?

V. Brazil

Brazil is the fifth-largest nation in the world, and the fifth-most populous. It covers half of the South American continent and contains several of the continent's key geographic areas. Its wealth of resources and vibrant culture hold the promise of a great future.

Brazil is unique among Latin American nations. It is the only nation in the Western Hemisphere that once belonged to Portugal and has Portuguese as its official language. It is also the largest Roman Catholic nation in the world, with 73 percent of the population claiming some affiliation with the Catholic Church. Protestant churches, however, have grown rapidly in recent years, particularly among Charismatic denominations.

Evangelical Christians represent 26 percent of the Brazilian population and have grown from 2 million in 1960 to 51.3 million as of 2010. The growth of Evangelical congregations has also led to extensive missionary activity. Nearly 2,000 Brazilian missionaries have gone to unevangelized areas in Brazil and abroad and planted new churches.

The Atlantic Coast

The Treaty of Tordesillas gave Portugal all lands east of the Line of Demarcation. Pedro Cabral's discovery of Brazil in 1500 affirmed Portugal's claim to the eastern tip of South America.

Because of the rough terrain and the hostile Indians of the interior, however, the first settlements were only along the coast. As was the case with the colonies of North America, the first European settlements in Brazil were often at harbors and tied to Atlantic trade with the Old World.

Portuguese Settlers

Portuguese settlers built sugar plantations all along the east coast of Brazil. Within two years, **São Vicente** (soun vee-SEHN-teh), near the southern city of Santos, became the first colony and oldest city in Brazil.

If you look at the map of modern Brazil, you will see that Portugal settled quite a bit more of the coast than they were supposed to. In 1669, Portuguese settlers crossed the treaty line and founded

Manaus (muh NOUSE) far up the Amazon River. Another group of settlers founded Pôrto Alegre on the southern coast in 1740. The westward movement required a new treaty with Spain. The Treaty of Madrid, signed in 1750, gave Portugal almost all the land of modern Brazil.

Independence

In 1822, **Dom Pedro**, the son of the Portuguese king, whom the king had placed in charge of Brazil, declared independence for Brazil and became its king. Brazil remained a monarchy for sixty-six years under Pedro and his son, Pedro II. Dom Pedro opened the door to thousands of European immigrants, and he freed the black slaves in 1888. However, angry slave owners, who received no money for compensation, overthrew Pedro II and declared Brazil a republic, modeling its constitution after that of the United States. The republic has been interrupted by periodic dictatorships and military rule.

Brazil is also unique in other ways. It shares borders with seven Spanish-speaking nations and has won a sliver of territory from each of them. Brazil was the first Latin American country to develop nuclear capability and the only one to send an army to Europe during World Wars I and II.

Modern Coastal Cities

As is typical of South America, the large cities of Brazil are very modern. Cars and buses fill the streets. Operas, plays, and orchestras entertain the people, and schools are good. Houses and apartments might be small and crowded, but they have basic appliances, such as refrigerators, toasters, and televisions.

Cities in the South—The biggest cities are in South Brazil, the nation's heartland. Most of the region enjoys a humid subtropical climate, similar to that of the southern United States. But Rio de Janeiro (zhah NEH roh), the nation's second-largest city and one of the largest on the continent, has a pleasant tropical climate on the coastal plain. Orange groves in the area make Brazil a leading producer of oranges.

"Rio" is considered by many to be the most charming city of the New World. Dom Pedro made Rio de Janeiro his capital, and it remains the cultural center of the nation. Its harbor is internationally

The *Christ the Redeemer* statue, which overlooks Rio de Janeiro, is on a 2,329-foot mountain and is 125 feet high and 92 feet wide from fingertip to fingertip.

acclaimed, surpassing the beauty of San Francisco Bay. Sugar Loaf, a granite dome-shaped mountain, is a famous landmark.

Life on the Northeast Coast—Most other major coastal cities of Brazil lie on the eastern "bulge," known as the Northeast. Eight state capitals, from São Luís to Salvador, are clustered on this crowded coast. Salvador, Fortaleza (fort uhl AY zah), and Recife (reh SEE fuh) are the largest cities in the region, each with more than two million people. Recife is the major industrial city of the Northeast. Farmers from the drought-stricken interior have poured into the coastal cities to find work. Unfortunately, most of them end up in one of the cities' huge slums, called *favelas* (fah VEH lahs).

The northeast coast has a large population of descendants of the African slaves who once worked on the sugar plantations. Descendants of Europeans still own and supervise most plantations, but hired workers enjoy moderately good living conditions. In addition to sugar cane, the modern plantations raise cacao, bananas, and cotton. Brazil leads the Western Hemisphere and is one of the world's top ten producers of bananas. In 2009 Brazil was the world's leading producer of sugar cane.

The Brazilian Highlands

Above the narrow coastal plain rise the **Brazilian Highlands**, a rugged plateau that dominates the east side of the continent. Near the Atlantic coast, the highlands form a steep wall-like slope called the Great Escarpment. It reaches its highest point at 9,482 feet above sea level at Pico da Bandeira (PEE-koh dah bahn-DEH-rah), just west of Vitória.

Like the Andes, the Brazilian Highlands greatly influence river drainage on the continent. Most waters flow down the highlands into two great water systems—the Amazon in the north and the Rio de

Brasilia

In an effort to move some of its population westward into the interior, Brazil built the new capital city of **Brasília** (brah SEEL yah) in 1956. By 1960, it was a large, working city. The carefully planned, modern city was carved out of the Brazilian Highland about six hundred miles from the coast.

Everything about the city, including the architecture of individual buildings, was designed to be in harmony. The economy of the capital is slowly developing, but most people prefer to remain on the coast. The government of "the United States of Brazil" is a federal republic, with twenty-six states and the federal district of Brasília.

West of the Brazilian Highlands is the **Mato Grosso** (MAH-toh GROH-soh) **Plateau**. Swamps cover the plateau along the borders with Paraguay and Bolivia. Although it is remote, this region undoubtedly holds great potential wealth.

Every building and street in Brasília, including government buildings such as the Congress building (pictured here), was planned to demonstrate architectural harmony.

Iguaçu Falls

"Poor Niagara," cried the visiting wife of an American president when she first beheld Iguaçu (ee gwah SOO) Falls. Iguaçu Falls is about eighty feet higher than Niagara Falls and twice as wide, making it the widest waterfall in the world. Although Iguaçu is less powerful than Niagara on most days, the rainy season turns it into a raging torrent. Its flow has been recorded to be as high as 452,059 cubic feet per second.

Some 275 cataracts, separated by stony outcroppings, fall over a semi-circular cliff that is 1.8 miles wide. The rushing falls plunge 237 feet into the canyons below, sending up clouds of mist in a lush jungle setting.

After the Iguaçu River flows over the Falls, it joins the Paraná twelve miles downstream. Near this point is Itaipu (ee TYE poo) Dam, one of the largest dams in the world. Built in 1982 to harness the mighty Paraná

River, Itaipu's concrete wall is five miles long and seventy-five stories high. Brazil and Paraguay jointly constructed the massive hydroelectric plant, which in 2012 was tied with the Three Gorges Dam in China for the highest kilowatt output in the world.

The building and operation of Itaipu Dam exemplify how the people of many countries can benefit from the peaceful cooperation of countries.

Iguaçu Falls dwarfs North America's Niagara Falls, especially during the rainy season.

la Plata in the south. One other major river, São Francisco, cuts east through the highlands. Paulo Afonso Falls, where the river drops toward the coast, is one of the world's most powerful high falls.

Although the Brazilian Highlands lie in the tropics, the climate is not like that of the Amazon Basin. The Amazon, which straddles the equator, is rainy all year, but heavy rains fall only half the year in the highlands farther south. The Amazon always receives direct sunlight, which heats the surface and causes regular afternoon showers (by convection precipitation, which you studied in Chapter 3). But in the highlands, the direct rays of the sun shift every six months. The rainfall begins in February, when the sun shifts over the highlands. When the sun shifts back north in August, the land cools, cold air rises, and the rains cease.

Cities in the South

Two hundred miles west of Rio is São Paulo (soun POW-loh). Including its metropolitan area, São Paulo is the largest South American city and the ninth-largest city in the world by population.

São Paulo includes ethnic populations from all over the world. Liberdade is the largest Japanese community outside Japan. But the minorities of Brazil—including Japanese, Germans, and Arabs—now speak Portuguese and have adopted Brazilian culture.

Imperial topaz

São Paulo arose in one of the most fertile areas of the country. Plantations raise coffee, sugar cane, and cotton. São Paulo's coffee has made Brazil a world leader in coffee exports. Brazil is second in beef cattle production, with much of the cattle raised in the dry savanna around São Paulo.

The sixth-largest city in Brazil, Belo Horizonte, is also located on the Brazilian Highlands in the southern heartland. It is the capital of **Minas Gerais** (MEE-nuhs zheh-RICE), one of Brazil's largest states. This highly industrialized state has some of the largest deposits of iron ore in the world and is a leading producer of iron ore. Other mineral resources in Minas Gerais include diamonds, manganese, and gold. Brazil is one of the largest producers of gold in South America. It also produces most of the world's finest imperial topaz.

Poverty of the Northeast

Unlike the southern heartland, the northeast portion of the Brazilian Highlands has poor soil and long dry seasons. While the coastal cities afford decent living conditions, the interior is a virtual desert, and its people are very poor. The primary crop of that region is cassava, a root similar to a potato that can be eaten or used to make tapioca. Brazil is a leading producer of this root.

Section Quiz

1. What country colonized Brazil?
2–3. What is Brazil's largest city? Which city is its cultural center?
4. Why are southern cities more prosperous than northeastern cities?
5. Brazil is a leading producer of what three products from the Brazilian Highlands?
∗ Why did the Spanish colonies break up after independence, but not the Portuguese colonies? What advantage has unity given Brazil?

The Amazon

The **Amazon River** is the greatest river system in the world. Not only does it drain the largest area, but more water flows out of the Amazon than out of the next ten largest rivers combined. The Amazon is also the longest river by some estimates. Even the lowest figures put it within 160 miles of the Nile.

The flat basin of the Amazon River is covered by a steamy rain forest, called **selva**. Spreading over one-third of the continent, it is the largest tropical rain forest in the world. The high canopy of trees supports a host of exotic animals: the anaconda, the world's longest snake; the capybara, the world's largest rodent; colorful toucans and parrots; jaguars; tapirs; and sloths. The waters teem with electric eels, the razor-toothed piranha, and the ten-foot-long pirarucu. Even dolphins and sharks have appeared as far upstream as Iquitos, Peru!

Life of the Remote Indians

Few people live in the Amazon rain forest. It has a very steamy, uncomfortable climate. Temperatures hover between 75°F and 95°F throughout the year. Many areas receive more than one hundred inches of rain annually.

Earth Matters: Amazonia, the Lungs of South America

You may think that rain produces rain forests. Actually, it's the other way around. Rain forests produce rain as the leaves on trees "exhale" both water vapor and oxygen. This water vapor produces clouds that make rain. Though some rain comes from other places, the Amazon rain forest generates up to half the rainfall in the area.

But when we cut down too many trees in a rain forest, there's a point at which the rainfall that the remaining trees produce isn't enough to keep them alive. In fact, cutting down too many trees could eventually shrink the mighty Amazon. Cutting down 40% of the trees in the Amazonian rain forest could reduce precipitation in the area by 43%!

People need rain forests, not just for the health of the environment, but also because they are beautiful. God wants us to enjoy and thrive in His resource-filled world. But He also wants us to wisely use those resources to meet the needs of people who bear His image while keeping a mind toward the future. When Brazil began monitoring the Amazon with satellite images in 2007, deforestation dramatically dropped. But in 2013, there was an uptick in deforestation as the Brazilian government loosened restrictions on protected lands around the Amazon.

Consider how a Christian worldview can shed light on the problem of deforestation in the Amazon.

However, the interior began experiencing significant growth in the 1990s, mainly because of the *cerrado*, fertile savannah rich in agricultural promise. The region is flat, so it can be industrially farmed, and it has adequate rainfall. The area still needs to develop transportation to complement these opportunities.

Several small, scattered Indian tribes live deep in the forests. Each Indian group generally lives together in one large community structure, called a *malocas*, covered with woven palm leaves. The only significant piece of furniture is the hammock—an invention of the Amazon Indians. Sailors adopted it the world over, and hammocks are a common sight in most homes of coastal Brazilians.

Many tribes practice shifting or **slash-and-burn** agriculture. They cut down a plot of forest, burn the vegetation to fertilize the soil, and then plant cassava. In most cases, they have replaced their ancient stone tools with modern steel. The women turn the cassava into flour and store it in baskets. When the soil is depleted, they cut down a new plot. Cassava is not high in nutrients, but it grows well in the poor, acidic soil. Europeans spread cassava to tropical colonies worldwide.

The Indians supplement their diet by hunting, using some of the longest bows in the world (some more than six feet tall). In recent centuries, the use of blowguns has spread through the western selva. In thick brush, it is easier to aim blowguns than bows to hit birds and monkeys. Using tubes eight to twelve feet long, skilled blowers can hit targets as high as 120 feet in the trees. Their poison darts fly through the air in deadly silence. The tribes make poison from the sap of the *strychnos* vine. (We get *strychnine*, a poisonous chemical, from that plant.)

Missionaries have contacted most tribes of the selva and have convinced the native peoples to end the practice of cannibalism. Although some Indians have accepted Christ and are learning to read, others remain bound by spirit worship and superstitious practices. Some anthropologists have urged the Indians to retain aspects of their traditional lifestyle that the anthropologists believe to be in harmony with nature. "Foreigners tell us to reject the missionaries and

Missionaries on the Amazon

Michael and Katrina Geurink have an unusual if not unique ministry in Brazil. They live on a houseboat and minister to native peoples along the upper Amazon River. During the course of their ministry, God has allowed them to adopt four Brazilian children.

They began working in Brazil in a local church ministry about sixteen years ago. Gradually they developed a relationship with several members of the Ticuna tribe and began to disciple believers from this group. Moving to a houseboat about ten years ago, the Geurinks began to visit several villages and developed Bible training classes for the Ticunan believers as well as others.

As the Lord permits, the Geurinks plan to settle in one central village along the Amazon and minister to people from other tribes who come to this village. Since the government prohibits most people from going from one tribe to another, the Geurinks are planning to train people from these tribes so they can take the message of God's Word back to their own people.

Michael has another opportunity for outreach because of his status as a missionary pilot. Given the travel restrictions, he is hoping to be able to fly government officials into restricted areas. This would provide him with additional contacts for future ministry.

go back to our old ways," said one Yanomamo Christian. "But they do not have Christ in their hearts. Our old ways were evil. We will never go back."

Modern Development and Deforestation

As part of its program to develop the rich potential of the Amazon, the government has divided it into seven states. The largest states (in area) in Brazil are Amazonas and Pará. They share the land along the main channel of the Amazon River. **Amazonas**, with its capital of Manaus, governs the western half of the river. Pará, with its bustling capital of Belém on the coast, governs the eastern half. Pará is slightly smaller than Amazonas, but it has more than twice the population. Five other remote states include chunks of the Amazon Basin and are the least populated states of Brazil.

An increasing number of Brazilian settlers are moving into the rain forest, both legally and illegally, to exploit its riches—minerals, farmland, and lumber. The Amazon has a valuable supply of mineral resources. Pará has Brazil's second major iron ore deposit, located about 250 miles south of Belém. South America's leading bauxite and tin mines are located in the Amazon. The state of Rondônia (rohn DOHN yah), along Brazil's southern border with Bolivia, is the world's fifth-largest producer of tin.

Farmers have attempted to grow crops in the rain forest. A few cacao and rubber plantations thrive along the banks of the Amazon. You might think that heavy rainfall would make productive soil, but the soil is actually very thin. Insects and rapid decay deprive the soil of humus. In a process called **leaching**, constant rains dissolve nutrients in the soil and carry them away.

Increasing numbers of lumberjacks are felling the forests to extract valuable hardwoods, such as mahogany and ebony. But because the trees hold the soil in place, **deforestation** is depleting the soil, rendering the land useless for future generations. Environmentalists are also concerned about the loss of these oxygen-producing forests.

Section Quiz

1. What word refers to the steamy rain forest of the Amazon basin?
2–3. Which records does the Amazon River hold: most volume, longest river, largest drainage basin, or highest waterfall?
4–5. What mineral products come from the Amazon Basin?
   ★ Why is the soil poor in the Amazon?

Chapter Review

Making Connections

1. What role did the Creoles play in the history of South America?
2. What piece of land joins North and South America?
3. Why is much of South America's Pacific coast so dry?
4. Which countries of South America were not settled by the Spanish?

Developing Geography Skills

1. Pick a city in South America where you would like to live. Describe how your life would change if you moved there.
2. Compare Brazil's settlement of the Amazon with the U.S. settlement of the West.

Thinking Critically

1. Why do those concerned about the environment want Brazil to stop developing the selva? Should other nations have a say in Brazil's decisions?
2. What does the presence of advanced civilizations in South America long before European contact demonstrate about the nature of the people who lived there? How would your conclusion contradict non-Christian philosophies?

Living in God's World

1. Imagine that you are a Christian missionary working among indigenous people in South America. Write a letter to an anthropologist who opposes your work on the grounds that you are corrupting these people's culture.
2. Compose a brief paragraph that explains why Christians should support the use of the earth's resources while also being concerned about the damaging effects of activities such as deforestation.

People, Places, and Things to Know

Andes
Simón Bolívar
Cordillera Occidental
Cordillera Central
Cordillera Oriental
Bogotá
Llanos
Caracas
Lake Maracaibo
Orinoco River
Guiana Highlands
tepuis
Cotopaxi
Quito
Amazon rain forest
Incas
Cusco
Francisco Pizarro
Quechua
Peru Current
Lima
landlocked
Altiplano
Lake Titicaca
La Paz
Yungas
Amazon Basin
Atacama Desert
Aconcagua River
Santiago
Salvador Allende
Augusto Pinochet
Tierra del Fuego
Drake Passage
Río de la Plata
estuary
José de San Martín
Juan Perón
Pampas
Buenos Aires
Patagonia
Gran Chaco
Montevideo
Asunción
Guaraní
Paraná River
São Vicente
Dom Pedro
Brazilian Highlands
Brasília
Mato Grosso Plateau
Minas Gerais
Amazon River
selva
slash-and-burn
Amazonas
leaching
deforestation

Unit Five
EUROPE
AND RUSSIA

*T*his vast region that spans over seven thousand miles has been the birth-place of many modern nations, languages, and cultures. It varies in geo-graphical features, climates, languages, and forms of government.

British Parliament on the River Thames in London

WESTERN EUROPE

I. Northern Europe
A. United Kingdom
B. Ireland
C. Scandinavia

II. Continental Europe
A. France
B. Low Countries
C. Germany
D. The Alpine Region

III. Mediterranean Europe
A. Iberian Peninsula
B. Italian Peninsula
C. Greece

Europe is a peninsula on the Eurasian (the continents of Europe and Asia) landmass. Because it is one large peninsula with many smaller peninsulas, it has been called a "peninsula of peninsulas." Europe is also noteworthy as the only continent with no deserts. The good climate and rich soils support productive farms and industry.

Europe illustrates the idea of the nation-state (see p. 92). For several centuries, there has been a strong desire among Europeans for every nation to have its own state. This desire drives current movements for independence, such as that of the Basques in Spain. Remembering the distinctions between nations and states (ch. 5), see if you can spot examples of nations, states, and multinational states throughout this unit.

Western Europe has less than 5 percent of the earth's landmass, but its people have dominated much of world history. Many nations in Western Europe have enjoyed a golden age of influence and prestige, followed by a decline into relative insignificance. As a result of these past periods of influence, Western European traditions and institutions are found on every continent. Three continents—North America, South America, and Australia—are populated primarily by descendants of Western Europeans.

I. Northern Europe

Northern Europe consists of the British Isles and Scandinavia. With the exception of Ireland, northern Europe is primarily Protestant. Looking at a map, one might assume that most of northern Europe would be extremely cold because of its distance from the equator. However, this is not the case. Coming off the coast of Canada, the **North Atlantic Drift** warms northern Europe so that even the harbors of Norway remain ice-free year-round.

United Kingdom

Great Britain, the largest island in Europe, lies at the heart of the United Kingdom. The United Kingdom also includes land on the neighboring island of Ireland as well as numerous smaller islands surrounding Great Britain. The United Kingdom sits astride northern Europe's major water routes. Off the east coast lies the North Sea, the main route to the peninsulas of Scandinavia. Between Great Britain and Ireland lies the choppy Irish Sea. South of Great Britain is the English Channel, a narrow body of water between the island and the European mainland. In the past, merchant ships had to pass through this channel to reach the ports in northern Europe.

The United Kingdom has four political divisions—England in southern Great Britain, Wales in western Great Britain, Scotland in northern Great Britain, and Northern Ireland. In 1707, the kingdoms in Great Britain were officially united, with one parliament, forming the United Kingdom. In 1801 the entire island of Ireland was brought into the United Kingdom, but most of Ireland became its own nation in 1921. At that time, Northen Ireland voted to remain in the United Kingdom. You will sometimes hear the United Kingdom loosely called Great Britain or just Britain.

Sixty percent of the population of the United Kingdom identify with some form of Christianity, but that number is in decline. Evangelical Christians make up 9 percent of the population, and many of these are ethnic minorities. Having in previous centuries been the

Find It!
London
51.500° N, 0.126° W

British English
Sometimes speaking the same language does not ensure communication. The Standard English of Great Britain is quite different from the Standard English in America. To the British, gasoline is petrol, and raising the hood of a car is looking under the bonnet. The trunk of a car is the boot. Here are a few more examples.

American Word	British Word
cookies	biscuits
biscuits	scones
truck	lorry
sink	basin
closet	cupboard
candy	sweets
dessert	pudding
elevator	lift
horn	hooter
radio	wireless
pharmacist	chemist

"Angles' Land"

Early England had its share of invaders. Among them were the Jutes, Angles, and Saxons. The name England, in fact, is from two Old English words meaning "Angles' land."

center of missionary outreach, the UK is now in need of missionaries itself.

England

England is the largest division of the United Kingdom. England's agricultural heartland is the rolling plains and hills of southern England. The United Kingdom is among the world's top producers of flax fiber, hops, sheep, green peas, carrots, sugar beets, and raspberries. The **River Thames** (temz) flows through the center of this region. The largest city on the Thames is London. Off the southeast coast of England, the English Channel separates Great Britain from

the continent. The narrowest point in the channel, at only twenty-one miles wide, is called the Strait of Dover. The turbulent channel has been called England's "first line of defense" against enemies from the mainland.

Downs are another feature of southeast England. These chalk hills cannot support trees, but they have plenty of grass for cattle and sheep. Two parallel ranges of rolling hills run along the interior. The South Downs run near the channel, and the North Downs run just south of the Thames.

South-central England lies west of the downs. The ancient kingdom of Wessex was once in this area. It divided its kingdom into shires, which is evident in the names of some of its counties (e.g., Hampshire [HAMP shuhr]). A range of limestone hills called the Cotswolds adds scenic beauty to this region.

Several good ports lie on the coast of south-central England. The deep Bristol Channel, an arm of the Atlantic Ocean, extends into the western side of Great Britain. The important port of Bristol lies on the River Avon, which flows into the channel. East of Bristol, visitors can examine the ancient ruins at Stonehenge. There are many theories regarding the purpose of these structures, but scholars are limited to speculation at the present.

Unlike south-central England, southwestern England consists of a low plateau with scattered granite highlands. Two national parks, Dartmoor and Exmoor, protect the **moor**—a wasteland on a high, treeless plateau. The land cannot be cultivated, although a tangle of low shrubs does grow on it. Because fields of heather are so common, moors are often called heaths. Moors also have patches of peat bog or sphagnum moss. Most moors are farther north in the uplands of Scotland. Lizard Point is the southern extreme of Great Britain, and Land's End is its western extreme.

Central England is the home of the Industrial Revolution. The Industrial Revolution started here in the eighteenth century for several reasons: easy access to iron and coal, productive farms that

Stonehenge may date as far back as 2000 BC.

Windsor Castle

Western Europe Fast Facts						
Country	Capital	Area (sq. mi.)	Pop. (2013) (M)	Pop. Density (per sq. mi.)	Per Capita GDP ($US)	Life Span
Andorra	Andorra la Vella	181	0.09	497	$37,200	82.5
Austria	Vienna	32,382	8.22	254	$41,600	79.91
Belgium	Brussels	11,787	10.44	886	$37,800	79.65
Denmark	Copenhagen	16,639	5.56	334	$37,000	78.78
Finland	Helsinki	130,559	5.27	40	$36,000	79.41
France	Paris	211,210	65.95	312	$35,100	81.46
Germany	Berlin	137,847	81.14	589	$38,100	80.19
Greece	Athens	50,942	10.77	211	$26,300	80.05
Iceland	Reykjavík	39,769	0.32	8	$38,100	81
Ireland	Dublin	27,135	4.76	175	$40,800	80.32
Italy	Rome	116,306	61.48	529	$30,500	81.86
Liechtenstein	Vaduz	62	0.04	645	$89,400	81.5
Luxembourg	Luxembourg	999	0.51	511	$80,600	79.75
Malta	Valletta	122	0.41	3,361	$25,600	79.85
Monaco	Monaco	0.75	0.03	40,000	NA	89.68
Netherlands	Amsterdam	16,033	16.85	1,051	$42,000	80.91
Norway	Oslo	125,182	4.72	38	$53,400	80.32
Portugal	Lisbon	35,672	10.80	303	$23,400	78.7
San Marino	San Marino	24	0.03	1,250	$36,200	83.07
Spain	Madrid	194,897	47.37	243	$30,500	81.27
Sweden	Stockholm	173,732	9.12	52	$40,700	81.18
Switzerland	Bern	15,942	8.00	502	$44,500	81.17
United Kingdom	London	94,526	63.40	671	$36,500	80.17
Vatican City	Vatican City	0.17	0.001	NA	NA	NA

Commonwealth of Nations

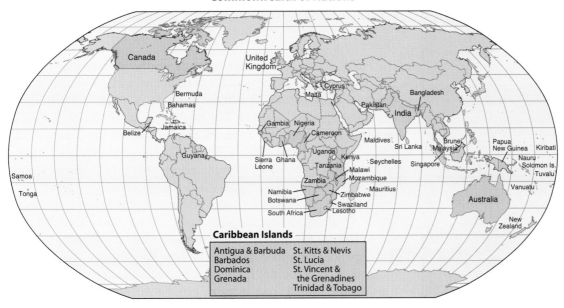

Caribbean Islands

Antigua & Barbuda	St. Kitts & Nevis
Barbados	St. Lucia
Dominica	St. Vincent &
Grenada	the Grenadines
	Trinidad & Tobago

produced flax and wool for textiles, plentiful rivers for transportation, colonies that supplied raw materials from around the world, and political freedom that encouraged new ideas and inventions.

Northern England includes all the counties north of the River Trent and has some of England's most beautiful scenery. **The Pennines** (PEN eyenz), a mountain system extending south from Scotland to the Midlands, form the backbone of England. Sherwood Forest—the fabled haunt of Robin Hood—is located at the southern tip of the Pennines, around Nottingham.

> ### Commonwealth of Nations
>
> The Commonwealth of Nations was formed in 1931 to facilitate the conversion of the British Empire into an association of free and equal countries. Today, the Commonwealth consists of over fifty countries encompassing about 30 percent of the world's population and about 25 percent of its land area. Most of the countries were once part of the British Empire, and the British monarch retains a symbolic role in the Commonwealth. Mozambique is the only member that was not ruled by the United Kingdom at some time. The Commonwealth promotes democracy, human rights, and economic development among its members.

The Pennines

Manchester, located at the foot of the Pennines, is the third-largest metropolitan area in the British Isles. It was once the textile capital of the world. West of Manchester on a major estuary of the Irish Sea is Liverpool, one of England's largest ports.

Sadly, England is the most secular nation in the United Kingdom. Only 6 percent of the population attends church, and atheism is filling the void left by declining Christian influence. Ethnic minorities

Hadrian's Wall, completed in AD 136, protected Roman England from the northern barbarians. Seventy-four miles long and twenty feet high, it is the largest Roman ruin in Britain.

constitute nearly 60 percent of those who do attend church, and outreach appears to be most effective among ethnic groups.

Wales

Wales occupies a broad peninsula on the western side of England. The climate of the country is mild and wet, similar to that of England, but less than 10 percent of the land is arable. Dairy cattle and sheep graze the grassy but treeless uplands. Wales is mostly mountainous except for a narrow coastal plain in the south. Snowdonia is the northern range and includes Snowdon (SNOHD n), the tallest mountain in Wales. The central range is the Cambrian Mountains, and the southern range is the Brecon Beacons.

Another geographical feature is the Rhondda Valley in southern Wales. Coal mines began operating in the Rhondda Valley during the Industrial Revolution, and for many years the Welsh economy was dependent on the coal industry. However, the coal has been exhausted, and the country has been forced to find alternative incomes. Cardiff, the capital, and Swansea are the main ports on the south coast.

One in five people still speak the Celtic dialect of Wales, along with the main language—English. Outsiders find the complex Welsh language hard to pronounce and spell, however, because it has so many double consonants. Wales joined the Anglican Church when it was first founded, but the Welsh remained open to the preaching of nonconformists, who refused Anglican rule.

Many churches in Wales have been closed, and church attendance has declined to 7 percent of the population. Most Welsh churches have 25 or less in attendance. However, some evangelical congregations have experienced growth through a clear presentation of the gospel and interaction with the community.

Scotland

Scotland lies north of England. It is known for green **glens** (narrow valleys carved by glaciers) and blue **lochs** (loks; deep, narrow lakes carved by glaciers). The Scots, descendants of the Celts, held off many invaders who tried to take their rugged and isolated homeland. Though part of the United Kingdom, Scots have preserved a culture distinctly their own.

Scotland's border with England's Pennines is called the Southern Uplands. It consists of barren hilltops, fertile slopes, and foggy moors. The range that divides Scotland from England is the Cheviot Hills and is crowned by Hadrian's Wall, which Rome built to stop raids from the unconquered Scots north of Britannia.

North of the border, a belt of lowlands stretches across central Scotland. The flat lands and relatively fertile soil make it Scotland's most populated area. About 75 percent of the Scottish people are crowded around Glasgow, Scotland's largest city, in the west and Edinburgh, Scotland's capital, in the east.

North of the populous lowlands are the Grampian Mountains, the principal range of the Scottish Highlands. They include **Ben Nevis**, the highest mountain in the British Isles (4,406 ft.). North of this mountain system is a deep valley, called Glen More or the Great Glen. The Caledonian Canal cuts through this valley and includes the waters of Loch Ness. Beyond the Great Glen are more highlands and the Hebrides (HEB rih deez) Islands, where isolated people still speak a Celtic dialect.

Membership in the Church of Scotland has dropped to half of what it was fifty years ago. Even worse, only a small percent of those who are still members attend church on a regular basis. Some evangelical churches remain strong and continue to minister, but there is a national need to evangelize the Scottish people.

Northern Ireland

Northern Ireland, also called Ulster (UL stuhr), is on the island of Ireland, the second-largest island in the British Isles. This Protestant country, first populated by Protestants from Britain in the early seventeenth century, shares the island with Catholic Ireland. Northern Ireland consists of six counties on the northeast corner of the island. It is a land of rugged coasts and rolling hills. Many crystal lakes, called **loughs** (LOKS), dot the interior. Lough Neagh (NAY) is the largest freshwater lake in the British Isles. It covers over 150 square miles and is also the center of Northern Ireland, with five counties bordering it. The plentiful lakes and rivers provide fishermen with salmon and sea trout. Among the region's many bays are the excellent harbors of Londonderry and Belfast.

Belfast, the capital and largest city, is an industrial city once famed for shipbuilding. Belfast shipyards built many warships and ocean liners, including the *Titanic*. Aircraft construction is now an important part of the economy. The textile mills are known for their fine Irish linen.

Many churches in Northern Ireland have experienced a decline in attendance, although attendance is greater in this country than in any other nation in the United Kingdom. Belfast and the area around this city remain a bastion of strong evangelical churches. Northern Ireland also maintains a missionary burden beyond anything found in the rest of the United Kingdom.

Ireland

The Republic of Ireland covers five-sixths of the island of Ireland. Ireland's thin, rocky soil was apparently caused by massive glaciers—the same forces that scraped New England. Although farther north than New England, Ireland's climate is much warmer because of the North Atlantic Drift, which carries warm water from the Gulf Stream. Ireland is consistently humid; about half of the time the weather is overcast. Regular rains drench the green countryside of the Emerald Isle.

A rim of mountains surrounds the coast of Ireland. As of 2009, Ireland ranked tenth in the production of zinc, found in the mountains west of Dundalk. The River Shannon, which flows through the rolling plain in the center of Ireland, is even longer than the Thames. The grasslands support cattle and horses. In the central and western parts of the island are many bogs, where the water sits without access to the ocean. Here, partly decayed mosses have been compressed to form thick layers of peat. Since Ireland lacks coal, many people burn peat for heating and cooking.

Around 87 percent of the Irish population is Roman Catholic. Most Irishmen speak English, though they do so with a brogue (BROHG), or soft accent. Gaelic (GAY lik), also called Irish, is their

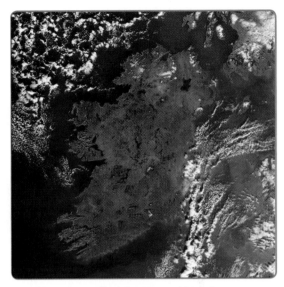

Ireland is often called the "Emerald Isle."

Giant's Causeway

According to legend, Irish giant Finn McCool (Fingal) made a pier, or causeway, out of rock so that he could walk across the Irish Sea from Ireland to Scotland. Around thirty-seven thousand columns, some of them twenty feet high, descend into the ocean on the coast of Northern Ireland. Similar columns rise up out of the sea in Scotland. The rocks are basalt, formed from lava. When the lava cooled, it cracked into prism-shaped pillars having four to eight sides.

ancient Celtic language. The constitution calls it the "first official language," and street signs and official documents must be bilingual. However, only about one-quarter of the people speak Gaelic with some proficiency.

The history of English-Irish relations has been tragic. Over the centuries England instituted harsh measures discriminating against Catholics, including a law that once prevented them from buying or inheriting land. Ireland was joined to the United Kingdom in 1801. However, in 1921, the Anglo-Irish Treaty created an Irish Free State, and in 1949, the Republic of Ireland cut all ties with Britain.

For centuries Ireland was a land of poor farmers. Their young men left the farms and went to the cities seeking jobs. They often continued on, emigrating to other countries to find a "better life." Then, in the 1990s, there was a great turnaround. Ireland became known as "the Celtic Tiger" for its rapid economic progress. Young people of Irish ancestry returned to Ireland, where there were many good factory jobs and desirable living conditions. Recent economic downturns due to declining demand for exports have forced government leaders to cut spending and balance budgets using austerity measures.

Ninety-two percent of the population identifies with some form of Christianity, and 7 percent claim no religious affiliation. Evangelical Christians form a tiny minority of 1.5 percent and number around 71,000. With 21 percent of Ireland's population under the age of fifteen, there is a burden to reach these young people before they are consumed by alcoholism, suicide, and the consequences of broken families.

Section Quiz

1. What river runs through the heart of Southern England?
2. What is the "backbone of England"?
3. What is Gaelic?
* Why do you think Ireland is referred to as the Emerald Isle?

Scandinavia

Scandinavia is the Land of the Midnight Sun. There are five countries in Scandinavia: Norway, Sweden, Finland, Denmark, and Iceland. Iceland and Finland are republics, while the other three Scandinavian nations have constitutional monarchies. Parts of Scandinavia lie above the Arctic Circle, where the sun never sets for more than two months each summer and where it never rises for two months each winter. During the sun's absence, the northern lights (*aurora borealis*) are visible. Norway's view is especially famous. Vacationers in Hammerfest, Norway, can see the midnight sun hanging over the Arctic Ocean.

The people are called Scandinavians from an ancient center of the Norsemen called Scandia. During the Middle Ages, the Scandinavians converted to Christianity, but they never had close ties to Rome. When Martin Luther sparked the Reformation in the sixteenth century, they became Protestants. Today, over 90 percent of all Scandinavians are Lutherans. Unfortunately, as is true in most of Europe, many Nordic people no longer attend services except for baptisms and religious holidays.

Norway

Scandinavia is known for its peninsulas. Norway and Sweden share the largest peninsula, the Scandinavian Peninsula, with Norway facing the North Sea. Norway's mainland coastline stretches for more than sixteen hundred miles. The coast is splintered by numerous fjords. Other major fjords around the world are in Alaska, Patagonia, and New Zealand; but the most famous are in Norway. Norway's longest fjord, **Sogne** (SAWNG nuh) **Fjord**, cuts 127 miles inland.

Including long fjords, numerous small islands, and minor indentations, the full length of Norway's shore stretches 15,626 miles, or more than half the circumference of the earth. Norway includes

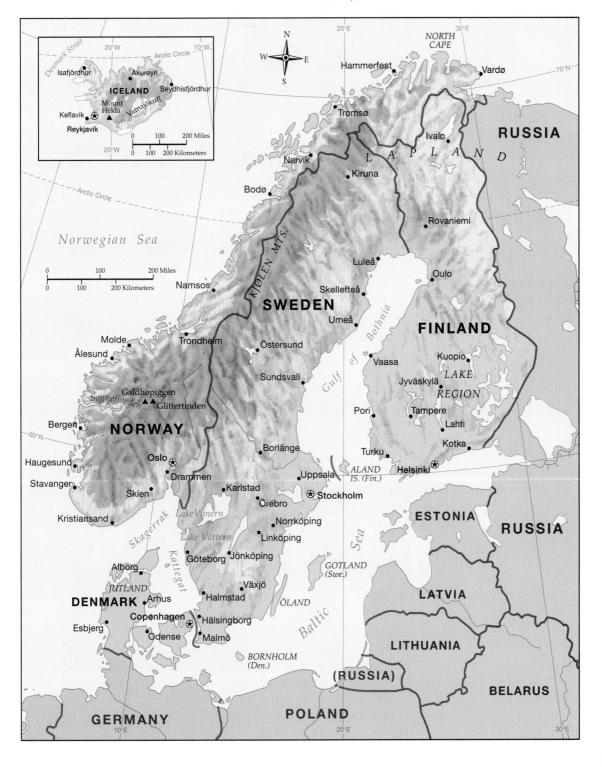

One of the many fjords in Norway

about 50,000 islands. Many streams drop into the fjords to create beautiful waterfalls. Norway has five of the world's fifteen highest waterfalls.

Norway's important cities lie on the coast, where the ocean moderates the climate. Most Norwegian cities also take advantage of fjords as natural harbors. The area surrounding Oslo Fjord is the largest lowland in the country and contains most of the arable land.

A high plateau covers most of Norway. Glaciers cover many mountains and have scraped the rocky surface. About one-quarter of Norway is forested, and only 3 percent is arable. Nordic, or cross-country, skiing was developed in this wasteland. Skiing is a national sport.

The plateau includes several mountain ranges. The Kölen (CHUHL uhn) Mountains form Norway's border with Sweden. **Galdhøpiggen** (GAHL huh[r] pig uhn; 8,100 ft.), the highest peak in Scandinavia, rises in the south. Jostedals Glacier to the west of this peak is the largest glacier in continental Europe, covering 188 square miles.

Bergen, the principal port, lies on the southwest coast. Norway's fishing industry ranks as one of the most productive in the West. The merchant fleet, one of the world's largest, transports goods around the world.

Norway's cultural center is its capital, Oslo. Oslo refines oil from large deposits in the North Sea. Oil exports have helped make Norway rich. It enjoys one of the world's highest standards of living. To ensure an educated population, Norway requires children to attend at least ten years of school.

Most Norwegians are employed in service industries, which make up a large portion of the country's economy. Only a small percentage of the workforce is involved in oil industries, but they produce 20 percent of the annual GDP.

While the Lutheran Church is the official church in Norway, the country allows freedom of religion. Ninety-one percent of Norwegians affiliate with some form of Christianity, and six percent have no religious affiliation. Evangelical Christians represent 8 percent of the population. Many of the Lutheran churches in Norway as well as the Evangelical churches maintain a strong influence and continue the nation's tradition of sending out missionaries.

Sweden

Sweden is the largest Scandinavian country and the fourth-largest country in Europe. About one-third of Sweden is lowland plains in the south. A mild climate and fertile soil make it Sweden's best agricultural region. As a result, Sweden remains a leading producer of mixed grains. A low plateau in the center of the plain has poor, rocky soil that is useful for dairy cattle.

Stockholm, the nation's capital, is the largest city in Scandinavia. The city covers fourteen islands and is connected by fifty bridges.

The port city of Göteborg has been influential in the growth of Sweden since its founding in the seventeenth century.

While the North Atlantic Drift keeps Norway's harbors ice-free year-round, many ports on the Baltic Sea, including Stockholm, freeze in winter. Ships enter only with the help of icebreakers.

Most of Sweden's western border is shared with Norway. In the south, however, the west coast lies along the Skagerrak (SKAG uh rak) and Kattegat (KAT ih gat), two arms of the North Sea. Göteborg (yuh tuh BAWR ee) is the second-largest city in Sweden. Ice-free year-round, Göteborg has become Sweden's leading port. The Göta (YUH tuh) Canal provides the eastern ports with a year-round trade route through the interior lakes of Vänern and Vättern.

Sweden's sparsely populated Northland is considered the last frontier of Europe. Mountains line the border with Norway, and rugged hills cover the rest of the region. Rivers flow southeast through deep gorges that broaden into valleys near the Gulf of Bothnia. Great forests of pine and spruce cover these hills and provide timber for the pulp mills and sawmills on the coast. Sweden is a major exporter of timber products.

Sweden joined the European Union in 1995, but it does not use the euro. The country has one of the highest life expectancies in the world while having one of the lowest birth rates. The decline in the population growth rate, in Sweden as well as in other European countries, has caused concerns regarding the "graying" of the population and the economic challenges that may result.

About 70 percent of Sweden's GDP is based on services. Almost 80 percent of the workforce is unionized. Its industries have a reputation for quality, high-tech engineering and metallurgy. They make everything from ball bearings to surgical instruments. Sweden is also a major producer of automobiles, including Volvos and Saabs.

Sweden's welfare state set the example for all other Nordic countries by providing "cradle to grave" benefits, including most major expenses from childbirth to burial. The "Swedish model" was a mixed economy that allowed businesses to stay in private hands, but the state taxed and regulated businesses heavily. It also adopted one of the highest income taxes in the world. In the 1990s, the people began to see the damage this system can do to private enterprise. In recent years most industry has been allowed to operate with reduced government regulation. This has resulted in a growing and prosperous economy.

European Union

The European Union (EU), an organization of twenty-eight countries, seeks to form a single European community that can compete on the world stage economically and politically. Each country in the EU relinquishes some of its sovereignty when it joins the EU. The EU was formed in 1992 with the Maastricht Treaty, but early forms of cooperation existed before 1992. Since 1951, economic organizations existed among major European powers. In 1967, the unity of these countries was advanced through the creation of a European Parliament. The Maastricht Treaty expanded these developments with more interaction between the governments of the countries. The EU introduced the euro (€) in 2002 as a common currency. The EU is divided between those who use the euro (e.g., France) and those who do not (e.g., United Kingdom). In the early twenty-first century, the EU proposed a new constitution that would strengthen the EU considerably but diminish the sovereignty of the member countries. Support, however, has not been strong in some key countries. In addition, recent economic downturns have significantly weakened the economic strength and stability of the EU.

Sweden has had a significant religious history, but recent decades have witnessed a decline in religious fervor accompanied by a rise in secularism. Fifty-seven percent of the Swedes affiliate with some form of Christianity, while 38 percent consider themselves non-religious. Evangelical Christians represent 7 percent of the population, although this group has also suffered a slight decline. Many Christians in Sweden are responding by reaching out to plant new churches, help people with addictions to alcohol, assist victims of physical abuse, and meet other needs of people in their community.

Finland

Finland has been independent only since 1917. Prior to that time, the Finns spent a century under Russian control and seven centuries under Swedish control. Unlike the rest of Scandinavia, Finland's language and physical features are related to those of northern Russia. The difficult Finnish language is not Germanic, or even Indo-European, but Uralic. To improve their ability to trade, many Finns are learning English or German.

Finns work hard to keep their environment one of the cleanest in the world. Their love of nature is reflected in their favorite recreational activities of fishing, hunting, and camping. However, relaxing in a hot sauna is the national pastime. Most apartment complexes have saunas, as do many homes.

Finland's only access to the ocean is the Baltic Sea. It has a long coastline along the Gulf of Bothnia. Most of Finland's population clusters in the southern coastal lowlands, which enjoy the mildest climate and the best farmland. Less than one-tenth of Finland's land is arable, but Finland's farms are self-sufficient. The ports freeze during the long winters, but the shipbuilding industry builds over half of the world's icebreakers to keep the ports open. Helsinki is the nation's capital, main seaport, and largest city. The city often hosts peace talks between warring nations.

Finland has been called the "Land of Ten Thousand Lakes" because of its southern interior. Like Minnesota, Finland has many glacial lakes, perhaps one hundred thousand. Thick forests cover three-fourths of Finland, and timber products account for 13 percent of its exports. The shimmering lakes and rivers are called "white coal" because the running water produces cheap hydroelectricity to run the mills and other industries.

Northern Finland contains the heart of Lapland, which extends into Sweden, Norway, and Russia. The regional capital is Rovaniemi. The **Lapps**, who call themselves Sami, have tended reindeer in this region for thousands of years. In summer, they take the reindeer north to feed on the moss and lichen of the tundra. In the winter, they return south to the forests. But since many Lapps have moved to villages to work as fishermen or lumberjacks, the Lapps' nomadic customs and culture are fading.

Finland recognizes the Evangelical Lutheran and Finnish Orthodox Churches as national churches, while granting freedom of religion to other faiths. As in many other European countries, Finland has been secularized and negatively influenced by humanism. This has resulted in a serious decline of church attendance by the Finnish people. Eigthy-four percent claim to practice some form of Christianity, and 16 percent have no religious affiliation.

A few Laplanders continue to herd reindeer in the Arctic.

Denmark

Denmark has been an independent country since 950 and even ruled England from 1013 to 1042. Its islands and mainland peninsula lie farther south than the rest of Scandinavia, making its winters less severe. Lacking mineral resources, the country depends heavily on agriculture and trade. The Danes are firm believers in welfare; they pay one of the highest tax rates in the world. After taxes and duties are added to a new car, its cost triples!

The Jutland Peninsula extends northward from Germany and accounts for about 70 percent of Denmark's land area. Dunes along the west coast protect the peninsula from winds off the North Sea. A rocky plain covers the far north, and a sandy plain covers the southwest. Low hills roll gently across the rest of the peninsula. Farmers grow barley and raise both beef and dairy cattle. About half of Denmark's people live on ninety islands east of Jutland. Hills cover the islands, as on Jutland, but the deep soils are more fertile.

The capital city, Copenhagen, is on Denmark's largest island, Zeeland. Copenhagen houses nearly one-quarter of the country's population and is one of the largest metropolitan areas in Scandinavia. The name Copenhagen means "merchant's harbor," and it is indeed a strategic port. The Danes are also known for elegant design and fine quality in their exported furniture, machinery, and silverware.

Denmark's overseas territories have included Iceland, Greenland, and the Faeroe Islands, a group of seventeen inhabited islands north of Scotland. Denmark granted Iceland independence in 1918 but retained the other islands. The Faeroe Islands and Greenland are currently self-ruling provinces within the kingdom of Denmark.

Greenland is the largest island in the world, fifty times larger than Denmark and thirteen hundred miles west of Denmark in North America. Vikings deceptively named the island Greenland to attract settlers. In reality, 75 percent lies under an ice cap. Colonists settled on the southwest coast, the island's warmest region. In the fifteenth century, the entire colony perished, but the Danes resettled in the eighteenth century. Today, Greenlanders are a mixture of Eskimo and Danish ancestry. Around one-third of the work force is employed in the fishing industry.

As in other countries in this region, the Lutheran Church is the national church of Denmark. However, there is freedom of religion in this country, and 10 percent of the population has no religious affiliation. Out of the 85 percent of the people who identify with some form of Christianity, 3.5 percent are Evangelical Christians. Despite the spiritual stagnation that often accompanies traditional churches, new congregations are forming, especially among Christian immigrants. In addition, recognition of the need to reach the largely unreached immigrant population is stirring some to evangelize the lost.

Iceland

About 650 miles west of Norway is the "Land of Fire and Ice." Large glaciers glide down the active volcanoes on Iceland. The glacier-carved fjords are reminiscent of Norway, but not the island's two hundred volcanoes, one of which erupts about every five years. Surtsey, an island off the south coast, was created by an undersea volcano

Mount Hekla is one of the most active volcanoes in Iceland.

Greenland has more ice than green, and Iceland, to the southeast, is greener.

in 1963. **Mount Hekla** (4,892 ft.) was once thought by some to conceal the gates of hell.

As elsewhere in Scandinavia, the North Atlantic Drift flows around Iceland, warming the southern coast. Temperatures similar to those in New York City keep the ports open all year.

Icelanders are proud of their heritage. The **Althing** (AHL thing), their national assembly founded in 930, is the oldest parliamentary assembly still in existence in the world. The Icelandic language is the only Scandinavian tongue that remains essentially unchanged from the Viking era. Without too much difficulty, many Icelanders can read the medieval chronicles of their Viking ancestors. Desiring to keep their language pure, a special committee creates new Icelandic words for such things as telephones and computers instead of adopting foreign words.

Almost all the population and the island's 1 percent of arable land is found along Iceland's fjords. The main crop is hay for the sheep, which in turn provide food and clothing. Potatoes and turnips also withstand the cool climate. Iceland's fishing fleet is one of the world's most modern. Nearly 40 percent of Iceland's exports are fish products.

The capital, Reykjavik (RAY kyuh veek), houses half the population. Geothermal energy provides heat for hot water, heated outdoor swimming pools, greenhouses, and nearly 80 percent of the homes. The greenhouses enable Icelanders to grow flowers, tomatoes, and fruit during the long winters.

Iceland is known for its rugged beauty. The barren interior plateau is twenty-five hundred feet above sea level. The plateau has the largest glacier in Europe, **Vatnajökull** (VAHT nah yuh koot ul). Glacial lakes dot the region, and glacier-fed rivers create beautiful waterfalls.

Iceland has more hot springs than any other country in the world. The English word *geyser* comes from Iceland's most spectacular hot spring, the Great Geysir, which spews water almost two hundred feet in the air.

While the Lutheran Church is considered the state church in Iceland, other groups enjoy freedom of religion. Ninety-one percent of the people embrace some form of Christianity, and 8 percent identify with no religion. Evangelicals represent nearly 4 percent of the population and are experiencing some growth. The Bible society and Christian radio programs have dispensed the Word of God through written and oral means, and some who would not visit a church have trusted Christ through these outreach efforts.

Section Quiz

1. What peninsula contains both Norway and Sweden?
2. Greenland belongs to which country?
3. Where do most Icelanders live? Why?
* Why might geographers exclude Finland from Scandinavia? Why might they exclude Iceland?

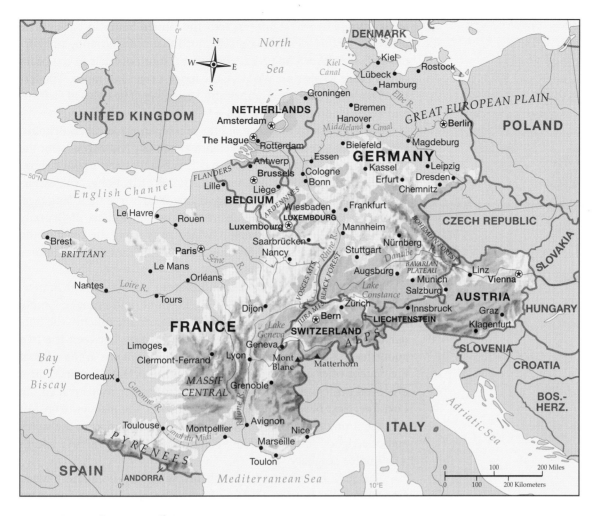

II. Continental Europe

Continental Europe refers to the main landmass of Western Europe, as opposed to the islands and peninsulas. Much of the continent is a wide coastal lowland with a marine-west-coast climate. The countries on this continent have greatly influenced the history and culture of the world. The Reformation divided the continent. Today Roman Catholicism dominates the south and west, and Protestant denominations are prominent in the north.

France

France is the largest country in Europe (by landmass). Over four-fifths of the people are Roman Catholic. France has few Protestants and Jews but has a growing Muslim population. Since 1815, France has gone through four kings and five republics. It has been a parliamentary republic since 1870. The present constitution was passed in 1958. Today, France retains only a small portion of its once mighty empire that spanned four continents.

Generally, northern France is lower and flatter than the southern regions. The Great European Plain extends across the north of the European continent, from France to Russia. Three of the five major French rivers flow through northern France. On the **Seine** (sayn) **River** lies the capital of France, Paris. With 2.2 million people, Paris is among the largest cities in Europe.

The plains around Paris produce wheat, barley, and sugar beets. France is second (Russia is first) in sugar beet production. It also

The Arc de Triomphe in Paris memorializes Napoleon's brilliant victory at the Battle of Austerlitz (1805), when he crushed a combined Austrian and Russian army.

leads Europe in wheat and exceeds the United States in barley. The plains of northern France continue northeast of Paris, along the border with Belgium. The plains also extend south of Paris to the basin of the **Loire River** (luh WAHR), the longest river in France. The fertile river valley produces grapes and vegetables. The cities of Orléans and Tours lie on the Loire River.

The far western province of France is a peninsula called Brittany. The north coast on the English Channel is rocky and rugged, but the south coast on the Bay of Biscay has fine beaches and major fishing villages. Bretons (BRET ns), the inhabitants of Brittany, are descendants of the Celts. The Bretons are trying to preserve their language, similar to Welsh, and some desire independence. East of Brittany is the historic **Normandy** region, which runs along the coast to the Seine River. This region is famous for the Allied invasion of France during World War II on June 6, 1944.

Three provinces lie on a broad plateau in east central France. The provinces are Alsace (al SAYCE), Lorraine, and Franche-Comté (frahnsh con-TAY). The plateau of Alsace-Lorraine touches the border of Germany and has been a disputed region between the two countries in the past. The Vosges (VOHZH) Mountains at the edge of the plateau offer forest products as well as important deposits of iron ore. Steel centers process the ore at Nancy, the key industrial city in Lorraine. East beyond the Vosges Mountains, the plateau drops off into the Rhine River valley. Alsace includes France's part of the valley and offers good farmland. The people speak Alsatian (al SAY shun), a Germanic language.

The Jura Mountains lie south of the Alsace-Lorraine plateau along the Swiss border. The low Jura Mountains are the dominant feature in the province of Franche-Comté. Few mountains rise above the timberline, which is around 5,300 feet. The Jurassic period in evolutionary geology is named after the Jura Mountains, which display "Jurassic" dinosaur fossils.

Southern France has a complex geography of mountains, rivers, and lowlands. All three main regions in southern France have mountains exceeding ten thousand feet. But they each have lowland valleys and coastal plains as well, where large populations thrive. Southeast France is a favorite vacation spot.

The Alps divide France from Italy, and the border has been disputed between the two countries. **Mont Blanc** (mawnt blangk) is the highest mountain in the Alps at 15,771 feet. It lies near the Italian and Swiss borders. Nearby is the deepest cave in the world, the Jean Bernard Cave, which reaches depths of about one mile below the surface.

The water from the snowcapped Alps drains west into the Rhone River, which flows south into the Mediterranean Sea. The valley and adjacent coasts are unique in Continental Europe because of the mediterranean climate. The region is a major producer of grapes and wine. Lyon (lee OHN), the third-largest city in France, lies in the Rhone River valley. This valley, which cuts deep into France, was historically the main overland route between Mediterranean Europe and Northern Europe. Near the mouth of the Rhone River is the oldest and second-largest city in France: Marseille (mahr SAY). Between the Rhone River and Italy lies the French Riviera, Europe's answer to Hawaii as a vacation paradise.

The Alps descend into the Mediterranean Sea and form the island of Corsica. Corsica's mountains rise to 8,878 feet at Monte Cinto. Corsicans speak a unique language similar to Italian, and they are trying to preserve it. Corsica's beaches are favorite French resorts. The island's most famous native was Napoleon, whom the British called the Corsican Ogre.

The capitals of the four central provinces, Toulouse (too LOOZ), Limoges (lee MOHZH), Clermont-Ferrand, and Montpellier (mohn pel YAY), lie at the corners of the **Massif** (ma SEEF) **Central**. This mountainous plateau in south-central France has poor soils that make the region useful only for grazing livestock.

Toulouse is an important transportation center on the Garonne (gah RAWN) River, which flows into the Atlantic. The Garonne is important because of the Canal du Midi, which completes a link between the Atlantic Ocean and the Mediterranean Sea. By sailing up this canal and the Garonne, French vessels can bypass the long trip around the Spanish peninsula.

The **Pyrenees** (PEER uh neez) **Mountains** rise south of Toulouse and form the border with Spain. The region boasts many deep caves, including the Cave of Pierre-St. Martin. These caves descend three times deeper than the deepest caves in North America. The **Basques** (BASKS) live in this mountainous area. Members of this ethnic group also live in Spain. The Basques are fiercely independent and work hard to maintain their language and culture in both countries.

The Pyrenees are a natural boundary between France and Spain. Few passes cross these mountains.

The two provinces of southwest France are mostly lowlands. The region is called Aquitainian Lowlands. The Lascaux (la SKOH) Cave is famous for its prehistoric cave paintings. Bordeaux (bore DOH), the main city, lies near the mouth of the Garonne River. The fertile river valley produces grapes and corn.

Historically, France has been a staunchly Roman Catholic nation. Many Protestants died for daring to preach and witness in this country. That changed in 1789 with the French Revolution. Since that violent upheaval in France, the country has remained a secular state and has avoided supporting any form of organized religion. As of 2010, 61 percent of the French people affiliate with some form of Christianity, and 26 percent have no religious connection. Muslims, primarily immigrants, make up about 11 percent of the population. Evangelical Christians now represent about 1 percent of the French population, a significant increase in the last fifty years. There are about 2,500 groups or congregations that meet throughout France, and more are being planted each year.

The Low Countries

The Low Countries are so named because they lie entirely on coastal lowlands and low plateaus. The Low Countries are located at the crossroads of Western Europe, between the French and the Germans. Because these countries are small in area and are situated on desirable plains, they are some of the most densely populated countries in Continental Europe.

The Netherlands

The Netherlands has fought a great battle against the sea. Sand dunes twenty feet high protect the inland regions from the North

The Netherlands or Holland?

The name Holland is sometimes used for the entire country of the Netherlands, but it is only part of the country. The terms to describe the people can be very confusing also. The people of the Netherlands call themselves Nederlanders or Hollanders, but the English call them the Dutch. Their language is also called Dutch. Adding to the confusion, the Kingdom of the Netherlands once included all three Low Countries.

The new name for the modern economic union of the Low Countries, Benelux, is not so confusing. Can you guess where they got this name?

Abraham Kuyper

The Netherlands has not always been in such a state of religious decline. During the late nineteenth and early twentieth centuries, a man named Abraham Kuyper (1837–1920) challenged the way Christians thought about their lives. Converted while a pastor in the Dutch Reformed Church, Kuyper advocated the idea that the Christian faith should shape every aspect of a believer's life. He founded the Free University of Amsterdam to train Christian leaders with this worldview. He later led conservative Christians to separate from the Dutch Reformed Church and form a more conservative denomination in 1886. Believing that every area of society should be influenced for Christ, Kuyper undertook a life of politics along with his pastoral ministry. His political life reached its height when he became prime minister of the Netherlands from 1901 to 1905. Despite Kuyper's fervent activity and evident desire to see the Netherlands serve Christ, the country has embraced a blatantly ungodly stance.

At least three reasons exist for this decline: (1) the generation after Kuyper did not have the biblical discernment necessary to engage in cultural matters; they emphasized cultural conformity rather than the need for Christians to remain culturally distinct from the unbelieving culture. (2) Kuyper taught that children born to Christian parents should be presumed to be regenerated. This led to a weakening of the church since many of these children were not regenerate. (3) Related to this, Kuyper's emphasis on cultural engagement continued in the next generation but without the warm, personal walk with God that he had. A personal walk with God is the heart of the Christian life out of which the rest of the Christian life flows.

Sea. Much of the land farther inland is below sea level. The Dutch have built strong walls of stone and earth, called dikes, to hold back the seawater. Big electric generators pump out the water to keep the land inside dry. At one time, windmills were used to generate power, but only a few windmills still operate.

Parcels of land reclaimed from the sea are **polders**. The polder region of the Netherlands covers a wide strip of territory behind the dunes and dikes. Polders have good fertile soil, and tulips and daffodils are important cash crops, but living on polders presents many dangers. The Dutch must wage a ceaseless battle against the sea, constantly pumping out rainwater and maintaining the dikes.

Two of the Netherlands's twelve provinces form the region of Holland, which contains 40 percent of the population and all three of the nation's largest cities. Amsterdam, the capital and largest city, is on a polder in the province of North Holland. The same tolerance that made the Netherlands a refuge for Protestants in Catholic Europe has secularized the nation today. Though there is no official religion, the monarch traditionally belongs to the Dutch Reformed Church. Just over 13 percent of the people are Dutch Reformed or Lutheran, about 25 percent are Catholic, just over 5 percent are Muslim, and over 50 percent have no religion at all.

The province of South Holland includes both Rotterdam and The Hague (HAYG). Amsterdam has been called the capital since Napoleon moved it there, but the national government of the constitutional monarchy meets in The Hague. One of Europe's busiest ports, Rotterdam lies in the delta of the busiest river on the continent, the **Rhine River**. The Rhine River is one of the most important rivers in Europe and flows through or borders six countries. Rotterdam is also a major industrial town with oil refineries and steel manufacturing.

The two northern provinces, Friesland (FREEZ lund) and Groningen (GROH ning uhn) lie in the polder region. The dunes rise as a chain of offshore islands. The Netherlands controls the West Frisian (FRIZH un) Islands, but Germany owns the East Frisian Islands. Frisian is the language of Friesland. Like Dutch, Frisian is a Germanic language. Large deposits in this area make the Netherlands the world's eighth-largest producer of natural gas.

Three other polder provinces lie immediately east and south of Holland. The most important is Zeeland to the south. This region is a series of islands and peninsulas in the delta of the Rhine River. The Oosterschelde Barrier has enabled the Dutch to convert some of this marshy area into productive ground.

The five provinces along the eastern border are slightly above sea level and do not have polders. However, these sand plains do not have fertile soil either. Fertilizers are used to make them productive. The eastern provinces have salt deposits, and there are coal mines in the Ardennes.

During the Reformation, the people of the Netherlands bravely fought against Spain to obtain religious liberty. However, during the last few decades this country has embraced almost every form of moral vice and sought freedom from moral restraint, with dire consequences. Freedom to practice deviant lifestyles has limited the liberty of Christians to teach about many topics from the Bible because the state has instituted anti-discrimination legislation. This decline is further demonstrated in a population that is 47 percent

High-Tech Dutch Dikes

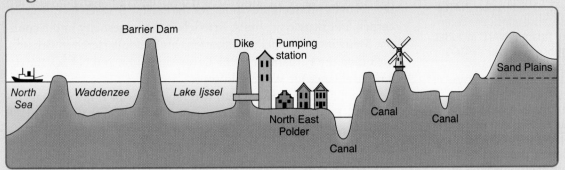

The Dutch and dikes go together. The Dutch have been building them for centuries. However, two daring projects in the twentieth century have far surpassed any previous attempt to capture land from the sea.

The first challenge was to control the floods along the Zuiderzee (zide-uhr ZEE; Southern Sea), an arm of the North Sea that reaches into the heart of the country. Storm surges in the North Sea would sometimes fill this inlet and flood the coast. In 1931 the Dutch completed a nineteen-mile-long dam called the "Enclosing Dike," which crossed the Southern Sea. Rivers slowly turned the enclosed portion of the sea into a freshwater lake called Lake Ijssel (EYE suhl;

Inner Lake). The portion beyond the dam became known as the Waddenzee (VAHD-en zee; Outer Sea).

The next challenge was to drain parts of the IJsselmeer to obtain more land for housing and farming. Building

Land Reclaimed from the Sea

Wieringermeer Polder
Northeast Polder
Waddenzee
Lake Ijssel
Amsterdam
The Hague
Flevoland
Rotterdam
Ijssel R.

■ Lands protected by dikes and dams

the dikes, draining the water, and preparing the land for settlement took many years. Now, four large polders exist that a few years ago were covered by the salt waters of the Zuiderzee. The Flevoland Polder, the largest, covers over one hundred thousand acres.

Another great project was to protect Zeeland, farther south, from sea storms that might break dikes and flood homes. As much as the Dutch liked their new freshwater lake farther north, they did not want another one. If they did that to all of their estuaries, they would lose bird migrations as well as the shrimp, mussels, and eels used for food. Conservationists thus persuaded the Dutch to undertake an even greater engineering feat. The Oosterschelde Barrier allows 80 percent of the normal tides to flow through the barrier, but the gates can be shut during storms to keep out squalls.

Oosterschelde Barrier

nonreligious and 47 percent who embrace some form of Christianity. Muslims constitute nearly 6 percent of the population. In the Netherlands, Evangelical Christians represent 4 percent of the population. However, a large majority of these Evangelicals are immigrants, and growth is most significant among the immigrants and the congregations they are planting.

North Atlantic Treaty Organization

The North Atlantic Treaty Organization (NATO) was formed in 1949. Because it includes countries close to the North Atlantic, NATO includes more countries than those in Europe. NATO's original purpose was to counter the agressiveness of the Soviet Union. Since the Cold War, though, NATO has developed into a peacekeeping organization, contributing troops to conflicts in Darfur, Iraq, Afghanistan, and the Balkans. Notable additions to NATO since the Cold War have been several countries from Eastern Europe. The twenty-six countries of NATO have pledged to come to each other's aid in the case of an attack on any of them.

Belgium

Belgium has one of the most developed free market economies. Perhaps the country's best-known product is Belgian chocolate, and several of its products are named for the capital: Brussels lace, Brussels carpet, and Brussels sprouts. **Brussels** is the largest city in the country. Many international organizations are headquartered in Brussels, including the Parliament of the European Union and NATO, the defensive alliance for Western Europe.

The nation is divided into two regions, with three official languages—Dutch, French, and German. **Flanders** in the north, much like the Netherlands, is a region of polders and sand plains where people speak Dutch. The people are called Flemings; Belgian Dutch was once known as Flemish. Antwerp, the largest city in Flanders, is one of the busiest ports in the world and a major center for the cutting and setting of diamonds. The Flemish school of painting is also world famous.

The northern lowlands of Flanders give way to a low plateau in central Belgium. In the far south is a series of rolling hills called the **Ardennes** (ahr DEN). The forest of the Ardennes covers southern Belgium and much of Luxembourg, extending into France.

Belgium's southern district is called **Wallonia**. The Ardennes is dotted by many villages and hiking trails; most of the cities are on

Secularism

Secularism emerged in Europe as a response to the wars of religion. Secularists thought that if religious reasoning could be excluded from politics, law, education, and anything else that a society does together, then religious wars would cease. Religious people could still attend places of worship, and they could talk about their religions among themselves. But religion would be banished to the private sphere. In public, religion would have no place. A neutral secularism would keep the peace between warring religions.

Proponents of secularism also proposed a "secularization thesis," which stated that as the world modernized, religion would wither away. Religion would no longer be needed to explain how the world works or to give moral reasons for how people ought to live. Science could provide these answers. But in the last decades of the twentieth century, several prominent sociologists noticed that the secularization thesis simply was not true. At first the United States was singled out as the exception to the rule. Though modern and technologically advanced, large

numbers of Americans are not only religious but also believe that their religion (often evangelical Christianity) speaks to every aspect of their lives. But it soon became clear that Western Europe was the real exception in the world. The rest of the world is becoming more religious while Western Europe (and American higher education) clings to secularism.

This raises the question of why secularization has failed. In the first place, secularization is not inevitable, as its proponents claimed. Where secularization has flourished, it has done so because its supporters gained positions of influence and power. This highlights the second failure of secularism. Secularism claims to be a neutral place of common ground in contrast to various religions. But secularism is not neutral. It has its own ideology. It dictates to religions what areas of life they can speak to and in what areas they must be silent. It bars some voices from speaking in the public square. Secularism is willing to protect religion as long as religion is irrelevant. But when a Christian case is mounted in public, the secularist

shuts down the discussion. But this raises a third problem with secularism. Secularists want to refer to justice, equality, liberty, and other such concepts. But what do these concepts mean? Secularism cannot answer this question. There is no value-neutral formula for determining what is just. Moral and religious meaning must be smuggled in somehow.

Philosopher and Harvard professor Michael Sandel notes, "Asking democratic citizens to leave their moral and religious convictions behind when they enter the public realm may seem a way of ensuring toleration and mutual respect. In practice, however, the opposite can be true. Deciding important public questions while pretending to a neutrality that cannot be achieved is a recipe for backlash and resentment. A politics emptied of substantive moral engagement makes for an impoverished civic life. . . . To achieve a just society we have to reason together about the meaning of the good life, and to create a public culture hospitable to the disagreements that will inevitably arise."

the Meuse River system, which begins in France and flows through central Belgium. The people, called Walloons, speak French. The Flemings and Walloons have had difficulty creating a united country, and a split is sometimes debated. Steel was once the chief industry in the south, but crude steel is now imported and the steel plants have moved to the northern ports in Flanders. Liège (lee AYZH), the largest city of Wallonia, continues to produce guns and glassware.

Citizens of Belgium enjoy freedom of religion, and 63 percent associate with some form of Christianity. However, 32 percent have no religious affiliation. Islam is also a growing religious movement in Belgium, representing 4 percent of the population. Belgium now has at least 380 mosques. Evangelical Christians make up 1 percent of the population, and their numbers are growing through church planting and personal witness. About 50 percent of the Evangelicals are immigrants, and they are active in planting international (rather than immigrant) churches to reach people from all nationalities living in Belgium.

Luxembourg

Luxembourg is one of Europe's oldest settlements, dating back to 963. Luxembourg is also one of the few remaining duchies. A **duchy** is a country ruled by a duke, and the Grand Duke is Luxembourg's hereditary monarch. The official title of the constitutional monarchy is the Grand Duchy of Luxembourg. The capital is also called Luxembourg.

Seventy-nine percent of the people are Catholic, and most people speak all three official languages. Letzeburgesch, the local dialect of German, is used commonly. German is used in elementary school, while French is used in high school. Although villages still huddle around medieval castles, Luxembourg is now one of the world's most industrialized countries. It has the highest GDP per capita of any country in the world.

Luxembourg plays a leading role in Europe today. Its small size and central location make it a prime neutral location for international endeavors. Luxembourg is an international financial and banking center. It hosts both the secretariat (administrative staff) of the European Parliament and the European Court of Justice.

Freedom of religion is guaranteed in this country, and 82 percent profess some form of Christianity, while 18 percent have no religious affiliation. Evangelical Christians are a tiny minority, representing 0.5 percent of the population, and many of them are immigrants. Evangelical services are conducted in one of nine different languages, reflecting the different nationalities that make up the Evangelical community in Luxembourg.

Section Quiz

1. What is France's capital city, longest river, and highest alpine peak?
2. What does the Netherlands do to reclaim land?
3. What city in the Low Countries is home to the headquarters of the European Union?
★ Why do you think the Low Countries have been at the center of efforts to unite Europe?

Protestantism

Protestantism is a major group in what is broadly defined as Christianity. Finding its roots in the Protestant Reformation of the sixteenth century, Protestantism "protested" against some of the doctrines and practices of the Roman Catholic Church. Among other things, Protestantism's historic beliefs have included the authority of Scripture over tradition, salvation by grace alone through faith alone in Christ alone, and a renunciation of the authority of the pope. Protestantism is characterized by denominations such as Lutherans, Anglicans, Presbyterians, Baptists, Methodists, Pentecostals, and many more.

Parts of Luxembourg seem to belong to a different time.

Combining Religion and Secularism

Belgium and Luxembourg are fairly young, independent countries by European standards, having gained their independence in the 1830s. They are both wealthy countries and have relatively small populations.

These countries have something else in common: they are predominately Roman Catholic. Many of the people continue to celebrate religious holidays, and their festivals often have a religious theme. However, the people of both nations tend to limit their religious activity to an occasional church service or festival. For the most part, the people do not allow traditional religious beliefs to guide their decisions. As a result, the cultures of Belgium and Luxembourg have virtually no Christian influence. This has led the people to place their trust in international organizations, education, and material prosperity.

Germany

Germany is the birthplace of the Reformation. Martin Luther was born in northern Germany, studied in its schools, was converted, and spent the rest of his life preaching to and teaching the German people. Protestant leaders, including Luther, used the printing press to spread the ideas of the Reformation around the world. Today, about 29 percent of the German people are Protestants. About 30 percent of the people are Catholic. Most Lutherans live in the northern plains, while most German Catholics live in the southern uplands. This division is even reflected in their languages. They speak different dialects of German: High German and Low German.

Berlin is the heart of Germany, both ancient and modern. With 3.5 million people, it is one of the largest cities in Western Europe. The city was founded on the Spree River, a tributary of the Elbe (EL buh) River, in the thirteenth century.

After World War II, Berlin lay in ruins—isolated within Soviet-occupied territory. The peace agreement allowed the Allies in the West—the United States, Great Britain, and France—to occupy the western part of Berlin. Refugees escaping the Communists flooded into West Berlin, prompting the Soviets to build a wall around that part of the city in 1961. The Berlin Wall became a hated symbol of the division caused by the Cold War, until its removal in 1989.

The first chancellor of West Germany, Konrad Adenauer (AD n ow ur; 1949–63), utilized free-market ideas, the natural waterways and strong ports of the land, and funds from the Marshall Plan to create the *Wirtschaftswunder* (VIRT shahfts vun duh), meaning "economic miracle." He rebuilt German industry and revived the German economy. By 1955, the nation was producing more goods than it had before the war, despite the loss of East Germany.

LET'S GO EXPLORING

Land Use of Western Europe

1. Besides manufacturing, what are the two most common ways land is used in Continental Europe?
2. What kind of agriculture is most common on the southern peninsulas of Europe?
3. How is agriculture in the Alps different from the surrounding areas?
4. Where is the center of forestry in Europe?
* What would you expect to be the greater regional difference in Western European culture: between the north and the south or between the east and the west?

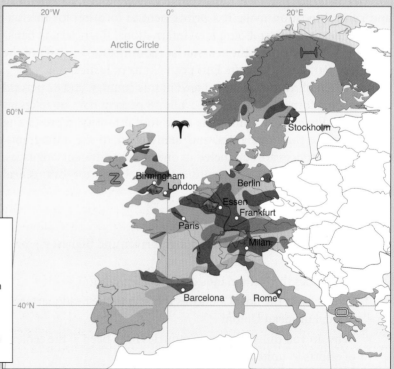

In contrast, East Germany fell further and further behind. Its Communist government greatly hindered economic development. As the 1980s drew to a close, protests started all across Eastern Europe and could not be stopped. In October 1989, East Germany's Communist leader resigned and was later placed under house arrest. Protesters, joined by the wall's guards, tore down the Berlin Wall in November. The two Germanies formally reunited into one nation on October 3, 1990.

Germany's northern plains are part of the Great European Plain that stretches from France to Russia. The deciduous forests of France and the Low Countries give way to a mixture of broadleaf trees and evergreens in Germany, especially as you move east and south into the interior of the continent. The Elbe River and its tributaries flow through the heart of eastern Germany. Upriver from Magdeburg is the town of Wittenberg, where Martin Luther posted his ninety-five theses. By using the northern dialect, High German, Luther's Bible helped to establish the standard for the German language.

The northern plains in western Germany cover five states. Two of them are city-states—Bremen and Hamburg. Hamburg, located downstream from Berlin on the Elbe River, is the main seaport and the third-largest city in Germany. Another important harbor lies on the north coast at Kiel (KEEL). The important **Kiel Canal** directly links the North Sea with the Baltic Sea. This gives German vessels a shortcut to avoid going around Denmark's Jutland Peninsula.

The people of the plains, whether east or west, produce the same products. The western plains in particular have some of the best soil in Europe, formed by a thick layer of loess, a fine-grained soil deposited by the wind. Germany is a large producer of rye, barley, wheat, potatoes, sugar beets, and hogs. Germany's northern plains have the largest concentration of cities and industry in the nation. Germany is now the most populous country in all of Europe (excluding Russia). Diverse industries and great wealth make Germany potentially the most powerful and influential country on the continent.

Farthest west is Germany's most important river, the Rhine River, which flows through several important regions of Germany before it winds west into the Netherlands. At the lower end of the river, where the Ruhr (ROOR) River flows into the Rhine, is an industrial megalopolis called the **Ruhr**, the largest industrial region in Europe and perhaps in the whole world. The Ruhr, centered on the city of Essen, is one of the most crowded regions in Europe. The coal mines in this "smokestack region" make Germany one of the world's largest coal producing nations.

Farther up the Rhine River are the major river ports of Cologne (kuh LOHN) and Bonn. Bonn served as the capital of West Germany while Germany was divided; but after the fall of communism, the government decided to move the capital back to Berlin. Cologne is the largest city in this industrial district, even larger than Bonn, with a population of one million people.

Germany has made up for its lack of important minerals by importing or synthesizing man-made materials. By importing iron from Sweden, Germany has become the top-ranking producer of crude steel in Western Europe. Germany is also a leading Western European country in producing refined copper and refined lead.

The Black Forest covers 2,320 square miles, almost 1,500,000 acres.

Neuschwanstein Castle is one of Europe's most frequently photographed castles.

The provinces of Southern Germany lie on hilly plateaus. Germany's plateaus are part of a wider system of plateaus that begins with the Massif Central of France and stretches through the low Jura Mountains and Ardennes eastward through Germany into the Czech Republic. The whole system is sometimes called the **Central Uplands**.

The rivers in Germany's Central Uplands flow into two major rivers: the Rhine in the west and the Danube in the east. Four of the south's five provinces lie mostly in the drainage basin of the Rhine. The main tributary of the Rhine in southern Germany is the Main River. The Main flows past Frankfurt, the banking center of Germany and home of Germany's stock exchange.

The Black Forest along the French border is the best-known feature in the southwest. Mountains rise east of the Rhine. Dark forests of spruce and fir cover the mountains, which contain the headwaters of the Danube River. Lumber mills and granite quarries provide work. Tourists come to health resorts at the mineral springs near Baden-Baden or to obtain handcrafted toys and cuckoo clocks.

The largest state in Germany, Bavaria lies in the southeast. Bavaria was a duchy throughout the Middle Ages, but Napoleon made it a kingdom in 1805. After the unification of Germany in 1871, Bavaria became a state. Bavaria contains Grosser Arber (4,780 ft.), the highest peak in the Bohemian Forest (known locally as the Bavarian Forest) along the Czech border.

Dairy cattle roam the hills of Bavaria. Hops, used in beer making, are a major cash crop. Munich is the center of the beer industry, celebrated at the annual festival called Oktoberfest. With almost two million people, Munich is the fifth-largest city in Germany. Its great collection of baroque, rococo, and neoclassical architecture makes it one of the finest cities in Europe.

The **Bavarian Alps** stretch along Germany's entire southern border with Austria, not far south of Munich. The range reaches 9,718 feet on the Zugspitze, a popular skiing area. Several famous castles adorn the area.

While Lutheran and Roman Catholic Churches enjoy a special relationship with the German government, freedom of religion is guaranteed. However, the decline in traditional religious groups is evident in the statistics showing that only 64 percent are connected to some form of Christianity, while 31 percent are nonreligious. Islam is also a growing religious presence, representing 4 percent of the primarily immigrant population. Against this backdrop, Evangelical Christians make up 2 percent of the German population. Despite the overall decline in religious activity, Evangelicals are growing and continue to plant new congregations in Germany.

The Alpine Region

The Alpine Mountain system forms a great snowy barrier severing the southern peninsulas of Europe from the rest of the continent. The system runs from France all the way to Albania. It forms the third-largest mountain system in the world (after the Himalayan system of Asia and the Western Cordillera of the Americas).

The primary range in the system is the **Alps**, up to 160 miles wide and 660 miles long, which curves across Italy's northern border.

These mountains display the splendor of God's creation in many ways. They are home to golden eagles, marmots, and exotic mountain goats, such as chamois and ibex.

The Alps are grouped into three main divisions: the Western Alps, Central Alps, and Eastern Alps. The Western Alps lie in France and Italy, while Switzerland contains the Central Alps. The Eastern Alps spread south from Germany across Austria and into Eastern Europe. Few passes cross this barrier, and they can be dangerous, especially in winter.

Switzerland

The rugged Jura Mountains of France and Germany cross over into the northern part of Switzerland. Rhine Falls in this area is the most powerful falls in Europe. The third-largest city in Switzerland, Basel (BAH zuhl), is located in the Rhine River valley. Basel contains part of the vital canal system that links Germany's Rhine River and France's Rhone River.

The Swiss Plateau, or Mittelland, lies between the Jura Mountains in the north and the Swiss Alps in the south. The average altitude is 1,902 feet. The Jura Mountains protect the plateau from cold northern winds, while a warm, dry wind, called a **foehn** (FUHRN), blows from the Alps in the south. Although the winds keep the climate mild, they can cause sudden avalanches.

Glaciers apparently gouged out several long, narrow lake basins on the plateau. The two largest are Lakes Constance and Geneva, at each end of the plateau. The country's two most important rivers—the Rhine and the Rhone—flow from these lakes, respectively. Other large lakes include Lake Neuchâtel (noo shuh TEL), Lake Lucerne, and Lake Zurich. Lake Geneva borders France, and the Rhone River flows west from the lake into France. All of the Mittelland except Lake Geneva drains into Germany's Rhine River.

Switzerland's second-largest city, Geneva, lies on the lake. As you might expect, the people speak French. The Red Cross is one of several international organizations that have made their headquarters in Geneva.

German, spoken by about 64 percent of the people, is one of four official languages. The people speak Schwyzerdütsch, or Swiss German, at home and in public. But standard German is used in the schools, churches, and the media.

Bern, the capital of Switzerland, is on the Aare (AHR uh) River, a tributary of the Rhine. Emmentaler, or Swiss, cheese originated near here. Throughout Switzerland, some watch companies still have their headquarters in the villages that first manufactured the precision watches for which Switzerland is famous. The largest city in Switzerland is Zurich, located at the northern tip of Lake Zurich. Unlike French-speaking Geneva, the citizens of Zurich speak German. Zurich is the hub of international investment and gold trade.

The Alps cover 60 percent of Switzerland, but less than 10 percent of the population lives in that area. The **Swiss Alps**, or Central Alps, stretch across southern Switzerland and consist of four principal ranges. The first major range, the Bernese Alps, lies between the Swiss capital, Bern, and the upper Rhone River. Visitors to the resort of Interlaken enjoy the highest waterfall in the Alps, the Giessbach, which spills 1,982 feet down the mountainside.

A Unique Blend

Switzerland is a unique country in Europe. Surrounded by larger countries and having no natural boundaries, Switzerland has thrived by tolerating diversity and maintaining strict neutrality.

The language you hear in Switzerland depends largely on which region of Switzerland you are visiting. For example, German is the predominant language used in northern Switzerland, while French is the dominant language spoken in western Switzerland. Then there is the southern region of Switzerland, where Italian is spoken.

In addition, the nation is evenly divided between Roman Catholics and Protestants. As a result, both are prominent and equally influential.

Switzerland is also unusual in its granting a privileged status to farmers. Although only about 5 percent of the population is employed in agriculture, the Swiss government provides them with some of the highest subsidies in the world. They do this for several reasons, including the desire to maintain Switzerland's magnificent landscape to continue the thriving tourist industry. Other nations benefit from Swiss farmers because they produce delicious cheeses including Emmental and Gruyere. Another delightful export is Swiss chocolate.

Giessbach Falls

The triple-cirque Matterhorn pierces the sky.

St. Bernard Dogs

St. Bernard Pass, between Mont Blanc and the Matterhorn, links France and Italy. Armies and merchants have crossed this pass for hundreds of years. It is named for the monastery at the pass, which bred the St. Bernard dogs to rescue travelers lost in the snow.

Swiss Banking

Switzerland is famous around the world for its banks. These banks are considered the safest in the world, and laws ensure utmost secrecy. This secrecy has sometimes created controversy, such as that created over the discovery that Nazis had stolen gold and hidden it in Swiss banks.

The other three major ranges in the Swiss Alps lie farther south along the Italian border. The Pennine Alps in the west include both Monte Rosa (15,203 ft.) and the **Matterhorn** (14,692 ft.). Monte Rosa is the highest mountain in Switzerland, but the Matterhorn is more famous because of its rare triple-cirque peak. The peak forms a three-sided pyramid with that has bowl-shaped basins (or cirques) on each side.

East of the Matterhorn are the Lepontine (li PAHN tine) Alps. Italy is easy to reach from this canton of Ticino, but the Alps separate the people from the rest of Switzerland. Engineers have bored through the Alps here to make some of the longest highway tunnels in the world. The St. Gotthard highway tunnel is over ten miles long, and the Simplon railway tunnel is over twelve miles long. People in this area speak Italian. Italians constitute about 10 percent of the Swiss population.

The Rhaetian (REE shun) Alps cover southeast Switzerland. In addition to pockets of Italians, Romansch-speaking people live in the small communities of this canton. Less than 1 percent of the Swiss people speak this quaint language, similar to ancient Latin.

Switzerland is divided into **cantons**. The cantons were once Catholic Church districts, like parishes, but they later became self-governing districts. These cantons eventually joined together into the country of Switzerland. In 1515, Switzerland adopted a policy of neutrality regarding Europe's wars. France violated this neutrality in 1798 by invading Switzerland. Swiss neutrality was guaranteed by the victorious countries following Napoleon's defeat in 1815. Since this time, the Swiss have refused to join organizations that could jeopardize their neutrality. The Swiss government is one of the most democratic in the world. The cantons are united as a federal republic, but the people can demand a popular vote on any issue by submitting a petition with sufficient signatures. At one time, people in each canton met in an open-air assembly, called a *Landsgemeinde*, to conduct government by a show of hands. Today five cantons still elect their magistrates in this way.

As in many countries in Europe, religious freedom is guaranteed in Switzerland. Seventy-six percent of the people identify with some form of Christianity, 15 percent are nonreligious, and 6 percent are

Muslim. Evangelical Christians represent just under 5 percent of the Swiss population, and local congregations are supporting more than 1,700 missionaries to other countries. In addition to foreign missions, there is a growing recognition that the more than one hundred foreign nationalities in Switzerland constitute a nearby mission field.

Liechtenstein

Between Switzerland and Austria is the tiny principality of Liechtenstein (LIK tun s[h]tine), located on the east side of the Rhine. A prince from Vienna first bought land in the area in 1699, and his descendants—the von Liechtensteins—have ruled ever since. The prince now serves under a constitutional monarchy.

Liechtenstein uses Swiss currency and lets Switzerland represent it internationally. Like Switzerland, it has remained neutral in wars and has not even had an army since 1868. The official language is German, but most people speak a dialect called Alemannic (al uh MAN ik). About 76 percent of the people are Catholic.

Before 1950, Liechtenstein was primarily a farming country. Today, only 1 percent of the people farm. Now highly industrialized, it has one of the highest standards of living in the world. Over five thousand businesses have headquarters in Liechtenstein because of its reasonable tax rates. The government also earns a large portion of its money from the sale of beautiful postage stamps.

Religious freedom and religious equality are part of the modern state of Liechtenstein. Various forms of Christianity are embraced by 79 percent of the population, while 14 percent are nonreligious, and 7 percent are Muslim. Evangelical Christians represent 0.5 percent of the population and number less than two hundred people.

Austria

Austria adopted a strict policy of neutrality in the Cold War because of its precarious position between the East and the West. The country maintains close cultural and economic ties to Eastern Europe. Austrians speak German, and over 70 percent of them are Catholic. Most people live in the north, where the **Danube River** winds through the foothills of the Alps.

With almost two million people, **Vienna**, Austria's capital, is the largest city in the country. Vienna is known for baroque architecture and its outstanding musicians, including Franz Haydn, Wolfgang Mozart, Franz Schubert, and Johann Strauss. Concerts, festivals, and operas are performed regularly all over Austria, enjoyed by tourists and natives alike. Vienna is also home to the headquarters of the Organization of Petroleum Exporting Countries (OPEC) and the International Atomic Energy Agency.

The Alps dominate southern Austria. Most people in this region live in the mountain valleys. Austria's forests have allowed it to become

Lipizzaner Horses

One of the highlights of tours in Vienna is a stop at a majestic hall, decorated with ivory and gold and lighted with chandeliers. But tourists don't come to see the architecture. All eyes are turned to events on the dirt floor. The hall has been the home of the Spanish Riding School for over 250 years. The world-famous performers are a troupe of Lipizzaner (LIP it SAH nur) horses, "dancing horses," whose performances are unmatched for their combination of grace and strength.

The Spanish Riding School has been training the Lipizzaners for over four hundred years. It usually takes six or seven years before a horse and rider are ready to perform. They move as one, while the orchestra plays the great music of Vienna. The horses perform several ballet movements, such as a *capriole*, in which they take a flying leap in the air. They stand on their hind legs in a pose called the *levade*. Only the very strongest horses can complete a *courbette*. The horse hops into the air and completes three or more leaps without touching its forelegs to the ground.

The Danube River is Europe's second longest river and runs through or touches the borders of ten countries.

Missionaries Raising Children in Austria

Todd and Sarah Hudson, Vienna, Austria

In Vienna, as in so much of the world, it is a rapidly growing trend to have children call their parents by their first names. Discipline, if existent, is minimal. Children are little people with their own agendas that cannot be quenched by the adult establishment. Demanding obedience and honor is considered the height of a parental ego trip. The converse, however, is the truth. We are not requiring honor because it makes our lives easier. In fact, it is a demanding job to be "demanding." It takes time, patience, and great effort to hold children to a standard. It is much easier to bring a child up "in the way he wants to go." Resistance to the child's will is tiring. Yet God wants and expects children to honor their parents.

a leading exporter of wood in continental Europe. Austria was the world's fifth-largest producer of tungsten as of 2009. The main city in the western panhandle is Innsbruck. It stands on the Inn River, a tributary of the Danube that forms most of Austria's northwestern border with Germany.

The highest and most famous mountain in Austria is Grossglockner (GROHS GLAHK nur; 12,461 ft.), located southeast of Innsbruck. It lies in a central Alpine range called the Hohe Tauern, the hub of the many other ranges in Austria. The primary mountain pass that German invaders and merchants have used to reach Italy is **Brenner Pass**, south of Innsbruck. It is the lowest major pass through the Central Alps, and warm foehns keep it open all year long. Several roads, railroads, bridges, and tunnels now cross Brenner Pass, linking Innsbruck and northern Italy (South Tyrol).

Roman Catholic and Reformed Churches enjoy a special status in Austria. Other religious groups are allowed but operate at a disadvantage. Eighty-three percent of Austrians align with some form of Christianity, just under 12 percent have no religious affiliation, and around 5 percent are Muslim. As in some other European countries, Evangelical Christians constitute only 0.5 percent of the Austrian population but are growing as believers continue to plant new congregations. Accompanying the growth is the need for trained leaders. The Evangelical Academy currently has a Bible college with several campuses to train Christians for leadership positions in these new churches in Austria.

Section Quiz

1. What is the best-known feature of southwest Germany?
2. What river dominates the most populated region of Austria?
3. Which tiny European country transitioned from farming to industry and has no army?
* Why do you think the Alpine countries have traditionally stayed out of European politics?

III. Mediterranean Europe

Mediterranean Europe consists of three large peninsulas jutting into the Mediterranean Sea. The sea offers food, provides harbors,

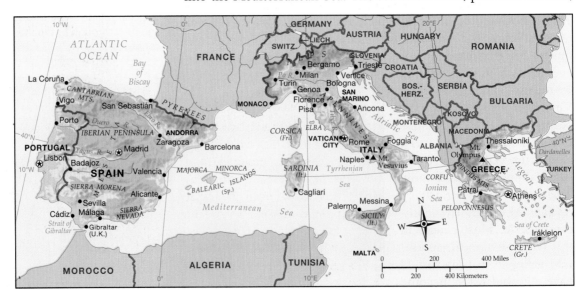

and moderates the climate. Mediterranean Europe has a subtropical mild climate with rainy winters and hot, dry summers. Because of the easy access to trade, this region was the cradle of Western civilization, which eventually spread across the globe.

Iberian Peninsula

The Iberian Peninsula contains the modern-day countries of Spain, Andorra, and Portugal. The waters of the Atlantic Ocean and Mediterranean Sea surround almost 90 percent of the peninsula. The short land border on the north runs through the rugged Pyrenees Mountains.

Spain

Over 80 percent of the Iberian Peninsula lies in Spain. Spain's main provinces were united in 1469 when Isabella I, queen of Castile, married Ferdinand II of Aragon. Most Spaniards are Roman Catholic, and Castilian Spanish is the primary language of business and government.

In 1936, the country was engulfed in a bloody civil war when Spain's military revolted against the country's newly formed Republican government. The fascist victor, Francisco Franco, ruled as a dictator from 1939 to 1973. After Franco's death, Juan Carlos became king of Spain. He pushed democratic reforms, and in 1978 Spain adopted a constitution. The government began to increase local control by allowing the election of regional parliaments. In an attempt to bolster the country's economy, Spain joined the European Economic Community (now the EU) in 1986.

The capital city of Spain, **Madrid**, perched on a plateau over two thousand feet high, is the highest capital in Europe and the most populous among Europe's Mediterranean nations. Madrid is uncomfortably hot in summer and freezing cold in winter. During August, the Spanish government actually relocates to a cooler location on the north coast.

A high plateau extends from Madrid across most of interior Spain. The plateau is called the **Meseta**, meaning "tableland." The Meseta, sprinkled with rocky hills and mountains, is the heartland of Spain. Although the higher elevations are forested, most of the plateau supports only small shrubs and flowering plants. The hot, dry summers, bitterly cold winters, and poor soils make farming difficult. The medieval ruins and small villages of the Meseta are celebrated in Spain's greatest novel, Cervantes's humorous *Don Quixote de la Mancha*.

Spain's longest river, the **Tagus** (TAY gus), cuts the Meseta in half as it flows west to the Atlantic through Portugal. Madrid lies on a tributary of the Tagus upstream from the historic city of Toledo. North of the Tagus, the Meseta stretches to the Pyrenees Mountains. To the south, the Meseta reaches the Sierra Morena. Near Portugal, this mountain range contains Spain's primary mineral resources.

The mountains of the Sierra Nevada rise in the far south. This part of Spain is separated from North Africa by the eight-mile-wide **Strait of Gibraltar**. The narrowness of this strait makes Spain a land bridge between Africa and Europe.

Two rivers, the Ebro and Guadalquivir, flow from the Meseta into fertile lowland basins. Most of Spain's olives come from these basins. In the north, the Ebro River drains east to the Mediterranean.

Basques

There are three small Spanish provinces in "Basque Country": Álava, Vizcaya, and Guipúzcoa. But the heart of their ancient land was Navarre, on the border with France. More than two million Basques live in Spain, and over one-half million live across the border in France. Not much is known about their origins, and their language, Euskara, is unrelated to any known language. The fiercely independent Basques have clung to their way of life despite foreign invaders.

Many Basques make their living from the sea. The adventurous Basques were the first Europeans to hunt whales in the Bay of Biscay during the sixteenth century. Two centuries ago the whales disappeared, so now the Basques fish for tuna and cod instead.

Euskara is very difficult and has several dialects. The first "unified Basque" Bible was not translated until 1995. Most Basques speak Spanish, and only a minority speak Basque. But the Basque speakers are a vocal minority, and many want independence from Spain. A terrorist group, called ETA, began a campaign of bombings and political assassinations in 1968. They have killed over eight hundred people.

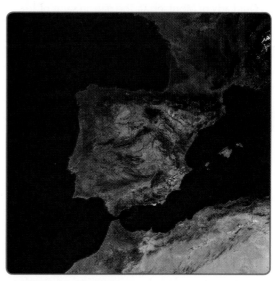

Viewed from space, the narrow Strait of Gibraltar is a striking feature of the earth's surface.

The broad plain of the Ebro Basin includes the province of Aragon. The river delta is well suited for growing rice, a Spanish staple.

In the south, the Guadalquivir River flows west to the Atlantic just beyond Gibraltar. The whitewashed houses and narrow, shaded streets of Seville (say VEEL), Spain's fourth-largest city, make it the epitome of what foreigners think Spain is like. Cádiz is an Atlantic port sixty miles downstream from Seville. Founded by Phoenician traders in 1100 BC, the city claims to be the oldest continuously inhabited city in Europe.

Several ancient ports were established on the narrow coastal plain along Spain's Mediterranean coast. In these fertile lowlands, farmers diverted rivers to irrigate their crops. Spain leads the world in the production of olives. It is also a leading producer of almonds, grapes, strawberries, apricots, lettuce, cauliflower, lemons, limes, oranges, tomatoes, watermelons, oats, and rye.

The seaport and resort city of Alicante, known for its bright skies, was built on the site of the Roman city of Lucentum, or "City of Light." Valencia is located about midway up the coast. Located on the Turia River about three miles from the Mediterranean, it is the third-largest city in Spain. Valencia's rows of white houses reflect its long period of Moorish occupation.

Located in the northeast corner of Spain, **Barcelona** has been an important seaport throughout Spain's history. Today it is the nation's most important manufacturing and trading center. During the Spanish Civil War, Barcelona was a stronghold of opposition to Franco's Nationalists. The people of this region speak Catalán, similar to Provençal, used across the border in France. When Franco forbade the speaking of Catalán, the fiercely independent people continued to use it during soccer matches to cheer for their local team. Today, **Catalonia** is one of three regions of Spain in which there is a second official language. The people here, who think of themselves as Catalonians first and Spaniards second, continue to seek independence.

Montserrat (4,054 ft.), meaning "serrated mountain," is an apt name for this fantastic peak in the foothills of the Pyrenees. On its slope is a popular shrine to Our Lady of Montserrat, the patron saint of Catalonia.

The mountainous north is the only part of Spain that receives adequate rainfall. Its marine-west-coast climate benefits from the moist winds that blow off the Atlantic. The poor-quality soil does not support crops, but the rain provides adequate pastureland. The pastures and woodlands in this region support thriving dairy and paper industries.

In the summer, Spaniards flock to the cool mountains and the northern beaches. The forested mountain slopes are broken by short, swift rivers that flow into the Atlantic. Although these rivers are not navigable, they are harnessed to generate electricity. The river mouths provide harbors for fishing fleets.

The **Cantabrian Mountains** rise from the northern and northwestern edge of the Meseta and run parallel to the Atlantic. In the far west, the people speak Galician, a Portuguese dialect. The Basques live in the eastern Cantabrian Mountains near the port of Bilbao. This area provided iron during the early Industrial Revolution. Today Bilbao is densely populated as a result of industrial development. To the east, the towering Pyrenees rise to over eleven thousand feet and form a formidable barrier between Spain and France.

Until 1992, religious groups not recognized by the state were subject to persecution. Modern Spain is rapidly becoming a multi-religious society in a secular state. Spaniards who associate with some form of Christianity represent 77 percent of the population, while those who consider themselves nonreligious represent nearly 20 percent. Muslims constitute 2 percent, and Evangelical Christians make up 1 percent of the Spanish population. Many of the Evangelicals in Spain are immigrants, and they have increased the Evangelical population from 40,000 to around 450,000 in the last five decades. They meet in 3,000 congregations throughout Spain.

Andorra

Nestled high in the Pyrenees Mountains, Andorra lies between Spain and France. Its name may have come from an old Moorish word meaning "thickly wooded place," but it is indeed a mixture of Spain and France. The official language is Catalán, and both French francs and Spanish pesetas were legal tender until the euro was adopted.

Isolated by steep mountains in their fertile valleys, the Andorrans lived as farmers and shepherds when Charlemagne, according to tradition, granted them independence in exchange for help in fighting the Moors. When roads to Spain and France opened in the 1950s, tourism developed. Today, tourists come to view historic sites and to buy Andorra's rare postage stamps. The low tax rate also lures bargain hunters.

While the Roman Catholic Church remains the established church in this tiny state, freedom of religion has been guaranteed since 1993. Ninety-one percent of the people affiliate with some form of Christianity, 6 percent are nonreligious, and 2 percent are Muslim. Evangelical Christians are believed to represent 0.4 percent of the population and may number around three hundred.

Portugal

The country of Portugal lies on the west coast of the Iberian Peninsula. This small country once ruled large regions of the world. During the sixteenth century, Portugal's empire included Brazil, much of India, and colonies in Africa, the East Indies, and a few ports in China. Today only three small terriories remain from the once great Portuguese empire.

The Spanish Meseta extends into Portugal almost to the coast. North of the Tagus, the climate is cool and rainy. This populous region supports many small farms that produce grapes, olives, and grains. Deposits of tungsten in this area enabled Portugal to rank as the sixth-highest producer of this mineral worldwide as of 2009.

South of the Tagus River, the climate is warmer and the terrain less rugged. Forests of cork oak trees in this region produce large quantities of cork for export. Wealthy landowners have large farms in the area. Because of the forests and large farms, the population is small.

Missions in Europe

Missionaries to Europe face a unique challenge. The people of Europe have had the gospel preached among them longer than any other part of the world except for the Middle East and North Africa. Of these three regions only Europe successfully resisted Muslim invasions. As a result, Europe has a long Christian heritage. The Reformation took place in Europe. Christians from Europe stood at the forefront of Christian missions in the eighteenth and nineteenth centuries. But at that time many Europeans began to doubt the Bible's truthfulness. In the last half-century, church attendance has dropped in many European countries. In Roman Catholic countries, such as Poland, church attendance may be higher, but the need for the gospel is just as great. Missionaries to Europe, as well as Christian pastors in those countries, face the challenge of bringing the gospel to people who think they already know what Christianity is and therefore are not interested in it.

The value that Europeans place on community and compassion provides an open door for Christian ministry. Europeans believe that churches should be involved in compassionate outreach to societies' most vulnerable. Christians who show the love of Christ in meeting people's temporal needs are therefore able to open up opportunities to minister to people's eternal needs. While the former ministry should never replace evangelism, it is a valid means of displaying the love of Christ in a way that opens doors for evangelistic ministry.

Cork oak tree after the lower bark has been removed

The great port at Lisbon is prone to floods and other disasters. Its greatest tragedy was an earthquake in 1755 that leveled the city and killed sixty thousand inhabitants.

With a metropolitan population of almost three million, **Lisbon** is Portugal's capital and largest city. Lisbon's harbor, at the mouth of the Tagus River, is one of the finest natural harbors in the world. The official language is Portuguese, and most people are Roman Catholic.

The government at Lisbon was tyranical in the past. From 1928 to 1968, a dictator denied the people basic civil rights. In 1974, a military group seized control of the government and vowed to restore democracy. Two years later Portugal held its first free elections in more than fifty years. The standard of living improved as some state-owned industries were privatized. The country's future growth is now tied to the growth of the European Union, which it joined in 1986.

Porto is Portugal's second-largest city, and it stands at the mouth of the second-most important river, the Duero River. Like Lisbon, it is a canning center for sardines, but it is also famous for port wine. The beautiful beaches from Porto south to Lisbon have earned this area the name Silver Coast. Men from Porto and the fishing villages along the coastal plain fish for tuna, sardines, and cod. Dried cod, called *bacalhau*, is one of the nation's favorite foods. The Portuguese claim that a good cook can prepare it 365 different ways, one for each day of the year.

Freedom of religion was granted in Portugal in 1974, and the nation remains a nominally religious state with 94 percent of the Portuguese identifying with some form of Christianity. Five percent of the population considers itself nonreligious. Evangelical Christians represent 3 percent of the Portuguese population, and they are experiencing modest growth. As in many countries, the need for church leaders continues to outpace the number of people being trained. Bible institutes and Bible correspondence courses are being used to help meet this need.

Section Quiz

1. What peninsula contains Spain and Portugal?
2. What mountainous plateau covers most of Spain, including the capital, Madrid?
3. Which river cuts the Meseta in half as it flows through Portugal to the Atlantic Ocean?
* Why has Portugal's government been unstable at times? What event ended this instability?

Italian Peninsula

Italy

Italy occupies a long and narrow boot-shaped peninsula. The Alps form the top of the boot, while its toe stretches almost to Africa. Although Italy usually has a sunny and mild climate, its extremes are exceptional. Winter is cold in the north, while the *sirocco* (winds) may bring to the south the intense heat of the Sahara. The name *Italy* comes from the ancient Romans, who referred to the southern part of the peninsula as *Italia*, meaning "grazing land."

Italy's coastline stretches for 4,722 miles and is known more for its beautiful beaches and resorts than its natural harbors. Nearly three-fourths of the country's land is either hilly or mountainous. Areas isolated by the mountains have their own unique customs, dialects, and cuisine. The main lowland areas lie along the west coast and on the boot heel.

The Alps form the northern border of Italy. Lake Garda and Lake Como are two of the large alpine lakes that attract many tourists. People who live along the Austrian border speak German rather than Italian.

The **Apennine** (AP uh nine) **Mountains** stretch the length of the Italian peninsula. The highest peak, Corno Grande, reaches only 9,554 feet, and its once-thick forests have been indiscriminately cleared for crops, resulting in serious erosion. Though lower and less picturesque than the Alps, the Apennines form the backbone of Italy and separate northern Italy from the Italian peninsula.

The **Po River** is the longest river in Italy. From its origin in Italy's northwest corner, the Po flows east until it empties into the Adriatic. The broad plain of the Po is the largest in Mediterranean Europe. The Alps and the Apennines on either side of the valley provoke rains, which wash soil and minerals into the drainage basin. The resulting good soils make this valley the most heavily cultivated part of Italy. Vegetables, grapes, and grains such as wheat, corn, and barley are grown here.

Large ships navigate inland on the Po as far as Turin. The region from Turin to Milan is the industrial center of Italy. Large power plants on the upper reaches of the Po provide electricity for factories producing cars, chemicals, and candy. Milan, Italy's second-largest city, is also a banking center and contains the world-famous opera house La Scala. North of the Po River Delta, the Adriatic Coastal Plain extends to the eastern border. Venice is the most famous city in this area.

A wide coastal plain lies along the west coast of the Italian Peninsula. The coastal plains rise into foothills as they move inland toward the mountains. The southern regions are the most populous with the cities of Rome and Naples. The northern region, Tuscany, contains the cities of Pisa and Florence.

Rome, the capital, stands along the Tiber River, surrounded by seven steep hills. Rome blends the ancient and the modern. Each year

Venice

Unlike most cities, Venice is built on over one hundred low islands in a swampy lagoon of the Adriatic Sea. The people do not ride in cars and busses over paved streets. Instead, they ride in motorboats or in gondolas (long black boats). The seaside buildings are built on piles of mud and supported by debris, logs, and rocks. Many of these foundations were built during the Renaissance. Approximately four hundred footbridges cross the 150 canals, and a major road links the city to the mainland.

The sea, which once contributed to Venice's greatness, now poses a threat to its existence. Experts are working on ways to save the foundations of Venice's buildings, which are slowly eroding under the constant washing of seawater and the vibrations from motorboats. In the twentieth century, authorities noticed that the entire city was sinking about one inch every five years. They forbade drawing water from Venice's underground wells, and the sinking slowed considerably.

Portions of eastern Tuscany lie in the Apennines.

St. Peter's Basilica is almost the same height as the Great Pyramid at Giza.

Mount Vesuvius

Mount Vesuvius (vih SOO vee us) (4,190 ft.), mainland Europe's only active volcano, is about seven miles southwest of Naples. Tourists hike thirty minutes to the volcano's top. It has erupted eighty times since its most famous eruption in AD 79, which buried the ancient Roman cities of Pompeii and Herculaneum. Volcanic ash and mud preserved the ruins of these cities.

The elevation of Mt. Vesuvius changes with each major eruption—a low of 3,668 feet in 1906 compared to its current elevation of 4,202 feet.

thousands of tourists flock to the "Eternal City" to view the antiquities that testify of Rome's past greatness. The city boasts the Colosseum, the remains of luxurious Roman baths, and the foundations of opulent palaces built for Roman emperors. Today these antiquities exist in the midst of modern office buildings and dawn-to-dusk traffic jams.

Although a parliamentary republic was established in 1946, competing interests in the country have prevented the government from forming a lasting coalition. Over fifty governments rose and fell in the first fifty years after World War II. Recently, leaders in the rich north have even called for independence from the poorer south, which wants the government to increase socialist programs that would redistribute the nation's wealth.

The heel of the boot is called **Apulia** (uh POOL yuh). This region is cut off from the rest of Italy by the Apennines. Most of Apulia is a plateau which ends in steep cliffs that drop into the Adriatic Sea. Italy produces about one-sixth of the world's olives, mostly on large estates in Apulia and Sicily. Bari and Taranto are the main ports and support a large fishing industry.

Italy controls several islands in the Mediterranean Sea. The large islands of Sicily and Sardinia are very important. Sicily, the most populated island in the Mediterranean Sea, is situated just two miles from mainland Italy's toe. Mount Etna, Europe's highest volcano, rises to a height of 10,902 feet on the east coast of Sicily. The fertile volcanic soils surrounding Mount Etna encourage farming, but the rough terrain covering 80 percent of the island provides only limited arable land. Sicily was a primary setting for the imaginative journey of Homer's *Odyssey*. It also was the biblical site of Syracuse, where Paul spent three days on his way to Rome (Acts 28:12).

The island of **Sardinia** is located about one hundred miles off Italy's west coast and nine miles south of the French island of Corsica. Its mountainous terrain makes for a strikingly beautiful and sparsely populated island. Some consider Sardinia's beaches the finest in the Mediterranean, especially the exclusive Costa Smeralda (Emerald Coast). Tourist attractions on these islands include many historic sites.

While religious freedom is the law of the land in Italy, it is not consistently enforced. Eighty-two percent of the Italian people identify with some form of Christianity, 14 percent have no religious affiliation, and nearly 3 percent are Muslim. Evangelical Christianity represents just over 1 percent of the population. Despite religious opposition and the growth of secularism in Italy, Evangelical congregations are experiencing modest growth, and a few Italians are taking up the mantle of foreign missions. As in other European countries, many of the Evangelicals are immigrants from Eastern Europe, Africa, and other regions.

Monaco

Monaco is a tiny principality on the French Riviera about ten miles from the Italian border. Much of Monaco is built on cliffs overlooking the sea.

Italians from Genoa first ruled the area in the twelfth century and built a fort in 1215. Since 1308, the Italian prince has been from the Grimaldi family. Although the prince of Monaco has Italian ancestry, he speaks French. The official language is French, most of the citizens are of French anscesty, and France is their main trade partner. In 1918, the prince signed a treaty permitting France to annex Monaco if Monaco ever lacks a male heir to the throne. The mixed French and Italian peoples of Monaco are known as Monégasques.

The palace and fortress is called Monaco-Ville. To the west lies the industrial area of Fontvieille, while to the east lies the secluded harbor and port area of La Condamine. Beyond the port lies Monte Carlo, an area famous for its luxury hotels, shops, beaches, and gambling casinos.

While the state religion is Roman Catholicism, freedom of religion exists in this tiny state. Eighty-five percent of the population identifies with some form of Christianity, 11 percent consider themselves nonreligious, and Evangelical Christians represent just over 1 percent of the population. Christian radio broadcasts are being used to spread the gospel in this state.

San Marino

San Marino is located in the central Apennines. **Mount Titano** (ti TAHN oh; 2,424 ft.) lies at the heart of the country. The people speak Italian, and most are Roman Catholic. Grapes, leather, and cheese are the main products. According to tradition, a Christian stonecutter named Marinus and his followers used this mountain refuge to escape religious persecution by Emperor Diocletian in the year 301. San Marino remained independent during the unification of Italy, and it now claims to be the world's oldest republic.

Vatican City

The pope leads the Roman Catholic Church from Vatican City, sometimes referred to as the Holy See. The tiny country, completely surrounded by the city of Rome, obtained independence by the Treaty of Lateran in 1929. With less than one thousand residents and an area of only one-sixth of a square mile, it is the smallest country in the world. Most of those who work in the country live in Rome.

Vatican City also has its own bank, post office, newspaper, and even a rarely used jail. The Vatican's radio station broadcasts in forty different languages. Its unique police force consists of Swiss guards whose sole duty is to protect the pope. These brightly costumed guards patrol with swords and halberds.

Malta

The island country of Malta is located about sixty miles south of Sicily in the Mediterranean Sea. The country consists of the two

Ministates Near Italy

Four small countries lie in or near Italy. These countries share Italy's mediterranean climate and are popular tourist destinations. All include historic sites, medieval buildings, and museums. Their economies depend on tourism and their rare and valuable postage stamps. Some of these ministates also have limited agriculture similar to adjacent regions of Italy.

Collectors prize stamps from Monaco (shown here), San Marino, Liechtenstein, Malta, and other ministates.

islands of Gozo and Malta as well as a few smaller islands. On Malta, a series of low hills dominates the terrain. Gozo is primarily a flat island with rocky soil and few rivers. Farmers struggle to grow grapes, onions, potatoes, wheat, and flowers. Most islanders work in the dockyards.

Around AD 60 the apostle Paul was shipwrecked on Malta (Acts 27:27–28:11) in the bay which now bears his name. Legend has it that Paul converted the entire population to Christianity during his stay on the island. Today most Maltese are Roman Catholic, and Catholic doctrine is required teaching in the public schools.

Malta's harbors and its location in the Mediterranean Sea have given the country tactical importance. Malta was long held by the British as a naval base, but the British colony gained its independence in 1964. Though the British navy has departed, English remains an official language together with Maltese.

The state religion is Roman Catholicism, but freedom of religion is guaranteed in the state's constitution. Ninety-seven percent identify with some form of Christianity, 2 percent are nonreligious, and 1 percent are Muslim. Evangelicals make up just over 1 percent of the population. Since British officials did not allow Evangelicals to minister in the country, this movement has only existed since independence was granted in 1964. Fewer than twenty congregations and house churches exist in Malta, and the fledgling Evangelical groups are laboring to increase in numbers and spiritual influence in Malta.

Greece

Greece occupies the southern tip of the Balkan Peninsula that juts out of Europe at the eastern end of the Mediterranean. Greece's terrain is mostly rough and mountainous, but about 30 percent of the country has arable soil. Farmers must work hard to get anything to grow in the rocky soil. In the country's many mountainous regions, the population is sparse, with most people residing in small villages. The largest and most productive farms are located either along the coast or on interior plains where irrigation is common.

The ancient Roman province of Achaia occupied the heart of Greece around the city of Athens. The mainland portion is Central

The Parthenon crowns the Acropolis at Athens. Even in ruins, it has moved generations of Western poets.

Greece. Achaia also included a large peninsula in the south, called the **Peloponnesus** (pel uh puh NEE sus).

Today, small villages are scattered across Central Greece. Farmers grow cotton or raise sheep and goats on the hillsides. Lamb is a central feature in many Greek dishes, such as gyros. Goat's milk is used to make a cheese called feta.

Athens sits on a plain in southeastern Greece. About a third of the population resides here, a city which sprawls over 165 square miles. One-half of the nation's industry takes place in the city, and the pollution is very harmful, both to the people and to the ancient ruins. With its nearby port, Piraeus, Athens is the commercial center of Greece.

The Peloponnesus is the large, hand-shaped peninsula in southern Greece. Though rugged, it is less mountainous than Central Greece. Crops including citrus fruits, grapes, and olives grow mainly on the coastal plains.

The ruins of Mycenae stand on the northeast side of the peninsula. Mycenae was the first civilization on mainland Europe and was the center of culture recounted in Homer's epic poem the *Iliad*.

On the mainland north of Central Greece is Thessaly, a valley coveted by cities in Achaia and people farther north. Its importance arises from the fertile farmland, which produces most of the wheat grown in Greece. The valley is ringed by mountains. The highest and most famous is Mount Olympus (9,570 ft.) at the north end of the valley. The Pindus Mountains border the valley on the west and rise to over eight thousand feet. Modern Greece took Thessaly from the Ottoman Turks in 1881.

North of Thessaly is a region known as **Macedonia**. It is one part of a larger historical region where Alexander the Great rose to power. It is now divided between Greece, Bulgaria, and the modern nation of Macedonia. The Macedonian region of Greece stretches along Greece's northern border east to a three-fingered peninsula on the Aegean coast, called Khalkidhiki Peninsula. The coastal plain of Macedonia is Greece's most productive agricultural area. Major crops include maize, sugar beets, olives, cotton, rice, and wheat. Tobacco is grown here for sale in other parts of Europe.

Macedonia's excellent seaport, Thessaloníki, is the second-largest city in Greece. It was named after a sister of Alexander the Great. The apostle Paul preached in three cities of Macedonia, including Thessaloníki (Acts 16:9–17:13).

Throughout its history, Greece has had trouble with the territories that lie on its outer edges. The ancient kingdom of Epirus lay west of Macedonia in the Pindus Mountains, and Thrace lay east on the coastal plain that touches the Black Sea. Greece took Epirus and much of Macedonia from Turkey during the Balkan War of 1912. It received part of Thrace from Turkey in 1919 after World War I. The eastern half of Thrace remains in Turkish hands. A small minority of Albanians still live in Epirus, Slavs live in Macedonia, and a large number of Turks live in Thrace. The nations of Albania, Macedonia, Bulgaria, and Turkey still covet these lands.

About one-fifth of Greece's territory consists of more than 500 islands—166 of which are inhabited. Ever since Greece obtained independence, it has fought to regain control of the islands off the coast of Turkey. The Greeks have a name for their goal—the Megali Idea,

Ruins of the North Portico in Knossos, Crete

meaning "Great Idea." Only a couple of islands in the northeast are still held by Turkey, and the eastern island of Cyprus is an independent country divided between Greeks and a Turkish minority.

The island of Crete lies southeast of mainland Greece at the south end of the Aegean Sea. The largest of the Greek isles, it is known as the "Great Island." Mountains rise sharply from the sea along the south shore and provide a scenic backdrop to the cities and beautiful beaches in the north. The most interesting tourist stop is the ruins of the ancient Minoan capital, Knossos, possibly destroyed by a volcano.

The Ionian Islands lie off the west coast of Greece in the Ionian Sea. These fertile islands receive more rainfall than the rest of Greece. The main crops include figs, citrus fruits, olives, and grapes. Ithaca, the island home of Odysseus in Homer's *Odyssey*, is a popular destination. The island of Corfu is strategically located at the north end of the chain near Italy and Albania. It has changed hands many times. This beautiful island, the second-largest in the chain, is known for its wildflowers.

The majority of Greece's islands are Aegean Islands in the sparkling Aegean Sea. These rocky and sparsely inhabited islands are divided into three groups. The Cyclades, a group of 220 islands owned by Greece since its independence, form a circle in the Aegean Sea. The group includes the island Thíra (or Santorin). Its huge volcanic crater indicates that the island once exploded in the largest eruption in history, perhaps accounting for the demise of Minoan civilization.

The Sporades stretch across the center of the Aegean to the Turkish coast. Throughout the Aegean, islanders fish for mackerel and harvest sponges. Greece obtained the last of these islands in 1913 as a result of the Balkan Wars.

The Dodecanese ("twelve islands") lie southeast of the Cyclades off the coast of Turkey. The largest Dodecanese island is Rhodes. It has many streams and natural harbors, where ancient ships anchored for the night (Acts 21:1). Rhodes made a massive bronze statue of the sun god Helios in the fifth century BC that was as tall as the Statue of Liberty. This statue, called the Colossus of Rhodes, was one of the Seven Wonders of the Ancient World.

Historically the Greek Orthodox Church has enjoyed a special relationship with the Greek government, but that is gradually changing. Ninety-one percent of the Greek people affiliate with some form of Christianity, 6 percent are Muslim, and 3 percent are nonreligious. Evangelical Christianity represents about 0.4 percent of the Greek population.

Section Quiz

1. What mountain range forms the backbone of the Italian Peninsula?
2. What is the smallest country in the world?
3. What peninsula contains such famous sites as Mycenae and Olympia?
★ Compare and contrast Mediterranean Europe and Continental Europe.

Chapter 11 Review

Making Connections

1. What two nations have the highest population densities in Western Europe?
2. Why do you think Roman Catholicism is the dominant religion in southern and Western Europe?
3. Why is Protestantism significant in Germany's history?
4. How has Germany made up for its shortage of natural resources?
5. Why did Austria maintain a strict policy of neutrality during the Cold War?

Developing Geography Skills

1. Many of the countries of Western Europe have rivers. How do the rivers in Western European countries contribute to their prosperity?
2. What effect do the Alps have on European culture and geography?

Thinking Critically

1. What are two cultural geographic reasons that Western Europe has been so influential in world history?
2. Western European countries are generally considered secular, though many have tax-funded state churches. In contrast, the United States is not considered a secular nation and does have separation of church and state as part of its constitution. What distinguishes separation of church and state from secularism?

Living in God's World

1. Compose a paragraph that describes the guidelines a local church will want to consider in developing programs to meet people's temporal needs. Specify the goals that they should have with such programs. Note potential dangers of such programs.
2. Choose a public policy topic that is currently debated and formulate an argument for the Christian position that is both distinctively Christian and potentially persuasive to the wider public.

People, Places, and Things to Know

North Atlantic Drift
River Thames
downs
moors
the Pennines
glens
lochs
Ben Nevis
loughs
Sogne Fjord
Galdhøpiggen
Lapps
Mount Hekla
Althing
Vatnajökull
Seine River
Loire River
Normandy
Mont Blanc
Massif Central
Pyrenees Mountains
Basques
polders
Rhine River
Brussels
Flanders
Ardennes
Wallonia
duchy
Berlin
Kiel Canal
Ruhr
Central Uplands
Bavarian Alps
Alps
foehn
Swiss Alps
Matterhorn
cantons
Danube River
Vienna
Brenner Pass
Madrid
Meseta
Tagus
Strait of Gibraltar
Barcelona
Catalonia
Cantabrian Mountains
Lisbon
Apennine Mountains
Po River
Apulia
Sardinia
Mount Titano
Peloponnesus
Athens
Macedonia

EASTERN EUROPE

I. Baltic Region
   A. Poland
   B. Baltic States

II. The Carpathians
   A. Czech Republic
   B. Slovakia
   C. Hungary

III. The Western Balkans
   A. Slovenia
   B. Croatia
   C. Bosnia and Herzegovina
   D. Montenegro
   E. Albania

IV. The Eastern Balkans
   A. Macedonia
   B. Serbia
   C. Kosovo
   D. Bulgaria
   E. Romania

V. The Eastern Plains
   A. Moldova
   B. Ukraine
   C. Belarus

𝐀fter our study of Western Europe's pleasant climate, rich soils, and bustling cities, we turn to Eastern Europe. This region is quite unlike Western Europe. For much of the twentieth century, this area was under the control of the Soviet Union. As a result, it generally lacks the material prosperity that is characteristic of Western European nations.

Since the collapse of communism in 1989, some countries have made great strides in establishing themselves politically and economically. Others have degenerated into civil war and struggled to settle long-standing disputes in order to achieve peace.

Eastern Europe has appropriately been called a **shatter belt**. The size, shape, and number of countries have frequently changed. The borders of some countries shifted back and forth, depending on the military success of their powerful neighbors. Each time a nation revolted against its conquerors and set up a new country, it was conquered again and divided among the victors. Some countries even disappeared from political maps for a period of time.

Eastern Europe Fast Facts						
Country	Capital	Area (sq. mi.)	Pop. (M) (2013)	Pop. Density (per sq. mi.)	Per Capita GDP ($US)	Life Span
Albania	Tiranë	12,000	3.56	250.95	$7,800	77.59
Belarus	Minsk	80,155	10.30	120.09	$15,000	71.48
Bosnia and Herzegovina	Sarajevo	19,741	4.03	196.33	$8,100	78.96
Bulgaria	Sofia	42,823	7.45	163.03	$13,800	73.84
Croatia	Zagreb	21,831	4.50	205.01	$18,000	75.99
Czech Republic	Prague	30,450	10.24	333.76	$27,100	77.38
Estonia	Tallinn	17,461	1.33	72.53	$20,400	73.58
Hungary	Budapest	35,919	10.01	276.72	$19,600	75.02
Kosovo	Pristina	4,204	1.8	439.51	$6,500	----------
Latvia	Riga	24,938	2.29	87.35	$16,800	72.93
Lithuania	Vilnius	25,174	3.60	139.66	$19,100	75.55
Macedonia	Skopje	9,781	2.05	213.39	$10,500	75.36
Moldova	Chişinău	13,067	4.46	277.03	$3,400	69.51
Montenegro	Podgorica	5,416	0.63	120.66	$11,500	----------
Poland	Warsaw	120,728	38.64	317.94	$20,200	76.25
Romania	Bucharest	91,699	23.33	237.63	$12,500	74.22
Serbia	Belgrade	34,116	9.40	212.31	$10,400	74.56
Slovakia	Bratislava	18,859	5.43	291.02	$23,300	76.03
Slovenia	Ljubljana	7,828	2.01	254.56	$28,800	77.48
Ukraine	Kiev	233,090	47.43	191.23	$7,200	68.74

I. Baltic Region

Four nations in Eastern Europe—Poland, Lithuania, Latvia, and Estonia—have ports on the Baltic Sea. The latter three countries are known as the **Baltic States**. The dominant land feature of all four countries is the Northern European Plain, which rolls across northern Europe from France to Russia. Numerous rivers drain this agricultural belt.

The warm marine-west-coast climate of Western Europe gradually gives way to a colder climate in the heart of the Eurasian continent. The term for this type of cold, wet climate is a *humid continental* climate. Precipitation averages between twenty and thirty inches a year. Summer temperatures often reach the eighties, and freezing temperatures endure through much of the winter.

Poland

Poland lies almost entirely within the Northern European Plain. Unfortunately, the Polish people have suffered from a lack of natural barriers. The Poles, who account for 97 percent of Poland's population, are descendants of the western Slavs, who migrated into Europe from Asia around two thousand years ago. The Slavic language has evolved into a dozen languages.

The Poles were among the first Slavic tribes to convert to Christianity. In the great division of 1054 between the Eastern Orthodox and Roman Catholic (western) Churches, Poland sided with Rome. Later, during the Reformation, Protestantism showed strength initially, but Catholicism eventually prevailed in Poland because of military victories by Roman Catholic forces.

The eighteenth century found Poland caught between three growing empires—Prussia, Austria, and Russia. In a series of three agreements, the foreign emperors agreed to divide up Poland's territories. In 1795 Poland ceased to exist as an independent country. After World War I, President Woodrow Wilson of the United States insisted that the Poles be given their own nation again.

Then came Hitler's German armies in World War II, followed by the Soviet armies that "liberated" Poland from the Germans. Russia forced Poland to join the **Soviet bloc**, a string of semi-independent countries behind the Iron Curtain. Puppet rulers, like puppets on strings, took orders from the Soviets.

The "year of surprises"—1989—showed the world just how unpopular the Soviet system was among the people. In a few remarkable months, all the countries within the Soviet bloc cast off communism and threw open their borders to the West. Poland started the movement in April 1989, when it legalized a labor union called Solidarity and a few months later held the first free elections in Eastern Europe in forty years. Today, Poland is slowly transitioning to a free-market economy. Poland joined the North Atlantic Treaty Organization (NATO) in 1999 and the European Union (EU) in 2004.

In Poland all religions enjoy equal rights, although Roman Catholicism enjoys a preeminent position in a nation where 90 percent of the people identify with some form of Christianity. Ten percent of the people are nonreligious, and 0.3 percent are Evangelical Christians. Growth in the number of Evangelicals has been slow, but some congregations are supporting missionaries to neighboring countries. Christian literature, including a Polish Bible, is available and provides a powerful opportunity for the spread of the gospel.

Warsaw

With a population over 1.7 million, Warsaw is Poland's largest city. This historic city has seen many conquerors. The last invaders, the Nazis, leveled the city in 1944 during the sixty-three-day Warsaw Uprising, killing over one-quarter million of the city's inhabitants. In an unusual gesture of kindness, the Soviets restored the quaint buildings of Old Warsaw after the war, using old photographs and written accounts. The rest of the city now has a modern appearance, with

Farmers in Poland have tilled the land of the Northern European Plain for centuries.

plain rectangular apartments and high-rise buildings. A monument remains in Castle Square honoring Sigismund III Vasa, the king who first moved the capital to Warsaw in 1596.

Central Plains

Larger than either Italy or the United Kingdom, Poland has played a central role in the history of Europe. The best farmland and most of the nation's major cities lie on the Central Plains. Warsaw lies on the **Vistula** (VIS chuh luh) **River**, the major artery of shipping through the Central Plains. Poland's farms are leading producers of rye, potatoes, oats, and hogs. Poland's sausages are world renowned.

Few people live on the plains near the coast, where glaciers have left many lakes and rocky moraines. The Masurian Lakeland lies east of the Vistula on the coastal plains, and the Pomeranian Lakeland lies in the west. These lakes, nestled among low hills, are popular among campers. The Great Poland Lakeland is located west of Warsaw.

Near the mouth of the Vistula is Gdańsk (formerly Danzig), Poland's largest port and once its most populous city. The hardworking shipbuilders of Gdańsk formed Solidarity, the first trade union in the Iron Curtain. In the 1980s **Lech Walesa**, the head of the union, demanded changes that helped to bring about the end of communism in Eastern Europe. He later became the first president of free Poland, introducing many reforms to the economy.

Southern Uplands

The Polish plains rise into a series of hills and scattered mountains in southern Poland. Mines there produce zinc, lead, and sulfur; Poland ranks tenth worldwide in copper and sixth in silver production. A coal field that crosses the border with the Czech Republic is the largest source of coal in Europe outside the German Ruhr.

Galicia—Southeastern Poland consists of hills and low mountains, rising into the Carpathian Mountains on the border. Farms cover the uplands, although they are not as productive as farms on the Central Plains.

This region, drained by the upper Vistula River, is known as Western Galicia. (The Soviet Union took Eastern Galicia away from Poland during World War II.) **Kraków** (KRAK ou), the third-largest city in Poland, is located on the upper Vistula River. Kraków was the first capital of Poland. Here King Casimir the Great (r. 1333–70) built the magnificent Wawel Castle on a rocky hill above the Vistula River. Kraków was the only major city in Poland that escaped destruction during World War II. Tourists still enjoy visiting the city because of its fine castles and medieval architecture.

Today many foreigners visit a rail center thirty-three miles west of Kraków, called **Auschwitz** (OUSH vits) (Oświęcim in Polish). Auschwitz was the largest of several Nazi "death camps" where the Nazis killed over 2.5 million Jews and Poles, whom Hitler considered "inferior races." Many Jews had lived in Poland, a haven for oppressed peoples who were forced to flee other countries in Europe. In 1933, on the eve of Hitler's rise to power in Germany, the Jewish population of Poland was about three million—the largest concentration of Jews in Europe. By 1950, this number had decreased to about forty-five thousand. (Some survivors of the Holocaust left Poland when the national state of Israel was founded in 1948.)

Gdańsk, formerly called Danzig, has been an important trade center on the Baltic Sea for a thousand years.

Wawel Castle in Kraków, Poland

Auschwitz today

Silesia—The Sudeten Mountains lie on the southwest border of Poland. Waters from the Sudeten Mountains flow into the **Oder River**, which flows west and then north along the German border into the Baltic Sea. The industrial city of Wroclaw, located on the upper Oder, processes minerals from the mountains.

The region drained by the Oder River is known as **Silesia** (sigh LEE zhuh). Many emperors have fought over this valuable piece of property. Frederick the Great's invasion in 1740 sparked a major war fought on three continents. (In America it was called the French and Indian War.) Until World War II, most of the Silesian people were Germans. When the Soviets gave this land to Poland in return for the land it took from eastern Poland, over three million Germans left their homes in Silesia, and many Poles resettled there.

Baltic States

Located on the Northern European Plain, the Baltic States of Estonia, Latvia, and Lithuania have low rolling hills with many shallow lakes and swamps. Besides rye, farmers grow potatoes or raise dairy cattle.

The Baltic States have a rich heritage, which they celebrate with annual festivals that display traditional dress and recall the glorious deeds of the past. After centuries of occupation by foreigners, they received independence after World War I. But in 1944, the Baltic States were incorporated into the Soviet Union. Recalling their independent spirit, they were the first of the fifteen republics in the Soviet Union to declare independence in 1991. Their bravery helped to hasten the breakup of the Soviet Union.

While the Baltic States were a part of the Soviet Union, the Soviets invested a great deal of time and resources into strengthening the economies and transportation networks of these states. After the Baltic States achieved their independence, they retained the infrastructure that the Soviets had built.

Lithuania

Lithuania is the largest of the Baltic States and the farthest from Russia's capital. Over 50 percent of Lithuania is cultivated land, and almost a third is forest. The country is mostly flat, but the eastern portion is more hilly. Eighty-four percent of its people are ethnic Lithuanians. Poles and Russians each make up about 6 percent of the population.

About 77 percent of the people are Roman Catholic. While Lithuania was part of the Soviet Union, devout Roman Catholics opposed the Soviet Union's atheistic government by setting up crosses on a place called the **Hill of Crosses**. Although the Soviet authorities destroyed the crosses numerous times, the Lithuanians continued to replace them. The Hill of Crosses provides an excellent example of the Lithuanians' religious fervor and nationalistic spirit.

Lithuania has the oldest documented history among the Baltic States. Tacitus (c. 55–c. 120) mentioned that this Baltic region sold amber to the Romans. Lithuania united with Poland in the twelfth century when its king converted to Catholicism and married the heir to the Polish throne. Russia later ruled Lithuania after the partitioning of the kingdom of Poland, except for the brief respite between

World Wars I and II. It has made great progress in developing a free republic.

Lithuania joined both NATO and the EU in 2004. Its trade has shifted from a focus on Russia to a focus on Western Europe. The country benefits from Klaipėda, its major warm-water port on the Baltic and has developed a thriving economy. Its industries include machinery, fabrics, transportation equipment, and paper products. Lithuania's two most abundant crops are potatoes and wheat.

As in Poland, Lithuania allows religious freedom but gives preference to Roman Catholicism. Eighty-five percent of the people affiliate with some form of Christianity, and 14 percent consider themselves nonreligious. Evangelical Christians make up 1 percent of the population, and their numbers grow around 3 percent each year. As is often the case, steady growth has led to a shortage of trained church leaders, and a few denominational schools are attempting to meet this growing need.

Latvia

Latvia is the middle Baltic State. Its landscape includes plains and forests with few hills. Latvia has over twelve thousand rivers, but few are very long. The Daugava River flowing through the country divides the north and east from the south and west. The Daugava has been used very effectively for hydroelectric power. There are also over three thousand lakes throughout the country. Riga is the capital and major city of Latvia.

About 61 percent of the people are ethnic Latvians, who are similar to Lithuanians, and about 27 percent are Russians who immigrated during the Soviet era. Latvian is the official language. Russian is still widely used since it was the official language during the Soviet era. However, recent laws require candidates for citizenship to pass a Latvian language examination. As a result, tensions between Russia and Latvia have increased.

Latvia became a member of both NATO and the EU in 2004, and its trade reflects this shift towards the West. Potatoes, sugar beets, wheat, and barley are the most abundant crops, and Latvia's major industries include transportation, agriculture, and electronics.

Religious freedom was granted to the Latvians in 1988, and 60 percent of the people affiliate with some form of Christianity. One of the results of the secular influence of the Nazis and the Communists in the twentieth century is that 38 percent of Latvians identify as being nonreligious. However, Evangelical Christians represent 7 percent of the population. Most of this growth occurred in the 1990s, and recently growth has slowed significantly.

Estonia

Estonia is the northernmost of the three Baltic States. It is bordered by the Baltic Sea on its north and west shores, and most of its eastern border is taken up by Lake Pskov. The mainland has marshes, lowlands, and few hills but is rich in oil shale, which provides much of Estonia's energy needs. The major port and capital city, Tallinn, lies on the northern coast. The Baltic Sea moderates the climate of the port, which averages 25°F in the winter and 58°F in the summer. Estonia's fifteen hundred islands make up 10 percent of its land area. The two largest, Saaremaa and Hiiumaa, have cities.

Estonia has much in common with Scandinavia. The people speak Estonian, a Finnic language, and many people understand Finnish. Though controlled successively by Germany, Denmark, Sweden, Poland, and Russia, Estonia has kept a separate identity. Today, ethnic Estonians compose almost 69 percent of the population, and ethnic Russians make another quarter. The Estonian government has also made learning the Estonian language a requirement for citizenship, heightening tensions between the ethnic Estonian majority and the sizeable ethnic Russian minority.

Electronics, telecommunications, and engineering make up the bulk of the country's industry. The major agricultural products are barley, potatoes, and wheat. Estonia joined NATO and the EU in 2004, and it plans to adopt the euro as the national currency.

As in other countries in this region that broke away from Soviet domination, Estonia gained political independence and granted freedom of religion in 1988. Decades of Communist rule left a terrible legacy in Estonia as 54 percent of the people consider themselves nonreligious. Only 45 percent identify with some form of Christianity. Evangelical Christians make up 5 percent of the Estonian population, but their annual growth is less than 1 percent each year. Effective outreach tools include radio, television, and Christian literature.

Section Quiz

1. Why is Eastern Europe considered a shatter belt?
2. What are Poland's two most important rivers?
3. What two regions of Poland lie in the hills along the southern mountains?
4. Name the Baltic States. Which state is predominantly Roman Catholic?
★ Why have two of the Baltic States enacted laws requiring a knowledge of each country's native language for citizenship? What are the benefits and disadvantages of these requirements?

II. The Carpathians

The Alps are the dominant mountain system in Western Europe, cutting the region in half. But they diminish in Austria. The **Carpathian Mountains** (kar PAY thee uhn) pick up on the east side of the Danube River, becoming the dominant system in Eastern Europe. They divide the northern plains from the south.

There are many subranges within the Carpathian system. The highest subrange, the **Tatra Mountains**, rises in the far north along the border of Poland and Slovakia. The Tatra range is the continental divide, separating the rivers that flow north into the Baltic Sea and the rivers that flow south and east into the Black Sea. Most people on the Carpathian Divide live in the river valleys, not in the mountains. Three landlocked nations share parts of the Carpathians—the Czech Republic, Slovakia, and Hungary.

The dominance of the Soviet Union had a lasting effect on the religious life of these three nations. Before World War II, these countries had a strong Roman Catholic presence. The leaders of the Soviet

The Nizke Tatry (Low Tatra) National Park is located in Slovakia.

Religion in the Czech Republic

Many of the churches in the Czech Republic are empty or used for other purposes, and the Czech people are regarded as among the most secular in Europe. This dubious distinction has resulted in part from a history of repressive rule by the Roman Catholic Habsburgs. The Czechs responded with a strong anticlerical movement. In addition, the atheistic influence of communism during the Cold War took its toll on religious life in this country. The result is a society largely devoid of any Christian influence. (Evangelical Christians make up 0.7 percent of the population.)

Family, Friends, and Home

The Czech people place great importance on spending time with family and friends. They pride themselves on being a friendly people and welcoming visitors to join them for conversation at a local restaurant or other public place. They are generally well-educated and knowledgeable about foreign events and politics. However, it is most unusual for Czechs to invite strangers or acquaintances to their homes. This is considered a private place and generally off-limits for visitors, unless they are invited.

Union, however, tried to discourage religion. As a result of Soviet influence, countries within the Iron Curtain also discouraged religion. The result is evident in the religious demographics of some Eastern European countries.

Country	Roman Catholics	Protestants	Unaffiliated/ None
Czech Republic	10.3%	0.8%	88.9%
Slovakia	68.9%	10.8%	20.3%
Hungary	51.9%	21%	27.1%

Czech Republic

The Czech Republic was formerly part of Czechoslovakia, a union of Czech and Slovak peoples. These two peoples, like the Poles, are Western Slavs. The Allies created Czechoslovakia after World War I when they broke up the Austria-Hungary Empire. The Allies hoped this union would give the Slavic people enough strength to defend themselves against future threats. But Czechoslovakia fell to Hitler's armies in 1939 and then to the Soviet armies in 1945. The overthrow of the Communist Party in Czechoslovakia in 1989 was so swift and peaceful that it was called the **Velvet Revolution**.

After Czechoslovakia's independence, the Czech and Slovak representatives differed over the nature and pace of economic reforms. In 1993, these differences caused the two parts of the nation to split peacefully into the nations of the Czech Republic and Slovakia in what is called the **Velvet Divorce**.

LET'S GO EXPLORING

Climates of Eastern Europe

1. What climate occurs east of Europe's marine-west-coast climate?
2. Which nations have three different climates within them?
3. Which nations have a mediterranean climate?
4. For which country or countries is the climate entirely marine west coast? humid continental?
★ What geographical feature characterizes the northern regions of the marine-west-coast and humid continental climates in Eastern Europe? (Compare this map with the one on page 287.)

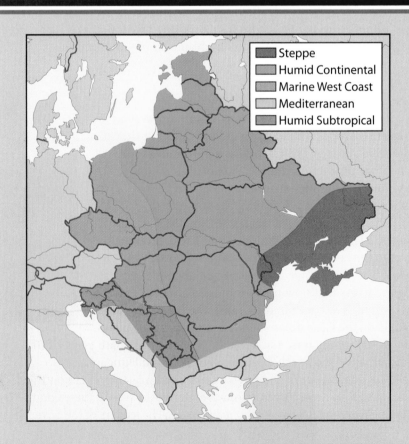

Legend:
- Steppe
- Humid Continental
- Marine West Coast
- Mediterranean
- Humid Subtropical

The government of the Czech Republic introduced reforms that strengthened the ecomony rapidly. To get property back into the hands of the people, leaders handed out vouchers to private citizens in an experiment called **mass privatization**. Each adult became a shareholder in the nation's various industries. After a brief period of economic hardships, the country swiftly regained its vigor. Today, the Czech Republic has one of the strongest economies in Eastern Europe. The Czech Republic joined NATO in 1999 and the EU in 2004.

Bohemia

The western half of the Czech Republic, called Bohemia, is a large basin ringed by highlands. Its waters drain north into Germany's Elbe River. Farmers raise cattle as well as barley, wheat, sugar beets, and potatoes. The entire country enjoys a marine-west-coast climate, similar to that of Western Europe.

Protected by the mountains, the Bohemians cultivated an independent spirit over the centuries. Today, the capital of the Czech Republic, **Prague** (PRAHG), has nearly 1.3 million people. Known as the City of a Hundred Spires, Prague has many churches, bridges, and historical landmarks that were spared from bomb attacks during World War II.

Prague Castle, which stands on a hill overlooking the Vltava River, was the home of the kings of Bohemia. Today the president of the Czech Republic lives in a portion of the castle.

The Sudetenland

The Bohemian Basin is ringed by the Sudeten Mountains on the northern border with Poland and the Bohemian Mountains on the western boundary with Germany. The Bohemian range includes the famed Bohemian Forest in the west and the Erzgebirge (EHRTS guh bier guh), meaning "Ore Mountains," in the northwest. The coal mines of the Erzgebirge make the Czech Republic one of the world's major producers of coal. Uranium is also mined there.

Many Germans used to live in this valuable mountain region, called the Sudetenland. The Allies gave it to the Czechs after World War I to guarantee them a defensible border against Germany. But Hitler invaded in 1938, claiming a right to recover German lands. The Nazis killed or displaced many Czechs; in retribution after World War II, the Czechs forced over half a million Germans out of their homes.

The Tatra Mountains are a major mountain range in the Carpathian Mountains.

Moravia

The eastern part of the Czech Republic is Moravia. About 4 percent of the Czech population is Moravian. Moravia takes its name from the Morava River, which drains south into the Danube.

Slovakia

Slovakia, in the heart of the Carpathian Mountains, is separated from the Czech Republic by the White Carpathians. A spruce-fir forest carpets these mountains. The Tatra Mountains separate Poland and Slovakia. The mountains of Slovakia hold a wealth of resources, such as iron ore, copper, lead, and other metals. In the southwest, crops are grown on a plain

Religion in Slovakia

While the people of the Czech Republic are known for their secularism, a majority of the people of Slovakia embrace religion and their religious traditions. While most Slovaks are at least nominal Roman Catholics (70 percent), about 7 percent are Protestants. Four percent of the Slovak population affiliate with the Greek Orthodox Church or the United Reformed Church. Only about 13 percent of the Slovaks claim to be atheists.

In further contrast with the Czechs, many of the churches in Slovakia are well attended on Sunday. This is especially true in the small towns and villages throughout the country. (Evangelical Christians constitute about 1 percent of the Slovakian population.)

Minorities in Slovakia

As in many Eastern European countries, Slovakia has several ethnic minorities that make up its population. While about 85% of the population is Slovak, many Hungarians, Roma (Gypsies), Ukrainians, Czechs, and Poles also live in Slovakia. In the past, this has led to periodic persecution of minorities. More recently, the Slovaks have sought to embrace these groups. However, living conditions continue to be very difficult for the large Roma communities, where people live in great poverty with few opportunities for improvement.

Buda + Pest = Budapest

Buda was founded on one side of the river by Romans in the second century. It became the capital of Hungary in the fifteenth century. In 1872 Buda merged with the town of Pest across the Danube, forming the present city.

The Danube River with the Chain Bridge in the foreground and the Hungarian Parliament and Buda Castle in the background.

called the **Little Alföld** (AHL fuhld), which extends into the northwest corner of Hungary. Farmers in this lowland area raise wheat, cattle, and hogs. Bratislava, the capital, lies within the Little Alföld, just downstream from Vienna on the Danube River.

Slovakia's government is a parliamentary democratic republic, supported by a multi-party system. Slovakia joined NATO and the EU in 2004, and its economy has continued to grow. Wheat, sugar beets, and other grains are the top agricultural products of the country. Some major industries include automobiles, chemicals, metal, energy, transportation, and textiles. Slovakia and the Czech Republic continue to cooperate in economic alliances.

Hungary

The Hungarians are not like their neighbors. They are descendants of Magyar tribes from the East who invaded Central Europe in AD 896, enslaving the Slavic and Germanic peoples. They speak a Uralic language associated with the Ural Mountains, the border between Europe and Asia.

Hungary is part of a basin within a sweeping curve in the Carpathian Mountains, which reach into the north of Hungary. The country is divided by the Danube River, Europe's second-longest river. The capital of Hungary, **Budapest**, lies on the Danube River at the foot of the mountains. With more than 1.7 million people, it is one of the largest cities in Eastern Europe.

East of the Danube, the **Great Hungarian Plain** (also known as the Great Alföld) dominates the landscape. This plain spreads through other countries in Eastern Europe. The Tisza River, a tributary of the Danube, runs through the middle of this plain, making it useful for both pastureland and cropland. Hungary's farmland, some of the best in all of Eastern Europe, is sufficient to meet Hungary's food demands. The chief crops are maize, wheat, beets, barley, sunflower seeds, apples, potatoes, and grapes.

Hills roll west of the Danube to the foothills of the Austrian Alps. Much of this land is used for crops. Forests cover the northeast and southwest corners of Hungary. Lake Balaton, the "Hungarian Sea," is the largest lake in the basin and a favorite vacation resort. Major products from the foothills include timber and uranium. Hungary's mines are major producers of bauxite.

Hungarians have enjoyed freedom of religion since 1990, and 88 percent of the people affiliate with some form of Christianity. Eleven percent of the Hungarians identify as being nonreligious. Evangelical Christians represent 3 percent of the population, but the rapid growth of the 1990s has slowed to an annual growth of about 1 percent. There is an urgent need for trained Christian leaders.

Section Quiz

1. What mountain system extends from the Alps across Eastern Europe?
2. What people group settled the Czech Republic and Slovakia?
3. Compare and contrast the Czech Republic and Slovakia.
4. What important plain covers a large portion of Eastern Europe?
★ How is Hungary different from all its neighbors?

III. The Western Balkans

The **Balkan Peninsula** is a mountainous region that juts down from Europe into the eastern end of the Mediterranean. Ten countries of Eastern Europe, called the **Balkans**, lie on the peninsula. They share the peninsula with Greece and Turkey.

The Balkans' rugged ranges once isolated numerous tribes that migrated into the region, causing them to develop separate cultural identities. The terrain encouraged disunity and conflict between these peoples. The Balkans are a complex knot of two dozen separate nationalities in ten countries. The tendency of such diverse territories to break up into small, hostile nations is called **Balkanization**.

The **Dinaric** (di NEHR ik) **Alps** run down from the border of Italy along the western edge of four countries—Slovenia, Croatia, Bosnia and Herzegovina, and Montenegro—and end in northern Albania. The Dinaric Alps divide the waters that flow into the Adriatic Sea from the waters that flow east into the Great Hungarian Plain. Few good ports are available on the rugged coast of the Adriatic.

Most of the people in these four Balkan countries belong to the language group of the Southern Slavs—including Slovenes, Croats, and Serbs. But they are divided by religion and culture. The Slovenes and Croats once belonged to the Austrian Empire, and they share its Western culture, Roman alphabet, and Catholic religion. But the Serbs belonged to the Byzantine Empire and share its Eastern culture, Cyrillic alphabet, and Orthodox religion. The uniting factor between these peoples was their common enemy in the south—the Ottoman Turks, who at one time conquered all their lands. During the Cold War, these countries, with Macedonia, were part of the Communist country of Yugoslavia.

Where Are the Balkans?

Many students wonder where the Balkans are and what nations make up the Balkans. To find the Balkans on a map, take a map of Europe and place your two index fingers at the top of the Adriatic Sea. Move your right finger east until you reach the Black Sea and stop. Then move both fingers down into the form of an upside-down triangle. This peninsula is the Balkan Peninsula, and all of the nations on this peninsula (except Turkey and Greece) are collectively called the Balkans.

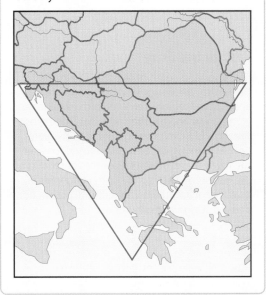

Gypsies

One of the largest ethnic minorities in Europe is the **Gypsies**. Gypsies call themselves "Roma" and their language "Romany." Although the precise origin of Gypsies remains uncertain, they have been genetically linked to people from northwest India. This dark-complexioned people migrated to Europe by the fourteenth century. They were mistakenly thought to be Egyptians, thus the term *gypsy*.

Gypsies limited their contact with the outside world and consequently preserved their own tribal language, laws, and customs. Their work reflected the life of wanderers. Some took seasonal jobs as circus performers, musicians, and acrobats. Others worked as peddlers, smiths, tinkers, woodcarvers, hangmen, undertakers, dogcatchers, or horse traders. Gypsy women, who had fewer alternatives,

A Gypsy girl in Warsaw, Poland

begged or took up fortunetelling with crystal balls and palm reading.

Gypsies developed a bad reputation because of the few who were tricksters or thieves. Even today, the verb *gyp* derives from *Gypsy* and means "to cheat." Hitler targeted Gypsies as "undesirables" and ordered the execution of about 400,000 of them during the Holocaust.

Today, many Gypsies have settled down and joined the modern world. Others have replaced their wagons with campers and now follow traveling circuses. Governments throughout Europe are seeking to incorporate the Gypsy population into the general populace. While Gypsies have spread to every continent, the three main tribes are in Europe. The Gitanos are in Spain, southern France, and North Africa; and the Sinti are in France and Germany. The largest tribe is the Kalderash of the Balkans.

Alcoholism in Slovenia

Slovenia has distinguished itself in many areas. However, one tragic distinction is its position at the top of the worldwide list of alcohol consumption. Every fifth man and every twenty-fifth woman in Slovenia is an alcoholic. The Slovenian government is finally taking action to make alcohol harder to get. However, the government is also labeling alcoholism a disease. Failure to address the root cause of alcoholism will result in failure to overcome what is ultimately a moral issue.

Above the Fray

Following the death of Marshal Tito in 1980, the territories of Yugoslavia began to break apart. Many regions renewed old hostilities and went to war against their enemies. The Serbs, Croats, and Bosnians engaged in this violent upheaval. However, Slovenia refused to enter the fray and devoted its resources to rebuilding the nation's infrastructure, attracting foreign investment, improving agricultural production, and reducing unemployment.

Slovenia

The Alps extend down from Austria and Italy into most of Slovenia. The highest peak in Slovenia is Triglav (9,396 ft.) in the Julian Alps at the northwest corner of the country. From here, the Sava River flows southeast across the country and later enters the Danube. The Dinaric Alps rise south of the river. Koper is an important commercial seaport on Slovenia's tiny Adriatic coastline.

The Karst (or Kras) region, famous for its sinkholes and limestone caves, lies in the southwestern section of the country. Postojna, located east of the Italian city of Trieste, boasts the largest caverns in Europe. The name **karst** has come to refer to any exotic limestone landscape. Another tourist attraction in Slovenia is Lipica, the town for which Lipizzaner horses are named. Tourists can visit the farm where these dancing horses are still trained.

The karst caves in Slovenia contribute to the nation's tourism industry.

Slovenia, a democratic republic, has a president and a prime minister. The president chooses the prime minister, but the choice must be approved by the ninety-seat National Assembly, the chief legislative body. There is also a forty-seat National Council that functions as an advisory group. Slovenia was the first Yugoslavian republic to demand independence. After a ten-day war in 1991, the European Union negotiated a cease-fire.

Since its independence, the mostly-Catholic Slovenia has become a leading example of free-market economics in Eastern Europe. Even while it was a part of Yugoslavia, Slovenia produced more than any other part of the country, partially because of its ties to Western Europe. Today, it has one of the highest per capita GDPs in Eastern Europe. Wheat, watermelons, and maize are the top crops. Metallurgy, electronics, and transportation vehicles are three of the top industries. Slovenia joined the EU and NATO in 2004 and began using the euro in 2007.

Slovenians enjoy freedom of religion, and the country is almost evenly divided between those identified with some form of Christianity (54 percent) and those indicating no religious affiliation (44 percent). Muslims make up 2 percent of the population, and Evangelical Christians represent a tiny minority of 0.1 percent of the Slovenian people (less than 2,000).

Croatia

Croatian is so similar to Serbian that linguists consider it a single language called Serbo-Croatian. However, the Croats have a long history of rivalry with the Serbs. When Slovenia declared independence from Yugoslavia, Croatia followed suit. During the war that followed, Croatia endured most of the suffering. This suffering resulted from the large Serb minority in Croatia declaring independence from Croatia and receiving assistance from the Yugoslav army. Over ten thousand people died in the fighting. The fighting ended when the United Nations negotiated a cease-fire and sent in thirteen thousand soldiers to keep the peace. Since 2000, Croatia has taken significant steps toward a stronger democracy.

Croatia is shaped like a boomerang. Forests cover more than a third of the country. The southern wing of Croatia includes most of **Dalmatia**. The Dalmatian Coast has large beach resorts on the mainland as well as on hundreds of islands. The mediterranean climate and the scenic backdrop of the Dinaric Alps draw many tourists. Dalmatia has been proposed as the origin of the dalmatian dog breed, but this claim is disputed.

The eastern wing of Croatia lies on the Pannonian Plains, part of the Great Hungarian Plain. Low mountains roll across most of the plain. Zagreb, the capital and largest city, lies on the Sava River. The most fertile plain is Slavonia in the east along the border with Serbia. The top agricultural products for the country are maize and sugar beets. Two of the top imports for the country are cattle and pork, and the top export is refined sugar.

Croatia is a secular state that allows freedom of religion, and 92 percent of the people associate with some form of Christianity. Six percent of the Croatians consider themselves nonreligious. Evangelical Christians constitute 0.4 percent of the population and have an annual growth rate of only 0.6 percent. Despite these bleak stastics, leaders are being trained, and groups are planning to form new congregations.

Bosnia and Herzegovina

Muslims controlled the Balkans for about five hundred years. During that time, many Slavs embraced Islam. Most of them were located in Bosnia. Croats and Serbs make up the majority of the population, but slightly less than half of the people are followers of Islam. They are sometimes listed as **Bosniaks**.

A bitter civil war erupted in 1991 after Bosnia declared independence and the Serb minority refused to join the new nation. The fighting between Serbs, Bosniaks, and Croats dragged on until 1995, when U.S. president Bill Clinton invited the warring leaders to sit down at a military base in Dayton, Ohio, and work out the **Dayton Peace Accords**. The agreement, however, did not result in a complete unification. Troops (first from NATO and later, the EU) remained to enforce the fragile peace.

Bosnia consists of the northern and central portions of the country. The central portion of the country is dominated by the forested Dinaric Alps. The hilly northern portion of the country is pastureland in the northeast and forests in the northwest. The top agricultural products are maize, wheat, and a variety of vegetables.

Plitvice, Land of the Falling Lakes

Festivals in Croatia

Since gaining independence from the Soviet Union, Croatians have celebrated their traditional culture through songs, dances, and festivals. Women wear their traditional long dresses with aprons, and children wear masks, face paint, and hats. Each town hosts a carnival, and many merchants shut down their shops and enjoy a week of traditional festivities.

Many festivals are religious in nature and coincide with Lent and Easter. However, as in other parts of the world, Christmas is the favorite time for Croats to celebrate. In addition to appearances by the Croat version of Santa Claus, Croats fill their churches for Christmas services and walk through their neighborhoods singing Christmas carols.

Lingering Consequences of War

During the civil war in Bosnia, nearly two million land mines were buried by the warring parties. As of 2008, these weapons had injured or killed 5,005 people. After the war, groups such as the UN's Mine Action Centre (MAC) were tasked with discovering and removing the mines. As of 2003, there were more than one million mines and unexploded ordnance to be located and removed or detonated. Complicating matters, many of the mine fields are not marked or have not been mapped. The goal was to have all land mines and unexploded ordinance cleared by 2015.

Herzegovina consists of the southern portion of the country. The Dinaric Alps continue into this region. The wartorn capital of the country, Sarajevo, lies between Bosnia and Herzegovina in the south. There are a number of mining industries in the Dinaric Alps, such as steel, iron ore, coal, lead, and zinc. Other industries include furniture, refining, textiles, and transportation.

This country has a Muslim majority representing 54 percent of the population and a 41 percent minority comprising those who identify with some form of Christianity. Five percent of the people consider themselves nonreligious. Evangelical Christians represent a tiny minority of 0.1 percent but are growing at about 2 percent each year.

Montenegro

The Serbs are the most dominant Slavic people in the Balkans. After the breakup of Yugoslavia in 1991, two of the six regions, Serbia and Montenegro, united and retained the name of Yugoslavia. In 2003, the country was divided into two semi-independent states that were united politically under the name Serbia and Montenegro.

Much poorer than Slovenia and Croatia, Serbia and Montenegro followed an authoritarian path under the leadership of Slobodan Milosevic. He won popular support by calling for a "Greater Serbia," which would include all the bordering lands where Serbs live. He played a game with the Western powers, promising to stay out of the surrounding civil wars while secretly supplying the Serb minorities. While on trial at The Hague for war crimes, Milosevic died in 2006. Later that year, Montenegro voted to become independent.

Montenegro (mon tuh NEG roh), meaning "Black Mountain," is a coastal region whose settlement goes back to the time of the Roman Empire. In the seventh century, the Slavs settled there. By the thirteenth century, the area was under the control of the Serbian Empire. With its new independence, Montenegro has the opportunity to develop independently for the first time in centuries.

The landscape of Montenegro is mostly forested mountains. However, there is some land suitable for pastureland along the coast, and sheep are a major product of that area. Metallurgy, engineering, and mining are three major industries in Montenegro.

Religious freedom is guaranteed in this country, but most people remain connected to traditional faiths. Seventy-seven percent identify with some form of Christianity, 15 percent are Muslim, and nearly 8 percent are nonreligious. Evangelical Christians make up less than 0.1 percent of the Montegregan population but are growing in numbers and spiritual maturity.

Albania

The mountainous country of Albania lies to the west of Kosovo and Macedonia facing the Adriatic Sea. The Dinaric Alps extend into northern Albania, where they are called the North Albanian Alps. The Pindus

The Tara River is a major river in Montenegro.

Mountains, which are not forested like the northern mountains, extend from southern Albania into Greece. Two major industries are forestry and mining. Like Dalmatia, Albania's west coast has warm, dry summers. Durrës is the country's major port. Off the coast in the south is the Strait of Otranto, which connects the Adriatic Sea to the Meditarranean.

Albanians are not Slavs but speak a unique Indo-European language. Albanians are divided into two groups that speak different dialects: the Gegs in the north and the Tosks in the south. The long influence of the Ottoman Empire resulted in a population that is about 56 percent Muslim, one of the few Muslim majorities in a European nation.

Albania is unique in the history of the world because the Communist leader Enver Hoxha established what he claimed was the first truly atheistic country in the world. After the Communists were finally ousted in 1992, Albania opened its doors to the world. In the years that followed, missionaries of all types poured into the country. While Islam dominates the country, Eastern Orthodoxy has an estimated 20 percent minority, and Catholicism has an estimated 10 percent minority. Other groups, such as Protestantism, have gained footholds in the country's religious life.

The economy of Albania has struggled after the fall of communism. Steps have been taken to strengthen the economy, but the country's infrastructure is underdeveloped. Unlike the city dwellers crammed into the capital, Tiranë, most Albanians live on small farms, raising agricultural products such as livestock, wheat, and watermelons. Agriculture makes up nearly one fourth of the GDP.

Albanians have only enjoyed religious freedom since 1998. A majority of the Albanians are (primarily Sunni) Muslim (62 percent), while 30 percent affiliate with some form of Christianity, and 7 percent identify as nonreligious. Evangelical Christians constitute 0.5 percent of the population and are experiencing steady growth. Evangelistic outreach and church planting efforts are underway.

The Shkodër is one of the few well-watered valleys in mountainous Albania.

Section Quiz

1. Name the mountain range that runs along the Adriatic coast in the Balkans.

2–3. Compare the Croats and the Serbs.

4. Which two countries discussed in this section have a Muslim majority?

 ✶ Why is Slovenia the most prosperous country in Eastern Europe?

IV. The Eastern Balkans

Much like the western Balkans, the eastern Balkans are dominated by mountains. Macedonia is almost completely covered by mountains. Two mountain ranges dominate Bulgaria. Romania has portions of the Carpathian Mountains. Despite the prevalence of mountains, the eastern Balkans also include plains that allow many agricultural products to be grown.

Macedonia

Macedonia is a small landlocked country in the middle of the Balkan Peninsula, and 80 percent of the country is mountainous. These mountains are forested, but limited mining and grazing are possible in some portions of the mountains. Other agricultural resources include cotton, wheat, and fruit, which grow in the valley of the Vardar River. The capital, Skopje, lies in the north on the Vardar as well. The official language is Macedonian, a Southern Slavic language, but minority languages are taught in certain areas of the country along with the official language.

After the decline of the Ottoman Empire, the Balkan countries fought for control of this region. In the Balkan Wars of 1912 and 1913, Greece, Serbia, and Bulgaria joined together to defeat the Turks, but then they fought among themselves. The northern part went to Yugoslavia and became one of that country's republics.

When Macedonia declared independence after the breakup of Yugoslavia, Greece refused to let the European Union formally recognize its independence. Greece feared a movement to reunite the old lands of "Greater Macedonia." When the UN first admitted the nation in 1993, it did not grant approval for the country's new name because Greece opposed it. Instead, the United States and the United Nations officially designated Macedonia as "The Former Yugoslav Republic of Macedonia."

Sixty-five percent of Macedonians identify with some form of Christianity, and 31 percent are Muslim. Evangelical Christians

WORLD RELIGIONS

Eastern Orthodoxy

The Eastern churches, led by Constantinople (modern-day Istanbul, Turkey), followed an increasingly different path from the Western churches, led by Rome. The Eastern churches finally broke from Rome in 1054, when the pope demanded that they acknowledge his supreme authority. The Eastern churches became known as the Eastern Orthodox churches. The two churches refused to cooperate until 1965, when they agreed to restore friendly relations.

Eastern Orthodoxy agrees with Roman Catholicism and traditional Protestants on several points. All three groups hold to the Trinity, the two natures of Christ, and the inspiration of Scripture.

Roman Catholics also share some beliefs with the Eastern Orthodox that are distinct from many Protestant groups. For instance, both groups have a hierarchy that includes deacons, priests, and bishops. In both groups the Eucharist (Lord's Supper) is a central part of worship. Both groups also differ from Protestants in giving church tradition an authoritative role alongside Scripture and denying that salvation is by grace alone through faith alone in Christ alone. Instead, they teach that God and humans cooperate to bring about salvation.

Serious differences also exist between the Roman and Eastern churches. In Eastern Orthodoxy a church is a body of Christians overseen by a bishop. The bishops are all equals, although some are more highly regarded than others. In the West the Bishop of Rome, or the pope, claims authority over all other bishops. This was one of many factors that led to a split between the Western Church and the Eastern churches.

The Eastern Orthodox also reject the doctrine of original sin, as held by both Protestants and Catholics. The apostle Paul taught that all humans are born guilty because of Adam's sin (Rom. 5:12); the Eastern Orthodox deny this. The Orthodox Church also denies Paul's teaching that the human will was corrupted by the Fall (Rom. 3:11) so that people will not come to God apart from grace (Eph. 2:8–9). Instead, they teach that humans are affected by sin but remain basically good.

Along with Protestants and Catholics, the Orthodox Church teaches that Christ was offered as a sacrifice in His death. But unlike Western churches, the Orthodox deny that Christ's sacrificial death was offered to the Father to satisfy divine wrath over sin.

The Orthodox Church suffered a serious setback when Islam pushed its way up from the Middle East and into Eastern Europe. This shift, however, has caused some peoples in Eastern Europe to hold tightly to the Orthodox Church. For instance, over 90 percent of Greeks belong to the Greek Orthodox Church.

represent only 0.2 percent of the population, but their churches are growing at a steady rate. Congregations are actively reaching out to their communities, and church leaders have established ambitious goals for planting new congregations.

Serbia

The agricultural heart of Serbia is the northern plains, or Pannonian Plains. This fertile farmland is part of the Great Hungarian Plain. The agricultural products of this region are sugar beets, various grains, grapes, and sheep. The region of Vojvodina covers most of the Pannonian Plains in Serbia. Serbia received this province after the breakup of the Hungarian Empire.

Belgrade, the capital since 1402, lies near the edge of the Pannonian Plains where the Sava River joins the Danube. The centrally located city has been conquered and destroyed more than thirty times. With 1.2 million people, it is the second-largest city in the Balkans.

Much of Serbia is mountainous. The Dinaric Alps cross into the southwest, and the **Balkan Mountains** rise in the southeast before crossing into Bulgaria. Between the Dinaric Alps and the Balkan Mountains lies a complex maze of minor mountain ranges. The central ranges contain some of the largest lead deposits in Europe. Forests cover the areas farthest south. Vineyards and fields of grain also make up part of the landscape of southern Serbia.

While the Serbian constitution guarantees freedom of religion, the Orthodox Church receives special treatment. Eighty percent of the Serbian people affiliate with some form of Christianity, 16 percent are Muslim, and nearly 4 percent are nonreligious. Evangelical Christians represent 0.6 percent of the population and are slowly growing in number despite persecution, which is increasing because they are viewed as a sect. Evangelical congregations are still being planted and are reaching out to their communities to meet needs and demonstrate the love of Christ.

Kosovo

Kosovo, with a population that is 90 percent Albanian, was formerly a large Albanian province in the south next to the border of Albania. Like Vojvodina, this ethnic region enjoyed self-rule under the Communists, but when the Soviet Union dissolved, Serbia removed Kosovo's special rights. As a result, Kosovo declared independence in 1992. Continuing tension resulted in the Kosovo War in 1999. The UN brokered a peace agreement and sent in UN forces to govern Kosovo. In 2008, the people of Kosovo established the Republic of Kosovo and declared themselves an independent nation. As of this date, Serbia has refused to recognize Kosovo's independence.

Kosovo continues to experience economic expansion and a low inflation rate. Although this young state still requires financial support from Kosovars outside the country, Kosovo is striving to lower its dependence on foreign assistance.

While accurate statistics are difficult to obtain, an estimated 80 percent of the population identifies as Muslim, 10 percent affiliates with some form of Christianity, and 10 percent is nonreligious. Evangelical Christians may number around two thousand, and many are active witnesses despite the hostile environment toward Christianity.

Macedonian Call

On their first missionary journey, Paul and Barnabas traveled in the area we now call Turkey. God blessed their efforts to win converts and plant churches.

Paul and Silas, on Paul's second missionary journey, intended to return to this region, but God intervened and directed Paul to travel to Macedonia (Acts. 16:9). Responding to this "Macedonian call," Paul and his party crossed the Aegean Sea and founded the first churches in Europe—Philippi, Thessalonica, and Berea, all in the area formerly known as Greater Macedonia. From there Christianity spread into Athens, Corinth, Rome, and finally, all of Europe. For almost eighteen centuries, Christianity influenced European laws, architecture, educational institutions, customs, values, and economies.

Today, Christianity in Europe is in drastic decline. However, Christianity is thriving in Africa, South America, Central America, and parts of Asia—places traditionally considered as the unreached mission fields of the world. Perhaps the people of God need to hear the Macedonian call once again and return to Europe with the gospel.

Bulgaria

The Bulgars probably moved to the present region of Bulgaria in the seventh century. They then settled on the western shore of the Black Sea, mixing with the Slavs, who had arrived from Poland a little earlier. Bulgars account for 85 percent of the people, and Turks account for another 9 percent. Fifty-nine percent of Bulgarians are Bulgarian Orthodox, a branch of Eastern Orthodoxy. Eight percent of Bulgarians are Muslim.

Northern Bulgaria is a fertile valley along the Danube River. The river forms most of Bulgaria's northern border, but it winds northward into Romania just before it enters the Black Sea. Ruse is Bulgaria's major port on the Danube. Bulgaria's main port on the Black Sea, Varna, also lies in this northern portion of the country. Farm products from the valley include barley, millet, livestock, wheat, and grapes.

Mountain ranges rise south of the plain. In central Bulgaria, the Balkan Mountains dominate the landscape, cutting across the country to the Black Sea. Sofia, the capital, lies in this range on a mountain tributary that flows into the Danube River. In the southwest, the **Rhodope** (ROD uh pee) **Mountains** dominate the countryside. These mountains reach 9,596 feet at **Mount Musala**, the highest peak in the Balkans. Between the Balkan and Rhodope Mountains in the east is a large region of cropland. Several cities lie in this river valley.

Rhodope Mountains

Freedom of religion is not yet a reality in Bulgaria, although conditions have improved since the 1990s. Eighty percent of Bulgarians identify with some form of Christianity, 12 percent are Muslim, and nearly 8 percent are nonreligious. Evangelical Christians make up 2 percent of the population and are experiencing slow numerical growth. Evangelical congregations have a growing percentage of believers who are maturing. One example of this maturing is an increasing number of Bulgarian Christians who are involved in short-term foreign mission trips to other countries.

Romania

Romania is a large country at the crossroads of Eastern Europe. It shares mountain features with the nations in the Carpathian region, a long border on the Danube River, and cities near the Black Sea. Although it does not share any of the Dinaric Alps or a border with Greece, Romania is still on the Balkan Peninsula. Unlike the Catholic nations of the Carpathians, its people are Eastern Orthodox.

Romania means "land of the Romans." It was the last province captured by the Roman Empire. Modern Romanians are descended from a mixture of Roman soldiers and the native peoples. Their language is the only one in Eastern Europe that developed from Latin.

Romania gained independence from communism in 1989, but the effects of the Communists' poor stewardship continued to hinder development for a decade. Following extensive reforms, Romania has enjoyed economic growth. Romania joined NATO in 2004 and the EU in 2007, and the country's efforts to join the EU helped to strengthen the economy. The chief agricultural products are maize, wheat, potatoes, melons, and plums. Major industries include textiles, timber, and mining.

While Romania is a secular state, the Orthodox Church has a great influence in the country. Ninety-seven percent of the people identify with some form of Christianity, and 2 percent are nonreligious. Evangelical Christians represent 5 percent of the population and are experiencing an annual growth of 2 percent, despite Romania's decline in population. Romania is currently considered one of the most spiritually receptive nations in Europe.

Piatra Craiului is a mountain in the Romanian portion of the Carpathian Mountains.

Transylvania

Nearly half of Romania is a section of the Carpathian Mountain system called **Transylvania**. The range extends from Slovakia into northern Romania and then curves west across the center of the country, where it is known as the **Transylvanian Alps**.

The heart of Transylvania is a hilly plateau in the west encircled by the Carpathian ranges. Hungary ruled the principality of Transylvania for much of its history; consequently, Hungarians are Romania's largest minority. Romania received Transylvania after World War I. The forested hills and gloomy castles of this region have long intrigued Western Europeans, who view Transylvania as a place of mystery and danger.

Wallachia

The Danube flows east from the Great Hungarian Plain through a break in the Carpathian Mountains called the **Iron Gate**. Steep rock walls, 530 feet apart, guard both sides of this gorge. The Danube then flows east through a broad fertile plain, shared by Romania and Bulgaria.

The populous plain below the Iron Gate is called **Wallachia** (wuh LAY kee uh). Farms there produce flax, wheat, and livestock. Romania's capital, Bucharest, is located on a tributary of the Danube. It is the largest city in Romania.

In the east, the slow-moving Danube loops northward along the coast and flows into a broad swamp land before entering the Black Sea. During Communist oppression, workers were forced to build a huge canal that bypassed the swampy loop and connected the Danube directly with the seaport of Constanța. Over one hundred thousand men died constructing the Canal of Death (Canalul Morti).

The Canal of Death

Moldavia

In the east lies the Moldavian Plain and the region of Moldavia. If you look at the map on page 287, you will see the Moldavian Plain and its many valleys. The plain continues east into the country of Moldova, which Romania owned until the Soviets seized it in World War II.

Section Quiz

1. Name the three main mountain ranges of the eastern Balkans.
2. How does the United Nations refer to Macedonia?
3. What is the highest peak of the Balkans?
4. How is Romania unique among the Eastern Balkan nations?
5. What are the three main regions of Romania?
* Why are two landlocked nations—the Czech Republic and Hungary—so much richer than Romania, which has a Black Sea port?

V. The Eastern Plains

A huge plain extends east from the Carpathian Mountains and connects with the Northern European Plain. Together, these plains form the **Great European Plain**, which stretches over one thousand miles east into Russia.

Three countries lie on the eastern plains: Moldova, Ukraine, and Belarus. Like the three Baltic States, these countries were once among the fifteen republics, or soviets, in the Soviet Union. Most of the people who settled the eastern plains are Eastern Slavs, including Ukrainians, Belarusians, and Russians.

Moldova

Moldova is a hilly, landlocked country between Romania and Ukraine. Moldova is the eastern part of Romania's historic principality of Moldavia. Two-thirds of the people speak Moldovan, a language related to Romanian. It is the fourth most densely populated country in Eastern Europe. The Soviets took control of the region

The Commonwealth of Independent States

during World War II, but the country gained independence along with the other Soviet republics. A minority wants to rejoin Romania.

A third of the population consists of Slavs, both Ukrainians and Russians, who live on a sliver of land east of the Dniester (NEE stuhr) River. This valuable **Transnistria** region, which is heavy in industry, once belonged to Ukraine. In 1990, the Slavs declared themselves a semi-independent republic. Fighting erupted in 1992, and Russia sent its army to restore peace. Russia's failure to remove its troops has resulted in increased tensions between the two countries.

Despite the economic and human rights failures that brought about the end of communism in 1991, Moldova became the first part of the former Soviet Union to elect a Communist as its president in 2001. Economic pressures have forced the government to adopt some aspects of free enterprise, while authorities have retained some brutal measures of repression for any who object to government policies.

The land of Moldova is very fertile, resulting in a predominantly agricultural economy. The major agricultural products are maize, sugar beets, wheat, and grapes. Grapes are used to produce the chief export, wine. Moldova's industries focus mainly on agricultural-related equipment, but there are some basic manufacturing industries as well. The largest hindrance to Moldova's economy is a lack of natural resources. While Moldova produces some electricity, the country imports much of its energy resources. Consequently, in parts of the country there is not always enough energy to heat homes.

Commonwealth of Independent States

After the breakup of the Soviet Union, the former republics created the **Commonwealth of Independent States** (CIS) on December 21, 1991. All of the republics eventually joined, except the Baltic States. The original emphasis of the agreement was an alliance of independent states for the purpose of promoting economic ties between them. Since the group's inception, Russia has attempted to tighten its control over the CIS republics, which it calls the "**near abroad.**" Russian leaders became alarmed, though, at the willingness of some CIS members both to distance themselves from Russia and to embrace trading partners in the West. While Russia remains a major trading partner with most members, the economies of CIS members are slowly expanding beyond a reliance on Russia.

Seventy-three percent of Moldovans affiliate with some form of Christianity, 22 percent are nonreligious, and 5 percent are Muslim. Despite opposition by the Orthodox Church, Evangelical Christians have grown to represent 4 percent of the population and enjoy a sustained growth. Poverty has proven to be a greater hindrance in Moldova and has forced many pastors and laymen to leave the country in search of work to support their families. This has resulted in a great need for trained leaders to guide the growing congregations.

Ukraine

After Russia, Ukraine is the most important industrial and agricultural center in the CIS. It is also the largest nation completely on the continent of Europe. After its independence in 1991, the transition to a democratic form of government proceeded slowly. The elections of 2004 and their aftermath were watched by the world. During this campaign, one candidate (Viktor Yushchenko) was poisoned and survived, though he was severely scarred. The election day itself was tainted with charges of fraud when Yushchenko lost despite widespread support. Consequently, large groups of Ukranians protested the results. Due to the persistence of the people, another election was held, and this time Yushchenko won. This became known as the "**Orange Revolution**" because Yushchenko's supporters wore orange as a sign of their support. Since that time, Ukraine has continued to shift its focus from Russia to Western Europe and the EU.

Except for two small strips of mountains, the entire country lies in the eastern plain. Low plateaus cross the center but give way to lowlands in the north and south.

Ukrainians finally received freedom of religion in 1990, but not all groups receive equal treatment. Seventy-nine percent of the people identify with some form of Christianity, 19 percent consider themselves nonreligious, and one percent are Muslim. Evangelical Christians make up 4 percent of the Ukranian population and continue to grow numerically. An indicator of maturing Ukranian believers is the growth of the number of missionaries being sent from Ukraine to other nations of the former Soviet Union.

Viktor Yushchenko in 2008

Orange Revolution, November 2004

Northern Lowlands

Ukraine's northern lowlands include swamps and marshes along the border with Belarus. These waters flow into the **Dnieper** (NEE puhr) **River**, the third-longest river in Europe, which continues south through the heart of Ukraine. **Kiev** (KEE ev), the most populous city in all of Eastern Europe, lies at the junction between the Dneiper and Desna Rivers. It is the cultural center and capital of Ukraine.

Central Uplands

The Central Uplands cut across central Ukraine. With adequate rainfall and rich soils, these vast uplands produce many agricultural products. Ukraine ranks among the top producers in the world for over two dozen agricultural products. Among these are blueberries, potatoes, barley, cherries, honey, apricots, rye, cabbage, wheat, oats, and sunflower seeds.

East of the Dnieper River lies the valuable **Donets** (duh NETS) **Basin**, or Donbas. On a tributary of the Donets River is Kharkov, Ukraine's second-largest city. Three other cities—Odessa, Dnipropetrovsk and Donetsk—have around one million people each. Donetsk, Ukraine's fifth-largest city, is a major coal-mining center, and iron ore comes from the adjoining Krivoi Rog. Ukraine ranks eleventh in the world as a producer of coal, sixth in iron ore, and eighth in manganese. The Communists, who developed many of the region's industries, also created a pollution disaster that will take years to clean up.

Southern Coasts

Almost all of Ukraine's southern coast is a low plain. Because of the arid climate, farms must divert water from the Dnieper River. Odessa, Ukraine's largest port, lies on the coast of the Black Sea.

The most valuable southern region is the **Crimean** (kry MEE uhn) **Peninsula**, which juts out into the Black Sea. Crimea is barely attached to Europe by a narrow 2.5-mile-wide isthmus. A long series of conquerors have held the peninsula. Russia took Crimea from the Turks in the late eighteenth century and converted it into the "jewel in the crown" of the Russian Empire.

What makes Crimea unique is the Crimean Mountains, which rise from the sea along the southern tip of the peninsula. The mountains block the cold northern air and permit a pleasant mediterranean climate on the southern shore. Wealthy Russians flock to this coast, known as the "Russian Riviera." The czars even had a palace at Yalta, the best seaside resort in Crimea. Russia's main naval base in the Black Sea is Sevastopol, just west of Yalta.

The Crimea has been a sore spot between Russia and Ukraine. As a gesture of friendship, the Soviet Union gave Crimea to the Ukrainian soviet in 1954, and it passed to the independent country in 1991. But most of the natives are Russians who would like to rejoin Russia. Both Russia and Ukraine harbor their fleets at the strategic port at Sevastopol.

The Dniester River flows through Ukraine.

Belarus

Belarus, or "White Russia," has old ties with Russia, and those ties have continued since Belarusian independence. Alexander Lukashenko, who became president in 1994, fashioned an increasingly authoritarian government. Throughout his term in office, Belarus continued to be closely linked to Russia economically and politically. **Minsk**, the capital and the largest city, is the headquarters of the CIS.

Although they are related to Russians, Belarusians have their own distinctive culture and language. For many centuries they belonged to the Lithuanian Empire and its successor, the Polish-Lithuanian Empire. During the partition of Poland in the eighteenth century, Belarus fell into Russian hands. The Russian czars and later the Soviets tried to replace Belarusian with the Russian language. Today, most people, especially in the cities, speak Russian.

Most farms and cities are in the center of the country on the Northern European Plain. There are some areas of farmland in the south, but much of that area was harmed by the fallout from the Chernobyl disaster. Belarus ranks fourth in the world for the production of rye, fifth for flax, and eighth for potatoes. The far north has large forests, consisting of mixed deciduous and coniferous trees. The Belovezha Forest, a large natural preserve on the western border, is noted for the only surviving herd of wisent, or European bison.

The Pinsk Marshes as depicted in a nineteenth century painting

Few people live south in the **Pinsk** (or Pripet) **Marshes**. This is the largest marshland in Europe, extending about three hundred miles on the drainage basin of the Pripyat (or Pripet) River, a tributary of the Dnieper River. The swamps and marshes yield potash for fertilizers; Belarus is third in potash production after Canada and Russia. With environmental issues, a weak economy, and an increasingly authoritarian government, Belarus has many obstacles in its quest to become a strong, independent nation.

Although the constitution of Belarus guarantees freedom of religion, such freedom does not exist. However, nearly 71 percent of the population affiliate with some form of Christianity. Twenty-eight percent are nonreligious, and about 1 percent are either Muslim or Jewish. In this hostile environment, Evangelical Christians represent just over 1 percent of the population and are steadily growing at about 3 percent each year. These Christians must overcome numerous obstacles placed before them by a hostile government. They have to find new ways to assemble since it is almost impossible to get permission from the government to meet or own property as a church.

Section Quiz

1. To what country does Moldova have the closest cultural ties?
2. What is the main river of Ukraine?
3. Why is central Ukraine so valuable to the country?
4. What is the largest marshland in Europe, and in what country is it located?
* What disputed region lies in Ukraine? Why has a final solution been so difficult to reach?

Chapter Review

Making Connections

1–2. What two Christian religions are most common in Eastern Europe? Which of the two is associated with Western Europe?

3–4. Contrast the Baltic States and the Balkans.

5–7. What three countries seized control of Poland prior to World War I?

Developing Geography Skills

1. Based on the map on page 307, why would Russia have an interest in the countries of the Eastern Plains?

2. Find a source that maps populations' religious affiliations over time and compare the religion graphs for three Balkan countries. Explain why religious affiliations might have shifted over the time mapped. Also, identify the strengths and weaknesses of these graphs for charting a nation's religion.

Thinking Critically

1. How have the Balkans exhibited Balkanization? How have the many mountains of the Balkans contributed to Balkanization?

2. What are the potential benefits and problems resulting from Latvia and Estonia enacting laws requiring a knowledge of each country's native language for citizenship?

Living in God's World

1. God created His world with laws built into it. Some of these laws, like gravity, have been modeled by scientists. Built into God's world are also laws about how families and marriages work and laws about how economies function. Explain what laws of creation communism may have broken. Think about both Scriptural teaching regarding money and the effects of communism on economies.

2. What violations of creation law are nations newly freed from totalitarian Communist governments prone to that Christians should identify and warn against?

People, Places, and Things to Know

shatter belt
Baltic States
Soviet bloc
Vistula River
Lech Walesa
Kraków
Auschwitz
Oder River
Silesia
Hill of Crosses
Carpathian Mountains
Tatra Mountains
Velvet Revolution
Velvet Divorce
mass privatization
Prague
Little Alföld
Budapest
Great Hungarian Plain
Balkan Peninsula
Balkans
Balkanization
Dinaric Alps
Gypsies
karst
Dalmatia
Bosniaks
Dayton Peace Accords
Eastern Orthodoxy
Balkan Mountains
Rhodope Mountains
Mount Musala
Transylvania
Transylvanian Alps
Iron Gate
Wallachia
Great European Plain
Transnistria
Commonwealth of Independent States (CIS)
"near abroad"
"Orange Revolution"
Dnieper River
Kiev
Donets Basin
Crimean Peninsula
Minsk
Pinsk Marshes

Skyscrapers in Moscow

RUSSIA

Russia Fast Facts					
Capital	Area (sq. mi.)	Pop. (2013 est.) (M)	Pop. Density (per sq. mi.)	Per Capita GDP ($US)	Life Span
Moscow	6,592,772	142.5	21.6	$17,709	66.5

With more than one-tenth of the world's land area, Russia is easily the largest country on earth. From east to west, Russia is approximately 4,800 miles across. From north to south, Russia is about 1,850 miles. Russia borders fourteen countries; the only other country to join Russia in this achievement is China. These neighboring countries range from very stable to potentially explosive. Like the shatter belt in Eastern Europe, Russia is "lost" in a vast expanse of lowlands without clear natural borders, except the frigid ocean in the north and the Caucasus Mountains in the southwest.

With great size has come great opportunity. Russia has a vast wealth of natural resources. Though many of these resources are found in inhospitable climates, Russia has sought to utilize these resources. Russia has several obstacles, however, that affect its ability to use these resources properly.

Perhaps its greatest obstacle is its Soviet past. Russia was the largest part of the Union of Soviet Socialist Republics for most of the twentieth century. The Soviets misused many of Russia's physical and human resources. As a result, Russia has faced the dual tasks of cleaning up the mismanagement of the Soviet era and learning how to manage the land well.

I. History and Government

Russia looks both east and west. Its culture has borrowed elements from both—the authoritarianism of Asia and the longing for individual rights in Europe. The Great European Plain, which has played such a major role in European history, extends into Russia and has played a decisive role there as well. The plain covers only 20 percent of Russia, but over 80 percent of the population lives there.

Like the countries of Eastern Europe, Russia has suffered under the heel of many Asian tribes, including Scythians, Huns, and Slavs. Modern Russians are descendants of the Slavs and speak a Slavic language. Russia encompasses over seventy different nationalities, but 80 percent of the people are ethnic Russians.

From the Czars to the Present

Czarist Russia

A total of twenty-four **czars** (also spelled *tsars*) ruled Russia from 1547 to 1917. The czars and czarinas (female rulers) were **autocrats**; they had no established limits on their authority and power. During World War I under the last czar, Nicholas II, Russia experienced humiliating defeats. In the resulting confusion, **Vladimir Ilich Lenin** led the Russian Revolution in 1917 and executed the last czar the following year.

Russia and Climate Change

Russia may be at the epicenter of world-shaking climate change. Conflicting reports of melting glaciers and ice caps in the Arctic convince many that the global climate could really be changing.

But would climate change be bad for Russia? Maybe such change would actually be positive for a country that is mostly locked in permafrost. Siberia is the part of Russia closest to the Arctic. Most of the year this undeveloped region is frozen land—land that has abundant resources. While Siberia makes up around 77 percent of Russia, only 28 percent of the country's population lives there. A warming climate could make more Russian land habitable, unlock vast resources, and create great wealth for Russia, a country that has groaned under the weight of ice.

Despite its size, Russia has only a handful of ports that are ice-free for the whole year. This lack of warm-water ports has influenced Russian foreign policy historically. The desire for a warm-water port on the Mediterranean Sea has led Russia into many European wars. Perhaps climate change could expand the number of warm-water ports for Russia as well.

Lenin, shown here addressing a crowd, led the Russian Revolution in 1917, but the Communists did not have firm control until 1920.

Soviet Rule

In 1922, Lenin created the Union of Soviet Socialist Republics (**USSR**). This union gave limited power to several "republics." Communists claimed Russia was no longer an empire but a land of equals. Joseph Stalin, Lenin's brutal successor, extended the empire deeper into Europe than any czar could have dreamed possible. After a secret agreement with Adolf Hitler, Stalin seized Moldova, Lithuania, Latvia, and Estonia in 1940, bringing the total number of Soviet republics to fifteen. After the defeat of Hitler during World War II, Stalin extended the "Iron Curtain," the area under Soviet control, to lands as far west as Germany.

After World War II, the USSR (also known as the Soviet Union) was in competition with the Western Allies. Soon the competition involved primarily the USSR and the United States. As the USSR expanded Communist influence, the United States sought to limit this expansion. Both powers built up weapon arsenals, including nuclear weapons. Both the United States and the USSR feared that the other power would attack. This period was known as the **Cold War**.

Soviet Collapse

By the 1980s the Soviet economy lagged far behind the West. Soviet premier Mikhail Gorbachev instituted the reforms known

WORLD RELIGIONS

Russian Orthodoxy

The dominant religion in Russia is the Russian Orthodox Church. Russian Orthodoxy is a branch of Eastern Orthodoxy (see Chapter 12). The head of the church is the patriarch of Moscow. After Peter the Great, Russian Orthodoxy enjoyed a place of special privilege as a branch of the Russian government, but this privilege brought with it a large degree of government control. Under the Soviets, Russian Orthodoxy was variously honored and persecuted, yet it remained firmly under Soviet control. Today,

Russian Orthodoxy is reasserting its role as the religion of the Russian people. Now, though, it must compete with various other religious groups. Still, Russian Orthodoxy has regained some of its former privileged status. As it has grown in influence and power, it has become increasingly aggressive against other churches.

Saint Seraphim-Diveevo monastery near Sarov town, Diveevo, Russia

A Nation Suffering from Population Decline

Russia's population decreases by about a half million people every year. Multiple issues have caused this destructive trend. Russia has a low birthrate, one of the lowest in the world. In addition, Russia has a high rate of abortion, with more babies being aborted than allowed to live. Due to the low quality of health care, many of the women in Russia who undergo an abortion die as a result of complications during the abortion procedure.

Other issues leading to premature deaths in Russia include alcoholism, drug addiction, and HIV/AIDS. Russians buy over two billion liters of vodka each year and suffer from the dire consequences of alcohol consumption, including disease, homicide, and suicide. As many as 2.5 million people in Russia are addicted to drugs.

Russia also has one of the highest and fastest-growing rates of HIV/AIDS. This epidemic primarily affects Russia's young people.

as *perestroika* (pehr ih STROY kuh), or "restructuring," and *glasnost* (GLAHS nawst), or "openness." Perestroika brought more free-market policies and some private ownership of property. Glasnost opened the Soviet Union to the West. However, instead of stabilizing the Soviet Union, these reforms hastened its demise. The people of the Soviet Union had tasted freedom, and they wanted more.

The whole system collapsed in 1991, as the leaders of the various republics declared independence. Boris Yeltsin, the president of the largest republic—Russia—joined the others. By December 25, Gorbachev was a ruler without a country, and he quietly resigned. In the place of the Soviet Union, Yeltsin formed the Commonwealth of Independent States (**CIS**) to retain economic ties among the former Soviet states.

Yeltsin's tenure was marked by political and economic turmoil, and those conditions (along with declining health) led to his resignation in 1999. His successor, Vladimir Putin, increased the power of the president and moved Russia back toward a more centralized government.

Even after the fall of communism, people wait in long lines to see Lenin's tomb in Red Square, Moscow.

A Nation in Transition

The Soviets were poor stewards of the rich resources that Russia contained. Instead of managing the land, they abused the land for their own immediate desires. This misuse has left the country in ruins, with deteriorating buildings, antiquated machinery, and polluted lakes and rivers. Even in Russia, the wealthiest of the CIS states, living conditions are poor. Some people live in areas that have been contaminated by nuclear waste from the Soviet era. Air pollution in industrial cities is also a major problem. The quality of health care in government facilities is very poor.

A major concern among Russians is the strength of criminal elements. Although it has declined by about half in recent years, the murder rate in Russia is 10.2 per hundred thousand people, double the rate of the United States. Corruption remains a major problem in this country and includes police and other government officials as well as businessmen. Bribery is considered a standard business practice and accepted as the cost of doing business in Russia.

Power station in Russia

Federation Government

Russia is experiencing problems of **devolution**, a passing down or "de-evolution" of power. Under the Soviet Union, Moscow regulated everything. Even the train schedules in Siberia used Moscow time. With the breakup, Moscow has shifted some responsibilities to local governments. This transition, though necessary, threatens to tear Russia apart because some local areas enjoy their new powers and want more, perhaps even independence.

Political Divisions

Whereas the United States has states as its main political divisions, Russia has many different names for these divisions. An **oblast**

Missions—Ambassadors for Christ

Russian believers suffered severe persecution under the Soviets, who imprisoned, tortured, and even killed some pastors. Of the many changes in Russia after the fall of the Soviet Union, religious freedom was the most important. Unfortunately, since that time, Russian Orthodox leaders have pressured Moscow to pass new restrictions on religious groups. Some of the ethnic republics have imposed their own severe restrictions as well.

A major reason for the new restrictions was the flood of cults and rich Western missionaries, who appeared to be winning converts by simple virtue of the money they could spend. Orthodox churches argued that the national church needed a breathing space to reestablish its rightful role as the unifying force in the nation. In

truth, some missionaries used poor judgment.

Missionaries are not ambassadors of the United States or any other earthly country. Both they and we should represent Christ and be "ambassadors" for Him (2 Cor. 5:20). We are not ministering to make people Western in their thinking but are seeking to win people for Christ and cause them to think biblically. Western thinking and biblical thinking are often in conflict. For example, Westerners tend to be very individualistic. But churches in other cultures often place a high value on the community of believers—as does the New Testament. Western entertainment styles have overtaken American worship. These are often exported to other countries with little care that they are displacing

rich traditions of worship that small groups of Christians have nurtured over centuries.

Christians from different cultures can often alert each other to cultural blind spots. Sometimes Christians in a particular culture do certain things because that is what everyone in their culture does. It has not occurred to them that these practices may be contrary to Scripture.

The gospel and Christlike living have a home in every culture because each culture is built from the building blocks of God's good Creation. But the gospel also challenges every culture at points where it is sinful and fallen. The Christian missionary should conform to the host culture whenever it honors God but challenge it whenever it dishonors Him.

is a large region or administrative district similar to a state or province. Russia has fifty oblasts, one of which is autonomous. There are also ten large, sparsely populated areas, mostly in the north, that are called **okrugs** (areas). Moscow and St. Petersburg stand alone as Russia's two federal cities. Russia also has six **krais**, or territories, governed by Moscow.

Over thirty ethnic minorities have their own districts and have signed treaties with the government that give them a measure of self-rule. But the twenty-one **autonomous republics** (*autonomous* means "self-ruling") have the most population, power, and status. Since the autonomous republics were formed around ethnic groups within Russia, they are also called ethnic republics, internal republics, or Russian republics. These terms distinguish them from the republics of the USSR, which were external republics or Soviet republics.

The political divisions are distinguished by the degree of autonomy that they enjoy. The autonomous republics have the most freedom, followed by the oblasts, krais, okrugs, and federal cities. The administration of these different divisions was cumbersome. To deal with this difficulty, Putin grouped the various political divisions into seven **federal districts** based on geography. These federal districts allow Moscow to govern Russia more effectively.

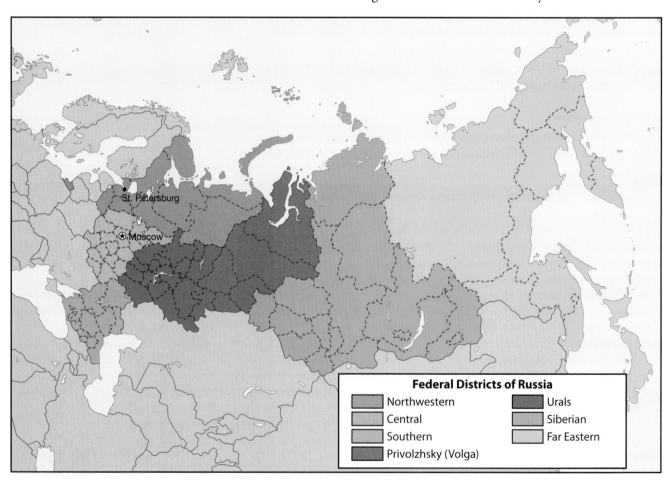

Federal Districts of Russia

Northwestern	Urals
Central	Siberian
Southern	Far Eastern
Privolzhsky (Volga)	

Branches of Government

The United States has had various levels of government throughout its history—each with its own clearly defined responsibilities and taxing powers. In contrast, the Russian government has generally been centralized throughout its history. The same leaders passed the laws, interpreted the laws, and enforced the laws. In 1993, the people voted for a new constitution, which separated powers among three branches of government. The new country is called the Russian Federation. The Communists still retain a substantial part of the vote, but other groups also have a large voice in the Russian Federation.

Most of the power resides in the executive branch. The executive branch is led by a president, but there is no vice president. Instead, the president chooses a premier with the consent of the State Duma. The government is run by the premier and cabinet. In the event that the president dies, the premier takes charge until the next election, which must be held within three months.

In 1996, each oblast began electing its own governor. In 2005, Putin gained the authority to appoint the governors in lieu of elections. The pretense for this power grab was an increase in terrorist attacks. This move by Russia's executive branch greatly increased its power and weakened the independence of the oblasts.

The **Federation Assembly**, the legislature, is divided into two houses. The Federation Council consists of two representatives from each political division in the Russian Federation. The State Duma is composed of elected representatives from throughout Russia. Russia's judicial branch of government has a **Supreme Court** that functions much like the Supreme Court of the United States. It also has a Constitutional Court that examines the constitutionality of Russia's laws.

The State Duma is the Russian Federation's lower house.

Section Quiz

1. What religion is dominant in Russia?
2. What was the title of those who ruled Russia for over 350 years before the Russian Revolution?
3. What kind of government did Lenin initiate?
4. What was Putin's solution to the problem of administrating the various political divisions throughout Russia?
* Why has Russia sought a warm-water port throughout its history?

II. Northern European Russia

Moscow

With about 11.5 million people, **Moscow** is the largest city in all of Europe. Its architecture, landmarks, galleries, and theaters display the great achievements of Russian culture.

Moscow is colder than most capitals of Europe. Its climate is determined by its location in the interior of the continent, far from the moderating influence of the oceans. During the summers, temperatures average in the sixties. Winters are harsh and snowy, with an average January temperature of less than 20°F. In most summers, adequate rainfall reaches this far inland, but rains are unpredictable and crops often fail. Deciduous forests lie south of Moscow, with aspen, oak, and linden; but much of this has been cleared for agriculture, settlement, and industry. Evergreen trees grow in increasing numbers north of Moscow.

St. Basil's Cathedral is probably the most colorful landmark in Moscow.

The Kremlin

The Kremlin is a massive fortress at the heart of Moscow. Many kremlins (walled enclosures) are located throughout Russia, but the one in Moscow has special significance. Its red brick walls enclose sixty-five acres. Surrounded by a moat, the Muscovite Kremlin became the greatest citadel in Europe.

The highest building in the Kremlin, the onion-domed Bell Tower of Ivan the Great, is more than 260 feet tall. Ivan recruited Italian architects from the West to build the Palace of Facets, completed in 1491. Both the Terem Palace and the Palace of the Patriarch were built in the seventeenth century. Workers finished the Grand Kremlin Palace in 1849 and the Armoury in 1851. After the Russian Revolution, the Palace of Congresses was built in 1961.

Besides palaces, the architects also built cathedrals. Ivan the Great built the Cathedral of the Assumption, where the czars were crowned.

The carved walnut throne of Ivan the Terrible, made in 1551, can still be viewed in the cathedral. Ivan the Great also built the Cathedral of the Annunciation, whose domes are made of gold, and the Cathedral of St. Michael the Archangel, where some of the czars are buried. All three cathedrals display valuable frescoes and icons.

These Russian Orthodox cathedrals formed the heart of the Kremlin, the place of royal weddings, coronations, and burials.

Outside the Kremlin is a large open area called Red Square. Once a marketplace, it now hosts parades and public entertainment. Lenin's tomb stands outside the Kremlin wall in Red Square. Also on the square is St. Basil's Cathedral, now a museum, with its ten colorful, onion-shaped domes. Ivan the Terrible built this Russian Orthodox church and then blinded the architect so that he could never design a more beautiful building. Ivan was infamous for his brutality, even killing his own son in a fit of rage.

The Kremlin

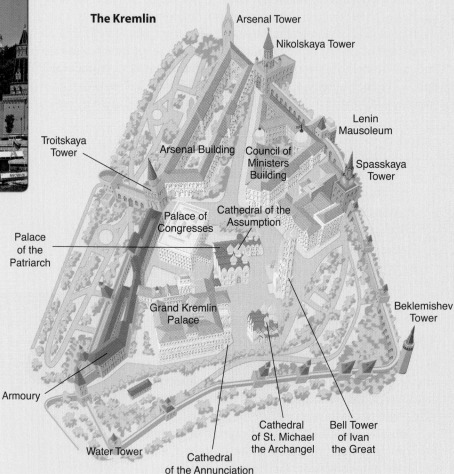

Moscow lies in the center of Moscow Oblast. Moscow and seventeen other oblasts compose the **Central Federal District.** With thirty-eight million people, around 35 percent of Russia's population, the Central Federal District is Russia's most important industrial area and is referred to as Central Russia. Central Russia developed around the headwaters of three river systems: the Dnieper, Don, and Volga. These allowed access to trade with both the north and the south.

Northwest Russia

The northwest includes all of Russia's European holdings north of Greater Moscow. The climate permits dairy farms. The main crop is flax, which is raised for both flaxseed oil and fiber.

St. Petersburg

Russia's second-largest city and main port is **St. Petersburg**, with a population of over five million. Peter the Great hired Italian architects to design the city. The ornate buildings and waterways of St. Petersburg closely resemble those of Venice. St. Petersburg has been a major center for shipbuilding since 1704, and this industry remains an important part of Russia's economy today.

St. Petersburg displays the unusual phenomenon of "white nights." No other city of over one million people is as far north as St. Petersburg (60° N). At such a high latitude, it has virtually no sunsets from the middle of June to early July. During those days, for about five hours each day, the city has a whitish twilight instead of a sunset. In contrast, the winter nights are long and dark.

Volga-Baltic Waterway

In spite of its great size, Russia has very few good ports with access to oceans and world trade. St. Petersburg's importance was enhanced by the completion of the **Volga-Baltic Waterway** and an interior network of railroads in the eighteenth century. Ships can reach inland to Moscow and beyond. Improved in 1964, the waterway connects several rivers in the interior, including the outlets of Lake Onega and Lake Ladoga. Located east of St. Petersburg, these two lakes are the largest in Europe.

Lake Ladoga is the largest lake in Europe.

Karelia

Karelia is a flat glaciated plain north of St. Petersburg. Karelians are much like the neighboring Finns in language and culture. However, because of Russian dominance in the region, ethnic Karelians now constitute only a small part of the population. For sixteen years (1940–56) Karelia enjoyed a status equal to Ukraine or Russia itself as a sixteenth Soviet republic.

With the completion of the **White Sea–Baltic Canal** in 1939, Russia successfully linked Karelia's Arctic coast to St. Petersburg. The

Russia's Second Capital

The energetic czar **Peter the Great** towers above all other czars in Russian history. From his youth he was fascinated by the West and its bustle. In 1697, he became the first czar ever to tour Western Europe, learning all he could about modern shipbuilding, warfare, and industry. Upon his return he reorganized the army and embarked on a program of Westernization, which included forcing the noblemen to pay a tax if they refused to shave their beards. His plan included new lands and a new port on the Baltic Sea. He marched west and defeated Sweden in the Great Northern War (1700–1721). On the marshy shores of the Baltic he founded a new Russian capital, St. Petersburg, which remained the Russian capital for over two centuries.

Peter the Great (1672–1725) built St. Petersburg to be his new capital.

Russia's Western Outpost

Besides St. Petersburg, Russia has only one other port on the Baltic Sea—**Kaliningrad**, far to the west and separated from the rest of the country. Russia captured this region from Germany and has kept it as an ear in the West, where a radar system can provide early warning of attack. Kaliningrad used to be known as Königsburg but was renamed after a Soviet official.

141-mile canal links the White Sea to the Volga-Baltic Waterway. Ships carry timber from Karelia through the canal to St. Petersburg. Russia is a leading producer of sawn wood. Use of the canal reduces the length of the trip by 2,500 miles when compared to a journey around Scandinavia.

Kola Peninsula

The **Kola Peninsula** lies north of Karelia. Murmansk is the key arctic port because the currents of the Barents Sea keep the port free of ice most of the year, and icebreakers break through even when there is ice. Murmansk is north of the Arctic Circle and is the world's northernmost large city. The Barents Sea provides herring and cod, two of the world's most important commercial fishes, as well as other fish.

Russian icebreaker near the North Pole

The Kola Peninsula is sparsely inhabited by Lapps, who also live in Finland, but it has important mineral resources. Geologists have found an assortment of metals and minerals on the peninsula. Among these are phosphates, zinc, nickel, and lead. Russia is a leading producer of nickel. Russia also produces large quantities of uranium, the most important resource of the peninsula.

Vast forests and tundra stretch from the city of Archangel east across northern Russia. Among the ethnic minorities who herd reindeer in these wastelands are the Komi, a Finnic people, and the Samoyeds, whose breed of furry dogs bred to herd reindeer is popular in the United States.

Section Quiz

1. What is the most important industrial area in Russia?
2. What is Russia's main port?
3. What two canal systems link the northern ports with Moscow?
4. What Russian port is separated from the rest of the country?
★ St. Petersburg was called Leningrad during the Soviet era. Why do you think the name has been changed back?

III. Southern European Russia

The Volga River

The **Volga River** is the longest river in Europe at 2,193 miles long. Canals make it the hub of Russia's shipping system. Central Russia lies along the Upper Volga River. Russia's second great industrial area, the Greater Volga, includes most of the rest of the Volga and its major tributary, the Kama River.

Middle Volga

The Middle Volga extends from Nizhniy Novgorod to Samara. **Nizhniy Novgorod** (NIZH-nee NAHV-guh-rod; formerly Gorki) is the third-largest city in Russia with over one and a half million people, while Samara ranks sixth with over one million people. The region is well-known for manufacturing automobiles.

Though Ivan the Terrible conquered the Tatars and tried to destroy their culture, Tatars remain the most numerous ethnic minority in Russia. Tatars compose about one-half of the population of **Tatarstan**, one of six Greater Volga republics. Their capital, Kazan, near the confluence of the Kama and Volga Rivers, is the eighth-largest city in Russia.

Bashkortostan, like Tatarstan, is a key ethnic republic with a large population. Ethnic Bashkorts constitute about 20 percent of the population, and Tatars account for nearly 25 percent. The republic's main economic resource is oil. Russia is one of the leading producers of petroleum in the world.

An elderly Russian couple who live in Suzdal, Russia, a popular tourist site

Lower Volga

The Lower Volga begins below Samara and flows to the Caspian Sea. **Volgograd**, called Stalingrad during the Soviet era from 1925 until 1961, has about one million people. Volgograd ranks after Moscow and St. Petersburg in importance because it is Russia's southern shipping hub. It produces much of the country's steel. Downriver from Volgograd is the port of Astrakhan in the Volga River delta, which allows Russia to trade with other countries on the Caspian Sea.

Novgorod, the First Russian City

Older even than Moscow, Novgorod was a key link at the north end of the ancient fur trade route between the Baltic Sea and the Black Sea. According to tradition, a Viking raider named Rurik gained control of Novgorod in 862, establishing the first ruling dynasty of Russia. This little nation, far from the centers of life in Europe, repulsed later attacks by Tatars from the east, Swedes from the north, and Teutonic Knights from the west. The Grand Duke of Moscow, Ivan the Great, finally conquered Novgorod in 1471. His grandson, Ivan the Terrible, became the first czar of Russia in 1547.

Russian Foods

Every Russian meal starts with a first course of soup. The most famous kind is called *Schi*. Schi is cabbage soup made with carrots, onions, potatoes, and beef. Russians eat lots of potatoes—boiled, mashed, or fried. Potatoes are often served with homemade pickles. Wild mushrooms are a specialty in Russia. There are many delicious ways to serve mushrooms, such as fresh mushroom soup or mushrooms fried in sour cream. For a truly special occasion, Russians love caviar served on white bread with butter. Caviar also tastes good with *blini*, a traditional dish similar to crepes. Appetizers such as beet salad or Olivier salad are fairly common. Olivier salad, also known as "Russian salad," is made with diced potatoes, beef, pickles, carrots, peas, and mayonnaise. Russians also love *pelmeni* and *pirozhki*. Pelmeni are small dumplings filled with meat. Pirozhki are bread rolls filled with cabbage, mushrooms, fish, meat, or apples and then baked. Every meal ends with hot tea plus chocolate candies, pastry, or homemade cakes. As in many other cultures, meals in Russia provide an excellent opportunity for fellowship.

Courtesy of Lilia Naprienko Kielmeyer

Cossacks

The steppes are famous for the **Cossacks**, fiercely independent nomads whose place in Russian lore is very similar to that of the Plains Indians in America. Novocherkassk near Rostov was the major city of the Cossacks.

The name Cossack comes from the Turkic word *Kazakh*, or "adventurer." Tracing their Slavic and Tatar origins is impossible, but their communities were independent and their elite cavalry units widely feared. The Cossacks finally fell to the Russians during the reign of Catherine the Great, an eighteenth-century czarina whose empire extended across the Caucasus. Later czars often turned to these skilled horsemen to defend the Motherland.

Chechen Cossacks in the late 1800s

One of the locks on the Volga-Don Canal

The Don River Basin

The 1,224-mile-long **Don River** is second only to the Volga in importance. Flowing south through a fertile region of Russia very similar to neighboring Ukraine, it loops east and then west before emptying into the Sea of Azov. This important region includes part of the Donets Basin (also called the Donbas), Ukraine's mineral-rich eastern territory.

Russia's Agricultural Heartland

The Don drainage basin consists of grasslands called **steppes** (STEPS). Rich in humus and nutrients, this productive land is called the **Black Earth** region of Russia. The semiarid climate of the steppes provides less than twenty inches of rain annually. As a result, farm production soars in rainy years, but only irrigation can prevent disaster in drier years.

The Black Earth region helped make Russia the world's fourth-largest producer of wheat in 2011. Russia is also a leading producer of rye, oats, and barley. The abundant grains make this area the "Breadbasket of Russia."

Shipping

The vital port at the mouth of the Don is Rostov (or Rostov-on-Don). Much of the Don is shallow, but large ships sailing on the Black Sea can reach over three hundred miles upriver to the Volga-Don Canal.

The **Volga-Don Canal** links the Don with the Volga. Completed in 1952, this sixty-three-mile-long canal with thirteen locks is Russia's final link in its European shipping system. Ships from Moscow can now reach any Russian port in Europe.

Caucasus Mountains

The Caucasus Mountains divide Europe from Asia between the Black Sea and the Caspian Sea. Catherine the Great conquered this area, which lies south of the Don and Volga Rivers. The Russian part of the region consists of two large krais (territories) and eight autonomous republics. The name *Caucasian republics* generally refers to these eight republics of the Caucasus region.

The northern half of the region is lowland, part of the Great European Plain. Besides the two territories, this region includes Kalmykia. Almost half of the people are Kalmyks, a nomadic people that keep livestock and speak a Mongol language. Their religion is Tibetan Buddhism, but some have converted to Islam.

The mountains along the southern border are the highest in Europe. The highest of these is **Mount Elbrus** (18,510 ft.). This mountainous region is a haven for ethnic minorities and includes seven of the eight Caucasian republics.

Mount Elbrus is the highest mountain in Europe.

LET'S GO EXPLORING

Land Use of Central Eurasia

1. What economic activity occurs north of the Arctic Circle?
2. What economic activity is most common among the nations south of Russia?
3. What is the most common economic activity along the Baltic Sea?
4. How is the economy different along the Black Sea than anywhere else in Russia?
★ What does the map reveal about the agricultural conditions of eastern Russia?

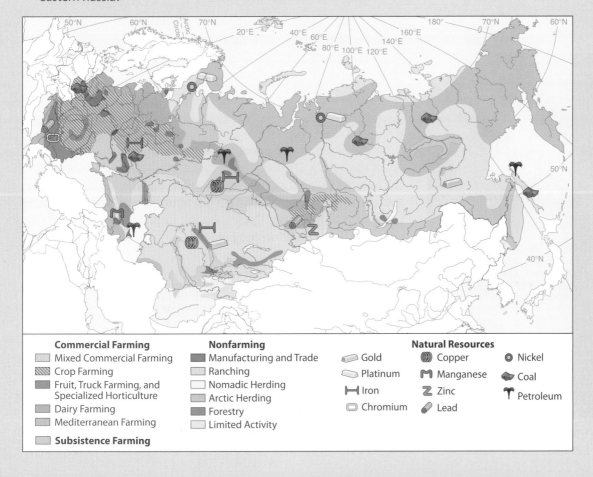

Commercial Farming
- Mixed Commercial Farming
- Crop Farming
- Fruit, Truck Farming, and Specialized Horticulture
- Dairy Farming
- Mediterranean Farming

Subsistence Farming

Nonfarming
- Manufacturing and Trade
- Ranching
- Nomadic Herding
- Arctic Herding
- Forestry
- Limited Activity

Natural Resources
- Gold
- Platinum
- Iron
- Chromium
- Copper
- Manganese
- Zinc
- Lead
- Nickel
- Coal
- Petroleum

Freedom of Religion in Russia?

Under the rule of communism, Russia incarcerated and executed up to twenty million people. Many of those who suffered were Christians. Perhaps as many as two hundred thousand Christian leaders were murdered by the Communists. Russian Christians suffered from discrimination and imprisonment or were subjected to psychiatric treatment.

Today, the Russian constitution guarantees freedom of religion and declares all religions to be equally protected. However, the Orthodox Church retains a clear advantage, and the 1997 federal religion law empowers the government to restrict the activities of religious groups. Foreign-based religious groups are especially subject to governmental intrusion and harassment.

Sixty-seven percent of the Russian population identifies with some form of Christianity, 19 percent are nonreligious, and around 12 percent are Muslim. Evangelical Christians compose just over 1 percent of the Russian population and are growing in numbers and influence. Evangelical groups continue to plant churches and reach unevangelized areas of the country.

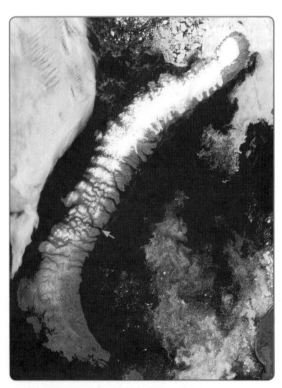

Novaya Zemlya's two main islands are separated by a very narrow strait.

The greatest challenge to the Russian Federation came from a small republic called Chechnya. When the Soviet Union broke apart in 1991, the Chechens took the opportunity to secede from the Russian Federation. The czars had spent thirty years trying to subdue these people, who never willingly bowed to Moscow. Russian parents would scare their children, saying a Chechen might come and get them in the night. While Yeltsin was distracted with politics in Moscow, lawless gangsters flocked to this "refuge" in Chechnya.

In 1994, Yeltsin made a fateful decision to send in his army, but the campaign was a disaster. When Russian columns became bogged down outside the capital, Russian planes started bombing innocent civilians. Generals refused to obey orders and openly criticized the attack. The Russians eventually withdrew but invaded again in 1999 after a series of terrorist attacks in Russia and Chechnya's invasion of Dagestan. That conflict ended in 2000. Today, tensions are high in Chechnya with the region's future still in doubt.

Thirty people groups live in neighboring Dagestan. Located on the Caspian Sea, Dagestan has important oil resources, but these resources are in a sensitive area of mixed ethnic groups between volatile Chechnya in the west, Buddhist Kalmykia in the north, and the Shiite country of Azerbaijan in the south.

Section Quiz

1. What is Europe's longest river?
2. Name two ethnic republics where descendants of the Tatars now live.
3. What group of people had their cultural center near the mouth of the Don River?
4. In what range is the highest mountain in Europe found?
5. What ethnic republic in the Caucasus declared independence after the fall of the Soviet Union?
★ Why do you think so many ethnic minorities survived on the Volga, despite Russian conquest?

IV. Asian Russia

Russia's supply of mineral and fuel resources is among the greatest in the world. Deposits of almost every industrial mineral from aluminum (bauxite) to zinc are found in Russia. Many of these resources, however, lie in remote parts of its vast Asian landmass. Compared to European Russia, Asiatic Russia is sparsely populated with very few population centers.

Ural Mountains

The **Ural Mountains** form a geographic border between the continents of Europe and Asia. The highest peak, Mount Narodnaya in the north, reaches 6,217 feet. While mineral resources lie in this part of the range, they are less utilized than those farther south. The range continues north into the Arctic Ocean to form the two large islands of the archipelago Novaya Zemlya. These two islands are the largest islands in the Eurasian Arctic. During the Soviet era, Novaya Zemlya was used as a nuclear weapons test site.

The Ural Mountains are low with several passes that enable people to cross freely. The southern Urals are more populous and have a

Cold Climates

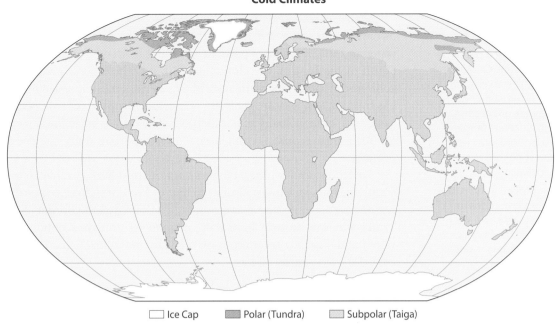

☐ Ice Cap　■ Polar (Tundra)　☐ Subpolar (Taiga)

unique culture. The most important mineral deposits in the Urals are iron ore and copper. Mining in the Urals also enables Russia to rank among the top producers of potash, bauxite, and silver.

Important industrial cities have grown up near the mineral resources. **Yekaterinburg** and Chelyabinsk each have over one million people and rank as Russia's fourth- and ninth-largest cities, respectively. Yekaterinburg, named after Catherine I, the wife of Peter the Great, manufactures many products, notably turbines and ball bearings. Yekaterinburg was also the city where the last czar of Russia, Nicholas II, and his family were executed in 1918.

Siberia

All of Asian Russia east of the Urals is broadly termed **Siberia**. Russia's interior has no east-west mountain ranges to block cold fronts that push down from the Arctic.

Earth Matters: Tower in the Taiga

Ecologist Ernst-Detlef Schulze clips into a safety harness as he rests on a platform almost 1,000 feet above the treetops of the Siberian taiga. He takes a dizzying look down. Schulze spearheaded a group of German researchers that have erected and man a "sniffing" tower almost as tall as the Eiffel Tower called the ZOTTO in the Siberian taiga.

The taiga is actually the largest land biome in the world, home to many of the longest rivers in the world. The Siberian taiga is the lungs of Europe, similar to Amazonia in South America. The goal of these researchers from the Max Planck institute is to "smell" gases generated and used by the Russian taiga, the largest continuous forest on Earth. And they set their sights high.

These scientists are trying to see if the forests of northern Russia are speeding up or slowing down climate change. Trees consume carbon dioxide, but climatologists are concerned that thawing bogs in Siberia could release large amounts of methane, another greenhouse gas like carbon dioxide. They are also concerned about massive logging in Siberia. But it is difficult for scientists to fully understand what is really happening on such a large scale. This is one of the challenges of science.

Celebration and Singing

Russians love to celebrate, whether it is a birthday, wedding, or some other event. Celebration calls for food and singing. If the conversation around the table begins to wane, someone from the family will often break out in song, and the others quickly join. Subjects range from traditional Russian songs to Soviet ballads. Many favorite Russian songs are about love, especially unrequited love.

One form of Russian song is called a *chastushka* (chast OO shka). It is usually a humorous improvisation based on recent local news, sung by two competing performers. The singers are accompanied by a stringed instrument similar to a guitar or by a Russian accordion.

Walruses and seals feed along the Arctic coast, while reindeer browse the mosses and lichens of the tundra. The polar climate keeps water and soil in a state of permafrost, that is, frozen most of the year. South of the tundra, the climate warms slightly. Wolves prowl the coniferous forests that blanket most of Siberia. The subpolar climate has freezing temperatures half the year, which drop to -60°F on occasion, and summer highs as hot as 100°F. The taiga—great coniferous forests of spruce, pine, fir, and larch—is an important source of wood products.

Southwest and southeast Siberia, where most Siberians live, have a more hospitable climate similar to that of Moscow. These populous regions are separated by Asian mountains that cross the border. The **Trans-Siberian Railway** links these regions, resulting in a ribbon development. Farmers grow crops on the scattered prairies, and loggers cut trees from nearby forests.

Omsk Railway Station near the Kazakhstan border

West Siberian Plain

The West Siberian Plain is possibly the largest plain in the world and covers over one million square miles, amounting to about one-seventh of Russia's area. Extending from the Ural Mountains to the Yenisey River, it is a vast marshy plain drained by the Ob River and its tributaries. The Gulf of Ob and the Kara Sea in the north remain frozen, while snow melts in the south. The ice blocks the water flow, causing annual flooding along the Ob.

Nenet reindeer herders in the Western Siberian Yamal Peninsula in Russia

Novosibirsk (New Siberia), with about one and a half million people, is the largest city in Siberia. Situated on the Ob River, it has experienced phenomenal growth because of natural resources available nearby. Petroleum and natural gas deposits lie north. To the southeast lie deposits of lead, zinc, and iron ore. The region contributed to Russia's status in 2011 as the fifth leading producer of coal worldwide.

Central Siberian Plateau

The Central Siberian Plateau covers one-third of Siberia and stretches between the Yenisey and Lena Rivers. It averages about two thousand feet in elevation. The lower north coast, or **Taymyr Peninsula**, is the northernmost mainland area in the world. Near the mouth of the Yenisey, miners dig nickel, cobalt, and platinum. Russia provides over 13 percent of the world's platinum. Diamonds come from the remote central part of the plateau. The Trans-Siberian Railroad enters the central plateau at Krasnoyarsk, the largest city of the plateau with almost one million people, which lies on the Yenisey River.

Two ethnic republics of southern Siberia—Altaya and Tuva—retain their ethnic majority. Remote Altaya is especially interesting because it is at the sensitive border between four large nations: Russia, China, Mongolia, and Kazakhstan. Altaya contains Mt. Belukha (14,783 ft.), the highest peak of the **Altai Mountains**. The mountainous republic also contains the headwaters of the Ob. There are four Altaic republics in this region of Siberia.

East Siberian Upland

The East Siberian Upland is a mountain wilderness between the Lena River and the Pacific Ocean. The Lena River is the eleventh-longest river in the world.

Interior—The largest Russian republic is **Sakha** (formerly Yakutia); it has the world's harshest climate of any inhabited area. It contains much of the Lena and Kolyma River basins as well as the New Siberian Islands in the Arctic. Covering about 1.2 million square miles, it would be the eighth-largest country in the world if it obtained independence.

Ethnic Yakuts speak a Turkic language and constitute over one-third of the population, while Russians constitute over one-half. Yakutsk, the main city, was founded in 1632 and has grown to become the largest city of northern Siberia. The growth has come from mining in the **Yakutsk Basin** along the Lena and in the mountains. The Sakha gold fields made Russia the fourth-largest producer of gold in the world in 2012.

The Far East—Russia has more Pacific coastline than any other country. The Pacific coast has a more moderate climate and includes some farmland. The ports still freeze in winter, but some ports, such as Vladivostok, can be opened with ice breakers. Russian leaders are hopeful that its Far East will share in the booming trade of the Pacific Rim.

Russia's Far East has land within a few miles of all the great Pacific powers. Its land borders China and North Korea, while Japan is across a narrow channel from Russia's **Sakhalin Island** (SAK uh leen). The island has both coal and petroleum resources. Russia's **Kuril Islands** also extend in a chain from the Kamchatka (kam

Lake Baikal

Lake Baikal is the deepest lake in the world and the seventh-largest lake in the world. Over one mile deep, 395 miles long, and up to fifty miles wide, it contains more water than all the Great Lakes combined.

Baikal seals, a freshwater species, sunbathe on the shore. Over nine hundred animal species in the lake are found nowhere else in the world. These include many unusual fish that swim near the lake's surface. The black and frigid depths are virtually lifeless and little-explored.

Over 330 rivers feed the lake, but only the Angara River drains it toward the north. The Angara provides hydroelectric power to the city of Irkutsk, an ancient trading post located on a vital pass through the mountains near the lake. The large haul of fish from the lake is loaded on trains at Irkutsk.

Lake Baikal has beautiful blue waters, like the Great Lakes in the United States, but it lacks many other advantages. It has no navigable outlet to the ocean. While the climate is better than much of the area around it, the lake surface remains frozen from January to May.

Chuvorkusky Bay is one of the many beautiful bays on Lake Baikal.

Kuril Islands

A continuing disagreement over the ownership of the Kuril Islands has prevented Russia and Japan from signing a peace treaty to end World War II. The Kuril Islands were given to Russia after the war, but Japan still claims several of the southernmost islands.

CHAT kuh) Peninsula to Japan. The United States (Alaska) is just across the **Bering Strait**.

The Trans-Siberian Railway links **Vladivostok**, Russia's main Pacific port, with Russia's European ports. Russia's fishing fleet catches enough fish for Russia to rank seventh worldwide.

Two peninsulas dominate the far northern coast. The Chukchi Peninsula reaches toward Alaska and divides the Bering Sea from the Chukchi Sea. The **Kamchatka Peninsula** extends south into the Pacific. Kamchatka contains twenty-nine active volcanoes, including Siberia's highest peak, snow-capped **Mount Klyuchevskaya** (15,584 ft.). Its southern end has the Russian port city of Petropavlovsk.

The Russian Empire once crossed the Pacific, including Alaska and trading centers as far south as California. The first permanent settlement in Alaska was founded in 1784. Russia did not have the means to protect these distant lands, however, and sold them to the United States in 1867. Instead, it concentrated its energies on expanding its empire in Central Asia, closer to home.

Section Quiz

1. What mountain range divides Europe and Asia and forms the western border of Siberia?
2. On what group of islands did the Soviets conduct nuclear testing?
3–5. What are the three major geographic regions of Siberia?
6. What is the main seaport in Siberia?
 ✶ Why is Asiatic Russia so important to European Russia?

Chapter Review

Making Connections

1. Why are Russia's European lands more populous than its Asian lands?
2. What have been the results of the Soviets' misuse of Russia's resources?
3–4. What has been the result of devolving central authority in Russia? Why is it important?
5. Why does Russia's development have a ribbon pattern in Asia?

Developing Geography Skills

1. Examine the map on pages 314–15 and list three geographic features that provide barriers between Russia and neighboring countries. How might these barriers have influenced the distinct history of Russia?
2. What geographic features would make the effective governing of Russia difficult, if not impossible?

Thinking Critically

1. Why do you think the Communist Party is still strong in Russia?
2. How would a warming climate benefit Russia?

Living in God's World

1. Write an essay that defends the human population as a nation's most valuable asset. How should this position affect government policy?
2. Imagine you are a Russian Christian with the opportunity to petition the government to protect Russian citizens from religious suppression. How would you frame your case?

People, Places, and Things to Know

czars
autocrats
Vladimir Ilich Lenin
USSR
Cold War
CIS
devolution
oblast
okrugs
krais
autonomous republic
federal districts
Federation Assembly
Supreme Court
Moscow
the Kremlin
Central Federal District
Peter the Great
St. Petersburg
Volga-Baltic Waterway
Karelia
White Sea–Baltic Canal
Kaliningrad
Kola Peninsula
Volga River
Nizhniy Novgorod
Tatarstan
Volgograd
Cossacks
Don River
steppes
Black Earth
Volga-Don Canal
Mount Elbrus
Ural Mountains
Yekaterinburg
Siberia
Trans-Siberian Railway
Lake Baikal
Novosibirsk
Taymyr Peninsula
Altai Mountains
Sakha
Yakutsk Basin
Sakhalin Island
Kuril Islands
Bering Strait
Vladivostok
Kamchatka Peninsula
Mount Klyuchevskaya

Unit Six

ASIA

The nations of Asia developed from ancient civilizations and diverse people groups. As in other parts of the world, many Asian civilizations formed around rivers, which provided food, transportation, and irrigation. While China is the best-known kingdom in Asia, many other cultures also developed and thrived there.

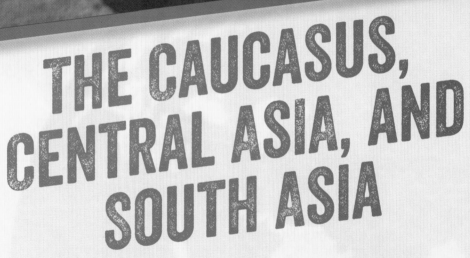

14

THE CAUCASUS, CENTRAL ASIA, AND SOUTH ASIA

View of Tbilisi, Georgia, from the ancient Narikala Fortress

I. The Countries of the Caucasus
A. Georgia
B. Armenia
C. Azerbaijan

II. Central Asia
A. Kazakhstan
B. Turkmenistan
C. Uzbekistan
D. Kyrgyzstan
E. Tajikistan
F. Afghanistan

III. South Asia
A. India
B. Pakistan and Bangladesh
C. Nepal and Bhutan
D. Sri Lanka and Maldives

The area covered in this chapter extends from the Caucasus Mountains east of the Black Sea to the Western and Eastern Ghat Mountains along the southern borders of India. This region extends to the Himalaya Mountains along the southern border of China. Between the mountain ranges, the land displays a great variety of surfaces, including deserts, steppes, valleys, more mountains, and plains.

Some of the countries are landlocked, while others have access to large bodies of water. Rivers of various sizes also thread their way through this region and flow to a sea or ocean.

These countries also vary in the percentage of land that is arable. Mountainous regions have very little land that can be farmed, while many of the plains and plateaus contain large regions of productive land.

This area is populated by people with deeply held religious beliefs. Islam has a strong influence in many of these countries. However, Buddhism, Hinduism, and other religions also have many followers in this region. Christians make up a minority of the people.

The peoples of this region also share another characteristic—conquest or attempted conquest by foreign powers. Many fell to Muslim conquerors at some point in their history. Others became the battleground between Western imperialists and other Asian states. A few proved impossible to conquer.

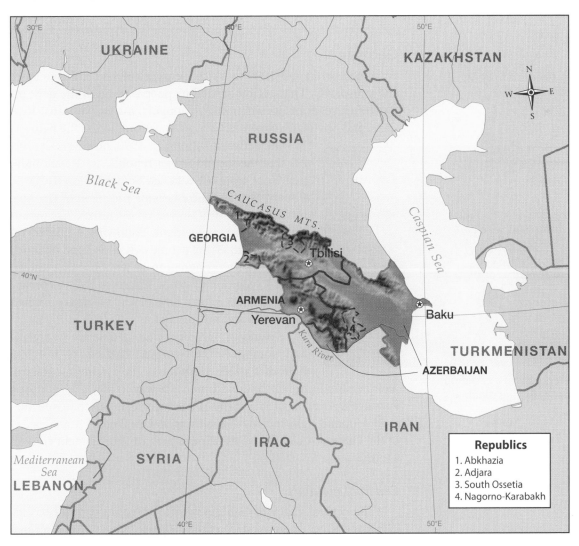

Republics
1. Abkhazia
2. Adjara
3. South Ossetia
4. Nagorno-Karabakh

I. The Countries of the Caucasus

The **Caucasus Mountains** lie at the crossroads between Europe, Asia, and the Middle East. The western border of the mountains runs along the Black Sea. The eastern border touches the coast of the Caspian Sea, which was settled by Asian nomads and by Muslim conquerors from the Middle East.

A diversity of peoples arose in the isolated valleys of the Caucasus Mountains. The Arabs call the Caucasus the "mountains of a thousand languages." The people are fiercely independent and frequently fight among themselves.

Caucasus Fast Facts						
Country	Capital	Area (sq. mi.)	Pop. (M)	Pop. Density (per sq. mi.)	Per Capita GDP ($US)	Life Span
Armenia	Yerevan	11,483	2.98	260	$5,600	73.49
Azerbaijan	Baku	33,436	9.60	287	$10,700	71.32
Georgia	Tbilisi	26,911	4.56	169	$5,900	77.32
Tajikistan	Dushanbe	55,251	7.91	143	$2,200	66.38
Turkmenistan	Ashgabat	188,456	5.11	27	$8,500	68.84
Uzbekistan	Tashkent	172,742	28.66	166	$3,500	72.77

Georgia

From about AD 1000 to 1212, Georgia enjoyed independence and prosperity. That period carried its people through the dark intervening years of domination by Mongols, Turks, Persians, Russians, and Soviets. Frequently, Georgia was trampled as the pathway in wars between nations. In 1990, however, Georgia became the second Soviet republic to declare independence from a weakened Soviet Union. In 1995, Eduard Shevardnadze became president of Georgia, but his administration was characterized by corruption and mismanagement. Following a tainted re-election in 2003, the people demanded and obtained Shevardnadze's resignation in what became known as the Revolution of Roses. Efforts to reduce corruption and enact reform have placed Georgia on a path to stability and prosperity.

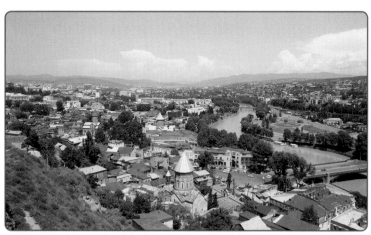

Villages in flat, fertile valleys against a backdrop of high, snow-topped mountains are common throughout Georgia.

Seventy-six percent of the people are Georgians and worship in the Georgian Orthodox Church, a type of Eastern Orthodoxy. For many Georgians, membership in the Orthodox Church is a way to identify with their ancestors. As such, it is a form of patriotism rather than spiritual faith. Hopeful signs include a small spiritual awakening among a few of the Orthodox clergy and the slow growth of Independent congregations.

Central Lowlands

The central valley of Georgia is formed from two river basins. The Rioni River drains west into the Black Sea. The surrounding area has a mild marine-west-coast climate in which citrus fruits and grape products are grown. Georgia is the only Caucasian country with ocean ports. Those ports on the Black Sea permit greater opportunities to trade with Russia and Ukraine, Georgia's main trade partners, as well as other nations.

Tbilisi (tuh BIL eh see) has been the capital of Georgia for more than fifteen hundred years. It is on the Kura (kuhr RAH) River, which flows southeast into Azerbaijan (az ur bye JAHN). Irrigation in this drier region supports tobacco and wheat. The main industries of the city involve food processing.

Highland Rebels

Dissatisfied Muslim minorities are concentrated in two breakaway regions on the northern borders. Abkhazia (ab KAHZ ee ah) lies along the Black Sea, and South Ossetia (ah SEE shah) is located across the border from Russia's republic of North Ossetia. When Georgia tried to exert control of South Ossetia in 2008, Russian forces invaded Georgia, humiliated the government, and briefly occupied the country. Russian interference remains a troubling issue in the region.

Armenia

The **Armenians** (ahr MEE nee uns) live in a landlocked mountainous region in the Caucasus Mountains. In the fourth century, their nation became the first in the world to officially adopt Christianity. During the fifth century the Armenians developed a unique language with its own alphabet. Today they enjoy a literacy rate of 99.4 percent.

History

Throughout most of Armenia's history, it has endured frequent invasion and conflict as Byzantine forces opposed Turkish forces and Russian forces fought with Persians. Current tensions result from concern over the status of ethnic Armenians in Nagorno-Karabakh, Azerbaijan. A disputed border with Turkey and a violent past also contribute to instability in the region.

Leading up to World War I, Turkish leaders decided to eliminate the possibility that Armenians would side with Turkey's enemies, the Russians. By 1917, Turkish forces and their allies had murdered up to 1.5 million Armenian men, women, and children. This became known as the Armenian Genocide. Part of Armenia's tension with Turkey stems from Turkey's continued denial of these atrocities.

Life

Despite Armenia's dry climate that provides only twenty inches of rainfall annually, farmers grow barley, wheat, and potatoes. Mineral resources include copper and bauxite.

Armenia is a densely populated nation in the Caucasus with nearly 98 percent of the population consisting of native Armenians. A tragedy occurred

This Georgian shepherd tends his sheep.

Holidays and Festivals in Georgia

During the Soviet era, Georgians celebrated Labor Day, Soviet National Day, and other secular Soviet holidays. However, after the fall of the Soviet Union, the people of Georgia returned to their traditional folk and religious holidays.

Basil was one of the spiritual fathers of the Eastern Orthodox Church, and a feast is held in his honor on January 1. Along with many other countries, Georgians celebrate Christmas. However, they celebrate Christmas on January 6 because their religious calendar is 13 days later than the Gregorian calendar.

The most important festival in Georgia is Easter. People prepare Easter eggs as a symbol of renewal and rebirth and hold an Easter feast in the church. On Ascension Day, forty days after Easter, they extinguish candles to symbolize the physical departure of Christ to heaven.

Mt. Ararat towers over the mountains that form the border between Armenia and Turkey.

Shiite Versus Sunni Muslim

Following the death of the third Caliph in 656, Islam split into two groups. A minority group declared that Muhammad had intended Ali, Muhammad's cousin, to rule. They took the title of of **Shiite** ("follower") because they claimed to be the true followers of Muhammad. The Shiites insisted that the right of rule was limited to members of Muhammad's family and a certain group of his descendants. They also believed that their ruler should retain Muhammad's dual role of political and religious leader. They called this individual their *imam* ("leader").

The majority of Muslims, however, continued to support the practice of appointing a caliph ("leader"). They took the name **Sunni** ("adherent"). The Sunnis believed that any worthy Muslim could become the ruler of Islam. In addition, they divided the leadership between a political leader (caliph) and a local religious leader (imam). (Abu Bakr, the successor of Muhammad and the first caliph, had created this division of power.)

War between these competing views resulted in the Sunnis retaining the dominant position in the Muslim world (80–90 percent) and the Shiites representing about 10 percent of the Muslim population. Today, Shiites have a majority population in Iran, Iraq, Azerbaijan, and Bahrain.

Much of the Muslim-on-Muslim violence stems from the division between these two major interpretations of Islam. Each group considers the other to be apostate.

Ancient Religious Practice in Armenia

"Although Armenia was the first state to adopt Christianity as a national religion, some older customs have persisted. For example, in ancient times, Armenians considered trees to be sacred plants with the power to grant special requests. By tying strips of cloth to a tree, one could ask for help or heal sick relatives and friends. Some Armenians continue this practice today."

Cultures of the World: Armenia, 79.

in 1988 when an earthquake killed twenty-five thousand people and left half a million others homeless. Recovery has been slow due to an economic blockade by Azerbaijan and Turkey.

The legacy of the Armenian Apostolic Church has endured for over 1700 years. While many Armenians identify with the church for traditional reasons, a growing number of Armenians are embracing the truth of the gospel. Thanks to the efforts of The Armenian Church-Loving Brotherhood, Bible study groups and the publishing of Christian literature and Bibles are thriving in Armenia.

Azerbaijan

Iran (formerly Persia) has had the greatest influence over Azerbaijan. Persians controlled the region from 700 BC to AD 600 (except for the brief interruption of the Greek Empire) and from the sixteenth century to 1813 (except for a brief period under the Ottoman Turks).

The people of Azerbaijan speak Persian, and about 88 percent practice Shia Islam. About 9 percent of the population has no religious connection, and nearly 3 percent practice some form of Christianity. Despite persecution and the assumption that Christianity is tied to Russian imperialism, the number of Azerbaijani believers has grown from less than fifty in 1991 to at least 3,000 as of 2010.

Recent conflict with neighboring Armenia has left this state unsettled and ready for war. Military spending remains at an all-time high, and the economy has suffered as a consequence. Although a small elite segment of the population enjoys great wealth, most Azerbaijanis have been excluded from these economic benefits.

A long plain runs southeast across the nation. The Kura River flows through this lowland valley of the Caucasus, where farmers grow cotton, grain, and tea. Some raise silkworms in the semiarid

Baku, the capital of Azerbaijan, sits on the western shore of the Caspian Sea.

temperate climate. This area is known for its beautiful rugs and shawls.

The Kura River, which provides water for textile and chemical plants, empties into the **Caspian Sea**, the largest lake in the world. This lake provides key resources, such as fish and salt. Azerbaijan's capital, Baku (BAH koo), is the leading port. Unfortunately, rising waters have threatened the lowland city with floods.

Several other rivers also flow into the Caspian Sea, which is ninety-two feet below sea level, but no waters flow out. The resulting "deadness" makes the Caspian Sea salty, although it is not as salty as ocean water.

The most important resource of the Caspian has been an abundance of oil and natural gas reserves. The region could become a major battleground in the twenty-first century, as nations—including China, a nearby international giant—compete for the Caspian's oil wealth. The big problem for Azerbaijan, however, is how best to get its oil and natural gas to the rest of the world. It must use oil pipelines across other countries—often a difficult diplomatic task.

The Caspian Sea viewed from orbit.

Section Quiz

1. Why are there so many languages and cultures in the Caucasus?
2. Which country in the Caucasus became the first to officially adopt Christianity?
3. Why do Shia and Sunni Muslims persecute one another?
4. What gives Azerbaijan an economic advantage over the other two Caucasus nations?
★ Why do you think Russia is concerned about conditions in the Caucasus?

II. Central Asia

Central Asia is a wide-ranging term that includes all of the arid plains between the Caspian Sea and western China. This region is isolated from other regions by deserts and high mountains. Various tribes of fierce nomads left an imprint of war and conquest on Central Asia. The Huns from this region threatened ancient Rome in the fourth and fifth centuries AD. The Mongols briefly dominated the

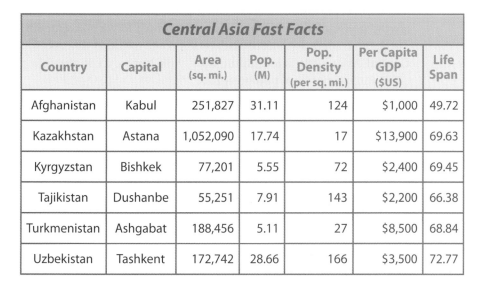

Central Asia Fast Facts						
Country	Capital	Area (sq. mi.)	Pop. (M)	Pop. Density (per sq. mi.)	Per Capita GDP ($US)	Life Span
Afghanistan	Kabul	251,827	31.11	124	$1,000	49.72
Kazakhstan	Astana	1,052,090	17.74	17	$13,900	69.63
Kyrgyzstan	Bishkek	77,201	5.55	72	$2,400	69.45
Tajikistan	Dushanbe	55,251	7.91	143	$2,200	66.38
Turkmenistan	Ashgabat	188,456	5.11	27	$8,500	68.84
Uzbekistan	Tashkent	172,742	28.66	166	$3,500	72.77

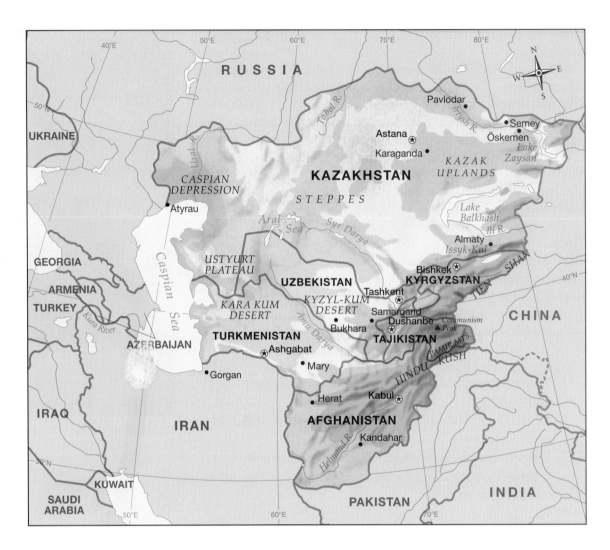

region when they terrorized all of Eurasia during the thirteenth and fourteenth centuries. But it was the Turkic peoples, who migrated across most of Central Asia between the fifth and tenth centuries, that had the longest-lasting impact. Because so many of the modern-day countries in Central Asia have mainly Turkic populations, the entire region is sometimes referred to as Turkistan.

Central Asia was once a major trade route between the East and the West. The **Silk Road** linked the two great ancient empires: Rome and China. Europeans gladly traded gold, silver, wool, jewels, and anything else of value to the Chinese in return for silk. Eventually, European traders discovered a new water route to China that avoided Central Asia. Little is left on the dusty Silk Road except struggling cities and memories of past greatness.

The new nations of Central Asia are struggling to find their place in the modern world. They suffer from a devastating shortage of water and landlocked borders that isolate them from international trade. To make matters worse, former Communist rulers continue to exercise power in Central Asia.

Kazakhstan

Kazakhstan (KAH zahk stan), the "giant" of Central Asia, is the only Central Asian nation that borders Russia. The histories of the two nations are closely linked. For years, Russian farmers settled in northern Kazakhstan. A major problem, however, is that while northern Kazakhstan is heavily Russified, the southern part is influenced more by its Turkish background. When the country was under Soviet rule, the capital was Almaty (ahl MAH tee) in the south, which put strong Russian authority in the heart of Kazakh territory. When the Soviet Union fell, however, Kazakhs feared that the Russians in the north would try to become part of Russia, so they moved the capital to Astana (uh STAH nuh) in the north, putting Kazakh authorities in the heart of the Russified area.

The country is about 54 percent Muslim, with 34 percent identified as nonreligious. The Christian population is around 12 percent, having grown from virtually nothing to around fifteen thousand believers during the last twenty years. These Christians have multiplied despite growing persecution by Muslims and increasing governmental oppression.

The Ministry of Transportation and Telecommunications, the tallest building in Astana, shows the modernity of that growing city.

Europeans on the Northern Steppes

Kazakhstan's northern steppes are good for grazing sheep and cattle. Russian and Ukrainian farmers began arriving on the northern borders in the 1730s, and Russian armies had conquered the region by the 1850s.

The move of the capital to the north in post-Soviet years sparked one of the world's most ambitious building projects as oil income was used to erect government buildings, a presidential residence, parks, and monuments.

Eastern Kazakh Uplands

The Kazakh Uplands cover the eastern lake regions around Lake Balkhash and Lake Zaysan. The climate is similar to that of the northern steppes. Karaganda and Ekibastuz are important industrial centers. Large lead mines have made Kazakhstan the second-leading smelter of lead, behind the United States.

The major industrial city at the south end of the uplands is Almaty. With 1.3 million people, it is Kazakhstan's largest city and its cultural center. Dense orchards provide one of the country's main products—fruit.

Southern and Western Deserts

Most of the south is a desert that contains great wealth. Copper comes from Betpak-Dala, the desert north of the country's main river, Syr Darya. Uranium is mined south of the river.

In the middle of these deserts, the Syr Darya flowed into the **Aral** (AHR ul) **Sea** until the Soviets diverted it for irrigation in the 1960s. Like the Caspian Sea to the west, the Aral Sea was a salt lake with no outlet to the ocean. Although it was once the world's fourth-largest lake, diverting the water flowing into the lake reduced it to a tiny fraction of its former size. The diverted water was originally used to increase agricultural (especially cotton) production, but the declining waters of the Aral Sea left salt deposits as they evaporated, and crop production has dramatically fallen as the soil quality in the area has

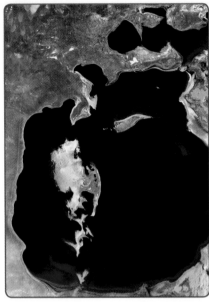
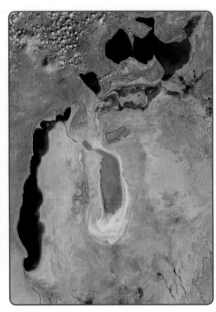

The Aral Sea in 1989 (left) and 2013 (right)

deteriorated. The draining of this lake is considered by many to be one of the greatest environmental disasters in history. The loss of income and productivity has devastated the region around the Aral Sea.

Western Kazakhstan consists of lowlands on the Caspian Sea. Unlike Azerbaijan, Kazakhstan has no major cities on this salt sea. There are no Caucasus Mountains to create orographic rainfall. Instead, the region is a barren wasteland. The lowland forms a deep bowl, or depression, in the earth. At its lowest spot, the **Caspian Depression** is 433 feet below sea level.

Kazakhstan is a corridor between the oil-rich Caspian Sea and China. China is seeking ways to gain the fuel it needs for its expanding industrial economy and to end its dependence on long ocean routes, so Kazakhstan is of great strategic importance. Kazakhstan has granted China sole rights to exploration and exploitation of oil along its border with the Caspian.

Turkmenistan

Uzbekistan (ooz BEHK ih stan) and Turkmenistan (turk mehn ih STAN) lie south of Kazakhstan. Like Kazakhstan, these two desert nations were settled by Turkic peoples, speak Turkic languages, and follow the Turkish branch of Islam, Sunni Islam.

The Turkmens account for about 82 percent of the people of modern Turkmenistan. Uzbeks constitute 9 percent and Russians 2 percent. The rest are smaller minorities, such as Kazakhs, Tatars, Ukrainians, and Armenians.

Turkmenistan, which is about the size of Utah and Nevada combined, lies south of Kazakhstan and east of the Caspian Sea. Turkmenistan's most important border is on the south with Iran. It is the only former Soviet republic bordering Iran. Its major hindrance to trade, however, is its relative inaccessibility to other countries.

This country is 96 percent Sunni Muslim with a Christian population of around 2 percent. Although the country's constitution guarantees freedom of religion, Christians, Jews, and non-Sunni Muslim groups are severely persecuted and strictly forbidden. Perhaps as many as one thousand Christians live in Turkmenistan, and many of them are Russian, Ukranian, or Armenian. The New Testament has been translated into the Turkmen language, and the translation of the Old Testament is under way.

The **Kara-Kum** (kah-rah KOOM) is a desert that covers 80 percent of Turkmenistan. Summer temperatures can exceed 122°F. The desert's most important resources, petroleum and natural gas, make Turkmenistan one of the richest Central Asian nations. As in Kazakhstan, the petroleum lies along the Caspian Sea. Natural gas is found throughout the desert.

Uzbekistan

Uzbekistan is in the heart of Central Asia, completely surrounded by other Central Asian nations. It borders every other

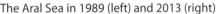

Turkmen man in traditional garb with camel

nation in the region and is the only double landlocked state in Central Asia. Its population is made up of Uzbeks (78 percent), Russians (2.5 percent), and small minorities of Tatars, Kazakhs, Tajiks, and Karakalpaks. It is the most populous nation in Central Asia.

The nation has several religious groups, but 85 percent of the people are Muslim. About 1 percent of the population constitutes a Christian minority. Despite the persecution and political opposition Uzbek Christians face, their numbers have grown to more than ten thousand.

When Central Asia broke from the Soviet Union, Uzbekistan hoped that the Turkic peoples of Central Asia would unite into a single nation called **Turkistan**. Uzbekistan, with its large population, had much to gain from a union because of its weak economy and lack of trade opportunities. However, no other nation shared Uzbekistan's enthusiasm.

Uzbekistan has natural resources in the form of oil, natural gas, and mineral deposits. However, processed resources must be transported across one or more national boundaries to reach foreign markets. In addition, this country has a fragile water supply, made worse by the draining of the Aral Sea. Crops, including cotton, will grow in this country but must be irrigated. This further depletes the nation's water supply.

Desert Oases

The **Kyzyl-Kum** (kih-ZIL KOOM) is a vast desert that covers 80 percent of Uzbekistan, except for a few mountains on the eastern edge. Most of the Kyzyl-Kum is wilderness, but it does have a few oases and mining towns. The greatest oasis lies at **Bukhara** (BOO kah rah), north of the Amu Darya. Bukhara served as a crucial juncture of the Silk Road as caravans crossed eight hundred miles through the deserts.

In the tenth century, Bukhara was the capital of a Muslim dynasty, the Samanids, and was second only to Mecca as an Islamic holy place. It still boasts Ulugh Beg madrasah (mah DRAH suh; an Islamic seminary), the oldest in Central Asia, dating from 1418. It is also the home of the largest madrasah in Central Asia, with over two hundred domes, dating from the sixteenth century. Today, Bukhara is a center of Tajik culture in the middle of an Uzbek nation.

The Crowded Foothills

Most of Uzbekistan's population lives in the foothills of the great Asian mountain system. Its two largest cities are there.

The capital, **Tashkent**, has 2.2 million people and is the largest city in the Caucasus and Central Asia. Tashkent has a rich heritage that dates back at least to the second century BC, according to Chinese sources. Unfortunately, a 1966 earthquake destroyed most of the historic buildings. The region around Tashkent contains some of the world's greatest uranium mines.

Samarqand (SAM er kand; sometimes spelled Samarkand) lies near the eastern

> ### Landlocked
>
> Nations that do not have access to some form of navigable water, such as a river or ocean, or whose coastlines are on closed seas are called landlocked nations. Two nations, Uzbekistan and Liechtenstein, are surrounded by other nations that are landlocked. These nations are classified as double landlocked.

Grain and spice merchants display their products for sale in this bazaar in Tashkent, Uzbekistan.

border of Uzbekistan, where the Kyzyl-Kum Desert reaches the first spur of the mountains. Ancient Arab manuscripts called it "the Gem of the East." It is famous for its excellent examples of various types of architecture. Alexander the Great defeated the local tribes and destroyed the city in 329 BC, but it was rebuilt and became a leading city on the Silk Road between Rome and China. The Mongol conqueror Tamerlane, the last ruler to unite Turkistan, made Samarqand his capital in the fourteenth century.

Section Quiz

1. What product ruled trade across Central Asia?
2–3. What desert covers most of Turkmenistan? Why is Turkmenistan the richest nation in Central Asia?
4. What is the most populous nation in Central Asia?
✶ What role did the Silk Road play in Central Asia in the past? What caused this route to become insignificant?

Kyrgyzstan

Kyrgyzstan (KIHR gee stahn) is dominated by the **Tien Shan** (tee-EHN SHAHN), or the "Celestial Mountains." This northern range runs one thousand miles from Tashkent to Urumqi in China and divides Kyrgyzstan from China.

The population is made up of Kyrgyz (64.9 percent), Uzbeks (13.8 percent), Russians (12.5 percent), and other ethnic groups. A major problem for the country is that its boundaries divide similar ethnic groups and put dissimilar groups together, yielding a situation that is ripe for friction and conflict.

Kyrgyzstan's population is 89 percent Muslim, 5 percent nonreligious, and 5 percent Christian. Muslim evangelists have been sent into the country to radicalize the traditional Muslims, with two thousand new mosques being constructed between 2000 and 2005. The struggling Christian population continues to grow despite religious and political opposition.

The people of Kyrgyzstan are primarily involved in pastoral occupations—raising yaks (for both milk and meat), sheep, and cattle. Irrigated valleys produce wheat and a variety of fruits and vegetables. Industry is limited primarily to textiles and food processing.

Shepherd children pose in the Pamir Mountains of southeastern Tajikistan.

Tajikistan

Tajikistan (tah JEEK ih stahn) is the mountain hub of Central Asia. About the size of Iowa, it shares borders with China and Afghanistan and is only a few miles north of Pakistan.

The **Pamir** (pah MEER) **Mountains** cover the eastern half of Tajikistan. This range is sometimes called the Pamir Knot because it ties together the great ranges: the Tien Shan, the Hindu Kush, the Himalaya (and Karakoram), and the Kunlun.

Tajiks constitute 69.7 percent of Tajikistan's people, and Uzbeks form the largest minority (23 percent). Tajikistan is unique in Central Asia. Its language is more Iranian than Turkic. Also, most of its people, 94 percent, are Sunni Muslims, as are most

Families such as this (left) eke out a living from the soil of Tajikistan.

A Tajik woman (right) shops in the spice market in Dushanbe, Tajikistan.

Iranians. The tiny, struggling group of believers in this country numbers around 1,000.

Tajikistan has few resources except its rivers. Some of the world's highest dams, Rogun Dam (1,099 feet) and Nurek Dam (984 feet), harness waterpower for industries at the capital, Dushanbe.

Afghanistan

The mountains of Afghanistan harbor more than twenty ethnic groups, including Turkic, Mongol, Arab, Aryan, and Persian peoples. The two largest, the Pashtuns and Tajiks, constitute about three-quarters of the Afghan population. Local rivalry, ethnic diversity, and isolation resulting from the mountainous terrain prevented the development of a strong central government in Afghanistan.

Following decades of wars during the nineteenth century, Afghanistan became a **buffer state**, a neutral state between two rivals who agreed to keep their armies out. But worries about Russia led the British into a futile war (1878–80). Later, Britain ended its efforts to control this region, and the world recognized Afghanistan as a sovereign nation.

Afghanistan became independent but remained politically weak. From 1978 to 1989, Russia waged a costly and ultimately unsuccessful campaign to set up and maintain a Communist dictatorship in Afghanistan. The United States supported the opposition to the Soviets, a coalition of Muslim tribes known collectively as the **Mujahideen** (moo jah heh DEEN; "strugglers"). After the Soviet Union gave up and withdrew its troops, Afghanistan broke into warring factions, and anarchy reigned. Islamic extremists known as the **Taliban** (TAL ih ban; "seekers," or "students") eventually prevailed and restored order by enforcing rigid adherence to sharia (severe Islamic law), including such punishments as amputation of hands and arms. They also allowed Islamic terrorists to set up training camps in the country, and some of their students carried out attacks against the West, including the attack on the World Trade Center and the Pentagon on September 11, 2001. Consequently, the United States invaded Afghanistan, overthrew the Taliban, and chased

Some Taliban Rules

The Taliban banned music, TV, and many other entertainments.

They ruled that girls and women

- could not be educated, work outside the home, or go out without a male relative, and
- had to cover themselves from head to toe in the burqa.

Global Hotspots: Afghanistan, 20.

Leaflet dropped by coalition forces into Afghanistan showing how the Taliban treated women and asking "Do you want this future for your children and women?"

Afghan girls are now allowed to go to school following the U.S. ouster of the Taliban from Afghanistan in 2002.

Opium

The major export of Afghanistan has been opium. In fact, Afghan farmers grew poppies in such large quantities that in 2007 they produced 90 percent of the world's opium. Afghan opium production generated $2.8 billion a year and represented more than 60 percent of Afghan GDP. Cultivation increased by 64 percent in 2004 and was present in all of the country's thirty-four provinces. However, extensive efforts to eradicate this crop and billions of dollars of foreign aid have substantially reduced the growing of poppies. Farmers are now growing other products, including potatoes, and as of 2010, twenty-four out of thirty-four provinces were considered free of poppy growth. While this progress could easily be undone by long-term instability, the Afghans have an opportunity to move away from growing this destructive crop.

Poppy field

down terrorists who had taken refuge in the mountains along the Afghan-Pakistani border. Despite thousands of American and Afghan casualties and billions of dollars devoted to rebuilding this country, Afghanistan will probably remain an unstable country for years to come.

Islam is the official religion of Afghanistan, representing 99.85 percent of the population. This percentage is further divided between Sunni (79 percent) and Shia (20 percent). Christianity is not recognized or tolerated in this country, so Christians must meet in secret. While accurate numbers are not available, indications are that some Afghans are converting to Christianity. The Afghan church is slowly growing, despite persecution and certain death upon discovery.

Geographic Divisions

Geographically, Afghanistan is divided into three zones: the fertile northern plains; the rugged, earthquake-shaken central highlands (the Hindu Kush); and the desert of the southern plateaus.

The **Hindu Kush**, Persian for "Hindu Death," is a mountain barrier extending southwest from the Pamirs and across central Afghanistan. It has thirty-four seven-thousand-meter-high peaks. All of them lie in the eastern **Wakhan** (wah KAHN) **Corridor**, a narrow panhandle that Russia and Great Britain created to stretch the buffer zone to China.

Most Afghan people live in these central and eastern mountain regions. The Pashtun (PUSH toon) people predominate. Their domain includes the nation's largest city and capital, **Kabul** (KAH bul), which lies in one of the many mountain valleys of the Hindu Kush. Its small industries include afghans, rugs, and jewelry made from locally mined gems. Afghanistan mines more lapis lazuli, a dark blue semiprecious stone, than any other nation in the world.

Kabul became important because of the thirty-three-mile **Khyber** (KYE ber) **Pass**, one hundred miles southeast of the city, which allows easy passage through the Hindu Kush. At its narrowest point, the pass is around fifty feet wide. Great conquerors and their armies came through the pass, including Genghis Khan and possibly Alexander the Great. A southern extension of the old Silk Road brought goods from India to Samarqand through this pass.

A semicircle of less rugged land borders the Hindu Kush on the north, west, and south. The northern plains support crops and livestock. In the valleys, farmers grow wheat, barley, corn, and cotton. Between the valleys, herders graze sheep and goats for milk, mutton, and wool. Many Tajiks, the other major ethnic group, live in this northern region, which borders Tajikistan. In the southwest lies the Rigestan Desert, Afghanistan's least populous region.

Section Quiz

1. What mountains cross into Kyrgyzstan? Tajikistan? Afghanistan?
2. Which nation speaks a language closer to Iranian than to Turkish?
3. What famous pass links Central Asia with India?
* Why has Afghanistan had so much difficulty building a strong nation?

III. South Asia

Asia is an exotic region of contrasts between wealth and poverty, high culture and demonic paganism, insurmountable peaks and broad river plains. Mountains and deserts have long isolated Asia from the West, creating distinct differences in culture and history. Because South Asia is separated from the rest of Asia by the formidable **Himalayas** on the north and by the Indian Ocean on the south, and because it is bigger than a peninsula and smaller than a continent, it is sometimes called a **subcontinent**.

The Himalayas dominate the weather system of the region. Because the cold air north of the mountains cannot rise over them to spill into South Asia, the cold temperatures do not reach into the subcontinent. As the summer heat rises in the south, a low-pressure

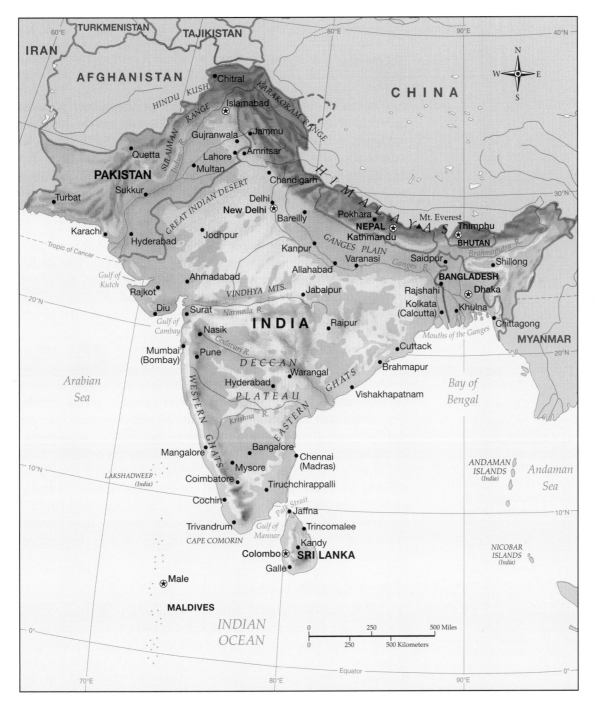

South Asia Fast Facts						
Country	Capital	Area (sq. mi.)	Pop. (2013) (M)	Pop. Density (per sq. mi.)	Per Capita GDP ($US)	Life Span
Bangladesh	Dhaka	55,598	163.65	2944	$2,000	70.06
Bhutan	Thimphu	15,210	0.73	48	$6,500	67.88
India	New Delhi	1,269,219	1,220.80	962	$3,900	67.14
Maldives	Male	116	0.39	3,362	$8,700	74.69
Nepal	Kathmandu	56,827	30.43	535	$1,300	66.51
Pakistan	Islamabad	307,374	193.24	628	$2,900	66.35
Sri Lanka	Colombo	25,332	21.68	856	$6,100	75.94

system results, drawing warm, moist air from the Indian Ocean in the form of winds called **monsoons**. South Asia has the strongest monsoon winds in the world. The Himalayas cause the airborne moisture to fall as rain. Eighty percent of India's total rainfall comes during the four-month monsoon season. A reverse monsoon pushes cool, dry winds across the mountains into South Asia, causing a dry season. Some islands escape the dry season because the ocean provides moisture regardless of wind direction.

The monsoon rains begin in June or July and supply the rain necessary for the agriculture on which all South Asian countries depend. If the monsoons come late or with too little rain, the plants wither and die. If the rains are early or cause floods, the rice rots. Either way, the subcontinent often experiences famine since it is largely a subsistence economy.

India

India, the largest country in South Asia, is also the seventh-largest country in area in the world and the second-largest in population. Of India's 1.2 billion people, about 382 million live in cities; the rest live in small villages or in the countryside. India is predicted to overtake China as the world's most populous country by 2050.

India is often called the world's largest democracy. It is a federal republic with twenty-five states and six territories. Each state represents at least one of the major languages in India. Although Hindi is the national language, English is an associate language used in commerce and diplomacy. Bengali, Urdu, Punjabi, Kashmiri, Sanskrit, and many other languages are also spoken.

Major Geographic Features

India resembles a giant triangle or an upside-down pyramid. It is bounded on the southeast by the Bay of Bengal, on the south by the Indian Ocean, and on the southwest by the Arabian Sea. Other countries provide India's border in the north: Pakistan on the northwest, China and Nepal on the north, and Bhutan and Bangladesh on the northeast. Its physical geography can be divided into

Indian Subcontinent

Because India covers three-fourths of the region, South Asia is also called the Indian subcontinent. The name is appropriate because India's influence is felt throughout the region, and several of the countries were once part of India. Today, the region includes not only India but also Pakistan, Bangladesh, Nepal, Bhutan, and the island nations of Sri Lanka and Maldives.

several different major features or regions: mountains, rivers, a plateau, and a desert.

India is bounded by three major mountain ranges: the Himalayas on the northeast and the Eastern and Western Ghats, which run down either coast of the country.

The Himalayas—The northeastern limit of South Asia is delineated by the Himalaya Mountains, the highest mountain range on earth. The name *Himalaya* is Sanskrit for "House of Snow." It is an appropriate name for the greatest mountain range on earth. It includes **Mt. Everest** (29,028 ft.), the highest mountain in the world. The Himalayas also boast most of the world's highest individual mountains: 150 tower almost 23,000 feet and 10 reach more than 26,000 feet.

The *Himalayan Mountain System* forms the great mountain barrier that runs fifteen hundred miles along the south border of China. It is the only mountain barrier in the world with peaks exceeding 26,246 feet. The Himalayas are the highest and most rugged mountains in the world, and many of them have never been climbed.

The Indus and Brahmaputra river valleys divide the Himalayan system into three distinct ranges. North of the Brahmaputra in China is the Trans-Himalaya, which contains three peaks over 22,965 feet. West of the Indus River is the Karakoram (kar uh KOHR uhm), which extends three hundred miles across Kashmir to the Pamir Knot.

The Himalayas proper extend twelve hundred miles from the Indus River to the great eastern curve of the Brahmaputra River. The Karakoram and the Trans-Himalaya are not technically part of the range.

The Western and Eastern Ghats—The **Ghats** are two ranges of long, low, hardwood-covered mountains that run along the coasts of India. The Western Ghats, as the name indicates, run for about a thousand miles along the west coast from just north of Mumbai southward to the southernmost tip of the country. They are home to numerous rare species of plants and animals, and they contain many wildlife sanctuaries and national parks designed to protect those species. Only one break exists in the range, the Palghat Gap. The ocean side of the Western Ghats gets heavy rainfall and therefore has lush tropical vegetation and dense forests of hardwood trees. The inland side is dry.

The Eastern Ghats stretch for about nine hundred miles along the east coast from the Mahanadi Valley in the north, where rice cultivation is a major economic activity, to the Nilgiri Hills in the south. The word *Nilgiri* literally means "Blue Mountains." The area is famous for its production of mild Nilgiri teas. Many rivers cut through the Eastern Ghats and are used for electricity production.

The Vindhya Mountains—The remaining major mountain range cuts from just north of where the Western Ghats begin, inland from the Gulf of Cambay and the city of Surat, almost due east into the heart of India. Actually more like high hills (approximately 3,000

The Himalayas viewed from orbit

Mt. Everest is the highest mountain in the world.

The Importance of Family in India

"The family plays a vital role. An Indian family is usually a home of three generations, rooted in a particular community. The family is also where traditional arts, handicrafts, and trades are learned and passed down. The cohesiveness of the family fosters a strong sense of belonging, and belonging is a serious and exacting concern in India. The family belongs to a particular lineage or *gotra* (go-trah) within a specific caste of a region or *kul* (kool). Through marriage, usually planned by collective choice over individual preference, families strengthen their bonds of lineage.

Family connections are seldom lost, even when a person leaves the village for the city in pursuit of a higher education or better job prospects."

Cultures of the World: India, 63.

feet in elevation), the sandstone **Vindhya** (VIHN dyuh) **Mountains** have historically been the natural dividing line between northern India and southern India.

The Ganges River—Rivers also play an important role in India's geography. The northern portions of the country are delineated by the great river systems and the plains that they drain: the Indus River in the northwest, the Ganges River in the north and northeast, and the Brahmaputra in the extreme northeast.

The **Ganges** (GAN jeez) **River**, one of the world's longest rivers, begins in an ice cave in the Himalayas. It flows southeast more than fifteen hundred miles across north central India. It ends its journey by emptying into the Bay of Bengal from multiple mouths of a 200-mile-wide delta on the India-Bangladesh border.

The Ganges is very muddy and deposits an estimated 1.5 billion tons of sediment a year. In 2007, this river was also ranked among the five most polluted rivers in the world, and subsequent efforts to reduce the level of pollution have had little success. Nonetheless, the river supplies much of the water needed to irrigate the farms in northeast India. Because its delta is so fertile, the Ganges is the most important river in India. It also holds great significance in **Hinduism**, the largest religion in India. (See p. 355.)

The Brahmaputra River—The headwaters of the **Brahmaputra** (brah muh POO truh) **River** are in Tibet. The river flows about 1,864 miles through four countries (Tibet, China, India, and Bangladesh) before joining the Ganges in the Ganges delta and emptying into the Bay of Bengal. It discharges about 725 million tons of sediment a year, and it provides water and irrigation for the state of Assam in

Bathing in the Sacred Ganges

According to Hindu legend, the Ganges River is the goddess Ganga, who took physical form. Hindu temples line the banks of this sacred river, and stairs lead down to the water. Pilgrims believe this water is holy and cleanses their souls. Many pilgrims come for healing, and others come to die, hoping to enter paradise immediately. The smoke from cremated bodies rises above the riverbanks of the Ganges. In spite of the filth resulting from this activity as well as industry, Hindus use the river water for drinking, cooking, and washing. As a result, diseases such as cholera are common.

Many religions throughout history have worshiped water as a source of life and healing, as Hindus do the Ganges and ancient Egyptians did the Nile. Christianity recognizes water as a gift from God to be used wisely. God is displeased when people worship the things He has created rather than worshiping Him (Deut. 4:15–17; Rom. 1:25).

Akshardham Temple in Delhi, India

northeastern India. The rich soil aids the production of tea, the region's leading product. India is the world's leading producer of tea.

The **Jumna** (JUHM nuh) **River** is another important tributary of the Ganges in the plains. It begins west of the Ganges in the Himalayas of Uttar Pradesh but then forms the boundary between Uttar Pradesh and the central state of Haryana. **Delhi** (DEL ee), India's second-largest city, stands on the Jumna River between Uttar Pradesh and Haryana. The city is a major manufacturing center. Its suburb, **New Delhi**, is the national capital. These two cities are not part of any state but lie in the separate capital territory of Delhi.

The Indus River—The **Indus River** flows from its headwaters in China through the states of Jammu and Kashmir and the entire length of Pakistan, emptying into the Arabian Sea. Although only a small portion of the river is within the borders of India, the valley holds great significance in history as the birthplace of one of the earliest civilizations.

The Great Indian Desert—Within the bounds created by the major Indian mountains and rivers are two other geographic features: the Great Indian Desert south of the Indus River and the Deccan Plateau in central India.

Southwest of where the Indus flows through India and into Pakistan is a region called the Thar (TAHR), or the **Great Indian Desert**. Other than palm trees near springs, only small desert plants grow without irrigation there.

The city of Ahmadabad, former capital of the state of Gujarat, is a manufacturing center with 5.6 million people. To the southwest, the Kathiawar Peninsula sticks into the Arabian Sea. A saltmarsh called the Rann of Kutch and the Gulf of Kutch are on the northwest side of the peninsula. The Gulf of Cambay is on the southeast side. The peninsula produces one-third of the world's peanuts, making India the leading producer of peanuts worldwide.

The state of Punjab (pun JAHB), north of the Thar, contains the Punjab Plains. These plains cross into India from northeast Pakistan and extend to meet the Ganges Plain. The Sutlej River, a tributary of the Indus River in Pakistan, drains the plains.

Most people there speak Punjabi and worship as Sikhs (SEEKS). Sikhs are followers of Guru Nanak (1469–1539), who sought to

A Sikh in traditional garb

Sacred Cows

Hindus consider cattle to be especially sacred, the symbol of all life. Cows pull plows and carts and supply milk and butter. Their manure is fuel for cooking and building material for village homes. To show thanks, Indians occasionally leave small offerings of food for the cows. They allow cattle to roam freely through India's villages and city streets, eating whatever they wish. Hindus allow the animals complete freedom because they

believe them to be reincarnations of past lives. Hindus refuse to eat beef to avoid the possibility of eating a deceased family member in his present incarnation.

In 2009, the number of cattle in India was estimated to be more than 281 million. By comparison, that same year United States had an estimated 96.7 million cattle.

Superstitions in India

Many Indians make decisions based on the astrological calendar. To further strive for success, they buy property or start a business on even numbered days. For example, eight is a good day, but day seven is not a good day to make a transaction. Travelers try to make their journey on a Wednesday, and sacred matters should be conducted on a Friday. However, Friday is considered a bad day to visit a barber or the home of someone who has lost a loved one.

Make sure you do not have a cold or allergy in India. If you happen to sneeze before a project starts, the project is doomed to failure. And watch out for falling lizards! If one falls on your head, death is considered imminent.

The origin of these superstitions is unknown, but Indian elders recite examples of the terrible consequences of disregarding these ancient beliefs.

reconcile Islam with Hinduism; their religion is known as **Sikhism**. Sikhs now number more than 16 million, about 2 percent of India's population. About 80 percent of Sikhs live in Punjab, where they make up about two-thirds of the state's population. (See p. 356 for more information about Sikhism.)

The Deccan Plateau—The **Deccan** (DEK uhn) **Plateau** is the heart of the Indian peninsula. The Deccan includes eight states, parts of two others, and three territories. It is bounded on the west by the Western Ghats and on the east by the Eastern Ghats.

Mumbai (muhm BYE), formerly called Bombay, is located on the northern half of the coast. With 19.85 million people, Mumbai is the largest city in India and is the capital and major manufacturing center of the state of Maharashtra. Cotton is the major crop there; India is the world's third-largest producer of cotton.

Many people in Mumbai live in poverty.

About three-fourths of the way down the peninsula on the western coast of India is an area called the Malabar Coast. Its tropical climate makes it an ideal location for growing mangoes and bananas, and India is the world's leader in producing those fruits.

Inland, the tropical climate changes abruptly to a dry climate. The city of Mangalore on the Malabar Coast receives more than 120 inches of rain a year, but the rainfall diminishes to less than 40 inches a year at Bangalore, which is inland due east of Mangalore, almost halfway between the east and west coasts. Bangalore is a manufacturing city of more than 8.5 million people and the only inland capital of the four west Deccan states.

Much of the Deccan has a dry climate. Scattered trees punctuate the tall grasses of its savannas. Although it is semiarid, the plateau's high altitudes keep the temperatures cooler than those in the tropical lowlands.

The eastern half of the Deccan Plateau increases in elevation from the Bay of Bengal to the highlands of the Eastern Ghats. The coastal plain is somewhat wider than that in the west. The coast on the Bay of Bengal is called the **Coromandel** (kohr uh MAN dul) **Coast**. All of the major rivers of the plateau flow to that coast. Three states cover the east coast.

The Deccan has most of India's mineral resources. The largest of several deposits of iron ore and coal are in the northeast portion of the plateau. Some iron ore is exported, but India does produce its own iron and steel using its own coal to fuel the steel mills. India also mines large deposits of bauxite, manganese, and mica from that part of the plateau. Although India does have some oil, it still imports much of its supply.

Chennai (chuh NYE), formerly known as Madras, is India's fourth-largest city, with a population of 8.9 million. It is a famous source of spices, such as turmeric and cardamon. It is India's major southeastern port, although its harbor is totally man-made. (The British took almost forty years—from 1862 to 1901—to complete it.) It is also a major rail center. Through this city flow exports of animal hides, cotton, textiles, and other products.

With Mumbai and Kolkata, Chennai was a center of the British East India Company from its inception in 1600. In fact, the city was founded by the East India Company. Expanding from these centers, the company gained control of most of India by 1763. The company relinquished rule to the British government in 1858.

Disputed Border Regions—India's border regions lie at the extreme edges adjacent to other nations. Some of them are remote wilderness areas. The cultures of those areas are influenced by India's neighbor nations, especially in religious worship.

Uniting such a mixed bag of religions and peoples into one nation has not been easy, and religious violence has racked the border regions of the nation from its birth. A Hindu assassinated **Mahatma Gandhi** (muh-HAHT-muh GAHN-dee) in 1948 because Gandhi wanted to make peace with the Muslims in India. Hoping to stop the killing, the first prime minister, Jawaharlal Nehru (jah-wah-HAHR-lahl NAY-roo), a close associate of Gandhi, established a "secular" federal republic in 1949. But religious fighting only increased. Since 1980, an extremist Hindu party called the Bharatiya Janata Party has

Mahatma Gandhi

resorted to violence in its efforts to replace the secular state with a pure Hindu kingdom, or *Hindutva*.

South of the Brahmaputra, in the eastern hills, lie five of the seven smallest states (in both area and population) in all of India. This region is the only region in India with a Christian majority. People there converted to Christianity after the days of William Carey. India has about 25 million professing Christians (2.3 percent of the total population). The wet and dry monsoons create a humid subtropical climate in this region. Instead of rain forests, deciduous trees such as maple, walnut, and birch grow in the hills, along with some tropical fruit trees and palms. However, many of the trees of the region have been cut for fuel and other needs.

The Himalayas follow the border of China from Pakistan to Myanmar (formerly called Burma). Many of India's Himalayan peoples practice the Lamaistic form of Buddhism common in neighboring Nepal and Tibet. It is the only region in India with a Buddhist majority, which is somewhat surprising because Buddhism began near the Ganges. The Himalayas cover three widely separated states of India in addition to the disputed area called **Kashmir** (kazh MIHR), which is claimed by both India and Pakistan.

Section Quiz

1. What geometric shape does India resemble?
2. What three major bodies of water border India?
3. Which mountain range forms much of India's northern border?
4. Which two mountain ranges frame the coasts of the Indian peninsula?
5. Which three rivers are of greatest importance to India?
* What issue more than any other divides India and its neighbors?

Religions

Hinduism—Seventy-four percent of the people of India are Hindus, so religious traditions greatly influence life there. For Hindus, two of the most sacred things are cattle and the Ganges. India has more cattle than any other nation in the world, and they are allowed to wander unhindered wherever they choose to go. Hindus also see great spiritual significance to bathing in the Ganges. Hindu tradition assigns people to different classes, each with its own privileges and responsibilities but also limitations. Each class, called a **caste**, strictly determines one's social status. According to the Hindu caste system, a Hindu must fulfill his or her role. **Brahmins** (BRAH mihns; priests and teachers) and Ksatriyas (kuh SHAT ree uhs; rulers and warriors) occupy the highest castes. Merchants, skilled craftsmen (artisans), and farmers—the Vaisyas (VYE shuhs)—belong to the mid-level caste. Sudras (Soo druhs; unskilled laborers) are the lowest caste. Some despised occupations, such as tanners and garbage

BRAHMINS
(priests, teachers)

KSATRIYAS
(rulers, warriors)

VAISYAS
(merchants, artisans, farmers)

SUDRAS
(unskilled laborers)

UNTOUCHABLES
(polluted laborers, outcasts)

WORLD RELIGIONS

Hinduism

Hinduism is often used to describe the religion of India. Though not every religion in India is considered Hindu (Buddhism for example), the Hindu religions do not all share the same beliefs or practices. Sometimes the beliefs of various Hindu groups contradict each other. These contradictions do not bother Hindus. They think what seems contradictory may actually harmonize in another dimension of reality.

The Hindu belief in god provides an example of these contradictions. Some Hindus believe in a personal god. Other Hindus believe that god is not a person but a divine being that pervades everything. They are pantheists. Brahmin is the name given to the divine being. Whatever view is taken of Brahmin, Brahmin is both the cause and the material of creation. There is no creation out of nothing as in the Bible's record of creation.

Most Hindus do agree on two key beliefs: **samsara** and **moksha**. Samsara is the law of **reincarnation**—a cycle of birth, death, and rebirth—governed by **karma** (KAHR muh). Doing good works gives a person good karma. Bad actions give a person bad karma. A Hindu accepts the caste into which he is born as the reward or punishment for his works in his past lives, and he tries to do good works so that his future lives will be better. Hindus believe that good karma might allow them to be reborn as a Brahmin or a rich man. Bad karma would cause them to be reborn into a lower caste, as an untouchable, or even as an animal. Moksha means "release" and refers to freedom from the law of samsara. Hindus wish to be freed from the cycle of reincarnation. Freedom from reincarnation means the person is absorbed back into full oneness with Brahmin.

Hindu beliefs vary greatly because Hinduism has three sets of holy books and no single founder or teacher. The first book, *Rig-Veda*, was written approximately 1200 BC and is the basis of the caste system. The *Upanishads*,

Vishnu

Shiva

written a few centuries later, teach about the Hindu gods—Brahma, Vishnu, and Shiva—as well as reincarnation and karma. The *Bhagavad-Gita*, which appeared even later, focuses on Krishna (a human manifestation of Vishnu). Some Hindus believe in one god; others believe in many gods. Many gurus (GOO rooz; spiritual leaders) attract followers to their own teachings. Their followers try to escape reincarnation by repeating prayers, by seeking spiritual wisdom from the gurus, by helping others, or by enduring strict discipline and self-denial (asceticism).

Hindus claim to be very tolerant of other religions. A Christian who shares the gospel with a Hindu may find him ready to accept that Jesus is a god and that Christianity contains much truth. But in fact Christianity and Hinduism are incompatible at their foundations. The Christian concept of God differs greatly from the Hindu conceptions of Brahmin. The Christian God is personal and exists apart from His creation. Brahmin is not personal for many Hindus and is both the material of creation as well as its cause. For the Christian, the fundamental problem is not being trapped in the material

world. The fundamental problem is sin and broken fellowship with God. For the Christian the human person is sinful. For the Hindu he is part of the divine being. This leads to a different conception of salvation. The Hindu seeks to escape life in this world so he can be absorbed back into Brahmin. The Bible teaches that God will redeem His fallen Creation. The Christian hopes for a resurrected body, a new earth, and a restored relationship with God for all eternity. The means of salvation is also different. For much of Hinduism, salvation is achieved by performing the right deeds to gain good karma or by achieving the right state of meditation to know Brahmin. Though some strands of Hinduism stress grace from a god as a means to escape samsara, the need for redemption from sin is not present. According to the Bible, human sinfulness places mankind under divine condemnation. But God made a way of salvation by the incarnation of Jesus, by His righteous life, by His death on the cross, and by His resurrection.

A Christian Wedding in India

Kim Hibberd, Bibles International missionary to India

This spring I saw living illustrations of the cost of discipleship. In May, a friend got married. Normally a wedding is a community affair, with all the neighbors and relatives pitching in to help. In this case, because my friend and her immediate family are the only believers in their village, her church family had to fill this role. Church people built the shelter in front of their home to keep rain and sun off the ceremony, decorated, served at the reception, and cleaned up after.

Normally, whenever there's a feast of any kind, for instance for a wedding or memorial or birth celebration, the hosts hire a Brahman to cook. This way Hindus of any caste will be willing to eat the food. Christians follow this practice too when they want unbelievers to feel comfortable attending. However, the Brahmans in the area my friend is from refused to cook for Christians. Although church people were willing to do the cooking, this would have been counter-productive to the goal of having unsaved neighbors attend. In the end they had to bring in a Brahman from more than an hour away to cook.

Although only one or two neighbors attended the wedding, a generator and sound system ensured that they all heard the message and several Manipuri gospel songs. Hopefully, they also saw the love of Christ in practice.

This family is one of many who have willingly accepted ostracism because of their love for Christ. Others have faced decisions about which funeral observances they can participate in and which they will not attend because of the religious ceremonies involved. At times of joy and at times of grief, I have seen believers choose to follow Christ instead of their culture or family. I thank God for these believers who truly are willing to leave all to follow Christ.

collectors, are considered so low that they are beneath caste. They are called "**untouchables**" and make up approximately one-seventh of the Indian population. Today, the basic castes are divided into hundreds of subcastes, called *jatis*. A Hindu is born into the *jati* of his parents, and he must marry someone from that jati. He must also hold an appropriate occupation and can never change his caste, so the system allows for little, if any, upward mobility in society.

Islam—The second-largest religion in India is Islam, with approximately 172 million adherents, representing 14.2 percent of the population. The introduction and early growth of Islam in India were primarily by violence. Arabic Muslims invaded the country in the eighth century and forced people to convert to Islam or be killed. Although relations between Muslims and people of other religious groups have never been totally peaceful, until fairly recently Muslims in India have chosen to tolerate the majority to avoid a backlash. With the worldwide rise of militant Islam, however, many Indian Muslims have become increasingly aggressive.

Christianity—According to tradition, the apostle Thomas came to India in AD 50 and established several churches on India's west coast before being martyred. European explorers of the fifteenth century were surprised to find groups of Christians, called the St. Thomas Christians, in India. Other people believe that St. Bartholomew was the one who introduced Christianity to India. Over the years, however, the Indian churches became bound by ritual and tradition with no real understanding of the gospel. A renewal of Christian outreach has recently occurred. One thousand Indian mission organizations and other church-based groups have sent more than one hundred thousand church planters, evangelists, and Christian workers. They have started and nurtured thousands of local congregations throughout India. Over one thousand Bible schools train Indian students and prepare them for current and future ministry. Today, about 70 million people in India, or about 5.8 percent of the total population, profess some form of Christianity.

Sikhism—The religion of Sikhism arose in the early sixteenth century in the northern Indian state of Punjab when a guru named Nanak sought to combine the teachings of Hinduism and Islam. He believed that both religions taught essentially the same thing. His disciples compiled his teachings in the *Guru Granth Sahib*, which became the holy book of the Sikhs. They teach reincarnation and karma but reject the existence of original sin and Satan. Salvation, they teach, is liberation from the cycles of rebirth, at which point the soul merges with God. This state is achieved by repeating prayers, meditating, giving alms, and performing other good works.

About 22 million Indians, or 1.9 percent, profess Sikhism as their religion. About 80 percent of all Sikhs live in Punjab, making up about two-thirds of that state's population. The Sikhs there have long pressured the Indian government to recognize them as an independent nation called Khalistan. In 1984, Sikh terrorists assassinated India's prime minister, Indira Gandhi. The continued terrorist activities had cost 47,000 lives as of 2009. However, recent peace talks between India and Pakistan have resulted in a significant decrease in violence.

Jainism—**Jainism** (JYE nihz uhm) is another religion of the region and is thought to be related to both Hinduism and Buddhism. Some people classify it as a heretical version of Hinduism. Jains believe that humans can become gods, or Jina, by being "enlightened" through the worship of twenty-four Jinas who serve as inspirational bridges. Until that point, one's soul is continually reborn through reincarnation.

Jainism has even more rigorous practices than Hinduism, including the rule of no violence against any life form. For instance, Jains cannot kill any living creature and must not eat meat. Some Jains wear cloths over their mouths to avoid accidentally inhaling and killing an insect.

Statue of Adinatha, the traditional founder of Jainism

Today there are about five million Jains in India. The religion started about 500 BC near the Ganges east of Varanasi, but today most Jains live on the west coast of India.

India has numerous other minority religions. Hinduism and all of the other competing worldviews make religion pervasive throughout the country. India has an estimated 2.4 million places of worship (temples, mosques, churches, etc.), more than the number of schools, colleges, and hospitals combined.

Government and Economy

Britain increased Indian representation in the government in appreciation for India's help in World War I and continued to grant Indians an increasing role in government. The minor changes, however, caused uncertainty and unrest. The most famous leader in the protests that resulted was Mahatma Gandhi, the Father of the Nation. He led the people in nonviolent protests, encouraging the people to destroy British power nonviolently simply by making their own goods rather than trading for them (i.e., economic self-sufficiency). One of his most famous marches was a march to the sea in 1930 to protest a salt tax. The protest resulted in more than sixty thousand imprisonments. Gandhi himself was imprisoned many times.

When Japan conquered Burma and then invaded eastern India in the early years of World War II, India joined the British cause. Britain granted the country full independence in 1947. The long British occupation had given Indians many practical benefits. It spread English

These followers of Jainism are wearing scarves over their mouths lest they inhale—and thereby kill—a tiny insect.

Rice is a major crop of India.

Poverty in India

Poverty is pervasive in India. As of 2010, one third of the malnourshed children in the world lived in India. Up to 42 percent of Indian children are underweight due to malnutrition, and 56 percent of children under five are stunted in their growth. Even with recent economic growth in India, an estimated 400 million people still live on less than $1.25 a day. While the poverty rate is expected to drop to 22 percent by 2015, India's grinding poverty will have long-term effects.

This photo of the homeless sleeping on the street in Pondicherry depicts a common scene in India.

Members of the Nuclear Club

India began developing the technology to build a nuclear weapon in 1962. Indian scientists tested their first nuclear weapon in 1974. Pakistan responded by initiating its own nuclear weapons research in 1972 and successfully detonating nuclear devices in 1998. Today, both nations are nuclear powers, further increasing the regional tensions. In 1999, to reduce the possibility of war, India issued a "no-first-use" policy, promising not to initiate a nuclear attack. Under this policy, India would respond only if attacked. This was designed to lower the level of tension while reminding its neighbors of India's nuclear capabilities.

among the educated, and English is still used for administrative purposes. The British also developed a vast railroad transportation network and established a strong judicial and administrative tradition.

Today, India is a federal republic: a national government, with its capital in New Delhi, that shares ruling powers with twenty-eight states and seven territories, each with its own government and capital. A president is the chief of state; a prime minister is the head of the government; and a bicameral parliament fills the legislative role. India has dozens of political parties, many of them representing religious factions, and even several Communist groups.

India has a growing economy in spite of widespread poverty and frequent natural disasters. Occupations range from subsistence farming to modern commercial agriculture and from modern industry to various service industries.

Although India is an economic powerhouse in South Asia, it faces its share of problems, all of which affect its economy in some way. It is susceptible to natural disasters, including the extremes of drought and flooding (especially during the monsoons). Such problems intensify the ever-present risks of disease. Health issues are further complicated by India's growing population, poverty, and industrial pollution.

On the other hand, India's economy is rapidly becoming more diverse, with increasingly more emphasis on industry and services. Although 53 percent of the labor force is involved in agriculture, services are responsible for 56.5 percent of the GDP. The country has become heavily involved in computer software development and production as well as telephone customer services for U.S. companies. India's major international trading partners include China, the United States, and the United Arab Emirates.

Section Quiz

1. What religious belief prompts Indians to give cows free rein to do as they please?
3. Which river holds special significance to Hindus, and by what practice do they show that regard?
4. Which Indian leader promoted nonviolent protest as a means for political reform?
5. What type of government does India have?
★ What are some of the effects of poverty in India?

Pakistan and Bangladesh

The histories and cultures of India, Pakistan, and Bangladesh are very closely linked because they were all India until 1947. Britain's offer of independence for India depended on India's deciding on a system of government. When Hindu and Muslim conflicts prevented agreement, Britain separated the main Muslim regions from Hindu India to form the nation of Pakistan. One-half million people died in the conflict that followed, as Muslims and Hindus fled to their respective countries.

Pakistan (PAK ih stan) initially consisted of two parts: East Pakistan and West Pakistan, indicating the opposite sides of northern India. Both regions were populated by Muslims, but they were about a thousand miles apart. The capital was located in West Pakistan, but most of the people lived in East Pakistan. Communication was difficult, and the people felt little national unity. India and Pakistan went to war over Kashmir three times (1947–48; 1965; 1971). Following the third war, East Pakistan, encouraged by India, sought and gained independence from West Pakistan and became known as Bangladesh (bahn gluh DESH). Since this change, the western part has been known simply as Pakistan.

Pakistan

Pakistan is often in the news because of both its ongoing dispute with India over control of Kashmir and its support of the Western allies in the war against terrorism. It also has been the site of much anti-Western violence and many earthquakes.

Physical Features and Society—The Indus River valley makes up most of Pakistan. Flowing southwest from the Himalayas, the river waters a very dry region. Only those areas that can be watered from the river are suitable for agriculture. The remaining land east of the river to the border with India is part of the Great Indian Desert. Most Pakistanis live in the two provinces along the Indus River system.

The province of Punjab contains Pakistan's portion of the Punjab Plains. The province includes the capital, Islamabad (pop. 1.15 million), and the cities of Lahore (pop. 7.1 million) and Multan (pop. 1.7 million). The people who live in Punjab control the government, economy, and military. The region supports wheat and cotton crops.

To the south, the river flows through the province of Sind. The delta at the mouth of the Indus supports large rice crops. Karachi (kuh RAH chee), west of the delta, is the provincial capital and the nation's leading port. With a population of 13.4 million people, it is also the largest city. The province extends north beyond Hyderabad and Sukkur, areas that have major natural gas deposits.

About fifty miles downstream from Sukkur lies a ruined city now known as **Mohenjo-Daro** (moh-HEN-joh DAHR-oh). The ancient civilization that flourished there along the Indus Valley from 2500 to 1700 BC was one of the earliest on earth.

In some nations, the remote areas offer important natural resources. Unfortunately for Pakistan, its remote regions have only

One of the world's earliest civilizations developed at Mohenjo-Daro in modern-day Pakistan.

U.S.-led coalition forces (above) ousted the Taliban from Afghanistan.

The inhospitable terrain (right) around the Khyber Pass on the Pakistan-Afghanistan border has long been a refuge for terrorists and criminals.

minor deposits of coal and petroleum. As a result, most of the people there herd sheep or goats.

The largest province, Baluchistan, is also the least populated. Elevations on this large plateau reach more than eight thousand feet and give some relief from tropical heat. However, the area is so arid that few plants exist there. Many of the people are nomads, leading their sheep or goats from one oasis to another. The large province includes all of the coast west of Karachi and north to the provincial capital, Quetta, and beyond.

The people of North-West Frontier Province are called Pashtuns (PUHSH toonz). They live in the mountain valleys where precipitation is adequate. The capital of the province, Peshawar, is south of Chitral and just east of the Khyber Pass, the only opening for travel through the rugged and formidable Hindu Kush Mountains. When Russia invaded Afghanistan in the 1980s, many Afghan refugees crossed into Pakistan using the Khyber Pass. The region also became a haven for the Taliban and other terrorists when the United States invaded Afghanistan following the September 11, 2001, terrorist attacks on the United States.

Government and Economy—About 96 percent of all Pakistanis are Muslims. Of this group about three-fourths are Sunni and 15–20 percent are Shia. While Pakistan has laws guaranteeing religious freedom, persecution of Christians, minority Muslim groups, Hindus, and others is common and tolerated by the government. Despite the constant possibility of persecution, there are around 4.5 million who claim some form of Christianity. Missionary analysts estimate that about 10 percent of this group could be considered committed believers.

The Pakistani government is officially designated a federal republic, with a president, a prime minister, a bicameral parliament, and, like India, dozens of political parties. In reality, however, it was a modified military dictatorship ruled by General Pervez Musharraf from 1999 to 2008. Since 2008, Pakistan has been ruled by a coalition government.

About 45 percent of the Pakistani population is involved in agriculture. Major crops include cotton, sugar cane, wheat, rice, milk, beef, mutton, and various fruits and vegetables. Industry (textiles/apparel, food processing, pharmaceuticals, paper products, and fertilizer) accounts for more than 21 percent of the labor force and services for more than 34 percent. Unfortunately, Pakistan is also a crossroads for both terrorism and Afghan opium and heroin.

Bangladesh

Poor. Overpopulated. Ill-governed. These words probably best describe the tiny nation of Bangladesh. Surrounded by India, Myanmar, and the Bay of Bengal, the country is essentially the delta of the Ganges, Jamuna, and Meghna Rivers. The rich delta soils hold potential for many crops, but the country's location also makes it susceptible to frequent natural disasters, including **typhoons** (tye FOONS; hurricane-like storms), **tsunamis** (soo NAH mees; sometimes called tidal waves), drought, and floods, especially during the monsoons. It is considered one of the poorest countries in the world.

Physical Features and Society—Bangladesh is slightly smaller than Iowa, but it is one of the most densely populated countries in the world. About 14.6 million people live in Dhaka (DAH kuh), the capital. Another 5 million people live in Chittagong (CHIHT uh gahng). Bengali is the official language of this crowded country.

Living conditions in Bangladesh are terrible, poverty is rampant, the risk of disease is extremely high, and medical care is scarce. Since two-thirds of the people rely on agriculture for their livelihood, the limited farmland and destructive weather patterns cripple the country. Rice and jute are the main crops, but production is minimal. The country cannot afford to import food, so the people depend on millions of tons of food donated by other nations to stave off famine. The country suffers from inadequate port facilities and inefficiently run, government-owned businesses. Economic reforms seem to be perpetually stalled by bureaucrats, and the government is plagued with corruption. As a result, Bangladesh seems to be trapped in a cycle of poverty.

Eighty-nine percent of Bangladeshis are Muslim. Nine percent are Hindu. The remaining 2 percent represent a variety of tribal religions, animism, and Christians. Radical Muslims have increased their persecution of minority groups, including Hindus, moderate Muslims, and Christians. However, the result of persecution of Christians has been growth at a pace that is greater than the staggering population growth. Churches are being shaken out of their lethargy and are reaching out to the tribal people, Hindus, and others with the gospel.

Government and Economy—Bangladesh is a parliamentary democracy. Its government is run by a president, a prime minister, and a unicameral parliament. The country has eight to ten political parties. Although the ruling party has sufficient numbers to push through the economic reforms necessary for improving the country, fundamental changes have not been made. As a result, the country continues to depend heavily on charitable donations from other countries to survive.

Nonetheless, Bangladesh has an economy that is growing slowly. Although 45 percent of the national labor force is employed in

The rickshaw-filled streets of Dhaka are nearly impossible to cross safely on foot.

Festivals in Bangladesh

Bangladesh is predominately a Muslim country, and priority is given to Islamic holidays. However, in addition to Ramadan, where the feasting begins at sundown after the day-long fast, there are many other festivals. Most are religious in nature. Hindus celebrate the festival of colors in March and throw colored water and powder on one another. In October, Hindus honor the Hindu goddess Durga Puja. On the last day of this festival, married women apply a red substance called *Sindoor* to each other's faces as a sign of greeting.

Bangladesh also celebrates two secular holidays. *Shaheed Dibosh* (Martyr's Day) is celebrated on February 1 to commemorate the death of four martyrs who were killed by Pakistani police during a protest. Independence Day is observed on March 26 to celebrate Bangladesh's fight for independence from Pakistan in 1971.

Serving in Bangladesh

(A young woman serves in a hospital and cares for the needy people of the region around her hospital. Her name cannot be used in order to protect her work in this Muslim country. This an excerpt of her story.)

Two very frightened parents brought their child down from the hills. Village doctors had tried to heal an abscess under the little girl's jaw with homeopathic herbal remedies.

However the infection had grown worse. The doctors at the hospital successfully operated and treated the girl with antibiotics. She began to heal.

Workers at the hospital befriended the mother and told "her about the Good News." They also shared with the father that God's miracle had saved their daughter. The parents were invited to a private showing of a film about Jesus. Before the film ended,

both parents "fell on their knees and met the God of Heaven Who had healed their daughter."

The parents took their daughter back home, knowing they might face persecution. Their tribe has not yet accepted the Good News and often persecutes those who have turned from Islam.

---

agriculture, it only produces 17.5 percent of the nation's GDP. The 30 percent who are employed in industry contribute 28.5 percent of the GDP. The remaining 25 percent of the workers are in services, which contribute more than half of the GDP.

Despite the country's minimal resources, Bangladesh is a major producer of several agricultural products, including jute, spices, rice, pulses (finely ground bean seeds), and tea. Major industries include paper, cement, cotton textiles and garments, and chemical fertilizers.

Section Quiz

1. What is the major religion of both Pakistan and Bangladesh?
2. From what country did Pakistan obtain independence?
3. Which region is the object of dispute between India and Pakistan?
4. What are the major products of Pakistan? Bangladesh?
5. Which country is known for its high population density?
* Why is Bangladesh unable to make full use of its natural resources?

Nepal and Bhutan

Nepal

The nation of Nepal (neh PAHL) is landlocked, technologically backward, poverty stricken, and prone to natural disasters, and its people are at high risk of disease. Its government is tenuous, its economy weak, and its prospects for improvement grim.

Physical Features and Society—A little larger than Arkansas, Nepal contains eight of the world's ten highest peaks, including Mt. Everest. Because of its overall altitude (even its lowest peaks are in the alpine zone), it has cool summers and severe winters. It is also susceptible to floods, landslides, droughts, and famine, depending on the timing, intensity, and duration of the monsoons.

South of the Himalayas is a strip of hills and valleys that are high enough to remain cool but low enough to be forested. Along the border with India is the Tarai, a region of tropical lowlands (only 150 feet in elevation). Crocodiles, elephants, and tigers roam the Tarai. Farmers raise sugar cane and tobacco there and wheat in the nearby hills. Corn and rice grow in both regions.

Only 49 percent of the Nepalese are literate, and Nepal is the only official Hindu state in the world, with 75 percent of its people being Hindus. Sixteen percent are Buddhist, 4.4 percent are Muslim, and nearly 3 percent are Christian. As in other countries in this region, Christianity has thrived despite persecution, or perhaps because of it. As of 2010, all seventy-five districts of Nepal have at least one church, and there are believers in every people group of Nepal.

Perhaps the most famous Nepalese are the Sherpas, renowned for their strength and endurance, and the Gurkhas. **Sherpas** (SHUR puhz) are frequently hired as guides and porters by the approximately 600,000 foreign tourists who come to climb Nepal's peaks every year. **Gurkhas** (GOOR kuhz) are famed for their fighting abilities. Great Britain first recruited Gurkhas for its army during the Age of Imperialism, and the Brigade of Gurkhas is still a part of the British army today.

Government and Economy—The capital is Kathmandu, with a population of just over one million. The country has at least eight political parties, including the Communist Party, which is heavily influenced by China. Since 1991, Nepal has been a parliamentary democracy and a constitutional monarchy in which the parliament rules under the ultimate leadership of the king. In February 2005, however, the king abolished parliament, signaling a move back to absolute monarchy. Public unrest in 2006 forced the king to recall parliament and surrender the throne. A Maoist-dominated government took office in 2008, but continued internal conflict led the prime minister to resign in 2010. Since that time the government has been effectively insolvent.

The economy is one of the poorest in the world. Seventy-five percent of the labor force is involved in agriculture, although it contributes only 38 percent of the GDP. Leading agricultural products include sugar cane, potatoes, and wheat. The most-produced crop is rice. Seven percent of the people are employed in industry, which contributes 15 percent of the GDP. Tourism is the leading money-maker for the country, but the volatile political situation makes that income tenuous.

Bhutan

Bhutan (boo TAN), landlocked like Nepal, is about half the size of Indiana. It is bordered by China and India, but it controls some key passes in the Himalayas. Also like Nepal, it is technologically backward and economically challenged.

Physical Features and Society—The climate of Bhutan ranges from severe cold in the Himalayas to tropical in the southern plains. Its climate is notorious for its sudden and violent thunderstorms. In fact, its very name means "Land of the Thunder Dragon." Its terrain is mostly mountainous, so it has frequent landslides, especially during the rainy season. Associated with the landslides is the problem of soil erosion. The country also has limited drinking water.

Bhutan's population is 75 percent Buddhist, 22 percent Hindu, and 2 percent Christian. Under a Buddhist monarchy and the predominant Buddhist influence, other religions are barely tolerated. Christians cannot build churches, and it is illegal to lead a person to Christ. Bhutanese who become Christian may lose their citizenship as well as access to education, health care, employment, electricity,

Sherpas are renowned for their skills as guides for mountain climbers.

Bon and Buddhism

"Bon was an ancient religion that existed throughout the Himalayas before Buddhism arrived in Bhutan in the seventh century. Mostly because Buddhism does not prohibit the simultaneous embrace of two (or more) religions, Bon beliefs and practices became fused with Buddhism.

Certain warlike Bon deities are . . . bloodthirsty in appearance. Such 'Buddhist gods' take on this visage to scare away evil spirits—precisely what the old Bon gods did to help its followers. Likewise, the Bon practice of praying to their gods to bring rain, cure illness, overcome poverty, and obtain objects of desire continues today, although this has nothing at all to do with Buddhist thought."

Cultures of the World: Bhutan, 84.

and water. As a result, Bhutan remains one of the world's least evangelized nations. However, despite religious and political hostility, churches are forming and Christianity is spreading across the county.

Government and Economy—Bhutan is officially an independent state, but in practical terms it is very closely linked to India. It remained essentially isolated until 1959, when it sought help from India to stave off threats from China. It is a monarchy ruled by a hereditary king, but its king promised to allow the country to move toward democracy. A draft constitution was completed in 2001 and was ratified in 2008. Buddhist priests and Indian merchants continue to exert great influence on the government. The country has a treaty with India whereby Bhutan controls its own domestic affairs and India controls its foreign policy.

Bhutan has one of the world's smallest economies, and even that is closely linked to the Indian economy. It is based on subsistence farming, animal husbandry, and forestry. Agricultural products include rice, corn, root crops, citrus, grains, eggs, and dairy products. Its industry is backward, and most of it is cottage industry. Major industries include cement, wood products, processed fruits, alcoholic beverages, and calcium carbonate. Bhutan's major trading partners are India and Germany.

Section Quiz

1. What political/religious fact makes Nepal unique?
2. Which two groups of Nepalese are famous, and for what special skills is each known?
3. What do Nepal and Bhutan have in common that make them unique among the countries of South Asia?
* What does Bhutan's name literally mean, and why is it called that?

Sri Lanka and Maldives

Several islands lie off the Indian subcontinent in the Indian Ocean. Two of them are independent nations, while several others are territories. The two nations are the only South Asian nations with normal life expectancies and high literacy rates.

Sri Lanka

The island country of Sri Lanka (sree LAHNG-kuh) lies twenty miles off the southeast coast of India. It is a little larger than West Virginia and is strategically located near the subcontinent and the shipping lanes of the Indian Ocean.

Physical Features and Society—The terrain is low, flat-to-rolling plains with mountains in the south-central interior of the island. The climate is tropical monsoon, and the natural vegetation is rain forest. The island is hit occasionally by fierce cyclones and tornadoes. Combined with the monsoons, these storms cause a great deal of soil erosion. Sri Lanka was hit by a devastating tsunami in December 2004 that left 31,000 dead, 6,300 missing, and 443,000 homeless and caused an estimated $1.5 billion in property damage.

Buddhist Sinhalese from northern India settled on the northern plains of Sri Lanka about 400 BC. Tamils, Hindus from southern India, began arriving three hundred years later. They finally won the

---

"Walking" Trees?

The banyan is a very large and interesting tree found in South Asia. The trees grow from the top down. Branches send out roots through the air until they reach the ground. Each root thickens into a new trunk and sends out more branches, which in turn grow roots. Each root becomes a new leg as the tree grows and expands across the countryside. Roots that grow down through the air are called aerial roots.

As the tree grows, it begins to look like a whole forest. The largest banyan tree has 350 large trunks and three thousand smaller ones. This record tree is in Sri Lanka.

Honoring the Dead in Sri Lanka

Muslims in Sri Lanka bury their dead within 24 hours. However, other Sri Lankans have their dead embalmed and keep the body in the house so relatives and friends can pay their last respects.

Buddhists have a special ceremony where they chant a verse about the brevity of life. Then the nearest relatives pour water from a jug into a bowl with water spilling over to symbolize the depositing of merit to the dead. They believe the better the merit the better the chance of reincarnation to a pleasant place as a human being.

northernmost point of the island, Jaffna, from the Buddhists. Today they make up about 14.3 percent of the island's population.

Most Sri Lankans (70 percent) are Buddhists. Hindus and Muslims make up 12.8 and 8.5 percent of the population, respectively. Various forms of Christianity represent 8 percent of the population. While Sri Lankan law declares the right to exercise freedom of worship, political and religious leaders restrict the actual practice of this freedom. The government supports an anti-conversion program, and Buddhist extremists persecute Christians. Despite this opposition, the number of evangelical Christians has grown significantly in the last fifty years.

The island has been influenced somewhat by both Portuguese and Dutch traders, but the greatest European influence was exerted by Great Britain, which claimed the island in 1796. At that time, the island was known as Ceylon. The British controlled it until they granted it independence in 1948. The name of the island was changed to Sri Lanka in 1972. Conflicts between the Sinhalese and the Tamils, who want independence, have been ongoing for decades. The warring factions finally signed a Norwegian-brokered cease-fire in February 2002. Fighting broke out again in 2006, and the Sri Lankan military defeated the Tamil forces in 2009. Sri Lankan leaders have since worked to bring about reconciliation between the warring parties.

Government and Economy—Today Sri Lanka has a republican form of government, with a president, a prime minister, and a unicameral legislature. The capital is Colombo (pop. 752,993 in 2011). The country has twenty or more political parties, and strong influence is exerted by Buddhist priests, labor unions, and radical separatist groups.

Thirty-two percent of the Sri Lankan work force is engaged in agriculture, producing 11 percent of the GDP. The largest sector of the economy, however, is services, employing 42 percent of the work force and contributing 58 percent of the GDP.

Rice and coconuts are the two major food crops of Sri Lanka. Plantations in the south produce the main exports of tea and rubber. Sri Lanka's tea is world famous, and its mines produce rubies and sapphires. Insurance, banking, and oil refining are other major industries. In addition, many Sri Lankans work in the Middle East and send much of their earnings back to their families.

Maldives

Maldives (MAWL deevz) is the smallest nation in Asia, not quite twice the size of Washington, D.C. Its 1,190 coral islands, arranged in 26 atolls, sprinkle the sea southwest of India over a region 475 miles long and 80 miles wide. About 200 islands are inhabited; another 80 are tourist resorts. The nation is strategically located on the Indian Ocean shipping lanes.

Physical Features and Society—The islands of Maldives have a hot, humid climate. The northeast monsoons are dry; the southwest monsoons are rainy. The terrain is flat, with beaches of white sand. The highest point is only about eight feet in elevation. The islands have a limited supply of fresh water.

Ninety-nine percent of the people in Maldives are Sunni Muslims, descendants of Sinhalese people from Sri Lanka, and the

Marriage in Sri Lanka

"Arranged marriages are still practiced in Sri Lanka. Originally a . . . marriage broker, would visit the parents of an eligible young man or woman and help the parents 'fix up' their son or daughter. These days . . Sri Lankans turn to relatives and friends for assistance on matchmaking and advertising in the newspapers for potential wives and husbands.

Marriage mediators propose candidates and look into their morals and credentials. Dowries are settled discreetly. Though the groom would like his bride to bring a dowry, he prefers not to ask for it.

Cultures of the World: Sri Lanka, 80.

Sri Lankan teas are world famous.

The islands of Maldives (left) are flat and densely populated. Maldives (right) was badly damaged by the 2004 tsunami.

national language is Divehi, which is related to Sinhalese. The remaining 1 percent is divided among Buddhists, Hindus, and Christians. The open practice of anything other than Islam is forbidden, and Sunni Islam is promoted in order to foster national unity. The government denies the existence of Christianity among the Maldivians and arrests any believers when they are discovered. This has resulted in the Maldives being one of the least evangelized nations in the world, with a tiny Christian population of less than 600.

Government and Economy—The history of Maldives was influenced by first the Dutch and then the British. It obtained its independence from Britain in 1965 and became a republic three years later. The government operates by secular Muslim law. It has a president and a unicameral legislature of fifty representatives, forty-two elected by the people and eight appointed by the president. The same president has dominated the government since he was elected in 1978, but riots in Male (MAH lee; pop. 70,000), the capital, in 2004 forced him to pledge reforms and greater freedoms. Four political parties, including three opposition parties, were allowed in June 2005. A multiparty democracy resulted from the 2008 election. Limited political freedoms have resulted.

The economy is dominated by fishing and tourism. Tourism contributes 28 percent of the GDP. Agricultural products grown include coconuts, corn, and sweet potatoes. Shipping, boat building, handicrafts, and coral and sand mining are important industries.

The islands of Maldives suffered extensive damage when they were hit by a tsunami in December 2004. With aid from India, the United States, and other nations, Maldivians have recovered and now enjoy the highest GDP per capita among south Asian countries.

Section Quiz

1. Which European nation exerted the most influence over Sri Lanka?
2. What two groups were at war in Sri Lanka until they signed a ceasefire in 2002?
3. What is the majority religion in Sri Lanka?
4. What fishing nation occupies a group of coral islands near India?
5. Of what religion are almost all of the inhabitants of those islands?
* What conditions make life difficult in Sri Lanka and Maldives?

Chapter Review

Making Connections

1. Why could India be called the world's largest democracy?

2–3. What country split from Pakistan in 1971? Why?

4. What is considered the poorest nation in the world?

5. What mountain range contains 250 of the highest mountains in the world?

6. Which group left the longest-lasting impact on Central Asia: Huns, Turkic peoples, or Mongols?

Developing Geography Skills

1. How do the mountains along the northern borders affect the climate of South Asia?

2. Why could the Caspian region become a battleground in Central Asia? What countries are likely to become involved should a conflict occur?

Thinking Critically

1. In what major ways does Hinduism differ from Christianity?

2. What are two conditions common among Christians in this region?

Living in God's World

1. Write a prayer for Christians in this region of the world. Be sure to take into account the specific challenges they face.

2. Write a paragraph identifying the differences that American Christians and Indian Christians have in discerning what parts of their culture are consistent with Christianity and what parts are opposed to it.

People, Places, and Things to Know

Caucasus Mountains
Armenians
Shiite
Sunni
Caspian Sea
Central Asia
Silk Road
Aral Sea
Caspian Depression
Kara-Kum
Turkistan
Kyzyl-Kum
Bukhara
Tashkent
Samarqand
Tien Shan
Pamir Mountains
buffer state
Mujahideen
Taliban
Hindu Kush
Wakhan Corridor
Kabul
Khyber Pass
Himalayas
subcontinent
monsoons
Mt. Everest
Ghats
Vindhya Mountains
Ganges River
Hinduism
Brahmaputra River
Jumna River
Delhi
New Delhi
Indus River
Great Indian Desert
Sikhism
Deccan Plateau
Mumbai
Coromandel Coast
Chennai
Mahatma Gandhi
Kashmir
caste
Brahmins
samsara
moksha
reincarnation
karma
untouchables
Jainism
Mohenjo-Daro
typhoons
tsunamis
Sherpas
Gurkhas

15

SOUTHEAST ASIA

The region known as Southeast Asia is as large as the contiguous United States. It borders both India and China and stretches from the Indian Ocean in the west to the Pacific Ocean in the east. The countries within the region have many similarities, such as climate and resources; but they also have many contrasts, ranging from primitive tribal societies to modern, computer-driven societies.

The population centers of Southeast Asia tend to cluster around rivers, especially the fertile delta regions of the Mekong and Irrawaddy Rivers, and along the narrow coastal plains where available harbor facilities make trade more feasible. Even steep highland areas, however, are heavily terraced to enable production of abundant crops. More than half of the total population of the region lives on islands. Dense forests, steamy jungles, and rugged mountains tend to inhibit land travel between the various countries. Most immigrants to the region are from China.

The region is part of the Pacific "ring of fire," experiencing numerous earthquakes, volcanic eruptions, and tsunamis. Because of the seasonal changes that accompany the monsoons—heavy rains and sometimes severe droughts—much of life in the region is regulated by the climate. But the rains also make possible the region's abundant crops, especially rice.

Rice can be grown in large quantities in relatively small spaces. The people of Southeast Asia rely daily on their rice production, and many more in other areas eat it regularly, too. In fact, more people in the world rely on rice than on any other staple. Five of the top ten

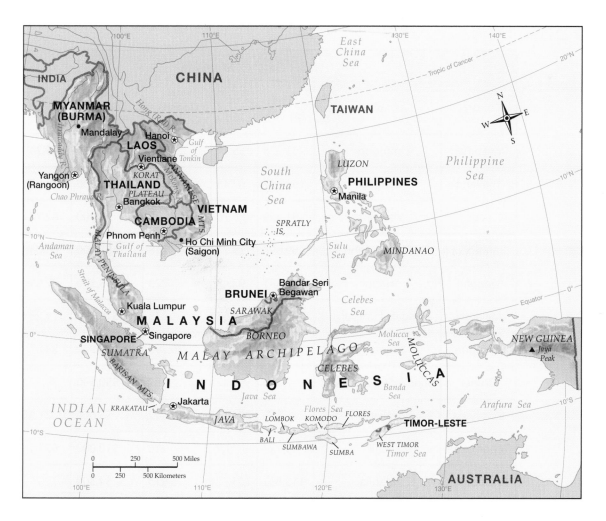

rice-producing countries of the world are in Southeast Asia. (Nine of the ten are in the broader Asian region.)

Southeast Asia has also been the focus of intense competition and power struggles among European colonial powers. Of the Southeast Asian countries, only Thailand remained free of European colonialism. Yet Thailand was instrumental in the era of imperialism as a buffer zone between British forces in Myanmar and French forces in French Indochina (encompassing Laos, Cambodia, and Vietnam). Japan coveted the riches of the region and conquered much of it before and during World War II. In the decades following the war, all of the countries of the region gained independence from colonial powers. One positive effect of colonialism was the unifying influence exerted among various tribal groups throughout Southeast Asia, which made independence possible and practical. Today, the region is developing into an economic powerhouse, although poverty continues to abound and political instability remains a concern.

I. Indochina

Southeast Asia is divided into two major subregions. The mainland portion is called **Indochina**, so named because of the dominant neighbors on either side of the region: India and China. These two countries exert strong influence on the culture, politics, and economy of the entire region. Indochina is composed of Myanmar, Thailand, Laos, Cambodia, and Vietnam. South of Indochina is the second subregion, the **insular countries** of the **Malay Archipelago**: Malaysia, Singapore, Indonesia, Brunei, Timor-Leste, and the Philippines. An **archipelago** (ahrk uh PEHL uh goh) is a large group of islands.

Southeast Asia Fast Facts						
Country	Capital	Area (sq. mi.)	Pop. (M)	Pop. Density (per sq. mi.)	Per Capita GDP 2012 ($US)	Life Span
Myanmar	Yangon	261,228	55.17	211	$1,400	65.24
Thailand	Bangkok	198,117	67.45	340	$10,000	73.83
Laos	Vientiane	91,429	6.70	73	$3,000	62.77
Cambodia	Phnom Penh	69,898	15.21	218	$2,400	63.04
Vietnam	Hanoi	127,881	92.48	723	$3,500	72.65
Malaysia	Kuala Lumpur	127,355	29.63	233	$16,900	74.28
Singapore	Singapore	269	5.46	20,297	$60,900	84.07
Brunei	Bandar Seri Begawan	2,226	0.42	189	$50,500	76.57
Indonesia	Jakarta	735,358	251.16	342	$5,000	71.9
Timor-Leste	Dili	5,724	1.2	210	$10,000	67.06
Philippines	Manila	115,831	105.72	913	$4,300	72.21

Myanmar

As one moves eastward from India, the first country of Indochina one enters is Myanmar (myahn MAHR), formerly known as Burma, which is the largest country in Indochina and the second largest in Southeast Asia. Slightly smaller than Texas, it shares a border with China in the north and Laos and Thailand in the east. It has a coast on the Bay of Bengal in the southwest and the Andaman Sea in the south.

Most of the people of Myanmar live along the coastal lowlands, where the rain forest offers sufficient water for rice paddies. The country ranks seventh in the production of rice. The capital, Yangon (formerly called Rangoon), and its four million residents (2007) are in the lowlands of the delta of the **Irrawaddy** (ihr uh WAHD ee) **River**, which runs from the rugged eastern highlands down to the Andaman Sea.

The Irrawaddy River, seen here in Mandalay, is the main river of Myanmar.

Seventy percent of the work force is employed in agriculture, which contributes 39 percent of the GDP. In addition to rice, Myanmar produces vegetables, sesame, groundnuts, sugar cane, hardwoods, and fish. Commercial farming is done in the lowlands. Tribal peoples in the highlands are subsistence farmers. Sadly, farmers in the "**Golden Triangle**," where the borders of Myanmar, Laos, and Thailand meet, also grow poppies for opium production.

Industries include food processing, clothing, wood products, copper, tin, tungsten, iron, fertilizers, cement, and pharmaceuticals. Nineteen percent of the GDP is from industry, but only 7 percent of the work force is employed in that sector.

Since Myanmar gained its independence in 1948, much of its history has been a succession of military dictatorships. Free elections were held in 1990, giving the opposition a landslide victory and control of the legislature, but the military junta refused to relinquish control for several years. Finally, the country transitioned to a new government in 2011. As a result, the regime that routinely harassed and arrested those who promoted democracy and human rights is being replaced with one whose human rights record is improving.

Eighty percent of the people of Myanmar are Buddhists. Nine percent practice a form of Christianity, and 7 percent are Muslims. Despite the improvement in human rights, Christians are still targeted by the military and referred to as "the C-virus." Foreign workers were expelled in 1996, and Christians were left without mature leaders or organization. Over three thousand villages of Karen, Chin, Shan, Mon, and Wa Christians have been burned out in the last decade. Yet a faithful group of believers still thrives in Myanmar.

Myanmar was once the richest country in Southeast Asia, but its military regime adopted socialistic economic practices that hindered productivity and prosperity. Oppressive government controls, inefficient economic policies, and economic sanctions imposed by nations who oppose the regime's human rights violations have crippled the economy. To date, the government has failed to change current policies in spite of rampant poverty, especially in rural areas.

Adoniram Judson

Adoniram Judson became America's first foreign missionary, arriving in Burma in 1813. In spite of various severe afflictions, including temporary blindness, imprisonment, and the deaths of his first and second wives, he completed a Burmese Bible translation that is still used today.

Role of Women

Women in Myanmar have many opportunities that are not available to women in many parts of the world.

Upon marriage, a woman keeps her own name. During the marriage she may continue to live with her parents or live with her husband's parents. She is expected to show deference to parents and in-laws but is not required to remain at home, as in the past.

Wives typically handle the household finances and are entrusted with their husband's paychecks to spend the money wisely. If additional income is needed, the wife is expected to operate some type of business out of the home. Of course, the most important role for the woman is to supervise the raising of her children.

While divorce is not common in Myanmar, divorced women are protected from being left penniless or treated as outcasts. The woman is allowed to keep half of the property gained during the marriage plus anything she brought to the marriage. She is also free to remarry.

Many professional careers, including teacher, accountant, secretary, nurse, and medical doctor, have become an option for women. The most recent careers open to women include lawyer and politician.

WORLD RELIGIONS

Buddhism

Buddhism is a religion that promotes the teachings of Siddhartha Gautama, who lived about five hundred years before Christ. *Buddha* means "enlightened one." Gautama gained this title as one who claimed to be enlightened and one who could help others become enlightened.

Buddha lived in India and was influenced by Hindu ideas such as *karma* and *samsara* (the cycle of reincarnation). But Buddhism is not considered a Hindu religion because Buddhists reject the Hindu scriptures. Buddhists use collections of Buddha's sayings as their scriptures. Buddhists also reject the idea of a soul or even of self. The soul, or *atman*, is an important concept for Hindus because the soul is reincarnated. Buddhists believe that what are thought of as persons are really the aggregates of matter, sensation, cognition, mental formations, and consciousness. When the body dies these aggregates affect the cycle of *samsara*, but no soul moves from one being to another.

Buddha's denial of the soul is important to his teaching about salvation. Buddha's diagnosis of the world's problem and the way of salvation is called the Four Noble Truths.

First, Buddha taught that suffering, impermanence, dissatisfaction, and emptiness (*dukkha*) afflicts everything. Second, the reason *dukkha* afflicts everything is desire. The existence of desire leads to suffering. Third, the way to escape suffering is to cease from desiring. This is one of the reasons that Buddha denied the existence of souls. This denial is important to cease from desiring. Fourth, desire and suffering cease when one follows the noble Eightfold Path: (1) right view, (2) right intention, (3) right speech, (4) right action, (5) right livelihood (do not work in an occupation that harms others), (6) right effort, (7) right mindfulness, (8) right concentration (meditation).

The goal is to escape from *samsara* into **nirvana**. *Nirvana* is not a place where souls go. Buddhists do not believe souls exist; nor is *nirvana* mere nothingness. It is ultimate reality. But because of this, Buddhists teach that nothing can be said about it.

Christians would say that Buddha recognized an important truth when he said that suffering, impermanence, dissatisfaction, and emptiness afflict everyone. Solomon made precisely this point in the book of Ecclesiastes. But Buddha made a grave error when he traced the root of suffering to desire. It is easy to see how he made this mistake. A person is most disappointed when he loses something he greatly desires. But the Bible points out that the root cause for suffering, impermanence, dissatisfaction, and emptiness is sin. Desire remains good. Love for God and love for others are the two great commandments, according to Jesus. Obedience to these commands includes desire for God to be glorified and desire for the good of others.

How can someone escape suffering and emptiness? First the root cause, sin, must be dealt with. By His death on the cross, Jesus paid the penalty for sin. By His resurrection He conquered death. Christians look forward to the return of Christ when He will restore the earth to a place of no suffering, death, or dissatisfaction. The souls of those who have died and been present with God in heaven will receive perfected, resurrected bodies. The Christian hope is not escape from this world. Christians look forward to the return of Christ and the redemption of God's good creation.

Buddhist monks in meditation

Thailand

East of Myanmar is Thailand (TYE land), which until 1939 was known as **Siam** (sy AM). It is the only country of Southeast Asia that was never controlled by a European colonial power. It is also the strongest economic power in Indochina because it has not only abundant resources that it has developed wisely but also a sound free market economy.

The Thai military staged a bloodless coup in September 2006 while the prime minister was attending the opening session of the United Nations. This led to political instability that proved difficult to resolve. However, during the national election in 2011, the opposition party, Pheu Tai, won a clear majority and formed a coalition government that has restored stability and international recognition.

A little more than twice the size of Wyoming, Thailand borders Laos, Cambodia, and Malaysia. Like Myanmar, Thailand has a major river, the Chao Phraya (CHOU prah-YAH), flowing from the northern highlands. It empties into the Gulf of Thailand near Bangkok, the capital. The river valley lies between two mountain ranges and is the most populous area of the country. Rice farming is prevalent in the valley.

Much of Thailand's territory encompasses the Malay Peninsula, which is almost one thousand miles long. Although Myanmar shares the northern section and Malaysia owns the southern portion, Thailand has the central section and therefore controls the only land route between Asia and Malaysia/Singapore. On the west side of the isthmus is the Andaman Sea; on the east is the Gulf of Thailand. The peninsula is sparsely populated, but it has many mines and rubber plantations and produces teak, bamboo, and other woods.

Bangkok is Indochina's second-largest city (behind only Jakarta, Indonesia) with a population of about 8.3 million. It is a bustling modern city, and its industries include refineries, textiles, auto assembly plants, and electronic equipment.

In the mid-fourteenth century, what was then known as Siam was founded as a kingdom. It switched from an absolute monarchy to a constitutional monarchy in 1932 and remains so today. Although the country has a hereditary king, its effective head is the prime minister, who is elected from among the members of the House of Representatives. The bicameral legislature has a corresponding Senate. Four political parties vie for dominance in the government.

Thailand's natural resources include tin, rubber, tungsten, tantalum, timber, lead, fish, gypsum, lignite, and fluorite. Thirty-eight percent of the work force is engaged in agriculture and produces 12 percent of the GDP. The remaining 88 percent of the GDP is divided almost equally between industry and services.

Eighty-five percent of Thais are Buddhists. The next-largest religion is Islam, representing 8 percent of the population. The greatest problem facing the government today comes from three Muslim-majority provinces in the south, which are in armed rebellion, most likely spurred on by the spread of radical Islam around the world. While the Christian population is currently 1 percent, congregations are growing, and as many as 65 percent of Thai church members are first-generation believers. Thus the Thai church is poised for significant growth.

The Shwe Dagon

"The Shwe Dagon, on Singuttara Hill in Yangon, is Myanmar's most sacred pagoda. It enshrines the Buddha's hair and other holy relics. Originally only 27 feet (8m) high, it is now 326 feet (99 m) in height after successive renovations and additions that were made by kings and queens.

"Gold and precious gems adorn the pagoda and are also buried in the main treasure chamber under the spire. Four staircases (each with about 130 steps) lead to the pagoda, which is surrounded by numerous smaller spires and monasteries. The main platform and surrounding terraces are always full of worshipers who are meditating or praying, and offering flowers, food, candles, and water."

Cultures of the World: Myanmar, 17.

The Shwe Dagon Pagoda

Reinforcement of Buddhism

Thai men are expected to spend time in one of the many Thai monasteries each year. They are taught that there are several benefits to this practice. The Thai are taught that if "a boy becomes a novice monk, his mother will not enter hell; if he becomes a full monk, his father will also not enter hell." Imagine the pressure many Thai families place on a son to become a Buddhist monk so that his parents will be spared from hell.

Even for those who do not become monks, this annual stay is considered of great value because each man spends time studying Buddhist teachings. These reviews serve to reinforce the laws of Buddhism.

Elephant Roundup

The elephant, Thailand's national symbol, is used in the timber industry of the country. Workers gather many elephants once a year in a big roundup that is something like a Western rodeo—but using elephants rather than horses. People from near and far come to watch the huge animals display their skills.

Opening the activities, more than one hundred elephants parade before the crowds. Their trainers, called *mahouts* (muh HOUTZ), sit proudly on the shoulders of the beasts, giving commands by nudging the beasts behind the ears with their feet.

A small group of elephants demonstrates the way wild animals are caught and trained. A few of the animals are used to play the role of wild elephants. The others chase them until the mahouts rope the wild beasts by their hind legs.

In other events the elephants show off their speed, skill, and agility. Many spectators volunteer to lie on the ground and let four or five of the 8,000-lb. beasts step over them. Between races and log-lifting demonstrations, dancers in colorful costumes perform traditional Thai dances.

In the most exciting event, elephants race to a line several yards away, pick up a banana or another small article with their trunks, and then return to the starting point, where they place the article in a small circle. They gallop back and forth picking up articles until the last article, a red flag, is returned. The first elephant to return with its red flag wins.

ASEAN

Thailand was one of the original nations involved in the founding of the **Association of Southeast Asian Nations (ASEAN)** and the only member nation from Indochina. The organization was started in 1967 to promote political and economic cooperation and regional stability through consultation, consensus, and cooperation. The founding member nations were Thailand, Indonesia, Malaysia, the Philippines, and Singapore, but today all of the nations of Southeast Asia are members. The organization's Secretariat is located in Jakarta, Indonesia.

Section Quiz

1. Which country in this region has a modern history characterized by military dictatorships?
2–3. Which country in this region is the only one never colonized by a European power, and what is that country's former name?
4. Which country has an elephant roundup?
* Why has Myanmar gone from the richest country in Southeast Asia to one characterized by ineffiency and poverty?

Laos

The only landlocked country in Southeast Asia is Laos (LOUSE). It is surrounded by Myanmar and Thailand on the west, Cambodia on the south, China on the north, and Vietnam on the east. It is a largely undeveloped mountainous country. Little of its land area is arable, and it rivals Myanmar as the poorest Southeast Asian country. Much of its border with Thailand is the **Mekong** (MAY KONG) **River**.

A little bigger than Utah, Laos was once much larger than it is now, but its power and influence gradually declined. It came under the control of Thailand in the seventeenth to nineteenth centuries. It was also part of French Indochina during the colonial period. In 1975, a Communist organization called the Pathet Lao, took over and closely aligned the country with Communist Vietnam. In recent years, Laos has tried to move back toward a free market economy with positive results. But the Communist Party retains control of the government, and freedoms are severely limited. In addition, the country's infrastructure is primitive. It has no railroads to speak of, telecommunications are limited, and the country has a poor road system.

People live in this long, narrow boat on the Mekong River in Laos.

Seventy-five percent of the labor force is engaged in agriculture, which, dominated by rice production, contributes 25 percent of the GDP. The other 75 percent is about evenly divided between industry and services. In addition to rice, the country's major agricultural products include sweet potatoes, vegetables, corn, and sugar cane. Its exploited resources include copper, tin, gypsum, and timber. Other industries include food processing, garment manufacturing, and cement production.

Fifty-seven percent of the Laotian people are Buddhists. Thirty-seven percent follow animism or other indigenous religions. About 3 percent profess Christianity. The Christians in Laos have endured cycles of persecution since the 1970s. As is often true in history, persecution has purified the Laotian church and resulted in growth. Despite the lack of trained leaders, Christians continue to worship in formal congregations and house churches.

Cambodia

South of Laos is the country of Cambodia (kam BOH dee uh). It also shares borders with Vietnam on the east and Thailand on the north and west. Its southern border is the Gulf of Thailand.

The terrain of Cambodia, which is slightly smaller than Oklahoma, is primarily low, flat plains, although it does have some mountains in the southwest and north. More than one-fifth of its soil is arable, and its natural resources include oil, natural gas, timber, gemstones, manganese, phosphates, and hydropower potential. The key term is *potential*; historically, the country has not capitalized on its great potential.

The country was under the colonial authority of France from 1863 until it gained independence in 1953. The Communist **Khmer Rouge** (kuh-MEHR ROOZH) took over in 1975 after a five-year struggle. The Communist leader, **Pol Pot**, had the idea that the solution to the country's problems was to erase all memories of colonial times and return everyone to a rural, agricultural lifestyle. In the process, the Khmer Rouge sought to eliminate all opposition. To accomplish this goal, the Comunists murdered all military personnel, civil servants, doctors, teachers, and their family members as well as anyone who had a basic education or who was wealthy. When they

This collection of skulls represents the millions of Cambodians murdered in the "killing fields" under the Khmer Rouge.

finished, the Khmer Rouge had killed nearly two million Cambodians. The Communists in Vietnam became involved when Cambodian forces attacked and massacred Vietnamese villagers. The Vietnamese army invaded Cambodia in 1978, drove the Khmer Rouge into the countryside, and occupied Cambodia for the next ten years. The Khmer Rouge finally surrendered in 1999, and the United Nations put the leaders on trial for crimes against humanity.

Today, the country has a king who rules with a bicameral legislature composed of representatives of three recognized political parties. They are working to make Cambodia a more vibrant country that is conducive to free markets. Foreign aid toward this goal has been tied to official efforts to reduce corruption. One area of concern is the great increase in drug abuse and drug trafficking over the last two decades.

During the reign of terror by the Khmer Rouge, 90 percent of Buddhist monks (along with most Christians) were killed in an effort to eradicate religion. However, these efforts failed, and 83 percent of the Cambodian people still identify with Buddhism, while about 3 percent practice some form of Christianity. Since 1990, limited religious tolerance has been granted, and Christians have begun to worship openly. Perhaps the most encouraging development is that most of the growth of the church has occurred under indigenous church plants and evangelists.

The prospects for improvement are bright. The GDP of Cambodia is about equally divided among the three sectors (agriculture, industry, and services). Although 56 percent of the work force remains in agriculture, most of it is subsistence farming. However, Cambodia can produce rice, rubber, corn, vegetables, cashews, and other products well. Its growing industries include tourism, apparel, rice milling, gem mining, and wood products. Another factor of great potential is the young population; 53 percent of the population is twenty-four years of age or younger.

Vietnam

The country of Vietnam (vee eht NAHM) can be visualized as a long, thin *S* reaching from southern China in the north to the Gulf of Thailand in the southwest. In total area it is slightly larger than New Mexico.

The northern third of the country is shaped like an inverted triangle with the Gulf of Tonkin on the east and Laos on the west. It is bisected from northwest to southeast by the **Hong (Red) River**, which flows through the capital, **Hanoi** (ha NOY), and empties through a low, flat delta into the **Gulf of Tonkin** (TAHN kihn). The chief seaport is **Haiphong** (hye FONG) in the northern portion of the delta.

The middle of the country, which makes up a little less than one-third of the length, is a thin band of narrow coastline and central highlands running southeastward from about Vinh to about Da Nang. In this central region, the narrowest point is only thirty-one miles wide; the widest point is only about sixty miles.

The southern portion is a little more than one-third of the total length of the country. It widens, and the coast, washed by the **South China Sea**, curves first southward and then southwestward near Cam Ranh. The western border of this third is Cambodia. The upper

The Human Toll

Following the Communist takeover of South Vietnam, millions of Vietnamese paid a terrible price for their efforts to remain free of communism. At least one million people were sent to "re-education" camps, with around 165,000 of them dying as a result of the dreadful conditions and brutality. Two hundred thousand South Vietnamese people were executed for various reasons, including their role in the South Vietnamese government or support of American forces. Another fifty thousand died in labor camps. Millions of Vietnamese fled the country in boats that were not seaworthy, and hundreds of thousands of them died at sea. Some did manage to survive and travel to the United States.

and central portions of southern Vietnam are dominated by central highlands. The lower portion is mostly a flat delta around the mouth of the Mekong River, which flows through the heart of Cambodia. The largest city in the southern portion of the country, **Ho Chi Minh** (hoh chee mihn) **City** (formerly Saigon), is at the northern edge of the delta.

The culture of modern Vietnam reflects a variety of influences, both Western and Oriental. It became a French colony in 1858. Although the Vietnamese declared their independence at the end of World War II, they did not break free of French control until 1954, when Vietnamese rebels led by Communist **Ho Chi Minh** defeated the French forces at **Dien Bien Phu** (dyehn byehn FOO).

More than two million motorcycles—and even more bicycles—jam the streets of Ho Chi Minh City.

Not everyone, however, wanted to live under communism. The United Nations proposed free elections to allow the Vietnamese to determine their country's future. Vietnamese living in the southern half of the country voted to remain free. However, when the Communists who controlled the northern half of the country refused, the UN divided the country at the 17th parallel, creating North and South Vietnam.

Not willing to let the richer South remain free and separate, the North Vietnamese invaded the South, supported by a guerrilla group known as the Viet Cong. Based on the **domino theory** (the idea that if one country of Southeast Asia fell to communism, the others would soon fall too, just like dominoes), the United States sent progressively more troops to help the South. However, the Vietnam War proved to be so divisive in the United States that U.S. troops were withdrawn in 1973. In 1975, the South fell, and millions of Vietnamese people were killed or imprisoned or died trying to escape the country.

For the next twenty years, Vietnam struggled economically. Under international pressure to improve its human rights record, Vietnam finally began to liberalize its economic policies in 2001, and the country is making vast improvements economically. Forty-eight percent of the work force is employed in agriculture, which contributes 22 percent of the GDP. Although other countries produce more rice than Vietnam, that is still its top agricultural product. It is a leading producer of cashews and coffee. Other products include fish, rubber, cotton, and tea. Industries such as food processing, garments, shoes, mining, cement, chemical fertilizers, and tires contribute 40 percent of the GDP.

Vietnam still has a Communist government that allows no opposition party. The president is elected by the unicameral National Assembly.

Vietnam is considered closed to formal missionary activity. However, despite more than thirty years of atheistic communism, only 23 percent of Vietnamese profess to be nonreligious. The largest religion is Buddhism, and 52 percent of Vietnamese embrace this religion. Just over 9 percent of the Vietnamese practice some form of Christianity. Although the Vietnamese constitution guarantees freedom of religion, the Communist bureaucracy continues to carry out or allow persecution.

Ho Chi Minh (1890-1969) led the Communist defeat of the French at Dien Bien Phu.

Section Quiz

1. Which river not only forms much of the border between Laos and Thailand but also flows through Cambodia and Vietnam?
2. What group came to power in Cambodia and used extreme violence to return the nation to an agricultural lifestyle?
3. What European country was defeated in the battle at Dien Bien Phu?
4. Vietnamese in which half of the country desired to be free of communism?
* Did the fall of South Vietnam prove or disprove the domino theory?

II. The Malay Archipelago

The Malay Archipelago is the largest group of islands in the world. It begins near the lower half of the Malay Peninsula and encompasses two major groups of islands: the East Indies and the Philippines.

Most of the islands are volcanic, and mountains dominate many of them. Apart from those highland areas, all of the islands have a tropical wet climate. Some areas get as much as 200 inches of rain a year; most places get at least 100 inches.

Malaysia

The first country a person traveling southward from Thailand enters is Malaysia (muh LAY zhuh). Part of it is on the lower portion of the Malay Peninsula, and the rest of it is on the northern side of the island of Borneo, located to the east of the peninsula.

Like Thailand, Malaysia is a major leader among the developing countries. It is also in a strategic location along the shipping lanes of the Strait of Malacca and the southern end of the South China Sea. It is slightly larger than New Mexico.

Eighty percent of Malaysia's people live on the peninsula. The capital, **Kuala Lumpur** (KWAHL-uh loom-POOR; pop. 1.6 million), is there. A distinguishing landmark of the city is the tallest twin buildings in the world, the two Petronas Towers, each at 88 stories, or 1,483 feet. Two of Malaysia's states, Sarawak (suh RAH wahk) and Sabah (SAH bah), are on the island of Borneo, which is about 400 miles east of the peninsula. Much of this area remains undeveloped, but its rich oil is being developed. The official language is Bahasa Melayu; but English, Chinese, and numerous other languages are also spoken.

Sixty-three percent of Malaysians are Sunni Muslim. Around 9 percent of Malaysians profess some form of Christianity. Six percent are Buddhist. As in many other countries, the Malaysian constitution proclaims freedom of religion. However, the reality is different. It is illegal to convert a Muslim, and sharia law is gaining support among the Muslim groups. The presence of over one hundred radical Islamic groups threatens the stability of the country and the safety of Christians. Despite

Importance of Family

Malaysians take their family relationships seriously, and elders are treated with honor. Muslim children show respect for their parents at the end of Ramadan by kissing their parent's hands and asking for forgiveness. Chinese children give their elders oranges and bow before them to receive a blessing. Indian children submit to their parents for major decisions such as whom they should marry. Malaysians of all backgrounds show respect for their parents by caring for them as they age.

Find It!

Petronas Towers in Kuala Lumpur

3.159° N 101.711° E

(Go to the ground-level view and enjoy the computer-generated image of these massive towers. Make sure your 3D building box is checked.)

This aerial view of Kuala Lumpur includes the Petronas Towers, the tallest twin-buildings in the world.

these threats, the Malaysian church is maturing and growing numerically and spiritually.

Malaysia was a British colonial power in the eighteenth and nineteenth centuries and was occupied by Japan during World War II. In 1948, the Federation of Malaya was formed, and in 1957 the country gained full independence. Singapore was part of the federation until it seceded in 1965. Then Sabah and Sarawak joined the federation in 1967, forming what became known as Malaysia. The country has a constitutional monarchy ruled by the Paramount Ruler, who is elected from among the hereditary leaders of the nine states that make up the country. It has a bicameral parliament, with members of the lower house being elected by the people and members of the upper house being appointed by the Paramount Ruler and the state legislatures. The country has dozens of political parties.

Malaysia has experienced an economic revolution. Although it was once heavily agricultural and merely a supplier or exporter of raw materials, in the 1970s it became a major electronics manufacturer. Today, 48 percent of its GDP is from services, and more than 40 percent is from industry. In addition to electronics, major industries include rubber processing, oil refining, and food processing. Only 11.1 percent of its work force is now employed in agriculture, producing 11.4 percent of the GDP. Among its agricultural products are rubber, palm oil, cocoa, and rice.

Singapore

At the southern tip of the Malay Peninsula is an island that is only a little more than three and a half times the size of Washington, D.C. But its influence far exceeds its size. Singapore (SING uh poor) is the name of not only the island but also the country and the capital. It has been a major trade and shipping location since the time of Christ, and it remains the focal point of trade in the region today. In fact, it is rated as one of the most competitive countries for business in the world. It is also one of the busiest seaports by volume in the world.

The population of Singapore is heavily Chinese (74 percent). Native Malays make up only 14 percent of the population. Indians make up 8 percent of the population. The largest religious groups are Buddhists (40 percent), Christians (16 percent), and Muslims (14 percent). Fourteen percent profess no religious affiliation, and the rest of the population practices a number of other minority religions. As diverse as its religions are its languages, which include Mandarin, English, Malay, Hokkien, and numerous others, totalling 31 languages. Christianity in Singapore has developed to the point of sending long-term missionaries out to other countries. In addition, thousands of Singaporean Christians embark on short-term mission trips each year. As a result, Singapore is becoming known as the Antioch of Asia.

Singapore has taken steps to increase its amount of space by reclaiming land from the sea (resulting in a 10 percent increase in its space). Because of its lack of land, agriculture is responsible for almost none of its GDP, although it does produce rubber, copra, fruit,

The Port of Singapore is one of the busiest seaports in the world.

The downtown business district of Singapore is a beautiful sight at night.

orchids, poultry, eggs, and ornamental fish. Its economy depends heavily on exports. Twenty-seven percent of the GDP is industry, mostly manufacturing and construction. Singapore is the financial and high-tech hub of Southeast Asia. Seventy-three percent of the GDP is service oriented, and more than half of that comes from financial services and transportation/communications.

The government of Singapore is a parliamentary republic with a president and a unicameral parliament led by a prime minister. It has numerous recognized political parties. The people have accepted restriction of certain freedoms in order to enjoy the stability and economic growth encouraged by this political system.

Brunei

Nestled between the Malaysian states of Sabah and Sarawak on the north central coast of the island of Borneo is the tiny (a little smaller than Delaware) country of Brunei (broo NYE). It is a flat coastal plain rising to mountains in the east and hilly lowland in the west.

Brunei has been important for traders since the seventh century. In 1888, the British made it one of their protectorates to stop pirates there who were preying on British shipping. It gained independence from Britain in 1984.

Less than half a percent of the land in Brunei is arable, so only about 0.6 percent of its GDP comes from agriculture. It does produce some rice, fruits, vegetables, and chickens. Industry, mostly extraction and refining of oil and liquefied natural gas, makes up 72 percent of the GDP. Approximately one-third of the work force is employed in government positions.

The government is a constitutional sultanate. It has a legal system based on English common law, but Islamic sharia law supersedes civil law in some areas. The sultan and the prime minister have hereditary positions; there are no elections. A legislative council is appointed by the sultan.

Islam is the official religion of Brunei; 65 percent of the people of Brunei practice it. Eleven percent of the people identify with various forms of Christianity, and Buddhists make up 9 percent of the population. Despite a constitutional guarantee of freedom of religion, it is against the law to witness to a Muslim or for a Muslim to convert to another religion. Handing out Christian literature is not allowed, and foreign Christian workers cannot legally enter the country. However, the church continues to grow numerically and across ethnic groups.

Indonesia

By far the largest country of not only the Malay Archipelago but also all of Southeast Asia is Indonesia (ihn doh NEE zhuh). It is a nation of 17,508 separate islands, but only about 6,000 of them are populated. They stretch across more than three thousand miles, from the Indian Ocean in the west to New Guinea and the Pacific Ocean in the east. (That is about the same distance as from New York City to Seattle, Washington.) Indonesia also has the fourth-largest population in the world (behind only China, India, and the United States).

As one might expect of such a far-flung nation, it is multi-ethnic and multilingual. Ethnic groups include Javanese, Sundanese, Madurese, coastal Malay, and various minority groups. The population speaks more than seven hundred languages and dialects.

The important factor that tends to unite so many different peoples of such different languages and cultures over such vast distances is religion. With 80 percent of Indonesians being Muslims, Indonesia is the largest Islamic country in the world. Radical Islamists are present in several areas of Indonesia. Despite the strong influence of Islam and periods of intense persecution from religious groups, about 16 percent of Indonesians practice some form of Christianity. It is remarkable that, in this environment, the number of evangelical Christians has expanded from 1.3 million to 13 milllion during the last fifty years.

The hub of Indonesian civilization has been the island of **Java** (JAH vuh), which is southeast of Sumatra and due south of Borneo. It has been at various times under the control of Arab traders, who spread Islam throughout the islands as they sought spices and other trade items; the Netherlands, which called the region the Dutch East Indies; the Japanese in World War II; and various regional warlords, dictators, and military juntas. Today, Java is the most densely populated of Indonesia's islands, and the capital, **Jakarta** (juh KAHR tuh; pop. 9.2 million), is one of the largest cities in the world.

Indonesia includes all or part of four of the world's eleven largest islands. Java ranks thirteenth worldwide, but four other Indonesian islands are even larger, of which New Guinea is the largest. The other three, with Java, are collectively called the Greater Sunda (SUHN duh) Islands.

The world's sixth-largest island is Sumatra (soo MAH truh), which is northwest of Java and southwest of Malaysia. It is the second-most-populated Indonesian island, and most of its people live in the eastern lowlands. Borneo, the third-largest island in the world, includes, as we have discussed already, the two Malaysian states of Sarawak and Sabah and the nation of Brunei. The eleventh-largest island in the world is Celebes

Marriage in Indonesia

Indonesians expect everyone in their country to get married at some point in life. Many Indonesians marry during their teenage years. Even an older man who is not yet married is still expected to find a wife.

Weddings in Indonesia are elegant and colorful. The participants wear elaborate ethnic clothing and exchange generous gifts, such as gold, money, fruit, and beautiful flowers. The couple getting married sit on elevated thrones and remain aloof from guests except to thank them as they walk by. The number of people invited to attend a wedding can vary from a hundred to a thousand, depending on the resources of the family. Some families go into debt to stage a grand wedding.

A tsunami devastated Banda Aceh, Sumatra, Indonesia, in December 2004.

Death and Funerals in Indonesia

"It is believed that when a person dies his spirit must be properly 'managed' or it will cause havoc in the world of the living. To prevent the soul from returning to Earth, some rites are designed to confuse it. In Sumatra the body is sent out of the house through a small gap in the floor, which is then sealed. In Bali and Sulawesi the hearse is jolted and jarred to prevent the spirit from finding its way back. For the soul to successfully make it to the land of the ancestors—usually in the form of a bird or insect—proper funeral rites are essential. Although these vary by region and ethnic group, they are often colorful and extravagant spectacles.

"If a family cannot afford this expense at the time of death, the body is either kept wrapped in shrouds in the house or temporarily buried until enough money is saved for the rites. In Bali the bereaved wait for more deaths so they can have a joint cremation. The bones are then exhumed, cleaned, and given a proper send-off."

Cultures of the World: Indonesia, 78–79.

Latex harvested from rubber trees is used to produce many rubber products.

(SEHL uh beez), also known as Sulawesi, which is east of Borneo. And the second-largest island in the world is New Guinea, but only the western half, an area called Irian Jaya (IHR-ee-ahn JAH-yah), belongs to Indonesia.

The rest of Indonesia consists of two island chains, the first of which is the Lesser Sunda Islands east of Java, which stretch from Bali to Timor. Timor (TEE mohr) is the largest of the Lesser Sunda Islands. Bali (BAH lee) is the most famous of the Lesser Sundas. It is a Hindu refuge in a sea of Muslims.

The second chain of islands is the **Moluccas** (muh LUHK uhz), which were at one time called the Spice Islands. This archipelago is located between the Philippines in the north, New Guinea in the east, Timor in the south, and Celebes in the west.

Although 39 percent of the Indonesian work force is employed in agriculture, that sector provides only about 15 percent of the GDP. Indonesia is second in the world in coconuts and fourth in the world in coffee. Other important crops include rice, cassava (tapioca), peanuts, rubber, cocoa, copra, and palm oil. The bulk of the GDP, however, is provided by a balance of industry and services. Major industries include oil and natural gas, textiles, apparel and footwear, mining, cement, chemical fertilizers, plywood, and tourism. Indonesia's biggest trade partners are Singapore and Japan.

Indonesia is a republic with a unicameral legislature as well as a president and a vice president who are elected by the people for five-year terms. Several political parties vie for influence in the government.

Timor-Leste

Timor (TEE mohr) is the largest of the Lesser Sunda Islands. Following the end of Portuguese rule in 1974, civil war between West and East Timor and Indonesian supression resulted in the death of one hundred thousand Timorese people. In 1999, the Timorese people in East Timor began to demand independence from Indonesia and West Timor. In response, Indonesian forces in league with local militia from West Timor destroyed about 75 percent of the region's infrastructure and economy before the UN intervened to stop the fighting. The new country **Timor-Leste** ("East-East") gained international recognition in 2002.

This young country is quickly developing its great potential in agriculture, minerals, and oil and gas deposits. However, about 37 percent of the population lives in extreme poverty, and half of the population is illiterate. This has resulted in a huge gap between the very wealthy and the very poor, with virtually no middle class. In addition, the new government is struggling to rebuild infrastructure and reduce corruption.

Timor-Leste, one of only two nations in Asia with a Roman Catholic majority (80.5 percent), had four centuries of Portuguese rule. The Catholic Church also retained strong support as a result of its support of independence. Traditional spiritism also has a strong presence at 11 percent of the population. Evangelical Christianity represents about 2 percent of the population and has experienced a modest growth. One of the most effective ministries to date has been from foreign Christians who witness as they work in this war-ravaged country, helping the people with medical and educational needs.

The Philippines

The Philippine (FIHL uh peen) Islands lie due east of Vietnam across the South China Sea, south of Taiwan, north of the Moluccas, and west of the Philippine Sea. The 7,107 islands stretch across more than a thousand miles and make up a land area a little larger than Arizona. The two largest islands are like bookends for the other islands, Luzon in the north and Mindanao in the south.

Luzon (loo ZAHN) is the largest and most populous island. It includes both the capital, Manila (muh NIH luh; pop. 1.7 million), and the largest city in the country, Quezon City (pop. 2.8 million). Luzon and the islands around it produce rice, tobacco, sugar cane, coconuts, bananas, and mahogany. **Mindanao** (mihn dihn NOW) is the second-largest island, and its largest city is the port of Davao (dah VOW; pop. 1.5 million). It is a leading producer of abaca, a strong fiber used to make rope.

Only about nine hundred of the seven thousand islands between Luzon and Mindanao are inhabited. The seven largest islands produce rice, corn, and coconuts. The oldest and largest city among those islands is Cebu (say BOO; pop. 2.6 million), a port to which professional fishermen bring their catches.

The islands of the Philippines are in the middle of the "typhoon belt." They are usually affected by fifteen typhoons a year and are hit directly by about five or six a year. The various islands also are susceptible to landslides, volcanoes, earthquakes, and tsunamis.

The Philippine Islands were a Spanish colony from the time of their discovery by Ferdinand Magellan in 1521 until the Spanish Empire was defeated in the Spanish-American War in 1898, giving the United States control of the country. Japanese occupation during World War II delayed the Philippines' scheduled independence, but it was finally gained in 1946. The influence of Spain is still heavily felt, as 77 percent of the people identify with the Roman Catholic Church. Thirteen percent are Evangelical Christian. Six percent are Muslim. The Christian population has increased at rapid rate, and churches have matured to the point of sending thousands of missionaries and evangelists to spread the gospel abroad. Missionary efforts are enhanced by the number of Filipinos who live and work in many Asian and Middle Eastern countries.

Although 32 percent of the work force is employed in agriculture, that sector provides only about 12 percent of the GDP. The Philippines is a top producer of coconuts, pineapples, and bananas. Fifty-three percent of the work force is in services, and that sector provides 57 percent of the GDP. Industry—including electronics, garments, footwear, pharmaceuticals, chemicals, wood products, oil refining,

Residents of Davao participate in a holiday parade.

Cebu City

Body Talk

"Filipinos are a 'touchy' people in that relatives and close friends make a lot of physical contact in greeting and in conversation. A young Filipino greets an older person with a gesture of respect called *mano* (MAHN no), or 'hand.' The young person puts the back of the older person's hand on his or her forehead. . . .

"Filipinos do everything with a smile—they praise with a smile, criticize with a smile, condole with a smile, take life's trials with a smile. A confrontation is best avoided, but if it is necessary, a smile is the best way to start."

Cultures of the World: Philippines, 94–95.

Missions in Southeast Asia

Many countries in Southeast Asia are very poor nations. Missionaries to these countries face the challenge of knowing how to obey the Bible's commands to be generous to those in need and how to avoid the dangers in providing financial support to needy people. One danger is the perception that converting to Christianity is a means of moving up in the world. Such conversions are quickly abandoned when the person gains financial stability. Another danger is that Christianity is perceived as a religion only for poor people who need help. Another danger is that churches in these countries may not become independent and accept the responsibilities that a body of believers should take on if they remain dependent on foreign money.

A missionary to Cambodia who has thought about these matters explains how his family navigates these tricky decisions. For instance, if someone in his church is ill and racking up bills, he will not bail them out. He will wait for the church to act. If the church comes along and helps the person out, he will contribute as part of the church. Because he has more, he will contribute more, but not a great deal more. He does not want the missionary to be the solution to the problem. He wants the body of believers to minister together.

This does not mean that Christians cannot be generous in helping those in need. In some countries disaster strikes and people are found in dire and immediate need. Christians have often reached out and helped people with these pressing needs. The same can happen to individuals as well. One missionary met a woman with a tumor that placed her in dire need. He gave her significant financial help so she could receive medical care. She made a profession of faith and joined the church. Later, however, the tumor returned. The missionary asked the people of the church what should be done. They said that he should not provide the funds to help her this second time lest the unbelievers around think that becoming a Christian was tied to getting money from missionaries. Instead, the church people themselves ministered very generously to the woman.

These are the kinds of difficult situations that missionaries must think about as they minister among poorer people.

and fishing—brings in about a third of the GDP. The two major trade partners of the Philippines are Japan and the United States.

The Philippines is a republic with an elected president. It has a bicameral legislature with a House of Representatives and a Senate. A dozen or so political parties vie for influence in the government. The country's most stable period was the twenty-one-year rule of president Ferdinand Marcos, but it ended in 1986 with widespread accusations of corruption. Since then, the country has had several presidents and periodic coup attempts, the latest of which occurred in 2006. A vexing problem of the twenty-first century is the threat of Muslim terrorists in the southern regions of the nation.

Section Quiz

1. Which two Malaysian states are located on the island of Borneo?
2. Which country in the Malaysian archipelago is one of the busiest seaports by volume in the world?
3. What tiny country is located on Borneo's northwest side between the two Malaysian states?
4. What is the largest country (in both area and population) in Southeast Asia?
5. What are the names of the two largest islands of the Philippines?
★ Why does Singapore enjoy the highest GDP in Southeast Asia?

Chapter Review

Making Connections

1. Why are the monsoons important to Southeast Asia?
2. What crop is critical to all Southeast Asian countries?
3–5. Which three Southeast Asian countries were ruled by the French?
6. Which European country colonized the Indonesian islands?
7–9. Which three countries controlled the Philippines before it gained independence?

Developing Geography Skills

1. Based on the map on page 369, why would it be difficult to have a cohesive government and economy in Indonesia and the Philippines?
2. Why do you think five of the top ten rice-producing countries are located in Southeast Asia?

Thinking Critically

1. Evaluate the status of Christianity in five of the countries mentioned in this chapter.
2. What do the atrocities committed by the Khmer Rouge reveal about human nature?

Living in God's World

1. Family is very important for many who live in Southeast Asia. Elders are treated with honor, and parents are consulted about important decisions even by their adult children. Write a brief paragraph comparing this view of family life to the role of family in American culture. Evaluate both cultures from a biblical perspective.
2. This chapter contains a brief description of basic Buddhist beliefs. Other books provide discussions of greater depth. But when a missionary travels to Southeast Asia, he may find that the people he meets do not believe exactly what the books say Buddhists believe. They have many other folk beliefs as well. Write out a plan for how a missionary should learn about the actual beliefs of those he seeks to evangelize.

People, Places, and Things to Know

Indochina
insular countries
Malay Archipelago
archipelago
Irrawaddy River
"Golden Triangle"
nirvana
Siam
ASEAN
Mekong River
Khmer Rouge
Pol Pot
Hong (Red) River
Hanoi
Gulf of Tonkin
Haiphong
South China Sea
Ho Chi Minh City
Ho Chi Minh
Dien Bien Phu
domino theory
Kuala Lumpur
Java
Jakarta
Moluccas
Timor-Leste
Luzon
Mindanao

EAST ASIA

16

$\mathcal{T}$he countries of East Asia (with the exception of North Korea) are vibrant economic giants that compete with the best of the Western nations. Millions of people have been lifted out of poverty with the rise in industrialization. Although the Far East has adopted many Western ideas about industry and government, this openness has resulted in high levels of industrial pollution. Sadly, it is often the poorest people who are most affected by the pollution. In the case of China, relaxed economic controls have resulted in a degree of political and personal freedom, but by Western standards the Chinese still are not free.

Geographically, East Asia is the area bounded by the Pacific Ocean on the east, Russia on the north, the Indian subcontinent and Southeast Asia on the south, and Southwest Asia on the west. The region, which has coasts on the Yellow Sea, the East China Sea, the South China Sea, and the Pacific Ocean, is sometimes called the **Pacific Rim**.

It is a region of extremes and contrasts. Its climate ranges from tropical to subarctic. Its terrain ranges from fertile valleys to dry deserts. Its economic condition varies from modern countries similar in material wealth to the United States to the most backward, most secretive country in the world. The governments of the region range from those that allow great personal liberties to those that repress all individual freedom or initiative. Attitudes toward religion range from toleration and openness to total closure to the gospel. For these and other reasons, East Asia makes an interesting study.

History of Relations Between East and West

Until the last few centuries, the West knew very little about the exotic lands of the Far East. The customs, religions, and even appearance of the East Asian people differed from those of Western people. Towering mountains, harsh deserts, and treacherous seas isolated the nations of East Asia from the rest of the world. Left alone, these nations built advanced civilizations that endured for centuries.

During the nineteenth and twentieth centuries, however, the ancient societies of the East came face to face with the industrialized West, which resulted in revolutionary changes to every area of life in the Far East. The nations responded in vastly different ways to the perceived threat of the West, and they are still reaping the consequences of their choices. Two nations—China and Korea—split in two, between Communist and republican governments.

East Asia Fast Facts						
Country	Capital	Area (sq. mi.)	Pop. (2013) (M)	Pop. Density (per sq. mi.)	Per Capita GDP ($US)	Life Span
China	Beijing	3,705,407	1,349.59	364	$9,100	74.84
North Korea	Pyongyang	46,540	24.72	531	$1,800	69.2
South Korea	Seoul	38,502	48.96	1,271	$32,400	79.3
Japan	Tokyo	145,914	127.25	872	$36,200	83.91

I. China

China is slightly smaller in area than the United States. Only Russia, Canada, and the United States surpass its immensity. Like America, it has some of its continent's richest farmlands and driest deserts. Also as in America, most of China's most populous cities are in the east. However, China has almost five times the population of the United States. Indeed, one out of six people in the world lives in China.

About 92 percent of the people in China are called **Han** (HAHN). Their language is one of the oldest in the world. Although it has many spoken dialects (e.g., Mandarin, Cantonese, Shanghiese, Fozhou, and Hokkien-Taiwanese), the written language is the same throughout China and helps to unite the nation. To improve communication, the government has made Mandarin the official spoken language.

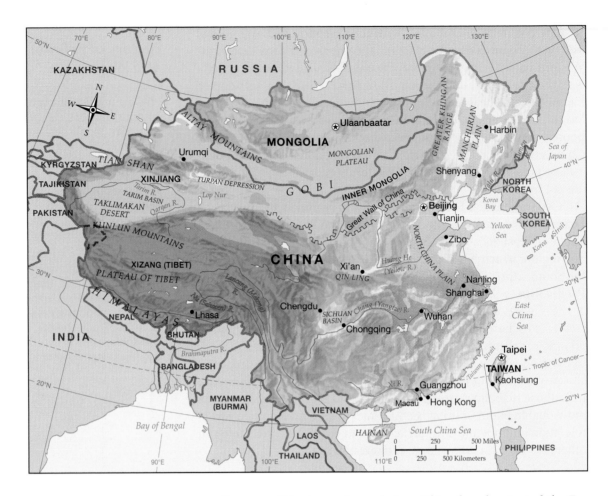

The Threat of Christianity

When foreign missionaries were forced to leave China in 1949 as the Communists seized power, there was great concern about the fledgling Christian church. However, six decades of brutal Communism and severe persecution have failed to halt the tremendous growth of Christianity in China. Currently there are just over one hundred million Chinese people who embrace some form of Christianity. Since persecution continues and the Chinese government has vowed to eliminate underground churches, the Chinese church is made up of those willing to endure such persecution.

Why are the Communists so concerned about the growth of Christianity? One answer lies in the fact that the Communist Party in China boasts a membership of eighty million. Thus, Christians outnumber Communists. The leaders of China know that if Christians united for any political reason, including support for a representative government, they could overthrow the Communist regime. While no such effort is known to exist, the mere possibility worries those in power. This fear fuels their determination to stamp out a growing Christian presence in China.

Because of its size and population, China has dominated the Far East. The ancient Chinese viewed their land as the "Middle Kingdom"—the geographical and cultural center of the universe, surrounded by barbarians. China has a recorded history of over four thousand years, longer than that of any other nation. Although China has been conquered at times, the conquerors have adopted Chinese ways and not vice versa. The Chinese have made a number of important contributions, including gunpowder, paper, printing, and the magnetic compass, although the West later developed these discoveries to their full potential.

The climate of China ranges from tropical in the south to subarctic in the north. It is susceptible to frequent typhoons (about five a year), floods, droughts, earthquakes, and tsunamis. Its terrain is mostly mountainous, but it also has high plateaus, deserts (in the west), plains, deltas, and hills (mostly in the east).

The North China Plain

The **North China Plain** is the heart of the People's Republic of China and is sometimes called the "real" China. It extends from just north of Beijing southward to just below Shanghai and inland approximately 500 miles. The plain supports countless villages and many of the forty-nine Chinese cities that exceed one million people. The plain also offers petroleum and coal. China is the world's leading coal producer, and it ranks fifth in petroleum.

Chinese farmers practice intensive farming, a form of subsistence farming in fertile areas that allows many individuals to raise crops on a small plot of land. The crops differ, however, depending on the climate. A major climate barrier is the **Qin Ling Mountains**, which run east to west across the middle of the plain, rising to 13,474 feet. The two main rivers of China, the **Huang He** (HWAHNG HEH; formerly the Yellow River) in the north and the **Chang Jiang** (CHAHNG JYANG; formerly the Yangtze River) in the south, flow on either side of the range.

The Huang He

The dry north is good for growing wheat, corn, and soybeans. China is a leading producer of all these crops. Because of the monsoons, the climate south of the Qin Ling Mountains is much wetter than the climate to the north. The people there grow rice and tobacco and raise swine. China is the world's top producer of both rice and tobacco. It is also a leading producer of cotton, apples, peaches, and pears.

The Huang He flows through five of China's twenty-three provinces. According to legend, Chinese civilization began in this river valley about 2200 BC but was made up of several small, warring states. Finally, in 221 BC, one of the local rulers defeated the other states and united all of China for the first time. Emperor Qin Shi Huang, the "first emperor," founded the Qin (CHIN) dynasty, from which the name *China* is derived. A **dynasty** is a series of rulers who come from the same family. Qin Shi Huang ruled with an iron fist and burned books that he feared might cause rebellion, so the government censorship so prevalent in China today is nothing new to the Chinese.

The city that is now Xi'an (SHEE AHN), on a tributary of the Huang He, was the capital of the Chinese dynasties for more than a thousand years, with only brief interruptions. The temples and tombs around the city include the tomb of the first emperor, which is guarded by the now-famous terra cotta army. The city was the eastern end of the Silk Road, and Marco Polo arrived there in 1275.

The Extended Family in China

The extended family is a vital part of Chinese culture. In China's crowded cities three generations often live together. In rural areas the extended family includes cousins, aunts, uncles, and those related by marriage. In Chinese culture, the greater the age, the greater the respect. So the elderly are treated with great honor and are cared for until they die.

Babies are also considered a treasure in China. One of the results of China's disastrous one-child policy is the special attention given to the family's child. The child receives almost royal attention, and many families generously provide for the wishes of their child.

A life-size terra cotta army guards the tomb of the emperor in Xi'an.

Three Gorges Dam

Both the Huang He and the Chang begin high on the Plateau of Tibet in Qinghai, the largest and least populated of China's provinces. As the Chang River drops down into the North China Plain, it passes through a series of three gorges, known as the Ichang Gorges. Scenic limestone cliffs rise two thousand feet above the rushing water.

In the 1990s, Communist China began a controversial project to dam the river and flood the gorges. The Three Gorges Dam became fully operational in 2012 (with the exception of a ship lift). When it reaches capacity, it will generate electricity equivalent to eighteen nuclear power plants. At 1.3 miles long and 607 feet high, it will be the most powerful dam in the world,

even more powerful than Itaipu (Brazil) and almost three times as powerful as America's most powerful dam, Grand Coulee.

The project is controversial in that it involved the involuntary displacement of at least 1.3 million people, whose homes would be submerged by the reservoir. Several historical sites will also be lost. Some environmentalists have condemned the destruction of the beautiful scenery, the increasing threat of landslides in the region, and the loss of habitat for the river dolphin. Others have expressed concern about sewage from former factory sites that is polluting the reservoir. Upstream, the people of Chongqing are concerned about buildup of sediment in the city's harbor. The cost of constructing the dam has already exceeded its initial $17 billion estimate, and the final cost may approach $24 billion (although sources vary). Chinese authorities optimisticially predict that the cost will be recovered within the first ten years of energy production.

The Three Gorges Dam project has been called the largest construction project since the building of the Great Wall.

The Chang Jiang

The southern river of the North China Plain is the Chang Jiang, which flows through four provinces. Its enormous drainage basin encompasses an area nearly the size of Mexico. At 3,880 miles long, the Chang is the world's third-largest river, the longest river in Asia, and the most important river in China. It is known as China's "main street." Ocean liners can travel seven hundred miles inland to Wuhan (pop. 4.6 million), and smaller vessels are able to navigate as far as one thousand miles inland. The Chang is one of the busiest waterways on earth.

The upper Chang follows the western boundary of Sichuan (SEHTCH WAHN) Province, the most populous of all China's provinces. The Chang flows through the large **Sichuan Basin** before it leaves the mountains. The mountain-ringed basin contains two large cities, Chengdu (pop. 14 million) and Chongqing (pop. 29 million). The Sichuan Basin is one of the richest agricultural regions in China. Crops of rice as well as fruit, cotton, and tea grow on terraces cut from the hillsides.

Nanjing, with more than 8 million people, lies downstream on the Chang River, only about 150 miles from the coast. When the Ming dynasty came to power in 1368, the emperor moved the capital to Nanjing.

Downtown Shanghai is an ultramodern city.

Shanghai

China's largest city, **Shanghai** (SHANG HYE; pop. 23 million), lies on the Huang Pu River near the mouth of the Chang. Its textile mills make cloth from the cotton of the plain, and nearby iron mines provide raw materials for heavy manufacturing. Shanghai is now a center of world trade and banking.

The port at Shanghai is one of the busiest in the world by volume and handles much of China's international trade. The city's growth began in 1842, when the British forced China to open it to foreigners. Shanghai took on a Western appearance as foreigners built homes, churches, and office buildings. Shanghai was the headquarters of Hudson Taylor's China Inland Mission. Today most of Shanghai's residents are factory workers who dress and eat well by Chinese standards. Communist China has declared Shanghai and several other cities special economic zones for trade. Very little of the wealth being generated in such cities is making it into the interior of the country. However, the people in the rural interior, most of whom are farmers, are beginning to see economic improvement.

As a major fishing center, Shanghai contributes to China's ranking as the world's leading fish producer. China acquires much of its catch through aquaculture. Farmers raise fish and shellfish in tanks, ponds, reservoirs, estuaries, and shallow bays. China's coasts offer shrimp, salmon, eel, mackerel, and sardines.

Beijing

With a population of 20.7 million, **Beijing** (BAY ZHIHNG; formerly Peking) is China's second-largest city and the sixteenth largest in the world. Located on the North China Plain, it is only about thirty-five miles south of the Great Wall. It has served as China's capital since 1267, except for several brief periods. For centuries, Beijing has been and still is the country's educational and cultural center. Since the Communist takeover in 1949, it has become industrialized and now produces iron, tools, and textiles.

Death in China

Those who die in the crowded Chinese cities are cremated after being placed in a glass coffin for viewing. Following cremation, the loved one's ashes are placed in a container and stored at the crematorium or taken to the home of a family member.

In rural areas of China, burial is preferred rather than cremation. Families prepare for death by building ornate coffins several years before the oldest person is likely to die. Once the coffin is finished, the family stores it in the house. While this seems strange in our culture, it is intended to comfort the aging family member with the knowledge that the family will care for him when he dies.

Many Chinese take special precautions when a family member dies. The statues of deities are covered with red paper to avoid exposure to the deceased or the coffin. Mirrors are removed because many believe that a person who sees the reflection of the coffin will soon have a death in the family. Family and friends burn sacrificial gifts, including paper money, paper houses, and paper automobiles. They believe these gifts will ensure that the deceased is comfortable in the next life.

Earth Matters: "No Car Day" In China

Beijing celebrated "No Car Day" with a traffic jam!

September 22 is "no car day" in Beijing, China. Citizens in Beijing, Shanghai, and over 100 other Chinese cities are urged to bike, walk, or take public transportation to work. The problem is that most people drive their cars anyway! The first annual "no car day" was on September 22, 2007 in preparation for the 2008 summer Olympics held in Beijing. The purpose was to improve air quality for a country known for suffocating air pollution. In fact, 16 of the 20 most polluted cities in the world are in China.

This pollution initially comes from hundreds of power plants that burn cheap, dirty forms of coal. The goal is to economically generate electricity for an energy-hungry nation struggling to provide for its vast population. Pollution from these plants has already had a devastating effect. Some industrial communities in China now have cancer rates that are much higher than the national average, giving rise to the term *cancer villages*. As millions of Chinese continue flocking to the cities, the burden of power needs is concentrated in fewer places. This leads to more pollution in cities, often from automobiles. Despite China's strict environmental controls, there is little enforcement at the local level. A growing number of citizens in the cancer villages and in the big cities of China are imploring government officials to reduce the growing air and water pollution, but change is slow in coming. In the meantime, cancer deaths have increased in China by 80 percent in the past thirty years. Leaders must take action to wisely use God-given resources, with a mind for the future, in ways that help their most precious resource, their people.

China is a major producer of pollution.

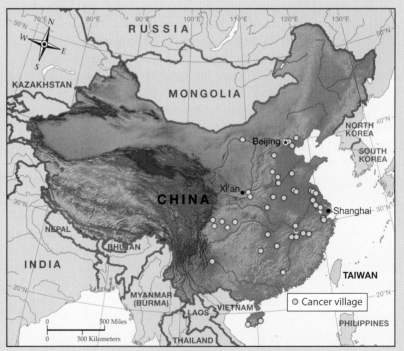

Most of the city walls have been torn down to make way for roads. The city streets are thronged with cars, buses, and bicycles as the people commute to and from work. In the heart of Beijing is the **Forbidden City**, where the Chinese emperors once lived. To

A moat and a wall separate the city of Beijing from the interior of the Forbidden City.

the north is the Gate of Heavenly Peace, which overlooks **Tiananmen Square**. Leaders review parades displaying the country's military might on the thirty-four-acre grounds, the largest square in the world. In 1989, Tiananmen Square became a symbol of the Chinese people's dissatisfaction with the Communist regime. (See the section on the government and economy of China.)

Tianjin

Tianjin (tee an JIN), the port for Beijing, lies at the mouth of the Hai River. Tianjin (pop. 13.55 million) is at the north end of the Grand Canal, which permits inland shipping to Shanghai. When it opened in 486 BC, the canal was the longest artificial waterway in the world. More than one thousand miles long, it linked China's two largest rivers. The canal has since fallen into disrepair, although one-third of it is still open to barges.

Shanghai, Beijing, and Tianjin are China's leading industrial centers. Each is a distinct political unit called a special municipality and is not part of any province.

Section Quiz

1. Which geographic region is considered the heart of the "real" China?
2. What are the two major rivers of China?
3. Which Chinese city has the greatest population?
4. What is China's capital city?
★ What are some of the environmental consequences resulting from construction of the Three Gorges Dam?

Manchuria

Because the three provinces of Manchuria—named for the **Manchus** (man CHOOS), the last non-Han Chinese to control China—are located northeast of the Great Wall, the Chinese commonly refer to them as the Northeast. The broad Manchurian Plain is an extension of the North China Plain. Crops such as soybeans, millet, corn,

> **Find It!**
> **Tiananmen Square**
> 39.903° N, 116.391° E
> (Make sure you have the 3D buildings box checked.)

Chinese police wrestle a man to the ground after chasing him through Tiananmen Square in Beijing on July 20, 2001.

The Great Wall of China

Of the architectural wonders of the world, the Great Wall of China is certainly one of the most impressive. It was built primarily during the fourteenth to the seventeenth centuries to protect China from invasions by the Mongols and Turkic tribes. It could not prevent invaders from scaling the wall, but it could prevent them from entering China with war horses or from escaping easily with plunder.

The wall began as several walls built in local areas of Mongolia and Manchuria in the third century BC. The bulk of the construction, however, was the joining of those walls where gaps existed. The wall is made of materials that were easily available in each region. In some places it is made of granite; in other places it is made of bricks; and in a few places it is made of double rows of logs tied together, with the space between tightly packed with soil. Because so

many workers died while building the wall, it has been called the longest cemetery in the world and "the long graveyard." Contrary to popular belief, however, the dead workers were not

buried within the wall but in graves nearby.

Watchtowers were constructed at intervals along the wall, and guards communicated among the towers using smoke signals. Battle forts were also constructed at strategic points along the wall, and guards assembled there if they were driven from the watchtowers. Ultimately, the wall was breached by the Manchus, who gained entry not by scaling the wall or tearing it down but by bribing a Chinese general to open the gates. Because of modern weaponry, of course, the wall is of no strategic value; it is merely a historical tourist attraction. Except in tourist areas, where preservation has been done, the wall is generally in disrepair.

The most recent measurements indicate that the Ming walls were 5,500 miles long when obstacles including trenches, hills, and rivers are included.

Find It!

Great Wall of China

40.676° N, 117.232° E

(Ground view is not available.)

China's Written Language

The next time you complain about having to study for a subject, remember that the Chinese have about fifty thousand characters in their written language. About three thousand of these are commonly used, and it is doubtful that anyone knows all fifty thousand.

Chinese students learn to write by mastering eleven basic strokes. These strokes are written in a proper sequence. Students spend many hours practicing dots, dashes, and strokes. Then they learn how to form words. Simple words can have a single stroke while complex words may have as many as thirty strokes.

apples, and spring wheat grow well in the relatively short growing season despite the severe winters and dry summers. The forested mountains to the north and east contain much valuable timber. Shenyang, with more than 8.11 million people, is Manchuria's largest city and its industrial center. Jonathan Goforth (1859–1936) was a missionary to Manchuria under the China Inland Mission.

Events of the nineteenth century humiliated the Manchu dynasty and angered many Chinese people. Defeats in the Opium Wars and the Sino-Japanese War caused much resentment of foreign intrusion in China. The Boxers, a secret society known for its ceremonial practice of shadowboxing, struck back in 1899 in a series of uprisings that became known as the Boxer Rebellion. Infuriated by anything they perceived as foreign or anti-Chinese, the Boxers attacked Christian missionaries and Chinese converts. Many believers were killed when they would not renounce Christ. Eight foreign nations, including the United States, sent in an armed force and put down the uprising. Although the Manchus attempted to maintain power by making reforms after the rebellion, the dynasty collapsed in 1912.

Manchuria has been a hotly contested region ever since. The Japanese invaded and occupied it in 1937. As the Japanese were driven out, the Communist Chinese occupied it, and it became a Communist stronghold. During the 1960s, when relations between the Soviets and the Chinese soured, the two countries massed troops along its border. Tensions were relieved once the Soviet Empire was dissolved.

The Southern Uplands

Eight populous provinces lie south of the Chang River basin in southeast China. The Southern Uplands harbor more ethnic groups and languages than any other region in China.

Green hills and mountains characterize the Southern Uplands. Rice grows throughout the region, but the region also contributes sweet potatoes, tea, and sugar cane. The hills and mountains produce large quantities of tungsten, phosphates, zinc, iron ore, lead, vanadium, tin, and manganese.

China's Southern Uplands are also one of the few places in the world that produce silk. Silkworms spin a cocoon consisting of one long, light, strong thread, which the Chinese weave into silk. The worms require a warm climate and a diet of leaves from mulberry trees. For many centuries, the Chinese kept the production technique secret.

The Southern Uplands include China's southernmost province, **Hainan** (HYE NAN), which is the largest island in China. It is the source of China's natural rubber. The island also produces bananas and pepper.

The **Xi** (SHEE) **River** (West River) is the transportation hub of the Southern Uplands. Its volume of flow is nearly three times that of the Huang He as a result of heavy monsoon rains. The river's delta is the largest arable plain in the Southern Uplands. The deep, rich soil and the warm, moist climate make the delta extremely productive. The year-round growing season allows farmers to reap two crops a year. Tea, fruits, and sugar cane are grown there.

Located on the delta of the Xi is **Guangzhou** (GWANG JOH; formerly Canton). With 12.7 million people, Guangzhou is the region's largest city. The people speak the Cantonese dialect. Westerners are familiar with Cantonese cooking, which offers a variety of steamed fresh vegetables.

Guangzhou is an important industrial and transportation center. The Xi River, railroads to the interior, and a deep-water port make it a center for international trade.

Foreign nations founded two colonies on China's southern coast. The British founded **Hong Kong**, which is about ninety miles southeast of Guangzhou. During the nineteenth century, the British forced China to cede Hong Kong Island and the tip of Kowloon Peninsula. Its deep-water port made it an ideal trading center for heavy sea traffic in the South China Sea. Business boomed under its low taxes and political freedom, and the colony grew rapidly. The colony reverted to China in 1997.

Hong Kong's economy is one of the strongest and most varied in Asia. Although it is only four hundred square miles in area (about six times the size of Washington, D.C.), its seven million people make it a bustling center of trade, finance, manufacturing, and tourism. Today, Hong Kong has one of the busiest ports (by total containers handled) in the world.

Hong Kong's people hope that China will keep its promise to protect Hong Kong's way of life for fifty years (the "one country, two systems" policy). For the most part, China has maintained a

Christian Influence in Hong Kong

While 60 percent of the people of Hong Kong follow traditional Chinese religions, such as Buddhism, and 22 percent have no religious affiliation, Christians have established a significant foothold in Hong Kong. Representing about 10 percent of the population, Christians operate most of the schools and about 25 percent of the hospitals. Christians in Hong Kong reach out to the elderly, the poor, and foreigners through their social organizations. To date, the government has not limited the opportunities for Christians to serve the people and witness to them as they meet their needs.

These social outreaches in addition to traditional outreach through local churches have led to numerical growth of believers and multiplication of congregations. However, Christian leadership remains a great need; up to one-third of the congregations lack a pastor. Thirty-five Bible colleges in Hong Kong are training future pastors and laymen to fill this void.

Hong Kong's streets are crowded, especially in the shopping district.

Sun Yat-sen

Chiang Kai-shek

Mao Zedong

hands-off policy regarding the economy and internal affairs. It has attempted a few encroachments on freedoms, however, and reserves all defense and foreign policy matters for the mainland government. Christians are particularly concerned about whether Communist China will soon restrict church activities as well.

The second colony was **Macau** (muh COW), the oldest European colony in Asia, which the Portuguese founded in 1557. It lies across an estuary from Hong Kong. Its six square miles (about one-tenth the size of Washington, D.C.) consist of a small peninsula and two small islands. The backbone of Macau's economy is apparel and tourism, especially gambling, which provides 70 percent of the government's revenue. Macau reverted to China in 1999.

Government and Economy

China has a Communist government and only one political party—the Communists. It has a unicameral legislature called the National People's Congress, but it is a rubber stamp for the Chinese Communist Party. Yet, China has the second-largest economy in the world (behind only the United States). It leads the world in the production of many products and industries. But almost half of its work force is employed in agriculture, which contributes less than 15 percent of the GDP. Large disparities exist between the income of coastal populations and rural populations. And overall, the GDP lags behind many less-developed economies. How did it come to this?

Although in 1912 **Sun Yat-sen** (SOON YAHT-SEHN) had established a republican form of government and was followed by **Chiang Kai-shek** (JYAHNG KYE-SHEK), corruption and strife within the Nationalist (Kuomintang) Party caused dissension in the country. **Mao Zedong** (MOU DZUH-DONG) led the Communist Red Army in a civil war that resulted in the defeat of the Nationalist army. Chiang, his army, and the Kuomintang escaped to Taiwan, an island about one hundred miles off the coast of China in the East China Sea. Mao proclaimed the birth of the People's Republic of China (also known as Communist China or Red China) on October 1, 1949, in Tiananmen Square.

He immediately began enacting ruthless programs he thought would strengthen the economy. First, he executed more than fifty thousand wealthy landlords, abolished private property, and redistributed the land to create collective farms, or communes, on which the peasants worked as virtual slaves under government supervision. In the **Great Leap Forward** of 1958, Mao further centralized farming and industrial activity. However, bad weather, discontented workers, and unwise decisions by inept bureaucrats resulted in poor crops and widespread famine.

To eliminate opposition, both real and potential, Mao launched the **Cultural Revolution** in 1966, sending overzealous gangs of young people throughout China in an anti-intellectual, anti-Christian rampage. Schools and universities were shut down. Millions of educated citizens died or were forcibly removed from the "corrupting" influence of the cities to be "purified" in rural communes and "re-education" camps. Schools did not reopen until 1970. Mao's programs proved to be disastrous failures.

After Mao died in 1976, his successor, **Deng Xiaoping** (DUNG SHOU-PING), began to change China's direction. He vigorously pursued economic modernization. Deng encouraged students to enroll in Western universities to learn how to improve industry and economy. He also permitted some citizens to own private gardens and businesses and opened China to foreign markets.

In the late 1980s, communism in Europe teetered on the brink of collapse. Chinese students began protesting in Beijing, seeking increased freedoms, especially political freedom and freedom of expression. In Tiananmen Square, they erected a thirty-foot replica of the Statue of Liberty. But on June 4, 1989, soldiers and tanks seized control of the square, wounding or killing as many as five thousand people. In spite of widespread coverage of the massacre by the world media, the Communists denied that anything had happened. Thousands of protestors were imprisoned in labor camps and re-education centers.

After Tiananmen Square, however, the Communists began to institute dramatic economic reforms in the major cities. They allowed private businesses to develop and promoted industry, especially in the high-tech computer fields. Communist leaders encouraged foreign investment. They opened Chinese markets and sought greater international trade. Business and personal wealth increased dramatically. Foreign capital came pouring into China. Major cities witnessed the opening of name-brand business franchises, such as McDonald's and Walmart.

Although some Chinese economic freedoms have increased, by Western standards the people are still repressed politically and religiously. They still have no voice in their government, and only one political party is recognized. Although they have access to much more information via the Internet, the government censors that too, the way it has always censored regular media (newspapers, television, radio, and theater).

China's recent history has been one of suppression or severe restriction of religious activity. When Communist authorities are able to do so, they arrest and outlaw religious groups such as the Falun Gong or underground church leaders. However, when suppression fails, the political leaders attempt to control religious activity through state-sanctioned groups, such as the Three-Self Patriotic Movement or the Catholic Patriotic Association. Protestants or Catholics have been pressured to join one of these groups or suffer persecution. Yet the number of Christians, who currently represent about 8 percent of the Chinese population, continues to multiply. Underground churches in China have matured to the point of sending missionaries to neighboring countries where Western missionaries cannot go. Many of these Chinese missionaries go to these fields anticipating a martyr's death.

This Walmart in Beijing is indicative of the economic changes taking place in China.

An American Teacher In China

The Bednarskis lived in China for a few years while Aaron served as a teacher. This is an account from Mrs. Bednarski.

As I reflect upon our time in China, I realize there weren't a lot of cognizant adaptations to the culture in order to minister effectively. Aaron's students were attracted initially because we were foreigners, and they wanted to learn our language and culture.

One pastor's wife there made a comment to me that struck my heart. She advised that I be willing to let the Chinese help me. Instead of always seeking to help them, I needed the humility to accept what they could offer.

We learned to appreciate their holidays, like the New Year. A group of teachers came to teach us how to make dumplings, the food always present at their gatherings. It takes hours to make these, and so we had plenty of time for profitable discussions.

We invited our students over to teach us some Chinese traditions. They loved sharing their origami, other childhood games, stories, etc. Listening to them builds trust, and they're more open to come to us with questions.

When we first got to China, our emphasis was on what we could teach them about America, but years down the road, our focus was on them and their lives. I wished we had known the benefit of valuing their culture earlier on.

Section Quiz

1. China is home to which of the world's architectural wonders?
2. Which geographic region of China has more ethnic groups and languages than any other?
3. Which former British colony did China regain in 1997?
4. Name two American businesses that have franchises in China?
* Describe the disastrous reforms of Mao Zedong.

China's Autonomous Regions

China has five autonomous (self-governing) regions, twenty-three provinces (one of which is disputed), three special municipalities, and several Special Economic Zones and Special Administrative Regions. Each **autonomous region** offers self-rule to a minority, but these minority groups have very limited powers. China has fifty-five ethnic minorities, but only five have been given autonomous regions. The island of Taiwan has never been recognized by the Chinese Communists as an independent nation—they consider it a recalcitrant province—and the United Nations admits only China, not Taiwan, to its membership. The United States government, although having good relations with Taiwan, operates on a "one China" policy as well.

Guangxi

The autonomous region of **Guangxi** (GWAHNG SHEE) is on the coast at the Tonkin Gulf and the border with Vietnam. China's largest minority, the **Zhuang** (JWAHNG), live in Guangxi, with an estimated population of 17 million. The Zhuang are ethnic Thai people who speak a northern Thai dialect. Many of the Zhuang also speak Cantonese.

This region is of one of China's least-developed areas and one of the least evangelized. Most of the people follow the traditional ancestral worship, while others pratice Buddhism. To date, one of the most effective means of evangelism has been a combination of radio outreach and showings of the JESUS film. The New Testament is being translated into one of the main dialects.

Tibet (Xizang)

The Plateau of **Tibet**, also known as **Xizang** (SHEE DZAHNG) rises west of China's Southern Uplands. Many high peaks are in Tibet, including Mount Everest, which is on the border with Nepal. Called "the Roof of the World," Tibet has an average elevation that exceeds sixteen thousand feet.

Many of Asia's great rivers begin on the plateau and cut through parallel gorges within a space of one hundred miles, including the Indus, the Brahmaputra, the Chang, the Huang He, the Irrawaddy, and the Mekong.

Tibet is quite rugged and is one of the world's most isolated regions; consequently, Tibet is the least populated of all of China's political divisions. In fact, about four times more people live in Beijing than in all of Tibet. Only a few scattered valleys, where the climate is milder and the soil is suitable for cultivation, are habitable. The capital, **Lhasa** (LAH sah), lies in one such valley, the Tsangpo Valley.

Defended by the rugged mountains, the indigenous Tibetans enjoyed independence for most of their history. However, in 1950, Chinese Communist troops invaded Tibet and seized control. The Chinese army crushed a Tibetan uprising in 1959, destroyed Tibetan religious shrines, and looted temples. In 1965, much of the plateau became the autonomous region of Xizang, usually called Tibet. In 1987 and 1993, Tibetans staged protests against Communist rule. In response, Deng Xiaoping, the leader of the Chinese Communist Party at the time, instituted a "population transfer" policy whereby Chinese are immigrating to Tibet, threatening to make native Tibetans a minority in their own country. The Communists subsidized the

This tiny village in Tibet is on the border of the Yunnan province in China.

Potala Palace

The title *Dalai Lama* means "Ocean of Wisdom." The ruler of Mongolia, the khan, conferred this title on the leader of the Tibetan Buddhists after the khan's own conversion in the sixth century. In 1951, Communist China occupied Tibet, which was then ruled by the fourteenth Dalai Lama. He escaped to India eight years later.

A Buddhist king of Tibet from the seventh century built the original royal residence at the city of Lhasa. His palace sits on the Potala, or "Buddha's Mountain," overlooking the city. The fifth Dalai Lama began rebuilding **Potala Palace** in 1645. The new palace far exceeded the old ruins and rose thirteen stories. When the Dalai Lama died in 1682, the monks kept his death secret until the building was finished in 1694.

The massive palace has one thousand rooms, ten thousand shrines, and twenty thousand statues. The top floor serves as a secluded place for the Dalai Lama to meditate. Other floors provide living quarters, meditation halls, libraries, storerooms, and a school for monks. The palace also contains armories, the tombs of eight Dalai Lamas, torture chambers, and the Cave of Scorpions dungeon. The palace is now a museum.

settlers, building homes and setting up shops for them. The growing Chinese presence was intended to muffle Tibetan dissent.

Intensely religious, Tibetans follow a branch of Buddhism called Lamaism, which is led by a governmental and spiritual ruler called the **Dalai Lama** (DAH-lye LAH-mah). Tibetans worship each Dalai Lama as a reincarnation of Buddha. Before communism, the Dalai Lama ruled as a **theocrat** (one who rules by religious or divine authority) from Potala Palace in Lhasa. When the Chinese took over, he escaped to India and became head of "the Government of Tibet in Exile."

The current Dalai Lama is Tenzin Gyatso, the fourteenth Dalai Lama. He was formally recognized at age two as the reincarnation of the thirteenth Dalai Lama. Like the Roman Catholic pope, he is referred to by his followers as "His Holiness." Other terms applied to him include "Holy Lord, Gentle Glory, Compassionate, Defender of the Faith," "The Wishfulfilling Gem," and "The Presence."

The number of Tibetans who follow some form of Christianity is estimated to be around three thousand. Of this number, about one thousand are Evangelicals and the other two thousand are Roman Catholics. As in Guangxi, the most effective means of evangelism has included a combination of radio outreach and showings of the JESUS film. In addition, the Tibetan Storytelling Project has been used to communicate the gospel using Tibetan art, songs, and rhythmic speech.

Xinjiang

Xinjiang (SHIN JYANG) covers an area the size of Alaska in northwest China, making it by far the largest of China's political divisions. Like Tibet, this large autonomous region has high mountains.

The Dalai Lama is revered in Tibet as a reincarnation of Buddha.

The Taklimakan Desert might be the driest area in Asia.

The Kunlun Mountains form its southern border with Tibet, and the Tien Shan (tee-EHN SHAHN), or Heavenly Mountains, cross the middle of the region.

Unlike Tibet, however, Xinjiang consists mostly of desert basins. The Tien Shan range divides the two large basins: the Tarim Basin in the south and the Junggar Basin in the north. Both basins are extremely dry because the high mountains almost completely block off any rain-bearing winds. Uyghurs and Kazakhs make up about 56 percent of the population and speak Turkic langauges. About 61 percent of the people identify as Muslim. In recent years, radicalization of Islam, along with discontent with Beijing's growing influence, has led to riots and talk of independence from China.

Christians represent about 4 percent of the population and number around 850,000. Most of these believers are Han Chinese, so they are culturally isolated from a majority of the people in Xinjiang. Despite opposition from the government on the pretext that conversion to Christianity will provoke the Muslim majority, house churches and congregations continue to grow.

Nei Mongol (Inner Mongolia)

The term *Mongolia* can refer to the region beyond the Great Wall of China. Inner Mongolia, or **Nei** (NAY) **Mongol**, is the part controlled by China, between the Great Wall and the country of Mongolia. Slightly smaller than Tibet, it stretches along two-thirds of the Mongolian border and southward to the Great Wall. The Gobi (GOH bee) Desert covers most of the region, but steppes (dry grasslands) mark its edges. The Chinese government has tried to increase the production of spring wheat, millet, and oats in this region. During the Middle Ages, the Mongol armies of Genghis Khan roamed the Gobi. Mongols still inhabit this autonomous region. They speak a Mongol language and are traditionally Tibetan Buddhists.

Ningxia

The last of China's five autonomous regions is **Ningxia** (NIHNG shee ah), a small region that lies just inside the Great Wall where the Huang He flows into Inner Mongolia. Sixty-five percent of the population is Han Chinese. The Hui people (34.5 percent of the population) who live in this region have the same physical features as the Han, but they follow Islam. Eighty percent of the Hui are Sunni Muslim.

The Hui people are the only minority recognized for religious rather than ethnic reasons. According to the government, to be Hui is to be Muslim. This makes conversion to Christianity extremely costly, because a Hui who becomes a Christian essentially loses his ethnic identity. Despite this obstacle, there are approximately one thousand Hui Christians in addition to Han Chinese Christians who make up 4 percent of the Ningxia population.

Taiwan

Taiwan (TYE WAHN) is an island in the South China Sea about one hundred miles off the coast of China. A mountain range reaching 13,113 feet forms the backbone of the island. The gentle western slopes descend to plains, which support most of the island's population of 23.3 million. Summer monsoons bring heavy rains and strong winds. Farmers have terraced many hills to make more land for growing rice. Chemical fertilizers and insecticides enable farmers to grow at least two crops of rice per year on the same field. Other crops include soybeans, sweet potatoes, bananas, and sugar.

In 1949, the Chinese Nationalists, led by Chiang Kai-shek, fled to Taiwan and reestablished their government at **Taipei** (TYE PAY). They also claimed two tiny islands off the coast of China—Quemoy (kwi MOY), which is due west of central Taiwan, and Matsu (maht SOO), which is northwest of northern Taiwan. Situated on the north end of Taiwan, Taipei is a busy industrial center of about 2.6 million people. Taipei's history reaches back less than three hundred years, but the city museums hold many priceless treasures of China's past, brought by Chiang Kai-shek from the mainland. Operating in a free market climate, the city and the island enjoy great personal and political freedom and economic prosperity.

The United Nations expelled Taiwan in 1971 and admitted Communist China. In 1978, the United States ended formal diplomatic relations with Taiwan. Nevertheless, U.S. warships continue to prowl the Taiwan Strait, guarding the former ally. Although the United States does not officially recognize its status as a country, Taiwan remains a major trading partner with America. Surprisingly, China is Taiwan's largest trading partner.

Although mainland China claims Taiwan, Taiwan insists that the legitimate government is in Taipei, not Beijing. Taiwan stops short of formally declaring independence for fear that China might invade. In fact, China has repeatedly warned Taiwan not to push for formal independence. While the potential for war with mainland China remains, the economies of these two states are intertwined. Taiwanese investment in mainland China has played a major role in China's recent economic success.

Taiwan allows freedom of religion, and most Taiwanese profess some form of religion. Sixty-one percent follow traditional Chinese religions, and 29 percent identify with Buddhism. About 6 percent follow some form of Christianity. Following several decades of little or no growth, churches have recently begun to experience sustained growth. Emphasizing personal evangelism and outreach, many congregations are overcoming resistance to the gospel and seeing many come to Christ, especially among migrant workers from the Philippines, Thailand, Indonesia, and Vietnam. There is great potential for these Christians to be trained and sent back to their countries as missionaries.

Mongolia (Outer Mongolia)

Mongolia is the ancestral home of a nomadic people called the Mongols. A hardy and independent people, they wandered over the grassy plateaus grazing their herds. They lived in portable round tents called gers. (The Russian term for the structures is *yurts*.) Made of layers of felt and covered with hides, these tents provided protection from extreme temperatures.

Genghis Khan and his grandson Kublai Khan ruled an area stretching from East Asia to Eastern Europe. The Mongols were among the most savage conquerors of all time. Skilled horsemen, they developed a system similar to the pony express, which linked

Taiwan Fast Facts					
Capital	Area (sq. mi.)	Pop. (2013) (M)	Pop. Density (per sq. mi.)	Per Capita GDP ($US)	Life Span
Taipei	13,892	23.3	1,677	$38,500	78.48

Taipei, the capital of Taiwan, is a thriving modern city.

These nomads are assembling their ger, and it will look like the lower photo when they are finished.

Mongolia Fast Facts					
Capital	Area (sq. mi.)	Pop. (2013) (M)	Pop. Density (per sq. mi.)	Per Capita GDP ($US)	Life Span
Ulaanbaatar	603,909	3.27	5.34	$5,400	68.63

the great khan in China with the outer reaches of his realm. The khan's heirs and his Mongol tribes never fully united, however, and the empire disintegrated.

Mongolia was controlled next by the Manchus. While China was distracted with its civil war, however, Russia stepped in to guarantee a measure of "independence" for Mongolia. The Communist Party came to power in 1924 and imposed harsh rule. As happened in other Central Asian countries, government authorities soon clamped down on Christian missionaries in Mongolia.

Mongolia's main urban center is the capital, **Ulaanbaatar** (OO lahn BAH tahr). A railroad now traverses the six hundred miles between Ulaanbaatar and the Great Wall of China near Beijing. The capital lies in the best grazing lands of north central and northeast Mongolia. Although few nomads remain, one-half of the people still raise livestock. The large farms raise mostly sheep but also camels, horses, cattle, and goats. Cattle and wool are the main exports.

The Gobi Desert covers five hundred thousand square miles in Mongolia and China. The desert averages an elevation of four thousand feet above sea level and extends over one thosand miles from southwest to northeast. The **Gobi Desert** is the world's coldest and most northerly desert. The soils are sandy but rarely form sand dunes. In the 1920s oviraptor eggs were discovered here, preserved by the dry soil. They were the first dinosaur eggs found.

Thirty-five percent of Mongolians are Buddhists, 26 percent have no religious affiliation, and 4 percent are Muslims. Prior to 1989 there were virtually no Christians in Mongolia. However, foreign missionaries have been very effective. There are currently at least forty thousand evangelical Christians in Mongolia, and the growth continues. Although the church is less than thirty years old in this country, congregations have matured to the point of sending missionaries to other parts of Mongolia. The rapid pace of establishing new church plants has left the churches short of trained leaders. Eight Bible colleges have been established in Mongolia to supply the great need for trained pastors and laymen. While there are some restrictions on foreign missionaries, Mongolia remains one of the greatest evangelistic opportunities in Asia.

Section Quiz

1. What region is called "The Roof of the World"?
2. Who leads the Tibetan Buddhists?
3. To what does the term *Mongolia* refer?
4. Which island does China claim as its own but exercise no control over?
5. What is the term for the portable houses in which many Mongolians live?
⋆ Why is it difficult for the Hui people to become Christians in Ningxia?

II. Korea

Korea is a peninsula that extends south from northeastern China. Mountains and hills cover most of the peninsula. The mountains provide mineral resources, and the two countries on the peninsula—North Korea and South Korea—rank among the leading producers of tungsten and smelted zinc. Both also produce coal, graphite, pig iron, and lead. South Korea is a major producer of cadmium.

Two rivers, the Yalu and the Tumen, divide the Korean Peninsula from China and Russia in the north. These rivers flow down from Korea's highest mountain, Mount Paektu, at the north end of the Hamgyong Mountains. South of the Hamgyongs are the Nangnim Mountains. Running down the east central portion of the peninsula are the **Taebaek Mountains**.

A minor coastal plain lies on the east coast in North Korea, but mountains dominate the eastern half of both countries. The most important coastal plain stretches along the western and southern coasts. It has most of the arable land on the peninsula, and its climate is

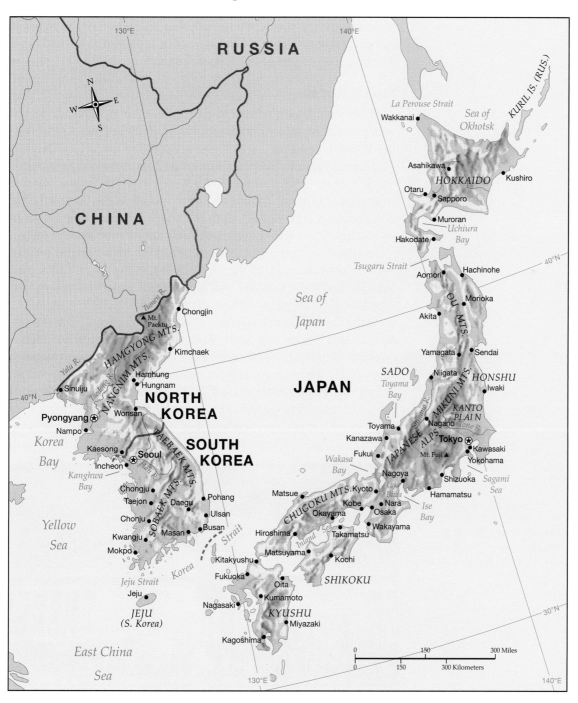

generally humid continental. Two-thirds of all Koreans live on that plain. All of the peninsula's major cities lie in that plain, including the respective capitals.

The turbulent history of the peninsula is due in part to its unfortunate geographic position. The Korean Peninsula is a bridge between the larger, more powerful countries on every side. It has been conquered at various times by China, the Mongols, Japan, and the Manchus. These invaders wanted not only to expand their borders but also to protect their respective countries from attack. However, the Koreans drove out each wave of invaders.

In 1910, Japan took control of Korea and began to govern it as a colony. The Japanese initiated an extensive modernization program, building railroads and developing industries. The Korean people, however, resented Japan's repressive government. After World War II, the country was divided at the thirty-eighth parallel. The United States supervised the southern half, and the Soviet Union oversaw the northern half. Free elections were then supposed to be held to set Korea back on its feet as an independent nation.

North Korea

The Soviet Union refused to give up its territory. Instead, the Soviets established a Communist satellite called the Democratic People's Republic of Korea.

Hoping to unify the peninsula under communism, the superior North Korean army invaded South Korea in 1950. United Nations troops, most of them Americans, were rushed to the peninsula just as the Allied forces were about to be pushed into the sea at Pusan in the southeastern portion of the peninsula and in time to avert certain defeat. Eventually, the UN forces repelled the invasion and pushed the North Korean army all the way back to the Yalu River. China then came to the North Koreans' aid, launching a massive invasion that forced the UN troops back down the peninsula.

After three years of warfare, a truce was declared. The boundary between North and South Korea, the thirty-eighth parallel, is a demilitarized zone (DMZ), a strip of land in which no troops or weapons are allowed. However, a peace treaty was never signed, so technically the two nations are still at war. Since the truce, America has continued to station thousands of soldiers in South Korea.

North Korea's Communist ruler, "Great Leader" Kim Il Sung, isolated his country from the rest of the world. The North Korean

Kim Il Sung is the central focus of Juche, or Kimilsungism, and the first stop of all visitors to Pyongyang is this 65-foot statue of him.

government owns all industries and farms and discourages all religion, except for worship of the state as represented by Kim Il Sung, a religion known as **Juche** (JOO chay), or **Kimilsungism**. His son, Kim Jong Il, succeeded him and continued his father's oppressive regime. North Koreans were required to refer to him as "the Dear Leader." Pictures of the two are everywhere in North Korea, from the sides of buildings to the front and rear interiors of every bus and streetcar in the country. Kim Jong Il, died in 2011. His son Kim Jong Un assumed the title of supreme leader and continues to lead the country in much the same direction as his father and grandfather did.

Despite opposition from most of the rest of the world—especially the countries of East Asia—North Korea continues to produce material for nuclear weapons. Most recently, the North Koreans have worked to produce multiple stage rockets with the potential of launching a nuclear warhead.

According to the *CIA World Factbook*, North Korea is "one of the world's most centrally planned and isolated economies." The capital, **Pyongyang** (pop. 3.14 million), has the only university. It is also the manufacturing center; all resources mined or produced are brought to factories there. The country has suffered food and fuel shortages every year for more than a decade, which has forced the North Korean Communists to seek foreign aid to survive a devastating famine.

About 15 percent of the land in North Korea is arable, and it has a temperate climate with rainfall being concentrated in the summer. The country, which is slightly smaller than Mississippi, produces vegetables, rice, potatoes, corn, cabbages, apples, fruit, soybeans, sweet potatoes, and beans. Yet, it cannot produce enough of these to feed its own people. Industries include military products, machines, chemicals, mining, metallurgy, textiles, and food processing. A large part of the GDP, however, is spent on the North Korean military rather than essential consumer goods.

The last six decades of Communist rule have resulted in the deaths of hundreds of thousands of Christians. There are an estimated 100,000 Christians in North Korean prisons or work camps. Yet the church survives underground and may number up to 250,000. Another 300,000 have fled North Korea and risked their lives traveling to China. There they must evade Chinese authorities who have orders to send them back to certain torture and possible death in North Korea. Radio ministries are transmitted to North Korea, and Bibles, New Testaments, and tracts are smuggled into the country. These tools, along with the witness of some foreign workers, are continuing to bear fruit in spite of the repressive and brutal regime.

Kim Jong Il

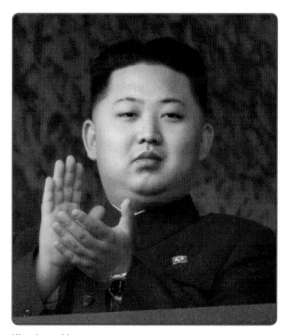
Kim Jong Un

South Korea

South Korea, also known as the Republic of Korea, is slightly larger than Indiana. The favorable climate and irrigation permit the rice fields to be double cropped (producing two crops per year). Since 1960, South Korea has undergone a rapid transformation from an agricultural society to a fast-growing industrial economy. In the 1960s, its economy was on par with those of the poorest countries of Africa and Asia. Today, it has a $1.64 trillion economy, the result of hard work and cooperation among business, government, and labor unions. Unlike North Korea, South Korea is free and not centralized.

Seoul is the fifth-largest city in the world in terms of population.

Korean ethnic dancers perform Buchaechum, a fan dance.

Korean Christianity and Missions

Christianity's growth in Korea at the end of the nineteenth century was due primarily to the work of North American Presbyterian missionaries. There are now more than twenty-one thousand South Korean missionaries in foreign countries. The majority of Christians may now live outside of Western countries. This provides several benefits to spreading the gospel because Asian missionaries often already know the cultures and languages of neighboring countries and thus do not have to spend as much time adjusting to the target country. They also often have access to countries where Western missionaries cannot gain entry. The growth of majority-world missionaries (those who live among the people in "developing countries") will likely direct the growth of Christianity in the coming decades.

Farms and industries are privately owned, and there are several universities.

People flocked to the cities for employment, and four cities now exceed two and a half million people: Seoul, Busan (formerly spelled Pusan), Incheon, and Daegu (formerly spelled Taegu). **Seoul** (SOHL), the country's capital and manufacturing center, is currently the eighth-largest city in the world by area and easily the largest on the Korean Peninsula. South Korea specializes in electronics, telecommunications equipment, automobiles, chemicals, shipbuilding, and steel. Busan is one of the busiest seaports in the world. Although South Korea has less arable land than North Korea, it has consistently produced more than enough food for its own people. Its main crops are rice, vegetables, watermelons, onions, and potatoes. It also produces pork, chicken, fish, eggs, and milk. It spends less than 3 percent of its GDP on the military.

After thirty-two years of military rule, South Koreans elected their first civilian government in 1993. They have a republican form of government with an elected president who appoints a prime minister. The unicameral National Assembly has 299 seats, and delegates are elected every four years. Five political parties and many labor and trade unions vie for influence in the government.

South Koreans also enjoy religious freedom. Christianity (31 percent) and Buddhism (24 percent) are the largest organized religions. About 31 percent of the population does not identify with any religion. In South Korea, Christianity is growing. In fact, there are more Christian converts in South Korea than anywhere else in East Asia. The capital has the largest church (by attendance) in the world. Unfortunately, cults are also growing.

Section Quiz

1. Which mountain range forms the backbone of the east central portion of the Korean Peninsula?
2. What do the letters DMZ refer to?
3. What are the names of the three Communists who have ruled North Korea?
4. What term refers to the centrality of and virtual worship of the state in North Korea?
5. What is the largest city in Korea?
* Contrast the effects of government policies in North and South Korea.

III. Japan

The Japanese refer to their country as **Nippon**, which means "source of the sun." According to their mythology, the rising sun first shone on the islands of Japan. Japan is a crescent of four main islands due east of the coast of Russia and the Korean Peninsula, along with thousands of smaller islands that stretch southwest to northeast for twelve hundred miles. Like the United States, Japan has four seasons, with colder winters in the far north. Only one-half of 1 percent of the people are of ethnic origins other than Japanese (most of those being Korean).

WORLD RELIGIONS

Shintoism

The Shinto religion is the national Japanese religion. Shinto mythology describes the formation of Japan itself. The gods, or kami, emerged out of a primordial chaos. In the seventh generation the brother and sister Izanagi and Izanami emerged. They created the islands of Japan. But they also quarrelled. The curses they pronounced on each other brought about the existence of death. From Izanagi emerged three of the most powerful kami: the sun goddess, the moon god, and the storm god. The sun goddess is the source of life and harmony. The storm god is the source of evil, but his evil comes about through ignorance rather than ill intent. The sun goddess's grandson descended to Japan, and his great grandson became Japan's first emperor. Thus Shinto has a very close connection to the state in Japan.

In the late nineteenth and early twentieth century, the Japanese government claimed that Shinto was not a religion. Religions were human creations, but Shinto was said to come directly from the gods. Shinto received a setback with Japan's defeat in World War II. The Americans required the Japanese emperor to confess that he was not divine, and Shinto became one of a number of religions. Nonetheless, it is the central religion for many Japanese.

Shinto identifies the disharmony with nature as the basic problem of the world. The world is pervaded with kami, which are gods or spirits. Humans themselves may become kami. They are basically good but are a great distance from becoming kami. Nature is permeated with the kami. Shinto ritual plays an important role in bringing about this harmony. The Shinto religion is not a philosophical religion, and it rarely involves ethics. It is a religion of tradition and ritual.

Shinto differs from Christianity in important ways. The Bible teaches that there is only one God who is the Creator of all things. This differs from the Shinto teaching that the kami permeate all reality. Christianity identifies human sin, not a quarrel between gods, as the reason for death. And the problem with the world, according to Christianity, is sin and its effects. This means that ethics is much more significant for Christianity than it is for Shinto. Christians would agree with proponents of Shinto that sin has affected our relation to creation (Rom 8:19–22). But the Christian anticipates a renewed earth at the return of Christ rather than depending on religious ritual to restore harmony with the kami that pervade nature. A final important difference between Shinto and Christianity is the breadth of their appeal. Shinto is a uniquely Japanese religion, whereas Christians call on all people everywhere to submit to the lordship of Christ as the Creator of all things and the One who atoned for the sin of the world.

Isolated by the 120-mile-wide Korea Strait, Japan was never invaded successfully before World War II. When Japan learned of China's advanced culture, writing, literature, and philosophy, it borrowed many Chinese ideas, including its system of government and provincial divisions.

Although the islands have few mineral resources, Japan has built a thriving industrialized nation by adopting an exemplary work ethic and importing raw materials and converting them into high-tech, high-quality goods that are in great demand. Japan leads the world in pig iron and cadmium production and is second in steel production (behind only China). Agriculturally, it is among the top five producers of strawberries, pears, and rice. Its automobiles have gained a well-deserved reputation for safety and quality of craftsmanship.

As in other Asian countries, many Japanese are blinded to the gospel by their traditions. The native religion of Japan, **Shinto** (SHIHN toh), promotes the worship of many gods called *kami*, who are believed to indwell mountains, rivers, trees, and other parts of nature. Most Japanese practice some Shinto ceremonies, one of the most common being offerings of flowers and cakes to appease the kami. Over time, the Japanese people have added elements of Buddhism and Confucianism to their native religion.

Itsukushima Shrine

The Itsukushima (iht soo KOO shee muh) Shrine near Hiroshima has Japan's largest *torii*, or gateway, marking a sacred Shinto site. The buildings of the shrine sit on an island in the Inland Sea, whereas the gateway stands offshore in the shallow waters of the bay. The two main supporting beams of the gateway rise fifty-three feet. The shrine dates from the twelfth century, and the magnificent gateway was added in 1875.

The sacred shrine is dedicated to three Japanese gods: Susano, Okinonushi, and Tenjin. No cemeteries defile the island, and dogs are prohibited so as not to disturb the deer. The wooded island has two pagodas, a treasury building, and the Hall of One Thousand Mats. But most of the white-and-red buildings stand on wooden platforms in the bay. The platforms make the shrine seem to float above the water. Bridges and covered walks link the buildings to one another and to the island.

Tokyo is not only Japan's capital but also part of a megalopolis.

The Japanese Constitution

Tokyo, the national capital, was the site of a dramatic change that occurred after the World War II. In 1947, the Allied occupation forces, particularly the United States, helped the Japanese write and adopt a new republican constitution that transferred the emperor's power to the people. The *Kokkai*, or Diet, Japan's parliament, has two houses (the House of Councilors and the House of Representatives) and selects a prime minister. The constitution forbids waging war; however, Japan maintains armed forces for defense. The emperor is still a symbol of Japan, but he has only ceremonial duties.

Estimates of the number of Christians range from 2 to 3 percent, yet conversions are rare because a new convert must break strong ties with family traditions and culture. Recently, economic stagnation, constant threats of a major earthquake, and a deadly tsunami (2011) have caused the Japanese people to begin to search for spiritual answers. Foreign missionaries to Japan must spend many years learning the language and the many nuances of Japanese culture. Over time they develop a relationship with the people and have an opportunity to witness. Remarkably, some Korean missionaries have moved to Japan and are contributing to the Christian witness in that land.

Honshu

Japan's population is just over one-third the size of the United States' population, but all of its people are concentrated in an area the size of California. Narrow coastal plains lie around the mountains and support most of the population. The precious arable land (13 percent) is intensely cultivated to produce some of the world's highest yields. **Honshu**, Japan's largest island, is home to more than 80 percent of the Japanese people. It contains thirty-four of the forty-seven prefectures and eight of the ten largest cities, including Tokyo.

Tokyo

With 13.23 million people, **Tokyo**, (meaning "eastern capital") is the largest city in Japan. **Yokohama**, Japan's second-largest city (pop. 3.70 million) and main port, is close to Tokyo. Another major city, Kawasaki, lies between them. This populous metropolitan area constitutes the Keihin Industrial Region, which produces ships, petroleum, steel, and electronic equipment. The entire industrial region is on Japan's largest lowland, the Kanto Plain, a major agricultural region that produces silk, wheat, and rice.

Tokyo is a state-of-the-art financial center. It has one of the world's leading stock exchanges. Its banks and industries make Japan one of the richest nations in the world. Land in Japan, however, is scarce and expensive, and rapid growth has brought traffic and pollution problems. Tokyo's crime rate remains lower than that of most Western cities, but random violent crime is on the rise.

Kyoto

Mountains cover about 85 percent of Japan. The loftiest peaks are found in the center of Honshu, at the Japanese Alps. Several peaks exceed ten thousand feet. The highest, **Mount Fuji**, reaches 12,389 feet. Earthquakes are common. The Japanese Alps provide zinc and lead, and tin deposits lie in the Chugoku Mountains to the west.

Japan's third-largest city is the Osaka-Kobe metropolitan area (pop. 2.59 million), which is called the Hanshin Industrial Region. Another large city nearby is Kyoto (pop. 1.47 million). Those two cities produce pharmaceuticals, textiles, and steel. (Japan is second only to China in steel production.)

Kyoto was Japan's capital for more than one thousand years in ancient times. Warriors called **samurai** protected estates of feudal lords (*daimyo*), whose rivalries escalated into civil war. When the Yoritomo clan established itself as the country's strongest clan in 1192, the emperor granted Yoritomo the title of *shogun*, meaning "great general" of the people. Shoguns ruled Japan in the emperor's name until 1867.

Mount Fuji towers over the Japanese landscape.

Other Industrial Centers

Honshu has three other major industrial regions. **Nagoya** is Japan's fourth-largest city at 2.18 million people, and the Chukyo Industrial Region around it produces many Japanese cars, synthetic fibers, ceramics, and aircraft. Only the United States has a greater ratio of car owners than Japan. The Hokuriku Region on the west coast extends from Niigata to Kanazawa and produces machinery and chemicals. The final industrial area is the Inland Sea Region. It lines both sides of the Inland Sea and produces rubber, trucks, and agricultural machinery. **Hiroshima** (heer oh SHEE muh), a city of 1.14 million people and the site where the first atomic bomb was dropped, is part of that industrial area.

Hiroshima

Shikoku

Shikoku, the smallest of Japan's four main islands, lies south of Honshu. With only 3 percent of the Japanese people, this mountainous and heavily forested island has only four prefectures. It has remained somewhat separate from the rest of Japan. Rice farms and villages nestled in the valleys appear as they have for more than a century. Japanese Buddhists still take pilgrimages to the island's eighty-eight sacred temples, hoping to be released from the cycle of rebirth.

In the past, travelers had to take a ferry across the Inland Sea to reach the island. That changed in 1988 with the opening of the 8.1-mile-long Seta Ohashi Bridge, which is high enough for ships to pass under. Most people on the island live on the north shore in the area known as the Inland Sea Industrial Region.

Kyushu

Southeast of the Korean Peninsula is **Kyushu**, the southernmost and second-most-populous of Japan's main islands. The earliest settlers built Japan's first cities there. The mild climate and lush green

Typical Japanese Home

"The traditional Japanese house has no tables or chairs. The Japanese sit on straw mats called tatami, and it is common to measure the size of the house and room in terms of the tatami, each about 3 feet by 6 feet (0.9 m by 1.8 m). Bedding consists of light mattresses and blankets that are put away into cabinets every morning so as not to clutter the small rooms. Since Japanese often sit on the floor, they remove their shoes as soon as they enter the house and put on house slippers. They change their house slippers for bathroom slippers before entering the bathroom."

Cultures of the World: Japan, 64.

Japanese Gardens

Japanese gardens are so famous that most public gardens in America have a section in the Japanese style. Japanese gardens often include arched footbridges, small pagodas, flowers, conifers, and ponds. Such gardens may include outdoor cafés that serve tea. These gardens are always clean, uncluttered, and carefully laid out. Tokyo has many such gardens. Two old and famous Japanese gardens are Korakuen Garden and Rikugien Garden.

One unique aspect of Japanese gardening is bonsai, the art of growing miniature trees. Grown in flowerpots or trays with carefully selected soil and fertilizer, the trees remain healthy, but their growth is stunted. Careful pruning develops branches in the desired places. A skilled bonsai gardener can shape the full-grown bonsai tree—by tying, bracing, or using copper wires—to look exactly like a normal tree, although it stands only one or two feet high. The gardener must also continually water, fertilize, prune, and shape the potted tree.

Japanese gardens are famous for their footbridges, ponds, and well-manicured walkways.

countryside support 10 percent of Japan's population in seven prefectures. On the north coast, the cities Fukuoka and Kitakyushu have a combined population of 2.46 million. The chief agricultural region in the northwest grows rice and tea. Northern coal fields produce about one-half of the coal mined in Japan.

On the west coast is the port city of Nagasaki (pop. 414,415), which is often referred to as the San Francisco of Japan. The United States dropped its second atomic bomb on Nagasaki in 1945 to end World War II.

Japan has many small islands. The United States captured the most strategic ones to use as bases for bombers during World War II. The Ryuku Islands form a curving chain of one hundred islands from Kyushu southwestward to Taiwan. Included among the Ryukus is **Okinawa**, Japan's fifth-most-populous island and the only prefecture not on one of the four main islands. The ninety-seven Bonin Islands are southeast of Japan. **Iwo Jima** is one of three Volcano Islands farther south.

Hokkaido

The northernmost of the four main Japanese islands is **Hokkaido** (hah KYE doh). The population is concentrated in Sapporo, a city of 1.93 million people, the fifth-largest city in Japan. Winters in Hokkaido are long and severe, and its summers are cool because of the influence of the cold Oyashio (or Kuril) Current. Surrounding waters provide a rich source of pollack and mackerel. Japan has the world's third-largest fish processing industry and the third-largest seaweed production industry.

Hokkaido compares to the American West as Japan's last frontier. Although it is the second-largest island and the largest prefecture, it has a relatively small population and is developed in pockets. Like the American frontier, Hokkaido has several natural resources. Lumber comes from the island's heavily forested mountains, and manganese comes from its southern peninsula. The Seikan Tunnel, the world's longest railway tunnel, transports these resources under the sea to Honshu. Hokkaido is a recreation and vacation destination, especially for skiers.

Hokkaido also has native peoples, the Ainu, Japan's original inhabitants. The Japanese have always considered the Ainu an inferior people. Over time, the Ainu retreated north to Hokkaido. They survived by hunting, fishing, and planting small gardens. Intermarriage with the Japanese has since made full-blooded Ainu rare. After World War II, social reforms assimilated the Ainu into the Japanese culture. As a consequence, their culture and their language—which were never fully studied—declined. The Japanese government has begun, however, to compensate the Ainu monetarily for the years of mistreatment and discrimination.

Section Quiz

1. What is the religion that influences all Japanese people?

2–4. Who are shoguns? samurai? Ainu?

5. What is the highest mountain in Japan?

★ What factors enabled Japan to recover so quickly from World War II to become the economic power it is today?

Chapter Review

Making Connections

1–3. Name three geographic and manmade features that helped isolate China from the outside world for centuries.

4. Why are the Qin Ling mountains important?

5. What key products come from the Southern Uplands of China?

6. In which part of Korea is Christianity oppressed?

7–10. What are the four main Japanese islands?

Developing Geography Skills

1. Using the maps and other information in this chapter, identify five differences between China and Japan.

2. Using the map of China, explain why most Chinese cities are located in the eastern section of the country.

Thinking Critically

1. Explain what is wrong with communism. Use countries in this chapter as positive and negative examples.

2. Why do you think God has allowed communism to become so powerful in China?

Living in God's World

1. If you were sharing the gospel with a Japanese person who adhered to the Shinto religion, how might you explain (graciously) its shortcomings compared to Christianity?

2. The Chinese often confuse American culture with Christian culture. If you were a missionary to China, what aspects of American culture would you identify as anti-Christian or un-Christian in comparison to Chinese culture?

People, Places, and Things to Know

Pacific Rim
Han
North China Plain
Qin Ling Mountains
Huang He
Chang
dynasty
Shanghai
Beijing
Forbidden City
Tiananmen Square
Tianjin
Manchus
Southern Uplands
Hainan
Xi River
Guangzhou
Hong Kong
Macau
Sun Yat-sen
Chiang Kai-shek
Mao Zedong
Great Leap Forward
Cultural Revolution
Deng Xiaoping
autonomous regions
Guangxi
Zhuang
Tibet (Xizang)
Lhasa
Dalai Lama
theocrat
Xinjiang
Nei Mongol
Ningxia
Taiwan
Taipei
Ulaanbaatar
Gobi Desert
Taebaek Mountains
Juche (Kimilsungism)
Pyongyang
Seoul
Nippon
Shinto
Honshu
Tokyo
Yokohama
Mount Fuji
Kyoto
samurai
Nagoya
Hiroshima
Shikoku
Kyushu
Okinawa
Iwo Jima
Hokkaido

Unit Seven

THE MIDDLE EAST

17 The Persian Gulf

18 Eastern Mediterranean

Post-Flood history began in this region. The descendants of Noah spread out across this area and great civilizations developed. According to the apostle John in the book of Revelation, history, as we know it, will also end in this important region.

Islam requires prayer several times a day and permeates culture in many parts of the world.

THE PERSIAN GULF

The **Middle East**, home to the Mesopotamian marshes, is the birthplace of the post-Flood world. The descendants of Noah founded the first civilization there. The Middle East will also be the focal point of the consummation of world history.

The three major monotheistic religions—Judaism, Christianity, and Islam—began there. Conquering armies have swept back and forth across the ancient trade routes, bathing the land in blood. The Middle East is at once a region of wealth and poverty, of beauty and terror, of ancient ways and modern industry.

This chapter examines the eastern half of the Middle East, where the **Persian Gulf** is the center of population and trade. The gulf has been a hub of activity since ancient times, as ships have sailed through the Arabian Sea to ports in Asia and Africa. Islam was

Mesopotamian Marshes

The disaster caused by the drainage of the Mesopotamian marshes in Iraq illustrates the destructive power of man. It also demonstrates the healing power of restoration built into creation by the Creator. This will be discussed in greater detail later in the chapter.

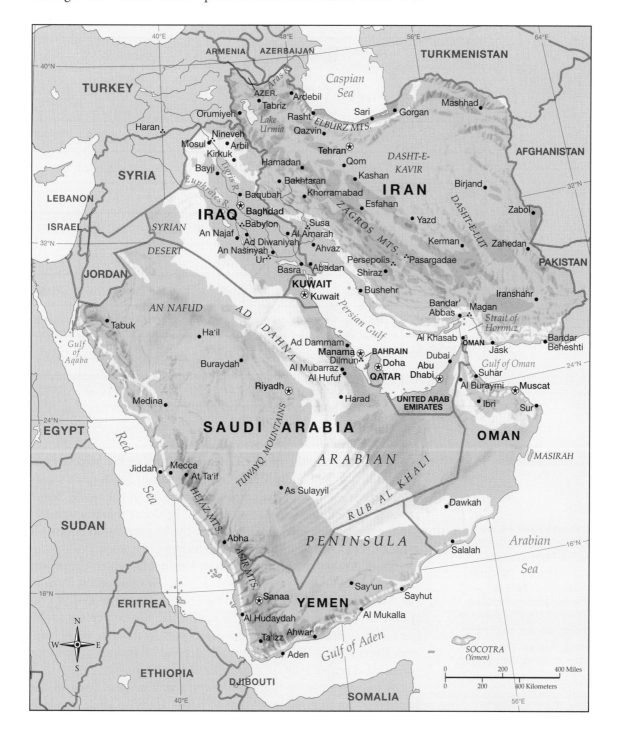

founded in this region during the first three decades of the seventh century AD, and it continues to dominate every aspect of life in this area of the world.

Although the great Islamic empires fell into decay long ago, the discovery of oil put the Persian Gulf back at the center of world politics. Money from oil has revolutionized life in the region. In countries where leaders exercise wise stewardship, this wealth has been used to provide improved health care, education, and economic opportunity for the people. In other countries, wealth has been used to suppress the people and support the spread of Islam.

Many nations have sought to bring peace to the Middle East. While human efforts will not ultimately succeed, the ruler who will bring lasting peace to this region and the world is coming soon. His name is Jesus.

Persian Gulf Fast Facts						
Country	Capital	Area (sq. mi.)	Pop. (2013) (M)	Pop. Density (per sq. mi.)	Per Capita GDP ($US)	Life Span
Bahrain	Manama	293	1.29	4,403	$28,200	78.29
Iran	Tehran	636,371	79.86	125	$13,100	70.35
Iraq	Baghdad	169,235	31.86	188	$4,600	70.85
Kuwait	Kuwait City	6,880	2.70	392	$40,500	77.28
Oman	Muscat	119,498	3.15	26	$28,500	74.47
Qatar	Doha	4,473	2.04	456	$102,800	78.09
Saudi Arabia	Riyadh	870,000	26.94	31	$25,700	74.35
United Arab Emirates	Abu Dhabi	32,278	5.47	169	$49,000	76.71
Yemen	Sanaa	203,850	25.41	125	$2,200	64.11

I. Saudi Arabia

Saudi Arabia is the most influential country in the Middle East. Besides being the largest Middle Eastern nation, Saudi Arabia currently exports more oil than any other country in the world. Some of the largest known oil reserves on earth lie under this country. But Saudi Arabia holds even greater sway in the Muslim world because it is the birthplace of Islam and home to its most holy sites.

Saudi Arabia lies on the **Arabian Peninsula**, which juts down from the Middle East into the Arabian Sea. Two important arms of the Arabian Sea—the Persian Gulf on the east and the Red Sea on the west—lie on either side of the peninsula. Ninety percent of the peninsula is desert or barren plateau. Saudi Arabia has no permanent rivers and no lakes. Since Saudis depend on springs or wells for water, most settlements are at oases or along the coasts.

A narrow strip of highlands rises near the west coast of the peninsula, forcing monsoon winds periodically to drop precious

Centrality of Islam

Islam permeates life in most Middle Eastern countries today, even those that, like Turkey, have secular governments. Every city has at least one **mosque** (Islamic worship building). Criers or loudspeakers call the people to prayer five times daily from the *minarets* (towers) beside the mosques. Businesses stop for prayer at dawn, noon, midafternoon, sunset, and night. On Friday, the Muslim holy day, people meet at noon in the local mosque to recite their prayers together.

LET'S GO EXPLORING

Climates of the Middle East

1. What is the most obvious contrast between the north and the south?
2. What is the predominant climate along the eastern edge of the Mediterranean Sea?
3. How many countries seem to be made up entirely of desert? (Compare this map with the one on page 415.)
4. What climate does Iran have on the southern end of the Caspian Sea?
✶ From what you have learned about monsoon winds, why does the entire coast of the Arabian Sea have a dry climate?

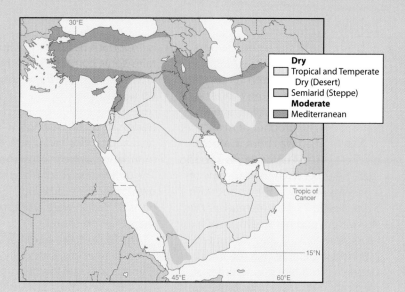

moisture. Terracing is possible on the mountain slopes to enable farming. However, the narrow coastal plain at the foot of the Asir Mountains in the southwest corner is the most fertile region in the country.

The primary highlands in the west are the Hejaz Mountains, which run parallel to the coast. Several important cities lie in the Hejaz region. Jiddah, meaning "Bride of the Red Sea," is the largest port on the Red Sea and has a population of 5.1 million people. It lies on the narrow coastal plain known as the *Tihamah*. Nearby in the highlands are the two holiest centers of Islam: **Mecca**, which is about fifty miles east, and **Medina** (meh DEEN ah), which is about two hundred miles north.

Officially, people of other faiths can live in Saudi Arabia, but they can not practice their faith openly, gather privately, or convert a Muslim to another religion. Muslims who become Christians face the death penalty. Despite the harsh penalties and brutal punishment of Christians, an estimated 88,000 Evangelical Christians live in Saudi Arabia and worship in small groups.

Deserts and Oases of Inland Arabia

The interior of the peninsula is even drier than the coast. Most of the land receives less than four inches of precipitation annually. About one-half of Saudi Arabia is tropical, and the rest is temperate, but freezing temperatures are rare. The heating and cooling of the rock and sand tend to make the climate uncomfortably hot, and temperatures over 100°F are common in the summer months. Hot, dry winds add to the discomfort.

The most desolate parts of Saudi Arabia are in the far north and the south. At least seven parts of the Arabian Desert have their own names. The most important one in the north is the An Nafud. The sands of the An Nafud eventually give way to the rocky Syrian Desert in the far north.

Women in Islamic Countries

In strict Muslim societies, women are expected to wear a cloak, called a *burqa*. Even in countries where these practices are not strictly observed, few jobs are open to women because they are not permitted to socialize with men other than their relatives. Education for females is discouraged or forbidden. Women are not allowed to vote or run for office. In Saudi Arabia, they are not even allowed to drive cars. Muslim women are taught to hold the family honor in the highest regard, and women are pressured to follow these cultural restrictions to ensure that they avoid any improper actions that might dishonor the family. Maintaining honor is very important in Muslim society. Bringing dishonor for any reason often results in the death of the offender at the hands of the head of the home. These deaths are known as honor-killings.

Muslim women face heavy restrictions, especially in countries with Muslim governments.

WORLD RELIGIONS

Islam

Islam, one of the world's largest religions, emerged on the Arabian Peninsula in the seventh century. At the center of Islam is the confession "There is no god but Allah, and Muhammad is the prophet of Allah."

Muhammad was born in Mecca, on the Arabian Peninsula. As a young man, he supervised the caravans of a wealthy widow in their trade with Syria. At age 25, Muhammad married the widow, and her wealth gave him more time for solitude and contemplation. He claimed that the angel Gabriel visited him during times of meditation in a cave. Muslims claim the **Qur'an** is the collection of the messages given to Muhammad by Allah. They declare that Muhammad is the last in a line of prophets that includes Adam, Abraham, Moses, and Jesus. Because Muhammad is the final prophet, Muslims insist that the Qur'an corrects corruptions in the revelations passed on from other prophets. Muhammad passed these revelations to his followers orally. This oral tradition was written down during his life and over the twenty years after his death. In its written form, the Qur'an has 114 suras, or chapters. The suras are arranged from longest to shortest, not in chronological order. And yet the chronology of the suras

is important because the Qur'an contains some contradictions. Muslims attempt to resolve these contradictions by saying that later revelation supersedes earlier revelation. The Hadith, collected sayings of Muhammad and stories about him, also play a foundational role in Muslim thought. The different sects of Islam have their own collections of Hadith. The collections of Hadith were written down in the late ninth century.

The Bible is also a significant holy book for Muslims, especially the Torah (Pentateuch), the Psalms, and the Gospels. Nevertheless, Muslims claim that the Bible has been corrupted and needs correction by the Qur'an. Muslim scholars disagree about whether this means that the actual text of the Bible has been corrupted or that Jewish and Christian interpretations of the Bible are corrupt. The Qur'an has suras that speak both positively and negatively about the Bible.

The oneness of Allah is one of the most important teachings of Islam. Muhammad grew up in a polytheistic society. Islam rejects polytheism. Islam also rejects the biblical teaching that the One God exists in three Persons: Father, Son, and Spirit. Muslims say that Allah has no companions and no Son. Though Muslims believe that

Rub al Khali

The key southern desert, the **Rub al Khali** (roob ahl KAH-lee), covers an area larger than California. It is one of the largest deserts in the world. The Rub al Khali is also one of the largest sand deserts in the world, with shifting winds whipping sand into dunes up to one thousand feet high. No one lives there, although nomads occasionally travel across it. This uninhabited wasteland covers one-quarter of Saudi Arabia and is aptly called the **Empty Quarter**.

The Capital

Between these wastes of the An Nafud and the Empty Quarter is a large central plateau called the Nejd. This desert is not quite as harsh because of its higher elevation.

The Rub al Khali, also called "the Empty Quarter," covers most of the Arabian Peninsula.

Muslim pilgrims (top) end their hajj by walking around the sacred Ka'bah in Mecca. People have been trampled to death in the huge crowds that gather to worship Allah.

The sheer size of The Mosque of the Prophet in Medina (bottom) shows the importance of the city to Islam.

Jesus was a prophet, they deny that He is God. They do accept the virgin birth and miracles of Jesus. Muslims teach that in the resurrection Muslims will appeal for a prophet to intercede for them with Allah. In Muslim teaching, Jesus is unable to intercede for people. Only Muhammad can successfully intercede between Muslims and Allah.

Muslims also deny that Jesus died for the sins of mankind. In Muslim teaching, everyone is responsible for his own sins. Humans are considered to be, at the root, good. However, people are weak, and they sin. Salvation is given by Allah to those who follow the path of Islam, although no Muslim can be sure of salvation apart from a martyr's death.

The religious practices of Muslims are often described as the Five Pillars. The first pillar is the daily recitation of the Shahadah: "There is no god but Allah, and Muhammad is the prophet of Allah." The second pillar is prayer. Muslims pray three to five times a day, facing toward Mecca. These prayers are set recitations that give glory and thanks to Allah in Arabic. Extemporaneous prayers may be given at other times in whatever the Muslim's native tongue happens to be. The third pillar of Islam is fasting. Muslims fast during the month of Ramadan. During this month Muslims do not eat or drink between sunrise and sunset. The fourth pillar is almsgiving. The *zakat* or alms can range from 2.5% to 20% of what one owns. Giving the alms is supposed to indicate that Allah owns all things as well as to benefit the poor. The fifth pillar is pilgrimage. Every Muslim is to make a pilgrimage to Mecca at least once if at all possible. Central to the pilgrimage is the circling of the Ka'bah. The Ka'bah is a black stone building believed to be located near the well that sprang up when Hagar and Ishmael faced death in the wilderness. Muslims teach that Abraham built this structure as a place of worship.

The most controversial Muslim practice is called *jihad*. Jihad is the Arabic word for struggle. It can be used to refer to the struggle that each Muslim wages against his sin. But it is primarily used to refer to the Muslim "holy war" to spread Islam throughout the world. Some modern Muslims argue that this spread of Islam should take place only through peaceful means. They teach that Muslims should seek to persuade others to become Muslims. But other Muslim groups practice a violent jihad against those they view as enemies of Islam, including other sects of Islam. The Qur'an and Hadith give mixed messages on this matter. Some Muslims stress passages in the Qur'an that teach toleration for Jews, Christians, and others if they pay a special tax. The Qur'an teaches "there is to be no compulsion in religion" (2:256). But the Qur'an also teaches that Muslims should fight Jews and Christians who will not submit to Muslim rule (9:29).

When considering this threat, Christians must balance a number of considerations. They must consider the real security issues that violent segments of Islam present while rejecting fear that prevents Christians from reaching out and evangelizing Muslims. Many of the Muslims that American Christians meet in their communities harbor no ill will toward them and would be willing to establish a friendship with a Christian. Christians should not neglect these opportunities.

Several oases dot the plateau. **Riyadh** (ree YAHD), the capital, was built around one such oasis. In the early twentieth century, Riyadh was just a mud village. Since it became the capital of a united kingdom, however, it has become the largest city in the country, with about 5 million people in its metropolitan area.

Ibn-Saud (IB-en sah-OOD) conquered the desert tribes of Arabia and formed the kingdom of Saudi Arabia in the early twentieth century. His descendants continue to rule Saudi Arabia. The country has no constitution. The king is bound only by Islamic law and tradition as interpreted by the **Wahhabi**, leaders of a religious sect that is noted for its strict adherence to Islamic law. Their influence has been great. Non-Muslim peoples are almost outcasts in such a society.

Black Gold on the East Coast

The eastern lowlands along the Persian Gulf are mostly sand and gravel, but there are several fertile oases. The Al-Hasa Oasis, at the

Bedouins

The nomads of the Arabian Desert are called **Bedouins**. Traditionally, Bedouins have lived in tents, "houses of hair" carefully woven by the women. Bedouins in Saudi Arabia make the outside of their tents from black goats' hair, but the inside is very colorful. Hand-woven curtains divide the interior, and carpets are laid on the dirt floor. The Bedouins wander between oases, seeking water for their livestock. Most Bedouins keep camels, sheep, and goats. They eat dates and dairy products and trade in village markets for pots, tools, and other household items.

Today there are about one million Bedouins, but very few of them wander all year. Many prefer the steady jobs and easier life that the oil-rich government has made available for them.

Bedouin tents are truly "mobile homes" in some of the most inhospitable areas of the world.

base of the Nejd, is fed by more than fifty springs and covers seventy square miles. The town of Al Hufuf lies in that oasis. The people grow such diverse crops as citrus fruits, rice, and wheat. Ad Dammam is the largest city on the coast, and Ras Tanura is the major port from which Saudi Arabia exports most of its oil.

The discovery of oil in 1936 created a new economy for Saudi Arabia. The oil boom enabled the country to advance rapidly in industry, education, and health care. It currently produces about 10 million barrels of oil per day. However, there is a growing realization that the nation must develop new industries for the time when its oil supplies diminish.

Section Quiz

1. Who founded Islam?
2. What are the two most holy cities of Islam?
3. What is another name for the Rub al Khali?
4. Who founded the Kingdom of Saudi Arabia?
5. Who are the Bedouins?
* Contrast the spread of Christianity in the first century (Book of Acts) with the spread of Islam during the seventh century.

II. Small States on the Arabian Peninsula

In the West, the Muslim world is sometimes called the "Arab world," although not all Muslims are Arabs. The Muslim religion began, however, on the Arabian Peninsula, and it was first spread by tribes of Arabic-speaking people called **Arabs**. The Arabs spread their language and writing as well as their religion. No matter what language they speak in daily life, Muslims in every Muslim nation study and memorize the Qur'an in the original Arabic language. Translations are not permitted.

Early in the history of Islam, the center of power shifted to the populous cities farther north, leaving the Arabian Peninsula forgotten in the dust. Only a few towns thrived on the coast of the peninsula, visited by rare caravans and adventurous merchant ships. Separated by harsh deserts from the rest of the Middle East, these distant towns developed an independent spirit, resisting the later invasions of other Arabic tribes, Turks, and Europeans.

Tent Making

What kind of work can you do well? Many missionaries have developed skills in trades such as carpentry or mechanics. Others have studied English and can teach it for high school or college courses. These missionaries sometimes have the option of going directly to the mission field without raising support. In this position, they have a great opportunity to assist full-time missionaries. This type of missions work is called *tent making*, after the apostle Paul's practice of earning his own way by sewing tents (Acts 18:1–3).

Muslim countries generally do not allow missionaries as such, but teachers and skilled technicians are welcome. Such missionaries can take comfort from Paul's example. Paul seldom received financial support from churches (Phil. 4:15).

Even if the missionary is honorably employed in his new country, he must be prepared to face serious opposition. Such missionaries should recall the Scripture passage that says that "all that will live godly in Christ Jesus shall suffer persecution" (2 Tim. 3:12). Are you willing to be a tent-making missionary somewhere in the world? Are you willing to suffer, if necessary, for the sake of the gospel?

Six small coastal countries border Saudi Arabia on the east and south. Most of these lie on the Persian Gulf, but two lie farther out on the Arabian Sea. The two nations on the Arabian Sea—Yemen and Oman—do not share the wealth from the Persian Gulf oil reserves. Though they have some oil, their economies revolve around farming and trade.

Yemen

The Arabian Peninsula rises sharply in the southwest corner. From these highlands, the rest of the peninsula slopes downward. Yemen occupies this corner. Most of its people are poor. Their meager subsistence involves farming or herding. They trade their goods at *bazaars* (open markets). Yemen has one of the lowest literacy rates, the lowest life expectancy, and the lowest per capita GDP in the Middle East. In addition, the country suffers from dwindling oil and water supplies while experiencing a rapid population growth. Wells as deep as 3,900 feet deep have been drilled to reach aquifers that supply fresh water, but this supply will be exhausted in one or two decades.

Islam is the official religion of Yemen, and 99.92 percent of the people are Muslim. Sunni Muslims (65.9 percent) live in the center and southern part of the country while Shia Muslims (34 percent) live in the north. About 19,000 Yemenis practice some form of Christianity, and an estimated 4,200 Evangelical Christians endure a hostile environment to worship, serve, and witness. Many Christians in this country are expatriates from Ethiopia and workers from Western and Asian countries. They work in business, education, and medical fields and cautiously witness to the Yemeni people they interact with.

Yemen has the highest peaks of the Arabian Peninsula. Rainfall in these highlands gives Yemen the only permanent river on the entire peninsula. Sanaa, the capital, lies in these highlands in the major agricultural area. The main cash crops are coffee and **khat** (KAHT), a shrub whose leaves are chewed in East Africa as a narcotic. Yemen is famous for mocha coffee, which is shipped from the coastal town of Mocha, west of Ta'izz.

This land on the Red Sea, once known as Sheba, has maintained a civilization for many centuries. The Queen of Sheba journeyed from here to visit Solomon (1 Kings 10:1–13). Sheba once contained gold and other minerals, but these resources have long since been exhausted. The Red Sea is the westernmost arm of the Arabian Sea. But before its waters enter the Arabian Sea, they pass through a narrow spot called Bab el Mandeb and then pass into the **Gulf of Aden** (AH dehn).

Yemen has several islands off the eastern horn of Africa. Socotra (suh COH trah), the most important, was a major stop on the early Arab shipping routes across the Arabian Sea. Today, most islanders live by spearfishing from single-sail boats called *dhows*.

Sultanate of Oman

Oman (oh MAHN) is among the hottest countries in the world, with daytime temperatures often reaching 130°F. Most of the country is part of the Rub al Khali desert. The people wear long white robes and turbans to protect themselves from the heat, wind, and blowing sand.

Sanaa is the capital city of Yemen.

Traditional Yemen Social Values

As is common elsewhere in the Arab world, family is the basic building block of Yemeni society. However, Yemenis have developed their own customs that include a polite reception of guests beyond their family. The guest is welcomed and treated like a member of the family. The host offers food, drink, entertainment, and even gifts to the guest.

Importance of Family

The extended family has been the central focus for Arabs for millennia. Prior to the existence of a central government, the typical Arabian family resolved most issues and punished most transgressors. Today the average extended family involves at least three generations and can include other relatives such as aunts and uncles.

In modern Saudi families, those who are financially able no longer live in the same house with their parents and grandparents. However, several charactistics of the extended family continue. The male leader of the family retains great authority and makes important decisions for the family. The welfare of the group continues to take priority over the desires of an individual in the family. In addition, social activities are largely contained within the extended family group. It would be unusual to see a family entertain others in a restaurant or gather at a public event. Another aspect of the traditional extended family that continues is the care given for family members in need. This would include the elderly, sick, divorced, widowed, or handicapped. Emotional and financial support is provided for these family members.

The mountains of Oman stand in stark contrast to the deserts of the Persian Gulf region but are just as dry.

Wadi Bashing

(Note: *Wadis* [WAH deez] are dry stream beds that fill up with water after rainstorms.)

"Off-road driving is known as wadi bashing in Oman, and it is becoming increasingly popular. In four-wheel drive vehicles, people simply take off on a wild ride through wadis and over towering dunes. The pastime has become so popular that tours are organized by hotels and private tour companies.

A successful drive requires great skill and some know-how. Tire pressure is lowered for sand driving but raised for mountains and rocks. Drivers learn not to shift gears in sand, a sure way to get stuck. They also know to keep their wheels straight when going up or down dunes. In addition to the thrill of a wild ride, veterans say there is no better way to appreciate Oman's wildly beautiful scenery."

Cultures of the World: Oman, 115.

A wadi and date palm oasis flanked by the Hajar al Gharbi mountains in the sultanate of Oman

Although the Portuguese captured several ports in 1507, they could not take all of Oman. Arab tribes forced the Portuguese completely out by 1650. Oman even took part of East Africa. The present line of sultans (Muslim monarchs) came to power in 1740. The government is called a **sultanate**. Because Oman's ships could not compete with modern vessels, however, its trade declined in the nineteenth century, and it lost its African territory in 1861. Since 1970, it has begun a major push to modernize and diversify to reduce its heavy dependence on oil. So far, the limited industry in the nation is subsidized by the government. However, tourism is increasing, and efforts to diversify the economy are expected to offset the decline in oil production.

Islam is the state religion in Oman. Eighty-nine percent of the population is Muslim, and 7 percent is Hindu. Those who embrace some form of Christianity constitute 3 percent. Christians are allowed to have churches and gather for worship, but converting Muslims to Christ is forbidden. While the percentage of Evangelical Christians (0.8 percent) is tiny, the number of Christians is growing. Most of the Christian population is composed of workers from other countries, and many other foreign workers are coming to Christ, but some Omanis are also trusting Christ. Christian radio broadcasts in Arabic and distribution of Bibles have been effective means of spreading the gospel in this Muslim country.

Dhofar

Southwestern Oman, around the cities of Salalah (suh LAHL uh) and Dawkah, is a plateau called Dhofar (doh FAHR). It is known for its many frankincense trees. The plateau gets slightly more rain than the surrounding desert.

Strategic Cities on the Gulf of Oman

The main population center is a stretch of highlands that rises at the southeast corner of the Arabian Peninsula. It is the heart of Oman and one of only two places on the peninsula where mountains cause some regular rainfall. A fertile coastal strip with date palms lies at the base of the mountains. The capital, Muscat (muhs KAHT), is on that coast.

The coast is important today because of its strategic location at the entrance to the Persian Gulf. Before the Arabian Sea enters the Persian Gulf, it passes through the **Gulf of Oman**. In addition to the main territory along this gulf, Oman controls Cape Musandam, at the narrowest junction of the Gulf of Oman and the Persian Gulf. The Omani town of Al Khasab on the cape guards the strategic Strait of Hormuz (hahr MOOZ), through which all oil tankers must pass as they leave the Persian Gulf.

Emirates on the Persian Gulf

In the nineteenth century, various rulers on the coast of the Persian Gulf asked Great Britain to protect them from their powerful neighbors. In return, they gave Britain control of their defense and foreign affairs. When Britain withdrew from the Persian Gulf in 1971, these tiny British protectorates became independent. Since the discovery of oil in the 1930s, all four minicountries on the Persian Gulf have profited greatly.

United Arab Emirates

Seven small states, each with its own traditions, lie along the southwestern shore of the Persian Gulf. Each is ruled by a prince, or *emir* (ih MIR), and its government is therefore called an **emirate**. During the nineteenth century, when Britain dominated the area, it enforced truces between the states to keep the naval lanes open; therefore, the area was called the Trucial (TROO see uhl) States. These states have retained sovereignty over local affairs but are now united into a single country called the United Arab Emirates (UAE). The seven emirs form the Supreme Council and appoint a president as head of state.

The UAE is the richest country in the Persian Gulf. This recent wealth has resulted from developing some of the largest oil reserves in the world. The sale of oil has brought riches (per capita GDP of $49,000). The prosperity has also drawn waves of immigrants both

Abu Dhabi is not only the capital of the United Arab Emirates but also a beautiful modern city.

Turning the Desert Green

Officials and average citizens have joined forces in the United Arab Emirates to plant trees and other outdoor plants to reclaim portions of the desert. Water from desalination plants (as well as groundwater projects, including the one in al-Khazna) is used to sustain the plants. As a result, Abu Dhabi now has around 3,700 acres of grass. The nearby al-Ayn oasis has forty parks with pools or fountains. The increased vegetation appears to have slightly moderated the intense heat and has resulted in additional birdlife.

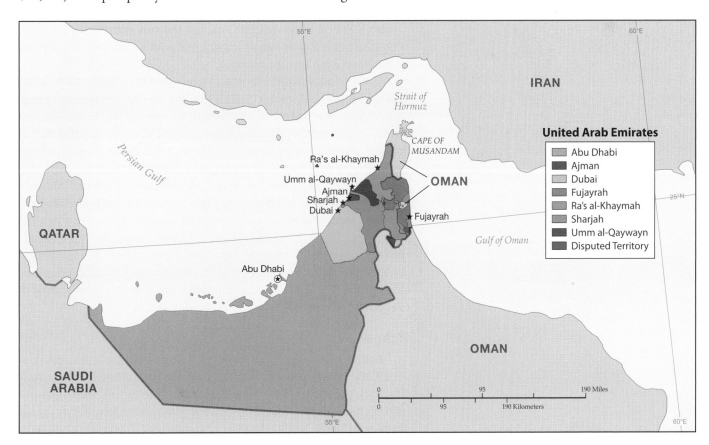

Burj Al Arab, Dubai, UAE, is 1,053 feet tall, one meter taller than the Eiffel Tower. The oblong structure about two-thirds of the way up the side of the hotel is a restaurant; behind it is a platform for landing helicopters.

Palm of Jebel Ali; under construction from land formed from reclaimed ocean sand

from neighboring Saudi Arabia and from as far away as India and Pakistan.

While Islam is the state religion, the UAE allows a significant amount of religious freedom, within limits. A combined Sunni majority and Shiite minority represent 68 percent of the population. Due to heavy immigration, Hindus constitute 15.5 percent of the population, and various forms of Christianity represent 9 percent. Evangelical Christians make up just over 1 percent of the population, and most are immigrants from Asia. Open evangelism and handing out of Christian literature can lead to arrest, imprisonment, and deportation of foreigners. However, discreet witnessing is bearing fruit, especially among foreign workers.

Qatar

For centuries the Arab peoples supported themselves by raising camels, diving for pearls, and fishing. Like the United Arab Emirates, Qatar (KAH tur) is an emirate that has recently grown rich from oil. This prosperity has drawn so many immigrants that about 65 percent of the people are foreign-born.

Qatar is on a peninsula that extends into the Persian Gulf. Most of the peninsula is stony desert, but the southern region consists of salt flats. Since there is little water, the people distill seawater to drink. The process of **desalination** (removal of salt from saltwater) is too expensive for most countries. However, it is less expensive than importing water from neighboring countries.

Islam is the state religion, and it is practiced in the strict Wahhabi interpretation of Sunni Islam (88 percent). Not surprisingly, Muslims in Qatar are forbidden to convert to Christianity. However, 6 percent of the population, largely immigrant, practice some form of Christianity. Evangelical Christians represent 1 percent of the population, with most being non-Qatari. Christian radio and Internet programs offer access to the gospel in Arabic, with the goal of reaching some of the Qatari people.

Bahrain

Bahrain (bah RAYN) consists of a large island and a number of small ones northwest of Qatar. Bahrain is an emirate led by a *sheik* (SHAYK), the male leader of an extended Arab family. Many natural springs provide the islands of Bahrain with a fresh water resource that is rare in the Middle East.

Many international companies have headquarters in Bahrain, which operates an oil refinery on Sitra (sih TRAH) Island. Pipelines bring crude oil from both Bahrain and Saudi Arabia. The business has enabled the country to become the leading banking and financial center in the Persian Gulf region. It is also a major port of call for U.S. warships traveling in the gulf.

Eighty-three percent of the population is Muslim in Bahrain, where Islam is the state religion. Conversion of Muslims to another religion is illegal. Ten percent of the population embraces some form of Christianity, and 6 percent is Hindu. The government of Bahrain allows greater religious freedom than most of the other Gulf nations. This environment makes it possible for immigrant Christians to meet and spread the gospel to other immigrants. While the number of Bahraini Christians is small, their number is increasing. The people have access to the Christian message through satellite broadcasts, Christian radio, and Internet sites. In addition, there are a few Christian bookstores where Scriptures and Christian literature are available in Arabic.

Kuwait

The barren land of Kuwait, at the north end of the Persian Gulf, was uninhabited until 1710, when Arab settlers found a water source at what is now the capital of Kuwait. Kuwait Bay, with its excellent harbor, soon became an important port. But its existence has been threatened by its two large neighbors, Saudi Arabia in the south and Iraq in the north.

Kuwait prospered immediately after the discovery of oil. Soon hundreds of oil wells dotted the east. In 1960, it joined Saudi Arabia and other oil-producing countries in the Organization of Petroleum Exporting Countries (**OPEC**). OPEC members decide how much oil they will produce in an attempt to control the selling price and make political statements designed to influence Western policies. This tactic proved most effective in 1973, when the availability of oil dwindled as a result of the Arab-Israeli War. Since then, however, OPEC nations have generally fought among themselves because of the glut of oil.

In August 1990, Iraq invaded Kuwait, claiming that it had exceeded OPEC production limits and that it was actually a territory of Iraq. The invasion sparked the **Persian Gulf War**, the most significant war fought on the Arabian Peninsula since World War I. Iraq not only seized control of the huge oil reserves of Kuwait but also threatened the safety of Saudi Arabia. The Arab nations dropped their typical opposition to Western powers and joined a grand alliance, led by the United States and Great Britain, to protect the flow of oil. The UN authorized "all necessary means" to liberate Kuwait if Iraq did not withdraw by January 15, 1991. The Coalition forces began a massive military buildup in the region with central headquarters in Saudi Arabia. When Iraq ignored the UN demand, the United States made its first official declaration of war since World War II. On January 16, the UN Coalition began five weeks of massive, around-the-clock air strikes, followed by a lightning-fast ground attack that lasted just one

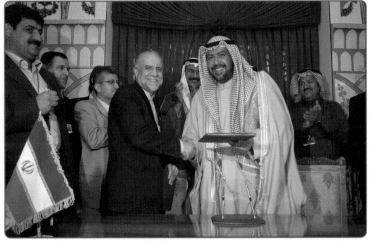

OPEC president Ahmad al-Fahd al-Sabah (left) and Iranian oil minister Bijan Namdar Zanganeh at an OPEC meeting in 2005

Missions in Muslim Countries

Missionary work in Muslim countries is difficult but not impossible. Some of the most effective missionaries come from Asian countries. For instance, in the United Arab Emirates a Filipino pastor, "Pastor Ben," started a church in a home. By law Christians must worship in designated places of worship, but worshiping there places them under certain limitations, especially with regard to evangelism.

Because he is Filipino, "Pastor Ben" has greater missionary opportunities than an American would. Americans are often viewed negatively in Middle Eastern countries whereas Filipinos are not. Because of their relational skills, English background, and cultural adaptability, Filipinos work all over the globe, and they are especially liked in Middle Eastern countries. Middle Eastern countries make up five of the top ten countries where overseas Filipino workers are found. Saudi Arabia and the United Arab Emirates are the top two destinations for these workers.

"Pastor Ben" works for the government of the UAE in a maintenance job. But his main reason for being in the UAE is to start a church. In two years he learned to speak Arabic. He cannot read or write well in Arabic, but he can speak it amazingly well. His church services also draw people from a wide variety of backgrounds. People from Africa, India, Pakistan, Bangladesh, and the Philippines all attend his services.

Because of the success of Filipino pastors in spreading the gospel in hard-to-reach places, some American missionaries have dedicated themselves to training Filipino pastors so that well-trained men can take the gospel into some of the darkest parts of the world.

hundred hours before Iraq agreed to a cease-fire. The war, however, could be considered a Pyrrhic victory. It did not remove Saddam Hussein from power in Iraq, and it prompted the growth of radical Muslim organizations, including al-Qaeda, because of Muslim resentment of a Western presence and influence in the Persian Gulf.

Despite the great wealth resulting from oil production, Kuwait, like many other countries in this region, lacks a key natural resource—fresh water. To provide enough drinking water, the Kuwaiti government burns millions of barrels of oil each day to produce electricity so they can extract fresh water from the sea. In addition, the Kuwaiti people consume 1.5 million cubic meters of water each day, and the **desalination** plants can barely keep up with demand. Over time, the discharged salt brine from desalination is increasing the salinity of the Persian Gulf, thus compounding the problem.

Eighty-two percent of the population is Muslim in this country, where Sunni Islam is the state religion. There is also a large Shia Muslim minority. Kuwait employs a large immigrant work force, and nearly 13 percent of these people affiliate with some form of Christianity. Other religions are tolerated and have some freedom to worship openly. As in other Muslim countries, conversion from Islam to another religion is forbidden. Therefore, most Kuwaiti Christians meet in secret. However, Evangelical Christianity (1.5 percent of the population) is growing in numbers, and Christians there are increasing in boldness.

Section Quiz

1. What Arab country has one of the lowest literacy rates and the lowest per capita GDP in the Middle East?

2. What is a sultan? an emir? a sheik?

3. What factors caused the Persian Gulf War?

✳ What do you think the role of the United States should be in the Persian Gulf?

III. Iraq

The **Tigris** and **Euphrates Rivers** are the most important rivers in the Middle East. They begin in the mountains of Turkey before entering Iraq. Rain and melting snow in the mountains provide a constant flow of water in spite of the low rainfall downstream—only ten inches annually. The lifeblood of Iraq, these rivers provide water for irrigation and hydroelectric projects. Also navigable, these rivers are as important to Iraq as the Mississippi River is to the United States.

The rivers flow almost parallel in Iraq for five hundred miles. Since ancient times, the land between them has been called **Mesopotamia**, meaning "(land) between rivers." This well-watered plain was the home of several of the world's early civilizations, including Sumer, Babylonia, and Assyria.

A ruthless dictator named **Saddam Hussein** took over the country in 1979. He proved his willingness to use any means to further his ends, including biological and chemical warfare. His efforts to win glory for himself and power for his nation led the country into chaos. Hussein's invasion of Kuwait sparked the Persian Gulf War, and his repeated violations of UN resolutions prompted the 2003 invasion that toppled him from power. Following the exodus of U.S. and allied forces in 2011, the country began to decline into civil war between Shia and Sunni Islamic groups who desire to exact revenge on one another.

An Iraqi farmer casts his ballot during the Diyara Agricultural Union elections in 2006.

This Muslim country is divided between Shias (65 percent) and Sunnis (35 percent), with a tiny group of Iraqis (1.59 percent) identifying with some form of Christianity. Evangelical Christians numbered 53,000 in 2010 (or 0.2 percent of the population). Christians continue to endure persecution and yet grow in number in the midst of suffering.

Iraq is surrounded by land, except for a thirty-six-mile coastline on the Persian Gulf. Its neighboring states are Turkey on the north, Syria and Jordan on the west, Saudi Arabia and Kuwait on the south, and Iran on the east. Its Persian Gulf access is in the southeast between Iran and Kuwait.

Iraq, which is a little more than twice the area of Idaho, may be divided into four general geographic zones: deserts, rolling uplands, northern highlands, and alluvial plain. Only about 13 percent of its land is arable.

Desert Zone

The Syrian Desert covers western Iraq, and the Arabian Desert sprawls across southern Iraq to the Euphrates River. Without adequate rain or rivers, a warm and dry desert climate prevails. The desert is rutted with numerous wadis, most of them dry, that can become raging torrents in the rainy season. The desert has only a few settlements at oases, some of which produce dates from palm trees. This area is populated by few people, mostly nomads.

Northern Highlands

The *northern highlands* near Turkey and in the northeast near Iran consist of rugged mountains that range from about 3,200 feet to more than 13,000 feet. As is true elsewhere in the Middle East, oil

Muslim Festivals

The Muslim calendar is based on a lunar calendar rather than a solar calendar. Therefore, the new year and other festival celebrations occur at different times of the year. During the first month of the Muslim calendar, Muslims honor the memory of Hussein, the grandson of Muhammed, who is believed to have been killed in battle. Shia Muslims in Iraq and Iran consider Hussein to be a martyr, and the men walk through the streets chained together and beat themselves in order to imitate the suffering of Hussein.

On the tenth day of the new year, Iraqis celebrate Ashura ("AH-shoo-rah") to honor the landing of Noah's ark. Their version of the story of Noah has some similarities with the biblical account but limits the time of the Flood and Noah's stay on the ark to 40 days. Even though the Islamic version of the Flood differs from that recorded in Genesis, the Muslims still teach of the animals being gathered by twos and a flood that destroyed everything on earth.

International Women's Day in Istanbul, Turkey

is the primary resource in Iraq, especially in the Upper Mesopotamia region, where the cities of Mosul (MOH suhl) and Kirkuk (kihr KOOK) are centers of the oil industry. The area is inhabited primarily by **Kurds** (a non-Arab ethnic group in the Middle East).

The high mountains in the northeast corner of Iraq are part of the range that is called the Zagros (ZAHG rohs) Mountains in Iran and the Taurus Mountains in Turkey. The Kurds have lived in that mountainous region for around four thousand years, enduring ancient and modern conquerors. Kurds have long fought for an independent homeland called Kurdistan. The Kurds have suffered in all four countries where they live, but especially in Iraq. The world was shocked during the Iran-Iraq War when reports surfaced that Saddam Hussein had used chemical and biological weapons to wipe out Kurdish villages.

Following the defeat of Hussein, the Kurdish region became autonomous, and the people have become prosperous. While many Kurds are Muslim, freedom of religion has allowed the spread of Christianity among the Kurdish people. As a result, Kurdish congregations are appearing and growing, with great possibilities for the future.

Rolling Uplands

The *rolling uplands* are located between the upper Tigris and Euphrates Rivers. The zone includes what became known during the Iraq War as the "*Sunni* (SOO nee) *Triangle*" or the "Triangle of Death" because it is heavily populated by Sunni Muslims, ardent supporters of Saddam Hussein, and because a large number of American

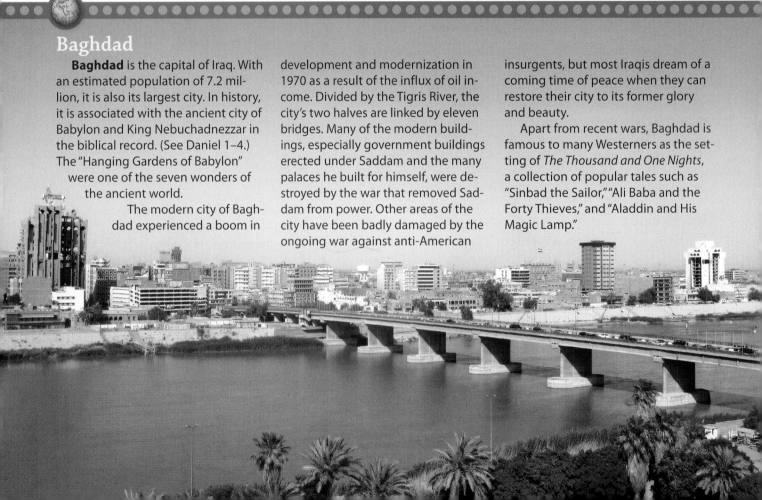

Baghdad

Baghdad is the capital of Iraq. With an estimated population of 7.2 million, it is also its largest city. In history, it is associated with the ancient city of Babylon and King Nebuchadnezzar in the biblical record. (See Daniel 1–4.) The "Hanging Gardens of Babylon" were one of the seven wonders of the ancient world.

The modern city of Baghdad experienced a boom in development and modernization in 1970 as a result of the influx of oil income. Divided by the Tigris River, the city's two halves are linked by eleven bridges. Many of the modern buildings, especially government buildings erected under Saddam and the many palaces he built for himself, were destroyed by the war that removed Saddam from power. Other areas of the city have been badly damaged by the ongoing war against anti-American insurgents, but most Iraqis dream of a coming time of peace when they can restore their city to its former glory and beauty.

Apart from recent wars, Baghdad is famous to many Westerners as the setting of *The Thousand and One Nights*, a collection of popular tales such as "Sinbad the Sailor," "Ali Baba and the Forty Thieves," and "Aladdin and His Magic Lamp."

Earth Matters: "Eden Again"

An Iraqi girl carries reeds gathered from the Mesopotamian marshes near Basra in southern Iraq.

Saddam Hussein used lack of water as a weapon of mass destruction against the Shia Muslims. The only thing holding back the desert from overcoming the Marsh Arabs was the waters of the Mesopotamian marshes. So he drained them.

At first, the rest of the world didn't notice because Hussein's shadow hung over Iraq. Then, in 2001, the United Nations Environment Programme (UNEP) published a document describing the drying of the marshes as "the worst engineered environmental disaster of the last century."

Azzam Alwash, an Iraqi engineer, devoted himself to restoring the waters to a region he had loved since childhood. He worked with his father to get flow-rate and soil data. The data showed that if waters were directed back to the marshes, the area would teem with life again. When Iraq was invaded in 2003, the Mesopotamian marsh restoration captured world attention, catapulting the project forward. As of 2013, over half the marshes were filled with water again, and wildlife and Marsh Arabs were returning home.

troops were killed there trying to subdue Iraqi insurgents. The northern point of the triangle is the city of Tikrit (tih KREET), Saddam's hometown. The other points of the triangle are Ar Ramadi to the southwest of Tikrit and Baghdad to the southeast.

Alluvial Plain

The final zone is the *alluvial plain* of the Tigris and Euphrates Rivers. The plain extends from just north of Baghdad through the area southeast of Baghdad, especially at the rivers' confluence, to where the rivers flow into the Persian Gulf near Basra (BAHS rah). About 75 percent of all Iraqis live in that region, which is also known as Lower Mesopotamia.

The two great rivers of Iraq join in the far south to form the **Shatt al Arab**, which continues about one hundred miles through marshy lowlands before it empties into the Persian Gulf. Many Shiites live in the swamps and cities of the Shatt al Arab. After the Persian Gulf War, the Shiites rebelled against Hussein and his Sunni government. The UN cease-fire enforced a no-fly zone south of the thirty-second parallel. But Hussein used ground troops to massacre the rebels. In 1992, he completed a 351-mile canal to drain the swamps, hoping to destroy the Shiite way of life and eliminate their hideout.

Behistun Rock

Along the caravan road between Ecbatana and Babylon is a high cliff that displays one of the greatest treasures from the ancient world. Behistun Rock is five hundred feet high. Darius ordered an account written there in stone, for all to read, of how he took the throne and organized the realm into satrapies (provinces). The inscription is important because it holds the key to reading the undeciphered letters of the ancient Babylonian language. Darius had the account of his accomplishments inscribed in three languages: Babylonian, Old Persian, and Elamite. The Behistun Rock ranks with the Rosetta Stone, which was used to unlock the mysteries of ancient Egyptian hieroglyphics.

Section Quiz

1. What two major rivers flow through Iraq and into the Persian Gulf?
2. What is the fertile region between those rivers called?
3. What cultural group dominates the population of northern Iraq?
4. What is Iraq's capital?
* Where would you, as a Christian, prefer to live—in Iraq or among the Kurds? Why?

IV. Iran

Geographic Overview

In area, Iran is the second largest country in the Persian Gulf (behind only Saudi Arabia). On the north, Iran borders Armenia, Azerbaijan, the Caspian Sea, and Turkmenistan. On the west, about one-fourth of Iran borders Turkey, and the rest borders Iraq. On the east, two-thirds of Iran borders Afghanistan, and the rest borders Pakistan. And on the south, Iran is washed by the waters of the Persian Gulf and the Gulf of Oman.

The climate of Iran is mostly arid and semiarid. The narrow plain along the Caspian Sea, however, is subtropical. The terrain ranges from a rugged, mountainous rim to a high central basin to narrow plains along the coasts. The combined factors of climate and terrain make only about 10 percent of the land arable.

The Zagros Mountains

Iran is an ancient kingdom. Its people are not Arabs but Persians. The ancient **Persian Empire** included all of modern Iran. In fact, Iran was called Persia until 1935. The name Persia originally referred to a small region in the southern **Zagros Mountains.** The rugged mountains cover most of the western third of Iran, extending along southern and western Iran and into northern Iraq. They offer a cooler climate than do the plains of Iraq. Major sources of income in the mountains are agriculture and livestock.

The rugged, snow-topped Zagros Mountains provide a natural boundary between Iran and Iraq.

The Elburz Mountains

Along the northern border of Iran run the **Elburz** (ehl BOORZ) **Mountains**, which connect the Caucasus Mountains on the west with the Hindu Kush to the east in Afghanistan. Like these neighboring mountain ranges, the Elburz Mountains are high, rising to 18,406 feet at Mount Damavand near Tehran.

Tehran is the capital and largest city of Iran. With more than twelve million people in its metropolitan area, it is also the largest city in the whole Persian Gulf region. Until the rise of the caravan route in the thirteenth century, however, it was only a small town. It did not become the capital until 1788. Most sections of the city were built after 1910, and many of them have a distinctly European flavor. The official language is Farsi (FAHR see; Persian), an Indo-European language.

The Khuzestan Plain

The Khuzestan (KOO sih STAHN) Plain is an extension of the fertile plains of Mesopotamia. The plain shares the same climate as Mesopotamia and contains Iran's major oil-producing area. It was the home of the Elamites in Bible times (see Ezra 4:9 and Acts 2:9) and the focus of fighting during the Iran-Iraq War (1980–88).

In the winter, the Persian kings moved to the Khuzestan Plain in the southwestern corner of Iran. The winter capital, Susa (or Shushan, as the Bible calls it), appears in Nehemiah 1:1 and Daniel 8:2. It is also the setting for the book of Esther. To help the movement of soldiers and messengers, the Persians constructed a Royal Road from Susa all the way to the Aegean Sea.

The Eastern Deserts

Eastern Iran is desert. The Dasht-e-Kavir and the Dasht-e-Lut together cover thirty-eight thousand square miles of the barren Plateau of Iran. The plateau averages three thousand feet in elevation and consists of barren rocky hills and large salt flats. Most cities stand on the western edge. The border city of Zabol (zah BOHL) lies beyond the plateau in the Rigestan Desert.

Religious Overview

Zarathustra (zahr ah THOO strah; Zoroaster in Greek) founded the ancient religion of the Persian Empire, **Zoroastrianism** (zohr oh AS tree uh nihz um). The Arabs defeated the last Zoroastrian forces in AD 635 near Baghdad. However, the religion is still practiced by a persecuted minority in the plateau cities of Kerman and Yazd (and in India, where adherents are called Parsis). Their sacred book is the *Avesta* (uh VES tuh), and they worship the god Ahura Mazda. Ahura Mazda is opposed by the evil spirit Angra Mainyu. Zoroastrians believe that Ahura Mazda will win in the end, but individuals are caught up in the battle between good and evil. The fate of the individual lies with his own choices. Whereas some religions promote cremation and others burial, Zoroastrians put the corpses on Towers of Silence, where vultures strip off the flesh within a few hours. Zoroastrians believe that burying the corpses pollutes the earth. Cremating them would pollute the fire, a symbol of Ahura Mazda.

The official religion of Iran is the Shiite branch of Islam, which about 90 percent of Iranians follow. The Sunni minority of 9 percent is subject to persecution in this country.

Iran has been increasing its persecution of Christians in recent years. It has forbidden the sale of Bibles in bookstores and barred Muslims from attending church services. In 1993, the Iranian parliament required all citizens to make public their religious affiliation. The government has used this information to remove Christians from government jobs, such as teaching and civil service. Converts from Islam are threatened with torture unless they deny their new faith in Christ. However, since the 1979 revolution, the number of those affiliated with some form of Christianity in Iran has grown to

Persepolis

Persepolis was the largest and greatest Persian capital. About twenty-five miles east of modern Shiraz, the ruins still dwarf visitors. The Audience Hall of Darius held ten thousand people, and Xerxes built the even larger Hall of a Hundred Columns. The gold, silver, ivory, and marble have long since been removed, but many fine relief sculptures remain. Naqsh-i Rustam, a cliff near Persepolis, contains four royal tombs cut into the rock, including that of Darius.

The Breakdown of Iranian Society

Iran is a land of extremes. Muslim religious leaders follow **sharia** law and mete out harsh forms of punishment. The government is flouting world opinion and pressing ahead on development of nuclear weapons. Meanwhile, there is a breakdown of Iranian society that lies just below the surface. A widespread though illegal underground party circuit exists where young Iranians defy Islamic restrictions and engage in destructive behavior. This has contributed to Iran's having the highest rate of opium addicts in the world, with five million drug addicts across the country. The breakdown in society has resulted in two hundred thousand children living on the streets. Prostitution is also on the rise.

Baha'i houses of worship, such as this one in Israel, look different from the typical mosque.

approximately 385,000 as of 2010. Evangelical Christians number around 118,000, and 100,000 of these are from a Muslim background.

Baha'ism (bah HIGH iz um) is a religion based on the writings of two renegade Shiites, the Bab and Bahaullah. In 1844, the Bab predicted the imminent coming of an imam who would bring truth and justice. The government executed the Bab in Tabriz in 1850 and imprisoned his disciple Bahaullah in the Black Pit in Tehran, where Bahaullah came to view himself as the predicted imam. He was later exiled—first to Baghdad (Iraq), then to Istanbul (Turkey), and finally to Acre (Israel).

In spite of bitter persecution, about three hundred thousand Baha'ists remain in Iran. Baha'ists have spread to Africa, India, and the United States and have their international headquarters in Haifa, Israel. Baha'ists promote the unity of all religions, and they offer no salvation from sin. In contrast to the one true God of biblical Christianity (1 John 5:20), the god of Baha'ism is unknowable.

Another Muslim minority that started in Persia is the Sufis, the mystics of Islam. **Sufism** (SOO fihz um) teaches that nothing exists except God. Other Muslim sects do not consider Sufis orthodox Muslims.

Section Quiz

1. From which mountain range did Persia emerge?
2. During what season did the Persian kings go to the palace in Susa on the Khuzestan Plain?
3. What ancient religion is still practiced in small pockets on the plateau of Iran?
4. What mountains cross Iran in the north?
5. Iran is the only country of the Persian Gulf that has an official language other than Arabic. What is it?
* Baha'ism emphasizes unity in all world religions, stating that we should accept the good in each religion and practice tolerance and acceptance of all religions. Was Jesus tolerant of false religion? What can we learn from Jesus's example and teaching regarding other religions?

Chapter Review

Making Connections

1. What language is spoken throughout most of the Persian Gulf region?

2–3. What are the two holiest cities of Islam?

4–5. What are the two main arms of the Arabian Sea?

6. What advantages does Bahrain have over the other Gulf States?

7. What natural resource has turned many Persian Gulf countries into wealthy nations?

8. What natural resource is scarce in most of the Persian Gulf countries?

Developing Geography Skills

1. Based on the map on page 415, what countries can Iran easily influence by merely crossing the border? What are some of the countries in this region where Iran is exerting an influence?

2. Based on the map on page 415, what countries would be adversely affected by the increasing salinity of the Persian Gulf resulting from desalination discharge?

Thinking Critically

1. How should Christians respond to Islamic nations closed to the gospel?

2. Why is the Muslim world divided against itself?

Living in God's World

1. The Muslim population in the United States is small but growing. Research where the nearest significant Muslim population is located near your hometown. Develop a plan for evangelizing Muslims in this community.

2. Research the kinds of tent-making jobs that are available in Middle Eastern countries.

People, Places, and Things to Know

Middle East
Persian Gulf
mosque
Arabian Peninsula
Mecca
Medina
Qur'an
Rub al Khali
Empty Quarter
Riyadh
Ibn-Saud
Wahhabi
Bedouins
Arabs
khat
Gulf of Aden
wadis
sultanate
Gulf of Oman
emirate
desalination
OPEC
Persian Gulf War
desalination
Tigris River
Euphrates River
Mesopotamia
Saddam Hussein
Kurds
Baghdad
Shatt al Arab
Persian Empire
Zagros Mountains
Elburz Mountains
Tehran
Zoroastrianism
Persepolis
Baha'ism
sharia
Sufism

18

EASTERN MEDITERRANEAN

*W*hile the jagged peninsulas of southern Europe have plentiful harbors and a mild mediterranean climate, the coasts along the eastern Mediterranean Sea have few good ports, scarce fresh water, and almost no natural resources. Yet the strategic location of this region has placed it at the center of the world stage.

The countries of the Eastern Mediterranean touch three continents. Turkey is anchored in Europe, Israel borders Africa, and the region as a whole is on the southwest border of Asia. Ancient cultures from all three continents have mixed in the Eastern Mediterranean for thousands of years.

While a primary source of controversy in the Persian Gulf has been oil, the primary cause of trouble in the Eastern Mediterranean has been religion. Whether the issue is oil or religion, however, terrorism has been and now is the method of expression most associated with this region. Muslims overran the area long ago, but in 1948 the United Nations allowed the Jews to establish an independent state in the heart of Muslim territory. The region has been torn by strife ever since. The presence in the region of Western powers that are trying to mediate or enforce peace seems only to have added fuel to the fire of hatred between the Muslims and the Jews. The challenge that the nations of the world now face is to find a just and merciful resolution to one of the most bitter conflicts in world history. Christians should be especially concerned to work toward that end because the Lord came to teach the peoples of the earth justice and mercy (Matt. 12:17–21).

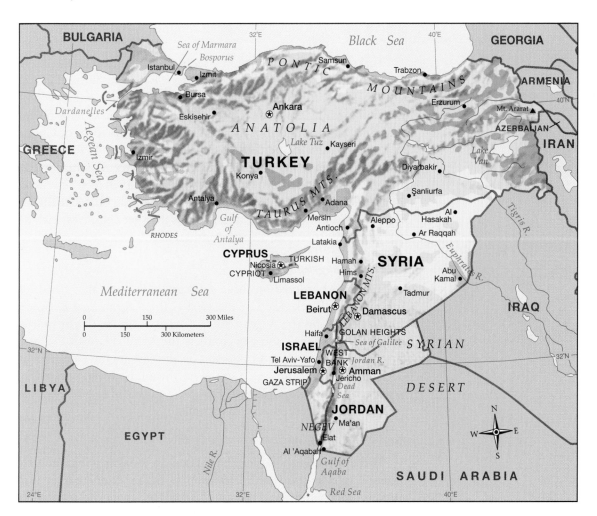

Eastern Mediterranean Fast Facts						
Country	Capital	Area (sq. mi.)	Pop. (2013) (M)	Pop. Density (per sq. mi.)	Per Capita GDP ($US)	Life Span
Cyprus	Nicosia	3,571	1.16	325	$26,900	78.00
Israel	Jerusalem	8,019	7.71	961	$32,200	81.07
Jordan	Amman	34,495	6.48	188	$6,000	80.18
Lebanon	Beirut	4,015	4.13	1029	$15,900	75.23
Syria	Damascus	71,498	22.46	314	$5,100	74.92
Turkey	Ankara	302,535	80.69	266	$15,000	72.77

I. Turkey

Overview

Turkey is the crossroads between Europe and Asia and the Middle East. It is part European and part Middle Eastern in its influences. Its location forms a "**chokepoint**," controlling movement of goods and peoples between the three great continents. As such, it has played a pivotal role in history. It is itself influenced by both its external and internal geography. It is often called **Asia Minor**, signifying both its size—it is much like a small continent—and its influence on history.

Turkey has technically been a secular state since the reforms of the 1920s. However, 97 percent of the people follow a form of Islam, with 70–80 percent identifying with Sunni Islam and 15–25 percent associating with Shia Islam. Three percent of the Turks have no religious affiliation, and those identifying with some form of Christianity constitute 0.2 percent of the population. While Evangelical Christianity represents less than one tenth of a percent of the population, this group has grown from as few as ten in 1960 to around four thousand by 2010. Despite being few in number, Christians in Turkey have sent around two dozen missionaries to other countries, including Germany, Romania, Bulgaria, and France.

External Geography

Turkey is bordered on three sides by bodies of water. North of Turkey is the Black Sea. On the west is the Aegean Sea. Between the Black Sea and the Aegean are two narrow straits, the Bosporus and the Dardanelles. On the south is the Mediterranean Sea and the countries of Syria and Iraq. And on the east are the countries of Georgia, Armenia, and Iran. On the northwest, however, Turkey extends across the Bosporus into Europe, and that area borders Bulgaria as well as Greece's western extreme.

Internal Geography

Turkey is slightly larger than Texas in area. It is rimmed by mountains, and its overall elevation is higher than that of any surrounding countries. Half of the land is above 3,280 feet in elevation; two-thirds of the land is above 2,625 feet. Turkey is home to the biblical **Mount Ararat**, which towers to 16,854 feet in an eastern area that juts between neighboring Armenia and Iran. The mountains of Turkey are susceptible to earthquakes.

Seven major river basins are within Turkey, each originating within its borders and flowing out of the country. Two of them flow into the Caspian Sea; one flows to the Arabian Sea via the Tigris and Euphrates Rivers, the Persian Gulf, and the Gulf of Oman.

Turkey's climate is temperate. It has hot, dry summers and mild, wet winters. Conditions are harsher in the interior region and in areas of greater elevations.

Mt. Ararat on the right; Lesser Ararat on the left

Politics and Demography

Although Turkey is predominantly Muslim, it has close ties to Europe. Turkey allied itself with Western Europe and the United States when it joined NATO in 1952. Like its European neighbors, Turkey has sought to become a secular (nonreligious) state. The Father of Modern Turkey, **Kemal Atatürk** (keh-MAHL at-ah-TURK), introduced this policy when he won control of Turkey in 1923. Atatürk introduced a long list of reforms, including a new non-Arabic alphabet, Western laws, the right of women to vote, a ban on polygamy ("many wives"), a ban on wearing veils and turbans, and the adoption of the West's solar calendar to replace the Muslim lunar calendar. These Western reforms remain in effect today, although support for sharia law and radical Islam is on the rise.

Turkey has the largest population in the Middle East and one of the largest populations in Europe. About 28 percent of the Turkish people live in rural areas, and they provide about 9 percent of the nation's GDP. Turkey's economy has traditionally revolved around agriculture and mining, but tourism, commerce and modern industry are increasing.

The great hope of Turkey's secular government is to trade with the rich nations of Europe and avoid the religious strife that has hurt the rest of the Middle East. The key to Turkey's hope is membership in the European Union (EU). But Europe continues to force Turkey to wait for three reasons: Turkey's weak economy, its historic conflict with Greece, and its history of human rights abuses against the Kurds. In addition, some people have questioned whether Turkey is actually more Asian or Middle Eastern than European.

To the Turks, the EU's hesitance to admit their country to full membership is evidence of prejudice. The citizens have grown increasingly bitter, and religious leaders are pushing for a return to the Muslim world. A radical Islamic Party came to power in 1996, hoping to replace Turkey's civil laws with sharia law and to withdraw Turkey from NATO. But the army intervened—as it has in the past—threatening to seize power unless the Muslim leaders promised to uphold democracy and to protect the secular constitution. Since 2003, Recep Tayyip Erdogan has served as prime minister of Turkey. In 2011, he was elected to a third term.

Recep Tayyip Erdogan is prime minister of Turkey.

Thrace

The European portion of Turkey is a small corner of the Balkan Peninsula, an area called **Thrace**. It is a hilly area with a mediterranean climate that is good for agriculture. Thrace includes **Istanbul**

Istanbul

The Hagia Sophia in Istanbul is an example of Byzantine architecture.

Among the architectural wonders in the ancient city of Istanbul are the Hagia Sophia, Topkapi Palace, and the Blue Mosque. The Hagia Sophia was the mother church of the Byzantine Empire. The interior moldings are covered with gold leaf, and the crucifix and altar are of pure gold. The Turks turned the Hagia Sophia into a mosque. They added four minarets, and covered the mosaics of Christ and the archangels because Muslims believe that such images are a form of idolatry. In the twentieth century, Atatürk turned the old church into a museum, and the mosaics have since been uncovered for visitors.

Topkapi Palace was the seat of the Ottoman Empire. Mehmet II, who conquered Constantinople, first built the palace, which includes fountains, three hundred rooms, and secret passageways. Adding to the splendor is a wealth of diamonds, rubies, and emeralds. At first, only government officials lived in the palace, but Suleiman the Magnificent made it his home in the 1540s. The palace included rooms for a harem of four thousand women. It is now a museum.

In 1609, Sultan Ahmed I commissioned a mosque to be built across from the Hagia Sophia. It became known as the Blue Mosque because of the twenty thousand blue ceramic tiles decorating the interior. The unusual design includes a series of half-domes leading up to the central dome. The mosque also has six minarets rather than the traditional four.

(is tan BULL), formerly called Constantinople, the largest city in the Middle East and the heartbeat of Turkey.

The water passage between Thrace and Asia Minor, the main part of Turkey, is the only route from the Black Sea to the Mediterranean Sea. In making that passage, ships leaving the Black Sea first enter the narrow strait called the **Bosporus** (BOS pohr us), passing Istanbul on the European side. A bridge spans that strait today. Next, the ships enter the small Sea of Marmara (MAR mohr ah). Finally, they enter the Aegean Sea by passing through a second strait, called the **Dardanelles** (dahr den ELS), which the Greeks called the Hellespont. From there, the ships enter the Mediterranean. This region has been important since the times when the armies of both Xerxes of Persia and Alexander the Great of Greece crossed at the Dardanelles.

Section Quiz

1. What strait separates Europe and Asia?
2. What religious group wants Turkey to withdraw from NATO?
3. Name the region of Turkey that lies in Europe.
4–5. What is the largest city in the Middle East? Give a former name for this large city.
   ✯ Do you think the European Union should allow Turkey to become a member? Why or why not?

Anatolia

The Asian section of Turkey, what is sometimes called Asia Minor, is **Anatolia**. Many historic cities lie on this crossroad between Asia and Europe. The ancient city of Troy once stood on the Asian side of the Dardanelles, near the Aegean. The German archeologist Heinrich Schliemann discovered the ruins of Troy in 1871, thereby proving that Homer's epic poem *The Iliad* was not a complete myth. Another ancient city is Troas, where Paul boarded ship on his missionary journey to Europe.

Several empires arose in Anatolia, the first being the Hittite Empire (c. 1700–1178 BC). The Hittites became proficient at ironworking. This advance enabled them to build war chariots and win many battles.

Capital on the Central Plateau

The high Central Plateau is the most dominant feature of Asia Minor. Because the Pontic and Taurus Mountains block most moisture, the plateau gets less than ten inches of rain annually. Irrigated portions are very productive, and Turkey is one of the largest producers of wheat and barley in the region. It also produces sugar beets.

Ankara, Turkey

Even today, a few nomadic herders roam with their flocks over the dry grasslands. The Seljuk Turks, who originally came from Central Asia, settled there in the eleventh century, bringing with them the Turkish language and Islam. Turkish remains the official language; most of the people speak it.

When Turkey became a nation in 1923, Atatürk moved the capital from Istanbul to Ankara (ANG kah rah), and it quickly became the most important city in the Central Plateau. Its population is 4.55 million.

Taurus Mountains in the South

The rugged **Taurus Mountains** cross southern Turkey, continuing east until they meet the **Pontic Mountains** near Mount Ararat, the highest mountain in Turkey. The Taurus Mountains form a barrier between the south and the rest of Turkey. Historically, the only pass between the Central Plateau and the coast was the Cilician Gates, north of modern Adana.

The Turquoise Coast—A narrow coastal plain lies on the southern coast at the foot of the Taurus Mountains. Both this area and the western valleys have a mediterranean climate and receive about twenty-five inches of precipitation annually. Farmers there grow grapes, citrus fruits, olives, tobacco, and cotton. The beautiful scenery has earned the south the title "the Turquoise Coast."

Kurds on the Southeastern Borders—The headwaters of the Tigris and Euphrates Rivers are in the eastern Taurus Mountains. These rivers wind their way through the plateau, then drop into the upper Mesopotamian Plain. Most of the region is dry, except for the fertile riverbanks, which allow farmers to grow grains and fruit. Abraham once stayed in the city of Haran, near Urfa (oor FAH). The main modern cities there are Sanliurfa and Diyarbakir (dy yahr bah KEER).

Turkey's largest minority group, the Kurds, live in southeastern Turkey, near the border with Iraq and Iran. The Kurds constitute

Cyprian Hospitality

"Hospitality is one of the cornerstones of the Cypriot way of life, and Cypriots are usually generous and gracious hosts. Even the poorest peasant feel[s] bound to honor guests as lavishly as they can afford to. Turkish Cypriots are far less exposed to foreigners than their Greek counterparts, and consequently treat guests, or in Turkish, *misafir* (mihs-ah-FEER), with lavish cordiality and generosity. Typically Cypriots will ply their guests with food and drink, especially coffee."

Cultures of the World: Cyprus, 72

about 20 percent of Turkey's population. Some Kurds have moved to cities, dropping their Kurdish language and customs; however, many still herd sheep in the mountains.

Section Quiz

1. Give two names for the part of Turkey in Asia.
2–3. What two mountain ranges border the Central Plateau?
4. What is the typical climate of the plateau?
5. What ethnic group makes up about 20 percent of the population of Turkey?
* Why are the Dardenelles and the Bosporus so important?

II. Cyprus

The island of Cyprus is a little bigger than half the state of Connecticut. It is the third-largest island in the Mediterranean Sea (behind Sicily and Sardinia). Two forested mountain ranges cross Cyprus from east to west, rising as high as 6,406 feet, with the **Mesaoria Plain** between them. Near the center of the plain on the northern half of the island is the capital, **Nicosia** (nik oh SEE ah).

The valley and the coasts have a typical mediterranean climate—mild, rainy winters and hot, dry summers. Only the mountains get snow in winter. Although only about 8 percent of the land is arable, the climate supports grapefruit, lemons, oranges, grapes, and olives.

The economy of Cyprus is heavily dependent on the tourist trade, which is susceptible to erratic swings caused by political and social instability. The economy also depends on its limited agriculture and government service, which combined represent more than half of the workforce. Natural resources of Cyprus include copper, asbestos, gypsum, timber, salt, and marble.

Cyprus has a rich history. Greeks, Persians, Romans, Byzantines, Franks, and Venetians have occupied it. The Ottoman Turks ruled it from 1571 until the British gained administrative control in 1878. Although Cyprus gained its independence in 1960, the British retain two military bases on the southern and southeastern coasts of the island.

The ethnic composition of the island's population makes it a volatile, divided country. Sixty-nine percent of its inhabitants are Greek Cypriots, who follow the Greek Orthodox religion. Twenty-three percent are Turkish Cypriots, who are Muslims (mostly Sunni). In addition, there are a number of foreign workers from Asia, Africa, the Middle East, and Eastern Europe. While 94 percent of the people identify with some form of Christianity, only tiny groups of Evangelical Christians exist in Cyprus. Most of these are foreigners; only a few are native to Cyprus. At the same time, Cyprus is the home base for several Christian organizations that work in nearby Middle Eastern countries. Christian radio programs and Christian literature are being used to spread the gospel to this divided country.

After gaining independence, Cyprus tried to balance the interests of the Greek and Turkish communities to bring stability to the island. Most of the people wanted to stay united, but a few Greek Cypriots wanted to reunite with Greece, and a few Turkish Cypriots wanted to partition the island into two countries. Fighting broke out in 1963,

Nicosia is the capital of Cyprus.

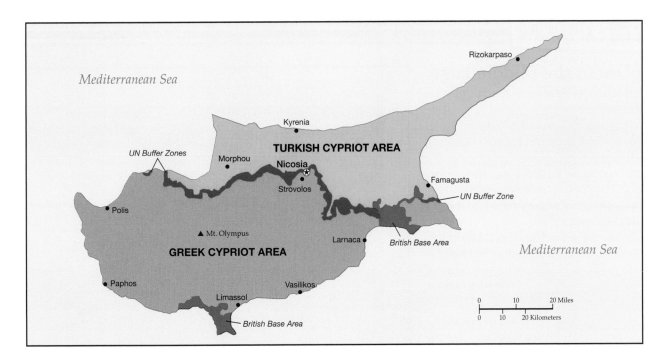

but the UN stepped in to restore peace. In 1974, Greece backed a coup that overthrew the president. In response, Turkey invaded the island and captured the northern one-third of the island for the Turkish Cypriots.

United Nations peacekeepers have remained in Cyprus since 1964. The UN's goal is to unite the island into one sovereign Cyprus, but events since the 1974 war have not been promising. In 1983, the northern portion declared itself the Turkish Republic of Cyprus, but only Turkey has recognized it as a legitimate government. The Greek Cypriots rejected a UN-brokered agreement in April 2004. A month later, the southern two-thirds of the island, known as the Republic of Cyprus, joined the EU. Turkey and the northern Cypriots resent the implication that the division of the island might be permanent and fear that the south and Greece will prevent Turkey's admission to the EU. While the potential for war is ever present, barriers to trade and free movement are slowly being removed, and communication between the two regions is improving.

Section Quiz

1. What two rival groups live on Cyprus?
2. What country retains two military bases on the island of Cyprus?
3. Which country supported a coup that toppled Cyprus's president?
4. Which country retaliated by invading and capturing the northern third of the island?
* Should Cyprus be partitioned permanently? Why or why not?

III. Former Mandate of Syria

The land southeast of Turkey along the eastern Mediterranean is often called the **Levant** (leh VAHNT). The lowlands and mountain ranges of the Levant have a mediterranean climate. These fertile lands contrast with the wastes of the Syrian Desert in the interior.

LET'S GO EXPLORING

Land Use in the Middle East

1. Which countries have some mediterranean agriculture?
2. Which two countries on the Arabian Peninsula have large areas of subsistence agriculture?
3. Find a continuous path of agriculture from Israel to Iran. Which countries share parts of this agricultural region, known as the Fertile Crescent?
* Which country in the Middle East seems to have the largest area of productive land?

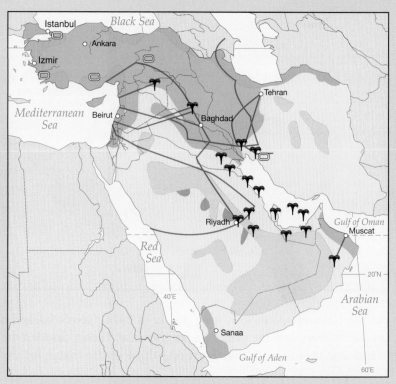

Commercial Farming
- Mediterranean Farming
- Specialized Horticulture (oasis)

Subsistence Farming

Nonfarming
- Nomadic Herding
- Limited Activity
- Chromium
- Petroleum
- Petroleum Pipeline

The Levant and the river valleys of Mesopotamia form a crescent-shaped area called the **Fertile Crescent**, which has been heavily populated since Bible times. For thousands of years, merchants and marching armies have passed through this fertile land route.

The Levant belonged to Turkey until Turkey's defeat in World War I. France and Britain took over these territories, called **mandates**, which they governed in the name of the League of Nations. Their goal was to prepare the people for self-government and independence. The French mandate was called **Syria**, and two countries were born from it: Syria and Lebanon. The British mandate was called **Palestine**.

Syria

Syria has arable lowlands along the Mediterranean coast, which rise to the Jabal an-Nusayriyah Range. Many farming towns lie in this region, where forty inches of rain fall each year. Arvad was the most important port in Bible times (Ezek. 27:8), but today the major port is Latakia (lat uh KEE uh).

The **Syrian Desert** covers most of Syria east of the mountains. Almost uninhabited, the rocky desert plateau slopes downward and eastward from the mountains to the Euphrates River valley. The desert provides phosphates, but the most important resource is oil. Syria also gets most of its precious water from the Euphrates.

Syria's second largest city, Aleppo, lies in the north on the dry side of the mountains, near the border with Turkey. Aleppo has been a major hub of transportation since ancient times. Many railroads in the Middle East meet in Aleppo, which also is the focus of cotton and wheat growing and is known for its textile industry. It ships most of its goods through the port at Latakia.

Syria's capital and largest city, **Damascus**, is also on the arid side of the mountains but in the south. The Barada River, which flows off the mountains, made Damascus a virtual oasis. In ancient times, the city was a convenient stop for caravans traveling through the desert to and from the Euphrates. Damascus claims to be the oldest continuously inhabited city in the world. It was already a city in Abraham's time (Gen. 14:15). Later, Paul became a Christian on the road to Damascus (Acts 9). Today, shoppers at the old marketplaces (*suqs*) can still buy beautiful samples of old-fashioned textiles and metalwork.

Northeast of Damascus are the ruins of Palmyra, another major stop on the caravan route between the Mediterranean Sea and the Persian Gulf. This ancient town arose at an oasis in the Syrian Desert. Solomon first fortified "Tadmor in the wilderness" (1 Kings 9:18; 2 Chron. 8:4). The name *Tadmor* means "palm." The Greeks later called the town by the Greek word for "palm," *Palmyra*. The city was destroyed after it revolted against Roman rule in 273. The ruins have been excavated near the modern town of Tadmur.

Today, 90 percent of all Syrians are Arabs, and the official language is Arabic. The remaining 10 percent are a mixture of Kurds, Armenians, and other ethnic groups. Syria is 90 percent Muslim (74 percent Sunni Muslim and another 16 percent other Muslim sects). About 6 percent affiliate with some form of Christianity. Until the outbreak of the civil war in 2011, Syrian Christians were guaranteed freedom of religion and a greater degree of protection than in most other Middle Eastern countries. However, persecution of Christians by Islamic militias has become one of the tragic consequences of the war. As of 2010, Evangelical Christians represented about 0.1 percent of the Syrian people and numbered around twenty-four thousand.

Syria claims to be a republic, but it has been ruled by a military leader since 1963. **Hafez al-Assad** (ah SAHD) took power in a 1970 coup. Upon Assad's death in 2000, his son **Bashar al-Assad** was elected president in a one-man race. As was the case under his father, Bashar al-Assad's government strictly controls the economy, limits personal freedoms, and suppresses opposition ruthlessly. Assad had promised changes when he succeeded his father but failed to deliver on those promises.

Lebanon

Southwest of Syria is the country of Lebanon. Two parallel mountain ranges, called the Lebanon and Anti-Lebanon Mountains, run down the length of the country. Their highest peaks are Qurnat as-Sawda (10,115 ft.) and Mount Hermon (9,232 ft.), respectively. Between the two parallel ranges lies the Bekáa Valley.

France received Lebanon as part of its mandate after World War I. In 1920, France separated Lebanon from Syria, and both remained under French control until 1946.

Damascus, Syria

Civil War in Syria

In March 2011, protests in Syria erupted into civil war. Government forces responded with brutal repression, including the use of chemical weapons, that resulted in the deaths of at least one hundred thousand Syrians, including many women and children. By late 2013, nearly two million Syrians had fled the country and were being housed in temporary camps in neighboring countries.

Mount Hermon, on the border between Syria and Lebanon, is the only mountain in the region with snowcaps.

A cedar tree in Lebanon

Beirut, Lebanon

Importance of Family in Lebanon

"Many Lebanese homes are organized around the extended family, with grandparents often living with one of their children and his or her family. Other married children and their families join this extended family on festive and holiday occassions, considerably enlarging the family group.

"Partly due to the disruption caused by the years of fighting, and partly because Lebanese people have a long tradition of traveling abroad for work and study, it is difficult for families to get together. . . . When there is a holiday or free time, families want to be together, and reunions become an important leisure goal for many Lebanese people, young and old."

Cultures of the World: Lebanon, 113.

Ancient Tyre

The major city of ancient Lebanon was Tyre. Built on an island, it was the capital of Phoenicia until 583 BC. Tyre was a great trading center in the ancient world. King Hiram of Tyre exported cedars to Solomon (1 Kings 5), and a park preserves the last major grove of the Cedars of Lebanon near the mountain Qurnat as-Sawda. As prophesied, God brought Nebuchadnezzar against Tyre in a destructive siege (Ezek. 26). Later, Alexander the Great built a causeway to take the island in 332 BC.

Modern Beirut

Beirut is the modern capital of Lebanon. With more than 1.9 million people, it is the largest city in the country. Beirut once had a thriving economy based on its resorts and its fruit crops (apples, cherries, grapes, lemons, oranges, and peaches). It was a city of splendor and was known as the "Paris of the Middle East." But that was before the civil war between Muslims and Christians.

Lebanon has a Muslim population of around 59 percent and the largest proportion of Christians of any Middle Eastern country. About 32 percent of the population embraces some form of Christianity. Most of the Christians are called Maronites (MAHR uh nites; descendants of a Syrian hermit named St. Maron). The Maronites later united with the Roman Catholic Church as a separate religious community, acknowledging the pope but following their own format for religious services. Evangelical Christians make up 0.5 percent of the Lebanese population at 21,400 believers. Following the disruptions of civil war, Christian ministries in Lebanon are trying to rebuild and regain momentum.

The 59 percent of Lebanese who are Muslim are members of competing groups. Shia Muslims are the largest group, representing 37 percent of the Lebanese. Next are the Sunnis, who make up 22 percent of the population. There are also about 250,000 **Druze** (DROOZ), or Druse, who broke from the Shiites in the eleventh century and followed some of the teachings of an Egyptian ruler named Muhammad bin Ismail Nashtakin ad-Darazī, who later claimed to be God. Although the Druze considered ad-Darazī a heretic for claiming to be deity, their opponents attached his name to their movement, and they have since adopted it.

Warfare between Maronites, Sunnis, Shiites, and the Druze erupted in 1975. Street fighting, bombings, and the taking of European hostages became commonplace. Terrorists assassinated the Sunni prime minister and the Maronite president. The war became more complex when the Israelis moved into the Bekáa Valley in the south to reduce terrorist bases. Israel eventually carved out a "security zone" in southern Lebanon. The Syrians also moved in to extend their own authority. Once beautiful, Beirut became a pile of rubble.

The people have begun rebuilding their country, but peace is by no means assured. In 2005, the popular prime minister was assassinated, and the outpouring of grief led to demonstrations that forced the Syrians to withdraw their troops. Islamic forces often use Lebanon as a base of operations against Israel and other neighboring states, and the Lebanese government has been unable to stabilize the country. Observers of the Middle East realize that Lebanon remains a powder keg.

Section Quiz

1. What is the Fertile Crescent?
2. What desert forms the interior of the Levant?
3. What is Syria's main resource?
4. What two parallel mountain ranges run the length of Lebanon?
* Why does Lebanon have a larger coastal population than Syria?

IV. Former Mandate of Palestine

Palestine was the British mandate formed out of the Ottoman Empire. The British kept the mandate until 1948, when the territory became the two nations of Israel and Jordan. In modern usage, the term *Palestine* refers only to this area from the intertestamental period through 1948. In ancient times, it included all of what is now Israel, as well as the part of Jordan called Gilead.

Both Jews and Christians call this area the **Holy Land** because most of the events recorded in Scripture took place there. Abraham, Joshua, David, and Elijah walked its dirt roads. Most importantly, Christ came to this corner of the earth two thousand years ago, and He will return to it at His Second Coming.

Israel

Three issues galvanize the countries of the Middle East: Islam, oil, and opposition to Israel. Of those three issues, perhaps the most volatile is Israel. As the only non-Muslim country in the region, it is clearly the "odd man out" among the nations of the Eastern Mediterranean.

Israel is the **Promised Land**, the place God gave to His chosen people. The Israelites conquered the Promised Land under Joshua and built a great nation that lasted about fifteen hundred years. But the Romans destroyed Jerusalem in AD 70, and the Israelites spent the next two thousand years dispersed in foreign lands and persecuted by all peoples. The modern state of Israel testifies to the Jews' undying dream of returning to their homeland.

This dream became a burning passion at the end of the nineteenth century with the rise of the **Zionist Movement**. Hardy pioneers began moving to Zion to build farms on the rough Palestinian frontier. At first, their numbers were few, and the Turks would not give them legal recognition of owning land. But after Palestine became a British mandate, Jewish immigrants began to pour into the area, especially during the Nazi persecution of the 1930s. Against overwhelming odds, the Jews won independence in 1948.

Since its independence, Israel has welcomed Jews from all over the world. They revived the Hebrew language and created words for modern items. Immigrants have come from at least one hundred nations and speak nearly as many languages. As part of the process of adapting to the new country, immigrants can take a five-month course on the nation's culture. In addition, the first job of most Israeli citizens is military service. Adult citizens, with few exceptions, must serve: women serve two years, and men serve three. Israel is surrounded by sworn enemies. Its very survival depends on the willingness of every citizen to defend Israel's right to exist.

Largest Cities of Israel	
City	**Population**
1. Jerusalem	801,000
2. Tel Aviv	410,000
3. Haifa	267,000
4. Beersheba	210,000
5. Ashkelon	113,000

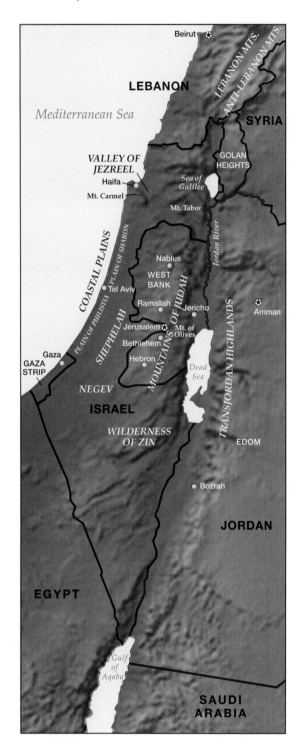

Israel is the home of Judaism and Christianity. From this region Jews were dispersed in the sixth century BC as punishment for their idolatry, and their descendants became instrumental in the spread of the gospel during the first generation of the Church. Christianity spread from Jerusalem to Judea and Samaria and continued to many nations of the world. Today, Judaism is practiced by 75 percent of the people in Israel, and Muslims represent about 17 percent of the population. Four percent have no religious affiliation, and 2 percent practice some form of Christianity. Evangelical Christians constitute about 0.4 percent of the people and number around thirty-one thousand. Sadly, most religious opposition and persecution in Israel comes from the ultra-Orthodox Jews, who want to limit the religious freedom of others and who support anti-conversion laws.

Physical Geography

At its widest point, Israel reaches only about seventy miles wide. At its narrowest point, Israel is only 9.3 miles wide. Its total land area is about the same as that of Massachusetts. Moving eastward from the Mediterranean Sea, one crosses several geographic landforms in relatively quick succession to the Transjordan Highlands on the east bank of the Jordan River.

The **Coastal Plains** are two lowland areas along the Mediterranean Sea: the Plain of Sharon in the north and the Plain of Philistia in the south. Proceeding inland from the Plain of Philistia, the land rises into an area of low hills called the **Shephelah** (shuh FAY luh). The land continues to rise east of the Shephelah into the mountains of Judah, which run north-south for the full length of Israel and are an extension of the Lebanon Mountains to the north. The ancient capital city of **Jerusalem** is at the top of these mountains; hence, the Bible always refers to going up to Jerusalem, even when traveling from north to south.

In the extreme south lies the arid **Negev** (NEHG ehv), which, although it is desert, produces abundant crops of fruits and vegetables with the help of irrigation. It also has rich deposits of potash, bromine, and copper. Northwest of the Plain of Sharon, the **Valley of Jezreel** (also known as the Plain of Esdraelon) extends inland just north of **Mount Carmel** from the Mediterranean to the Jordan River. In the extreme north, the waters from the mountains drain into Lake Hula and then southward into the Sea of Galilee and from there into the Jordan River, which continues flowing due south and empties into the Dead Sea. Between the Dead Sea and the Central Hills is the Wilderness of Judah.

Jewish Cities on the North Coastal Plain—The coastal plain along the Mediterranean Sea has Israel's best farmland. North of Mount Carmel, the coastal plain is called Acre (AHK uhr), or Acco, named for the ancient city by that name. The modern city of Haifa

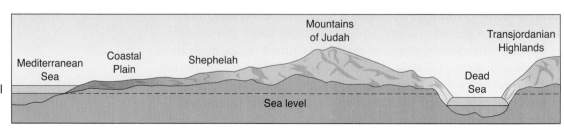

Side view of Israel

GEOGRAPHER'S CORNER

Bible Geography

Valley of Jezreel with ruins of Solomon's fortress in the foreground   *Valley of Jezreel*

A knowledge of geography is an invaluable tool in understanding events in the Bible because it helps to explain why some cities were so important, why Bible characters traveled the routes they did, and why battles were fought where and how they were.

Perhaps the single most important factor in Israel's history was the trade routes that crossed the country. Armies and merchants generally follow well-watered lowlands. Ever since ancient times, the main route from Egypt to Mesopotamia followed the coast until it reached Mount Carmel (1,789 ft.). Because the slopes of Mount Carmel descend directly into the sea, the mountain created a barrier to travel along the coastal plain. There, the ancient trade route veered inland to the Iron Pass, at the fortress of **Megiddo** (muh GID oh). Traders traveled east to the Jordan River before continuing north to Damascus.

The valley from Megiddo to the Jordan is the only valley through the mountains. It has two parts, divided by the narrowest spot in the valley near the town of Jezreel. The western part of the valley, from Megiddo to Jezreel, is called the **Plain of Esdraelon** (ez DRAY lon), or Valley of Megiddo. This plain will become the greatest battlefield in history, where Christ defeats the forces of Antichrist.

Beth-shan and Megiddo, guarding each end of the valley, were the most strategic cities in ancient Palestine. With Jezreel in the center of the valley, these cities controlled trade between Egypt and the Persian Gulf. Israel's enemies from the east gathered in the valley of Jezreel, where Gideon defeated them. The Philistines later controlled Beth-shan and displayed the body of King Saul on the city walls (1 Sam. 31:10). Josiah died at Megiddo while attempting to prevent an Egyptian army from using the pass on its way to Assyria (2 Kings 23:29).

These places will become important again, according to prophecy. The name *Armageddon* comes from *Har Megiddo*, or Mount of Megiddo. Revelation 16:12–16 tells about vast armies that will come from all nations to a battle at Armageddon. Revelation 19:11–21 tells how Christ will be the conqueror at this battle. His clothes will be blood-stained because of a slaughter compared to the trampling of grapes.

Using the passages indicated, answer the following questions, about this time period. Use the map on page 446 for place names.

1. Where will Jesus first arrive on earth when He returns for this battle (Zech. 14:4)?
2. What will happen when His feet touch the ground (Zech. 14:1–9)?
3. What city will be surrounded by these armies from all nations (Luke 21:20–28)?
4. How far south will they be trampled (Isa. 63:1–6)? (Find the city on the map on page 446.)
✯ How deep will the blood be from all of these troops? For what distance will this blood run (in modern units)? How far is it between the northern and southern extent of these armies, according to the map? (All answers can be found in Revelation 14:20.)

(HY fah) has far surpassed Acco and is now the third-largest city in Israel.

The Plain of Sharon stretches south from Mount Carmel to **Tel Aviv**, Israel's largest port and second-largest city. Tel Aviv is short for Tel Aviv-Yafo, which includes the ancient port of Joppa (or Yafo) in its city limits. Sharon is renowned for its fertility and flowers, especially the Rose of Sharon (Song of Sol. 2:1).

Gaza City

Independent Palestinian Cities in the Gaza Strip—The Plain of Philistia extends from Tel Aviv south to Egypt. The land is not as productive as the other coasts. In the Six-Day War, Israel won the coastal strip that is called the **Gaza** (GAH zah) **Strip**. This area covers about 140 square miles and has an estimated population of 1.76 million people. Most of the population is Sunni Muslim. In 2005 the Israeli military withdrew from this region, and elections were held in 2007. The terrorist group called **Hamas** came to power and has maintained power in the Gaza Strip to the present. Hamas has fired thousands of rockets into Israel from the Gaza Strip, and Israel has responded with precision attacks to destroy Hamas's leaders and headquarters.

Wadis in the Shephelah

The Shephelah is a region of low hills between the coastal plain and the mountains. Its average elevation is one thousand feet.

Wadis descend from the mountains and cross the Shephelah on their way to the coast. The parched ground soaks up little moisture from these infrequent torrents. In the ancient struggle between the Philistines and Judah, the main routes from the plain into the mountains of Judah followed the wadis.

Mountain System

The Lebanon and Anti-Lebanon Mountains continue south from Lebanon. They rise less than four thousand feet in this area, but between them is the northern end of the **Great Rift Valley**, which falls below sea level. The **Jordan River** flows through this valley from its headwaters on Mount Hermon south to the **Dead Sea**. (South of the Dead Sea, the Great Rift Valley continues to the Red Sea and into East Africa.)

The mountains of Judah (or Judea) lie west of the Jordan River. The main mountain in this range is the **Mount of Olives** (2,737 ft.). The main cities of ancient Judah, including Jerusalem, lie along the top of the mountain range. Many Palestinians live in these cities today.

Israel also occupies the **Golan** (GOH lahn) **Heights**, a small part of the Anti-Lebanon Mountains northeast of the Sea of Galilee. Israel took this region from Syria during the Six-Day War to stop Syrian attacks and provide a buffer zone, but Syria wants it back. In Bible times it was called Bashan (BAY shun), famous for its pastures and bulls (Ps. 22:12).

Mountains of Galilee—Galilee refers to the northernmost mountains of Israel. The main peaks are Mount Tabor (1,886 ft.) and Mount Meron (3,963 ft.), the highest mountain in Israel. Jesus lived most of His life in Galilee and preached in its synagogues (Mark 1:39). His childhood home, Nazareth, overlooked the Valley of Esdraelon.

This region includes the **Sea of Galilee** in the Great Rift Valley. The Jordan River pauses in this lake on its way to the Dead Sea. The lake is subject to strong winds, which swoop down from the north into the Rift Valley. Today the main town is Tiberias on the west coast. During Jesus' life on earth, Capernaum at the north end was more important.

Archeologists have excavated ruins all over Israel. As cities were destroyed, new ones were built on top of their ruins, creating huge

The Divided Capital

Jerusalem, the most populous city in Israel, sits in the mountains of Judah at the western edge of the West Bank. It has again become the heart of Israel. The Hebrew parliament, or **Knesset** (kuh NES eht), is located in the city. Israel established the first true democracy in the Middle East. The government guarantees Christians, Jews, and Muslims access to their holy sites in Jerusalem: the Temple Mount and the Wailing Wall for Jews, the Dome of the Rock for Muslims, and various sites in Jerusalem and Bethlehem for Christians. The country's industries have excelled. Israel's per capita GDP exceeds that of all of its neighbors and even that of many oil-producing nations in the Middle East. Israel's health

The Knesset

care and educational opportunities are excellent.

Jerusalem has two parts: the Old City and the New City. Israel took East Jerusalem, or the Old City, during the Six-Day War. It has small, winding streets and many ancient buildings. A wall built by Suleiman the Magnificent surrounds the Old City. The Knesset is located in West Jerusalem,

the more modern part of the city. The streets are wider, and the atmosphere pulses with new life. Other buildings in the New City include the Holocaust Museum and the Shrine of the Book, where the Dead Sea Scrolls are housed. Although the capital of Israel is Jerusalem, most foreign embassies are still based in Tel Aviv.

mounds called **tells**. Archeologists dig layer by layer, investigating the history of each time period. Hazor is one of the largest tells in Israel. Hazor was strategic because it guarded the entrance to the Jordan Valley from the northern trade route to Damascus.

West Bank—The **West Bank** is the mountain region west of the Jordan River and south of Galilee, which Jordan owned until Israel captured it during the Six-Day War. This region includes many of the famous biblical regions of Judah and Samaria.

The West Bank is a landlocked territory shaped like a backward capital *B*. The population is made up of 2.1 million Arabs and five hundred thousand Jewish settlers. This volatile mix periodically leads to violence.

Section Quiz

1–3. What three occupied territories consist mostly of Palestinians?

4. What occupied territory once belonged to Syria?

5. What mountain interrupts the north coastal plain?

☆ Why would Syria want to regain control of the Golan Heights?

Modern Negev

The Hebrew word *negev* means simply "south," and it refers to the southern part of Israel. It has three parts: historical Negev, the Wilderness of Zin, and Arabah.

Historical Negev—In the Bible, the Negev always refers to a small arid region around the towns of Beersheba and Ziklag. Because it supports marginal agriculture, it was sharply distinguished from the uninhabited wastes of the southern wilderness. In the best years, this region gets just enough moisture for some agriculture. Abraham and Isaac settled in Beersheba (Gen. 26:33), and David lived in

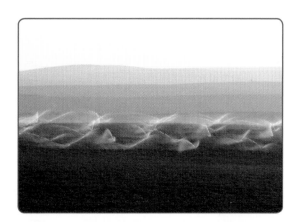

Farming in the Negev is made possible by extensive irrigation.

WORLD RELIGIONS

Judaism

The religion of **Judaism** emerged in the wake of the destruction of the Jewish temple in AD 70. Though the roots of Judaism reach back to Moses and Abraham, AD 70 proved to be a decisive turning point. With the temple destroyed, sacrifices ceased and the influential priestly class fell from power. The crushing response of Roman military power also led the rabbis to discourage messianic movements, which stirred up the people against Rome and led to the kind of retribution experienced in Jerusalem in AD 70. In addition, the emerging Judaism faced competition from followers of Jesus, who claimed that Jesus was the Messiah—the one who fulfilled the Old Testament Scriptures and inaugurated the era of the New Covenant.

Following the Jews' return from the Babylonian captivity, the Pharisees, a Jewish sect that focused on keeping the law of Moses, gained ascendency. The rabbis who emerged from this tradition developed rules for interpreting the Jewish Scriptures. These rabbis collected interpretations of laws about agriculture, holy days, ritual, and civic life in a collection known as the *Mishna*. The Mishna was completed in AD 200. Additional traditions about the application of the law can be found in the *Gemara*. Joined together the Mishna and the Gemara form the *Talmud*. Some Jews believe that the Talmud is inspired just like Scripture. Others deny its inspiration, but they do accept it as an authority for Judaism.

Central to Judaism are monotheism, the Torah, and the election of the nation Israel. Monotheism means that adherents to Judaism believe there is only one god. They believe God created all that there is and that His laws govern the way that all people everywhere ought to live. Evil exists in God's world, but God will one day raise all people from the dead. He will judge the world with justice and mercy. The wicked will be judged for their wickedness. The just will be rewarded. One authority on Judaism notes, "If the balance is equal, then God inclines the scale to forgiveness." Because of the future judgment, humans must choose to do right and repent when they do wrong. Many in Judaism believe that people who work hard enough to overcome sin will be able to do it if they ask God for help. Judaism teaches that God chose Israel to be His special people because of the merits of the patriarchs. They are unique because God gave them the Torah (Law) and because they worship the one true God instead of idols. Obedience to the Torah is thus a very important part of adhering to Judaism. It identifies a person as being a part of Judaism, which in turn marks him or her out as being specially related to God.

Orthodox Jews follow the teachings found in the Torah and the Talmud.

Judaism celebrates many holy days. Each week Jews observe a Sabbath. *Rosh Hashanah* begins the Jewish year (in September or October) with a time of reflection and repentance. *Yom Kippur*, the Day of Atonement, ceased being a day of special sacrifice with the destruction of the temple. Today it is a day of fasting, repentance of sins, and synagogue attendance. *Sukkoth*, or the Feast of Booths, occurs five days after Yom Kippur. It is a remembrance of the wilderness wanderings after deliverance from Egypt. Closely following Sukkoth is the celebration of *Simchat Torah*. This marks the completion of the yearly reading of the Torah in the synagogue. The Torah scrolls are brought out and carried in a procession. *Hanukah*, or the Feast of Lights, takes place in December. It celebrates the re-dedication of the temple after it was recovered by the Maccabees in 142 BC. In February or March the feast of Purim is held. This feast celebrates the deliverance of the Jews from Haman as recounted in the book of Esther. One of the most important feasts for Jews is Passover. The Passover is the remembrance of God's deliverance of Israel from Egypt. Fifty days after Passover is *Shavuot*, the feast that celebrates the giving of the law to Moses on Sinai.

Monotheism, the Hebrew Scriptures, the feasts, and a common history unite Judaism as a religion. Nonetheless, over time Judaism has split into distinct branches as Jews have struggled with how to relate to growing secularism. *Reform Judaism* seeks to accommodate a secular society as much as possible. They emphasize belief in one god and the need to live moral lives. But they are willing to pray in languages other than Hebrew, to discard distinctive ways of dressing, and to forego the strict dietary laws. *Conservative Judaism* also seeks to accommodate the prevailing culture. But it has held on to Jewish traditions more than Reform Judaism. Conservative and Reform Judaism both waver on the full inspiration of the Jewish Scriptures. *Orthodox Judaism* insists on the inspiration of the Jewish Scriptures. It retains Hebrew as the language for prayer and worship. It also retains the dietary laws and distinctive dress of Judaism, such as tassels and head coverings.

Jacob Neusner, *Judaism: The Basics*, 103

Ziklag before he became king (1 Sam. 30:1–2). Beersheba's position as the southernmost habitable city in Israel made it proverbial in the phrase "from Dan to Beersheba" (1 Sam. 3:20).

Wilderness of Zin—The Wilderness of Zin lies south of the biblical Negev. Steep wadis cut through its rugged mountains, and several craters gouge the landscape. The largest crater, Maktesh Ramon, is called the Grand Canyon of Israel.

Arabah—East of the wilderness and south of the Great Rift Valley is a wide barren valley called the **Arabah**. The Wadi Arabah descends through the valley northward into the Dead Sea. Elat (Eloth in 1 Kings 9:26), at the south end of the valley on the Gulf of Aqaba, is Israel's only port on the Red Sea. Solomon built a fleet at Eziongeber, next to Eloth.

> ### Find It!
> **Masada**
> 31.315° N, 35.354° E
> (If you look closely, you can still see the rectangular walls that surrounded the Roman camps two thousand years ago!)

Masada

Near the Dead Sea is a flat-topped, steep-sided mountain called Masada (mah SAH dah), which means "fortress" or "stronghold." It was the setting for the stirring story of the Jewish Zealots' last stand for freedom in their revolt against Rome, and it has become a patriotic symbol for Israel, much as the Alamo is a symbol for Texas.

King Herod built a major citadel on the summit of Masada about 35 BC. A Roman garrison took over the fort in 4 BC, but the Zealots seized control in AD 66 in the revolt against Rome. After the Romans took Jerusalem in AD 70, Masada became the last holdout of the Jewish revolt. Two years later, the fifteen thousand men of the Tenth Legion, led by Silva, arrived to quell the resistance. He surrounded the mountain with eight camps and built a siege ramp on the west side. After nearly two years, Silva's men breached the walls—only to find dead bodies. Rather than be tortured by the Romans, the 960 men, women, and children had committed suicide the night before.

Israeli archaeologists took great interest in studying the site at Masada. Excavations in 1955 and 1963 by Yigael Yadin restored the wall, cisterns, and palaces. The team found remains from each period: frescoes in the throne room of Herod's palace built on the northern cliffs; weapons and stone missiles used by the Zealots as well as fragments of scrolls of Genesis, Leviticus, Deuteronomy, Psalms, and

This view of Masada shows the ramp that the Romans built to break the seige.

Ezekiel; Roman coins left by a garrison stationed there until AD 111; and a Byzantine church dating from the fifth century.

Today, visitors can still see many of these ruins, but the frescoes have been moved to museums. Visitors can reach the twenty-acre plateau on the summit of Masada by cable cars or by climbing the siege ramp. One other path, the Snake Path, climbs the steep eastern face on a winding route that few visitors attempt.

Although the modern Negev is an apparent wasteland, the Israelis have devised a method using small amounts of salty water to grow hardy plants, such as tomatoes, peanuts, and cotton. This specialized farming, called brackish water agriculture, has allowed Israel to become a major exporter of these products to Europe.

The Palestinians

The term *Palestine* is probably derived from the Greek term *Palaistínē* or the Arabic *Filastin*. In the Bible the term *Philistine* is used and is similar to the Arabic term. Outside of the Bible, *Palestine* has historically been used to refer to the region between Egypt and Phoenicia. Gradually, the people who lived in this region became known as **Palestinians**. The name was associated with where people lived rather than their nationality or religion, since Jews, Christians, and Muslim Arabs lived in this region for centuries.

By the beginning of the twentieth century, the term began to be used to refer to the Arab population living in this region, and the transition was completed by the re-formation of the nation of Israel in 1948. After this time, Jewish people referred to themselves as Israelis and the term *Palestinian* was used almost exclusively by the Arab population of this area.

Palestinian students in Jerusalem

The Palestinians rejected the creation of the nation of Israel in 1948 and, along with neighboring Arab nations, began the first of four wars to drive out the Jews. In the first war, Israel conquered West Jerusalem and annexed it to their country. Thousands of Arab Palestinians were forced into exile. These refugees became a source of bitterness between the two sides, a constant "thorn in the flesh" for Israel. Another full-fledged war against Egypt in 1956 proved inconclusive when the U.S. and UN pressured Israel to return the land it had taken from Egypt in the Sinai Peninsula.

In 1967, three Arab nations—Egypt, Syria, and Jordan—began planning a new attack on Israel, but Israel learned about their plans and struck them first. In that **Six-Day War**, the Israelis easily routed the unprepared Arabs, capturing much land on Israel's borders, including Egypt's Sinai Peninsula, Syria's Golan Heights, and three Palestinian regions (the West Bank of the Jordan River, the Gaza Strip along the Mediterranean coast, and East Jerusalem). Egypt and Syria attacked Israel again in the **Yom Kippur War** (1973), but the Israelis narrowly repelled the invasion at great cost, with a massive resupply of military equipment provided by the United States.

While Palestinians in the West Bank and the Gaza Strip are predominately Muslim (88 percent), about 8 percent of the people are Jewish, and 1.6 percent affiliate with some form of Christianity. As of 2010, there were about four thousand Arab Evangelical Christians in these areas. Their lives are very difficult because of great poverty, poor treatment by the Israeli government, and persecution by the radical Islamists. Yet Arab evangelicals continue to meet in about thirty churches, and some Muslims are accepting Christ through the witness of believers. Bethlehem Bible College is training leaders to meet the needs of these struggling Christians.

The Dead Sea

The **Dead Sea**, fifty miles long and ten miles wide, lies at the bottom of the Great Rift Valley between Israel and Jordan. The Dead Sea boasts both the lowest shoreline and the saltiest water in the world. Its shore, 1,310 feet below sea level, has a lower elevation than any other point of land on the earth. Its waters are up to eight times saltier than ocean water, and they are about 25 percent more salty than the nearest rival, the Great Salt Lake. The Jordan River supplies most of the water, but desert wadis bring additional salts.

The Dead Sea is a lake with no outlet. Since the water evaporates quickly in the dry climate, salt deposits collect around the edges. Every ton of water from the Dead Sea contains about 125 pounds of common salt, potash, bromine, and other minerals. A peninsula called *Al Lisan* ("The Tongue") divides the Dead Sea into two parts. The larger northern section reaches a depth of 1,312 feet. The southern portion averages only twenty feet deep and is shrinking due to mineral mining.

The salty sea and surrounding desert make for a harsh environment, but

life persists. Brine shrimp and a few plants and bacteria live in the water. Springs in the rugged desert hills surrounding the lake create desert oases. One such spring, En-gedi, or Spring of the Goat, creates a large waterfall. The spring takes its name from the ibex, a wild goat living in the canyons.

People have lived in the area since ancient times. Masada, a fortress, overlooks the west shore. Bedouins found the oldest known manuscripts of the Old Testament, called the Dead

Sea Scrolls, in caves at Qumran on the northwest shore. The ancient cities of Sodom and Gomorrah also stood near the Dead Sea (or Salt Sea, Gen. 14:3). Many people believe that the ruins of these cities lie under the southern part of the sea. Today, people visit health resorts on the Dead Sea to float in the salty mineral water. Jordanians and Israelis are diverting so much water from the Jordan River for agriculture that the size of the Dead Sea continues to shrink.

The Dead Sea Scrolls

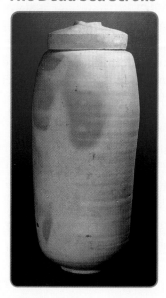

In 1947, a Bedouin shepherd threw a rock into a cave. It hit a clay pot and shattered it. When the shepherd went to investigate, he discovered one of the greatest archaeological finds of the century—the Dead Sea Scrolls. Subsequent investigations of nearby caves turned up more manuscripts, more than nine hundred in all. Some of these are mere fragments, whereas a few are complete scrolls.

Many manuscripts date from the first century BC, making them hundreds of years older than the former oldest-known copy, the Masoretic text. They were likely recorded and preserved by a Jewish sect called the Essenes. The Dead Sea Scrolls contain every book of the Bible except Esther and Nehemiah, along with worship hymns, commentaries, and rules regulating community life. The Isaiah scroll is the only complete copy among the scrolls. The veracity of the Scripture is attested to by the remarkable accuracy the modern copies show when compared with the ancient scrolls.

One of the clay pots that contained the Dead Sea Scrolls

Petra

The ancient ruins of **Petra** stand in a narrow canyon in what is now Jordan. The Edomites founded the city in the ninth century BC and took pride in the security of its easily defended entrance. However, as Isaiah and Obadiah prophetically warned, the Edomites were conquered by the Nabataeans in 300 BC. The Romans took over in AD 106 before the city fell into ruin after the rise of Palmyra. After a brief resurgence in the twelfth century, it fell into permanent ruin.

Posing as a Muslim, Swiss explorer Jakob Burckhardt discovered the ruins in 1812. The city's ruins include mysterious 130-foot-high tombs chiseled into the salmon-pink cliffs.

Petra, a city carved from the desert rock, is an awe-inspiring attraction in Jordan.

Importance of the Family in Jordan

"Families are the main focus of Jordanian life, and children are so important (especially sons) that fathers and mothers assume nicknames after the first child is born. For example, if the son is named Mahmoun, the father becomes known as Abu Mahmoun (literally, father of Mahmoun) and the mother becomes Umm Mahmoun (mother of Mahmoun). If no sons are born, the mother usually identifies herself as the mother of the first-born daughter; fathers rarely do this, however. Most Arabs feel that being without children and family is very tragic, and Jordanians are no exception to this."

Cultures of the World: Jordan, 76.

Jordan

Jordan, located east of Israel and south of Syria, is about the size of Indiana and consists mainly of uninhabited desert. Unlike some Middle Eastern desert areas, Jordan lacks petroleum. Furthermore, only 3 percent of Jordan can be farmed. Many Jordanians work abroad and send money home to their families. Adding to the difficulties are the many Palestinian refugees who fled to Jordan as a result of the Arab-Israeli wars. More Palestinians now live in Jordan than native Jordanians! In spite of these problems, Jordan has been one of the most stable and peaceful countries in the region. Its government is a constitutional monarchy.

Jordan's primary resources come from the Great Rift Valley. Deposits of potash, bromine, and salt are extracted from the Dead Sea. The rich soil of the Jordan River valley enables farmers to produce citrus fruits, cabbage, melons, eggplants, and cucumbers. At the south end of the Arabah lies Jordan's only port and its only major town in the Great Rift Valley, Al 'Aqabah (for which the gulf is named). The Syrian Desert, which covers the eastern half of Jordan, offers few if any resources.

Between the Great Rift Valley and the Syrian Desert is the **Transjordanian Plateau**, where most people live. The northern border of this plateau is the Yarmuk River, which runs through a wadi dividing Jordan from Syria in the north.

The Moabites and Ammonites, descendants of Lot, lived on the plateau (Gen. 19:36–38). The wadi called Arnon runs west to the middle of the Dead Sea. This wadi divided Moab in the south from Ammon in the north. Amman has always been the capital of the Ammonites. In ancient times, it was called Rabbah (1 Chron. 20:1) or Rabbath Ammon. Today, it has some industries, and nearby farms produce wheat, barley, grapes, olives, and nuts. But lacking oil, having little arable farmland, and being inundated with refugees, Jordan struggles with poverty. The stabilizing force was the forty-six-year reign of King Hussein, who died in 1999. His son, Abdullah II, is now king and is continuing the struggle to bring prosperity to the country.

While the state religion is Sunni Islam (96 percent), the Jordanian constitution guarantees freedom of religion. About 2 percent of the population adheres to some form of Christianity, and about 0.3 percent is made up of Evangelical Christians. With the huge inflow of Muslims from Iraq and Syria, Christians are under great pressure and face the possibility of persecution from radical Islamists. However, the Evangelical Christian population in Jordan is growing, numbering nineteen thousand believers as of 2010.

Section Quiz

1. Distinguish the modern and biblical Negev.
2. What geographic feature is common in Palestine, providing both strategic routes in the Shephelah and national boundaries on the Transjordanian Plateau?
3–6. Name four geographic features found in the Great Rift Valley.
   ✷ What conditions threaten the stability of Jordan?

Chapter Review

Making Connections

1–3. This region lies at the crossroads of what three continents?

4–5. What are the two factions that divide Cyprus?

6. Which of the four main factions in Lebanon claims to be Christian?

7–8. What plain contains the Gaza Strip? What people live there?

9. In what part of Israel are the Arabah and the Wilderness of Zin?

Developing Geography Skills

1. Based on the map on page 435, explain why Israel must constantly be ready for an attack from its enemies.

2. Based on the map on page 435, from what country is Hamas in the Gaza Strip supplied with rockets to launch against Israeli cities?

3. Based on the map on page 435, what countries are most likely to receive refugees resulting from a civil war in Syria or Lebanon?

Thinking Critically

1. Why has it been so difficult to bring peace to the Middle East?

2. Why is the United States allied with Turkey? What problems does this alliance create?

Living in God's World

1. American Christians are often noted for their support of the nation Israel in international politics. Write a brief paragraph evaluating this support from a biblical perspective.

2. Explain why Christians oppose secularism in the United States but might support it in Turkey.

People, Places, and Things to Know

chokepoint
Asia Minor
Mount Ararat
Kemal Atatürk
Thrace
Istanbul
Bosporus
Dardanelles
Anatolia
Taurus Mountains
Pontic Mountains
Mesaoria Plain
Nicosia
Levant
Fertile Crescent
mandate
Syria
Palestine
Syrian Desert
Damascus
Hafez al-Assad
Bashar al-Assad
Druze
Holy Land
Promised Land
Zionist Movement
Coastal Plains
Shephelah
Jerusalem
Negev
Valley of Jezreel
Mount Carmel
Megiddo
Plain of Esdraelon
Tel Aviv
Gaza Strip
Hamas
Great Rift Valley
Jordan River
Dead Sea
Mount of Olives
Golan Heights
Sea of Galilee
tell
Knesset
West Bank
Arabah
Judaism
Palestinians
Six-Day War
Yom Kippur War
Dead Sea
Petra
Transjordanian Plateau

Unit Eight

AFRICA

19 **Southern and Eastern Africa**

20 **Central and Western Africa**

21 **Northern Africa**

This continent, rich with history, people groups, and natural resources, is often misunderstood, and its history is little known by many in the West. Natural development was halted by imperialism and its aftermath. However, many African nations are developing at a rapid pace, and the continent's abundant resources are being put to effective use.

19

SOUTHERN AND EASTERN AFRICA

*A*frica is the second-largest continent. Its size is not as important as its location, however; 80 percent of Africa's land is between the Tropic of Cancer and the Tropic of Capricorn. This position makes the climate mainly warm, and it makes the climate in most areas consistent—there are no great temperature fluctuations. This position also determines the patterns of rainfall for the continent. Near the equator, there are heavy tropical rains on the west coast of Africa; this is not true in East Africa because of mountains and wind patterns.

The amount of rainfall decreases as you move north or south away from the equator, and near each end of the continent there are great deserts, the Sahara in the north and the Kalahari in the south. The Sahara is perhaps the single most important geographic factor in the history of Africa, dividing the continent into two regions with very different peoples and histories. Saharan Africa shows the strong imprint of Islam, while sub-Saharan Africa's history involves many tribal groups. **Sub-Saharan Africa** encompasses all of the lands below the Sahara.

The rainfall pattern influences vegetation in Africa as well. While there are rain forests near the equator in the west, most of the continent is grasslands, which are usually called **savannas**. About half of

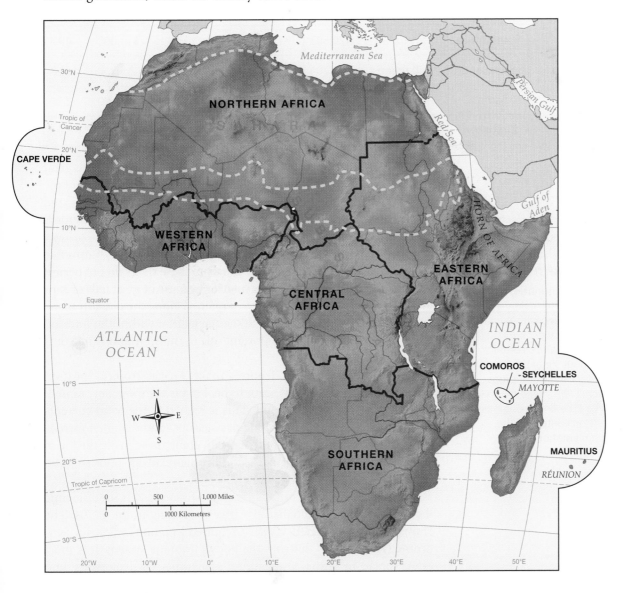

Southern Africa Fast Facts						
Country	Capital	Area (sq. mi.)	Pop. (2013 est.) (M)	Pop. Density (per sq. mi.)	Per Capita GDP ($US)	Life Span
Angola	Luanda	481,354	18.57	38.6	$5,900	54.6
Botswana	Gaborone	224,607	2.13	9.5	$16,100	55.7
Comoros	Moroni	863	0.75	871.7	$1,200	62.7
Lesotho	Maseru	11,720	1.94	165.2	$1,900	51.9
Madagascar	Antananarivo	226,657	22.60	99.7	$900	64.0
Malawi	Lilongwe	45,747	16.78	366.7	$900	52.3
Mauritius	Port Louis	788	1.32	1678.0	$15,000	74.7
Mozambique	Maputo	308,642	24.10	78.1	$1,100	52.0
Namibia	Windhoek	318,261	2.18	6.9	$7,500	52.2
Seychelles	Victoria	176	0.09	516.2	$25,400	73.8
South Africa	Pretoria	470,693	48.60	103.3	$11,000	49.4
Swaziland	Mbabane	6,704	1.40	209.3	$5,300	49.4
Zambia	Lusaka	290,587	14.22	48.9	$1,600	52.6
Zimbabwe	Harare	150,872	13.18	87.4	$500	51.8

Ethnic Diversity in South Africa

South Africa, like many other countries, is an ethnically diverse land. The Dutch colonists, and later the British, intermarried with the Africans. The people of mixed descent are called **Coloureds** (KUL uhrds), a recognized ethnic group that constitutes about 9% of the population of South Africa. Other ethnic groupings in South Africa are blacks (79%), whites (10%), and Indians/Asians (2%). (The British originally brought Indian laborers on contract in the 1860s to work on sugar plantations.)

Africa is covered by grasslands, and this helps to produce the great range of wildlife that has made Africa famous. About one-third of the land is considered desert; however, not all of this desert land is void of plant life. Some of the desert areas are home to nomadic herders and provide adequate food for their flocks.

Africa is also home to several mighty river systems; but unlike the Mississippi, the Rhine, or the Amazon, these rivers do not permit navigation from the coast to the interior because of great falls or rapids. This is why European settlers remained along the coast in many areas. The rivers, however, do allow navigation within the interior, and therefore they play an important role in transportation and communication.

Two other geographic features make Africa's tropical location less favorable than it might seem to be. First is the unreliable rainfall in many areas of the continent. This is related to the wind currents found in the tropics, but the long dry seasons (and the often torrential downpours when the rains finally do come) have made the life of African farmers very difficult. Second is the relatively poor soil that characterizes much of the continent.

Perhaps the biggest problem facing Africa today is the epidemic that spread across sub-Saharan Africa beginning in the 1970s. The Human Immunodeficiency Virus/Acquired Immune Deficiency Syndrome (**HIV/AIDS**) destroys the body's immune system. It is most often spread by sexual contact and sometimes by drug users who share needles. Sixty-nine percent of people living with HIV are in sub-Saharan nations, and 70 percent of AIDS deaths in 2011 occurred in this region.

I. Southern Africa

The region of southern Africa is located south of the rain forests of the Congo Basin. Southern Africa also includes the large island country of Madagascar as well as a few other island countries. The most important country in southern Africa is South Africa.

Southern Tip of Africa

The southern tip of Africa consists of the countries South Africa, Lesotho, and Swaziland. Of these, South Africa is the largest and most prosperous country in the area. Lesotho is surrounded by South Africa, and three of Swaziland's four sides border South Africa.

South Africa

The Portuguese rounded the **Cape of Good Hope** in 1488. By 1652, the Dutch East India Company had set up a supply station there. In the early nineteenth century, the British took over the Dutch station and made it the capital of a British colony. Over 3.3 million people live in **Cape Town** today, making it the third-largest city in southern and eastern Africa.

The Cape—Only a small part of the Cape region is coastal lowland. The region's climate varies radically, from desert west of Cape Town to marine west coast in the east. Most of the Cape is a large plateau with a steppe climate. The **Orange River** is the longest river in South Africa, flowing through the steppe to the west coast. It cuts across the middle of the region and forms the northwestern border with neighboring Namibia. Ships on the Atlantic Ocean cannot navigate up the river because the powerful Augrabies Falls drops a total of 625 feet near the coast.

Natal—The **Drakensberg Mountains** (DRAH kuhnz berg) (Dragon's Mountains) rise from the coastal plain of Natal to over eleven thousand feet above sea level in the tiny landlocked country of Lesotho. The mountains are actually an **escarpment**, a steep rise from a plain to a plateau. Ocean winds give Natal a humid subtropical climate. The second-highest waterfall in the world, **Tugela Falls** (too GAY luh), takes a 3,110-foot plunge on Natal's border with Lesotho.

In Natal are the **Zulu** (ZOO loo), the most famous of the Bantu tribes. In 1818, a fierce warrior named Shaka became chief and led the Zulu against all neighboring tribes. Under Shaka, a great kingdom called Zululand emerged. When Britain annexed the southeast Zulu territory in 1843, fighting began between Britain and the Zulu. In 1879, the Zulu demolished a British regiment, but the British won the war later that year. The British policy of indirect rule permitted the Zulu to govern themselves in Natal as a British colony. Today, KwaZulu-Natal is one of nine administrative provinces in South Africa. The Zulu continue to defend their unique identity. While the other tribes support a strong central government, the Zulu leaders in the Inkatha Party desire a weak federation.

Orange Free State—The original Dutch farmers, called **Boers** (BOORS), spread out from Cape Town across the fertile coastal plain.

Historical Background

Throughout the nineteenth century, European powers sought to increase their control of Africa. The United Kingdom outstripped the other European powers, controlling a nearly continuous path of land from Cape Town to Cairo. Not all Europeans sought an empire, though. Among the great British explorers and missionaries was David Livingstone (1813–73), who gave his life exploring the interior and striving to open Africa to Christianity. Others, like Cecil Rhodes, sought to advance the British empire and made fortunes at the expense of the colonies. Despite the efforts of the imperial powers, the European empires crumbled in the wake of World War II.

Post–World War II Africa was caught in the middle of another contest, between communism and democracy. Newly independent African colonies often experienced civil wars as the two political systems struggled for dominance. The collapse of Russian communism and the breakup of the Soviet Union relieved much of that tension. Today, widespread civil wars are being fought over religion and a variety of other issues. Diseases such as AIDS also hinder progress.

In the 1990s, most African states moved toward democracy and away from dictatorships and single-party states. Freedom of speech and political freedoms grew stronger, which enabled the African press to attack corruption.

The Drakensberg Mountains rise high above South Africa and Lesotho.

Bantu

Many tribes settled the diverse lands of South Africa. Almost all of them are of the Bantu tribes. The **Bantu** (BAN too) peoples include hundreds of tribes across sub-Saharan Africa. Linguistic studies trace the Bantus to the Benue River in Cameroon. Whether because of drought, war, or a need for more land, the Bantus are believed to have begun their Bantu migrations around 2000 BC and reached South Africa by AD 1000.

The largest group of Bantu in South Africa today is the Nguni, accounting for 60 percent of the black population. The Zulu and the Xhosa (KOH suh) speak the main languages of the Nguni, but the Swazi and the Ndebele are also included in this group. The other Bantus are divided among three smaller groups: 20 percent are Sotho, 4 percent are Tsonga, and 2 percent are Venda. The other 14 percent of blacks in South Africa are non-Bantus.

When the British took over, many Boers fled inland. In 1836, some left for the far interior. This Great Trek ended after they crossed the Orange River. They called their new nation the Orange Free State.

The Orange Free State eventually stretched east to the Vaal River, a tributary of the Orange River. Much of the plateau belongs to a vast savanna, called the **veldt**, that spreads across several countries in the interior of southern Africa. The Boers established their capital at Bloemfontein but faced opposition from both the British and the Zulu.

Over time, the Boers simplified the grammar of their High Dutch language and incorporated words from other languages, such as Zulu. The resulting language is quite different from Dutch and is called **Afrikaans** (af ri KAHNS). Today, the Dutch South Africans call themselves **Afrikaners** (af ri KAH nurs).

Transvaal—A number of Boers crossed the Vaal River to distance themselves further from Britain. The Transvaal ("across the Vaal") became the second independent Boer country in the veldt. It extended north to the **Limpopo River** (lim POH poh), the northern border of modern South Africa. It also reached east to the border of the Portuguese colony on the coast (Mozambique). Today, the region has been divided into several provinces. Some of the eastern border remains unsettled. A popular destination in the Transvaal is Kruger National Park, which has a great variety of animals. Visitors can observe elephants, lions, giraffes, leopards, antelope, and cheetahs. Rhinos and hippos are more common at Kruger than at Serengeti, a park in Tanzania.

In 1886, prospectors struck gold near Johannesburg in the Witwatersrand District. English-speaking foreigners poured in and staked claims. The influx of people made **Johannesburg** (joh HAN is burg) one of the largest cities in South Africa. It now boasts over seven million people and is the largest city in southern Africa.

The Boers clashed with Britain over the treatment of British immigrants. After a valiant stand, the Boers lost the Boer War (1899–1902). Four colonies later joined in 1910 to form the Union of South Africa. In 1961, the name changed to the Republic of South Africa.

After World War II, the Afrikaners gained control of the government. **Pretoria** (pri TOR ee uh), near Johannesburg and the nation's fourth-largest city, became the administrative capital of the nation to balance the legislative capital at Cape Town. These two cities are the major national capitals, while Bloemfontein is the judicial "capital."

Apartheid—About 79 percent of all South Africans are black. However, after winning an election in 1948, the Afrikaner minority began to institute **apartheid** (uh PART hite), an oppressive policy of ethnic separation. The Afrikaners contended that each ethnicity was culturally different from every other. They claimed it was best to keep all ethnic groups separate so that each could develop its own unique genius. Nevertheless, apartheid severely regulated life for blacks, Coloureds, and Asians. These groups could not vote in national elections and, after 1959, had no representation in the South African Parliament. Opposition groups, such as the African National Congress (ANC) and the Pan-African Congress (PAC), were banned, so the oppressed groups had no organized voice.

Under apartheid, every citizen was registered by ethnicity. Every area of life was segregated: restaurants, stores, buses, trains, and so forth. The apartheid government also forced black people to live in reservations called "homelands." Homeland citizens had to carry identity documents at all times. If employed outside the homeland, they had to carry a passport and a pass as well. Any protest was met with swift and brutal retribution. Even children were not exempt from the government's assaults. As a result of these policies, the international community condemned apartheid. In 1973, the United Nations called apartheid "a crime against humanity."

In 1989, F. W. de Klerk became president. De Klerk responded to foreign criticism and trade embargoes by easing the apartheid restrictions. In 1990, he released the jailed ANC leader, **Nelson Mandela**. De Klerk and Mandela began negotiations to make a smooth transition away from apartheid. In 1992, a referendum proved that even most white people supported the negotiations. The negotiations between de Klerk and Mandela won them a shared Nobel Peace Prize in 1993. The next year, Mandela was elected president of South Africa, and the old provinces were broken up into nine provinces. The number of official languages rose from two to eleven, and a new constitution went into effect in 1997.

After Mandela ended his term as president in 1999, Thabo Mbeki came into office. Mbeki was reelected for

Mined gold is refined in machines like this one.

South African President Nelson Mandela (center) applauds a new constitution approved by the Constitutional Assembly, 1996. With him are Thabo Mbeki (left) and F. W. de Klerk (right).

Jacob Zuma, president of South Africa

a second term in 2004. As president, he focused on improving the economic condition of the country's black population. Jacob Zuma became the fourth democratically elected president of South Africa upon his election in 2009.

Although apartheid ended two decades ago, South Africa still exhibits an uneven distribution of wealth. Unemployment remains high among black people, but more black families have entered the middle class, and the income disparity continues to decrease.

Another great challenge for the new government is the lawlessness throughout the country. Immediately after apartheid ended, the crime rate increased dramatically. The poor economic conditions of those who had suffered under apartheid combined with the new freedom of mobility contributed to the high crime rate. In the last few years, the crime rate has stabilized or decreased.

South Africans enjoy freedom of religion, and 75 percent of the people identify with some form of Christianity. Thirteen percent participate in ethnic African religions, and 8 percent are nonreligious. Evangelical Christianity has a strong presence and makes up 21 percent of the population. Local congregations are growing and sending out missionaries to unreached regions. Christian ministries are also reaching out to the poor, diseased, and helpless members of their society.

Lesotho

During the Zulu conquests, Chief Mosheshoe led the Basotho (or Southern Sotho) tribe to refuge in the Drakensberg Mountains. Later, the Basotho also defended the rugged terrain from the Boers and the British. Under attacks from the Boers, they asked for British help and became the protectorate of Basutoland in 1868. The kingdom gained independence in 1966. At that time Basutoland became Lesotho (luh SOH toh).

Most of the country is at a high altitude. **Thabana Ntlenyana** (tah-BAHN-uh ent-len-YAHN-uh) in the Drakensberg Mountains is the largest mountain in southern Africa, rising to 11,424 feet. Lesotho's high plateau contains the headwaters of the Orange River. These headwaters provide water for crops and livestock. Most farmers, however, remain poor. Lesotho has made use of its water supply by exporting water to South Africa and using the water to produce electricity. Lesotho produces enough electricity to be self-sufficient and to export excess electricity to South Africa.

Lesotho is entirely surrounded by South Africa and is one of only a few nations in the world that are surrounded by another nation. As a result, Lesotho has been at the mercy of the political situation in South Africa. But in the last few years, Lesotho has been racked by its own turmoil. Shortly after a disputed election in 1998, various young army officers mutinied and threatened to stage a coup. At the Lesotho government's request, foreign troops came into the country and restored order. However, just a few months after the troops left, disorder erupted again. Elections in May 2002 brought a restructuring of the government and added more positions in the country's legislative body. Since that time, the country has been more stable.

While 89 percent of the population affiliates with some form of Christianity, all citizens enjoy freedom of religion. Ten percent are involved with ethnic African religions, and those who consider themselves nonreligious constitute a mere 0.25 percent of the population. Evangelical Christians make up 12 percent of the people. They are facing the challenge of ministering to those afflicted with HIV/AIDS and the nearly 100,000 children who have become orphans because of this epidemic. As in other countries, there is an ongoing need for training of pastors and for additional national workers.

Swaziland

The country of Swaziland (SWAH zee land) borders South Africa and Mozambique. From west to east, there are four major geographic sections in the country—the Highveld, the Middleveld, the Lowveld, and the Lubombo region. The Highveld, in the west, reaches an average elevation of 4,500 feet while the Lowveld reaches an average elevation of 500 to 1,000 feet. The Lubombo region is the farthest east and swells sharply from the Lowveld to an average elevation of 2,000 feet. Most of the population lives in the Middleveld, which is about 2,000 to 2,500 feet in average elevation.

Swaziland continues to have the highest rate of HIV/AIDS among adults in the world. In 2004, 39 percent of pregnant Swazi women tested positive for the virus. As of 2012, the rate for all adults had dropped to 25.8 percent. In 2004, the population had an average lifespan of 32.6 years. This average has risen to 49.4 years. The improved percentages are, in part, the result of aggressive treatment of the disease. In addition, immoral traditional practices have been discouraged, and the biblical pattern of marriage of one man to one woman has been encouraged.

After being ruled by the Boers and then the British, Swaziland gained independence in 1968. Most of the people are Swazi. Mbabane is the administrative capital, but the traditional royal capital is the nearby village of Lobamba. The well-watered mountains and plateaus of Swaziland offer the same good agriculture and mineral wealth as in adjacent South Africa. Sugar products, especially soft-drink concentrate, greatly contribute to Swaziland's economy. Diamonds and coal constitute a small portion of the nation's GDP.

Eighty-five percent of the people identify with some form of Christianity, and 12 percent practice ethnic African religions. Evangelical Christians make up 25 percent of the population as a result of more than a century of faithful witness among the people. As in Lesotho, Christians are facing the enormous challenge of ministering to those suffering from HIV/AIDS and the families that have been devastated by this epidemic. The need for qualified leaders in the churches also remains urgent.

Section Quiz

1. Why is the Sahara the single most important geographic factor in the history of Africa?
2. What famous tribe has its home in KwaZulu-Natal?
3. What was the name of the South African government's plan of segregation during the twentieth century?
4–6. What is the largest mountain in southern Africa? What range is it in? What country?
  ✯ How can national Christians address the tragedies resulting from HIV/AIDS in countries such as Lesotho and Swaziland?

Southwest Plateau

Three nations lie on the plateau in southwest Africa—Botswana, Namibia, and Angola. The land is hot and dry. The coast and parts of the interior are desert, and the rest is grassland.

Botswana

The British protectorate of Bechuanaland became the independent nation of Botswana (bot SWAH nuh) in 1966. Botswana, a landlocked country, remains part of the British Commonwealth.

The southeast produces nickel and copper, but little development has occurred. Diamonds were discovered in Botswana in 1967, and diamonds account for a significant portion of the country's export income. The country is the largest producer of gem-quality diamonds in the world.

Bantus and Europeans drove the **San** (sahn), or Bushmen, out of South Africa and into Botswana. The San have survived as hunters and gatherers in the Kalahari Desert.

The **Kalahari Desert** (kah luh HAHR ee), the sixth-largest desert in the world, lies on the Tropic of Capricorn, much as the Sahara lies on the Tropic of Cancer. The desert spreads across southwest and central Botswana and into neighboring Namibia and South Africa. This large desert (over 200,000 sq. mi.) covers over half of Botswana. One of the largest diamond mines in the world is located in the northeast part of the desert at Orapa.

Northern Botswana consists of several basins with no outlet to the sea. One basin contains the Makgadikgadi Salt Pans, a large region of salt flats. The largest basin is the Okavango Basin. Rivers draining into this basin create the **Okavango Delta** (oh kuh VANG goh).

Although Botswana has a stable government and a growing economy, the country also has a tragic problem. Botswana has the second-highest rate of HIV/AIDS (24.8 percent) among adults in the world. However, aggressive treatment has reduced transmission of the disease from infected mothers to their children from 40 percent to 4 percent. This has increased the life expectancy from 34 years to 55.7 years.

Following 150 years of missionary activity, 65 percent of the people in Botswana have embraced some form of Christianity. Thirty-three percent practice ethnic African religion, but it is impossible to draw clear distinctions because many who claim to be Christian also adhere to ethnic African religion. Evangelical Christians represent 8 percent of the population and are playing an active role in dealing with the tragic consequences of HIV/AIDS. Botswana also has at least one hundred thousand AIDS orphans, and many Christian organizations are reaching out to these needy children.

The Okavango Delta is the largest inland delta in the world.

Namibia

Namibia (nuh MIB ee uh) is a country with deserts in the west and east. The barren **Namib Desert** (NAH mib) stretches eight hundred miles along the Atlantic coast. Mines provide most of the nation's resources: diamonds, zinc, lead, tin, and uranium. A cold ocean current keeps the air very dry and causes temperature inversions and thick fogs. The frequent fogs, resulting in many shipwrecks, have given the northern shore the nickname **Skeleton Coast**. In the west, the Kalahari Desert expands into Namibia.

In spite of several rivers on its borders, Namibia is a bleak and arid land. Most people live in the arid but cooler Central Plateau between the Kalahari and Namib Deserts. The plateau averages between 3,200 and 6,500 feet. Almost two-thirds of the small population survives on subsistence farming. The main port is Walvis Bay, west of the capital, Windhoek. Walvis Bay is one of the finest ports in Africa.

The German colony of South-West Africa became a South African mandate after World War I. After decades of negotiations, UN interventions, and Communist guerilla warfare, Namibia gained independence in 1990, but the government is not yet stable. Because of South African influence, English is the official language, but Afrikaans is spoken more commonly.

Namibia relies on South Africa for much of its economic trade. Most of its imports come from South Africa, which also receives many of Namibia's exports. The country is seeking to break away from its dependence on one country. Namibia's mining industry produces diamonds, uranium, lead, zinc, tin, silver, and tungsten.

While Namibia is technically a secular state, freedom of religion is guaranteed. Ninety-one percent of the Namibians affiliate with some form of Christianity, and 5 percent practice ethnic African religions. Evangelical Christians constitute 12 percent of the Namibian population, and a renewed emphasis on outreach and missions is underway. Christian leaders have developed a few Christian centers of education to meet the growing need for trained pastors and lay workers for the existing and newly planted congregations.

Angola

Angola (ang GOH luh), almost twice the size of Texas, lies mainly on a series of high plateaus with altitudes averaging 6,000 feet. The Bié Plateau in the west rises to 8,800 feet. Angola's coastal plain extends from 15 to 125 miles inland. Savanna covers most of the land except for the rain forests in the far north and deserts in the southwest.

The capital, Luanda, has 5.2 million people in the metropolitan area. Warfare has kept Angola from benefiting from its abundance of diamonds and its arable land, which once enabled the country to export large amounts of coffee. Diamonds and oil are the major exports today, accounting for over half of the country's GDP.

Angola is an important exception to British rule in southern Africa. Portugal had forts in the area dating to the sixteenth century. The Portuguese influence remains obvious in

> ### Discovery of a Vast Water Supply
> Namibians recently discovered an aquifer (underground water supply) and have named it *Ohangwena II*. Officials estimate that this vast supply of water can supply the needs of eight hundred thousand people (about 40 percent of the population) for the next four hundred years. This is an incredible discovery in one of the driest countries in Africa.

Luanda, Angola

The Living Dead?

In Angola and other African countries, many believe that the impact of one's life does not end at death. This has nothing to do with the Christian concept of resurrection or a future judgment. Rather, it is the conviction that family members should remember the deceased and thus keep his or her memory alive. Shrines to the dead often contain bones from the departed family member, and the living do everything they can to avoid offending the dead family member. If the family experiences misfortune, they may contact a "diviner" or witch doctor to determine if the deceased family member is angry about something the family has done. If the witch doctor determines that the family has indeed offended the departed, the diviner will carry out a ritual to satisfy the spirit of the deceased family member.

Angola, where Portuguese serves as the official language. In 1961, Angola revolted against Portugal, and most of the white settlers fled the country. After several years of fighting, Portugal granted Angola independence in 1975.

Angola has continued to suffer since gaining independence. It became the main battleground between Cold War superpowers in sub-Saharan Africa. The civil war claimed over half a million lives. Despite UN intervention, fighting continued even after the Cold War ended. Peace was negotiated in 2002, and the government has started to stabilize. Economic expansion has led to a growth of industry and job creation.

The first president was a Marxist who vowed to eliminate Christianity from Angola. However, his efforts proved unsuccessful, and today 94 percent of Angolans embrace some form of Christianity. Evangelical Christians make up 23 percent of the population and represent a four-fold increase since 1990, despite years of opposition and the devastion of four decades of war. As is true in so many countries, the need for trained and qualified Christian leaders is great, and many congregations have no trained pastor. Twenty-five Bible schools and two seminaries in Angola are striving to meet this urgent need.

The Zambezi River Nations

The **Zambezi River** (zam BEE zee) rises in southern Zambia and flows across southern Africa to the Indian Ocean. The Zambezi is the fourth-longest river in Africa and the longest in southern Africa. It runs through several southern African countries.

David Livingstone won renown after crossing the continent between 1853 and 1856. He started in Luanda, the capital of the Portuguese colony of Angola, and followed the course of the Zambezi to the far coast in Mozambique. Great Britain later claimed the lands between these two coastal colonies.

Victoria Falls is on the Zambezi River, which separates Zimbabwe and Zambia.

Mozambique

Like Angola on the western coast, Mozambique (moh zum BEEK) was a large Portuguese colony on the eastern coast. Although

Recognizing Cultural Differences in South Africa

Tony and Cathy Payne, Cape Town, South Africa

South Africa is the land of apartheid, and though apartheid was officially scrapped twenty-two years ago, its policy of racial prejudice still plays a role. South Africans distinguish between whites, blacks, and Coloureds, who are of mixed ethnicity. American missionaries can easily offend South Africans by failing to understand that certain actions can be interpreted as racist, prejudiced, or condescending. For instance, missionaries can offend the nationals by insisting on eating their own food that they bring to a braai (cookout), rather than adding their food to share with everyone else. Failure to mingle freely with the nationals at functions can be interpreted as rudeness. Sitting and chatting only with other Americans at the function, can be viewed as being racist or prejudiced against the nationals.

An interesting cultural difference between Americans and South Africans has to do with social etiquette during phone conversations. When Americans call one another, they get to the reason for their call right away. South Africans do not. They first ask about the family, ministry, etc., and eventually get around to the reason they called. Mentioning the reason for the call immediately is considered rude. The same is true when stopping by a home to get something. South Africans expect to be invited into the home for a visit before receiving the item and going home. It is considered rude to keep them on your doorstep and not invite them in, even if you are very busy.

Marxist rebel armies won the country's independence in 1975, Portuguese remains the official language. The country suffers from the loss of the skilled laborers who fled during the war for independence.

The Marxist rebels who won control of Mozambique did not enjoy a peaceful regime. They faced another rebel group called RENAMO (Mozambique National Resistance). As many as one million people died in the struggle between the two factions. After the fall of communism in Europe, the UN brokered a peace agreement. The UN insisted that both sides lay down their weapons before elections could occur. Elections were finally held in 1994. Soon after that, refugees from Mozambique began returning home. It has been estimated that almost six million people returned home after the war.

Mozambique's 1,535-mile coastline on the Indian Ocean is abundant with natural harbors. The Zambezi River divides the nation. In the north is the Mozambique Plateau. A wide coastal plain covers the southern region and supports many agricultural products, including sugar, cotton, cashews, tea, and copra. Coal is mined in the west.

The long coast makes Mozambique vital to shipping and transportation. Even in ancient times, Sofala served as a port for the interior kingdom of Zimbabwe, and later, the Boers shipped goods through the port city of Maputo. Today, Mozambique serves four landlocked neighbors.

Between 1975 and 1982, the Marxist regime ruthlessly persecuted Christians. However, Christianity survived, and religious freedom was granted in 1994. Forty-six percent of the people affiliate with some form of Christianity, and 32 percent continue to practice ethnic African religions. Eighteen percent of the population is Muslim, and 3 percent consider themselves nonreligious. Evangelical Christians represent 11 percent of the people and have a growing influence as new congregations are being planted at a rapid rate. As in other countries where the Christian assemblies are multiplying, there is a critical need for more trained leaders. At least twenty Evangelical schools are training leaders to fill this void. Extension education is also being offered via radio to those who cannot travel to the schools.

Victoria Falls

Victoria Falls ranks among the most spectacular waterfalls in the world. The falls drop 355 feet over a crest that spans more than one mile. The roar is audible twenty-five miles away. Even the twelve-hundred-foot-high mist is visible at that distance. The African people had named the falls *mosi-oa-Tunya*, which means "The Smoke that Thunders."

Livingstone visited the falls on November 16, 1855, while on his great

trek down the Zambezi River. He named it in honor of Queen Victoria of England, and the name has remained. He wrote in his diary that "scenes so lovely must have been gazed on by angels in their flight." He later described the falls as "the most wonderful sight I had witnessed in Africa."

Victoria Falls drops into a chasm on the border of Zambia and Zimbabwe.

Find It!
Victoria Falls
17.924° S, 25.856° E

The Great Enclosure on the plain can be seen from the Hill Fortress at Great Zimbabwe. This was the center of a great civilization in east Africa that traded with China, Persia, and Indonesia. Most of its history remains a mystery.

Zimbabwe

Zimbabwe (zim BAHB wee) lies on the veldt, the savanna that covers much of southern Africa. Its average elevation is one thousand feet above sea level. The prominent geographical feature is a ridge called the Highveld, which makes up about 25 percent of the country. The Highveld lies across the country from the southwest to the northeast. Along the Highveld is a series of hills and mountains. Zimbabwe has a wide array of mineral resources. The country produces gold, steel, nickel, and many other products. Yet gross mismanagement of the economy and forced redistribution of land by the government have led to an economic disaster, with unemployment at times reaching 90 percent.

On either side of the Highveld lies the Middleveld. While the Highveld averages 4,500 feet, the Middleveld plateau averages 3,500 feet. The Middleveld makes up about 40 percent of Zimbabwe. A feature of the south is the Lowveld, which reaches 600 feet at its lowest point. The Lowveld makes up about 23 percent of Zimbabwe. The two major rivers of Zimbabwe are the Zambezi at the northern border and the Limpopo at the southern borders. **Victoria Falls** lies on the Zambezi near the northwest corner. Downstream is Lake Kariba. Zimbabwe also has Mtarazi Falls, one of the highest waterfalls in Africa (2,500 ft.).

In 1890, Cecil Rhodes founded Fort Victoria and Fort Salisbury, hoping to find gold and to extend British influence north of South Africa. In 1895, the British South Africa Company named the colony Rhodesia after Rhodes. The white minority maintained control, refusing to accept the idea of black rule. For a time, between 1953 and 1963, Great Britain allowed the colony to form a federation with the other two landlocked British colonies north of the Zambezi River. But black people in the other colonies broke away.

When Britain criticized the white population's rule in Rhodesia, the leaders declared independence in 1965. This was the first full-fledged separation by a British colony since 1776. The act was declared illegal and unconstitutional by the United Kingdom and the United Nations. Economic sanctions were put into place soon after this. Black rebels fought the white rulers until they won in 1979. After officially gaining independence on April 18, 1980, the country changed its name from Rhodesia to Zimbabwe and renamed the capital Harare. Most white people fled the country after this change of power. To date, Zimbabwe has had only one ruler, Robert Mugabe. Mugabe has dominated the country, rigging elections to maintain power. The United States, the European Union, and other entities have imposed sanctions against Zimbabwe. However, the poor people suffer the most as a result of Mugabe's abusive leadership and the international sanctions.

Technically, Zimbabwe allows freedom of religion. However, government officials regularly interfere in church affairs by appointing religious leaders, disrupting religious events, and obstructing the activities of religious ministries on political grounds. Despite this interference, 78 percent of the people of Zimbabwe identify with some form of Christianity. Nineteen percent of the people continue to practice ethnic African religions, and 1 percent have no religious affiliation. Evangelical Christians constitute 31 percent of the population, and congregations are increasing in size and number despite the government-imposed trials. Given the dreadful economic conditions, congregations have taken it upon themselves to meet the needs of those in extreme poverty. The Christians in Zimbabwe offer a hope found in Christ that the government cannot take away.

Zambia

David Livingstone visited what is now Zambia (ZAM bee uh) in 1851, but Britain did not obtain the region until Cecil Rhodes negotiated treaties with the natives in 1891. The British named the area Northern Rhodesia, with the Zambezi River dividing it from Southern Rhodesia. Great Britain granted Northern Rhodesia independence in 1964, and the country adopted the name Zambia.

Western Zambia lies on the Angolan Plateau but supports forests. Most of the country averages about four thousand feet above sea level. In the west are also some swamps as well as the Kafue National

---

Cuisine of Zambia

In Zambia the staple food served at most meals is called *nshima* (en-SHEE-mah). Nshima is ground maize, or corn, boiled to make a mash similar to grits. Many Zambians consider a meal to be incomplete if nshima has not been served. Many will say they have not eaten all day if they have not yet had nshima, even if they have eaten fruit, vegetables, or a sandwich.

Zambians eat nshima by scooping up a handful in one hand and rolling it into a ball. The ball is then dipped in the accompanying dish, called *ndiwo* (en-DEE-woh). Ndiwo is a sauce made from vegetables or meat. It is never served by itself. Traditionally, a good Zambian wife would make a different type of ndiwo every day, never serving her family the same meal twice in a row. In addition, a wife would be careful not to run out of nshima. Therefore, the process of grinding corn was a group activity performed regularly by the women of the village. These traditions are less common today, and many women buy their nshima already ground.

Bible Colleges on the Mission Field

Phil Hunt, President of Central African Baptist College

A major goal in mission work is training local leaders (national believers) "for the work of ministry" (Eph. 4:12). The missionary has been given the specific task of making disciples through evangelism and by "teaching them to observe all things" that Jesus commanded (Matt. 28:18–20). In many countries around the world, national men who are called to pastor local churches have little or no opportunity to study God's Word and prepare for ministry. Because this urgent need exists, missionaries have begun Bible institutes and colleges. These schools

train national leaders for local church ministry within the local context. In this way, national pastors and missionaries are grounded in doctrine and trained in the practical application of

Central African Bible College in Zambia seeks to reach the English-speaking parts of Africa.

Scripture within their own people group. While foreign missionaries must spend time learning a language and a new culture, the local pastor or missionary knows the people and culture to which he is ministering. Theological training through Bible colleges is a critical component of missionary work and is vital to indigenous church planting movements around the world.

Remembering the Dead in Zambia

When there is a death, as many family members as possible come to the home of the deceased to visit. Before the age of cell phones, announcements of recorded deaths were made daily on the radio to inform relatives. Today most Zambians use cell phones to contact relatives. The gathering of extended family members may continue for several days, following which believers may conduct a Christian service. Poor Zambians often cannot afford to pay for the transportation of the body to the church and then to the graveside. They have a single service at the graveside.

Park. Sharing the great copper belt with Congo in the north, Zambia remains the largest producer of copper in Africa.

The Muchinga Mountains run through eastern Zambia. North of the mountains are two lakes in the Congo River drainage system. Lake Mweru is the deeper of the two. Zambia shares Lake Tanganyika with Tanzania and the Democratic Republic of the Congo. Maize and sugar cane are the country's largest crops, yet almost three-fourths of the population lives in poverty. In addition, up to 13 percent of the adult population lives with HIV/AIDS, although reports of new infections have declined by 25 percent in the last decade.

Zambians have enjoyed a guarantee of religious freedom since 1996, and 87 percent of the people affiliate with some form of Christianity. Eleven percent of the population continues to practice ethnic African religions, and 1 percent are Muslim. Evangelical Christians represent 26 percent of the Zambian people. This group has grown steadily from 3.8 percent in 1960, and the increase continues. Christianity is now widely accepted, and some public officials have openly declared themselves to be Christian. One result is the open door for Christian work and the spread of the gospel to the unreached in this country.

Malawi

Almost the size of Pennsylvania, the British colony of Nyasaland was nestled along Lake Nyasa in the Great Rift Valley. Britain granted the country independence in 1964, the same year that it gave independence to Zambia. The people renamed both the nation and the lake Malawi (muh LAH wee). In 1994, the first multiparty elections were held.

Lake Malawi, the third-largest lake in Africa, is the dominant geographical feature of the country. The lake lies on most of the eastern border. Much of the country is on plateaus. Elevations in Malawi range from 8,500 feet in the north to 200 feet at the southern tip. Mount Mulanje rises to 10,000 feet in the south. The climate varies with the elevation and the distance from Lake Malawi.

Malawi is one of the world's poorest nations. It lacks an array of natural resources, and its remote location hinders transportation and tourism. The economy depends heavily on agriculture. Tobacco and tea are two of its most important crops. In addition, many of Lake Malawi's tropical fish find their way to pet shops around the world. The lake is famous for its beautiful but feisty cichlids (SIK lids).

The people of Malawi enjoy freedom of religion. Seventy-six percent of the people affiliate with some form of Christianity, 17 percent are Muslim, and 7 percent continue to practice ethnic African religions. Evangelical Christians represent 20 percent of the population, and this group continues to experience steady numerical growth. The political stability in Malawi allows Christians many opportunities

Cichlids

to plant congregations and evangelize the unreached people of their country.

Indian Ocean Islands

Several islands lie in the Indian Ocean off the coast of Africa. France controlled each of these beautiful tropical islands at various times. Some of the people are Creoles, being of French descent mixed with African or Indian. However, there is a very cosmopolitan mixture of black Africans, Indonesians, Arab and Chinese traders, Indian laborers, and European settlers.

Madagascar

Africa's largest island, Madagascar (mad uh GAS kar), is separated from Africa's southeast coast by the Mozambique Channel. It is the fourth-largest island in the world. During the seventeenth and eighteenth centuries, pirates such as Captain Kidd hid there. Madagascar became a French colony in 1896 and gained its independence in 1960.

The land in Madagascar is diverse. A range of mountains parallels the east coast, leaving only a narrow coastal plain. The range reaches to 9,436 feet at the north end, and reefs block most of the east coast. To the west, the range drops gradually with long fertile valleys. The capital, Antananarivo (AN tuh nan uh REE voh), lies on the cooler crest of the range.

The southern end of the island is desert, and many of the forested places have been cleared for agriculture. More than half of the population works in agriculture, which produces 28 percent of the country's GDP. Rice is the major crop of the country, and Madagascar ranks among the top twenty nations in the production of this crop. As the population of the island grows, more wildlife becomes endangered. This is especially unfortunate because lemurs, aye-ayes, and other species live nowhere else in the world.

The people are probably a mixture of Africans and Indonesians whose ancestors arrived about two thousand years ago. The Malagasy language, similar to Malay and Indonesian, spread throughout the island. French and Malagasy are the official languages of the country.

Fifty-four percent of the people identify with some form of Christianity, and 38 percent continue to embrace ethnic African religions. Evangelical Christians make up 12 percent of the population, and Muslims represent 8 percent. Evangelicals continue to

Baobab trees are native to Madagascar.

Decline of Family Life in Madagascar

"The extended family has traditionally been the strength of Malagasy society. A family council that included the grandparents used to make decisions pertaining to children's upbringing, basing decisions on ideals such as family solidarity, respect for elders, and mutual help. Much of this has changed, however, and many Malagasy say that family life in the past was better than what it is now, the young were more respectful, and there was greater harmony. Today, the generation gap is being felt, and traditional family structure may not be able to withstand a more modern lifestyle."

Cultures of the World: Madagascar, 72–73.

Ring-tailed lemurs (left) and the aye-aye (right) are two of the many species endemic to Madagascar.

Religious Confusion in Madagascar

An odd mix of traditional beliefs and organized religion exists in Madagascar. The people of Madagascar believe that their ancestors, or razana, are the source of life and values. Therefore, nearly every aspect of life revolves around a "relationship" with the dead, who are believed to be the intermediaries between the living and a supreme god. Elaborate tombs are built to house the deceased, and diviners are regularly hired to consult with the dead about important family matters, such as marriage.

At the same time, over half of the population participates in an organized religion. Worshipers are divided between Roman Catholicism and some form of Protestantism. Some early missionaries built on traditional beliefs of a supreme god and the concept of an eternal soul. Unfortunately, natives often blended their traditional beliefs with forms of Christianity. Even today, many Roman Catholics and Protestants will hold a religious funeral for a loved one and then have the deceased blessed, believing that the dead relative has gone on to become an arbitrating spirit.

experience numerical growth, and efforts are being made to disciple new believers while laboring to train new leaders for the multiplying congregations.

Comoros

The Comoro Islands consist of four main volcanic islands and several islets northwest of Madagascar. The largest island, Grand Comore, consists of a high plateau with Mount Karthala, a volcano, at the southern end. When the Comoros (KAHM uh roze) gained independence in 1975, the island of Mayotte voted to remain part of France. Comoros still claims the island although France controls it. The economy is based on agriculture, tourism, and commerce; and the main exports are cloves, vanilla, and perfume oils. The official languages are Arabic and French, but Shikomoro, a dialect of Swahili, is spoken more widely.

Ninety-nine percent of the people are Muslim, and just under 1 percent identify with some form of Christianity. Evangelical Christians represent about 0.2 percent of the population and number less than 1,300. The government places severe restrictions on Christians, and evangelism is not allowed. Any native people who convert to Christianity are persecuted by the community and their own family. Yet the Christian community is gradually increasing as a result of the faithful witness of nationals and foreign workers.

Seychelles

The 115 tropical islands of the Seychelles (say SHELZ) are sprinkled in an archipelago northeast of Madagascar. About forty-one of these islands are granite mountains rising abruptly from the sea. The others are low coral islets and atolls. Mahé, the largest island, contains the capital and only town, Victoria. Ninety percent of the people live on Mahé, and most of the rest live on the nearby islands of Praslin and La Digue in the same northernmost group. The coral islands do not have any fresh water. The islands obtained independence in 1976 and have repelled attempts by rebels to overthrow the government.

The people of Seychelles are descendants of French settlers and African slaves that the French brought with them. Creole, English, and French are all official languages, but most people speak Creole. The education level is very high in the Seychelles, and 92 percent of the people are literate. Tourism and fishing are the backbone of the economy.

Religious freedom is enjoyed by the people of this country, and 96 percent affiliate with some form of Christianity. Evangelical Christians constitute 6 percent of the population, and many of these believers are working to plant new congregations throughout the country.

Mauritius

Mauritius (maw RISH us) is a volcanic island east of Madagascar. It is surrounded by coral reefs. Ruled in turn by the Dutch, French, and British, Mauritius opted to remain part of the British Commonwealth when it gained independence in 1968. Since independence, Mauritius has grown quickly in economic areas, such as banking, industry, and tourism.

WORLD RELIGIONS

World Religions: Prosperity Gospel

The prosperity gospel is an American phenomenon that has spread across the world. It is especially popular in the Global South, especially in parts of Africa. Proponents appeal to the lives of Abraham, Joseph, and David as people who rose from humble circumstances to wealth and prosperity. John's wish for Gaius's well-being in 3 John 2 has also become a key verse for prosperity preachers: "Beloved, I wish above all things that thou mayest prosper and be in health, even as thy soul prospereth." Wealth and health are the promises, but they are grasped by faith. Faith is the power that turns the promise of health and wealth into reality. Sometimes this is called "positive confession." A positive confession spoken in faith can make spiritual realties physical realities according to some prosperity teachers.

The prosperity gospel has provoked mixed reactions. For those who live a subsistence lifestyle and who see illness and death on a regular basis, the promise of health and wealth for the claiming is very attractive. But critics point out that the prosperity gospel is often used to make prosperity preachers wealthy off the backs of the poorer congregation. The very nature of their message makes it hard for the people to critique the lavish lifestyle of the pastor, since prosperity is claimed to be a sign of God's favor.

Sugar cane (the major crop of the island), tea, and molasses are exported. Both Mauritius and nearby Réunion, which voted to remain part of France, are tropical islands with booming tourist industries.

While there is religious freedom in this country, the government favors Hinduism. Therefore, it is not surprising that 49 percent of the population is Hindu, while 33 percent identify with some form of Christianity. Seventeen percent of the people are Muslim, and Evangelical Christians represent 10 percent of the people of Mauritius. Evangelicals are experiencing modest growth but must endure discrimination by government officials when they apply for permits and when they openly witness.

Section Quiz

1. What two major deserts lie in southern Africa?
2. What river divided Northern and Southern Rhodesia? What are Northern and Southern Rhodesia called today?
3. Between what two countries is Victoria Falls located?
4. Of the four island nations, which is the largest?
* How has European imperialism left its mark on African nations?

II. Eastern Africa

Africa's highest mountains and some of its most important ranges dot the plateau in East Africa. The most impressive feature, however, is the **Great Rift Valley**. Beginning in the Middle East, this gash in the earth continues southward through East Africa. The valleys and lakes in the Great Rift Valley have been important since ancient times. East Africa shares many other features with the Middle East, located just across the Red Sea.

Another significant feature in the region is the Nile River and its tributaries, which flow west of the Great Rift Valley. The Nile is the longest river in the world. The source of this mighty river was long

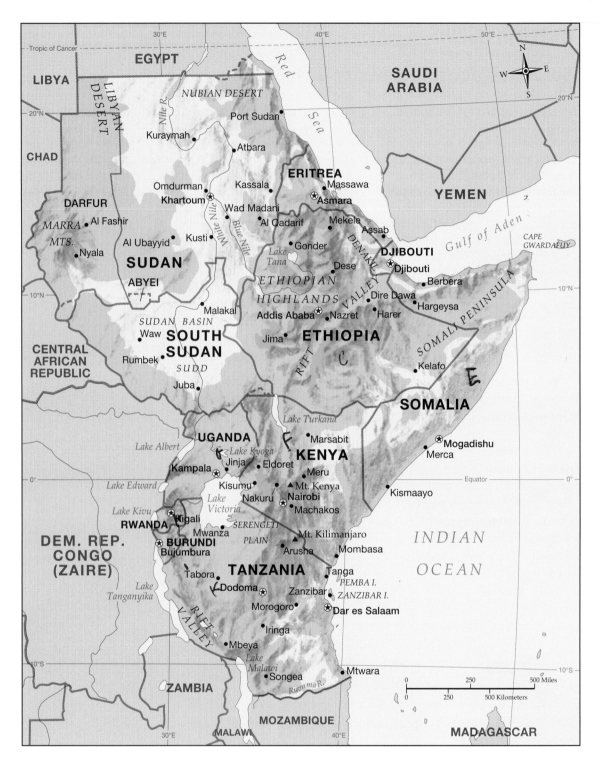

a mystery to Europeans. Two rivers join to form the Nile: the Blue Nile and the White Nile. In 1770, the daring Scottish explorer Robert Bruce found the source of the **Blue Nile** at the Geesh Springs in the mountains of Ethiopia. Bruce's book about his adventures sparked the modern exploration of Africa. The source of the **White Nile**, the longer of the two tributaries, lay hidden until 1862 when John Speke, a British officer, pushing ever deeper into the interior, traced the source to **Lake Victoria**. We now know that the Nile begins in Burundi on the Ruvubu River, which empties into Lake Victoria. From Lake Victoria, the water makes its way to Sudan, where it becomes the White Nile.

Eastern Africa Fast Facts						
Country	Capital	Area (sq. mi.)	Pop. (2013 est) (M)	Pop. Density (per sq. mi.)	Per Capita GDP ($US)	Life Span
Burundi	Bujumbura	10,745	10.89	1013.3	$600	59.2
Djibouti	Djibouti	8,958	0.79	88.4	$2,600	61.6
Eritrea	Asmara	45,406	6.23	71.2	$700	62.9
Ethiopia	Addis Ababa	426,373	93.88	220.2	$1,100	56.6
Kenya	Nairobi	224,081	44.01	196.5	$1,700	63.1
Rwanda	Kigali	10,169	12.01	1181.3	$1,300	58.4
Somalia	Mogadishu	246,201	10.25	41.6	$600	50.8
Sudan	Khartoum	718,723	34.85	48.5	$2,700	62.6
South Sudan	Juba	248,777	11.09	44.6	$2,100	N/A
Tanzania	Dodoma	365,755	48.26	132.0	$700	53.1
Uganda	Kampala	93,065	34.76	373.5	$1,800	53.45

Lakes Region

Think of wild lions, giraffes, elephants, zebras, and rhinoceroses roaming freely. If you've seen footage or photographs like this, chances are they were taken in the large nations of Kenya and Tanzania, which border the Indian Ocean south of the Horn of Africa. Although these two countries do not have a monopoly on wildlife, they are the location of many big-game safaris, Jeep tours, and wildlife documentaries. Grasses and scattered trees cover the savannas of these countries. In the west, Kenya and Tanzania share the lakes of the Great Rift Valley with three smaller countries—Uganda, Rwanda, and Burundi—where mountain gorillas roam.

The Great Rift Valley runs through the interior of this region, dividing into two parts at Lake Turkana in Kenya. The Eastern and Western Rifts extend south and rejoin at Lake Malawi in Tanzania. The largest lakes in Africa lie in this rift region, which is a hub of transportation, population, and industry.

The Eastern Rift runs from Lake Turkana south through such towns as Nakuru, Tabora, and Mbeya. Many salt lakes lie in the Eastern Rift, but Lake Turkana is the only one included in the seven "Great Lakes."

The Western Rift runs along the western edge of East Africa and contains five great lakes. Lake Edward drains north into Lake Albert and then into the Nile River. Lake Kivu drains into Lake Tanganyika and then west into the Congo River. Lake Malawi drains south into the Zambezi River.

The land between these rifts drops to form a large basin containing the Serengeti Plain and Lake Victoria. Lake Victoria is the second-largest freshwater lake in the world. Waters from Lake

Rift Valleys of Africa

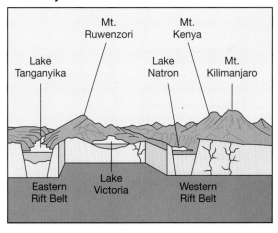

Over half of the world's flamingoes live in Africa. Flamingoes congregate at Lake Nakuru in Kenya.

Victoria flow north into the White Nile. Three countries have coastlines on this vital lake.

Kenya

Kenya is a little smaller than Texas, but its advanced cities make it the key to East Africa. The wildlife here draws tourists from all over the world. The equator crosses Kenya, and most of the country experiences hot temperatures. Most people live in the highlands located in the southwest, where the air is a little cooler and more comfortable than it is on the coastal lowlands.

Since Kenya's independence in 1963, the government has transitioned from a multiparty democracy to a one-party democracy and back again to a multiparty democracy. **Nairobi** (nye ROH bee), the capital of Kenya, is the center of trade, finance, and communication for East Africa. Kenya's economy is based on a variety of industries, from agriculture to mining and manufacturing. However, up to one million tourists visiting every year provide much of the nation's income. The tourists are drawn by the thirty-five parks and game reserves across the nation that the government has set aside to protect the wildlife. Nairobi National Park, on the outskirts of the capital, enables sightseers to photograph wild lions and giraffes with skyscrapers in the background.

The people of Kenya enjoy religious freedom. No comprehensive survey has been taken for several years, but there are estimated to be nearly 34 million people (83 percent) in Kenya who identify with some form of Christianity. The Muslim population is believed to be around 8 percent, and about 7 percent of the people continue to practice ethnic African religions. Nearly half (49 percent) of the Kenyans are believed to be Evangelical Christians. The Kenyan believers have matured to the point of sending missionaries to unreached areas of their country and abroad to other countries. More than seventy Christian schools are struggling to meet the need of multiplying congregations by training leaders and lay workers.

East Kenya—Mombasa is the largest port and capital of the Coast Province. The mangrove swamps, lagoons, and rain forests look much like coasts in West Africa, but they are interspersed with fine beaches and groves of coconut palms. The Northeastern Province lies along Kenya's

Languages of Africa

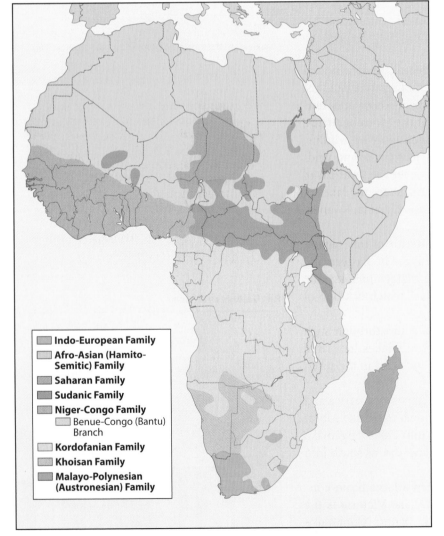

- Indo-European Family
- Afro-Asian (Hamito-Semitic) Family
- Saharan Family
- Sudanic Family
- Niger-Congo Family
  - Benue-Congo (Bantu) Branch
- Kordofanian Family
- Khoisan Family
- Malayo-Polynesian (Austronesian) Family

Swahili

The people on the east coast of Africa traded frequently with Arab merchants long before the first Portuguese ships arrived. The language that developed between the coastal people and the Arabs was a hodgepodge of Arabic and Bantu languages called **Swahili** (swah HEE lee). Later, Swahili incorporated some Portuguese and English words, such as *blanketi*. English has gained some words from Swahili too, such as *safari* and *impala*.

Swahili has since become a *lingua franca* in East Africa. It is one of the two official languages of Tanzania and Kenya and is spoken by at least thirty-five million people as a first or second language. Yet even Swahili has many dialects. Missionaries who translated the Bible into Swahili developed what is now the East Africa Standard version of Swahili. Although there is talk of making Swahili the common tongue of Africa, English is more common in colleges and printed media.

border with Somalia. These hot lowlands are dry except for the Lorian Swamp.

The Eastern Province rises from the low Coast and Northeastern Provinces in tiers. The grassy plains have the driest climate in the nation. The Chalbi and Dida Galgalu Deserts lie east of Lake Turkana at the northern border. The main towns of Meru and Machakos lie on the higher elevations (4,000 ft.) toward the west. The province has eight national game reserves and parts of seven national parks.

West Kenya—West Kenya is dominated by high plateaus and mountains. The agricultural lands in the highlands are very fertile. The production of coffee and tea in this area is very important, since it is the only part of the national economy (other than tourism) that provides significant foreign income.

Kenya's highest peak lies in the Central Province and is just north of Nairobi. Mount Kenya (17,058 ft.) is the second-highest mountain in Africa. In the west is the Nyanza (or Lake) Province on Lake Victoria. Kisumu, Kenya's third-largest city and the chief port on Lake Victoria, is located here.

Of Kenya's many national parks and reserves, two are famous. Amboseli National Park, on the southern border, offers spectacular views of Tanzania's snowcapped peak, Mount Kilimanjaro, which rises above the savanna. Masai Mara Game Reserve, Kenya's portion of the Serengeti, is home to the **Masai** (mah SYE) tribe. The nomadic Masai people are famous for their ritual dances and skills as warriors.

A Missionary Conducts a Masai Wedding

Jeannette Joyner, Kenya

My husband was conducting a wedding for a Masai couple. (The Masai are one of the more traditional/primitive tribes in Kenya.) We held a Christian ceremony in a school near the home. Afterward we went to the boma [fortified hut] of the groom's clan for the traditional ceremony. The bride and her attendants have to stand outside, and the bride has to literally cry because she is leaving her family. They often make her cry for a long time. Then some of the ladies from the husband's clan will go to comfort her and welcome her into their boma to become a part of their clan. They then give her gourds and small trinkets to make her feel welcome. After the ceremony we were served food. They had roasted a goat, so they took us outside the boma to the fire. A young man cut a leg off the goat with his *panga* (machete), which he used for every other outdoor use, and proceeded to cut off chunks for each of us. Then the portions that remained were placed in the branches of a thorn bush until we were ready to have some more. We entered the hut and were served stew and rice.

Mount Kilimanjaro dominates the horizon behind this portion of Amboseli National Park, Kenya.

Tanzania

Germany established a colony called German East Africa in the late nineteenth century, preventing Great Britain from controlling a

Serengeti Plain

The **Serengeti Plain** (ser un GET ee) has more large land animals than any other place on earth. It is also the only place left in the world where vast herds of large mammals still migrate.

All five of the famous African big-game animals—lions, elephants, rhinoceroses, cape buffalos, and leopards—are now protected in the 5,700-square-mile park. Elephants and rhinos are endangered because of poachers.

Wildebeest migrate one thousand miles north across the Serengeti every year to spend the dry season around Kenya's Masai-Mara Game Reserve. The wildebeest, or gnu, has a funny appearance, with the mane and tail of a horse, beard of a goat, and horns of an ox; but it can run fifty miles per hour. About two hundred thousand zebras often migrate with the over one million wildebeests, which provide safety in numbers. Nevertheless, danger lurks at every turn. Lions attack from the high grasses, cheetahs from rock outcroppings, leopards from trees, and huge crocodiles from the rivers and water holes.

Many other animals live on the Serengeti Plain, such as the impala, topi, eland, and dik-dik (the smallest antelope in the world). Foxes, jackals, gazelles, giraffes, baboons, and

Elephants on the Serengeti Plain in Tanzania

monkeys also roam the park, while vultures, storks, and egrets soar overhead. Hyenas compete with vultures for leftovers from lion kills. Packs of wild dogs are excellent hunters, succeeding even more often than lions. Cheetahs, which reach speeds of sixty miles per hour, are the fastest animals in the world.

Is the Serengeti National Park a waste of land that could be developed? Some people may think so, but the Christian has good reasons to support the park. First, the park protects natural wildlife in its habitat.

Preservation is an act of wise dominion that protects the natural resources God has given us. When the land is preserved, animals and plants can flourish with limited interference from humans and environmental intrusions. Humans can then admire the beauty of nature and observe the natural order God has implemented in this ecosystem.

Second, the tourism generated by the parks provides employment for the Kenyans. Thus, there are economic reasons for protecting this and other areas, in addition to wise dominion.

continuous string of land along Africa's east coast. Germany maintained control of the colony until the British took over after World War I. The land was known as Tanganyika when it became independent in 1961. The name changed to Tanzania when the island of Zanzibar joined it in 1964. Over 120 ethnic groups live in Tanzania, and Swahili is the common language. English is also an official language, and Arabic is commonly spoken in Zanzibar.

Tanzania is much like Kenya. Game reserves cover one-fourth of the country. The coastal region has mangrove swamps and beaches. Dar es Salaam is the largest port. In 1996, the Parliament moved inland from Dar es Salaam to Dodoma, making Dodoma the capital of the country. From the first inland plateau at Morogoro, the land rises to Iringa and Dodoma. North of Dodoma is the Masai Steppe, where the Masai live and herd their cattle.

Also as in Kenya, highlands cover western Tanzania. **Mount Kilimanjaro** (kil uh mun JAHR oh) rises to 19,341 feet near the border with Kenya. This massive volcanic peak is the highest mountain in Africa. Snow falls on this mountain even though it is near the equator. West of the city of Arusha are Serengeti National Park and Ngorongoro Crater.

Farther west lies the largest lake in all of Africa, Lake Victoria. Tanzania's main lake port, Mwanza, is located on the southern border of Lake Victoria. The best soils also lie around this lake. Farmers produce coffee, tobacco, rice, and maize. Tanzania's main port on Lake Tanganyika is the small town of Kigoma, near the border with Burundi. Four miles away at the town of Ujiji, the reporter Henry M. Stanley discovered David Livingstone, whose whereabouts had become a mystery. Their encounter on October 28, 1871, began with the now-famous words "Dr. Livingstone, I presume."

Zanzibar, Pemba, and Mafia are three large tropical islands off the coast. **Zanzibar** was once the Muslims' largest slave-trading port in East Africa. At one time it was also the largest producer of cloves, supplying up to 80 percent of the world's needs. Today, it is a resort area, and it guards its autonomy by making visitors from the mainland pass through customs. Unlike the rest of the country, Zanzibaris sometimes clamor for full independence.

Tanzanians enjoy religious freedom in a nation that has a variety of religious faiths. Those who identify with some form of Christianity represent 54 percent of the population, and Muslims make up 31 percent. Eighteen percent of the people are Evangelical Christians, and 13 percent of Tanzanians continue to practice ethnic African religions. Many new congregations have been planted since the 1980s, and this has contributed to the strong growth of the Christian influence in this country.

Uganda

Uganda (yoo GAHN duh) lies on a plateau averaging about five thousand feet of elevation in the south and three thousand feet in the north. The northeast has a volcanic range. Savanna covers the rest of the northern region, while the region around Lake Victoria in the south offers the best farmlands. The capital and main port, Kampala, lies on the northern edge of Lake Victoria. Owen Falls Dam at Jinja is a dam on Lake Victoria.

Highlands cover the southeast. The Ruwenzori Mountains, or Mountains of the Moon, are located on Uganda's western border and stretch from Lake Edward to Lake Albert. These mountains are very rugged, remote, and enshrouded by clouds most of the time. Many tourists visit this area to observe the mountain gorillas.

Uganda has been independent from Britain since 1962, but it has found little peace. A brutal dictator named Idi Amin ruled the land from 1971 to 1979, killing thousands of his opponents. After his overthrow, conditions continued to be unstable and oppressive. Yoweri Museveni, the leader of the National Resistance Army, took power in 1986. Museveni became president and, despite some claims of fraud, was reelected to his fourth term in 2011.

Museveni's government has strengthened the economy of Uganda. The inflation has stabilized at a low level, and foreign investment has risen. The economy is based on agriculture and related industries. However, there is an ongoing effort to shift from agricultural industries to construction industries.

Ngorongoro Crater

Near the Serengeti Plains, a volcanic crater, Ngorongoro Crater (en gore on GORE oh), rises above the plains, creating an isolated region bounded by rugged crater walls. The lakes in the crater provide homes for hippopotami, and the grasslands of the crater provide grazing for all the species of the Serengeti.

Marriage in Tanzania

As in many other African cultures, marriages in Tanzania are often "arranged." In such a marriage, the parents often make an agreement when the girl is still a child. The parents of the future groom, or the groom himself, must agree to an amount of "bride-wealth" based on the bride's parents' demands. This value is determined using the logic that the daughter has been doing a certain amount of work in her parents' home and the marriage will result in a loss for the family. Bride-wealth is calculated to make up for that lost labor. For centuries, bride-wealth was paid in goats, cattle, or other items of value. However, modern bride-wealth is more likely to be paid in payments of cash. A younger bride commands a higher price than an older bride does. The only one who has no say in this arrangement is the bride. She must accept her parents' decision or bring embarrassment on her family and village. Her only hope of escaping an arranged marriage is to convince her father to stop the procedure.

Mountain gorillas, like this young one, are at the brink of extinction.

What Is in a Name?

"Names are very important in Uganda, as they portray tribal and religious affiliations and sometimes signify what clan an individual belongs to. Due to religious influences, however, most people in Uganda have an Arab or European name, which is more commonly used than their traditional name.

"Traditional names vary from tribe to tribe. Just mentioning someone's name to a Ugandan is enough for him to know which tribe and what area of Uganda that person comes from."

Cultures of the World: Uganda, 96–97.

Rural water pump in Rwanda

During Idi Amin's rule, Christians were intensely persecuted. However, since 1986, Christian groups have enjoyed freedom of religion, and 85 percent of Ugandans identify with some form of Christianity. About 37 percent of the people are Evangelical Christians. Eleven percent of the people are Muslim, and nearly 3 percent practice ethnic African religions.

Rwanda

Landlocked Rwanda (roo AHN duh) is almost the size of Maryland. Plateaus cover the nation, rising highest in the west. The western border follows the Great Rift Valley. In the northwest corner, Volcanoes National Park provides a home to half of the world's remaining mountain gorillas. Farther south on Rwanda's western border lies Lake Kivu. About in the center of the country is the capital, Kigali. The Kagera River forms the border on the east. Agriculture is a major part of Rwanda's economy. Forty percent of Rwanda is arable, and another 20 percent is able to support livestock. Rwanda is heavily dependent on foreign aid.

Rwanda has a high population density, with nearly twelve hundred people per square mile. Most people speak Kinyarwanda (kin-yahr-WAHN-duh), a Bantu language, but French and English are also official languages.

The Hutus constitute 84 percent of all Rwandans, and most are subsistence farmers. One percent of the people belong to the Twa, a Pygmy tribe. The Tutsis (or Watusi), typically over six feet tall, were traditionally cattle herders who ruled as feudal lords over the Hutus. They now account for 15 percent of the population. In a bloody civil war in 1959, the Hutus wrested control from the ruling Tutsis. In 1962, the nation gained independence from Belgium, but tribal conflicts continued.

In 1990, the Tutsis began a civil war with the Hutus. A ceasefire was reached two years later. In 1994, following the murder of the presidents of Rwanda and Burundi, the killing began again and climaxed with one of the worst cases of genocide in recent years. Hutus began killing Tutsis and political moderates, even other Hutus. The genocide claimed over eight hundred thousand lives. With international assistance, the Tutsis managed to restore order. Rwanda has

Reconstruction of king's palace in Rwanda

LET'S GO EXPLORING

Land Use of Africa

1. What economic activity is most common in both East Africa and North Africa?
2. What type of farming is common on the Nile River?
3. Where can you find mediterranean agriculture?
4. What type of commercial farming is common in the Sahara?
5. What type of commercial farming is common in the Congo Basin?
✷ Which African country has the widest variety of economic activity?

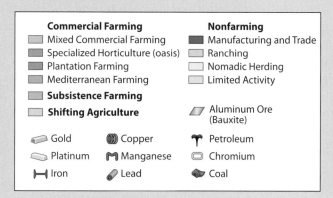

Commercial Farming	Nonfarming
▢ Mixed Commercial Farming	▢ Manufacturing and Trade
▢ Specialized Horticulture (oasis)	▢ Ranching
▢ Plantation Farming	▢ Nomadic Herding
▢ Mediterranean Farming	▢ Limited Activity
Subsistence Farming	
▢	◢ Aluminum Ore (Bauxite)
Shifting Agriculture	
▢	

🝙 Gold	Ⓒ Copper	⊤ Petroleum
▱ Platinum	M Manganese	▭ Chromium
⊢⊣ Iron	✏ Lead	◥ Coal

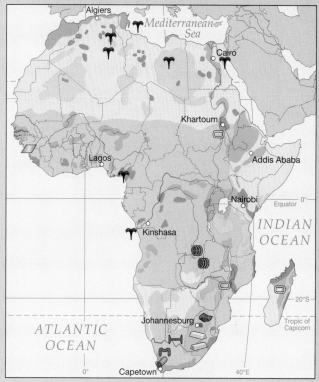

made great progress, and the country is rebuilding its infrastructre. The country is now considered safe for international travelers, and tourism is increasing.

Rwandans enjoy freedom of religion. Eighty-nine percent of the people affiliate with some form of Christianity, 5 percent are Muslim, and nearly 4 percent continue to practice ethnic African religions. Evangelical Christians represent 27 percent of the population and have experienced sustained growth since 1994. A partial explanation for this growth is found in the strong outreach ministries and aid programs to those hurt by the ethnic cleansing that left many in great need.

Burundi

Like Rwanda, Burundi (boo ROON dee) is a small country with a large population. Most of Burundi is a large plateau that rises to 9,055 feet. The Ruvubu River and the Rusizi River, at the western border, flow through the country. Lake Tanganyika lies on Burundi's western border, supplying the country with over ten thousand tons of fish annually. The capital, Bujumbura, lies at the head of this lake.

Swamps along the southern coast breed deadly insects, such as the tsetse fly. Coffee is the major exported crop for both Rwanda and Burundi, but overseas trade is difficult for both landlocked nations. Burundi has natural resources, but these resources have been largely untapped.

Burundi received independence from Belgium in 1962 and has two official languages: French and Kirundi, a Bantu language. It has the same tribal divisions as Rwanda. Unlike their Rwandan

Men carrying carrots

counterparts, however, Burundi's Tutsi minority retained rule until losing multiparty elections in 1993. The Tutsi army officers kept power in the army and restored Tutsi control in 1996. From 2001 to 2005, the government underwent a transition period and seemed to have stabilized. However, renewed fighting led to the flight of half a million civilians to refugee camps and the destruction of the nation's economy. Most of the refugees have returned home, but the nation has been reduced to one of the poorest in Africa.

The people of Burundi enjoy freedom of religion, and 90 percent associate with some form of Christianity. Twenty-seven percent of Burundians are Evangelical Christians. Five percent of the people are Muslim, and nearly 4 percent practice ethnic African religions. Evangelical Christian congregations continue to grow and multiply, although the pace has slowed since the rapid growth of the 1990s. A few Bible schools and theological colleges are endeavoring to fill the great need for trained leaders for the congregations.

Section Quiz

1. What are two significant geographic features of East Africa?
2. What city is the center of trade, finance, and communication in East Africa? What country is it located in?
3. What is Africa's highest mountain? What nation contains it?
4. What important mountain range lies on Uganda's western border?
* Why are national parks important in the Lakes Region?

The Horn of Africa

On the east side of Africa, the wide Somali Peninsula jabs toward the Middle East. Because the peninsula is shaped like an animal horn, the region is often called the **Horn of Africa**. The four nations in this area are closely linked. Some of the countries in this region have been devastated by war and famine, resulting in very poor economies.

The waters of the Red Sea actually lie in part of the Great Rift Valley, which continues down into the north coast of the Horn of Africa. Many places in the Great Rift Valley are far below sea level. The hot, dry lowlands near the coast are part of the **Denakil Desert**. One spot in Eritrea plummets to 246 feet below sea level. Another spot in Ethiopia is 410 feet below sea level. But the valley falls to its lowest point down the coast in the tiny country of Djibouti. Here beside Lake Assal, the Denakil Desert sinks 509 feet below sea level. It is the lowest spot in Africa.

Ethiopia

In Africa, only Nigeria and Egypt have more people than Ethiopia (ee thee OH pee uh). In addition to Ethiopia's large population, its unique history and geography have given it a special place in Africa's growing sense of pride. Ethiopia is one of only two nations in Africa that no foreign nation has ever successfully colonized. The rough terrain of the Ethiopian Highlands provided refuge from advancing empires. In 1896 at the Battle of Adwa, Ethiopia became the first black African nation to win a war against a European colonial power when

This boy is a herder in the Ethiopian Highlands.

it defeated Italy. In the 1930s under Mussolini, Italy sought revenge and invaded Ethiopia. The temporary conquest ended a few years later when Italy lost World War II.

Haile Selassie, the last emperor of Ethiopia, who ruled from 1930 to 1974, began developing modern industries. Discontent grew, however, because the people did not benefit equally. Several droughts and famines added to the turmoil. Marxist rebels supported by the Soviet Union overthrew Selassie, and Ethiopia endured a military rule from 1974 to 1991, when rebel groups united and overthrew the junta. Ethiopia held its first multiparty elections in 1995.

North and central Ethiopia are a rugged highland plateau. The **Ethiopian Highlands** rise to 14,928 feet at Ras Dashen in the far north. With such towering peaks, the highlands stay cool and receive large amounts of rainfall. The Blue Nile begins in Lake Tana and circles through the northern highlands before its descent west to the Sudan. Most Ethiopians live in the highlands because of the cooler climate and fertile soil. Farmers produce corn, wheat, cotton, coffee, and sugar cane. Ethiopia is the legendary home of the coffee bean, from the town of Kaffa in the southwest. Coffee is Ethiopia's top agricultural export.

Like other isolated highlands of the world, Ethiopia has a diversity of peoples—at least one hundred ethnic groups and eighty-five languages. Amharic, the language of the last emperors, is the official language. Sixty-one percent of Ethiopia's people affiliate with some form of Christianity, and 34 percent are Muslim. Evangelical Christians represent 20 percent of the Ethiopian population and have experienced strong growth since the 1970s, when a Marxist government came to power. This growth has occurred despite persecution and suffering. Ethiopian nationals are continuing an aggressive plan of church planting and evangelism and anticipate sustained growth.

The capital, **Addis Ababa** (AD-is AB-uh-buh), stands on the plateau at the center of the nation. With an estimated population of four million people, this city is the largest within the four nations of the Horn of Africa. The various heads of state in Africa met at Addis Ababa in 1963 and chartered the Organization of African Unity (OAU), to promote the common good of the continent. The OAU

Addis Ababa, Ethiopia

became the **African Union** (AU) in 2002, but the headquarters of the AU remain in Addis Ababa.

The Great Rift Valley cuts through Ethiopia south of the capital. Ethiopia has roads connecting it to all of its neighboring countries, but only one vital railroad links Addis Ababa to Djibouti through the Great Rift Valley. The part of the valley that continues southwest from the capital into Kenya contains several small salt lakes with no outlets.

The southeastern part of Ethiopia is called the **Ogaden**. This section is one of the hot, dry lowlands along the Ethiopian border. The Somalis who live in the city of Kelafo and the surrounding plains of Ogaden are Muslim. Britain allowed Emperor Selassie to annex the region in 1948, but after Somalia gained independence in 1960, Ethiopia had to fight Somalia to keep Ogaden. Even today, the Somalis living in this region desire independence. A lowland similar to Ogaden lies along the west border.

Eritrea

The geography of Eritrea (ehr ih TREE uh) is dominated by a central plateau that rises to almost ten thousand feet at Mount Soira. In the west, the elevation does not rise as high. A plain extends the length of Eritrea's coast on the Red Sea. Off the coast of Eritrea's mainland, the Dahlak Archipelago, consisting of more than one hundred islands, also belongs to Eritrea.

The Denakil Desert in the south has oil, which is refined at Assab. The economy is based largely on agriculture. Other prominent industries include ship repair and construction materials. Unfortunately, most of the people live in desperate poverty as a result of three decades of war.

In 1889, Eritrea became an Italian colony. After World War II, the United Nations made Eritrea an autonomous territory under the Ethiopian crown. But when Ethiopia annexed Eritrea outright in 1952, Eritrea revolted. A bitter struggle ensued for about forty years. After Ethiopia's Marxist government collapsed in 1991, Eritrea voted to gain its independence in 1993. However, Marxist leaders regained power and turned this poor country into such a restrictive state that even the UN is unwelcome.

Four religious groups are recognized by the government: Sunni Islam, Eritrean Orthodox Church, Roman Catholic Church, and Lutheran Church. All other religious groups face intense persecution. Fifty percent of the population is Muslim, and 47 percent identify with some form of Christianity. Despite the oppressive treatment by the government, 2 percent of the Eritreans are Evangelical Christians, and this group is growing in numbers. When the government closed most of the churches, Christians migrated to a house church movement, and these local congregations continue to multiply.

Djibouti

The little country of Djibouti (jih BOO tee), almost the size of Massachusetts, lies at a strategic spot on the coast of Africa. It guards the **Bab al-Mandeb** (bab ul MAN-dub), the twenty-mile-wide entrance to the Red Sea. Djibouti was once called French Somaliland, a strategic colony that France took in 1864. Djibouti received its independence in 1977. Though civil war plagued Djibouti from 1992 to

---

Families in Eritrea

The father is the head of the home and is expected to provide for his family. A father who cannot work is considered cursed. The mother feeds her family and, along with her daughters, performs the chores around the home. In many Eritrean homes, the women must walk for up to two hours each day to fetch clean drinking water from the nearest well.

Eritrean parents rarely play games with their children, but they do tell the traditional stories. They also teach the children about their ancestors in order to pass on their cultural heritage.

As in other African countries that have been scarred by war, many children in Eritrea have lost their parents. Most of these children live with relatives and receive a small amount of financial assistance from the government.

1994, the government has been generally stable since that time.

Most citizens of Djibouti live in the capital city, also named Djibouti. The capital is a convenient stop for ships sailing between the Indian Ocean and the Mediterranean Sea. International transportation is the backbone of the economy. In addition, the American base and the French military base provide a significant source of income for the country. Ethiopia relies on the railroad from Addis Ababa to ship goods, especially coffee, through this key port. The country's population is made up mostly of Somalis (61 percent) and Afars (28 percent).

With few natural resources, rural people eke out a living raising camels on the bleak and barren landscape. Very little of the land is suitable for farming. As a result, Djibouti imports most of its food from other countries.

Ninety-seven percent of the people embrace Islam, and about 2 percent identify with some form of Christianity. Evangelical Christians make up about 0.1 percent of the population of Djibouti, and most of these are immigrant workers who have moved to this country in recent years. While there are a few Somali and Afar believers, they are subject to great pressure from family members and are ostracized or even killed for converting to Christianity.

Djibouti, capital city of Djibouti

Somalia

Somalia (soh MAHL ee uh) occupies the east coast of the Horn of Africa. In ancient times, it was called Punt (or Put, as in Nahum 3:9). Italy gained control of much of Somaliland in the late nineteenth century. In 1960, the Italian and British Somaliland territories joined to form the nation of Somalia. Since then, Somalia has alienated all three of its neighbor nations by trying to annex portions where Somalis live. It invaded Ethiopia in 1977 and refused to sign a peace treaty until 1988.

Northern Somalia has many hills. Some of these reach as high as seven thousand feet above sea level. On the northwest coast of the Gulf of Aden lies the Guban, a coastal plain. Nomads herd livestock in this area. Southern Somalia is much more flat than the north. Average elevation in this area is less than six hundred feet. This southern area has some arable land watered by two rivers. The rivers join and empty into the Indian Ocean at Kismayu. The capital, Mogadishu, lies near the northern end of the arable region.

The people of Somalia share the same ethnic and cultural background. The vast majority are Somalis, a black African tribe that speaks the Somali language. Nearly all Somalis are Sunni Muslim and keep close ties to Saudi Arabia, which buys Somali fruit and livestock. There is a tiny Evangelical Christian presence in Somalia of around 4,200 people, but they continue to endure despite great suffering at the hands of radical Muslims. In many cases, persecution has resulted in a bold witness by these believers.

In spite of its ethnic unity, the region has suffered from constant internal strife between clans. In 1991, the government disintegrated, and clan warfare engulfed the south. Two years later, famine laid

Deforestation and Desertification

In many parts of Africa, including Somalia, there is a destructive cycle occurring. Trees are cut down to provide shelter, fuel, and income (as charcoal) at a faster rate than they can be replaced. This makes the soil vulnerable to erosion by water and wind. Desertification follows as the exposed soil becomes unable to support vegetation. Deserts form or grow in size, and the amount of life-supporting land is reduced. People are forced to move to other areas, and the cycle is repeated.

Many African countries are trying to reverse this cycle by planting trees and other vegetation to stop desertification. Since the damage is massive, the efforts to correct this problem will need to occur on a large scale as well.

waste to the land. Later that year, the UN sent troops into Somalia to restore peace. However, the United States pulled its troops out after eighteen Americans died in a raid to capture one of the clan leaders. The UN withdrew in 1995, and anarchy and famine returned to Somalia. In 2004, a transitional government was formed, bringing some hope for the war-ravaged country, but peace has eluded this land.

As the national government was disintegrating in 1991, northwestern Somalia—former British Somaliland—declared itself an independent nation, the Somaliland Republic, but no foreign country has recognized it. Somaliland has a stronger economy than the rest of Somalia, and leadership provided by clans has resulted in political stability.

Section Quiz

1. The Horn of Africa is the name for what peninsula?
2. What four nations compose the Horn of Africa?
3. What East African country was never successfully colonized by a European power?
4. What is the name of the entrance to the Red Sea?
* Have ethnic and religious differences been the primary causes of civil war in the Horn of Africa? If not, what has been the main cause?

Sudan

Sudan (soo DAN) shares many similarities with Egypt, its northern neighbor. Egypt controlled Sudan in ancient times. During the Middle Ages, Arab Muslims conquered Egypt and pushed south into Sudan, bringing their religion and language with them. Most Sudanese today speak Arabic, the official language.

Egypt regained control of Sudan in the early nineteenth century. The Sudanese threw off Egyptian rule briefly, but British and Egyptian forces combined in 1898 to subdue the rebels. Sudan gained independence in 1956, but military coups and civil war between the Muslims in the north and animists and Christians in the south hindered development for almost fifty years. The Muslims in northern Sudan were attempting to impose Islamic law, or sharia, in the southern highlands where the Christians primarily resided. In 2011, the civil war that had been waged between these two regions ended, and the people of southern Sudan voted to form a separate nation.

Beginning in 2003, Sudan was also scarred by genocide in the western Darfur region. The fighting took place between two Muslim ethnic groups. A ceasefire was signed in 2004, but the fighting persisted. Diplomatic negotiations continued into 2005. The struggle in Darfur has claimed over two hundred thousand lives and displaced about two million people.

Because of the various wars in Sudan, the country has struggled to establish its economy. The wars hindered the development of an infrastructure that could support the nation in times of peace. Sudan still has great economic potential, though, thanks to the discovery of oil in northern Sudan. The country also hopes to increase its hydroelectric power by building a new dam on the Nile. The chief crops in Sudan are grain, sorghum, millet, wheat, cotton, and gum arabic. Crop development is currently limited by a lack of irrigation.

North Sudan

Northern Desert—The land area of Sudan is equivalent to slightly less than one-quarter of the area of the United States, but large areas are desert or swamp. From Khartoum, the capital, the Nile flows north toward Egypt into the Sahara. The Libyan Desert lies to the west and the Nubian Desert to the east. Port Sudan is the only major port on the Red Sea in the northeast. The people are subsistence farmers, most of whom live along the Nile.

The Nile flows over six falls or rapids, called **cataracts** (KAT uh rakt). The First Cataract is at Egypt's Aswan Dam, but the rest are in Sudan. The cataracts prevent ships from sailing up the river, isolating Sudan from the civilization in Egypt.

Khartoum—Khartoum, a center of industry in Sudan, sits in the heart of the country, where the White Nile and Blue Nile branches join to form the main Nile River. The city has two main parts. North Khartoum lies across the Blue Nile, and Omdurman is located across the White Nile. Over five and a half million people live in this metropolitan area.

Central Savannas—Sudan gets its name from the Sahel, which rises in the center of the country, south of the deserts. The term *Sudan* originally referred to the entire Sahel. (Mali was called French Sudan in colonial times.) Herders raise sheep, goats, and cattle on the savannas of the Sahel. Camels provide transportation as well as milk and meat.

The El Gezira Plain lies in the central savannas between the Blue Nile and the White Nile. The Blue Nile flows from the highlands on the eastern border of Sudan, where heavy summer rains cause floods and carry silt downstream to Khartoum. The silt makes the plain the most fertile area in the country. Cotton is one of the country's chief agricultural products and a major export. The seasonal floods of the Blue Nile still affect Sudan.

Nearly 70 percent of the people in this country are of Arab descent, and Muslims make up 97 percent of the population. While it is believed that there are tiny groups of Christians in North Sudan, no reliable statistics are available. Christians in this state are at great risk because of the hostility of radical Islamic groups toward all non-Muslim religious groups.

South Sudan

In January 2011, the people in southern Sudan voted in a referendum about forming a new nation. Residents of this region, along with former residents who had fled the country, were allowed to vote on this historic question. When the votes were counted, 98.8 percent of the people voted for independence. Although open warfare between the people of South Sudan and the Muslim forces of Sudan had officially ended, tension remained, and many small outbreaks of violence continued. Nine of the ten states in South Sudan currently struggle with intermittent warfare between various groups and the South Sudanese government. Despite decades of abuse and ongoing uncertainty, the people of South Sudan are working diligently to rebuild what was destroyed by the civil war and to turn their new country into a thriving nation.

People of North Sudan

Arabic is the language most often spoken in North Sudan. Many of these people are the descendents of the Arab Muslims who migrated to this region around the twelfth century. The people live in communities, and homes are occupied by extended families. While they consider the home a private place, they are generally hospitable to visitors, even offering them a place to rest and eat.

Sudanese farmers have implemented irrigation plans in the El Gezira Plain.

Salva Kir Mayardit, first president of South Sudan

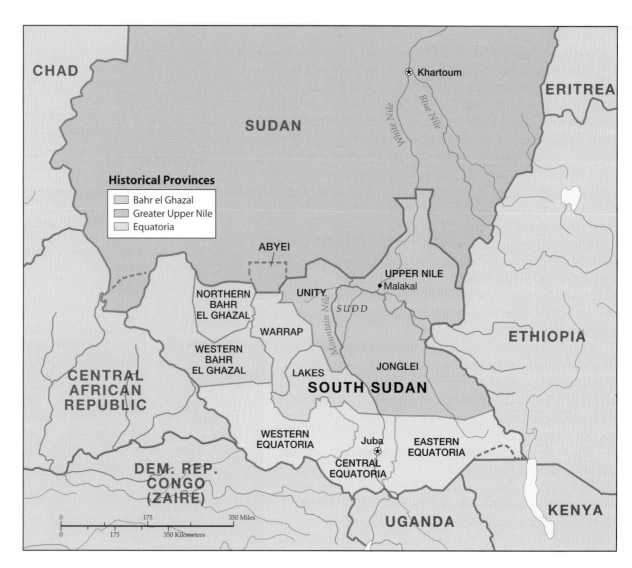

As many as 80 percent of the South Sudanese people identify with some form of Christianity, and the number of Evangelical Christians may be as high as six million, although accurate statistics are difficult to obtain given the recent formation of this country. One of the pressing needs for Christian congregations in South Sudan is the training of pastors. Continued planting of new congregations increases the urgency of this need for leaders.

The White Nile flows to the west of the Blue Nile across South Sudan and is called the Mountain Nile between Juba (the nation's capital) and Malakal. The White Nile does not flood because its waters spread out over a large marsh called the **Sudd**. These shallow wetlands cover an area the size of Maine, and much water is lost through evaporation. Rain forests lie along South Sudan's southern border.

Section Quiz

1. What is the youngest country in Africa?
2. What are the two main branches of the Nile?
3. What did *Sudan* originally refer to?
4. What swampy area borders the White Nile?
* How does Sudan form a transition zone between Egypt and eastern Africa?

Chapter Review

Making Connections

1. What geographical feature has divided Africa and, consequently, had the greatest effect on the continent?
2. Why did early settlers remain along the coasts of Africa rather than sail to the interior using the rivers?
3. Who are the Afrikaners, and where did they come from?
4. What is the significance of the Swahili language in East Africa?
5. Why has Somalia been unable to form a stable government?

Developing Geography Skills

1. Based on the maps on pages 462 and 476, what are three major deserts found in southern and eastern Africa?
2. Based on the map on page 476, what countries border Lake Victoria?

Thinking Critically

1. What role did Nelson Mandela and F. W. de Klerk play in ending apartheid in South Africa? Have all South Africans benefitted equally from the end of this practice? Explain your answer.
2. What are common characteristics of African nations that have a Christian majority?

Living in God's World

1. Evaluate a culture that requires a dowry of the man in order to marry his wife.
2. Imagine you are a pastor in an African country overrun with the prosperity gospel. You have been given the opportunity to write a column in a national newspaper about the prosperity gospel. What would you write?

People, Places, and Things to Know

sub-Saharan Africa
savanna
HIV/AIDS
Cape of Good Hope
Coloureds
Cape Town
Orange River
Drakensberg Mountains
escarpment
Tugela Falls
Zulu
Boers
veldt
Bantu
Afrikaans
Afrikaners
Limpopo River
Johannesburg
Pretoria
apartheid
Nelson Mandela
Thabana Ntlenyana
San
Kalahari Desert
Okavango Delta
Namib Desert
Skeleton Coast
Zambezi River
Victoria Falls
Great Rift Valley
Blue Nile
White Nile
Lake Victoria
Nairobi
Swahili
Masai
Serengeti Plain
Mount Kilimanjaro
Zanzibar
Horn of Africa
Denakil Desert
Ethiopian Highlands
Addis Ababa
African Union (AU)
Ogaden
Bab al-Mandeb
cataract
Sudd

Open air market in Nigeria

CENTRAL AND WESTERN AFRICA

℘xcept for a strip of the Sahel in the north (discussed in the next chapter), jungles and savannas dominate the landscape and lifestyles of the twenty nations in central and western Africa. The equator runs through the center of this region. Regular winds off the Atlantic continually dump rain along the equator, just as they do in the Amazon River Basin. A few degrees north and south of the equator, the winds shift, creating a rainy season and a dry season. A savanna rises there.

Unlike mediterranean climates and river valleys in the Sahel, tropical rain forests and dry savannas cannot generally support intensive agriculture. Typically, the people are hunters and gatherers, sometimes practicing slash-and-burn agriculture to supplement their meager existence. Their simple agriculture permits the existence of small villages, but there is not enough food to support large groups in one place.

The foundation of African society is the tribal village, such as this one in Rhoumsiki, Cameroon.

The **village** is an important concept in understanding life in Africa. In the traditional African village, each person plays a vital role in the survival of the whole community. Having more than one wife is a sign of wealth, so polygamy is common. Young children pull weeds or sort vegetables; older children herd livestock or do household chores. Loyalty to the village extends to larger social units. Several villages that are descended from a common ancestor form a clan. Two or more clans, in turn, form a tribe. A headman wields the highest authority in the village. A strong tribal **chief** unites several villages, using headmen as his administrators.

Whenever people are isolated in small groups, their speech patterns diverge quickly. Dialects arise and then turn into new languages. Africa has one-third of the people of the world and one-third of the languages. Strong identification with a tribe that speaks the same language or dialect is called **tribalism**. In spite of European influence, tribalism continues to be a central feature of sub-Saharan Africa. Individuals often feel more allegiance to their tribe than to their nation-state.

I. Central Africa

The equator crosses the heart of Central Africa. Most of the region has a tropical wet climate, with average temperatures of 80°F and one hundred inches of rainfall each year. Mangrove swamps, with their tangled vegetation and stagnant waters, barricade the

Initiation

At a certain age (twelve or thirteen in some cultures, fifteen to twenty in others), many young African men and women go through **initiation rites**. Those rites mark the transition into adulthood and usually involve a multiple-step process, including hunts, dances, and ceremonies with masks.

coastal lands. Where rivers or clearings break through this barrier, dense jungles line the path inland. Forest elephants, gorillas, and panthers roam these jungles, and pythons grow up to thirty-two feet long. Unlike the Amazon River, which flows through a low coastal plain and is navigable for one thousand miles, the rivers of Africa drop down from high plateaus to the coast.

Dense jungles, wild beasts, rough waters, and, worst of all, diseases plague Africa. Snails carry the disease bilharzia, which afflicts the Nile Valley as well as tropical Africa. More serious are the diseases spread by insects, such as *Aëdes aegypti* mosquitoes, which spread jungle **yellow fever**. Although treatments and preventative vaccines are available, epidemics still occur.

As it feeds on the blood of animals and humans, the **tsetse fly** spreads African sleeping sickness. Approximately sixty-nine million people in Africa are at risk of contracting African sleeping sickness. In the last ten years, cases of this sickness have dropped from twenty-five thousand cases annually to less than ten thousand each year. The disease occurs primarily in Africa between the fifteenth parallels north and south of the equator. It progresses from fever to seizures and finally to delirium and coma. Death results unless the victim seeks medical help in time. Sleeping sickness killed many explorers and left others stranded by killing their packhorses or oxen. Even today, farmers cannot raise cattle or horses in the regions infested by tsetse flies.

The anopheles (uh NOFF uh leez) mosquito infests many of the world's tropical areas, including most of the African continent.

The tsetse fly spreads the fatal African sleeping sickness that plagues much of Central Africa.

WORLD RELIGIONS

African Traditional Religions

African traditional religions are difficult to label and to describe. They are sometimes called primitive religions, but devotees of these religions find that label offensive. Christians reject it because it presumes that religions evolved from primitive beginnings toward more developed monotheism, whereas the Bible teaches that humanity began with knowledge of the true God and fell away. Furthermore, African traditional religions are often complex and developed over long periods of time.

Animism is another term used to describe African traditional religions. Animism is the belief that all things—rocks, trees, water, sun, owls, snakes, thunderstorms—have a spirit and that these spirits exercise great control over the world. A person must perform certain religious rituals or the spirits will become angry and he will experience bad luck. Worshiping the objects whose spirits are dominant in

his locality will supposedly please the spirits and bring him good luck.

There are many religions included under the broad category of African traditional religions. Each one is associated with a specific people group. Though these groups do not send out missionaries or proselytize, their beliefs and practices may spread as people intermarry with other groups or move to new areas.

Traditional religions do not have scriptures. They function by oral tradition and rituals that are carefully passed down from generation to generation. The rituals touch every aspect of life. This is a challenge for Christian missions. African converts to Christianity often attempt to merely add Christianity to their animistic beliefs. They may profess faith in Christ but then turn to a traditional healer to perform the traditional rituals if they become ill. Even true converts struggle to break with the religious

traditions of their people. For instance, they may struggle with superstitions about the evil influence of owls even though they know the superstition to be false.

African traditional religions often include a belief in a high god who is a personal spirit, the creator, omniscient, omnipresent, and eternal. But this god typically is not approachable. In some cases, only the community can pray to this god in dire circumstances. The individual may never appeal to him. Or it may be possible to appeal to this god through intermediary gods. Even when it is possible to pray to the high god directly, the spirits of ancestors and the spirits of objects and places are of greater concern. These religions do not focus on a right relationship with the high god. They focus, rather, on appeasing the spirits so that daily life progresses well rather than poorly.

AIDS and the Christian's Response

AIDS is a global epidemic that by 2009 had resulted in the deaths of about thirty million people.

Sub-Saharan Africa has the highest rate of AIDS in the world. Approximately 69 percent of the people infected with HIV/AIDS live there, even though their countries make up about 15 percent of the world's population. The first step for African countries has been to recognize the problem. Because of the stigma attached to the disease, many people were not being tested and some governments have, until recently, refused to acknowledge the enormity of the problem. For example, the president of South Africa initially denied that HIV causes AIDS. Education is an important part of the battle. Some countries, such as Uganda, have implemented programs that encourage sexual abstinence outside of marriage. Unfaithfulness of even one partner can affect an entire family. Many women get HIV through an unfaithful partner. Others contract it through sexual assault. Because of the physical method of transmission, women are more likely to get HIV than are their partners. Up to 60 percent of sub-Saharan Africa's AIDS patients are women.

The AIDS epidemic has taken a huge toll on the labor force in sub-Saharan Africa, devastating the economies of those countries. The average life expectancy in the region initially dropped to only forty-seven years, although that number is rising.

Nearly 18 million children in Africa have been orphaned by AIDS. And many children are infected themselves. Children can contract the disease simply by being born to an infected mother. Aggressive medical treatment has greatly reduced the number of children born with AIDS.

Certainly, Christians should be sympathetic toward those who have HIV/AIDS. Just as Christ healed the lepers of His day, Christians should be willing to minister to those from all levels of society. Could God be calling you to minister to AIDS victims in Africa?

It spreads the dreaded killer **malaria**. For some varieties of malaria there is no known remedy. Malaria kills up to a million people a year, nearly 90 percent of them in Africa. It is the single biggest killer of African children under the age of five.

The Congo Basin

The **Congo River** is the great river of Central Africa. The fifth-longest river worldwide, the Congo is second only to the Amazon in volume. The Congo pours more than one million cubic feet of water into the Atlantic every second. Like the Amazon, it drains a vast region, called the **Congo Basin**, which covers all or part of five countries. Tropical rains caused by evaporation replenish the river.

Central African Republic

The Central African Republic (CAR), only slightly smaller than Texas, is the only landlocked country in Central Africa. It is located almost exactly in the center of Africa on the southwest border of Sudan. The terrain ranges from flat to rolling hills. Plateaus averaging three thousand feet in height split the nation into two drainage basins. Savannas cover the northern plateau, where water flows into the Chari River and empties into Lake Chad. Only 3 percent of the land is arable, and the country is often threatened with the extremes of dust storms and floods.

More than half of the people are farmers who raise grains, beans, yams, peanuts, sesame seeds, and cattle. Natural resources include diamonds, uranium, gold, and oil.

The southern regions are equatorial rain forests and part of the Congo Basin. The Ubangi River forms the southern border. That populous region includes all of the main cities, including the capital, Bangui.

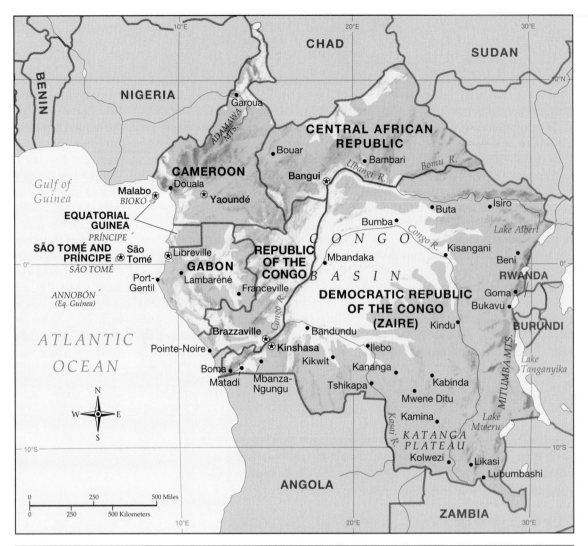

Country	Capital	Area (sq. mi.)	Pop. (2013 est.) (M)	Pop. Density (per sq. mi.)	Per Capita GDP ($US)	Life Span
Central African Republic	Bangui	240,533	5.12	21	$800	50.5
Democratic Republic of the Congo	Kinshasa	905,355	75.51	83	$300	55.7
Republic of the Congo	Brazzaville	132,047	4.45	34	$4,500	55.3
Gabon	Libreville	103,347	1.64	16	$16,300	52.3
Equatorial Guinea	Malabo	10,830	0.70	65	$20,200	62.8
São Tomé and Príncipe	São Tomé	372	0.19	511	$2,300	63.5
Cameroon	Yaoundé	183,567	20.55	112	$2,300	54.7

The people of the CAR enjoy freedom of religion, and 76 percent of the population affiliates with some form of Christianity. Muslims represent 14 percent of the people, and animism is practiced by 9 percent. However, statistics such as these can be misleading in many

African countries because animism has a strong influence among many who claim to be Christian or Muslim. Evangelical Christians make up 32 percent of the people, and they are growing at an annual rate of 2 percent each year.

Democratic Republic of the Congo

Three countries share the waters of the Congo River. The largest nation in the Congo Basin, the Democratic Republic of the Congo (DRC), is the third-largest country on the continent and the largest in sub-Saharan Africa. It is a little less than one-fourth the size of the United States and straddles the equator. It shares a border on the north with the Central African Republic and a western border with the Republic of the Congo. It has only a narrow outlet to the Atlantic Ocean at the mouth of the Congo River.

The DRC was the personal property of Leopold II, the king of Belgium, from 1885 until 1908, when he relinquished control to the Belgian government. The Belgian Congo, as it was then known, received its independence in 1960.

The country is made up of more than two hundred tribal groups. Four of those tribes make up 45 percent of the population. The largest tribes belong to the Bantu family of tribes. With such tribal diversity in the country, the government struggled for unity and stability. A military leader named **Mobutu Sese Seko** took control during a civil war that occurred after independence. He later renamed all of the country's geographic features with African names: the Congo River became the Zaire River; the country became Zaire. He even changed his own name from Desiré Mobutu to Mobutu Sese Seko. Mobutu also took over all businesses run by Europeans, but the national language remained French. A rebel leader from the eastern forests overthrew the aging Mobutu in 1996 and restored the name Congo, but instability continued. In 2013, the UN Security Council authorized the United Nations Force Intervention Brigade to enter the Democratic Republic of the Congo and disarm rebel forces.

The people of the DRC enjoy religious freedom, and 76 percent identify with some form of Christianity. Fourteen percent are Muslim, and nearly 9 percent practice ethnic religions. Thirty-two percent of the people are Evangelical Christians, and their numbers are growing. Nationals are becoming missionaries, and indigenous ministries are expanding.

Rain Forest—Throughout the jungle regions of the Congo Basin, cassava is a staple crop. The DRC has very little Atlantic coastline but enough to obtain a valuable resource—offshore oil wells.

Near the mouth of the Congo River are several rapids. The ocean port of Matadi lies just below the lower rapids. Above the rapids is **Kinshasa,** the capital. With nearly eight million people, it is by far the largest city in sub-Saharan Africa. Navigation is possible from Kinshasa upstream for over a thousand miles northeast to the city of Kisangani.

A thick rain forest lies in the northeast. Stanley (now Boyoma) Falls marks the end of navigation on the Congo River just upstream from Kisangani. This region is famous for isolated Pygmy villages.

Storytelling

"Storytelling remains popular in the DRC. The traditional folklore story conveys some piece of wisdom or social advice through a simple, often magical tale. The storyteller is usually elderly and respected, with the skill to create different characters with his voice and the noises of jungle animals as well if required. One favorite tale is the story of the Creator god and his four children: Raffia-palm, Liana, Wine-palm, and Oil-palm, his favorite."

Cultures of the World: Democratic Republic of the Congo, 113–14.

These children attend school in a UN-sponsored refugee camp in the Democratic Republic of the Congo.

Cassava roots

The okapi is a member of the giraffe family and is an endangered species.

The Ubangi River forms part of the borders of several Central African countries.

The quiet okapi, a short-necked giraffe with striped legs, also roams these dark forests.

The Congo River has a major tributary in the south, the Kasai River. The city of Ilebo lies at the farthest navigable point on this tributary. Kananga, the third-largest city in the DRC, lies on a branch of the Kasai.

Mineral Riches in the Highland Borders—Highlands mark the end of the Congo Basin along the eastern border: the Virunga Mountains in the north and the Mitumba Mountains farther south along Lake Tanganyika. The mountains produce tin but are better known as a haven for chimpanzees and the endangered mountain gorillas in Virunga National Park.

Great mineral wealth lies in the southern tip of the nation, at the **Katanga Plateau**. Lubumbashi, the DRC's second-largest city, is the capital of the important province of Katanga. Copper is the nation's primary export. The mining city of Kolwezi is the hub of Africa's largest copper deposits. This copper belt has some of the largest copper reserves worldwide. Other mines make the DRC one of the world's leading producers of cobalt. Additional products include diamonds, uranium, gold, silver, and zinc.

The Democratic Republic of the Congo's vast economic potential makes it the hub of Central Africa. Unfortunately, poor leadership and frequent wars have hindered its development.

Republic of the Congo

Africa has two Congos, which sometimes leads to confusion for a geography student. The "other Congo," on the west side of the Congo River, belonged to France. The capital of French Equatorial Guinea was at **Brazzaville**, across the river from Kinshasa. It is the largest city in the former French colonies. All of the French colonies in Africa became independent in 1960. This "other" Congo is simply called the Republic of the Congo, or Congo-Brazzaville.

The Congo River and its northern tributary, the **Ubangi River**, form the eastern border. Gabon forms the western border. The northeastern state of Likouala, west of the Ubangi, includes a remote swampy jungle, the largest and least-explored jungle wilderness in the world.

The population is made up of several tribal groups, including Bantu and Pygmy. Most of the people live in the hills and low plateaus along the southern border.

Freedom of religion was granted in 1992, and 90 percent of the people identify with some form of Christianity. Animists represent 5 percent of the population (although many who claim to be Christian retain animistic practices), 3 percent are nonreligious, and 1.5 percent are Muslim. Nearly 16 percent of the people are Evangelical Christians. Believers are struggling to overcome the nation's troubled past and take advantage of the country's great potential.

Subsistence agriculture is common throughout the country, although only 1 percent of the land is arable. The second-most produced agricultural product is cattle, used for meat. Plantations grow and export cassava, cacao, coffee, bananas, and peanuts. Although Congo-Brazzaville is not as rich as Gabon, it does produce a little petroleum. Other resources include potash, lead, zinc, uranium, copper, and phosphates.

Pygmies

The **Pygmies** are a distinct people group in Africa. Their average height is four feet six inches, and they continue to live in the jungle by hunting and gathering food. Pygmies travel in small groups of about ten to twenty families, building villages of sticks and leaves to live in for a few months before moving on. They have no chiefs but make decisions by group discussion.

Survival depends on their intimate knowledge of the jungle. Pygmies know the life cycles of more than one thousand species of plants: they know when to gather the food and what is edible or medicinal. They also know the habits of more than three hundred animals. Women dig wild yams and gather edible leaves, nuts, berries, and mushrooms. In the rainy season, men sometimes help the women gather caterpillars.

The men prefer, however, to gather honey and to hunt. Some tribes use

Baaka Pygmies in the Central African Republic

crossbows and typical arrows to shoot monkeys; others use small bows and poison-tipped arrows. A group of only two or three men can hunt porcupines and four-pound Gambian rats, but large groups of men are needed to

track elephants, red hogs, and gorillas. They bring them down using iron-tipped spears. Men, women, and children may form lines to drive duikers (the smallest antelope) into nets or into groups of waiting spearmen.

Pygmy tribes live in the various countries of the Congo Basin and its borders. Each tribe speaks the Bantu languages of the settled tribe in their area. The Pygmies' ability to survive in the jungle gives them a mystique even among Africans. The settled farmers attribute supernatural powers to Pygmies, especially as diviners and healers. Welcomed in farming areas, Pygmies often help clear fields and harvest crops. In return, they receive the right to gather bananas and manioc from the fields. They also trade meat to the settled tribes for iron knives and rice.

Section Quiz

1. What phrase is used to describe all countries south of the Sahara?
2. What is the most important concept that underlies most of African society?
3. What is the name of the country formed from the Belgian Congo?
4. What are the only two African capitals that face each other across a river?
✶ Why do you think the Democratic Republic of the Congo would keep French as the national language?

The Lower Guinea Coast

West of the Congo Basin is a region called the Lower Guinea Coast. It consists of three countries on the mainland and an island nation: Gabon, Equatorial Guinea, Cameroon, and São Tomé and Príncipe.

Gabon

A country the size of Colorado, Gabon gained its independence from France in 1960. It had been part of **French Equatorial Africa**, which also included the Republic of the Congo, the Central African Republic, and Chad. The Ogooué River, which drains the country, supports a vast, wild rain forest.

Central African countries are major producers of coffee.

Timber from Gabon's jungles, including ebony and mahogany, is an important product. Some other crops that grow in Gabon include plantains, yams, cassava, peanuts, cacao, coffee, sugar, and palm oil. Although only 1 percent of the land is arable, about 60 percent of the work force is engaged in agriculture. Fifteen percent of the work force is engaged in various industrial jobs. The export of manganese, gold, uranium, and petroleum supplements the lumber profits. Other important industries include chemicals, textiles, cement, and ship repair. Income from these industries is slowly helping to improve living conditions, education, and health care.

The population largely consists of the Bantu tribes. Less than 11 percent of the people are European or of other ethnic groups.

The people of Gabon enjoy freedom of religion, and 79 percent identify with some form of Christianity. Ten percent of the people are Muslim, and 8 percent practice animism (although many professing Christians and Muslims also retain animistic beliefs). Evangelical Christians make up 13 percent of the population, and they are growing numerically about 3 percent each year. Established churches are planting new congregations in formerly unreached interior regions. Islam is also growing at nearly 5 percent each year and has support from the current president of the country.

Equatorial Guinea

Equatorial Guinea is slightly smaller than Maryland and consists of several islands and a small mainland region (often called Rio Muni) that is sandwiched between the coast of Cameroon on the north and Gabon on the east and south. The capital, Malabo, is on the island of Bioko.

Portugal first claimed the region in 1471. Spain gained control in the mid-nineteenth century, forming the only Spanish colony in sub-Saharan Africa. After Equatorial Guinea gained independence in 1968, it became the only African country with Spanish as its official language.

Religious activity was severely repressed in the 1970s, but conditions have since improved so that the people enjoy a limited degree of religious freedom. Ninety percent of the people affiliate with some form of Christianity, 4 percent are Muslim, and 3 percent practice animism. Evangelical Christians represent 4 percent of the population and are growing at an annual rate of 5 percent. Christian leaders are being trained to meet the needs of this growing segment of the population and serve as pastors and evangelists in the country.

An oil boom in 1997 produced phenomenal economic growth of 71.2 percent, but because the president of the country, his family, and his close friends control the oil industry, little of that wealth has filtered down to most of the people. About 22 percent of the population is unemployed.

Most of the work force is engaged in industry, which is amazing for a third-world country. Only about 3 percent are in agriculture. In addition to oil, other industries include fishing, mining (gold, bauxite, diamonds, and tantalum), livestock, and timber. Major agricultural products include plantains, yams, coffee, cassava, bananas, and palm oil.

Cameroon

Previously a German colony, Cameroon was divided between France and Britain after World War I. Those two European powers ruled the country until 1960. Since colonial days, Cameroon's stable, autocratic government has made steady progress. The country has built manufacturing plants and mines. The most important industrial product is petroleum, drilled in the Gulf of Guinea.

Cameroon, which is about twice the size of Oregon, has an odd shape. A sliver of land extends seven hundred miles north of the Bight of Biafra to reach the swampy shores of Lake Chad, which Cameroon shares with Nigeria and two other nations. That narrow stretch of the country separates Chad on the east from Nigeria on the west. The Adamawa Mountains rise in the northwestern half of the country along the border with Nigeria. The highest mountain in West and Central Africa is farther south near the coast. Mount Cameroon rises dramatically to 13,255 feet just west of Douala, but most of the region is a rugged plateau.

Volcanic craters on Mt. Cameroon

Southern Cameroon, the most populous region of the country, consists almost entirely of lowlands clothed with rain forest. The village of Debundscha is one of the wettest places in the world, receiving as much as four hundred inches of rainfall annually. Several rivers flow southwest to the Gulf of Guinea. Both the capital, Yaoundé, and the largest city, Douala, lie on these rivers.

As a result of the French colonial influence, French is the official language of Cameroon, but 279 African languages are also spoken there, including several Bantu languages. Bantu is a subgroup of the **Niger-Congo family of languages**. Most Africans south of 5° N speak a language in this group. Bantu was probably first spoken somewhere in the mountains of Cameroon, and it later spread as the conquering Bantu moved south. Nearly three hundred tribal groups in Africa see themselves as Bantu, each with its own name, history, and language or dialect. The size of these tribes ranges from a few hundred people to millions.

Cultural Sensitivity in Cameroon

Jim and Jenna Wright, Cameroon

Two significant cultural aspects for daily life in northern Cameroon are what one wears and where one walks.

Particularly because we live among Muslim peoples, it is important that we do not offend by what we wear. Women are usually covered with a wrap-around skirt, a shirt, and an additional wrap around their shoulders that often extends down as far as their knees or ankles. A head covering is also mandated for a woman in public. Although we do not try to dress exactly like the local Muslims, we as missionaries follow the culture of covering up body and head. This conveys our respect to them and avoids immediately closing a door of witness and influence.

As we move about an Islamic culture, we must understand where one walks—and where he doesn't. Much of life in rural, desert, northern Cameroon, is lived on a mat or rug. You soon learn to take off your shoes when stepping onto a rug and never to step on a Muslim's prayer mat. In addition, it is rude to walk in front of someone who is praying. In a market area, you must learn to notice where certain areas have been set aside and designated for Muslim prayers. In this barren land, these are not always obvious; often the area is under a tree and given a rough border of rocks (if the rocks are available). Missionaries gain respect from the people as they learn to recognize and purposely go around such places that are sacred to them.

Festivals

"In Cameroon it is uncommon to find the kind of national public festivals like Christmas and Thanksgiving that have become institutionalized in Europe and North America. Instead, there is an astonishing diversity of local festivals for an equally diverse set of occasions. Major states in the life cycle, such as birth, marriage, and death, are celebrated as are important agricultural events. Yam festivals, for example, take place in parts of southern Cameroon when the yams are ready to be harvested."

Cultures of the World: Cameroon, 107.

Cameroon is a secular state that guarantees freedom of religion for its people. Fifty-four percent of the people affiliate with some form of Christianity, 26 percent are Muslim, and 19 percent practice animism. Evangelical Christians represent 9 percent of the population and have an annual growth of 4 percent. In addition to average citizens, many professionals and political leaders have embraced evangelical Christianity. This is expected to have a positive influence on a society that has been characterized by corruption.

São Tomé and Príncipe

About 150 miles off the coast of northern Gabon and Equatorial Guinea is the country of São Tomé and Príncipe. The islands of São Tomé (soun too-MEH) and Príncipe (PREEN see puh) are similar to the Cape Verde Islands. The islands were uninhabited until the Portuguese came in 1470. By 1500, the country was generally settled by the Portuguese. The nation gained independence from Portugal in 1975.

The Democratic Republic of São Tomé and Príncipe is a secular nation that guarantees freedom of religion, and 88 percent of the people identify with some form of Christianity. Seven percent are animists, 3 percent are Muslim, and 1 percent have no religious affiliation. Evangelical Christians make up 4 percent of the people, and their numbers are increasing at an annual rate of 6 percent. Missionaries from Portugal and Brazil have played a role in this strong growth.

The two main islands and the half-dozen islets are volcanic and have good soil. The dense mountainous jungle was cleared for large plantations. The work force is engaged in primarily agricultural

São Tomé is a contrast between the poverty of country villages and modern life in the cities.

LET'S GO EXPLORING

Climates in Africa

1. What are the only three climates found in North Africa?
2. What two climates appear in southern Africa and nowhere else on the continent?
3. At 20° N, what is the climate on the west coast? on the east coast?
4. At the equator, what is the climate on the west coast? on the east coast?
5. At the Tropic of Capricorn, what is the climate on the west coast? on the east coast?
★ Do you see a pattern in Africa's climate as you proceed north and south of the equator?

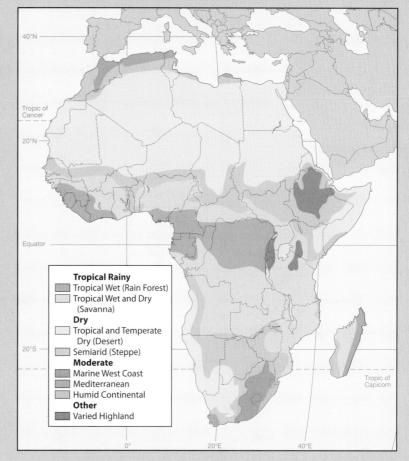

Tropical Rainy
- Tropical Wet (Rain Forest)
- Tropical Wet and Dry (Savanna)

Dry
- Tropical and Temperate Dry (Desert)
- Semiarid (Steppe)

Moderate
- Marine West Coast
- Mediterranean
- Humid Continental

Other
- Varied Highland

pursuits and fishing. Major crops include bananas, yams, cacao, copra (dried coconut), coffee, and various vegetables.

Major industries include textiles, soap, beer, timber, and fishing. Vast oil reserves are thought to exist as well, and the country hopes to tap into them soon.

Section Quiz

1. What enables the Pygmies to survive in the harsh jungle environment?
2. What Central African country exports gold, manganese, and uranium?
3. What Central African country suffers from high unemployment despite the discovery of oil deposits?
4. What is the official language of Cameroon? Why?
★ Why has Cameroon remained a stable country?

II. Western Africa

Thirteen countries cover the great western bulge of Africa. The largest, Nigeria, is bigger than Texas, but the others are quite small. Gambia, about the size of Connecticut, is the smallest country on the continent. All thirteen countries could fit into India. A majority of the people in the northern part of this region are Muslim. Most

Western Africa Fast Facts

Country	Capital	Area (sq. mi.)	Pop. (2013 est.) (M)	Pop. Density (per sq. mi.)	Per Capita GDP ($US)	Life Span
Nigeria	Abuja	356,669	174.51	489	$2,800	52.5
Benin	Porto-Novo	43,483	9.88	227	$1,700	60.7
Togo	Lomé	21,925	7.15	326	$1,100	63.6
Ghana	Accra	92,098	25.20	274	$3,400	65.3
Burkina Faso	Ouagadougou	105,869	17.81	735	$1,400	54.4
Côte d'Ivoire	Yamoussoukro	124,502	22.40	180	$1,800	57.7
Liberia	Monrovia	43,000	3.99	93	$700	57.8
Sierra Leone	Freetown	27,699	5.61	203	$1,400	57.0
Guinea	Conakry	94,927	11.18	118	$1,100	59.1
Guinea-Bissau	Bissau	13,946	1.66	119	$1,200	49.5
Gambia	Banjul	4,363	1.88	431	$1,900	64.1
Cape Verde	Praia	1,556	0.53	341	$4,200	71.3
Senegal	Dakar	75,955	13.30	175	$2,100	60.6

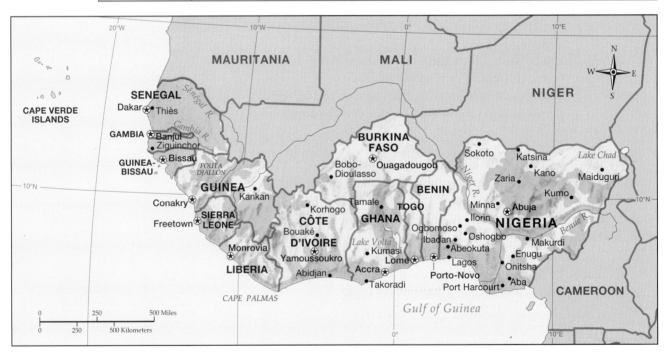

Christians and animists reside in the southern area. In this section, you will learn first about the countries on the southern part of the bulge, those that have a coast on the Gulf of Guinea. Later, you will read about those that are on the western part of the bulge and have coasts on the Atlantic Ocean.

The Gulf of Guinea Coast

The curved coast on the southern side of Africa's bulge from Côte d'Ivoire to Gabon bounds the Gulf of Guinea. Early traders gave various parts of that coast different names based on the types of trade conducted there: the Slave Coast, the Ivory Coast, and the Gold Coast. The long, curving eastern portion of this coast was called the **Slave Coast** because so many slave ships operated from the bays called **bights** in that area. The **Bight of Benin**, an extension of the Gulf of Guinea, extends north from the Gulf of Guinea into the coasts of three nations—Nigeria, Benin, and Togo—between the Volta and Niger Rivers.

Nigeria

With more than 174 million people, Nigeria is the most populous nation in Africa. Unlike most other West African nations, Nigeria was an English colony, and English remains its official language. Nigeria received independence from Britain in 1960, and it is an example of how Africa has struggled to rise above its troubled past.

Rivers divide the nation into three distinct geographic regions. The Niger River, the lifeline of Nigeria, flows into the country from Niger in the west and then proceeds southeastward to a point just below the center of the country. There, just south of the capital, Abuja, it is joined by the **Benue River** (BAYN way), the Niger's main tributary, which flows into Nigeria from Cameroon in the east. Thus enlarged, the Niger flows south into the Gulf of Guinea, effectively dividing the country into a northern half and two southern quarters. A different tribe has dominated the history and culture of each of those three regions.

Hausaland's Muslims in the North—North of the Niger and Benue Rivers rise the plateaus of the Sahel. The dominant **Hausa** tribe there is one of the three largest ethnic groups in Nigeria. About 16 percent of all Nigerians are Hausa. Unlike most other tribes, a majority of the Hausa are Muslim (45 percent of the national population), and their language belongs to the Afro-Asiatic family of languages, the same family as Arabic.

Christians in this region suffer persecution, and the Muslim majority is becoming radical. Hundreds of churches have been destroyed, and many Christians have been murdered. Government leaders have imposed sharia law in most of the northern states.

The Hausa built many city-states before the arrival of the Europeans, three of which are still important cities today: Katsina, Zaria, and Kano. Kano is the largest city in the north and the fourth-largest in Nigeria. The Fulani tribe took control in the nineteenth century and intermixed with the Hausa. The Fulani account for another 9 percent of the population.

Today, most of those northern people are rural, living in traditional ways on the savanna, grazing cattle or growing crops. Two of these crops are especially important. Nigeria is a leading producer of millet (a type of grain) and peanuts.

The Volta

The Volta River is a major river that empties into the Gulf of Guinea. The three main headwater streams are the Red Volta, the White Volta, and the Black Volta. Some of the headwaters flow through the interior country of Burkina Faso and then into the coastal nation of Ghana.

The Niger River is the lifeline of Nigeria.

Abuja National Mosque in Nigeria

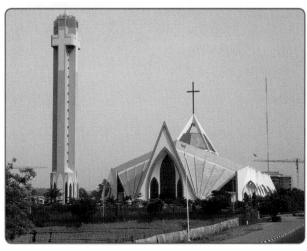
National Church of Abuja, Nigeria

Christians in the Southwest—The **Yoruba** dominate the lands south and west of the Niger. The Yoruba make up about 23 percent of the population of Nigeria as well as a major portion of Benin. The entire Slave Coast (basically the coastal region between the prime meridian and 10° E longitude, from Ghana to Cameroon) was once Yoruba territory. Unlike the Hausa, the Yoruba have adopted many Western ways, and about 50 percent of them identify with some form of Christianity. Three percent practice animism. Thirty percent of Nigerians are Evangelical Christians, and the growth (numerical and spiritual) is steady. Nigerian congregations currently support five thousand missionaries who serve in home and foreign missions.

Most of Nigeria's people live in the southwest. That region rises slowly from the coast through dense rain forests to the grassy Plateau of Yorubaland (2,000 ft.). The two largest cities in this region are Lagos (10.6 million) and Ibadan (2.8 million). **Lagos** was an important slave market and the capital of Nigeria. It is now the most important industrial center in Western and Central Africa.

To the east of Lagos lies Benin City, the former capital of the **Benin Kingdom**, one of the greatest kingdoms of Western Africa, which flourished between the thirteenth and eighteenth centuries. Its bronze and brass statues won international esteem, but the king's wealth depended on the slave trade, which declined after Europeans banned it.

Development of Nigeria's many resources has helped industries keep growing. Southwest Nigeria has the most resources of any region in the country. It has propelled Nigeria to a leading position in the production of cassava, cacao, and plantains. Nigeria is also a leading producer of hardwoods.

Petroleum is the most important natural resource of Nigeria. Its estimated reserves are some of the greatest in Africa. Most of Nigeria's oil comes from the Niger Delta. Unfortunately, the country's corrupt military dictatorship has siphoned off much of the wealth rather than using it to benefit the people. Polls of international businessmen indicate that Nigeria is one of the most corrupt countries in the world. To do business in Nigeria, foreigners are almost forced to join in the bribery and fraud. Compounding the problem are attacks by rebels, who disrupt the flow of production because they are envious of the wealth the oil has brought to the Niger Delta region. Western Africa will continue to suffer until Nigeria reforms its government, curbs corruption, and defeats the rebels.

The Igbo in the Southeast—The southeastern quarter of Nigeria is called **Biafra**, named for the Bight of Biafra, which lies east of the Niger Delta and continues south into Central Africa. Most of the region is lowland, but mountains rise over six thousand feet along the southeastern border with Cameroon. The region provides palm oil, hardwood, and rubber. This region is home to the Igbo people, the third largest ethnic group in Nigeria. The rural population is primarily employed in crafts, farming, and trade. Yam production is the most important crop, and annual celebrations take place following the yam harvest.

The Biafran War

In 1967, the **Biafran War** erupted as the **Igbo** people fought for an independent nation. Like the Yoruba, the Igbo have adopted Western ways and forms of Christianity. Both tribes have a similar language in the Kwa language family, which is common across the southern coast from Liberia to Nigeria. However, the Igbo wanted independence. A terrible famine compounded the suffering of war. After a million Igbo had died, the Igbo people finally surrendered in 1970. Instead of punishing the Igbo, however, the Nigerian government offered reconciliation.

During the war in Biafra, starvation and malnutrition affected thousands of innocent civilians.

Earth Matters: Drinking Water and Disease

It all begins with a simple drink of water. In contaminated water, small crustaceans called water fleas lurk, hosting the larvae of an even greater danger, the guinea worm. This parasitic worm can grow to a length of two to three feet and as thick as a strand of spaghetti. The scientific name for the guinea worm disease is Dracunculiasis, which means "affliction with little dragons," because of the fiery pain that guinea worms cause.

After the guinea worm mates in the body cavity, it migrates down to the leg or foot, where a blister forms on the skin. If the blister is popped, the end of the guinea worm is exposed. This causes intense, fiery pain. A person infected with a guinea worm often bathes the leg in water to seek relief. When the guinea worm contacts a body of water, it releases its eggs. A perverse cycle is created. There is only one treatment, and it is excruciating.

The only way to get rid of the worm is to wrap the end of it on a stick and turn it gradually until the worm is extracted.

But the good news is that this ancient disease that goes back to Ptolemaic Egypt may be on the verge of eradication. In 1985, experts estimated that there were 2.5 million cases of guinea worm in twenty countries across Asia and Africa. In 2012, only four countries reported over five hundred cases of guinea worm. The "affliction with little dragons" has been reduced by over 99 percent. Politicians, scientists, and especially Christians can get excited about this progress.

In the case of the guinea worm, no medications are needed. We can trace the dramatic reductions in guinea worm disease in the past few decades to just a little knowledge of geography and some simple science. Foreign

workers are teaching people to filter drinking water to remove the water fleas that host guinea worm larvae. People with guinea worm are taught to bathe their fiery wound in a bucket of water rather than in a stream, river, or pool. By not bathing their sore in streams and rivers, they keep guinea worm larvae out of the water supply. They can dump the bucket of water far away from a water supply to avoid contamination.

The guinea worm is not the only water pollution problem in Africa. Scientists continue to explore ways to filter and purify water and to make clean drinking water convenient for some of the poorest people in the world. We can value and appreciate the effectiveness of science and geography in meeting the needs of some of the world's poorest people. These people bear God's image, and they need Christ.

Benin

To the west, between Nigeria and Togo, is Benin, formerly known as Dahomey (duh HOH mee). Its northern neighbors are Niger and Burkina Faso. About the size of Tennessee, it is one of the smallest and most densely populated countries in Africa. Benin was once part of French West Africa. Porto-Novo is its capital.

Of the country's sixty ethnic groups, the southern Fon tribe is in the majority. The Bariba are the main group in the sparsely populated northern savanna.

The people of Benin enjoy religious freedom, and 40 percent affiliate with some form of Christianity. About 36 percent of the people practice a form of animism called **voodoo**, and nearly 24 percent are Muslim. Evangelical Christians represent 8 percent of the population and are growing at an annual rate of 4 percent. The country's religious freedom provides an open environment for witnessing, public worship, and planting new churches. The goal is to plant twenty thousand new congregations in Benin by 2020.

Eighteen percent of Benin's land is arable, producing cotton, corn, cassava, yams, beans, palm oil, and peanuts. It has small offshore oil deposits and some limestone and timber, but its main industries are textiles, cement, and construction materials. The country experimented with Marxism from 1970 to 1989, but the economy nearly collapsed and the government became a succession of military dictatorships. In 1991, Benin became the first Western African country to successfully transfer power from a dictatorship to a democracy.

It has also held free elections since 1996. To date, Benin continues to make great strides toward free and stable self-government.

Togo

Sandwiched between Benin on the east and Ghana on the west, with a small border on the north shared with Burkina Faso, is a country that is about twice the size of Maryland. Togo is only about fifty miles wide and about 325 miles long and is essentially covered by the Togo Hills, which are tallest near the central portion of the country, and savanna in the north.

Togo was a colony of both Denmark and Germany, under which the colony became known as Togoland. Following World War I, France and Great Britain were granted control of the region. After World War II, it was under the trusteeship of the United Nations. In 1960, the portion under British control voted to become part of Ghana. The French part declared independence. Gnassingbe Eyadema seized power in 1963 and ruled through a cult of personality until his death in 2005. The dictator's son, Faure Gnassingbe, assumed control and was elected to the presidency later that year. The country is now in transition from dictatorship to democracy and a multiparty political system.

Togo is a country of bare essentials and subsistence living in tribal villages.

Forty-six percent of the land in Togo is arable, and 65 percent of the population engages in agricultural work. Major crops include yams, maize, cassava, vegetables, sorghum, coffee, cacao, and millet. Another agricultural activity of Togo is raising livestock.

Only about 5 percent of the work force engages in industrial activities. Major industries include fishing, mining (phosphates), cement, handcrafts, textiles, and beverages.

Lomé, on the coast, is the capital of Togo and the country's only seaport. Few people live in the northern savanna. Native African tribes make up 99 percent of the population, with only 1 percent being non-African.

Following a period of great opposition to Christianity in the 1970s, the people of Togo now have religious freedom, and 45 percent identify with some form of Christianity. Thirty-seven percent of the people are animists, and 17 percent are Muslim. Evangelical Christians make up nearly 11 percent of the population and are enjoying sustained growth. Church leaders are seeking to visit every home and establish a congregation in every village in Togo.

Ghana

West of Togo is Ghana. Beginning in 1471, the people of Ghana had extensive contact with European traders, first the Portuguese and then the English, Dutch, and Swedes. The abundance of gold in Ghana prompted Europeans to call it the **Gold Coast**. Initially, the Portuguese paid rent to the Ashanti Empire for their coastal base. In 1820, the British took over and made the area a colony. Britain granted independence in 1957, and the new nation took the name Ghana after the ancient African empire based in the Sahel. Mines still produce some gold, and the Ashanti people display gold treasures on festive occasions.

The independent Ghana quickly aligned itself with China and the Soviet Union. It experienced a series of military coups between 1966 and 1979, however, which prevented the stability necessary for the development of a strong economy. Military dictatorship was replaced by civilian government, but the country suffered much turmoil and bloodshed for two years. Since 1996, however, Ghana has been one of Africa's most stable governments.

Ghana's chief export is cacao; the country is a leading producer of cacao beans. Ghana is also a leading producer of yams. It ranks among the top ten nations in the world in production of plantains and is also a major producer of cassavas.

While 56 percent of the people labor in agriculture, 15 percent of the work force is employed in major industries, including mining (bauxite, manganese, silver, gold, and diamonds), lumbering, light manufacturing, aluminum smelting, fishing, and ship building. Twenty-nine percent of the work force is engaged in various services.

The major river of Ghana is the Volta, which flows southward through Lake Volta to the Gulf of Guinea. Lake Volta was created when Ghana's government built Akosombo Dam. This is one of the largest man-made lakes in the world. The dam was a controversial project, however, because it flooded approximately seven hundred villages, displacing about eighty thousand people. The dam has failed to deliver the government's promises of benefits that its construction would bring to the nation, and it has also hindered transportation within the country.

Burkina Faso

Lying north of Benin, Togo, Ghana, and Côte d'Ivoire is the only landlocked country of Western Africa—Burkina Faso, a country slightly larger than Colorado. It shares an eastern border with Niger, and on the north and west is Mali. Burkina Faso lies in the Sahel but shares the Volta River with Ghana. As in the rest of the Sahel, savannas cover the land and droughts are frequent. The northern part of the country is desert.

The country was a French protectorate from 1897 to 1932. The French called it Upper Volta. In 1932, it was divided among Niger, Sudan, and Côte d'Ivoire. Then, in 1960, it gained its independence as a parliamentary democracy. In 1966, a coup toppled the government, and the country has been plagued with dictatorships and periodic coups ever since. In 1983, a Marxist leader took over, promising reforms and better living conditions. To break all connections to the colonial past, the new dictator changed the name of the country to

Cacao seeds (better known as "beans") are dried and used in the production of chocolate. Cacao is Ghana's chief export.

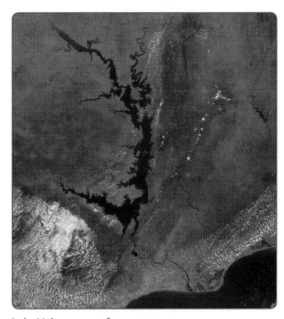

Lake Volta as seen from space

The Story of the Supreme Creator

The Akan people are the largest ethnic group in Ghana. Their elders tell a story about their supreme creator, Nyame, and how he moved up to the sky. In the beginning, Nyame lived on the rooftops of houses and remained close to men. However, as Nyame was going by some women one day he was bounced higher and higher as they pounded the *fufu* (cassava) into powder. Over time, their pounding bounced him up to the heavens, where he decided to remain. But this separated him from man, so Nyame used tall things to communicate with his people. As a result, the Akan people began to worship mountains and trees that they believed could carry their messages up to Nyame.

This man is processing millet.

Burkina Faso, which means "land of upright men." In 1987, however, the military revolted, assassinated the president, and set up yet another dictatorship under the ousted president's best friend. He put down an attempted coup in 2003. Political freedom remains severely limited in this country.

Much of the male work force migrates to other countries for seasonal jobs, but some industries are trying to gain a foothold in the troubled country. Major industries include textiles, cotton lint, cigarettes, and agricultural processing. Up to 90 percent of the people are poor cattle herders and subsistence farmers, but only 33 percent of the GDP comes from agriculture. The leading agricultural products are livestock, sorghum, millet, peanuts, sesame, rice, and maize. Natural resources include manganese, limestone, marble, phosphates, pumice, and salt.

Burkina Faso is sometimes described as a country that is "50 percent Muslim, 20 percent Christian, and 100 percent animist." Therefore, any statistics are tentative at best. Officially, 52 percent of the people are Muslim, 26 percent are identified with animism, and 21 percent affiliate with some form of Christianity. Evangelical Christians represent 4 percent of the population and are growing despite the strong influence of the occult in this nation. Several mission agencies labor to win the lost in this difficult field, and their work is warmly received by many of the people.

Côte d'Ivoire

West of Ghana lies Côte d'Ivoire. It is bordered on the north by Burkina Faso and Mali, on the northwest by Guinea, and on the southwest by Liberia. It is slightly larger than New Mexico and has dense forests in the center and savannas in the north.

French sailors arrived on its coast in 1483 and began trading with the people of the interior for ivory. This prompted the French name for the country, Côte d'Ivoire, meaning "Ivory Coast." Formerly part of French West Africa, the country gained independence in 1960 and made Abidjan, a major port city, the capital. The capital has since been moved inland to Yamoussoukro, which boasts a presidential palace with its own crocodile lake.

In contrast to many other countries of the region, Côte d'Ivoire became a relatively stable country, and economic prosperity naturally accompanied that stability. It did not experience its first military coup until 1999. Foreign aid essentially ceased at that point, however, and the economy began to suffer. The 2010 presidential election erupted into the Second Ivorian Civil War in 2011. Fighting ended four months later when UN and French forces intervened.

Because they had seized the opportunity to develop during the years of stability, numerous industries continue despite the uncertainties. Industries include beverages, wood products, oil refining, truck and bus assembly, textiles, fertilizer, and ship construction and repair. Côte d'Ivoire leads the world in cocoa bean production and is number two in yam production. It also produces much rice, coffee, and plantains. Its natural resources include oil, natural gas, diamonds, manganese, iron ore, bauxite, and copper.

Unlike many African countries that reject ties with former colonial powers, Côte d'Ivoire welcomes French businessmen, teachers, and other skilled workers. Although the foreigners seem to be the richest inhabitants, the entire nation benefits from growing businesses and industries.

The people of the Ivory Coast have religious freedom, and the government continues to welcome foreign missionaries. While accurate statistics are difficult to obtain, 42 percent of the people identify with Islam, 34 percent affiliate with some form of Christianity, and 24 percent practice animism. As in other African countries, animism permeates most of the population and is embraced by many along with Christian and Muslim beliefs. Evangelical Christians make up nearly 11 percent of the population, and the number is growing at an annual rate of 3 percent. Despite conflict and political instability during the first decade of the twenty-first century, as many as three thousand new congregations have been planted. Congregations are beginning to support home and foreign mission efforts.

Section Quiz

1. What West African country was an English colony?
2. What West African country was the first to move from a dictatorship to a democracy?
3. Through what two nations does the Volta River flow?
4–5. What was the main product of Côte d'Ivoire in colonial days? What is the main product today?
   ★ Why is the future of West Africa dependent on Nigeria's politics and economy?

Western Africa's Atlantic Coast

Black Africans populate the four mainland nations of the west Atlantic coast. Lying above the equator, the region has both a wet and a dry season.

Liberia

Liberia is one of only two African nations never colonized by Europeans. Furthermore, it was the first black republic in Africa and the second in world history (after Haiti).

Liberia's neighbors are Côte d'Ivoire on the east, Guinea on the north, and Sierra Leone on the northwest. It is similar in size to Tennessee and is mostly plateau with dense tropical forests. Hills rise

Ivorian Character

"Respect for one's family, elderly people, and women is a distinctive quality of Ivorians. Ivorians are very hospitable people—they are always ready to welcome strangers into their homes for some food and drink. They are also extremely polite and really enjoy inquiring about a visitor's health and family. Ivorians are a gentle and relaxed people. To the Ivorian, trust is very important in a relationship, whether one of business or friendship. Without trust, nothing much gets done."

Cultures of the World: Côte d'Ivoire, 70.

The Birth of Liberia

In 1822, the American Colonization Society sent a boat with freed American slaves to the Atlantic coast of Africa. They thought that they could establish the former slaves in a U.S. colony and eventually they would develop a free country of their own, thereby both improving their own lot in life and helping to solve the slavery issue in the United States. The former slaves named their country Monrovia first but later changed it to Liberia (based on the word *liberty*). They then named their capital city Monrovia after James Monroe, a U.S. president and one of the sponsors of the effort. In 1847, the black leaders of Liberia declared independence and established a republic modeled after the United States. Even their flag is similar to that of the United States. Over forty years, more than twelve thousand former slaves voluntarily relocated to Liberia. Today, descendants of freed slaves form only a small minority (only 5 percent of the population), but they have wielded the most influence. Ironically, in their constitution, they did not grant indigenous Africans equal rights with the former American and Caribbean slaves.

Monrovia, the capital of Liberia, was named for U.S. president James Monroe.

Thousands of Liberians became refugees during civil war in that country.

Typical Liberian Meal

Are you bored with typical American meals? Why not try some Liberian food? One of the normal ingredients is rice. It can be boiled or cooked in a broth containing meat and vegetables. Another option is to cook cassava into a thick soup, or form it into shaped cakes so you can scoop up *fufu* (FOO-foo), fermented cassava porridge, or *dumboy* (DUM-boy), unfermented cassava porridge. To this you could add *tumborgee* (tum-BOR-gee), fermented palm butter. If you are still hungry, you can enjoy a serving of frog soup or finish your meal with some *bugabug*, also known as termites.

into mountains along the border with Guinea. Liberia gets about 160 inches of rain per year.

People of sixteen native tribes, each with its own language, make up 95 percent of Liberia's population. About 2.5 percent of the people are Americo-Liberians, descendents of former U.S. slaves. Another 2.5 percent are Congo People, descendants of former Caribbean slaves.

Seventy percent of the Liberian work force is employed in agriculture. Major crops include cassava, rice, bananas, and vegetables. Liberia is also the world's ninth-leading producer of natural rubber. Only 8 percent of the work force is engaged in industry. Major industries are rubber and palm oil processing, timber, and diamonds.

In 1980, the opposition overthrew the government and killed the president. Another coup wracked the country in 1990, sparking one of the most horrifying civil wars in history and bringing to power a man named Charles Taylor. Taylor, who did little to improve conditions in Liberia, supported revolution in neighboring Sierra Leone and bankrupted the country. Rebels forced him out in 2003. In 2005, the Liberians elected Ellen Johnson-Sirleaf, the first female president in Africa. Taylor was captured and turned over to the UN in 2006 to stand trial for war crimes. A commission has been established to deal with past atrocities.

Natural resources of Liberia include iron ore, timber, diamonds, and gold. But Liberia's flag is also important to the country's economy. Liberia collects a fee from ship owners who wish to register their ships in Liberia and fly the Liberian flag. By this means, the ship owners avoid many regulations of industrialized nations. Because of this policy, Liberia has one of the largest commercial fleets in the world. (Panama also benefits from a similar policy. Greece's registry includes numerous cruise ships, which puts that country in competition with the commercial fleets of Liberia and Panama.)

Although Liberia was founded as a Christian state and freedom of religion is guaranteed, secret occult societies maintain a powerful influence in this country. Nearly 43 percent of the population practices animism, 41 percent affiliate with some form of Christianity, and 15 percent of the people are Muslim. Evangelical Christians represent 15 percent of the Liberian people, and their numbers are increasing at nearly 5 percent each year. New congregations are being planted, and Christians are reaching out to the large numbers of Liberians who were injured or displaced during the recent wars.

Sierra Leone

Northwest of Liberia is Sierra Leone, which is about half the size of Illinois. The coastal area is low-lying swamps, which give way to wooded hills and a plateau as one moves into the interior. The eastern region is mountainous. The country is bordered on the north and east by Guinea.

The Portuguese were the first Europeans to visit this land, and they gave the country its name, which means "lion mountains." In 1787, an Englishman named Granville Sharp established Sierra Leone as a settlement for freed slaves, and the capital was appropriately called Freetown. Today, only 2 percent of the people are descended from freed slaves, and most of them live near Freetown.

These workers are panning for diamonds near Freetown, Sierra Leone.

The British colony gained independence from Britain in 1961. Sierra Leone's development was brought to a halt by a bloody civil war in 1991 that began as a civil war in neighboring Liberia. The ensuing violence decimated the country and claimed up to one hundred thousand lives. The nation has been slowly recovering since 2002.

Sierra Leone is one of the leading producers of diamonds. The diamonds are found in gravel beds in the swampy rivers of the southeast. Other industries include ship repairing; petroleum refining; and manufacturing of beverages, textiles, and shoes.

Agriculture contributes 52 percent of the nation's GDP. Sierra Leone is one of the largest producers of citrus fruit. It also produces large quantities of rice, vegetables, cassava, pulses, and coffee.

The people of Sierra Leone enjoy freedom of religion, and 63 percent are Muslim. Animists compose 23 percent of the population, and 13 percent of the people identify with some form of Christianity. Evangelical Christians represent 4 percent of the people of Sierra Leone, and this group is growing at an annual rate of 4 percent. Local congregations are playing a vital role in rebuilding the country following the civil war.

Guineas

A *guinea* is a gold coin that was used in England from 1663 to 1813. It was named after the gold-rich Guinea Coast of Africa. Other kinds of "guineas" have remained in circulation.

Whereas merchants sought gold guineas, nations sought land "guineas." France, Portugal, and Spain each got one in Africa. But the countries couldn't have the same name, especially after independence. The first independent colony, French Guinea, became simply *Guinea.* Portuguese Guinea added the name of its capital,

becoming *Guinea-Bissau.* The former Spanish colony took a different tack, becoming *Equatorial Guinea* because it lies on the equator.

In Southeast Asia, the Dutch got a guinea. They colonized the island of *New Guinea,* which they thought looked like the "old" Guinea. To complicate matters, however, the island was later split, with half belonging to the independent nation of *Papua New Guinea* and half belonging to Indonesia.

Distinguishing Between Cultures

Several cultural traits have distinguished the culture of North Africa from that of sub-Saharan Africa, although many of these are changing. Sub-Saharan Africa is populated with black people who use slash-and-burn agriculture when necessary, live in villages, conduct initiation rites, are organized by tribes, and have a strong animist influence. Their rulers have tended to be autocrats, and most of the region has a history of Western colonialism. North Africa, on the other hand, is populated primarily by Arab peoples who use more traditional forms of agriculture, are a bit more modern and urbanized, and have a Muslim heritage.

Guinea

North of Sierra Leone is Guinea, the capital of which is Conakry. That city is one of only two major ports on Africa's Atlantic coast. Guinea also shares borders with Mali and Côte d'Ivoire on the north and east, Liberia on the south, Guinea-Bissau on the northwest, and Senegal on the north. Mangrove swamps cover the coastal plain. A plateau rises near the Atlantic and continues into the interior highlands. Forests cover the hills and low mountains in the eastern half of the country. The headwaters of two great rivers—the Senegal and the Gambia—lie in Guinea's mountainous north, called Fouta Djallon.

With large reserves of bauxite, Guinea ranks fifth (as of 2010) in bauxite mining. Most of the bauxite comes from the north. Guinea also has deposits of iron ore, gold, uranium, and diamonds. In addition to mining, Guinea's industries include fishing, light manufacturing, and agricultural processing.

Seventy-six percent of the work force is engaged in agriculture. Guinea is also a large producer of citrus fruit. Other major agricultural products include rice, peanuts, cassava, plantains, and cattle meat.

The people of Guinea enjoy a measure of freedom of worship although recent radicalization of some Muslims has put this freedom in jeopardy. Muslims represent 88 percent of the population, animists make up 7 percent, and those who affiliate with some form of Christianity make up 4 percent of the people. Evangelical Christians represent 0.7 percent of the population. More than twenty evangelical mission agencies labor in this country, and local congregations are beginning to send out their own missionaries.

Guinea was formerly a French protectorate called French Guinea and later French West Africa. The country gained its independence in 1958 and promptly became the first openly Marxist government in Africa. The rulers turned their backs on France and the West and turned to the Soviet Union for support. The country has been affected by not only the failure of Communist economic policies but also the political turmoil in neighboring Sierra Leone and Liberia. However, the nation has recently made significant progress as demonstrated by democratic elections in 2010.

Guinea-Bissau

Guinea-Bissau (gin ee-bih SOU), a country about half the size of South Carolina, lies on the coast between Guinea and Senegal. It is mostly lowlands with swamps, rain forests, and mangrove wetlands. It includes about twenty-five islands off the coast.

Portuguese exploration of the area began in the fifteenth century. By 1430, the Portuguese traded regularly along the coast of West Africa, and Guinea-Bissau became a major center of the Portuguese slave trade. It was also one of the few regions that remained in Portuguese hands throughout Europe's competition for global empire. Portugal did not give up the colony until 1974—and then only after years of bitter fighting. Marxist leaders kept a grip on the nation until the end of the Cold War, ensuring that it remained one of the poorest countries in the world. Between 1980 and 2003, the country experienced a series of military coups, further destabilizing the economy and hindering development. Conditions have improved, but the natural death of the most recent president in 2012 has left a power vacuum in Guinea-Bissau. The one who fills that void could have a great impact on the future of the country.

Subsistence agriculture dominates the economy (representing 82 percent of the work force) while large deposits of bauxite and oil lie unexploited. In addition to oil and bauxite, the country's natural resources include fish, timber, phosphates, clay, granite, and limestone. Guinea-Bissau is the world's eighth-largest producer of cashew nuts. It also produces rice, pork, cattle meat, groundnuts, plantains, and various roots and tubers.

The people of Guinea-Bissau have enjoyed freedom of religion since 1990, and 52 percent are Muslim. Thirty-five percent of the people practice animism, and 11 percent identify with some form of Christianity. Evangelical Christians make up 2 percent of the population and are experiencing strong growth of 6 percent a year. The presence and labor of many missionaries from Latin America and Asia are contributing to this solid growth. As is so often the case, there is a great need for trained national pastors and laymen to provide leadership for this growing body of believers.

Gambia

North of Guinea-Bissau and squeezed almost imperceptibly within the borders of Senegal is Africa's smallest country—Gambia. Averaging only twenty miles in width and stretching two hundred miles up the Gambia River, Gambia is about twice the size of Delaware. Mangrove swamps line the river. Banjul (pop. 455,000) is both the national capital and the country's only port.

The first explorers of Gambia were the Portuguese, who were followed by the French, but Great Britain was the country that colonized Gambia (1853). In fact, Gambia was Britain's first African possession. It became a major slave center until the slave trade to the West was abolished in 1807. It remained under the British imperial umbrella until it gained full independence in 1970. One civilian

Cashew apple with cashew nut attached

Giant ant hills are common in Guinea-Bissau.

president served from 1970 to 1994, when a coup toppled him. The military dictator kept his promise to return to civilian rule in 1997.

Seventy-five percent of the work force is in agriculture. Gambia's major agricultural products are peanuts, millet, cattle meat, rice, sorghum, and maize. Natural resources include fish, titanium, tin, zircon, silica sand, clay, and oil. Major industries are clothing, peanut processing, tourism, beverages, agricultural machinery, and woodworking and metalworking.

Gambians enjoy relative religious freedom, and a Muslim majority represents 89 percent of the population. Animists make up 6 percent, and 4 percent of the people affiliate with some form of Christianity. Evangelical Christians represent 0.8 percent of the Gambian people.

Cape Verde

The Cape Verde islands consist of ten main islands and five islets and have a combined area slightly greater than that of Rhode Island. They lie four hundred miles west of the coast of Senegal. One island is a still-active volcano.

The Portuguese discovered the then-uninhabited islands in 1460 and, recognizing that they were strategically located on the major trade routes, settled them with slaves. Today, 73 percent of the population is of mixed Portuguese-African ancestry; 25 percent are black Africans.

The Republic of Cape Verde is a secular state that allows freedom of religion. Ninety-five percent of the people identify with some form of Christianity, 3 percent are Muslim, and nonreligious and animists each represent 1 percent of the population. Evangelical Christians make up nearly 7 percent of the people.

Cape Verde became a province of Portugal in 1951. The people gained full Portuguese citizenship in 1961 and eventually gained complete independence in 1975. It was one of the last nations in Africa to gain independence. Unlike many other countries of Western Africa, Cape Verde has remained relatively peaceful.

Industries of the islands include food, beverages, fish processing, shoes and garments, ship repairs, and salt mining. Agricultural products include pork, pimiento, allspice, goat and cow milk, hen eggs, pulses, mangoes, and tomatoes. Since only 15 percent of the land is suitable for agriculture, the country must import 80 to 90 percent of its food.

Recent efforts to strengthen the economy include aggressive development of tourism, transitioning to a market economy, and developing fisheries. Wind farms constructed in 2011 now supply up to 25 percent of the electrical needs of these islands, thus reducing the nation's dependence on oil imports.

One of the major industries of Cape Verde is fish processing.

Senegal

The final country of what is considered Western Africa is Senegal, which is slightly smaller than South Dakota. The capital, Dakar, is the westernmost point of Africa.

Most of Senegal is lowlands and has a semi-desert climate. After all, much of it lies in the dry Sahel. It has suffered greatly from droughts and from an influx of refugees from its northern neighbor, Mauritania. Its advantage over Mauritania is the prominence of the Sénégal River and its tributaries.

Many of the people of Senegal are nomadic herders, tending cattle, sheep, and goats in the north and raising food crops in the south. Seventy-eight percent of the work force is involved in agriculture. Senegal is a leading producer of peanuts and millet. It also produces cattle and chicken meat, rice, maize, hen eggs, and cassava. Major industries include fishing, agricultural and fish processing, phosphate mining, fertilizer production, and ship construction and repair. Tourism has also increased.

Both France and Portugal had trading settlements along the coast of Senegal, but France capitalized on its situation, making Senegal a part of French West Africa in 1895. In 1958, the Senegalese voted for self-government. They gained independence in 1960. With independence, Senegal experimented unsuccessfully with socialism for twenty years. Although the country was politically stable, opposition

LET'S GO EXPLORING

Population Density of Africa

1. Which countries in Africa have two separate regions with high population density (over 250 per square mile)?

2. Which countries in Central and West Africa have a density that never rises above 25 per square mile?

3. Where is the only place in Africa that a dense population extends all the way across the Sahara Desert without a break?

4. What is the only coastal area that is completely uninhabited?

✷ What appears to be the shortest route through the Sahara from populated regions in West Africa (2–25 per square mile) to the populated regions in North Africa?

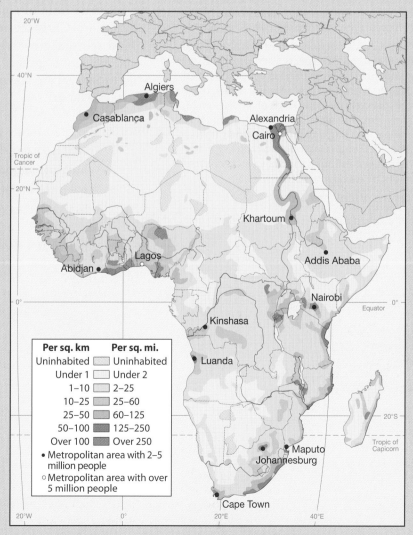

Per sq. km	Per sq. mi.
Uninhabited	Uninhabited
Under 1	Under 2
1–10	2–25
10–25	25–60
25–50	60–125
50–100	125–250
Over 100	Over 250

• Metropolitan area with 2–5 million people

○ Metropolitan area with over 5 million people

The notorious prison Mison des Esclaves, or "house of slaves," is located on the Ile de Goree in Senegal.

Superstitious Wrestling

"The traditional Senegalese sport is wrestling, or laamb. . . . Sometimes described as a combination of wrestling and judo, it is typical of traditional African wrestling. There are two types of laamb: one in which wrestlers are allowed to hit one another with their hands, and a more acrobatic type that does not allow hitting.

"But laamb is not only a sport; it is also valued for its ceremonial aspects. Each wrestler is accompanied by his marabout [religious leader]. In a ceremony that precedes the match, the wrestler wears various kinds of amulets on his arms, legs, and waist, and dances around the arena to the music of drummers and singers. All of this ritual is intended to protect the wrestler against evil spirits and any witchcraft that might be used by the other wrestlers."

Cultures of the World: Senegal, 112.

parties were illegal, the government strongly controlled the economy, and women did not enjoy equal rights. Only when the government allowed opposition, privatized industries, and granted equal property rights to women did improvements begin.

Senegal is a secular state whose people enjoy religious freedom. Ninety-one percent of the population is Muslim, 6 percent affiliate with some form of Christianity, and 2 percent practice animism. Evangelical Christians represent 0.3 percent of the people of Senegal. Most spiritual growth has been among the Serer, Bassari, Balanta, and Jola ethnic groups. It is also interesting to note that missionaries to Senegal are now coming primarily from Latin American and African countries.

Section Quiz

1. Which African nation elected the first female president?
2. Which two nations were settled by freed slaves?
3. What is the majority religion of Senegal, Gambia, and Guinea?
4–5. What west coast African nations tried to govern using Marxism?
★ Why did Marxism fail in African nations?

Chapter Review
20

Making Connections

1–3. What European languages are national languages in West and Central Africa? (List three.)

4–5. What tropical diseases plague Africa? (List two.)

6. Why is Côte d'Ivoire one of the most developed countries in sub-Saharan Africa?

7–8. What west African nations with a Muslim majority enjoy complete religious freedom? (List two.)

Developing Geography Skills

1. Using the maps on pages 496 and 504, determine what nation in West Africa is landlocked. Follow the same procedure for Central Africa.

2. What climate do you expect in the nations south of Central Africa?

3. Based on the maps on pages 496 and 504, which African nations have islands?

Thinking Critically

1. What are common problems many African nations struggled with following independence? How could European nations have helped prevent these problems?

2. What is the significance of missionaries to Africa coming from other African states and Latin America?

Living in God's World

1. If you were an African pastor in West Africa, what aspects of African tribal life would you, as a Christian, wish to see retained? What aspects of tribalism would you identify to your people as problematic?

2. Write a paragraph describing how the prosperity gospel addresses the concerns of those with a background in African traditional religions. Then explain which aspects of biblical teaching an African pastor would want to stress to guard the biblical gospel.

People, Places, and Things to Know

village
chief
initiation rites
tribalism
animism
yellow fever
tsetse fly
malaria
Congo River
Congo Basin
Mobutu Sese Seko
Kinshasa
Katanga Plateau
Brazzaville
Ubangi River
Pygmies
French Equatorial Africa
Niger-Congo family of languages
Slave Coast
bights
Bight of Benin
Benue River
Hausa
Yoruba
Lagos
Benin Kingdom
Biafra
Biafran War
Igbo
voodoo
Gold Coast

21

The Sahara dominates life in Northern Africa.

NORTHERN AFRICA

*N*orthern Africa is a unique region on the African continent. In many ways, the area has more in common with the Middle East than with the rest of Africa. As in the Middle East, the search for fresh water and adherence to the Islamic faith are central concerns.

The life and history of the region are dominated by the **Sahara**, the world's largest desert. It is about the same size as the United States and is the only desert in the world that spans an entire continent from shore to shore. The Arabs looked at this vast, barren expanse and called it simply "the desert," or Sahara. Annual rainfall ranges between one and five inches, and some parts are dry all year long. Average temperatures hover around 90°F but frequently exceed 120°F. Although it has few natural resources, the Sahara has served as a crucial trade route throughout history.

Northern Africa Fast Facts						
Country	Capital	Area (sq. mi.)	Pop. (2013 est.) (M)	Pop. Density (per sq. mi.)	Per Capita GDP ($US)	Life Span
Algeria	Algiers	919,595	38.09	41	$7,200	74.7
Chad	N'Djamena	495,755	11.19	23	$1,500	48.7
Egypt	Cairo	386,662	85.19	220	$3,900	72.9
Libya	Tripoli	679,626	6.00	9	$11,400	77.8
Mali	Bamako	478,840	15.97	33	$1,200	53.1
Mauritania	Nouakchott	397,955	3.44	9	$2,200	61.5
Morocco	Rabat	172,414	32.65	189	$4,200	76.1
Niger	Niamey	489,191	16.90	35	$900	53.8
Tunisia	Tunis	63,170	10.84	172	$8,300	75.2

I. The Sahel

Between the Sahara and the jungles of Central Africa lies a transitional region called the **Sahel**. This band of grass-covered plains is about three hundred miles wide. The northern part of the Sahel near the Sahara is the driest, often receiving as little as four inches of rain annually. Here the short grasses support scattered populations of Berber and Arabic nomads, who herd cattle and sheep. To the south, the grasses become more plentiful. This region sometimes receives up to twenty-four inches of rain per year. Most of the farmers are blacks, who settled the region long before Arab nomads came from the north.

Four countries—Mauritania, Mali, Niger, and Chad—are dominated by the Sahel. The Sahara covers only the northern part of these countries, and grazing lands cover much of the rest. Only the southern extremes can support crops and a large population. Unfortunately, the rain comes all at once, during the summer. Droughts often devastate the subsistence farmers, who do not have irrigation

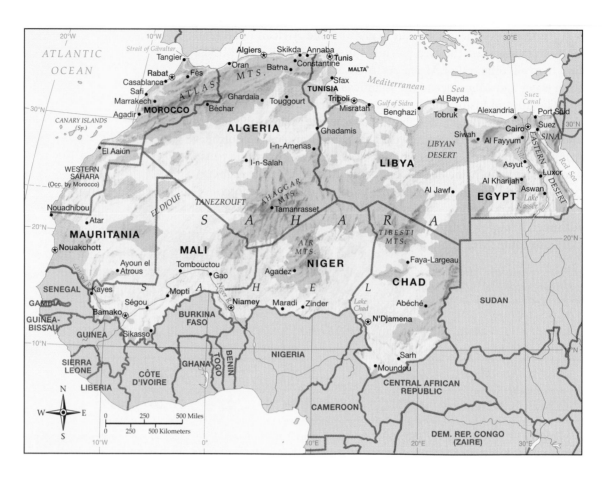

equipment. The people are so poor that children rarely attend schools. As a result, the Sahel has some of the lowest literacy rates in Africa.

The Sahel is a transitional zone in more ways than just climate and agriculture. The four countries of the Sahel display a complex mix of peoples and cultures. Mauritania, for example, has a significant Moor population (Arab and Berber mix), while the other three Sahel countries are composed of a variety of native indigenous groups. Islam is a leading religion in all four countries, but its influence progressively weakens in the south and east, where there are more black people.

The mix of languages in the Sahel is also complex. Arabic is the official language in the westernmost country, Mauritania. It is also an official language in the easternmost country, Chad, but 133 native languages are also spoken there. The Arabs had less impact on the two central countries, Mali and Niger, where tribal languages are common. Because these two countries were once part of French West Africa, French is the official language in both of them, and it is also an official language in Chad.

Mauritania

Mauritania is the only country of the Sahel that has a seacoast, which gives it access to shipping and the rich fishing waters of the Atlantic. Recently discovered offshore oil reserves are a welcome boost to the country's economy.

The Sahara covers most of northern Mauritania, where rainfall is rare due to the cold ocean currents. The region's only natural resource is iron ore, which constitutes 40 percent of the country's exports. The nomadic people who live in this region are called Moors. They account for over two-thirds of all the people in Mauritania. The Moors continue to engage in the prosperous slave trade, even though the government outlawed slavery in 1981 and made it a crime in 2007. Estimates of the percentages of slaves vary from 10 to 20 percent of the Mauritanian population.

The southern border, which is in the Sahel, is more hospitable. Black tribes farm the country's only fertile plain along the Sénégal River. However, recent drought, overgrazing, and deforestation have contributed to desertification. Many rural farmers and nomads have migrated to the capital, Nouakchott, located on the coast, living in makeshift camps and relying on foreign aid for survival.

Mauritania was not always so poor. The **Ghana Empire**, which may have risen to power as early as the fourth century, was centered in Kumbi Saleh, a city at the southeast corner of Mauritania. The empire controlled all the western trade routes across the Sahel into the thirteenth century, keeping all the gold nuggets and allowing the gold dust to continue north. The ancient capital now lies in ruins.

Mauritania's recent political history has been one of short-lived democracies followed by military coups. The Arab Spring of 2011 (when Arabs in many countries protested political and economic inequality) spread into this country, and future political stability remains uncertain.

WORLD RELIGIONS

Folk Islam

Religion as presented in a textbook and religion as practiced by people are often two different things. This is especially true of Islam in Africa. Officially, Islam centers on submission to the one god who controls all things. The Qur'an and the Hadith are the basis for Muslim teaching. Rites of prayer, cleansing, fasting, almsgiving, and pilgrimage are at the heart of the religion. Folk Islam maintains all of the teachings of official Islam, but it has other concerns, such as how to deal with sickness or famine or other negative events. Folk Islam is more concerned with spirits and ancestors. Often, folk Islam draws on the traditional religious practices of a region.

The Jinn play a large role in folk Islam. Jinn are believed to be spirits that stand between men and angels. They can be good or bad, but most are viewed as bad. For instance, in Egypt many Muslims believe there is a Jinn who will cause miscarriages. To be freed from a Jinn who has possessed a person or who is interfering with a person, a powerful person who can provide charms or curses is needed.

In Morocco one might go to the "old woman" who can make a magical drink to ward off or cure sickness. In West Africa one might go to a medicine man for a charm or amulet that can ward off evil powers. Often these amulets are made with verses from the Qur'an to give them power. Or a Muslim might go to a saint. In Asia, saints are often living and can intercede or bless a person. In Africa, the saints are typically dead. A pilgrimage is often made to the shrines of the saints. The saints and their shrines are believed to possess great power. Many Muslims believe they can heal people, make the future known, or provide protection.

Place and time are also important to Muslims. Even with a talisman, a Muslim might avoid going to a place where he thinks a Jinn might be present. Or he will take special precautions before going. In Egypt the Jinn are thought to inhabit toilets, so a person will call out for Allah's protection. In Morocco, the Jinn are thought to inhabit wells or rivers. On the other hand, the shrine of a saint is believed

to be an especially good place. Certain times can be good or bad. In some places the Jinn are thought to interfere with people more on Tuesday, Wednesday, and Saturday nights. Thursdays and Fridays are good days, though on Friday there is a bad hour in which misfortune may strike. The second month in the Muslim calendar is considered a bad month, but Ramadan is the best month since the Jinn are said to be bound that month.

African Muslims will often practice divination to help them make right decisions. For instance, they may open a Qur'an at random to see if the words on the page give them some direction. Or they might go to a fortune-teller to learn something of their future.

Many Muslims practice both official Islam and folk Islam without seeing any inconsistency. However, some Muslims see folk Islam as a corruption. They think shrines to saints promote idolatry. They reject the idea that saints can intercede with their god for people.

Desertification of the Sahel

At one time, scattered acacia, mahogany, and baobab trees made the Sahel a true savanna. But recent droughts and famines have raised fears that the Sahara is swallowing the savanna as it spreads southward. This process is called **desertification**, or desiccation. While it is hard to measure how much land is lost to the desert each year, desertification has caused food shortages that have killed thousands and forced many others to flee to the cities.

Two conditions may contribute to desertification. One is human abuse of the land. Since the 1960s, the number of people in the Sahel has more than doubled. Newly drilled wells attracted herders who settled permanently for the first time. With this increased population came an increased demand for pasture, firewood, and cropland. Poor farming techniques compounded the loss of soil through erosion. The loss of trees and soil opened the way for the desert to invade.

Desertification approaches Nouakchott, the capital of Mauritania.

Another often-ignored factor in desertification is the earth's natural cycles. During the time of its population increase, the Sahel also experienced extreme, prolonged droughts. Droughts are a fact of life, depleting soil and vegetation wherever they strike.

Some scientists think the earth may be in a warming cycle due to changes in the sun, changes in the earth's orbit, or changes in the earth's tilt. The Bible gives humans the responsibility to be good stewards over the earth (Gen. 1:26–28). Being good stewards can involve making difficult environments more livable. Some measures are now being taken to reduce desertification in the Sahel, such as new farming techniques and planting trees in rows to slow down wind erosion.

Dama Ceremony

One of the groups living in Mali are the Dogon people. They enact a ritual dance every twelve years called the Dama ceremony. Only men participate, and they prepare elaborate masks designed to honor dead relatives. The Dogon people believe these masks have great power because they contain the spirits of their deceased relatives. The men wear these masks and perform dramatic dances that are believed to protect their families and their crops. To prevent evil consequences, the women and children are required to remain a safe distance away from the dancers.

Dogon village, Mali

This country is officially an Islamic Republic, and the constitution names Islam as the state religion. Muslims represent 99.75 percent of the population, and those who affiliate with some form of Christianity make up 0.25 percent of the people. There may be up to two thousand Evangelical Christians in Mauritania, and most of these are immigrant workers from other African countries. Since the country has been dominated by Islam for a thousand years, and since it is illegal to convert to another religion, few native Mauritanians have trusted Christ.

Mali

Present-day Mali, which lies just east of Mauritania, stands in stark contrast to its own rich history. At one time, three great African empires—Ghana, Mali, and Songhai—occupied the region. Most early caravan routes in the western Sahara stopped at a desolate basin in the northern tip of Mali, where salts were plentiful. The salt mines of Taghaza provided traders with a valuable commodity, prized among the people of the southern rain forests, who gladly traded gold for salt.

Today, however, Mali is one of the poorest countries in the world. Because the country is mostly desert and is landlocked, 90 percent of the population is concentrated in the Sahel region in the south. Most people are engaged in subsistence farming or fishing. The main exports are cotton, rice, and livestock. Unfortunately, the country's economy is vulnerable because of constant fluctuation in the market prices for cotton.

Two major rivers, the Sénégal and the Niger, flow through this region. The **Niger River** is the third longest in Africa and the most important river in the Sahel. Most ancient and modern cities of Mali lie on this river. Mali's capital, **Bamako**, is the largest city in the Sahel. Local wildlife includes wart hogs, baboons, panthers, leopards, giraffes, elephants, crocodiles, and hippopotamuses.

Mali is a secular state that grants its people freedom of religion. Eighty-seven percent of the population is Muslim, nearly 10 percent practices animism, and nearly 3 percent identifies with some form of Christianity. Evangelical Christians make up 0.7 percent of the population and are experiencing modest growth, although not enough to keep pace with the country's rapidly expanding population. Christians are participating in relief efforts, supporting soil conservation, digging wells, and providing medical assistance to strengthen the country and provide opportunities to witness.

Boats gather at a small port along the Niger River in Mali.

Find It!
Timbuktu
16.775° N, 3.008° W
While a street view is not currently available, you can see the remnants of this ancient capital.

Timbuktu

Mali was once the center of the glorious **Mali Empire**, which arose when it conquered Ghana around 1200. By taking control of the gold trade, the empire increased its riches to mythic proportions. **Mansa Musa** gained a reputation as the richest man in the world. When he made a year-long pilgrimage to Mecca in 1324 with a caravan of sixty thousand people, he was preceded by hundreds of slaves, each bearing a staff of gold, and hundreds of camels, each bearing bags of gold. His lavish gifts flooded Mecca's economy and caused gold to drop in value for a decade.

After his trip to Mecca, Mansa Musa brought back Muslim scholars to teach the Qur'an and the Arabic language at new seminaries in his empire. He chose Timbuktu as the site of a new capital, and he built a large mosque. The city became the key university city in Northern Africa, known worldwide for its learning.

Timbuktu (now spelled Tombouctou) has become the epitome of remote and mysterious civilization. Europeans had no idea where the Mali Kingdom was located or where it got its riches. The Mali people guarded all the trade routes in the north, and water routes were impossible in the disease-ridden swamps and rapids to the south at the mouth of the Niger.

No European laid eyes on Timbuktu until 1826, though many tried.

A mosque in the ancient city of Timbuktu, where many buildings are made of mud

The Scottish explorer Alexander Laing finally reached Timbuktu after a two-year-long odyssey. Tragically, Laing was murdered before he could return. Hoping to sneak into the city, a Frenchman named René Caillié learned Arabic as a convert to Islam. In 1827 he posed as an Arab from Egypt and joined a caravan from Senegal. He reached Timbuktu a year later, but all he found was a town of mud houses and huts, long ago fallen into decline. He returned to Paris to report his findings, which earned him a prize of ten thousand francs offered by the Paris Geographical Society.

Tourists on a camel safari led by a Tuareg tribesman in the sand dunes of the Sahara

Niger

The Sahara covers two-thirds of Niger, Mali's neighbor to the east. The low **Aïr Mountains** in the north interrupt the vast sands of the desert. This "Switzerland of the desert" supplies lush vegetation in some valleys and oases. The Aïr Mountains have the largest uranium reserves in Africa, which provide mining jobs. Niger has almost no other valuable industry.

A wide savanna spans the southern border of Niger. In spite of average daily summer temperatures over 100°F, the Niger River in the southwest is the country's most attractive and populous region. The modern capital, Niamey, is on this river. Ninety percent of the people here are subsistence farmers, who are threatened by frequent droughts common to the Sahel.

Niger's living conditions are even worse than those in Mali. Niger is one of the poorest countries in the world and has the lowest per capita GDP and one of the lowest life expectancies in the Sahel. Niger's government provides very little service to its people; all aid is received from foreign countries. Foreign aid provides for education and healthcare, especially HIV/AIDS relief.

Like Mali, Niger has an interesting history. White desert nomads, called **Tuaregs**, came from the north and took control of ancient Niger's trade routes through the mountains. The largest oasis and market town, Agadez, was their capital. Today 9 percent of all Nigeriens are Tuareg.

The largest African empire, **Songhai**, was born along the Niger River in the eighth century. This black kingdom grew slowly at first, until its first great ruler, Sunni Ali, took over the declining Mali empire in 1464. However, Morocco blamed Songhai for its economic decline and invaded in 1591. Morocco won easily because it was the first country to use firearms in a battle on African soil. Although this defeat ended the last empire of the Sahel, a reduced Songhai kingdom remained until France invaded in the nineteenth century.

The people of Niger have a high degree of religious freedom and the government continues to permit mission work. Ninety-seven percent of the people are Muslim, 2.5 percent practice animism, and 0.33 percent identify with some form of Christianity. Evangelical Christians represent 0.1 percent of the population and are growing at an annual rate of nearly 4 percent. While the rise of radical Islam threatens the religious tranquility of this nation, Christians are impacting their communities through humanitarian efforts, including education, well-digging, leprosy control, and other health-related services.

Chad

Chad is one of the Sahel's most primitive countries. Roughly three times the size of California, Chad has only 166 miles of paved roads, the least in the Sahel. There are few cars, and most people walk for transportation.

The northern two-thirds of Chad is one of the driest regions in the Sahara. The far north has the highest elevations in the entire desert. Like the Aïr Mountains, the **Tibesti Mountains**, which are dormant volcanoes, rise up out of the sand. The highest Tibesti peak is Emi Koussi (11,302 ft.). The only inhabitants of this region are Arab nomads.

As in the neighboring countries, Chad's population is concentrated in the southern Sahel, away from the hot and dry Sahara. The Chari River and its tributaries, navigable only during the rainy season, provide a fertile region for agriculture. Eighty percent of the people are subsistence farmers, growing cotton and raising livestock. The Chari continues into **Lake Chad** on the western border. This lake is the most important body of water in the Sahel, and it harbors a wealth of fish. The capital, N'Djamena, lies near Lake Chad at the confluence of the Chari River and its largest tributary.

Chad has reserves of uranium and petroleum, but civil war between the Arab people of the north and the black peoples of the south kept the country from developing for nearly three decades. Libya invaded briefly on four occasions between 1978 and 1987, hoping to annex Chad, but was forced out by the UN. A form of peace was restored in 1990. Regional ethnic violence is still a problem, but Chad was able to begin development of its oil reserves in 2003.

Chad is a secular state that grants freedom of religion to its citizens. Fifty-three percent of the population is Muslim, 38 percent identify with some form of Christianity, and nearly 8 percent practice animism. Evangelical Christians represent 10 percent of the population and are growing at an annual rate of 3 percent. Missionaries are welcome, and their efforts have contributed to the growth of the Christian population. Outreach to Muslims is allowed and has had positive results, with a growing number of Muslims coming to Christ.

Shrinking Lake Chad

A full Lake Chad in 1963, as seen from space.

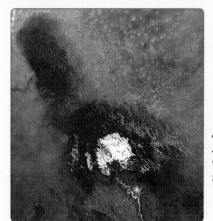

A depleted Lake Chad in 2013. The dark areas indicate vegetation that has grown in the former lakebed.

Lake Chad once had a surface area of approximately 9,600 square miles, or roughly the size of Lake Erie. Since 1963, however, Lake Chad has shrunk to one-twentieth of its former size. Two causes have been identified in this drastic change. First, because the surrounding region is susceptible to food shortages, water from Lake Chad has been used to irrigate massive areas of farmland in Chad and neighboring countries. In addition, the average rainfall has decreased since the 1960s. The lakebed is flat and shallow and is therefore naturally vulnerable to the slightest climate change. Scientists are concerned that Lake Chad will eventually disappear, and with it a vital source of water and wildlife.

Section Quiz

1. What term describes the expansion of the desert toward the savanna?
2. What country in the Sahel has been influenced the most by Islam? What country in the Sahel has the largest Christian population?
3. Through which countries of the Sahel does the Niger River flow? the Sénégal River?
⭐ What was the largest empire in Africa? What geographic advantages made a large empire possible?

Find It!

Lake Chad

13.136° N, 14.516° E

(Zoom out until you can see the current lake and the outline of its former size.)

II. The Maghreb

Most of North Africa's people live along the Mediterranean Sea. The **Atlas Mountains**, a fifteen-hundred-mile chain, lie along the northwest coast of Africa. The mountains, which rise to a maximum elevation of 13,661 feet at Jebel Toubkal in Morocco, have a major impact on the weather and culture. The Arabs call the mountains the

Jebel Toubkal, the highest point in the Atlas Mountains

Djezira el-Maghreb, meaning "Island of the West," because they are a haven of life in the bleak desert. The mountain barrier blocks winds blowing off the sea, causing orographic rainfall. The water flows down to the sea, bringing moisture to the valleys and coastal plains. Precipitation is near twenty inches annually, and this rainfall provides the only dependable water supply to support crops, livestock, and cities.

The coast enjoys a pleasant mediterranean climate and scenery comparable to southern Europe. Summers are dry but mild. Rains come in winter, with snow falling in the high mountains. Grapes, wheat, olives, and tomatoes are important crops. Northern Africa accounts for one-fifth of the world's phosphate mining.

The Arabs refer to the three countries of northwest Africa—Tunisia, Algeria, and Morocco—as the **Maghreb**, meaning the "West." The **Berbers** first settled the region over three thousand years ago. Some farmed the coastal plains and valleys, while others kept livestock on the mountainsides or at the edge of the desert. They traded with the Phoenicians, Greeks, and Romans, and major ports arose along the coast. These port cities—Tangier, Algiers, Tunis, and Tripoli—were the foundation of what later became known as the **Barbary Coast** states of Morocco, Algeria, Tunisia, and Tripoli (modern Libya).

As the Arabs spread across North Africa, they intermarried with the Berbers. The Arab-Berber ethnic group now accounts for over 80 percent of the population in the countries of the Maghreb. Arabic is the official language, and Islam (predominately Sunni) is their religion. A small minority still speaks the Berber language and continues traditional Berber farming practices, folk dances, and marriage customs. France gained control of the Maghreb during the era of European colonialism, and close cultural ties to France (such as language) remain, even though the Maghreb gained independence in the mid-twentieth century.

Morocco

Morocco has coasts on both the Mediterranean and the Atlantic. A narrow peninsula juts out between these coasts, almost touching Europe. It is only eight miles across the **Strait of Gibraltar** to Europe. Throughout history conquerors crossed this strait, through the border town of **Tangier**, to invade either Africa or Europe. Today it is still an important shipping point between the Mediterranean and the Atlantic.

Barbary Pirates

Pirates flourished along the Barbary Coast between the sixteenth and nineteenth centuries. Muslim raiders captured European ships and held sailors for ransom. Most countries, including the newly independent United States, paid tribute in return for protection. When the pasha of Tripoli demanded an increase in payments, the daring U.S. Navy sailed "to the shores of Tripoli" and won international respect with its victory in the Tripolitan War (1801–5). France ended piracy in these waters once and for all when it captured Algiers in 1830. This period of European domination lasted until the Barbary States gained independence in the mid-twentieth century.

The lush Mediterranean coastline of Northern Africa, as seen in Morocco, with the Strait of Gibraltar in the background

Morocco's two other major ports—**Casablanca** and Rabat—lie on the Atlantic coast. Casablanca has a population of 4 million people and is one of the largest cities in Northern Africa. It is also a popular tourist resort with a unique mixture of Spanish and French heritage. Rabat is the capital of Morocco. After gaining independence from France in 1956, the young Islamic country created a constitutional monarchy. The royal family claims direct descent from the prophet Muhammad. The king assumed broad powers, including the command of the army. In 1996, Morocco instituted a bicameral parliament.

Coastal lowlands provide rich farmland across northwestern Morocco. Beyond the coastal lowlands, the Atlas Mountains cover most of the rest of Morocco. The mountains provide water for hydroelectric plants as well as lead and phosphates.

Morocco claims a phosphate-rich area in the southwest known as the **Western Sahara**. When Spain gave up this territory in 1975, Mauritania and Morocco moved in. Algeria opposed this illegal land grab and supported the Polisario, a native independence movement. In the bitter fighting, Mauritania withdrew its claim, but Morocco then claimed the entire region. While Morocco's troops captured the coastal cities, they could not defeat the nomads in the interior. Disputes continued until the UN imposed a cease-fire in 1991. Sovereignty over the area has not yet been resolved, although Morocco effectively retains control of 70 percent of this region.

Morocco also faces the challenges of economic troubles. In 2006, it instituted a free trade agreement with the United States in hopes of encouraging more foreign investment. Increased revenues from tourism and financial aid from Moroccans living abroad are supporting education, creating new jobs, and improving living standards.

The state religion in Morocco is Sunni Islam (99.88 percent), yet Christianity (0.09 percent) has been tolerated until recently. Christian activity is now closely monitored, and the level of intimidation is rising. Evangelical Christians make up less than 0.01 percent of the population, but there are believed to be nearly five thousand believers, about two thousand of whom are Moroccans. While missionaries are not allowed, some Christians work as tentmakers in Morocco and discreetly witness to the Moroccan people they come into contact with.

Built by King Hassan II of Morocco, this mosque in Casablanca is one of the world's largest mosques and currently has the tallest minaret at 689 feet.

Traditional spice market in Morocco

Algeria

East of Morocco is Algeria, the one of the largest countries in Africa. It is approximately the size of Texas and Alaska combined. Because most of Algeria is desert, around 90 percent of the population lives along the country's 620 miles of Mediterranean coastline, even though the area is prone to devastating earthquakes. The capital, Algiers, is one of the largest cities on the Barbary Coast. The mild climate in this area supports the production of wine and citrus fruits, two of Algeria's important exports.

A hilly region called the Tell separates the coast from the Saharan plateau. Oaks, cedars, olive trees, and maquis grow in the fertile

Algerian Cave Art

Herodotus, a Greek historian who lived more than four centuries before Christ, described horse-drawn chariots that crossed the Sahara. Scholars scoffed at how naive Herodotus was. How could horses survive in the waterless Sahara?

However, in the twentieth century, several caves were discovered in the desert of Algeria that gave credibility to his story. Some four thousand paintings, now protected in an Algerian national park, adorn the walls of the many shelter caves at Tassili-n-Ajjer, just north of the Ahaggar Mountains. The drawings include chariots drawn by four horses. The earliest paintings, which may date from around 3000 BC, also show scenes of cattle, wild sheep, giraffes, and even hippos. Bones of hippos have been found as well, indicating that hippos may once have lived in this region. Hippos require standing water and do not live in the Sahara today. Apparently oases were once larger and more numerous in the Sahara, at least along some viable trade routes. Later paintings show camels, which are more suited to an arid climate.

The Flood could explain the source of this lost water. The land probably dried slowly after the Flood. For centuries, the Sahara could have been filled with standing ponds and lakes in its basins. Herodotus was not so naive after all.

Algerian cave art shows wild cattle living in the Sahara.

basins and plains of this area. A species of tailless monkeys, known as the Barbary apes, lives here, along with boars, antelopes, and jackals. Barbary sheep, the only wild sheep in Africa, roam the dry mountains.

South of the Atlas Mountains are the varied features of the Sahara. When most people hear the word *Sahara*, they think of sand deserts. These wide areas of drifting, blowing sand are called **ergs**. The Grand Erg cuts a swath across central Algeria. Its sands cover thousands of square miles, with only a few large oases to break the monotony. The discovery of oil and natural gas reserves in the Grand Erg Oriental (the eastern part of the erg) has provided the government with capital to develop industries, such as chemicals, machinery, textiles, and cement. Income from natural gas exportation has also made possible improvements in education and has resulted in a dramatic improvement in literacy (70 percent). However, unemployment remains high.

Ergs cover less than 20 percent of the Sahara. Much more common are **regs**, flat desert areas covered with pebbles. The Tanezrouft Reg, on Algeria's southern border, is a monotonous gravel plain that stretches hundreds of miles. Algeria also has **hammadas** along its southern borders. A hammada is a solid mass of barren, windswept rock. The bare rock of the **Ahaggar Mountains** seems to rise out of nowhere in the middle of the Sahara.

The central land between the Atlas and Ahaggar Mountains has no drainage to the sea and no permanent streams. Little vegetation grows in the desert. Coarse grasses, woody shrubs, and palm trees survive only at wadis and oases. Many oases are small and support only enough trees for a family or two, but several oases in the Sahara are large enough to support entire towns and cities. Wadis lead to shallow salt lakes called **chotts**. The chotts usually contain little or no water—just mineral deposits left behind after the water evaporates. The lowest such basin is Chott Melrhir, 131 feet below sea level.

Palms grow at this desert oasis.

Present-day Algeria has been shaped by its history of foreign invasions. Arab invaders, who first arrived in the eighth century, brought their Arabic language and the religion of Islam. French colonization, which began in 1830, created the country's modern borders. The French controlled every aspect of Algerian life, and natives who resented the rule revolted in 1954. More than one-quarter million people died before Algeria was granted independence in 1962. Many French colonists returned to France. The socialist Muslim government established after independence suffered continual terrorist violence. The most radical Islamic wing disbanded in 2000, and Algeria is currently governed by a small group of civilians and generals.

Technically, Algerians have freedom of religion. However, restrictive laws and increased persecution have all but eliminated this freedom. Ninety-seven percent of Algerians are Muslim, and radical Islam is becoming dominant, with calls for sharia law gaining greater support. Two percent of the people have no religious affiliation, and 0.28 percent of Algerians identify with some form of Christianity. Evangelical Christians make up 0.2 percent of the Algerian population, and this group is growing at an annual rate of 8 percent. Despite, or perhaps because of, persecution, Algerian believers are growing and winning many of their fellow countrymen to Christ. Algerians are producing literature in their own languages and have developed vibrant outreach ministries.

Tunisia

Tunisia, which is slightly larger than the state of Georgia, has several geographic advantages over its desert neighbors. It supports twice the population of Libya, its large neighbor to the east, because of a pleasant climate, consistent water supply, and productive land. Tunisia's life expectancy is one of the highest in Africa.

Most of the cities and farms are in the north, at the edge of the Atlas Mountains. The highlands rarely exceed two thousand feet, but that is enough elevation to cool the region and bring moisture. The average temperature in the north varies from 52°F in winter to 79°F in summer. This region produces wheat, olives, and tomatoes. Little rain falls in the southern desert, where temperatures are much hotter.

Part of Tunisia is a prominent peninsula that juts into the Mediterranean, almost cutting the sea in half. Tunis, the capital, is ideally located for trade, being only a short distance from Sicily and the Italian peninsula. Like Tangier in Morocco, Tunis has been used as a launch pad by invading armies. The ancient city of Carthage on this peninsula controlled trade passing through the western Mediterranean.

Tunisia's economy has recently seen growth in many major areas—farming, mining, tourism, petroleum production, and manufacturing. Liberal economic policies and privatization of industry have contributed to an average annual increase of 5 percent in the country's GDP since the 1990s.

While Islam is the official state religion of Tunisia, the government remains secular. Conversion to Christianity is discouraged, but religious minorities enjoy a degree of freedom, as do national Christians. Ninety-nine percent of Tunisians are Muslim, but the percentage of those who

Horse and Camel Festivals in Algeria

"In the desert regions, traditional horse and camel festivities are celebrated. Two of the better-known festivals are the Horse Festival of Tiaret and the Camel Festival celebrated in Metlili, near Ghadaia. During the Horse Festival, there are horse races and parades. . . . There is also a competition called Fantasia, in which the riders must aim and shoot at a target while their horses are in full gallop and then bring their horses to an abrupt stop.

"The Camel Festival at Metlili lasts two full days in March. There is a Fantasia at this one too. Another popular event is camel dancing, where the camel riders make their camels dance to the accompaniment of traditional instruments."

Cultures of the World: Algeria, 122–23.

Rades Harbor in Tunisia

GEOGRAPHER'S CORNER

Making Inferences

At this point, you have studied many kinds of maps. You should now be able to pick up maps of completely new areas and draw inferences, or reasonable conclusions, from what you see. Look again at the map of North Africa at the beginning of this chapter. Answer each question and make the inference.

1–2. What African capitals lie on the Mediterranean coast? Why do you think they are located there?

3–4. How many nations touched Lake Chad? Why were so many borders drawn to include this lake?

5–6. Where are the geometric boundaries in North Africa? Why are they used here and not in other places?

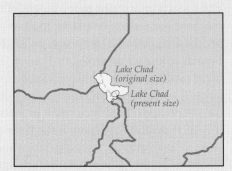

Lake Chad (original size)
Lake Chad (present size)

strictly adhere to Islam is much lower. Those who identify themselves as nonreligious represent 0.3 percent of the Tunisian population, and Tunisians who affiliate with some form of Christianity make up 0.22 percent of the population. Evangelical Christians constitute less than 0.1 percent of the population and may number around 1,100, but the number of believers is increasing and new congregations are forming.

Section Quiz

1. What mountain range provides water for much of the Maghreb?
2. What geographic feature in Morocco almost reaches Europe?
3. Distinguish an erg from a reg.
4. What high mountains form hammadas in southern Algeria?
✭ What is the status of freedom of religion in the countries in the Mahgreb?

III. Libya and Egypt

Libya and Egypt make up the remainder of Northern Africa and serve as a transitional area between Africa and the Middle East. They are the two most influential Northern African countries, and both continue to play important roles in world politics.

Libya

Like the other Northern African countries, Libya, which lies between Tunisia and Egypt, is primarily desert. Desert covers about 90 percent of Libya's land. Half of the country's population is urban and lives along the coastal plain, where there is a pleasant mediterranean climate. A small number of farmers and herders live in this area, surviving by raising crops or herding livestock, such as sheep. Their primary products are grains, dates, olives, and citrus fruits.

The **Gulf of Sidra** extends south into the center of Libya. Here the desert comes right up to the coast because there are no hills to bring rain. This gulf divides the Mediterranean coast into east and west, where the people live. The waters of the gulf are some of the warmest in the Mediterranean and are rich in tuna fish.

Historical Background

Libya became independent from Italy in 1951, but Colonel Muammar Qaddafi overthrew the new king in 1969. He removed all signs of Italian culture and instituted a military dictatorship. At one time he hoped to create a mighty new empire, attacking neighbors in Chad, Sudan, and Niger. He also funded terrorist activities around the world. The United States put a check on his work in 1986, when U.S. bombers struck several cities in retaliation for his support of terrorism. Since then, terrorist activities have decreased. After September 11, 2001, Qaddafi strongly condemned al-Qaeda terrorists. Beginning in 2003, Qaddafi agreed to end Libya's weapons programs and made an effort to improve dealings with Western nations. Qaddafi died in 2011 during a civil war that erupted during the Arab Spring.

Since the time of the Roman Empire, the hump on Libya's eastern coast has been called Cyrenaica, after the early capital of Cyrene. In New Testament times it was the home of Simon, who carried Christ's cross (Mark 15:21), and of Lucius, a church member at Antioch (Acts 13:1). Benghazi is the main eastern city today.

The western coast is known as Tripolitania. **Tripoli**, the capital, is the largest city in Libya. It was founded by the Phoenicians and became one of the major Mediterranean ports of ancient history. It also played a role in the later Barbary Wars with the United States. Today, Tripoli is the country's largest manufacturing center.

Hammadas rise from the desert in Libya.

Caravans, which have crossed the vast Sahara since ancient times, stopped at scattered oases to resupply. Libya's large oases, which lie in the west, became centers of trade. Black peoples in the south sold gold, ivory, and slaves in return for salt, cloth, and dates from the Mediterranean region. Arabs used camels to transport goods across the dry terrain, where horses or other draft animals would have perished. The sweet fruit of the date palm, which does not spoil as quickly as other fruits, provided convenient food for desert travel.

The eastern half of Libya has some of the most barren desert of the Sahara, where not even desert nomads wander. This area, called the **Libyan Desert**, extends east into Egypt and south into Sudan. Petroleum was discovered in this wasteland in 1959, just south of the Gulf of Sidra.

All the Barbary States have some oil in their desert regions, but Libya has the largest proven deposits in Africa. Libya's oil wealth gives it one of the largest per capita GDPs in Africa. Libya currently also has the highest life expectancy in Africa. The country has used its oil profits to develop agriculture, industries, and transportation. For example, the Great Man-Made River Project, begun in 1984, is being built to bring water underground from wells in the Sahara to the northern farmlands. The Man-Made River is the world's largest irrigation project and is projected to cost $25 billion. When completed, it could provide fresh water to Libyans for many years (estimates vary widely). No completion date has yet been given.

Oasis in Libya

The state religion of Libya is Sunni Islam, and 97 percent of the people are Muslim. Christianity is generally tolerated, and nearly 3 percent of the people affiliate with some form of Christianity. Evangelical Christians represent 0.3 percent of the population, and most of these are foreign workers. While Christians are allowed to worship in their own homes, congregations must meet in secret and are constantly on the watch for infiltrators who will report them to Libyan authorities. Despite official hostility and Muslim persecution, the number of Christians in Libya continues to increase.

Egypt

Egypt, one of the world's oldest and most fascinating countries, still thrives today along the Nile River. Located near the birthplace of civilization in the Middle East, Egypt seeks to maintain its rich ancient culture and heritage while surviving in the unpredictable Arab world.

Most people still associate Egypt with ancient pyramids and temples, which stand along the Nile Valley. As early as 2700 BC, Egypt was united as a state under one ruler. This began the long succession of dynasties and pharaohs who built the famous monuments. The dynastic period lasted until nearly five hundred years before Christ, when Egypt endured a series of invasions by Persians, Greeks, Romans, and Arabs, who each brought a new culture. The Ottoman Turks controlled Egypt beginning in 1517, until an Albanian officer named Mohammed Ali won control in 1805. Ali's rule ushered in the modernization of Egypt, which included the building of modern Cairo and the completion of the Suez Canal in 1869. Unfortunately, the process drained much of Egypt's resources, and the British occupied the country until independence was granted in 1922.

Egypt has the largest population in the Arab world, and it is struggling to find its place in modern civilization. A military coup in 1952 replaced the monarchy with a republic. Gamal Abdel Nasser became one of Egypt's most revered leaders, although other countries often disapproved of his policies. President Anwar Sadat succeeded Nasser in 1970 and reversed many of his policies. Most notably, he ended hostility toward Israel. In 1977, Sadat signed the Camp David Accords with Israel's prime minister. In the Accords, Egypt agreed to recognize Israel's right to exist and Israel agreed to return the Sinai Peninsula (which it had taken during the Six-Day War of 1967) and to remove its settlers.

In 1981, President Sadat was murdered by Islamic terrorists, and Hosni Mubarak succeeded him as president. After ruling Egypt for thirty years, Mubarak was forced to step down in 2011 during the Arab Spring. Despite great optimism initially, Egypt's political status has remained unstable, and intervention by the Egyptian military continues to be an option.

The state religion of Egypt is Islam, and 87 percent of the population is Muslim. While the government officially tolerates Christianity, persecution has been on the rise, and officials do little to prosecute those who kill believers and burn churches. Despite the growing persecution, those who identify with some form of Christianity make up nearly 13 percent of the population. Evangelical Christians represent 4 percent of the population and have been experiencing nearly 5 percent growth each year. Christian outreach in this country includes Bible distribution, websites, chat rooms, and satellite TV. Through these means and the personal witness of believers, many Muslims in Egypt are converting to Christianity.

Life Along the Nile

The **Nile River** is the lifeblood of Egypt. It is the longest river in the world, at 4,160 miles. Nearly all of Egypt's population lives along the river, where palm trees shade the houses and villages in the valley. The climate is hot and dry, with summer temperatures averaging 90°F in the north and reaching 110°F in the south. Only one inch of rain or less falls in the valley each year, but the delta region near the Mediterranean Sea may receive up to seven or eight inches.

Until the early twentieth century, the Nile flooded every year, bringing with it precious silt. The farmers channeled the floodwaters into their fields to sustain their crops of grain and cotton. The population was restricted to about ten miles on either side of the Nile, where the floodwaters could be channeled.

Beginning in 1902, new dams ended the flood patterns. The largest, **Aswan High Dam**, was finished in 1970. **Lake Nasser**, the

Cairo, Egypt, and the Nile River

reservoir behind the high dam, stretches southward about three hundred forty miles, entering Sudan, where it is called Lake Nubia. The dam and lake have stopped the flooding and allow year-round irrigation. About two million acres of land receive the waters automatically throughout the year. Now two or three crops can be raised in one year. However, the dam also traps the rich sediments in Lake Nasser, preventing the replenishment of soil downstream. Egyptian farmers must now rely on fertilizers.

The rural farmers are called **fellahin** (fel uh HEEN). They live in houses made of sun-dried brick and plow their fields with wooden plows pulled by buffalo. While they now have radios and other modern conveniences, they lack adequate health care. Sanitation is poor, and disease is rampant. Small worms called schistosomes live in the murky Nile and spread a disease known as bilharzia, which affects the liver and blood vessels.

The area between the Aswan High Dam and the Nile Delta is called **Upper Egypt**. Temples and tombs stand along the Nile in this region. The greatest ruins are at Thebes, which served as Egypt's capital during its early dynasties.

The Aswan High Dam as viewed from space

Valley of the Kings

Thebes was the great capital of Egyptian kings for fifteen hundred years, but only its ruins remain. The modern city of Luxor now stands in its place. Nearby in the desolate Valley of the Kings are more than sixty tombs of the pharoahs and their families. Most of the tombs were robbed long before archeologists explored them, but in 1922 an English archeologist discovered fabulous riches in the tomb of nineteen-year-old Tutankhamen, or King Tut. The most recent discovery, that of the mummy of Queen Hatshepsut, took place in 2007.

Other reminders of the ancient kings' glory are the ruins of their temples of worship. The Temple of Karnak is the most well known of these sites. Sphinxes once lined the avenue leading to the front gateway, flanked by towers 143 feet high. Inside, a colonnade enclosed the Great Court, and the 140 pillars of the Great Hall of Pillars supported an eighty-foot-high ceiling. Huge pylons, or gateways, led into the central court and then into the inner sanctuary, where the golden statue of Amun, god of the wind and air, stood in his sacred boat. The temple complex also had temples for Amun's consort Mut and for their son Khons. Also well known are the Colossi of Memnon, which guard the entrance to the temple of Amenhotep III. Each seated figure rises nearly sixty feet.

Entrances to the tombs in the Valley of the Kings

Sphinxes at the Temple of Karnak

About one hundred miles from the Mediterranean, the Nile River splits and fans out to a width of nearly one hundred fifty miles. Early geographers noted that this region was triangular in shape like the Greek letter delta. They called it the Nile Delta, and *delta* became the term for alluvial deposits at the mouth of any river. The Nile Delta is also called **Lower Egypt** because it has the lowest elevation of the river.

Alexander the Great established the city of **Alexandria** near the mouth of the delta. It was the site of the huge lighthouse called the Pharos, one of the seven ancient wonders of the world, and the largest library ever compiled in the ancient world. Today, Alexandria is the second-largest city in Egypt with 4.5 million people.

Muslim conquerors moved the capital from Alexandria to **Cairo** (KYE roh), near the start of the delta. With an estimated 17.8 million people, Cairo is Africa's largest city. Cairo has become a major tourist center because of the pyramids located across the river at Giza. Like most cities, Cairo mixes prosperity and poverty. Shantytowns stand across from modern business and industrial centers.

The three pyramids at Giza are located just outside of Cairo.

Deserts East and West

Deserts cover the rest of Egypt. The Sahara hems in the Nile Valley on both sides. However, the two sides are quite different. The **Eastern Desert** is rugged and covered by barren mountains reaching almost seven thousand feet high. It is sometimes called the Arabian Desert, but it should not be confused with the larger Arabian Desert that covers the Arabian Peninsula. The nation's largest petroleum deposit lies near the villages on the Red Sea coast.

The Western Desert, or Libyan Desert, is a low plateau covering two-thirds of Egypt. A few hills, salt flats, and depressions interrupt the flat sand horizons. Oases dot the vast wasteland, the largest of which is Al Kharijah. The **Qattara Depression** in the northwest drops to 436 feet below sea level. It covers an area almost as large as New Jersey. Egypt has considered digging a fifty-mile canal northward to the Mediterranean to flood the basin and create a new lake. This hydroelectric project would be more significant than the Aswan High Dam.

While most Egyptians are Muslims, a large minority of Coptic Christians live in the country, many of them in the deserts. The Coptic Church, which claims to have twelve million members (although others claim it is as low as seven million), has strong historical ties to the desert. Christianity spread throughout Egypt soon after the time of Christ, and it survived after the Arab conquest. Ancient historical sites, including monasteries, are scattered throughout the desert, especially at oases. The religion of the **Copts** is one of ritual and tradition, similar to Roman Catholicism and Eastern Orthodoxy. They follow the unscriptural belief that the divine and human natures of Christ mixed in a single nature.

Sinai Peninsula

Although most of Egypt lies in Africa, the **Sinai Peninsula** is part of Asia. It is divided from African Egypt by the Isthmus of Suez, a bridge of land between the **Gulf of Suez** and the Mediterranean Sea. The Gulf of Suez is the western arm of the Red Sea. The **Suez Canal** cuts through the isthmus to connect these two bodies of water. Egypt's largest port, Suez, is located at the southern end of the canal. The Sinai Peninsula borders Israel to the east and was a disputed territory during the Six-Day War. The main resources of the area are petroleum and manganese.

The mountainous Wilderness of Sinai lies at the south of the peninsula and takes its name from Mount Sinai, where Moses received the Ten Commandments (Exod. 31:18). Jewish, Christian, and Islamic traditions all identify Mount Sinai with Jebel Musa (meaning Mount of Moses, 7,497 ft.), although there is no physical proof. At the foot of Jebel Musa, Orthodox monks live in the Monastery of St. Catherine. Famous for ancient Bible manuscripts, it is also the oldest Christian monastery in the world (built c. AD 530).

Besides attracting religious pilgrims, the Wilderness of Sinai attracts divers to Ras Muhammad (Cape Muhammad). The Ras Muhammad Reef off the southern tip of the peninsula is among the greatest coral reefs in the world.

The Monastery of St. Catherine sits at the foot of Jebel Musa.

Origins of the Coptic Church

The Coptic Church claims to have been founded by Mark, the Gospel writer. During the fifth century, the Coptic Church broke with traditional Christian doctrine by claiming that the divine and human natures of Christ mixed in a single nature. There were some attempts to unify Christianity and the Coptic Church, but these were unsuccessful. The Coptic Church flourished until the Muslim invasion in the seventh century. Because of Muslim pressures, many Copts converted to Islam. Under Muslim rule, the Copts were persecuted, and their numbers declined. In the late-nineteenth and early-twentieth centuries, the Copts gained religious freedom and other privileges that had previously been denied, yet most Copts still feel oppressed.

Suez Canal

The Suez Canal was the longest canal in the world when it was opened in 1869. It stretches almost 120 miles from the Red Sea at Suez to the Mediterranean Sea, where a new commercial center, Port Said, was built. The canal is the shortest route between Europe and the Indian and Pacific Oceans. It is one of the busiest waterways in the world. The canal is 66 feet deep and 590 feet wide at its most narrow points, with wider spots every six miles for ships to pass. Thousands of workers took ten years to complete the job; many of them died in the arduous work of building the canal. The Suez Canal put Egypt back in the forefront of world affairs.

Interestingly, the French engineer Ferdinand de Lesseps was not the first to dig a canal here. Pharaoh Necho lost many slaves in his attempt to build the canal in the seventh century BC. King Darius of Persia conquered Egypt and completed the job around 522 BC. The Romans made improvements to the canal, but it eventually filled with silt.

Find It!

Monastery of St. Catherine (3D model)
28.5549° N, 33.9754° E

Africa's Uneven Progress

Now that you have finished reading about Africa, you may wonder why there seems to be so little progress or improvement in quality of life in some parts of Africa. The lack of economic and political development in some African countries can be somewhat explained by the problems that have plagued Africa in the past few centuries. Some problems are due to natural causes and cannot be helped; others are caused by man's broken nature.

Many of Africa's struggles are caused by the continent's geography. Much of the soil in Africa is infertile, especially in the Sahara and Sahel regions. As a result, proper nutrition is not always possible, affecting the physical well-being of all people. This in turn affects the available workforce. In addition to malnutrition, Africa has high concentrations of diseases such as malaria, typhoid, tuberculosis, and AIDS.

Africa has also suffered from outside invasions throughout its past. Early European colonists tended to protect the original inhabitants of the continent. However, over time, with the discovery of valuable natural resources such as gold and diamonds, many Europeans behaved more as owners of the land and people. The slave trade also removed a significant portion of the population from Africa each year until slavery was made illegal by Western nations. (Muslim slavery has continued.)

When colonies gained independence from European states, the Africans often had to establish their own national governments, and many learned the hard lesson that socialism does not work. Also, tribal loyalties made it difficult to find people who were interested in a federal government. As with any culture, access to power often exposed personal ambitions that ran counter to what was best for a nation. Thus some African governments have been prone to corruption.

However, a growing number of African countries are overcoming these obstacles, developing successful free market economies, and allowing private enterprise to grow their national wealth. Several countries, including China, Brazil, and India, are investing in Africa, a continent rich in raw materials and human potential.

Section Quiz

1. What body of water divides the coast of Libya in two?
2. What natural resource has transformed Libya's economy?
3. What is the most populous region in Egypt?
4. Which is farther north: Upper Egypt or Lower Egypt?
5. What are Egypt's peasant farmers called?
★ Why does Egypt have so much influence in the Arab world?

Chapter Review

Making Connections

1–2. What climate is common on the northern coast of Africa in addition to desert? What geographic feature makes this common climate possible?

3–6. What are four major sources of water in Northern Africa?

7–8. What two valuable natural resources are found in the African countries along the Mediterranean?

9–12. Name four ancient empires that influenced the development of the countries along the Northern African coast.

Developing Geography Skills

1. Using the map on page 522 and the text, explain why the Sahel's population is concentrated in the south of each country.

2. Using the maps on pages 522 and 532, determine which nations will be directly affected by the shrinking of Lake Chad.

Thinking Critically

1. What factors contribute to the process of desertification? What measures can be taken to slow or reverse this destructive process?

2. Why are missionary opportunities very limited in North Africa? What is an effective method of reaching the North African people with the gospel?

Living in God's World

1. Explain how folk Islam differs from official Islam, why this would matter to Christian missionaries, and how a Christian missionary could learn about folk Islam.

2. How should a Christian living in a prosperous country approach the issue of poverty in places such as Niger, one of the poorest countries in the world?

People, Places, and Things to Know

Sahara
Sahel
Ghana Empire
desertification
Niger River
Bamako
Mali Empire
Mansa Musa
Timbuktu
Aïr Mountains
Tuaregs
Songhai
Tibesti Mountains
Lake Chad
Atlas Mountains
Maghreb
Berbers
Barbary Coast
Strait of Gibraltar
Tangier
Casablanca
Western Sahara
ergs
regs
hammadas
Ahaggar Mountains
chotts
Gulf of Sidra
Tripoli
Libyan Desert
Nile River
Aswan High Dam
Lake Nasser
fellahin
Upper Egypt
Lower Egypt
Alexandria
Cairo
Eastern Desert
Qattara Depression
Copts
Sinai Peninsula
Gulf of Suez
Suez Canal

Unit Nine
THE AUSTRALIAN AND PACIFIC REALMS

This region was one of the last areas on the earth's surface to be explored, but its story is fascinating. The geography is challenging, and yet thriving civilizations existed prior to the arrival of Europeans. This area is home to some of the most inhospitable places and also some of the most beautiful places on the earth.

22

AUSTRALIA AND NEW ZEALAND

The Sydney Opera House, on the shore of Sydney Harbor, has become a symbol of modern Australia.

The remainder of the textbook explores the continent of Australia, its neighbor New Zealand, and the two most remote regions of the earth—**Oceania** and Antarctica. Hidden by the broad Pacific Ocean, the many islands of Oceania were probably among the last lands settled by Noah's descendants. When the Europeans began exploring the islands in the late eighteenth century, they discovered an interesting variety of isolated peoples who had not heard the gospel. Missionaries rejoiced when many of those people responded to the gospel.

English settlers also discovered rich soil and grassland on the islands of New Zealand and on the continent of Australia. There they planted a European culture and built a society very similar to their home on the other side of the world.

I. Australia

Australia is often referred to as "the land down under" because it lies on the opposite side of the earth from Europe and North America and in the Southern Hemisphere, where the seasons are opposite of those in the Northern Hemisphere. For example, Australian

Australia and New Zealand Fast Facts						
Country	Capital	Area (sq. mi.)	Pop. (2013 est.) (M)	Pop. Density (per sq. mi.)	Per Capita GDP ($US)	Life Span
Australia	Canberra	2,988,902	22.20	7	$42,400	81.98
New Zealand	Wellington	103,359	4.36	42	$28,800	80.82

This kangaroo family seems to be posing for the photographer.

families celebrate Christmas with picnics and other outdoor activities in the middle of the hot summer.

Australia is unusual in many other ways. It is the smallest and flattest continent. Its highest peak is less than half the height of peaks on the other continents. Australia is the driest inhabited continent, with an average annual rainfall of only seventeen inches. As an island continent, Australia is the only inhabited continent with no land bridge to another continent.

Australia has many exotic animals, many of which are unique to this island. The best known are kangaroos, although they are not unique to Australia; they are also found in New Guinea. Kangaroos raise their young in a pouch on the mother's belly and thrive in forest and plain alike. There are many species of kangaroos, ranging in size from the tiny muskrat kangaroo to the giant red kangaroo, which grows taller than a man and can hop at speeds up to thirty miles per hour.

The continent is also home to some peculiar birds. It has the second- and third-largest birds in the world—the emu and the cassowary. Like the world's largest bird, the ostrich, these birds cannot fly. The beautiful lyrebird has an amazing ability to mimic as many as forty different calls. Perhaps the most famous Australian bird, however, is the kookaburra, whose fiendish "laugh" is a familiar sound in the cities.

The Kookaburra

Growing up to eighteen inches long, the kookaburra is a loud and noisy bird that lives on the islands of Australia, Tasmania, and New Guinea. It is a member of the kingfisher family. Its cry sounds like human laughter. Kookaburras are carnivores, eating large insects, small reptiles, and amphibians, but they do not drink any water, getting all they need from their food.

The Platypus

This odd creature looks as though it might have been assembled by a committee. It is a furry freshwater mammal that lays eggs and has a tail like a beaver, a bill and webbed feet like a duck, and a streamlined body like an otter. The male has a spur on both of its hind legs that injects venom into its victims. The soft bill of the platypus is sensitive to touch as well as electrical charges and helps the platypus find prey as well as navigate. The platypus lives in lakes and rivers on the east coast of Australia as well as throughout Tasmania.

The Koala and the Eucalyptus Tree

Large forests of eucalyptus trees grow in Australia, especially along the east coast, and the koala, Australia's most-loved marsupial, dwells in them. Resembling a furry teddy bear, the koala gets all of its water and nourishment from eucalyptus leaves without ever having to descend to the ground. Fur traders once killed koalas in large numbers, but they are now protected by law.

Eucalyptus trees are useful for medicinal and aromatic purposes. The leaves are especially useful in treating colds, flu, bronchitis, muscle and joint stiffness, and some skin infections.

Australia has many unique plants too. In all, thirteen thousand plant species grow there and nowhere else in the world. Eucalyptus trees are the most common type of tree in Australia. There are six hundred varieties, ranging from dwarfs in the dry interior to three-hundred-foot giants in the northern rain forests—the tallest hardwoods on earth. The only other important tree is the acacia, which is pictured on the national coat of arms beneath an emu and kangaroo. Early settlers called acacia trees **wattles** because they wove, or "wattled," the trees together to build frames for their mud homes. English settlers also called the tall hardwood acacia trees "gums" because the sap dulled their axes.

Australia is unique for another reason. It was the last continent to be settled by Europeans. The first British colonists did not arrive in Australia until nearly two hundred years after Jamestown was founded in Virginia. In fact, Americans were ratifying the U.S. Constitution the same year that British settlers arrived in Australia.

Australia is still the most sparsely populated of the inhabited continents, and it is the only continent united under one national flag. In slightly more than two hundred years, pioneers created a thriving, industrialized nation with six states, each symbolized in the center of Australia's coat of arms.

Recently, however, Australia's economy has grown more slowly than those of some Asian neighbors, especially Japan and South Korea. The country's population makeup has also changed. Asian immigrants continue to increase, and about one in ten Australians has a non-English-speaking heritage. Japan is currently Australia's biggest trading partner, and Australia is becoming a vital member of the Asian economy.

The Australian National Coat of Arms incorporates the symbols of all the states on the shield held by a kangaroo and an emu.

States on the Great Dividing Range

Australia is divided into three broad geographic regions: the Great Dividing Range along the east coast; the Central Lowlands just

The Snowy Mountain Strategy

In an effort to bring more water to the thirsty interior, the Australian government began an ambitious program in 1949 to redirect the water that rushed eastward from the mountains to the ocean. The Snowy Mountain Scheme, as the program was known, consisted of fifteen large dams and one hundred miles of tunnels. They diverted the water westward through the mountains to the farms and sheep stations in the interior.

One of the generating stations in the Snowy Mountain project

Captain James Cook was the discoverer of Australia and other islands of Oceania.

west of the Great Dividing Range; and the Western Plateau, which is the western two-thirds of Australia.

The **Great Dividing Range** is a rugged complex of low mountains, plateaus, and hills that run parallel to the east coast of Australia. Although they are low, the mountains have played a central role in the development of the continent, much as the Appalachian Mountains influenced the history of the American colonies. Two of Australia's six states—New South Wales and Victoria—are located in eastern Australia, astride the Great Dividing Range.

The mountains influence the weather patterns of the whole continent. As winds blow off the warm ocean in the east, the moist air rises and cools over the mountains, depositing moisture by frequent rains. Several short, swift rivers flow down the eastern slope of the Great Dividing Range and empty into the ocean. The narrow coastal plains receive much more water than the vast, dry lands west of the mountains.

The first British settlements on the continent were near the rich alluvial soils of the coastal rivers. Australia's major cities and industrial areas arose on its eastern seaboard, just as America's first industries developed on the Atlantic seaboard.

New South Wales

Captain James Cook (1728–79), a famous British explorer, was the first European to map the east coast of Australia. He found fertile soil and one of the continent's few deep harbors at a place he named **Botany Bay**. Later, that harbor became the site of the first English settlement on the continent.

First Settlement at Sydney—At first, the king of England had little interest in this far-off land. A revolt by the American colonies in 1776, however, changed his view. No longer able to send prisoners to a prison colony in Georgia, England needed an alternative destination.

England selected New South Wales for its new prison colony. Captain Arthur Phillip, a retired naval officer, was appointed to lead the eleven ships of the "First Fleet" and to serve as governor of the new colony. After an arduous eight-month journey, the ships anchored in Botany Bay. On January 26, 1788, the captain hoisted the British flag and formally claimed the eastern half of the continent and the island of Tasmania. The territory was called New South Wales. Each year, Australians celebrate this date as Australia Day.

Of the one-thousand-plus initial settlers, 759 were convicts sentenced to "transportation." They included men, women, and children convicted of minor offenses, such as petty theft or failure to pay their debts. In the new colony of Sydney, they were given an opportunity to pay off their debts by farming. The rest of the First Fleet consisted of about two hundred British soldiers, approximately thirty wives of soldiers, and a few children.

Mother of States—Like Virginia, the first colony in America, New South Wales became a "Mother of States" in Australia. Over the years, its land was carved up into new states and territories. Although the modern state of New South Wales is only fourth in total area among Australia's six states, it remains first in industry, shipping, and agriculture. Numerous factories dot the coastal plain, manufacturing products from textiles to tractors.

Unlike their British cousins, to whom rank and privilege are still important, Australians consider themselves equals. Australia was settled by hard-working families who scratched out a rough existence in the new country. The continent offered plenty of land for everyone. Cities were not built up; they were built out. Tall buildings and apartments are rare. Most Australian families own their own homes.

Blue Mountains

Blue Mountains and the Australian Alps—Within view of the coastal cities is the Great Dividing Range. The mountains west of Sydney are called the Blue Mountains. Although they look blue to residents of the city forty miles away, they are actually covered with green eucalyptus trees, which secrete a bluish oil into the air. The Blue Mountains are actually a low plateau that has been eroded by water. Visitors there enjoy exploring the Jenolan Caves, the largest cave system on the continent.

South of the Blue Mountains is another part of the Great Dividing Range, called the Australian Alps. These snow-covered mountains are much higher than the Blues. The highest range in the Australian Alps is the Snowy Mountains, where **Mount Kosciuszko** (kahz ee US koh)—Australia's highest point—rises 7,310 feet above sea level. Covered with snow for half the year, it is the area's main attraction for skiers and hikers. It is also the site made popular by the

Jenolan Caves

LET'S GO EXPLORING

Climates of Australia and New Zealand

1. Which coast has a dry climate?
2. Which coast has a tropical climate?
3. Which coast has a mediterranean climate?
4. What climate appears directly west of the Great Dividing Range?
5. What is the most widespread climate in Australia?
6. What climate is found in New Zealand?
* Compare this map with the map on page 543 and determine the climate for each of the six state capitals of Australia.

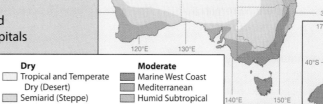

Tropical Rainy
Tropical Wet (Rain Forest)
Tropical Wet and Dry (Savanna)

Dry
Tropical and Temperate Dry (Desert)
Semiarid (Steppe)

Moderate
Marine West Coast
Mediterranean
Humid Subtropical

famous poem "The Man from Snowy River" by Australian Andrew Barton Paterson.

Jumbucks in the Interior—Just west of the mountains are fertile grasslands much like the American prairie. Wheat fields are common. But that area of Australia is most famous for its **jumbucks** (sheep), which are found in every region—on the coast, around the mountain slopes, and in the dry interior. Australia is a leading producer of wool and mutton.

Australia is becoming less dependent on "the sheep's back," however, as manufacturing increases. The mines near Broken Hill on the western border of the state are major producers of silver, zinc, and lead.

Canberra—During the nineteenth century, arguments over trade and taxes divided the six independent colonies on the continent. Late in the century, the militaristic emperor of Germany began planting colonies in the Pacific region and threatened the British colonies. As a result, the six colonies of Australia agreed to unite as a federation in 1901. As part of the settlement, the two largest states agreed to build a new seat of government midway between Sydney and Melbourne. New South Wales set aside nine hundred square miles for the capital.

The government sponsored an international competition to determine the best possible design for the new city. Of the 137 designs submitted, the design of architect Walter Griffin of Chicago won. He moved to Australia in 1913 to direct the construction of the capital. In 1927, the Australian Parliament met there for the first time. The federal government ran the Australian Capital Territory until 1989, when it was granted self-government. The capital city is named **Canberra** after the Aboriginal word *canburry*, meaning "meeting place."

Like the United States, Australia adopted a written constitution and a federal system of state governments. Like Canada, Australia has a constitutional monarchy with a parliament and claims the British monarch. The British monarch is the head of state and is represented

Sydney

The Sydney Opera House and the Sydney Harbor Bridge are icons of that large and beautiful metropolis.

For a city that began as an unpromising and inauspicious penal colony, **Sydney** has experienced remarkable growth. It is now Australia's largest city and its cultural heart.

The area that became Sydney was originally inhabited by Aborigines. James Cook discovered Botany Bay, which is now a suburb of Sydney, in 1770. In 1788, Sydney was founded as a penal colony and was named after the British Home Secretary at the time, Thomas Townshend, Lord Sydney. By 1847, however, the city had outgrown its penal colony reputation; only 3.2 percent of the population was made up of convicts. The first of several gold rushes occurred there in 1851, bringing an influx of immigrants. Sydney began the twentieth century with a population of more than one million and has grown to over 4.6 million. Among the world's cities today, it has one of the highest percentages of immigrants.

Sydney is the capital of New South Wales and is a major tourist destination. It hosted the 2000 Olympics. Its residents, known as "Sydneysiders," take great pride in the most widely recognized architectural feature of their city—the Sydney Opera House.

Sydney Opera House

Many consider the Sydney Opera House the most beautiful building in the world. Built on a point that juts out into Sydney Harbor, the opera house looks like a huge ship that is flying into the harbor with open sails. The "sails" are high partial domes.

A Danish architect provided the winning design in a worldwide competition. The original design called for wide sails, but they proved impossible to make. The engineering problems were finally overcome after thousands of hours of computer simulations. Unfortunately, the $7 million budget blossomed to $100 million. Queen Elizabeth presided at the formal opening on October 20, 1973.

One million ceramic tiles, specially made in Sweden to remain bright white and free of fungus, cover the concrete sails. The interior design mixes 67,000 square feet of Gothic tinted glass with space-age steel ribs and concrete fans. There are five performing halls, a theater, and two restaurants. The theater's wool curtains are the largest in the world. In addition, the world's largest mechanical organ—consisting of 10,500 pipes—sits in one of the concert halls.

---

by a governor-general in Parliament. The monarch also approves six governors, one for each state government.

Victoria

Victoria is located on the southeast corner of Australia. In 1851, it split from New South Wales and became a separate state. The two states have been competitors ever since. Although Victoria is Australia's smallest mainland state, it is home to nearly one-fourth of Australia's population.

Three-fourths of Victoria's population is located in **Melbourne**, the state capital and the nation's second-largest city. Originally, Melbourne was a prosperous mining port; however, its remote location has hurt its competition with Sydney for trade and commerce. It is too far away from world shipping routes. Nonetheless, its factories still play an important role in the Australian economy.

The city of Melbourne is the most "English" of Australia's cities. Stately buildings and beautiful parks display statues of prominent Australians. The world-renowned Victoria National Gallery is home to the finest collection of art in the nation.

Melbourne is also the sports center of Australia. The city hosts the Davis Cup tennis finals, international cricket matches, and Australia's richest horse race. Australians are able to enjoy outdoor recreation year-round in their mild climate.

Melbourne is within sight of the Great Dividing Range, which curls around Victoria's coast. The mountains near Melbourne contain great mineral wealth. In 1851, the discovery of gold at Ballarat started a gold rush, which increased the state's population sevenfold. After the rich veins of gold were mined out, the city became a major railroad junction and Australia's most populous inland city.

Victoria is home to Australia's largest oil field and a major natural gas field off the coast. Coal is also mined in the state. The Latrobe Valley holds one of the world's largest deposits of **lignite** (brown coal). Lignite is the lowest grade of coal, however, because its high

Melbourne, the capital of the state of Victoria, is the nation's second-largest city.

Australians and Sports

Australians are avid sports fans. Their most popular spectator sport is cricket. They also enjoy golf, tennis, lawn bowling, and water activities on the beaches. Sailing is popular in Sydney's beautiful harbor.

WORLD RELIGIONS

World Religions: Ecumenical Christianity

A distinctive feature of Australian religious life is the Uniting Church in Australia. The Uniting Church was formed in 1977 by the union of the Congregational, Presbyterian, and Methodist churches in Australia. It is an expression of the ecumenical movement, which was particularly strong in the 1960s and 1970s. The goal of the ecumenical movement is the external unity of the church. They argue that the Bible necessitates this unity because Christ prayed for the unity of the church in John 17:21. In addition, in the New Testament the church was unified in particular locations (e.g., the church of Ephesus). Ecumenists also make practical arguments. They claim that church union eliminates duplicated efforts made by the denominations, and it avoids competition among Christian groups. An example is found in missions. Ecumenists believe it is a scandal for different denominations to compete on the mission field for conversions. However, this argument has been weakened by those in ecumenical circles who teach that all religions lead to salvation.

Critics of ecumenism point out that the ecumenists' foundational text, John 17:21, is taken out of context. John 17 speaks as much about the calling out of disciples from the world and their sanctification in the truth as it does about unity. Thus it defines the people who are to be unified, and these people are Christians. They are unified because they are in Christ and believe the truth of the gospel. The ecumenical embrace of theological liberalism offends many Christians, since it denies the inspiration and authority of Scripture and ignores Christ's emphasis on truth and separation from the world. Critics of ecumenism readily admit that the early church was not divided into denominations, but they recognize that denominations can play an important role in carrying out the Great Commission (Matt. 28:19–20). In addition, Christians have often worked across denominational lines without sacrificing their convictions, recognizing that their unity in Christ enables cooperation in many areas. Unity is maintained within local assemblies where members hold the same views on issues such as church government and the method and significance of baptism.

moisture produces little heat but a lot of smoke. Four vast power plants in Latrobe Valley produce nearly 85 percent of Victoria's electricity.

Section Quiz

1. What mountain system runs along Australia's eastern coast?
2. What is the highest peak in Australia?
3. Where did the first European settlers land in Australia? What year did they arrive?
4. What are jumbucks?
5. What is the capital of Australia, and where is it located?
★ Why do most Australians live on the east coast?

The Central Lowlands

On the other side of the Great Dividing Range is the continent's dry interior, where rain is scarce. Runoff water from the Great Dividing Range is vitally important. This low area just west of the mountains is known as the **Central Lowlands**.

Waters flowing down the Great Dividing Range form long, leisurely rivers in the flat, inland terrain. The map on page 543 shows the three places where these rivers drain: the Gulf of Carpentaria in the tropical north, **Lake Eyre** (ayer) in the center, and the Great Australian Bight in the south.

Most rivers in the Central Lowlands dry up during the dry season. The major exception is the 1,476 mile-long **Murray River** and its tributaries, the most important water system on the continent. These rivers provide a steady supply of water for farms and pastures in the

Lake Eyre

Australia's largest lake is located in the northeast corner of South Australia. **Lake Eyre** is the lowest point on the continent, fifty-two feet below sea level. Most rivers of the Central Lowlands, including the Great Artesian Basin, drain into this lake. These rivers—and the lake itself—are dry most of the time. A few times each century, heavy rains fill the rivers and lake. Within a period of two years, however, the lake returns to a barren salt bed.

Paddle steamers still carry tourists on the Murray River, Australia's longest river.

south. A large wheat crop grows in the wide plains of the Murray drainage basin. Many varieties of fruit also grow in the fertile river valley that forms the border between Victoria and New South Wales.

Tasmania

Off the coast of Victoria is the island of **Tasmania** (taz MAYN ee uh), Australia's smallest and least populous state. Tasmania has so many apple orchards that it is sometimes called the Apple Isle. Apple trees, introduced in 1788, now produce Australia's most important fruit crop. The best orchards are located in the Huon Valley about twenty miles southwest of the capital, Hobart. In addition to exporting apples worldwide, the state also produces pears, berries, and potatoes.

The narrow Bass Strait separates Tasmania from Victoria. Like Victoria, Tasmania has low mountains and a pleasant marine-west-coast climate. Blessed with abundant rainfall, Tasmania is home to magnificent rain forests and powerful waterfalls. The fierce Tasmanian devil (a marsupial) lives in the rugged central plateau, which remains sparsely settled. Most Tasmanians inhabit the fertile coastal lowlands. The availability of cheap hydroelectric power has attracted many industries, such as pulp and paper works, a zinc refinery, and aluminum smelting.

Queensland

On the northeast corner of the continent is Queensland, Australia's youngest state. It was formed in 1859 when Queenslanders

The Tasmanian Devil

The Tasmanian devil is a mammal that is now found only on the island of Tasmania, although it once also lived on the mainland of Australia. Tasmanian devils prey on small- to medium-sized animals and can devour an entire carcass, including the bones, in a very short time.

Great Barrier Reef

Just off the northeast shore of Queensland is the largest coral formation in the world. The **Great Barrier Reef** stretches up to 1,600 miles—as far north as Papua New Guinea. The "barrier" makes travel hazardous for ships sailing to the coast. Even Captain Cook, the European explorer, ran aground on the reef and was nearly shipwrecked. Because of the navigational hazards, numerous lighthouses have been constructed.

This underwater garden is actually 2,900 separate reefs. It includes more than 900 islands, including 300 coral cays (keys), 213 unvegetated cays, 43 vegetated cays, and 44 low wooded cays. Similar to tropical rain forests, the reef is home to a large variety of life forms, including more than 1,500 kinds of fish, 400 types of coral, 4,000 kinds of mollusks, and at least two endangered species, the sea cow and the large green sea turtle.

Such variety provides unique research opportunities for many types of scientists. In the 1960s, scientists began warning that the reef was disappearing. It was under attack by a poisonous starfish that devoured the polyps by the millions. Also, insecticides from farms onshore were washing into the ocean and destroying the coral. Some fertilizer companies were even mining the reef for limestone. To protect the reef, the Australian government in 1975 set aside most of it as a national park. Up to two million people visit Queensland every year to see the reef, generating over $3 billion annually.

This aerial view shows part of the Great Barrier Reef near Cairns, Queensland.

Thousands of divers each year enjoy the variety of life forms on the Great Barrier Reef, such as this giant tridacna clam.

Artesian Wells

The livestock in Queensland get most of their water from a vast underground reservoir called the Great Artesian Basin. The landscape is dotted with **artesian** (ahr TEE zhun) **wells**, where water bubbles up to the surface without the need for pumps. Although the water is too salty for crops and people, cattle drink it without any problem.

As water flows west off the Great Dividing Range, some of it seeps underground into the Great Artesian Basin. This water moves through a layer of underground rock called an **aquifer** (AK wih fer, "water bearer"). The Great Artesian Basin is the largest reserve of underground water in the world.

There are two basic kinds of aquifers. The most common are *unconfined aquifers*, which occur where the layer of rock above the aquifer is permeable, allowing water to seep through. Permeable layers include gravel, sand, clay, and loose rock. If a well is dug to this aquifer, the water must be pumped to the surface.

The Great Artesian Basin, on the other hand, is a *confined aquifer*. It has an impermeable layer of rock above it that traps the water and keeps it from rising to the surface. As the water pressure builds, it pushes out through breaks in the surface. Natural artesian springs result. When someone digs a hole into a confined aquifer, water pushes up to the surface, creating an artesian well.

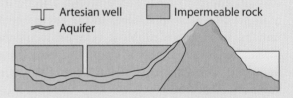

pressed for separation from New South Wales. A frontier spirit still exists in this sparsely populated state that is nearly two-and-one-half times the size of Texas. The majority of Queensland's residents are clustered along the eastern seaboard.

The Wet Coast—The capital, **Brisbane** (BRIHZ bun), is located in the southeast corner of the state on the Brisbane River. Originally founded as a prison colony, Brisbane grew rapidly to become Australia's largest river port. Because it is so near the tropics, the capital of the "Sunshine State" attracts many tourists each winter. Brisbane's numerous parks are filled with subtropical flowers.

South of the capital is the Gold Coast, which extends to New South Wales. Spectacular waves and beautiful beaches make it a surfer's paradise. The Darling Downs, a fertile plain in the southeast corner, produces pineapples and other fruits and vegetables.

The coast north of Brisbane reaches into the tropics. Frequent rains from moist trade winds make this Australia's wettest region. Sugar cane and cotton are grown along the narrow coastal plain. The northern tip of the east coast, Cape York Peninsula, is extremely hot and humid. Few people live in this tropical area. Climbing "tree kangaroos" feed on the leaves of the jungle canopy. Off the northeast coast of Queensland is the Great Barrier Reef.

The Dry Interior—To the west, beyond the low mountains and hills of the Great Dividing Range, the land becomes increasingly dry and grassy. Cowboys, called stockmen, live on large cattle **stations** (Australia's word for ranches). Some stations are the size of Delaware. More beef is produced in Queensland than in any other state. Australia exports most of the beef it produces to markets as diverse as the United States and the Far East.

Queensland also has great mineral deposits. During the gold rush of 1867, thousands of men poured into the state in search of

Australian cowboys, much like their American counterparts, participate in rodeo events.

instant wealth. Today, bauxite (aluminum ore) is mined on Cape York Peninsula, near Weipa (WEEP ah). North of Brisbane are large deposits of bituminous coal. Lead, zinc, silver, and copper are mined near the interior town of Mt. Isa (EYE zuh), Queensland's largest industrial complex.

Section Quiz

1. Why is runoff from the Great Dividing Range so important to the Central Lowlands?
2. What is Australia's smallest and least populous state?
3. What is the only island state in Australia?
4. What is a station?
5. What are the leading products of Queensland?
* What is happening to the Great Barrier Reef that should concern every Australian?

States of the Western Plateau

The western two-thirds of Australia is the dry, flat **Western Plateau**. Most of this region is desert or semiarid grassland. The only relief is provided by a few scattered mountain ranges. Two states, South Australia and Western Australia, and the Northern Territory were carved out of this plateau.

South Australia

The south-central state of South Australia, colonized in 1836, was the only state not settled by convicts. It is shaped like a keystone

LET'S GO EXPLORING

Land Use of Australia and New Zealand

1. What type of farming occurs in the tropics?
2. What is the most widespread type of land use in Australia and New Zealand?
3. What is the main commercial grain grown in Australia?
4. What two types of farming appear to be common in the Murray River basin?
* Compare this map with the map on page 543 and find the geographic names of the four main primitive hunting grounds (of the Aboriginals).

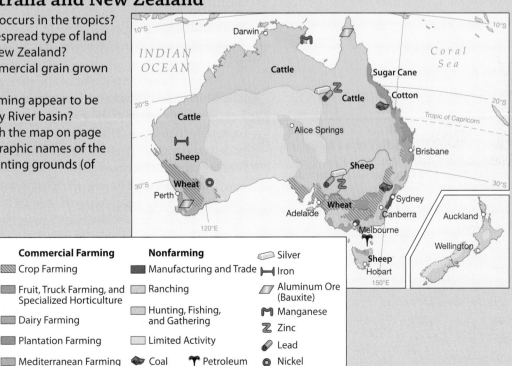

Australia's Transcontinental Railroads

Early in the twentieth century, Australians envisioned a railroad that would stretch across the continent from Adelaide in the south to Darwin in the north. The first portion was completed in 1927, but it stopped in Alice Springs, almost in the middle of the continent. It took about three-quarters of a century, but the rest of the transcontinental railroad was finally completed. The inaugural trip was made in January 2004. The railroad is one of the longest north-south lines in the world. The trip

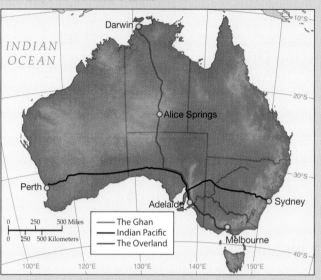

takes about 47 hours, but it facilitates getting goods from South Australia to ports in the Northern Territory and from there to the Asian markets. It also speeds Asian imports from those ports to the consumers in South Australia.

Australia also has a second transcontinental railroad that runs from Adelaide to Perth across the Nullarbor Plain. Completed in 1970, it includes the longest stretch of straight track in the world.

along the waters of the **Great Australian Bight**. The state is divided into two distinct geographic regions: the populous coast and the arid interior.

The Mediterranean Coast—The coastal portion of South Australia supports 98 percent of the state's population. Much of the coast enjoys an excellent climate similar to that of the Mediterranean. Cold Antarctic currents in the Great Australian Bight keep the land dry in the summer, but steady rains fall in the winter.

Adelaide (AD el ayd), the capital, has an ideal harbor protected by Kangaroo Island from the violent willy-willies (windstorms) that blow on the Great Australian Bight. The city, which is laid out with wide streets and many parks, boasts a warm climate and a relaxed atmosphere.

East of Adelaide is some of the nation's most productive land. The Murray River system drains into this part of the state and empties into the Great Australian Bight. The lush Barossa (buh ROH suh) Valley, thirty miles northeast of Adelaide, is known for its wine. The valley was originally settled by Lutheran immigrants from Germany seeking religious freedom.

The Outback—The sparsely populated areas beyond the coastal cities of Australia are collectively known as the **outback**. Life is hard and lonely for the stockmen and miners who live there. They tell many tall tales about the "blowies" (flies), sandstorms, and other common features of the outback. Although every state on the continent includes part of the outback, South Australia is known as "the gateway to the outback."

Mining and ranching have been two traditional industries of the outback. South Australia's outback is especially famous for its mineral wealth. The discovery of opals in 1915 attracted thousands to Coober Pedy ("hole in the ground"), from which most of the world's opals come. The first "diggers" not only dug holes in search of riches but

Australian English

Although Australia is thoroughly English in its customs and lifestyle, Australians have developed their own colorful dialect. The typical greeting is "G'day" (Good day). When meeting a friend, you say, "G'day, mate." Here are a few of the many other distinctly Australian words and expressions.

- barbie—barbecue grill
- billy—pan
- billabong—water hole
- up a gum tree—in trouble
- willy-willy—windstorm
- humpty do—all mixed up
- take a squiz—look over
- get all wet—get angry
- oscar—money

also made their homes in the ground to escape the intense heat. Even with the invention of air conditioning, many residents still prefer to live underground. Recent discoveries of vast deposits of shale oil in Southern Australia have the potential to add a third industry and make Australia an energy independent country.

Western Australia

Western Australia is Australia's largest but most sparsely populated state. Three-fourths of the people live in the southwest corner, where good land and tall evergreen forests abound. Blessed with a mild mediterranean climate, this region has beautiful wild flowers, many of which are unique to Australia. In the spring, tourists and residents flock to the countryside to view fields ablaze with color.

Perth—The capital of Western Australia is **Perth**, which is home to more than half of the state's population. With its ideal climate, Perth is often compared to cities in Southern California. Residents enjoy swimming at sandy beaches and boating on the Swan River. West of the business section is King's Park, the pride of Perth. It includes one thousand acres of natural bush vegetation. Driving through the park provides a spectacular view of the city, with the Indian Ocean to one's back and the Darling Range ahead in the distance.

The Inhospitable Interior—The dry and inhospitable climate did little to attract early settlers to the treeless interior of Western Australia. The discovery of gold in the late nineteenth century, however, changed everything. Gold mining camps sprang up east of Perth around the town of Kalgoorlie (kal GOOR lee), along the famed "Golden Mile." Veins of rich ore were mined to a depth of four thousand feet. As the gold began running out, nickel became the major source of revenue. Bauxite is also mined in the Darling Range.

One of the richest iron ore reserves in the world was discovered in the **Hamersley Range**. Towns, mining facilities, and railroads were built to exploit these resources. The ore is moved by rail to Port Hedland on the coast. Port Hedland ships more tons of freight than any other port in Australia, except Sydney.

The central part of Western Australia is covered with deserts. The Great Victoria Desert, the Gibson Desert, and the Great Sandy Desert combine to make up the second-largest desert area in the world. The deserts gradually give way to grasslands in the northern tropics and in the south near Perth. Large cattle and sheep stations are common in those areas.

Northern Territory

The Northern Territory is located at the heart of the desolate outback. Outside the capital of Darwin, the average population density is only one person for every five square miles of land. This territory, nearly the size of Alaska, is administered by the federal government.

The Tropical Coast—Most of the Northern Territory is located in the tropics. Tropical rain forests abound along the northern coast,

A Coober Pedy underground restaurant

Perth is Western Australia's population center, with more than half of the state's residents living there.

Uluru—Ayers Rock

The monotony of the outback is broken by the majestic **Ayers Rock**, the world's largest monolith, or free-standing rock. Jokingly referred to as the largest pebble in the world, it rises 1,142 feet above the surrounding desert. The rock forms an oval that is one and a half miles wide and four miles long. The monolith, composed of a kind of rock called conglomerate, changes color throughout the day. The early morning sun makes it look orange to deep red; it changes to violet and blue later in the day, and then back to red at dusk.

Erosion has cut deep gullies and basins in the rock that run from the top to the bottom. Rare desert rains create raging falls. The base of the rock is pocked with shallow caves that

contain many Aboriginal paintings of scenes from Dreamtime. Aboriginals consider this great rock sacred. They call it *Uluru*.

> ### Find It!
> **Ayers Rock**
> 25.353°S, 131.034°E

Aboriginal boys are taught to be skilled hunters and fishermen.

An example of Aboriginal art near the city of Darwin

gradually becoming grasslands and then desert farther inland. Trade winds bring heavy rains to the coast in the summer season, called "The Wet," but dry monsoon winds blow from the interior desert in the winter. Cyclones are common.

Nearly half the territory's population lives in Darwin, on the coast. Tourists fly to Darwin as the starting point for tours into the interior. Darwin is the only Australian city ever attacked by foreigners. During World War II, Japanese bombers based in New Guinea attacked the city.

The Interior—A major industry in the outback is mining. Scattered mountain ranges hold considerable mineral wealth, including gold, manganese, and iron ore. The world's greatest deposit of bauxite was discovered on Arnhem Land. Australia also has the largest known reserves of uranium.

The second major industry is cattle ranching. One cattle ranch covers six thousand square miles—an area larger than the state of Connecticut. Families in the outback sometimes live fifty miles from the nearest town and fifteen miles from their nearest neighbor. Obtaining medical care is difficult. To help solve this problem, doctors make "house calls" by plane, and children attend school over the Internet. The Royal Flying Doctor's Service and the School of the Air operate out of the central town of Alice Springs (often called "The Alice"), providing services to remote stations throughout the territory.

In the southeast corner of the Northern Territory lies the **Simpson Desert**, sometimes called the Red Center of Australia. No one, not even the hardiest stockman, lives there. Red sand is piled into dunes that can rise as high as 100 feet and stretch for up to 180 miles. The red color comes from rusted iron in the sand.

The Aboriginal Peoples—When the first British settlers landed in Australia in 1788, about five hundred tribes of dark-skinned people were scattered throughout the continent and nearby islands. These **Aboriginal peoples** (ab ohr IJ uh nuhl) may have migrated from Asia. (The term *aboriginal* refers to the earliest known settlers of a region. It comes from a Latin word meaning "origin" or "original.")

Although they spoke more than three hundred languages and lived in both the rain forests and the desert, the Aboriginal peoples shared the same basic culture. Each tribe was nomadic, frequently moving in search of food. Their only domestic animal was the dingo, a type of dog, and their weapons were the spear and the boomerang. One of the common foods in the bush was a fat, white grub that the Aboriginals ate raw.

Like the American Indians, the Aboriginal peoples developed a detailed knowledge of plants, animals, and natural cycles. They used this knowledge to survive in the harsh regions of Australia.

Aboriginals believed that spiritual beings created the world in a mythical era they called the "Dreamtime." These beings became a part of nature and mankind. The Aboriginal religion guided every aspect of the peoples' lives, including when they moved and where they camped. Their famous bark paintings depict scenes from their myths.

As the colonists' need for land grew, they drove the Aboriginal peoples away from the fertile river valleys and into the barren backcountry. Some were killed, and many others died as a result of diseases introduced by the European settlers. In time, many of the colonists considered the Aboriginal peoples to be a passing race, to be left alone to die out on reservations. Christian missionaries, however, had compassion and worked with the Aboriginal peoples while sharing the gospel with them.

As of 2006 there were 517,200 Aboriginal peoples living in Australia, approximately 2.3 percent of the Australian population. In the 1960s, Australian leaders responded to the Aboriginal peoples' call for civil rights and a return of ancestral land. They gave the Aboriginal peoples control of large tracts of land in northern and central Australia. The government has kept control of all mineral rights, however, even within the Aboriginal reservations.

The land-use map on page 553 shows where a few Aboriginal people continue to live as hunters and gatherers, like their ancestors. Only a few thousand of them maintain that lifestyle, however. Most Aboriginal people work on the large sheep and cattle stations in the outback of Australia's five mainland states and have adopted Western ways.

Australia is a secular state that guarantees its people religious freedom. Sixty-nine percent of the people affiliate with some form of Christianity, 23 percent are nonreligious, 2.6 percent are Buddhist, and 2.5 percent are Muslim. Evangelical Christians make up 14 percent of the Australian people, but they are struggling to remain a godly influence as the Australian society becomes post-Christian and multicultural. As of 2010, there were over 3,700 Australian missionaries serving in other countries. However, the number of missionaries has been declining since 2000.

The Aborigines are experts at throwing many kinds of boomerangs, each for a different specific purpose.

A boomerang must be thrown in just the right way to be effective, as this boomerang master demonstrates.

Dreamtime and Twinkling Stars

The Maung Aboriginal people tell a story about a group of women who went out one night in search of yams. Some were able to find yams, but others could not find any and were ashamed. The women returned to their camp, and those who had found yams began to cook them. However, the women who could not find any yams decided to live in the sky. When they began to rise, the other women joined them, and they all became stars. The Aboriginal people believe that if you look in the sky on a clear night you will see these women who turned into stars. The women who could not find any yams became dim stars, while those who found yams twinkle because they are eating their yams.

Missions: Australia

Tracy and Debbi Minnick, Cardwell, Queensland, Australia

Many Americans and Australians share a common British heritage, and they speak the same language (though with different dialects). One might think there is little cross cultural about missions work in Australia. But Australians have developed their own distinctive culture. This goes beyond learning that you need to visit the chemist rather than the drug store if you're sick and that a powerpoint is an electrical socket rather than a slide show. One difference is the Australian response to what they call the tall poppies. A tall poppy is someone who has more success than others and acts as though he might be better than others. Understanding this is very important when sharing the gospel. If an Australian thinks that you are condescending to him, he will resist the message of the gospel and seek to re-establish himself as your peer. Arguing over apologetics or attempting to out-talk the person will do more harm than good. A faithful friend who is concerned to serve him with God's truth goes a long way, however.

Section Quiz

1. Why do so few people live on the Western Plateau?
2. What type of climate is common on the coast of South Australia?
3. What are the two main industries in the outback?
4. What important product is mined in the Hamersley Range?
5. Who were the native people of Australia?
* What biblical commands did the colonists violate by their mistreatment of the Aboriginal peoples?

II. New Zealand

New Zealand is a beautiful island country isolated from the rest of the world. Its nearest neighbor, Australia, is twelve hundred miles to the west, across the stormy Tasman Sea. New Zealand has many similarities to Australia, including a British heritage and a similar history. However, New Zealand lacks the land area (it is about the size of Colorado) and mineral wealth of its continental neighbor. For its economic survival, New Zealand relies almost solely on agricultural exports. Meat, wool, and dairy products account for nearly half of what it sells abroad. New Zealand is one of the world's largest exporters of butter, cheese, and cross-bred wool.

New Zealand enjoys a marine-west-coast climate similar to that of Tasmania. Prevailing winds blow off the Tasman Sea, bringing warm, moist air that showers the islands 150 days of the year. Because clouds are so common, the native islanders called their home *Aotearoa* (ah oh tay ah ROH ah), or "land of the long white cloud."

Like Australia, New Zealand has unusual flora and fauna. Its variety of trees is especially noteworthy. More than 112 species live in the broadleaf evergreen forests that cover one-fourth of the country. The unique kauri (KOW ree) is New Zealand's largest tree. European shipbuilders once cut them down to make masts for their ships. Up to 90 percent of these trees were cut down before concerned New Zealanders pressured the government to protect the surviving forests.

New Zealand has some unusual native animals too, most of them birds. Several flightless birds once thrived on the island. Monster birds, called moa, sometimes grew to twelve feet in height, and are believed to have weighed up to five hundred pounds. Their kick

A kauri tree is believed to grow for one thousand years before reaching its full height.

could kill a man, but they were hunted to extinction. The smaller kiwi is New Zealand's national bird. About the size of a chicken, the kiwi has no wings, an extremely long beak, and feathers that look like hair. New Zealanders are nicknamed "kiwis."

Historical Background

The First Known Inhabitants

The **Maori** (MOW ree), a brown-skinned people from the islands of Polynesia north of New Zealand, were the first known humans to discover the islands. They arrived on magnificent warships made of hollowed logs. At first, they lived by hunting and fishing. After the "moa hunters" hunted the moas to extinction, they cleared forests and planted crops. They also became skilled woodcarvers using stone tools.

Frequent wars and superstitious rituals were central to Maori life. It was not uncommon for them to eat their defeated foes. The Maori proved to be a difficult challenge for Abel Tasman, who discovered the islands in 1642 while searching for a fabled continent south of Australia. When Tasman attempted to land, the Maori killed several of his men. Tasman did not try to land again. In 1769, Captain James Cook landed and established relations with the Maori. He succeeded in mapping the coasts of the two main islands.

British Settlers

The first European settlers on the islands were escaped convicts from Australia and deserters from British ships. Whalers and seal hunters also built small stations along the coast to resupply their ships. Christian missionaries soon followed. English traders gave rum and guns to the Maori in return for flax, a strong fiber used for ropes. The introduction of guns led to bloody fighting among Maori tribes and between the Maori and the whites. The settlers unknowingly also introduced diseases to which the Maori had no immunity, greatly reducing the Maori population.

In response to the growing violence, British settlers asked England to annex New Zealand and bring the law and order it needed so badly. On February 6, 1840, a group of Maori chiefs signed the Treaty of Waitangi in which they recognized the British monarch as their sovereign. In return, the Maori received full property rights over their land. They also agreed to sell land only to the British crown. New Zealanders celebrate the signing of the treaty each year in a holiday called National Day.

Tensions remained high on the North Island, where most of the Maori people lived. Complicating the situation, shiploads of settlers arrived and made illegal land purchases. In 1845, opposition to land sales resulted in a Maori uprising. This marked the start of the Land Wars. Much like the outnumbered American Indians, the Maori put up a stiff, though futile, resistance. When war ended in 1872, Maori power was broken, and the government seized the land.

After the Maori wars, the British colony grew rapidly. England gave it a large loan to attract one hundred thousand new settlers. The loan was also used to improve the transportation and communication systems. In 1872, the development of refrigerator ships enabled New Zealand to begin shipping meat to Europe. New Zealand has become one of the world's leading exporters of mutton. At New

An artist's reconstruction of an extinct moa bird (based on feathers and a skeleton)

The kiwi is a flightless nocturnal bird that burrows in the ground and sniffs out its food with nostrils on the end of its beak. These endangered birds mate for life and live as long as thirty years.

Maori Funerals

The Maori believe it is important to spend time with the body of a loved one after death. They take the body to the *marae* (mah-rye), a sacred area in the village, and watch over their loved one. They often leave the coffin open so family members can touch the body as they mourn. During the funeral, those making speeches talk directly to the body because the Maori believe the spirit does not leave the body until the burial. After the funeral service, the body is either buried in a nearby graveyard or cremated.

Family Life in New Zealand

As in many other societies, the image of a typical family is changing in New Zealand. While the traditional nuclear family is still important, more and more families are single-parent families. Divorce and remarriage are increasing, and many couples are opting not to have children. Those who do have children are often choosing to have fewer children, and one-child families are becoming predominant.

Zealand's request, Great Britain granted the colony dominion status in 1907.

The Government Today

The government of New Zealand is similar to those of other independent nations that make up the British Commonwealth. The British crown is represented by a governor-general. The legislative authority is the parliament. New Zealand's parliament consists of one chamber called the House of Representatives. Every three years, members are elected to represent ninety-one general districts and four Maori districts.

New Zealand has a long history of government programs. In 1890, the Liberal Party began implementing a welfare system. In 1893, it became the first country to give women the right to vote. New Zealand's benevolent socialism resembled its counterparts in Europe. But by the 1980s, it became obvious that the cost of welfare benefits was stifling initiative and driving businesses out of the country, so in 1985 the government began dismantling the socialist system, giving New Zealand one of the freest economies in the world. This has resulted in great economic improvements, increased productivity, and vastly improved efficiency in airports and shipping docks.

Geographic Divisions

North Island

New Zealand has two main islands and many smaller islands. **North Island** is slightly smaller than South Island, but it is home to twice as many people.

The Northern Peninsula—New Zealand is known for its scenic beauty and huge sheep stations. In 2010, 86 percent of the people in New Zealand lived in cities. **Auckland**, New Zealand's largest city and chief seaport, has nearly 1.4 million people. It is located on a beautiful harbor on the northern peninsula. In addition to shipping much of the region's dairy, sheep, and timber products, this colorful city is also the country's chief industrial center. Because it has an international airport, Auckland is the point of entry and departure for New Zealand's many visitors.

In recent years, thousands of Pacific Islanders have come to Auckland seeking a better life. The city now has the largest population of Polynesians in the world. Many of the country's Maori also live in the city and the surrounding region. The Maori population of New Zealand is relatively small (7.4 percent of the total population), but they have a powerful voice in the government. The Maori people believe that their rights, established by the Treaty of Waitangi, have been violated. Some leaders are demanding compensation and a return of all government lands.

The Geothermal Center—New Zealand is on the Pacific "ring of fire," the area of greatest volcanic activity in the Pacific. The center of North Island is a volcanic plateau with some still-active volcanic peaks. Near the town of Rotorua (roh tuh ROO uh) are hot springs, boiling mud pools, and spouting geysers. Two geysers, Pohutu and

Auckland's harbor and center city skyline show its beauty and modernity.

the Prince of Wales Feathers, spray hot water as high as one hundred feet into the air. A large geothermal plant nearby uses underground steam to generate electricity.

Lake Taupo (taw POH), New Zealand's largest lake, is located just south of Rotorua, near the very center of the island. It fills the crater of a dormant volcano. In fact, it is one of the largest volcanic lakes in the world. Fishermen from around the world come to fish for the large trout found there.

The Southern Hills—A series of low, rugged hills and mountains forms a V on the south and east parts of the island. On the slopes, sheep and beef cattle graze. As a result, New Zealanders are among the top consumers of red meat per person in the world.

Fruit and vegetables are grown on the coastal lowlands in the east. New Zealand is one of the world's leading producers of kiwifruit, a brown, fuzzy, egg-shaped fruit that has an emerald-green interior.

On the southern tip of the North Island is the city of Wellington, the capital and second-largest city in New Zealand. (The capital was moved from Auckland to the more centrally located Wellington in 1865.) Wellington is the southernmost national capital in the world. Its main office building, shaped in a series of stacked circles, is appropriately called the Beehive. Wellington has one of the deepest natural harbors in the world. Miles of docks receive oceangoing vessels from around the world. Ferries and hydrofoils transport people from the capital across the narrow **Cook Strait** to South Island.

Lake Taupo is ringed by volcanic mountains.

The kiwifruit contains many vitamins and minerals but is especially rich in vitamin C—a small kiwifruit has as much as a large orange.

This building, called "the Beehive," is part of the parliamentary complex of buildings that houses the New Zealand government in Wellington.

What Is in a Name?

The fruit we call kiwifruit is native to southern China and was brought to New Zealand during the early 20th century. Initially, this fruit was called *yáng táo*, but that name was soon changed to *Chinese Gooseberry*. After World War II, someone suggested changing the name to kiwifruit after New Zealand's national symbol, the kiwi bird.

South Island

South Island is known for its country atmosphere and relaxed pace. Because few Maori ever settled on this island, white settlers established a distinctly European lifestyle. The rugged west side of the island contrasts sharply with the plains on the east, where most people live.

The Southern Alps—The Southern Alps, a three-hundred-mile-long mountain chain, dominate the west coast. The magnificent alpine scenery includes snowfields, crevasses, and glaciers. Near the

Mount Cook on South Island is New Zealand's tallest peak.

center of the chain is snowcapped **Mount Cook**, New Zealand's highest mountain, rising 12,316 feet above sea level. Running westward to the sea are the Fox and Frans Josef glaciers. On the eastern slope is the great Tasman Glacier. Airplanes drop skiers at the heads of these glaciers, and the skiers can ski uninterrupted for stretches as long as sixteen miles. Farther south, glaciers carved a series of long valleys into the sea. These fjords create a jagged coastline similar to that of Norway. A highlight of the region is Sutherland Falls, where the water drops over nineteen hundred feet.

Rainfall is heaviest on the west slope of the mountains, averaging three hundred inches per year. The many swift rivers supply much of the country's energy needs at little cost. An underground sea cable carries surplus electricity from the South Island to the populous and industrial North Island.

The Canterbury Plains—East of the Southern Alps are the Canterbury Plains, which are dry because the prevailing westerly winds drop their moisture on the mountains before they reach the plains. Most of New Zealand's cereal grains—such as barley, wheat, and oats—are raised on these flat, fertile plains. Farther south, livestock graze on the plains and rolling hills.

About seven miles from the coast is Christchurch, the largest city on the South Island. Hydroelectric power has turned Christchurch into a major industrial center. Tourists who visit the Southern Alps come first to Christchurch. Named for a college in Oxford, England, Christchurch is well known for its parks, gardens, and British architecture. It is the most "English" of New Zealand's cities.

New Zealand has no established church and grants religious freedom to its citizens. Fifty-three percent of the people identify with some form of Christianity, and 41 percent have no religious affiliation. Evangelical Christians make up 18 percent of the population although Christianity's current growth is only half a percent each year. Despite this lack of numerical growth, congregations in New Zealand continue to send out missionaries (1,250 in 2010 to 150 countries). In addition, church leaders have set a goal of sending one missionary for every one thousand committed believers. This would result in three thousand missionaries from New Zealand.

Section Quiz

1. Why is New Zealand called "the land of the long white cloud"?
2. Who were the first known people to live in New Zealand?
3. What are the two main islands of New Zealand?
4. What is New Zealand's largest city?
5. What are the two main geographic regions of South Island?
* Why do you think New Zealanders opposed continued harvesting of the kauri trees?

Chapter Review

22

Making Connections

1–6. What are six features that distinguish Australia?

7. How did New South Wales become the "Mother of States" in Australia?

8. How do students who live in isolated regions of Australia receive an education?

9. How did the Aboriginal peoples respond to European settlement?

10. Who were the first known inhabitants of New Zealand? How did they respond to European settlement?

11. What fuzzy fruit is grown in New Zealand? What was one of its earlier names?

12. Contrast the state of Christianity in Australia and New Zealand.

Developing Geography Skills

1. What are three major geographic features of Australia? Locate them on the map on page 543.

2. Based on the number of cities shown on the map on page 543, what area of Australia is most densely populated? What makes this area able to sustain the large population?

Thinking Critically

1. How has Australia's location as "the Land Down Under" affected its history and economy?

2. Is it possible for recreation and sports to glorify God? Why or why not?

Living in God's World

1. What challenges do Christians face in an increasingly secular society? How can Christians rise to meet such challenges?

2. Imagine you are going to Australia as a missionary. What aspects of American culture might you need to adjust in your life to be an effective minister of Christ?

People, Places, and Things to Know

Oceania
wattles
Great Dividing Range
Captain James Cook
Botany Bay
Mount Kosciuszko
jumbucks
Canberra
Sydney
Melbourne
lignite
Central Lowlands
Lake Eyre
Murray River
Tasmania
Great Barrier Reef
artesian wells
aquifer
Brisbane
stations
Western Plateau
Great Australian Bight
Adelaide
outback
Perth
Hamersley Range
Ayers Rock
Simpson Desert
Aboriginal peoples
Maori
North Island
Auckland
Cook Strait
South Island
Mount Cook

OCEANIA: THE PACIFIC ISLANDS

I. Melanesia

  A. Papua New Guinea
  B. Solomon Islands
  C. Vanuatu
  D. Fiji
  E. New Caledonia

II. Micronesia

  A. Caroline Islands
  B. Mariana Islands
  C. Other Micronesian Islands

III. Polynesia

  A. Tuvalu
  B. Samoan Islands
  C. French Polynesia
  D. Other Polynesian Islands

$\mathcal{A}$lthough the Pacific Ocean (approx. 64 million square miles in area) is larger than all seven continents combined (approx. 57.4 million square miles in area), the twenty-five thousand islands that are scattered across its vast expanse have less combined land area than the state of Alaska.

The first Europeans to visit the islands sent home vivid descriptions of a paradise on earth, with warm breezes, sandy beaches, friendly natives, and abundant tropical fruits. Because most of the islands lie in the humid tropics, temperatures average a balmy 80°F.

Early reports of paradise were misleading, however. Islanders faced the threat of typhoons, volcanic eruptions, and earthquakes. Disease, superstition, and tribal warfare only made matters worse.

In the past two hundred years, the islanders have been thrust into the difficult process of **acculturation**—the exposure of one group of people to the values and lifestyles of a foreign group of people and their adoption of those ways as their own. Many people on those islands still eke out a living in small villages of thatched houses. Most islands lack

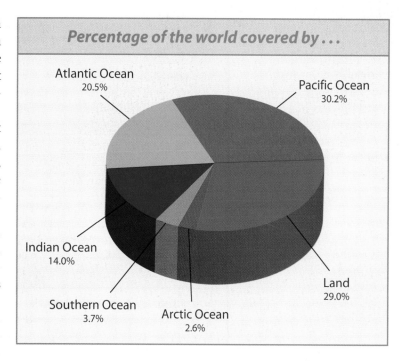

Percentage of the world covered by . . .

Atlantic Ocean 20.5%
Pacific Ocean 30.2%
Indian Ocean 14.0%
Southern Ocean 3.7%
Arctic Ocean 2.6%
Land 29.0%

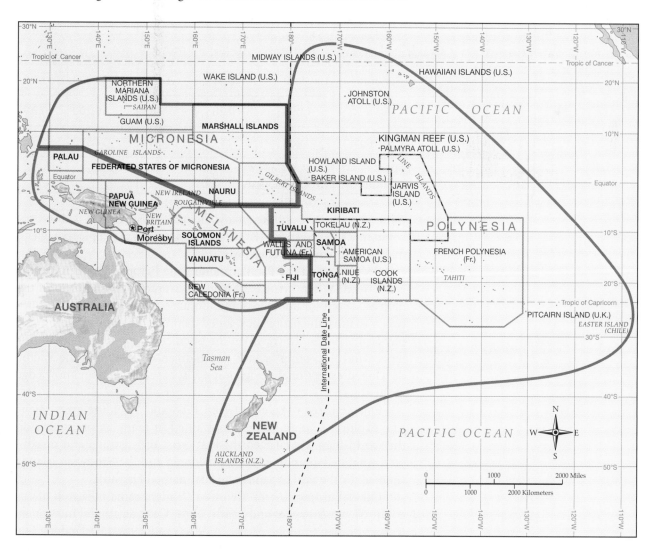

Pacific Island Fast Facts						
Country	Capital	Area (sq. mi.)	Pop. (2013 est.) (M)	Pop. Density (per sq. mi.)	Per Capita GDP ($US)	Life Span
Melanesia						
Fiji	Suva	7,055	0.90	128	$4,800	71.9
Papua New Guinea	Port Moresby	178,703	6.43	36	$2,700	66.7
Solomon Islands	Honiara	11,157	0.60	54	$3,400	74.7
Vanuatu	Port-Vila	4,706	0.26	55	$4,900	72.4
Micronesia						
Palau	Ngerulmud	177	0.02	119	$10,500	72.3
Kiribati	Bairiki	313	0.10	319	$5,900	65.1
Marshall Islands	Majuro	70	0.07	1000	$3,200	72.3
Federated States of Micronesia	Palikir	271	0.11	406	$3,000	72.1
Nauru	Yaren (District)	8.11	0.01	1,110	$5,000	66.0
Polynesia						
Tuvalu	Funafuti	10	0.01	1,100	$3,300	65.5
Samoa	Apia	1,093	0.20	183	$6,200	72.9
Tonga	Nuku'alofa	288	0.11	382	$7,500	75.6
French Polynesia	Papeete (on Tahiti)	1,609	0.20	124	$22,000	76.6

mineral resources, and for many, the only major export is dried coconut meat, called **copra** (KOH prah). Many of the people struggle to make a living in the modern world.

People settled the Pacific islands long before European explorers arrived. When one island became overcrowded, a group of the natives set out for another island. Because of the great distances between islands, the people developed distinct cultures, languages, and physical features. To travel on the open seas across these great distances and find other islands, the indigenous people of the Pacific developed exceptional navigation skills, based in part on knowledge of the stars.

During three voyages between 1768 and 1779, the great scientific explorer Captain James Cook filled in many empty spaces on the world map. He charted the east coast of Australia and discovered what he later named New Caledonia and the Sandwich Islands (named for the Earl of Sandwich; later named Hawaii).

Other Europeans soon followed. Traders came in search of coconut oil, sandalwood, and pearls. Next, Congregational missionaries and Roman Catholic priests came to evangelize the islanders. The missionaries provided medicine and education, and they encouraged the islanders to adopt Western dress and social norms. Although many islanders still worship their ancestors and believe in animism, the professed religion on most of the islands is Christianity.

With the rise of colonialism in the nineteenth century, foreign powers competed for control of the islands. During the 1930s, imperial Japan extended its control over many of the Pacific islands. American Marines later fought some of their bloodiest battles as they struggled to free the islands from Japanese control.

After World War II, the United Nations divided the islands among the Allied countries. They wanted to help the islands recover from their losses and develop stable governments. Most of the islands have since gained independence, although a few prefer to remain territories. For example, Guam, Wake Island, and the Midway Islands belong to the United States; New Caledonia and Wallis and Futuna belong to France; Niue and the Cook Islands belong to New Zealand; Easter Island belongs to Chile; and Pitcairn Island belongs to Great Britain.

Most of the thousands of islands of the Pacific Rim are very small. They can be divided into three broad groups: Melanesia, Micronesia, and Polynesia. We will study a few islands from each of these divisions.

I. Melanesia

Melanesia (mehl uh NEE zhah) is located south of the equator, near Indonesia and Australia. The French explorer Dumont d'Urville named the region *Melanesia*, the "Black Islands," in 1831 because he was struck by the dark appearance of the land rising from the green sea. A variety of short, black-skinned peoples settled Melanesia long ago. More than twelve hundred different tribes developed, each with its own language and rituals.

Skirmishes between rival tribes were once a normal part of life. A "big man" rose to power within a tribe based on his prowess in battle. Headhunting and cannibalism (the eating of human flesh) were common practices.

The Torres Strait and the Coral Sea separate Melanesia from the rest of Australia's continental plate. Like the continent, these *continental islands* have a rich variety of soils, rocks, and resources. Heavy rains produce vast tropical forests. Yams and sweet potatoes grow well in the acidic soil. **Taro** (TAH roh), a potato-like root, is a favorite food.

Melanesia was the last of all the Pacific regions to be visited by Europeans. Treacherous reefs and tricky currents fill the shallow waters near the shores. Good harbors are scarce. The first missionaries did not arrive until the 1830s at Fiji (FEE jee). Even then, few missionaries attempted to reach the rugged interior.

Papua New Guinea

Two countries occupy **New Guinea** (GIH nee), the second-largest island in the world. The western half is Irian Jaya, a province of Indonesia. The eastern half is part of Papua (POP oo uh) New Guinea (PNG), a young country that gained independence from

Ferdinand Magellan and the Pacific Islands

During his voyage around the world in 1519–21, Ferdinand Magellan became the first European to chart the Pacific. After battling the stormy seas on the southern tip of South America, Magellan reached a calm ocean, which he called the Pacific ("peaceful"). However, for ninety-eight days his men sighted only two islands, both of which were uninhabitable. Provisions ran out, and the crew was forced to eat rats and leather. Finally, the starving men reached the tiny island of Guam in the Marianas, where they took on fresh supplies. During the next two centuries, few expeditions braved this forbidding "empty" quarter of the earth.

Although Ferdinand Magellan did not survive to complete his voyage, he is generally credited with being the first man to circumnavigate the earth, and he discovered several Pacific islands in the process.

Islanders cultivate taro plants, which are the source of a favorite food in the Pacific islands. Taro is made from the root portion (inset) of the taro plant.

Australia in 1975. Papua New Guinea has several other tropical islands, but 85 percent of its land area is on New Guinea. It is slightly larger than California.

The people of PNG enjoy freedom of religion, and 96 percent affiliate with some form of Christianity. Even though only 3.5 percent identify with animism, the true influence of this ethnic religion is much greater in this country. Evangelical Christians make up nearly 26 percent of the population and are increasing by about 3 percent each year. While many of the Christians in PNG are poor, the congregations often have a strong outreach ministry.

Rugged Terrain

The most prominent geographical feature of New Guinea is the rugged mountain system that extends the length of the island and continues into the ocean. Although New Guinea is a tropical island, a few mountains, such as the 14,793-foot Wilhelm Mountain, remain cold year-round. Steep valleys lie between the mountain ranges. Numerous large, raging rivers flow through these ranges to the ocean.

The Papuan Mountains are scenic but very rugged.

New Guinea is a land of forbidding swamps and thick jungles. Tropical rain forests cover about 75 percent of Papua New Guinea; swamps occupy much of the narrow coastland. The seven-hundred-mile Fly River—the second longest river in Papua New Guinea—flows south through a vast swamp, which is the only major flatland on the island.

Papua New Guinea has several offshore islands. The largest is the Bismarck Archipelago, named after the nineteenth-century chancellor of Germany. New Britain, the largest island, is the most developed area in the country. The former provincial capital, Rabaul, is the

Wildlife of New Guinea

A variety of animals flourish in the isolation of New Guinea. As in Australia, the forests host many kinds of kangaroos and other marsupials. The swamps have both salt- and freshwater crocodiles, one species of which climbs trees! The Queen Alexandria butterfly is the largest butterfly in the world—as large as a small bird. The island's most famous faunas are its 660 species of birds—more than can be found on the entire continent of North America.

Saltwater crocodiles are abundant in Papua New Guinea, especially in the Sepik River area.

This eruption of a volcano near Rabaul, Papua New Guinea, nearly destroyed that city.

nation's export center. Tragically, nearby volcanoes destroyed most of the city, including the airport, in 1994. Following this eruption, the provincial capital was relocated to nearby Kokopo, and a new airport was built in Tokua.

Coastal Settlement

More people live in Papua New Guinea than in all the other Pacific islands combined. Many hundreds of tribes coexist, each speaking its own language. (These represent about 12 percent of the world's languages.) Papua New Guinea has three official languages: English (although few people speak it), a creole language called Tok Pisin (tahk PIH-sin), which most people speak, and Hiri Motu (HIH-ree MOH-too), which is spoken mainly in the southern region near the capital. The tribes are divided into two main culture groups: the lowlanders on the coast and the highlanders in the interior.

The Dutch claimed the western half of New Guinea in 1828, and Great Britain claimed the southeast in 1846. But no settlers came. Interest in settlement changed when imperialist Germany laid claim to the northeast coast of New Guinea and its nearby islands in 1884. The Germans established a post at the mouth of the great Sepik River in the north. But malaria-bearing mosquitos made life difficult on the German plantations. After Germany lost World War I, their lands came under Australian supervision.

The first British settlers came in 1874 after Captain Moresby discovered a deep harbor on the south coast of New Guinea. The settlers were Protestant missionaries who ministered to the local Motu people. Port Moresby is now the capital of Papua New Guinea, with modern buildings and paved roads.

The Baliem Valley

For decades, European explorers attempted to reach the interior of New Guinea, but difficult mountain ranges, torrential rains,

Indigenous people of Papua New Guinea take pride in their respective tribes' elaborate facial paintings.

WORLD RELIGIONS

World Religions: Cargo Cults

When Melanesians first faced Western culture, many of them were fascinated by its great variety of riches. They desired the goods that began to arrive by ship on their islands, but they had no idea how the goods were made or where they came from. They concluded that the goods or cargoes came from the spirit world. Late in the nineteenth century, their prophets promised a new age of plenty when tribal deities, ancient heroes, or dead ancestors would return with cargo for the Melanesians. Some leaders moved their tribes to the coasts where they built crude docks and outposts (and later airstrips) to prepare for the event. They built rows of warehouses to store the hoped-for goods. The tribes often imitated government flag-raising ceremonies and the like, hoping that such magic rites would hasten the arrival of the cargo.

These **cargo cults** also arose as a revolt against white colonial rule. Melanesians were often mistreated as slaves on plantations and in mines, and they never received the freedom and wealth that Europeans had. So the cult settlements refused to pay taxes, would not allow visitors, and would not work unless they were paid exorbitant wages. They abandoned their traditional wealth—gardens, pigs, and money—which they would not need in the age of plenty. These islanders expected their strange worship to bring justice, freedom, and plenty of eating, dancing, and kava (a narcotic beverage) drinking. However, because the cults threatened the European-based economy and government, their leaders were arrested. Most of the seventy or so cargo cults eventually dissolved.

While members of the cargo cults initially rejected the gospel, over time missionaries were able to win many of them to Christ. Their story should be a lesson to all who seek the empty treasures of this earth rather than the eternal treasures of heaven (1 Tim. 6:6–9).

and disease blocked their path. Most assumed that no peoples could survive in such an inhospitable land. Then, in 1930, a couple of gold prospectors from Australia stumbled upon a "lost civilization" of one million people. Hidden in the midst of the mountains of New Guinea was a great valley where Melanesian highlanders lived and fought. Because these people did not travel far from the safety of their own tribes, they thought that they were the only inhabitants on earth.

Almost all of the country's twelve thousand miles of roads are unpaved. Most travel is by plane or boat. Even today, few outsiders visit the remote villages. A new Highlands Highway connects some of the highland villages.

PNG's Economy

The heart of the economy is subsistence agriculture, the most common crops being taro and other root crops. Eighty-five percent of the labor force is engaged in agriculture, which accounts for about 25 percent of the GDP. The country is fifth in the world in production of both taro and other roots and tubers. Most land is owned by the whole clan; individuals do not buy or sell property. Coastal tribes grow two cash crops, cacao and copra. Plantations in the high altitudes grow coffee, the nation's most lucrative crop and one of its main exports. A significant portion of the population depends directly or indirectly on coffee income for living. Unfortunately, the shortage of fertile land (only 0.46 percent is arable) encourages fighting among the highlander tribes.

The nation is beginning to develop its natural resources. Large deposits of copper were first discovered in 1965. In 1991, the largest gold mine outside South Africa opened in Porgera. Recently, a mountain of copper was discovered at Ok Tedi near the head of Papua New Guinea's Fly River. Copper and gold account for nearly 75 percent of the nation's exports. The nation is also developing oil and natural gas deposits. Exxon Mobil has estimated that the country has at least 20 trillion cubic feet of natural gas reserves. In addition to refining oil, companies are planning to transport liquified natural gas from Papua New Guinea to Asian markets. The nation's major trading partners are Australia, Japan, China, and Singapore.

Chocolate is made from beans inside the cacao pods, which grow on trees.

Buying a Bride in Papua New Guinea

As in other cultures we have studied, a groom must pay a price for his bride in Papua New Guinea. This payment can be made in the form of kina shells (from a pearl oyster), pigs, cash attached to a pole, or flightless birds known as *cassowaries*. After the family examines the payment and accepts it, the marriage is complete. Even in the cities, these payments are common. The payments can also be very high, with the price consisting of dozens of pigs and thousands of kina shells. Then, if the marriage does not last, the entire bride price must be returned with interest.

Section Quiz

1. Define *acculturation*. Why has it been difficult for the Pacific islands?
2. What explorer first discovered Hawaii and many other Pacific islands?
3. What is the largest island in Melanesia?
4. What is Papua New Guinea's most profitable agricultural product?
* How would the large number of languages in Papua New Guinea impede the preaching of the gospel there? What can missionaries do to overcome this hindrance?

Solomon Islands

The Spanish explorer Alvaro de Mendaña first discovered these scattered islands in 1568. In anticipation of the riches he expected to find, he named the islands after the biblical King Solomon.

Europeans never found mineral riches, but they did discover plenty of dangers. Four active volcanoes belch smoke and fire, earthquakes pose a constant threat on the seven main islands, and the hot and humid climate breeds several deadly diseases, including malaria and tuberculosis.

Between 1870 and 1911, some planters used bribes or force to load their ships with Solomon Islanders to work on cotton and sugar plantations in Fiji and Queensland. To end these abuses and to protect the workers, Great Britain took control of the islands in 1893.

The Solomon Islands became independent in 1978, but the islanders have not yet developed a strong sense of national identity. Although English is the official language, native tribes speak over 70 indigenous languages.

These islands do not enjoy the same diversity of wildlife as New Guinea does. The only mammals native to the islands are some marsupials (kangaroos, wallabies, and wombats) and bats. Seabirds also thrive on the islands. The frigate bird, once considered sacred, is a national emblem.

The Solomon Islands are slightly smaller than Maryland. Forests cover more than 90 percent of the land, supplying valuable wood for logging industries. In contrast, less than 1 percent of the area is arable. Islanders clear land on a few narrow coastal areas and mountain valleys to raise copra and cacao. About 75 percent of the labor force is engaged in agriculture, which provides 54 percent of the GDP.

Guadalcanal (gwahd uhl kuh NAL) is the largest of the Solomon Islands. The capital city of Honiara is located on a deep port at the north end of Guadalcanal. Many tourists visit battlefields on the island, which was the site of one of the earliest U.S. offensives against Japanese forces in the Pacific in World War II.

Ethnic tensions that developed between the peoples of Guadalcanal and immigrants from Malaita became violent in 1998, and a civil war occurred between 1998 and 2003. The fighting ended when Australian forces intervened and disarmed the militias. Political instability remains a problem in the Solomon Islands as does corruption.

The people of the Solomon Islands have freedom of religion, with a strong Christian influence resulting from revivals in 1935, 1970, and 1982. Ninety-six percent of the people affiliate with some form of Christianity, and Evangelical Christians make up 33 percent of the population. During and following the civil war, congregations used their influence to seek the cessation of fighting, and Christian leaders have counseled thousands who were affected by the violence. Church leaders also convinced the government to form the Truth and Reconciliation Commission to help resolve issues between the warring factions.

Vanuatu

Southeast of the Solomon Islands is **Vanuatu** (vah noo AH too), a chain of twelve volcanic islands and approximately sixty smaller coral islands that together are slightly larger than Connecticut. Captain Cook named the islands New Hebrides after the Hebrides Islands in Scotland.

Several of the islands have active volcanoes. In these unstable conditions, nearly three-fourths of the people build rural homes made of bamboo and palm leaves. Bislama, a language that combines

This male frigate bird is putting on a show for a potential mate.

U.S. Marines invaded Guadalcanal on August 7, 1942, to drive out the Japanese.

mainly English words with Melanesian grammar, is the most widespread of the hundred different spoken languages. Most of the people survive on a subsistence economy based on copra, cacao, coffee, fishing, and cattle raised on the slightly more than 2 percent of arable land. Sixty-five percent of the labor force is engaged in agriculture, but it provides only 21 percent of the GDP. Sixty-two percent of the GDP is service oriented. Tourism and offshore financial services are also making a significant contribution to Vanuatu's economy.

The people of Vanuatu enjoy freedom of religion, and 94 percent identify with some form of Christianity. Evangelical Christians represent 46 percent of the population and are experiencing a 3 percent annual growth. Vanuatu's motto is "In God We Stand," and many of this tiny nation's leaders are Christians who played an important role in securing the nation's independence.

Fiji

The Fiji archipelago has more than eight hundred scattered islands and is slightly smaller than New Jersey. Only about one hundred of its islands are inhabited. Three-fourths of the country's population lives on the large volcanic island of Viti Levu (Big Island). Suva, Fiji's capital and largest city, lies on Viti Levu's southern coast.

Before the arrival of the Europeans, warring tribes of cannibals inhabited the islands. Cannibalism ceased in 1854 when the high chief Cakobau converted to Christianity. Twenty years later, Fiji became a crown colony when Cakobau petitioned Britain for protection from the other chiefs.

Great Britain imported laborers from India to work on sugar cane plantations. Nearly half of the islanders are descendants of those Indians.

Fiji has been called "the crossroads of the South Pacific." Airplanes frequently fly in and out of the airport at Nadi, and commercial ships dock at the natural harbors at Suva and Lautoka. Twelve percent of Fiji's GDP comes from agricultural activities (more than 10 percent of the land is arable), with sugar cane being the major export. Seventy percent of the labor force, however, is involved in agriculture. After gaining its independence in 1970, Fiji began diversifying its economy by encouraging tourism and striving to develop the country's manufacturing and forestry. Today, service industries supply 69 percent of Fiji's GDP.

When Fiji gained its independence, the government tried to balance Indian and Fijian representation. Both groups were given an equal number of representatives in the parliament. The minority voters (Europeans, Chinese, and various non-Fijian Pacific Islanders), with four representatives, held the balance of power. In 1987, the first Indian managed to gain a majority in parliament and became prime minister. That victory frightened the Fijians and led to the first coup ever to occur in the Pacific islands. Fiji has endured two more coups and remains an outcast nation because its leaders have failed to hold democratic elections as of 2013.

Religious freedom exists in Fiji, and 65 percent of the people affiliate with some form of Christianity. Hindus represent 28 percent of the population, and 6 percent are

---

Fijian Religions Before the Arrival of Missionaries

As in many cultures, the Fijian people worshiped a host of gods and spirits. They believed that most of these were malicious and had to be appeased with rituals and food offerings that kept the gods happy. Many Fijians also worshiped their ancestors and believed that the souls of these ancestors changed into what became local deities. The physical form of the gods to many Fijians was the local chief and high priest, whom they worshiped. The most barbaric form of Fijian worship was human sacrifice.

Conversion of a Cannibal King

Only 150 years ago, many tribes of fierce warriors lived on the islands of Fiji. Often the menus of their feasts included *bokolo*, another name for roasted enemies. One cannibal chief, Cakobau, who was born in 1817, gained power on the islands. He led his people to war against enemy tribes, murdered those who displeased him, and gave cannibal feasts. During his reign, however, Christian missionaries came to Fiji to preach the gospel.

In 1854, Cakobau accepted Jesus Christ as his Savior. He changed his ways, ended cannibalism on his island, and publicly told his people that he was a Christian.

Cakobau's power grew even though he was no longer a fierce cannibal warrior. In 1867, he became king of Fiji, and his people lived in peace on the islands. Today, most Fijians claim to be Christians.

Fishermen on Fiji cast a net.

Muslim. Evangelical Christians make up 25 percent of the people, and new congregations are forming as this group of believers grows about 2 percent each year. Fiji has been active in sending out missionaries to other Pacific Islands, and there is a renewed effort to expand this outreach.

New Caledonia

In 1774, James Cook discovered islands that he named **New Caledonia** (kal uh DOH nee uh). He thought that the islands resembled Scotland; hence, the name "Caledonia," which is Latin for "Scotland."

From 1853 to 1894, the French used the islands as a penal colony. However, they later discovered that one-third of the world's nickel reserves were buried beneath the mountains of the main island. Strip mines now dot more than half of the island's landscape. New Caledonia is one of the world's leading producers of nickel.

New Caldonia is divided along its length by a central mountain range. The east coast has a covering of lush vegetation dominated by evergreen trees, while the west coast has arable savannas and plains. This island also has a river and a large lagoon surrounded by the New Caledonia Barrier Reef.

In an increasingly secular society, the people of New Caledonia enjoy freedom of religion, and 81 percent affiliate with some form of Christianity. Those who identify themselves as nonreligious

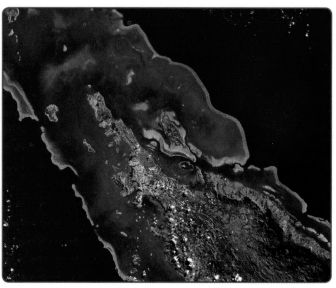

The New Caledonian Barrier Reef is one of the largest lagoons in the world.

Missionary Aviation

What three things do Arctic Eskimos, Amazon Indians, and New Guinea cannibals have in common? The answer is remoteness, primitive conditions, and hostile climates. Missionary pilots overcome these problems by using their airplanes to move people and supplies where they could not otherwise go, and they respond quickly to medical emergencies.

One such program was started in the Chuuk (CHOOK; also known as *Truk*) Islands in 1997. Three missionary couples pooled their money to maintain and operate the plane transporting them from island to island.

Becoming a missionary pilot requires great dedication. The typical flight training program at a Christian college includes five years of Bible and flight training. Many mission boards require a commercial pilot's certificate, an instrument flight rating (IFR, as opposed to a merely visual flight rating, or VFR), five hundred hours of flying time, and an aircraft mechanics certificate. Boards also demand that their candidates be debt-free—perhaps the hardest challenge because flight expenses add $12,000–$20,000 to the normal college bill. Once accepted, the missionary-aviator candidate must obtain financial support (typically through deputation), like any other missionary, except that he or she must raise a larger sum of money.

Missionary pilots face many challenges. Landings on small and remote airstrips can be dangerous. Dense fogs and precipitous mountains have claimed the lives of more than one missionary pilot. A pilot often must spend many days away from home. Mechanical skills are often in demand. Such busy schedules can take a toll on one's family, unless the missionary aviator makes time to provide spiritual leadership and family recreation.

Missionary aviation can also be dangerous for other reasons. For example, in April 2001, an American missionary and his wife and two children were flying over Peru when the Peruvian air force mistook them for drug smugglers and shot the plane down. The wife and her seven-month-old daughter were killed. But tragedies such as this should not discourage Christians from considering missionary aviation. God has called all His people to live lives of sacrificial service for the growth of His kingdom (Rom. 12:1–2; Matt. 28:18–20).

Missionary aviators can reach otherwise inaccessible peoples with God's Word.

represent 15 percent of the population, and nearly 4 percent are Muslim. Evangelical Christians make up 7 percent of the people. The indigenous Melanesian Kanaks make up nearly half of the population, and the spiritual needs of this group are significant. Congregations are reaching out to these people and, along with presenting the gospel, are being challenged to assist the victims of substance abuse and domestic violence.

Section Quiz

1. What sea bird is an emblem of the Solomon Islands?
2. Name the island in the Solomons where many American soldiers died in World War II.
3. Contrast Vanuatu's economy with that of the Solomon Islands.
4. What people live in Fiji besides the native Fijians?
5. What mineral is mined on New Caledonia?
★ Calculate the total land area of the four nations in Melanesia. What percentage of this total does each nation have?

II. Micronesia

North of Melanesia are the small, widely scattered islands of **Micronesia** ("small islands"). Although Micronesia covers an area of ocean about the size of the continental United States, its total land area is less than that of Rhode Island.

Unlike the continental islands of Melanesia, most islands in Micronesia are **atolls** (AY tohls), rings of coral on the submerged cones of volcanoes. Because they rise only a few feet above the water, coral islands are called **low islands**. Coral sand, which lacks organic material, is a poor soil. Few plants grow well. The islanders rely on fishing to subsist. Coral islands lack fresh water, except for what they receive from rainfall. Most of the islands have little hope for a brighter future. They depend on copra, tourism, and foreign aid to survive in the modern world.

Snorkeling and Scuba Diving

Two of the most popular ocean sports are snorkeling and scuba diving. (SCUBA is an acronym for "self-contained underwater breathing apparatus.") People from all over the world fly to the Pacific islands to enjoy these sports. Palau's reef, one of the "seven underwater wonders of the world," offers some of the best diving anywhere. Like Australia's Great Barrier Reef, its waters are filled with coral, exotic fish, undersea caves, lava tubes, and shipwrecks.

Snorkeling is an easy sport that can be done in as little as a foot of water. Snorkeling requires just a mask, flippers, and a snorkel. A snorkeler floats on the surface and watches crabs, eels, schools of colorful fish, and other creatures moving on the coral floor. Scuba divers wear oxygen tanks that allow them to stay underwater for as much as an hour. But scuba equipment is expensive and requires special training to use properly.

The islands of Micronesia present many excellent opportunities for exploring underwater wonders.

Micronesians are a little taller than Melanesians and have lighter skin and straight or woolly black hair. Only during World War II, when fighting devastated many of the islands, did Micronesia attract worldwide attention. Following the war, the United Nations gave most of the region to the United States to govern, aid, and defend. It was called the "Trust Territory of the Pacific."

The majority of those islands are now self-governed in "free association" with the United States. Under this system, the countries control their internal and foreign affairs, but the United States has promised to defend them. In return for this protection, the countries have agreed to keep out foreign military forces.

Micronesia is composed of three large island groups: the Caroline Islands, the Mariana Islands, and the Marshall Islands.

Caroline Islands

The **Caroline Islands** consist of more than 930 islands. In 1978, the Caroline Islands were divided into two groups—the Federated States of Micronesia and Palau.

Federated States of Micronesia

The Federated States of Micronesia are about four times the size of Washington, D.C., and consist of four major island groups: Kosrae, Pohnpei (formerly Ponape), the Chuuk Islands, and the Yap Islands. The 607 island states gained the status of free association with the United States in 1986.

Kosrae, a high volcanic island on the eastern corner of the Carolines, is one of the few important islands among mostly coral islands in the east. Known for its outstanding citrus fruits, Kosrae has the potential of becoming the vegetable and fruit basket of the Pacific.

The volcanic island of Pohnpei never suffered the ravages of World War II because armies avoided its forbidding terrain and heavy rainfall. The modern city of Kolonia on Pohnpei is the capital of the Federated States.

Kosrae International Airport is located on a man-made strip of land in the water off the mountainous island.

The government buildings in the Micronesian capital of Kolonia are a mixture of traditional and modern architecture.

The Chuuk Islands and the Yap Islands are predominantly volcanic. Both Chuuk and Yap were sites of Japanese bases during World War II. The U.S. bombardment of Chuuk created the best wreck-diving site in the world. More than a hundred Japanese ships and

The waters around Chuuk are filled with sunken ships from World War II, complete with their cargoes, including this Japanese tank.

planes, with their full loads of tanks, mines, and ammunition, sit on the lagoon floor.

More than 5 percent of the land is arable, and agriculture accounts for 14 percent of the GDP. As of 2011, two-thirds of the labor force was employed by the government.

Congregational missionaries have made a lasting impact on these islands, and 97 percent of the people profess some form of Christianity. The islanders reserve Sunday strictly for going to church. The women dress modestly, and bathing suits are not permitted—even for visitors.

Palau

Poverty-stricken **Palau** (pah LAU) is about two and a half times the size of Washington, D.C., but is composed of more than two hundred islands. It grows only enough food to provide for its rural population and is therefore heavily dependent on imports. Nearly two-thirds of the population lives in the capital of Koror. The government, assisted by U.S. foreign aid, remains a major employer of the population. Another 20 percent are involved in agriculture.

Mariana Islands

The **Mariana Islands** extend 350 miles from north to south and are part of a partially submerged mountain range in the Pacific. Of the fourteen islands in the chain, only the four largest are occupied in significant numbers: Guam, Saipan, Rota, and Tinian.

The Marianas are cooler and drier than most of their neighbors. The islands' terrain varies from grasslands suitable for grazing to tropical forests. Copra, sugar, coffee, and tobacco are the chief crops.

The Mariana Islands, located southeast of Japan, were bases for the U.S. bombing missions against Japan near the end of World War II. The base from which two B-29s dropped atomic bombs on Japan, ending the war, was located on the island of Tinian.

Guam (gwahm), the largest of the islands, is the most populous island in all of Micronesia with a population of 160,378 (2013 est.). Most of Guam's inhabitants are Micronesians, including the Chamorros (or Guamanians), the original inhabitants of the island, who speak an Indonesian language. Thirty-eight percent of the population is Asian. Guam is an independently governed territory of the United States. Residents of the Marianas, however, are U.S. citizens. Tourism is the major source of income on Guam, and American military bases are the second-leading source of income.

Ninety-seven percent of the people of Guam identify with some form of Christianity, and 14 percent are Evangelical Christians. Most of the numerical growth is among immigrant communities, including Chinese, Koreans, and Filipinos. Some congregations are beginning to send out missionaries to other Pacific nations, and the increase in tourism from Japan and Korea provides witnessing opportunities to these foreign visitors.

The other islands, collectively known as the Northern Mariana Islands, are a commonwealth of the United States and are administered by the U.S. Department of the Interior. The capital of the commonwealth is Saipan.

Tinian (TIHN nee uhn), eighty miles north of Guam, has a large population of 3,136 (2010) in the Mariana Islands but is one of the least developed. In addition to subsistence farming, tourism, government, and casinos employ most of the people.

Marshall Islands

The **Marshall Islands** lie east-southeast of the Mariana Islands. They are an island group of thirty-four low-lying atolls and islands that split into two parallel chains. The islands were named for John Marshall, a British sea captain who explored them in 1788. Many of the people in the Marshalls live in poverty.

The United States used the Bikini and Eniwetok (en ih WEE tahk) atolls from 1946 to 1958 to test nuclear bombs. The residents of Bikini vacated their islands after the military convinced them that the nuclear testing would benefit mankind. Although steps have been taken to rehabilitate the contaminated soil on these islands, as of 2013, the islanders were still waiting to return to their home.

Kwajalein (KWAHJ uh luhn), the largest atoll in the world, encloses a mammoth 839-square-mile lagoon. It is home to Reagan Test Site, a command and mission control center for intercontinental ballistic missiles and missile interceptors.

Kwajalein is part of the U.S. Strategic Defense initiative, which involves the research, testing, and development of missile defenses.

Other Micronesian Islands

Nauru

With an area of only 8.11 square miles, **Nauru** (nah OO roo) is one of the smallest and least populated countries in the world. The oval-shaped coral island is one-tenth the size of Washington, D.C. With more than thirteen thousand people, however, it has the highest population density in the Pacific.

The nearest neighbor, East Ocean Island, lies two hundred miles away. Nauru, which used to be called Pleasant Island, has no fresh water except for rainwater, and the soil is extremely poor; none of it is arable. Nauru's economy peaked in the 1980s due to the income from a large deposit of high-quality phosphate, an important fertilizer used by farmers around the world. However, this resource is nearly exhausted, and unemployment has risen to 90 percent. Excess profits from fertilizer exports that were to be set aside to meet the needs of the people have been mismanaged, and the government is becoming increasingly dependent on foreign aid to sustain basic services.

The people of Nauru enjoy freedom of religion, and nearly 92 percent affiliate with some form of Christianity. Five percent of the population are considered nonreligious, and 3 percent practice traditional Chinese religions. Evangelical Christians number 12 percent of the people and are growing at an annual rate of 2 percent. As the economy continues to decline, congregations are growing. The loss of material wealth has turned the hearts of many in Nauru to value the eternal treasures found in Christ.

One of the beautiful islands in Kiribati

Kiribati

The **Republic of Kiribati** (keer uh BAH tee), formerly called the Gilbert Islands, straddles both the equator and the International Date Line. Located at the juncture of Micronesia, Melanesia, and Polynesia, it contains both Micronesian and Polynesian peoples. Most islanders live in rural villages of crudely constructed houses and are heavily dependent on the sea to supplement the bananas, breadfruit, and sweet potatoes they grow. The islands are overcrowded. To help ease this problem, some inhabitants are migrating to other Pacific islands.

The people of Kiribati exercise religious freedom, and nearly 99 percent identify with some form of Christianity. However, many of these people do not regularly attend church, or they combine Christianity with traditional spiritist practices. Evangelical Christians make up 7 percent of the population.

Section Quiz

1. What is another name for a low island? Why is soil so poor on such islands?
2. The Caroline Islands are divided into what two nations?
3. What island chain in Micronesia is a U.S. commonwealth? What island is a U.S. territory?
4. Name the largest atoll in the world.
5. What mineral compound made Nauru rich?
* Was the U.S. government right to detonate nuclear devices on some of the Marshall Islands? Why or why not?

III. Polynesia

Polynesia ("many islands") encompasses a broad triangle that stretches from New Zealand in the west to Midway Island and Hawaii in the north and to Easter Island in the east.

Despite being separated by thousands of miles, the inhabitants of these islands are remarkably similar in both appearance and culture. The Polynesians have lighter colored skin and wavier hair than the inhabitants of Micronesia and Melanesia. Many of the different dialects are mutually understandable throughout all of Polynesia.

The beauty and natural wealth of the islands are the result of their volcanic origin. Volcanic islands, often called **high islands**, have beautiful hills and mountains. The rich volcanic ash provides fertile soil.

Many foreign countries vied for ownership of the islands during the nineteenth century. Three of the island groups have since become independent; the rest remain closely tied to their mother countries.

Tuvalu

Although **Tuvalu** (too VAHL oo) means "cluster of eight," it consists of a 360-mile chain of nine low-lying coral atolls, one of which is uninhabited. With a total land area of only ten square miles (one-tenth the size of Washington, D.C.), Tuvalu is the fourth-smallest nation in the world, just a little larger than Nauru.

Tuvalu, which gained its independence from Britain in 1978, is one of the most undeveloped countries in the world. The soil is poor (none of it is arable), and the islands have no mineral resources. Copra is the only major export. The country relies heavily on foreign aid from Australia, Great Britain, the U.S., Japan, and New Zealand. Some of this aid comes from fees paid by the foreign vessels that fish for tuna in the surrounding waters. Because young Tuvaluans lack opportunities at home, some of the young men are trained

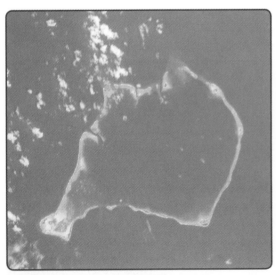

Funafuti is one of the nine atolls, eight of which are inhabited, that make up Tuvalu.

in seafaring skills, and many of the men of Tuvalu are employed on ocean vessels.

The people of Tuvalu practice religious freedom, and 98 percent affiliate with some form of Christiantiy. Evangelical Christians make up nearly 18 percent of the population. This island was first evangelized by missionaries from Cook Island and has had a strong Christian influence since that time. Given the dwindling resources and economic hardship, congregations are being challenged to help meet the material as well as spiritual needs of the people living on these coral atolls.

Samoa Islands

The **Samoa** (suh MOH uh) **Islands** are mostly volcanic. The soil near the coasts is fertile enough to grow bananas, taro, and cacao. Not much grows farther inland, however, because heavy rains leach the soil.

The first missionary to set foot on the islands, the Reverend John Williams of the London Missionary Society, arrived in the middle of the nineteenth century. Within a few years, Christianity completely changed Samoan culture, which had been very warlike. Much of Samoan life centers on the extended family. Some families still live in **fales** (FAH lays), framed houses that have a thatched roof and open sides. Fales remain open most of the time unless the owner lowers the coconut-leaf blinds.

The island chain has two parts. The islands west of longitude 171° W form the independent country of Samoa. The islands east of that line make up American Samoa, an unincorporated territory of the United States.

Samoans live in fales, which allow for breezes to ventilate the entire structure but also allow privacy when it is desired.

Samoa

Samoa has two large volcanic islands, Opolu and Savaii, and seven smaller islands. Most of the people live in small villages along the coast, raising their own food on small plots of land. Samoa became the first independent Polynesian state in 1962.

The people of the Independent State of Samoa are guaranteed freedom of religion, but local officials occasionally violate this right. Ninety-seven percent of the people are affiliated with some form of Christianity. Evangelical Christians make up 18 percent of the population, and the Evangelicals are maintaining a slight rate of growth (0.7 percent annually). During the twentieth century, missionaries from Samoa had a great impact on Pacific islands. Today, most Samoans who serve abroad are pastoring churches filled with Samoan migrants.

American Samoa

Eastern Samoa, or **American Samoa**, is a United States territory that is slightly smaller than Rhode Island. As nationals but not U.S. citizens, Samoans are able to enter the United States freely. Of the territory's seven islands, Tutuila is the largest and most populated. The capital city of Pago Pago (PAHN-goh PAHN-goh), located on Tutuila, overlooks one of the most beautiful harbors in the South Pacific.

Americans first used Pago Pago Bay as a refueling station for their ships in 1872. The U.S. Navy maintained a base there from 1900 to 1951.

Mutiny on the *Bounty*

The most famous mutiny in naval history occurred in the Pacific on April 28, 1789. William Bligh, commander of the HMS *Bounty*, had been sent to Tahiti to gather breadfruit plants and take them to Jamaica, where the British hoped to transplant breadfruit as an alternative to American flour. But Bligh's harsh discipline provoked the master's mate, Fletcher Christian, to seize the ship. Bligh and eighteen loyal crewmen were set adrift on a twenty-three-foot boat. The captain managed to sail 3,618 miles in forty-eight days to Timor, where he found a ship back to England.

Meanwhile, Christian and seven fellow mutineers left Tahiti with twelve island women and six island men to find a safe island on which to hide. Sailing southeast, they decided that uninhabited, isolated Pitcairn Island would be the ideal spot. Surrounded by jagged rocks and reefs, the island was a very forbidding destination. After managing to land, the crew

This tombstone on Pitcairn Island marks the resting place of the last surviving mutineer from the HMS Bounty.

burned the ship. The colony remained undiscovered for about eighteen years, until an American sealing ship landed there in 1808. By then, only one adult male remained with the many women and children. The volcanic soil proved highly productive, but soon the two square miles of land could not support the growing population, so in the 1830s and 1850s some of the people left. In 1857, the population dropped to zero when everyone moved to Norfolk Island. After people returned, the population peaked at 233 in 1937. In 2011 the population was only 67.

The inhabitants are under British jurisdiction. A supply ship comes three times a year. For medical attention, inhabitants must be transported to New Zealand, nearly four thousand miles away. Islanders make their living producing postage stamps, coins, honey, and handcrafts; by tourism; and by subsistence farming and fishing.

Although American Samoa is less than one-tenth the area of Samoa, it is in much better economic shape. In 1961, the United States launched a program to bolster the economy. Many people left their villages to take industry-related jobs around Pago Pago. The local tuna canning industry continues to provide the island's primary source of income.

The people of American Samoa enjoy religious freedom, and 95 percent identify with some form of Christianity, while 2.5 percent indicate they are nonreligious. Evangelical Christians make up 21 percent of the population and are growing at an annual rate of just under 2 percent.

Tonga

Tonga (TAHNG uh) is the oldest and last remaining kingdom in the Pacific. According to tradition, the most powerful chief extended his control over all of the islands during a civil war in 1845, declaring himself King George Tupou I. Converted by Methodist missionaries, he persuaded many of his subjects to accept a form of Christianity too. The king still wields great power in the constitutional monarchy.

The nation of Tonga considers itself a Christian nation and allows freedom of religion. Ninety-six percent of the people affiliate with some form of Christianity, and Evangelical Christians make up nearly 16 percent of the population. The Wesleyan Free Church of Tonga has strongly influenced the nation's culture. The country's constitution strictly prohibits all trade, games, and work on Sunday. Despite a need for money from tourism, the king and others discourage it for fear the nation will lose its identity: "We will become like Hawaii, where there are no more Hawaiians," warned King Tupou IV, who was crowned in 1965.

With a population of 103,036 (2010), Tonga suffers from overcrowding, especially on Tongatapu Island, where two-thirds of the people live. As land available for growing crops diminishes, the people have had few alternatives for making a living. Many Tongans have gone abroad to find work, and there are currently more Tongans living abroad than in Tonga. While corruption is rampant, plans are under way to develop a private sector that provides jobs in areas including tourism and transportation.

French Polynesia

French Polynesia includes five major island groups: the Society Islands, the Gambier and the Tubuai (Austral) Islands, the Tuamotu Archipelago, and the Marquesas Islands. About three-fourths of all French Polynesians live on the Society Islands, the largest islands in the territory.

French Polynesia is scattered over an area about the size of Western Europe. It has strong cultural, economic, and political ties to France. In 1958, the islanders voted to maintain their association with France rather than become independent. Its residents vote in French presidential elections and elect representatives to the French Parliament.

A majority of the islanders (183,645 in 2012) reside on the island of **Tahiti** (tuh HEE tee)—the geographical, social, and political center of French Polynesia. Two giant volcanic mountains unite to form the island. A coral reef surrounds most of the island, giving it a protected lagoon. Chief exports include copra, pearls, and vanilla. Papeete, the capital of the territory, is a bustling port city on Tahiti. Although exports, such as black pearls, provide a modest income in French Polynesia, tourism is a big part of the economy. Because of heavy tourism, Tahiti's 130 miles of roads experience traffic jams that rival those of many Western cities.

While the French Polynesian society is becoming increasingly materialistic and secular, the people enjoy religious freedom. Ninety-two percent of the people identify with some form of Christianity, and 5 percent are nonreligious. Statistically, Evangelical Christians make up 7 percent of the population, but their influence is minimal, and their outreach appears to be negligible.

Other Polynesian Islands

The volcanic Hawaiian Islands are the most important islands in the Pacific because of their size and strategic location. The United States also owns the Midway Islands west-northwest of Hawaii. New Zealand is another advanced, prosperous region of Polynesia and controls the Cook Islands, the Tokelau Islands, and Niue (NYOO ay).

> ### Cosmic Egg Creation
>
> Many Polynesian cultures, including Tahiti, developed a creation myth that involved a high god who initially dwelled in something like a cosmic egg. Although this egg was believed to have been constructed of gold or silver, it conveyed the idea of birth or creation that the indigenous people observed in nature. In Tahiti the high god was eternal and was called *Taaroa* (or *Tangaroa*). Taaroa also created other gods. In the Polynesian accounts, this high god took parts of the cosmic egg and parts of his own body to form the world. For example, he used part of the egg to form the sky, he took his own spine and made mountain ranges, and used his ribs to form hills. Taaroa had feathers that turned into trees and other plants when they fell from his body to the earth. Then Taaroa formed the first man from the earth and also created the first woman. He named the first man *Ti'i* and the woman *Hina*. She was good and protected mankind. However, Ti'i was bad and brought evil to men, such as storms and death. The Polynesians believed that Ti'i and Hina became gods and that Hina's intervention prevented the destruction of the world by Ti'i and other vindictive gods.

Tahiti is often portrayed as the ideal island paradise.

The Mystery of Easter Island

Easter Island is an unusual volcanic island over two thousand miles off the coast of Chile, far from the other inhabited islands of the Pacific. The Dutch admiral Jacob Raggeveen discovered the island on Easter, 1722. He found on the coast rows of mysterious stone heads, called *moai*. The massive heads had very long ears and flat noses. On the larger heads were red stones that looked like hats or crowns.

Most of the *moai* are ten to twenty feet tall and weigh up to fifty tons. The largest finished head is thirty-two feet high and weighs one hundred tons, but one of the unfinished heads is more than sixty feet high and weighs more than three hundred tons. How did the natives carve the *moai* out of the volcanic rock at the crater Rano Raraku, transport them to the coast, raise the heads to an upright position, and place the red stones on top?

In 1774, Captain Cook visited the island and talked to the natives. They told him that their Long Ear ancestors had made the statues twenty-two generations previously—around the thirteenth century. They called their island *Rapa Nui* and considered it the navel of the world. By that time the statues had been toppled. The natives said it happened during wars with Short Ear invaders from islands far to the west.

Where did the statue-builders come from? Where did the invaders who toppled the *moai* come from? If South American legends are true, perhaps the statue builders came from Lake Titicaca. A legend from the Gambier Islands, twelve hundred miles to the west of Easter Island, may explain the origin of the tribe that toppled the statues. The legend tells of a defeated chieftain who took his tribe in two large canoes to a solitary island in the east.

Easter Island has another mystery that has not yet been explained. It is the only Pacific island with an ancient writing system. But no one has been able to decipher the rongorongo tablets. Many of these tablets were hidden in caves, along with idols and skulls.

The Easter Island heads are immense, and the tallest head is thirty-three feet high.

Find It!

Easter Island

27.143° S, 109.360° W

(Zoom out until you can see the entire island. Zoom out further and note how remote this island is.)

Section Quiz

1. Describe how Polynesia differs from the other two Pacific island regions.
2. What is the smallest country in Polynesia?
3. Why is Samoa less developed than American Samoa?
4. What is the last surviving kingdom in the Pacific?
5. What European country controls Tahiti?
★ Should New Zealand and Hawaii be considered part of the Pacific island culture region? Why or why not?

Chapter Review

Making Connections

1–2. On which type of island would you best be able to survive if you were marooned in the Pacific: continental island, high island, or low island? Why?

3–4. Which is a major export for many Pacific islands? What is this product made from?

5. Nauru has prospered until recently because of which resource?

6. What role did Christians play in a civil war on the Guadalcanal Island?

7. Congregations on which Pacific islands mentioned in this chapter are currently sending out missionaries?

Developing Geography Skills

1. Based on the map on page 565, what is the most likely route of migration used to populate the Pacific Islands?

2. Based on the map on page 565 and the student text, explain why Fiji is known as "the crossroads of the South Pacific."

Thinking Critically

1. If a tribesman becomes a Christian, does he need to adopt Western styles of worship, or can he keep his tribal traditions?

2. In what ways does the Cosmic Egg story of Creation differ from the account in Genesis? What are some similarities? What is the significance of these similarities and differences?

Living in God's World

1. Respond to the critique that Christian missionaries were oppressors when they sought to convert islanders away from their traditional cultures to Christianity.

2. Respond to the critique that Christianity should concern itself with spriual things but should not try to change cultures.

People, Places, and Things to Know

acculturation
copra
Melanesia
taro
New Guinea
cargo cults
Guadalcanal
Vanuatu
New Caledonia
Micronesia
atolls
low islands
Caroline Islands
Palau
Mariana Islands
Guam
Tinian
Marshall Islands
Kwajalein
Nauru
Republic of Kiribati
Polynesia
high islands
Tuvalu
Samoa Islands
fales
American Samoa
Tonga
French Polynesia
Tahiti
Easter Island

Ice floe in the Antarctic

THE LAST FRONTIERS

*T*he Lord planted in the human heart an insatiable curiosity that will never be quenched. Many places in God's vast universe remain to be studied and colonized.

During the twentieth century, modern technology opened three new frontiers for scientific study: Antarctica, the ocean depths, and the heavens. Scientists discovered not only a wealth of new knowledge but also new areas of competition for scarce resources and military advantage. The Creation Mandate does not stop at the shores of the continents or on the beaches of Oceania. It invites man to extend his studies and to exercise his dominion over the unexplored areas of Antarctica, the undersea world, and the heavens.

Artist's conception of an iceberg

I. Antarctica

The psalmist declares, "The heavens are thine, the earth also is thine: as for the world and the fulness thereof, thou hast founded them. The north and the south thou hast created them" (Ps. 89:11–12).

At the bottom of the world is a remote region known as **Antarctica**. The Antarctic Circle, located at 66½° S latitude, marks the boundary of the region. For at least one twenty-four-hour period each year, the sun never sets in "the land of the midnight sun."

Because sunlight in Antarctica is either very slanted or nonexistent, temperatures there are extremely cold. Huge packs of permanent floating ice defied all attempts at systematic exploration until the twentieth century.

In the open seas, icebergs can be a major hazard. **Icebergs** are jagged chunks of ice that have broken off, or "calved," from a glacier as it reached the sea. Icebergs have been measured as large as two hundred miles long, sixty miles wide, and more than a thousand feet deep. Because nearly 90 percent of an iceberg lies hidden below the water, ships may crash into the underwater portion before the crew realizes the danger is there.

South of the Antarctic Circle is the forbidding continent of Antarctica. Technically, Antarctica is surrounded by three oceans—the Atlantic, Pacific, and Indian Oceans. Yet, a band of polar water circling the continent is much colder and less salty than the subtropical waters next to it. A gigantic ice pack covers this band. Pieces of the pack that break off the ice pack are called **ice floes**. The open water between floes is called a *lead*. In places, the ice extends as far as nine hundred miles from the coast.

In 2000, the International Hydrographic Organization (IHO) designated a fifth ocean from the southernmost portions of the Atlantic, Pacific, and Indian Oceans, calling it the **Southern Ocean**. They based their decision on the fact that the waters around the continent of Antarctica have characteristics that distinguish them from all other oceans. The area lies south of 60° south latitude and comprises

Scientists explore ice floes in Antarctica.

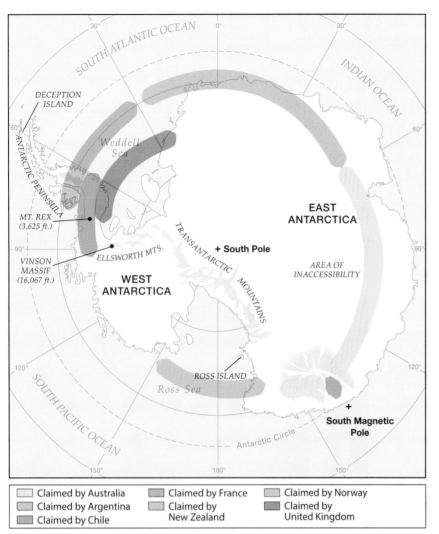

Claimed by Australia
Claimed by Argentina
Claimed by Chile
Claimed by France
Claimed by New Zealand
Claimed by Norway
Claimed by United Kingdom

Elephant Island is one of the northernmost islands on the Antarctic Peninsula.

an area more than twice the size of the United States. The waters are deep—from 13,123 to 16,404 feet (roughly two to three miles)—with the deepest point being 23,738 feet (more than 4.5 miles) at the South Sandwich Trench.

However, not everyone agrees that the Southern Ocean deserves to be a separate ocean. Some geographers disagree on the designation of this area as a distinct ocean, and others dispute what constitutes the northern boundary of such an ocean. Even the IHO has failed to ratify its original designation as of 2014.

Physical Geography

Antarctica is shaped like a pear. East (or Greater) Antarctica lies at the fat, rounded end. At the other end lies West (or Lesser) Antarctica. Dividing the two ends is the 1,900-mile-long Transantarctic Mountain Range.

East Antarctica

East Antarctica is a high plateau covered by a thick ice cap that is more than a mile deep. In fact, the weight of the ice has pushed the land down to form a great basin that is 9,840 feet (a little less than two miles) below sea level in one spot.

The Antarctic Plateau is famous for its cold cyclonic storms that whirl almost endlessly from east to west. Gales can reach two hundred miles per hour. The average temperature of the interior during the coldest months is ⁻94° F (compared to ⁻22° F on the coast).

The extreme cold of the interior prohibits life. Nothing lives here—not even a bush or an insect. However, the cold is a blessing. Because cold air cannot hold much moisture, the interior receives less than two inches of snow per year. The desert conditions prevent snow from building up and depleting the world's water level.

West Antarctica

In West Antarctica, the **Ross Sea** and **Weddell Sea** cut in on either side to form the neck of Antarctica's pear. Glaciers that flow into the Ross and Weddell Seas slide out onto the water to form solid **ice shelves**.

West Antarctica is mountainous rather than flat. The Ellsworth Mountains near the Weddell Sea—the highest mountains on the continent—peep up above the ice cap. Elsewhere, solitary mountains, called **nunataks**, stick up like rocky islands in an ice sea.

Birds That Wear Tuxedos

Penguins are curious birds whose dark backs and white fronts make them seem to be wearing tuxedos. These pudgy gentlemen look awkward on land as they waddle, and they cannot fly. But in water they are skilled acrobats with flipper wings. They can even leap out of the water like flying fish or dolphins. They have to be fast. Catching fish is not easy,

Penguins are a common feature of Antarctica.

and eluding leopard seals and killer whales is even harder.

Antarctica's mainland has two species of penguins. The emperor penguin is the largest of all penguins, growing up to four feet high and weighing up to one hundred pounds. The Adélie penguin is named for the coast first claimed by France. A third species, the gentoo penguin, lives on islands along the Antarctic Peninsula.

At the tip of West Antarctica is the **Antarctic Peninsula**, the most coveted piece of property on the continent. It is the only part of the continent that extends beyond the Antarctic Circle toward South America.

At the edge of this seeming desert, the coastal waters are teeming with life. Plankton forms the basis of the food chain. Small shrimp-like krill and many different species of fish thrive in the ocean. Squid, octopuses, whales, porpoises, seals, and dolphins are abundant. Penguins are the dominant birds.

Ross Sea and McMurdo Station

Between West Antarctica and East Antarctica is the Ross Sea. It is separated from the South Pole by the **Transantarctic Mountains**. About half of the Ross Sea is covered by the Ross Ice Shelf. On the side closest to East Antarctica is **McMurdo Station**, the largest settlement in Antarctica.

Exploration

The ice-choked seas surrounding Antarctica are the stormiest known to man. Until the nineteenth century, the continent eluded

> **Find It!**
> **McMurdo Station**
> 77.846° S 166.658° E

This sign at Scott Base, which is operated by New Zealand, indicates distances "back home" for the international community of scientists there.

Antarctica's harsh environment requires the use of special transportation equipment.

The Antarctic Explorers: Hall of Fame

Thaddeus von Bellingshausen (Russia): sailed around Antarctica; discovered Peter I Island (1819–20)

Sir James Clark Ross (Great Britain): made three expeditions to Antarctica (1839–43), during which he discovered Cape Adare, Ross Island, the Ross Ice Shelf, and McMurdo Bay

Carsten Borchgrevink (Norway): first explorer to winter in Antarctica (1899)

Ernest Shackleton (Great Britain): led first expedition (1908–9), traveling farther south than anyone else up to that time; discovered Beardmore Glacier and was only 97 miles from the South Pole when he had to turn back; his ship became locked in ice floes (1914), and he spent the rest of his expedition finding help and rescuing the crew.

Sir Douglas Mawson (Great Britain): member of Shackleton's 1908–9 expedition; led his own expedition in 1911, discovering Shackleton Ice Shelf; made two more expeditions (1929–31)

Sir Robert Scott (Great Britain): made his first expedition in 1902; in 1911 set out with the goal of being the first person to reach the South Pole, but Amundsen beat him; died on the return trip when only 150 miles from his final destination

Roald Amundsen (Norway) (right): became the first human to reach the South Pole (1911); left a letter for his competitor Robert Scott, who found it a month later

Jacques Cousteau (France) (far right): became the first person to dive beneath the ice of Antarctica (1975); filmed a TV series documenting his explorations

discovery. Captain Cook circumnavigated the Antarctic region in 1773 in search of a fabled southern continent, but his ship could not penetrate the ice pack. In 1820, an American sealing ship, a Russian sealing ship, and an English sealing ship each claimed to be the first to sight Antarctica. Finally, in 1895, a Norwegian businessman named Henryk Johan Bull became the first human to set foot on the continent.

The "heroic age" of exploration began in the twentieth century. On December 14, 1911, **Roald Amundsen** planted the Norwegian flag at the South Pole. At the same time, a British explorer named **Robert Scott** was struggling to reach the site. He did reach it; however, his entire party perished on the return trip.

Other records followed. Admiral **Richard Byrd** flew a plane over the South Pole on his 1928–29 survey expedition. In 1958, Vivian Fuchs successfully crossed the 1,550-mile width of the continent.

International Cooperation and Disputes

Foreign powers began establishing bases on Antarctica in the 1940s. Once they started, no seafaring nation wanted to be left out. Scientists from the United States and other countries prevailed on their governments to reserve the earth's last great wilderness for pure science, unspoiled by Cold War tensions. During an eighteen-month period from 1957 to 1958, twelve nations coordinated their efforts in building sixty scientific bases and sharing all their findings. The following year, twelve nations signed the Antarctic Treaty, agreeing to ban military bases and weapons testing on the continent, to freeze all land claims, to exchange all information freely, and to open all camps for inspection at any time. Many other nations later signed the treaty. In 1991, the "Antarctic Treaty Parties" extended the treaty indefinitely and agreed to ban mining for fifty years.

Scientists have studied all sorts of phenomena in Antarctica. Many of those scientists are looking for evidence that world pollution is increasing. The discovery of an ozone "hole" above the Antarctic has raised fears that the atmosphere might be warming. A warming of the earth could have serious consequences. About 90 percent of the world's ice is locked in the ice cap of Antarctica. This represents about 70 percent of the world's fresh water. Many scientists predict that if the ice cap were to melt, the sea level around the world would rise as much as two hundred feet, submerging many islands and every major coastal city.

Core samples and radio soundings provide tantalizing clues about what is under the ice cap. Extensive coal fields and mineral resources may lie under the ice, awaiting the development of economically feasible and environmentally safe methods of mining. Some nations have even set up sham research stations to ensure a right to participate in any bargaining over mining and land claims.

Volcanoes in the Antarctic

Many of the mountains in the Antarctic were created by volcanoes, and most are inactive. However, scientists have recently documented a chain of active volcanoes under the ice sheet along West Antarctica. They discovered seismic activity by accident and used airborne ice-penetrating radar to confirm the presence of volcanic activity near Mount Sidley. The heat produced by the volcanoes is being released below the mile-thick ice sheet and may not penetrate the ice. However, it is contributing a large quantity of melt water and causing sections of ice to break off. This could explain the melting of ice and increased number of ice floes along West Antarctica even as development of sea ice continues to increase along other parts of Antarctica. Such findings cast doubt on the popular claim that human-caused climate change is causing accelerated melting in parts of the Antarctic.

Section Quiz

1. What two large seas lie beside Antarctica's coasts?
2. What long, narrow peninsula extends from Antarctica?
3. What are ice shelves?
★ Do you think the United States should claim part of Antarctica?

Creatures that live at each level of the sea

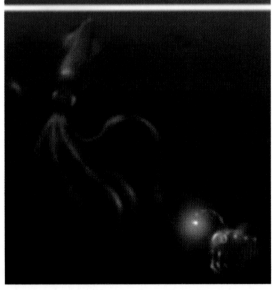

II. The Ocean Deep

The psalmist declared, "He gathereth the waters of the sea together as an heap; he layeth up the depth in storehouses" (Ps. 33:7).

God created the deep (Gen. 1:2), broke it up in the great Flood (Gen. 7:11), and put boundaries on the new oceans and deeps (Job 38:8–11). For thousands of years, the secrets of the deep have been hidden from human eyes. But new technology is finally allowing man to discover a whole new world of unusual life forms and valuable resources.

The Undersea Landscape

The Bible says that God covered the foundations of the earth with the deep (Ps. 104:6). Only in the twentieth century did deep-sea explorers discover what this means. The continents are thick slabs sitting on a foundation of rock. The submerged edges of these slabs are called the **continental shelf**. They slope gently down from the shore to a depth of about 650 feet. At the edge of the continental shelf, the continent drops off sharply. The steep sides of the continents, called the continental slope, descend to a depth of more than two miles (about thirteen thousand feet). Deep ocean basins stretch across the vast empty spaces between the continents.

The sea creatures that mankind harvests live in the upper seven hundred feet of the ocean, a region that is called the **photic zone** because it has enough light for photosynthesis. However, no plants grow below the photic zone. Some light filters down to two thousand feet—about the same amount of light that you see at dusk or on a starry night. This twilight region is called the mesopelagic (midsea) zone. Perpetual darkness reigns below that depth in the bathypelagic (deep-sea) zone, where man has discovered some unusual fish. The anglerfish, for example, has a light hanging in front of its mouth to attract prey.

The ocean floor consists primarily of deep **ocean basins**, which typically range from thirteen thousand to eighteen thousand feet deep. Soundings have uncovered a varied landscape, much more dramatic than the weathered landscape where people live.

Sediment from continental rivers and debris from landslides have caused a buildup at the base of the continental slopes. This buildup is known as the continental rise.

Like continents, the ocean basins have three major physical features: mountains, plateaus, and plains. The plains are known as **abyssal** (uh BIS uhl) **plains**. They begin at the edge of the continental shelf and continue in an extremely level and featureless plain that is covered by silt as deep as a few miles. They are the flattest areas on earth and make up about half of the ocean floor. A few plateaus and hills, usually extinct volcanoes, rise above the abyssal plains.

The sea floor map on page 591 shows that a number of deep canyons, called **trenches**, scar the ocean basins. The Pacific Ocean has more trenches than all the other oceans combined.

Less than 1 percent of the ocean floor descends below the ocean basin. The word *deep* refers to depths beyond eighteen thousand feet. The Milwaukee Deep, located in the Puerto Rico Trench, is, at about 28,560 feet below sea level, the deepest point in the Atlantic. The deepest deep in the world is the **Mariana Trench**, and its deepest

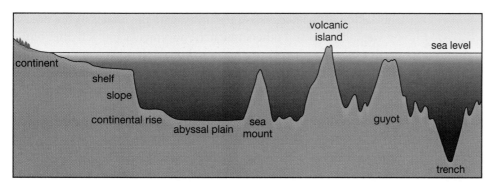

Undersea surface features

point is the **Challenger Deep**, which is up to 36,070 feet below sea level (according to the U.S. Center for Coastal and Ocean Mapping, in 2010).

Mountain ranges form along the **oceanic ridges**. Every ocean has ridges, but scientists have conducted the most studies on the Mid-Atlantic Ridge, a ridge of volcanic mountains that divides the Atlantic Ocean in half. Occasionally, the ridge rises above the surface to form islands. Iceland is such an island.

Isolated underwater volcanoes called **seamounts** dot the basins. Sometimes a new volcano breaks through the ocean surface, forming an island, such as Surtsey off the coast of Iceland.

Scarred areas on the ocean basin are creased by numerous earthquake faults. These regions are called fracture zones. Sometimes hot springs, or **deep-sea vents**, spew hot lava and sulfur into the dark, frigid waters. A wide variety of unique life forms are found around the vents.

Exploration

The psalmist proclaimed, "They that go down to the sea in ships, that do business in great waters; these see the works of the Lord, and his wonders in the deep" (Ps. 107:23–24).

Oceanographers are scientists who study the oceans in an effort to understand and use them better. Some of them study the plant and

> ### *Find It!*
> **Mariana Trench**
> 11.279° N 142.353° E
> (Note: You will need to zoom out until you can see the dark line of the trench.)

NOAA

The National Oceanographic and Atmospheric Administration (NOAA) was an outgrowth of the survey of the U.S. east coast that President Thomas Jefferson authorized in 1807.

Although NOAA is most commonly thought of as the organization that tracks and warns the United States of impending hurricanes, it does much more than that, as its name indicates.

In 2000, President George W. Bush formed a panel of "ocean explorers, researchers, and marine educators" to develop a national ocean exploration strategy. In *Discovering Earth's Final Frontier: A U.S. Strategy for Ocean Exploration*, the experts recommended an interagency program to explore in U.S. waters under the authority of the NOAA. The NOAA then organized

the Office of Ocean Exploration. They began cooperative explorations with the Woods Hole Oceanographic Institution and several colleges and universities. In 2002, they helped recover the turret and engine of the Union ironclad USS *Monitor*.

The National Ocean Service offices deal with coastal ocean science, studies of red tide, geodetic surveying, marine sanctuaries, coastal resource management, and response to natural (or man-made) disasters and restoration of the environment afterward.

NOAA scientists regularly collect water samples from the ocean to monitor the quantity of harmful algae.

animal life of the oceans; others investigate the effects of the oceans on weather; and still others research movements and activities of the earth under the oceans, such as earthquakes and volcanoes and the tsunamis they sometimes produce. Historical researchers try to find and raise (or study on-site) various shipwrecks and artifacts on the sea floor. Engineers help such scientists develop the equipment required to do those tasks safely and efficiently. A well-trained Christian working in any of these fields can do much to help mankind and honor the Lord by learning to be a better steward of this important resource.

As long as man had undiscovered or unexploited lands to explore and conquer, he tended to ignore the oceans, assuming that they held less value for him than the landmasses offered and using them as a mere transportation route. In fact, however, the opposite is true. Man has only begun to learn what the oceans can teach him and how this knowledge can benefit humankind.

Pioneers and Problems of Oceanography

History suggests that Alexander the Great might have been the first person to go underwater (in a glass barrel) to examine what was there. For centuries, sponge divers all over the world harvested their products without using any special equipment, but they were severely limited in both how deep they could go and how long they could stay down. (Even the best divers can hold their breath for only about two minutes and can descend only about one hundred feet unassisted by special equipment.)

The three biggest problems to be overcome were providing a reliable oxygen supply; preventing the divers from being crushed by the pressure, which increases with depth; and avoiding "the bends," a painful condition that develops when nitrogen bubbles form in the bloodstream as divers ascend. Over the centuries, people developed various kinds of suits and vessels (generally called diving bells) for going underwater safely.

Two underwater vessels became famous in the eighteenth and nineteenth centuries, but they were intended for warfare, not science. In 1776, early in the American War for Independence, **David Bushnell** built an egg-shaped submersible named the *Turtle* by which he hoped to slip under British warships, drill holes in their hulls, and attach and detonate explosive devices. His plan failed when the drill hit metal on the hull of the first British warship he tried to sink, the frigate HMS *Eagle*. (One theory is that the ship's hull was sheathed in copper, but it is more likely that the drill hit a metal band or a bolt.)

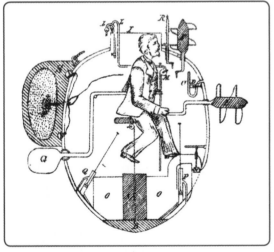

Bushnell's *Turtle* was an early attempt to construct an effective submersible for use in warfare.

The CSS *Hunley* was the first submarine to sink an enemy warship.

"The Pathfinder of the Seas"

Sometimes the people who make some of the greatest contributions to a field of study do not get the public honor they deserve. Such is the case with **Matthew Maury** (1806–73).

Maury grew up on a farm in Middle Tennessee. He followed his older brother's footsteps and joined the U.S. Navy. During ten years of sailing the seas, he rose in rank and conducted intensive studies of navigation.

While ashore between voyages, however, he was severely injured in a stagecoach accident that prevented his return to sea duty. Much to his dismay, he was reassigned to the Navy's Depot of Charts and Instruments.

Bored with being a mere caretaker of dusty maps, charts, and ships' logs, Maury began to study them closely. He noticed a pattern with the ships that had wrecked and were disabled

and consequently drifted aimlessly on the seas. He suspected that the ocean had continuous currents in certain locations. His naval colleagues laughed at his idea and dismissed it.

But then a ship lost its rudder off Sandy Hook and drifted out to sea. Most people gave up on ever finding it, but Maury obtained the last known coordinates of the ship and, using his theory, calculated where the ship should be. A rescue ship was dispatched. Using Maury's calculations, it found the otherwise doomed ship and rescued its crew. Maury became a recognized expert on currents and even published *The Wind and Current Charts of the North Atlantic* and *The Physical Geography of the Sea*.

Later, Maury served in the Confederate navy and taught meteorology at Virginia Military Institute.

In 1864, during the American Civil War, a group of Southern investors financed and built a submarine named the CSS *Hunley*. It became the first successful wartime submarine when it slipped out of Charleston Harbor under cover of darkness, attached an explosive device to the hull of the Union sloop of war USS *Housatonic*, and sank it. Unfortunately, the *Hunley* did not make it back to the Charleston shore; it sank, and the entire eight-man crew perished. (The *Hunley* was discovered in 1995 and raised in 2000. Scientists and researchers are examining and displaying the sub to the public at the Charleston Naval Yard.)

Twentieth-Century Undersea Explorations

The first humans to venture below the photic zone (beyond about seven hundred feet) were **William Beebe** and **Otis Barton** in 1930. They used a steel ball-shaped vessel called a **bathysphere**.

William Beebe contributed to undersea exploration with his bathysphere.

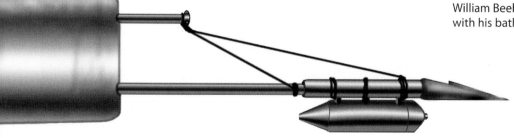

Descent into the Mariana Trench

Hundreds of people have summited Mount Everest or traveled into space, even walking on the moon itself. But only three men have descended into the deepest part of the ocean depths.

The Mariana Trench is the deepest trench in the world. The deepest place in the trench, the Challenger Deep, is 36,070 feet below sea level. The first people to descend into this spot were Jacques Piccard, son of the engineer

who invented the bathyscaphe, and Don Walsh of the U.S. Navy. The trip took nine hours. During their twenty minutes on the bottom, they spotted a flounder, which proved that certain fish can survive the tremendous pressures of the cold, dark deep.

Auguste and Jacques Piccard built Trieste, *the bathyscaphe, for deep-sea exploration.*

James Cameron

On March 6, 2012, film director and explorer James Cameron became just the third man to descend into the Mariana Trench, the first to do it solo. He traveled down to the trench in a machine he had designed and built, called the *DEEPSEA CHALLENGER*. Cameron's vehicle took two and one-half hours to descend to 35,756 feet and touch the bottom.

Initially, Cameron could see nothing other than sediment along the bottom of the trench. Using high-definition cameras and external lights, he recorded the terrain as he moved about using thrusters. Gradually, he was able to see tiny amphipods (flattened, shrimplike arthropods) floating by like tiny snowflakes. During the brief time that the hydraulics worked, Cameron collected sediment samples. Although he planned to remain at the bottom for five hours, failing batteries and thrusters forced him to shorten his stay by two hours. He jettisoned two 536-pound weights and returned to the surface in about ninety minutes.

Eight months after this dive, scientists announced that Cameron's sediment samples contained 20,000 microbes in addition to isopods (tiny arthropods with a single type of leg) and six kinds of amphipods. Scientists have since discovered that one of these amphipods produces a substance that may be used to treat Alzheimer's disease. More discoveries are likely to emerge from this historic dive.

In 1943, Frenchman **Jacques Cousteau** invented the Aqua-Lung, or self-contained underwater breathing apparatus (SCUBA), which dramatically increased the time one could spend underwater as well as the range of depth accessible for human study. He purchased and retrofitted a ship named the *Calypso* and used it for numerous underwater studies around the world. He filmed many of his expeditions and used them to develop documentaries that made his name almost synonymous with undersea exploration.

Another type of ocean exploration tool is the Floating Instrument Platform (FLIP). It is a 355-foot, spoon-shaped ocean laboratory. Developed in 1960, it is towed by boat to the site researchers

Jacques Cousteau, explorer and the co-inventor of the Aqua-Lung

FLIP is towed into place and then flipped into a working position.

Alvin is a three-person submersible exploration craft.

want to study. Ballast tanks in the handle-shaped end are flooded with seven hundred tons of water, causing that end to sink and flipping the bowl-shaped end into the air. The upper fifty-five feet remain above the surface of the water. Crew members live and work aboard this unique laboratory. *Alvin* is a much smaller, three-person submersible that is highly mobile under water.

Some undersea crafts, however, are unmanned and operate by remote control, photographing the sea floor and environment and sending the images to monitors aboard surface ships. *Jason/Medea* is a team of two vehicles, one large vehicle and one small vehicle, that are tethered together and work in tandem to take photos, collect temperature and other data, and gather physical samples from the sea.

Using another such device named *Argo*, **Robert Ballard** discovered the wreck of the HMS *Titanic* in 1985. Ballard has also used such equipment to locate and explore the wrecks of other vessels, including the Nazi battleship *Bismarck* and John Kennedy's famous patrol-torpedo boat, PT-109. Ballard's high-tech explorations continue into the twenty-first century.

Disputed Waters

Almost every speck of dry land on earth has been claimed by one nation or another, but claims on water have always stirred

Nautilus 90° North

In the summer of 1958, the USS *Nautilus*, the world's first nuclear-powered submarine, slipped into Seattle with a problem that threatened to doom its secret mission—a leaky condenser unit. The secrecy of the mission prevented its repair through normal channels, so Commander William Anderson resorted to unconventional methods. He ordered his sailors to don civilian clothing and to fan out through the Seattle area to gas stations and auto repair shops to find a product called Bar's Leak, which was normally used to repair auto radiator leaks. The sailors got every can they could find—one hundred forty of them—and poured half of the product into the condenser unit. The leak stopped. They prayed it would hold throughout the dangerous voyage ahead.

On June 9, under cover of darkness, the *Nautilus* headed northward and under the polar ice cap, traveling 1,830 miles to the North Pole. You can read Anderson's account of the experience in his book: *Nautilus 90° North*.

Earth Matters: Sustainable Fishing

A fleet of diving boats and tugboats jockey for position in the balmy waters of the Mediterranean Sea. A spotter plane has seen a school of bluefin tuna. Even a small school could bring in as much as half a million dollars.

Bluefin tuna are the sports cars of the marine world, reaching bursts of 55 miles per hour, and growing up to 10 feet long and weighing over a ton. They can dive thousands of feet down to pursue prey and avoid their predators, sharks and killer whales. Their torpedo-like bodies the color of hammered chrome are prized as sushi meat in Asia and around the world.

"He's fishing!" Galaz shouts. "He's shooting the net!" Txema Galaz Ugalde is a European marine biologist who runs a small tuna ranching operation in the Mediterranean. He uses a fishing method called a *purse seiner* to catch the bluefin tuna. This involves circling the school with a dragnet up to a mile long. Very few fish in the school can escape.

Marine biologists estimate that the number of fish in the world oceans may have reduced by as much as 80–90 percent in the past forty years. Fishing technology has maximized killing power for fishermen around the world. Fish factories—huge ships that patrol areas with large amounts of fish—can catch, fillet, and freeze several tons of fish a day. But the problem is that there are too many fishing boats and not enough fish. They seem to be catching and killing fish faster than the fish can reproduce and grow. Marine biologists wonder if bluefin tuna will suffer the same fate as the

American buffalo (bison). Pollution has also taken its toll on fish populations. Waters that once throbbed with life are falling silent.

But there is hope for the future. Government officials and marine biologists are teaming up to create rules and zones for sustainable fishing. They are capping the amount of fish that people can take from the ocean. Fishermen are returning to more primitive fishing practices such as harpooning and line-and-reel fishing, to avoid wiping out whole schools of fish. The result is a rebounding fish population in regulated areas where sustainable fishing is enforced, such as Alaska. Good and wise use of God-given resources involves thinking about how actions affect the future. Conserving world fisheries through sustainable fishing is an example of exercising good and wise dominion with a mind for the future.

Bluefin tuna

Territorial Claims in the North Sea

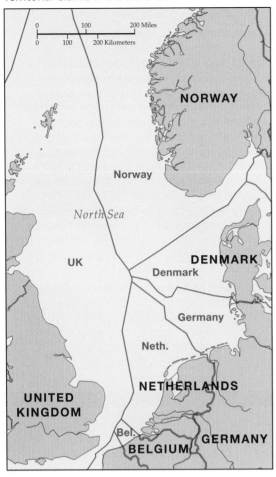

LOST

U.S. ratification of the Law of the Sea Treaty (LOST) has been periodically debated since 1982. Ronald Reagan was president when this debate began, and he opposed Senate ratification on the grounds that the U.S. would be turning over sovereign control of two-thirds of the earth's surface to the UN. As recently as 2012, this treaty was considered by the Senate, but conservatives rallied to defeat ratification. The concern that signing this treaty threatens U.S. sovereignty remains one of the main points of contention. Supporters argue that it is in America's best interest to sign this treaty. Opponents respond that a strong navy protects U.S. sovereignty more effectively than a UN treaty does.

controversy. The United States and many other countries support freedom of the seas, the view that any nation can fish and trade freely on the open seas. But this position has become complicated. Modern high-tech ships compete for a limited supply of fish to feed the growing world population. The discovery of offshore oil has given waters a value they never had before.

During the seventeenth century, seagoing nations developed the concept of **territorial waters**, the right of a nation to exclude ships of other nations from a three- to six-mile-wide strip of water along its coast. Ships of other nations enjoyed the "right of free passage" only if they came in peace to trade. Beyond the territorial waters were the **high seas**, which were open to vessels of all nations.

In the twentieth century, nations began extending their territorial waters to exorbitant distances from the shores. These claims often overlapped the valid claims of neighboring countries. One country's refusal to recognize the claims of another sometimes led to shooting. In 1958, nearly ninety nations agreed to limit territorial waters to a twelve-mile contiguous zone. However, narrow straits, such as the Strait of Gibraltar, were to remain open. Each nation was permitted to develop oil fields on its adjacent continental shelf, but the ocean basins were to remain free of claims. Disputes continued, however, because some countries did not want to comply with the agreement.

The United Nations drafted the Law of the Sea Treaty (LOST) in 1982 to address those problems. The treaty recognizes the territorial and contiguous zones and up to a two-hundred-mile **exclusive economic zone** (EEZ). Each signatory country has exclusive rights to fish and drill for oil in its own EEZ. The treaty went into effect in 1995 after sixty nations signed. Although the United States played a significant role in drafting the treaty, American leaders would not ratify it because of provisions in the final treaty concerning deep ocean mining and sovereignty. Nonetheless, the United States complied with all other treaty provisions as though it had signed. As of 2012, the U.S. Senate had postponed a vote to ratify this treaty.

Internationally Accepted Maximum Zones as of 1982

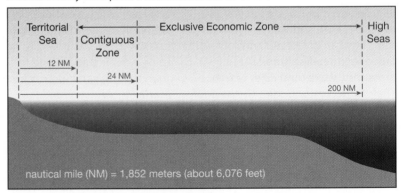

Section Quiz

1–3. Name the three ocean layers based on the amount of light received.

4–6. What are the three major geographic features that the sea floor shares with dry land?

7. What is the deepest trench in the world?

✶ Why have so few humans visited the Mariana Trench?

III. The Heavens

For thousands of years, the grandeur of the night sky has thrilled human observers.

In the twentieth century, man began to realize his dreams of exploring the heavens, both inner space (the atmosphere) and outer space. But space flight has introduced new problems. Nations now have another "border" to guard from enemy warplanes, missiles, and nuclear weapons.

The Troposphere

Psalm 147:8 says that God "covereth the heaven with clouds." This part of the heavens—the atmosphere—extends about seven hundred miles above the earth. It has various layers defined by differences in temperature, pressure, and gases.

The lowest six miles of the atmosphere is called the **troposphere**. It contains the air we breathe and the clouds that water the earth. The temperature drops about 3.6° F for every thousand-foot increase

The Ozonosphere

As the earth revolves around the sun, a delicate blanket of atmosphere protects the earth's inhabitants from much of the sun's deadly ultraviolet radiation. Particularly important is the ozonosphere, so named because of the relative abundance of ozone (though only six molecules in a million are actually ozone). Ozone is a rare form of oxygen in which each molecule contains three atoms rather than the usual two.

The ozonosphere stretches from an altitude of about six to thirty miles. Because air is so thin at that altitude, the total ozone would probably form a layer less than one inch thick were it brought to sea-level pressure.

As shortwave ultraviolet radiation from the sun passes through the oxygen in the ozonosphere, it produces ozone. Other radiation of a slightly higher wavelength then breaks down the unstable ozone. These chemical reactions help absorb most of the sun's dangerous radiation before it reaches the earth.

During the 1970s, officials became concerned because laboratory experiments demonstrated that ozone is destroyed by nitrogen oxide from car exhaust, aerosols, and certain refrigerants known as CFCs. In 1985, some scientists determined that dramatic changes were taking place in the

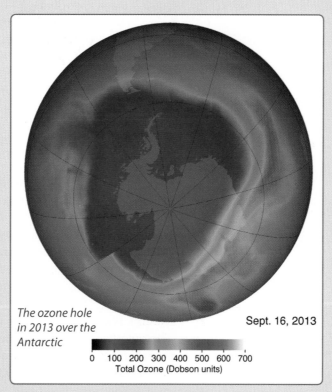

The ozone hole in 2013 over the Antarctic

Sept. 16, 2013

0 100 200 300 400 500 600 700
Total Ozone (Dobson units)

ozone layer above Antarctica. They discovered an ozone hole that appeared during the spring and grew until November, when it shrank. However, the size and fluctuation of the hole varied. For example, in 2003 the hole did not seem to develop at all.

Beginning in 1978, the U.S. and several other nations banned CFC production. In the Montreal Protocol of 1987, ninety-three nations agreed to regulate or ban chemicals that destroy ozone and to search for less damaging alternatives.

Yet the cause and significance of the hole is still uncertain. For one thing, no similar ozone hole occurs in the Arctic, even though continental air currents carry pollutants from temperate regions into the upper atmosphere. Theories about the culprits causing the ozone hole include volcanic eruptions, springtime upwelling of the air, and increased chemicals in the atmosphere (fluorocarbons, chlorine, and other trace gases).

Whatever the cause, humans must be good stewards of the earth and its resources. If possible, we should ensure that human activity does not contribute to the depletion of ozone in the atmosphere.

The ISS

Large enough to be seen with the naked eye from earth (at times), the International Space Station (ISS) is an inhabited man-made satellite that circles our planet every 92.9 minutes and thus orbits the earth 15.5 times each day. The ISS maintains an orbit that varies between 205 and 270 miles above the earth. This incredible scientific achievement is the result of cooperation between the United States, Russia, Japan, the European Space Agency, and Canada. Modular in design, the first component was

launched into space in 1998, and additional modules were delivered to the ISS via U.S. Space Shuttles and Russian rockets. In November 2000, three cosmonauts traveled to the space station on a mission called Expedition I and activated the station during a 136-day mission. Since that time, the space station has been continuously manned and is designed to house a crew of six. Cooperating nations have agreed to fund the ISS until 2020, and the station may remain active until 2028.

The ISS serves as a laboratory. It is used for many experiments from many different scientific fields, including biology, human biology, physics, astronomy, and meteorology. The ISS is also an ideal place to test equipment and systems that would make possible missions to other planets. One of the great benefits of the ISS to this book has been the many photographs taken from the station that have been provided for your viewing pleasure.

in altitude. God filled the troposphere with just the right mixture of gases for breathing—78 percent nitrogen, 21 percent oxygen, and 1 percent other gases, including carbon dioxide.

The Stratosphere, Mesosphere, and Thermosphere

The upper atmosphere consists of three regions. The stratosphere extends from six to around thirty-one miles above the earth. Unlike the troposphere, the stratosphere increases in temperature with altitude. It contains most of the ozone layer. The mesosphere extends about fifty miles from the earth. This region has decreasing temperatures; the coldest place in the atmosphere occurs at the top of the mesosphere. The thermosphere, extending up to about four hundred miles from the earth (although this number can vary significantly), is so named because it retains warmth from direct sunlight. The *ionosphere* lies within the thermosphere and protects the earth from harmful radiation and most meteors. Beyond the thermosphere lies the *exosphere* that reaches the limits of our atmosphere.

Section Quiz

1. How are the four main layers of the atmosphere distinguished?
2–3. In which region is the ozone layer? What does this layer protect the earth from?
4–5. In which region is the ionosphere? What does this layer protect the earth from?
   ✸ Based on how nations have solved disputes over territorial waters, how do you think they should resolve disputes over space rights?

Chapter Review

Making Connections

1–2. Describe two major differences between East Antarctica and West Antarctica.

3. Which nations claim part of Antarctica?

4–5. Fish are able to live in which layer(s) of the ocean? From which layer are most fish harvested?

6–7. Which nation has refused to sign the UN treaty known as LOST? Why?

8–9. Which layer of the atmosphere contains the air we breathe and the clouds? Which layer of the atmosphere is named for its ability to retain heat?

10. In which layer of the atmosphere does the ISS travel?

Developing Geography Skills

1–2. Using an outside resource (Google Earth, the Internet, or an atlas), identify the islands connected to the United States that are near the Mariana Trench. Which one of these islands is the largest?

Thinking Critically

1. What inspires humans to achieve feats such as reaching the South Pole or exploring the depths of the sea?

2. What can you do to protect the ozone layer?

Living in God's World

1. Why might fishermen overfish the seas when this puts their future livelihood at stake? What are some solutions that a Christian who is concerned about wisely stewarding God's earth might propose to solve this problem?

2. In what ways can a Christian who makes a career in a geography-related field bring glory to God?

People, Places, and Things to Know

Antarctica
icebergs
ice floes
Southern Ocean
Ross Sea
Weddell Sea
ice shelves
nunataks
Antarctic Peninsula
Transantarctic Mountains
McMurdo Station
Roald Amundsen
Robert Scott
Richard Byrd
continental shelf
continental slope
photic zone
ocean basin
abyssal plain
trenches
Mariana Trench
Challenger Deep
oceanic ridges
seamounts
deep-sea vents
David Bushnell
Matthew Maury
William Beebe
Otis Barton
bathysphere
Jacques Cousteau
Robert Ballard
territorial waters
high seas
exclusive economic zone (EEZ)
troposphere

Maps

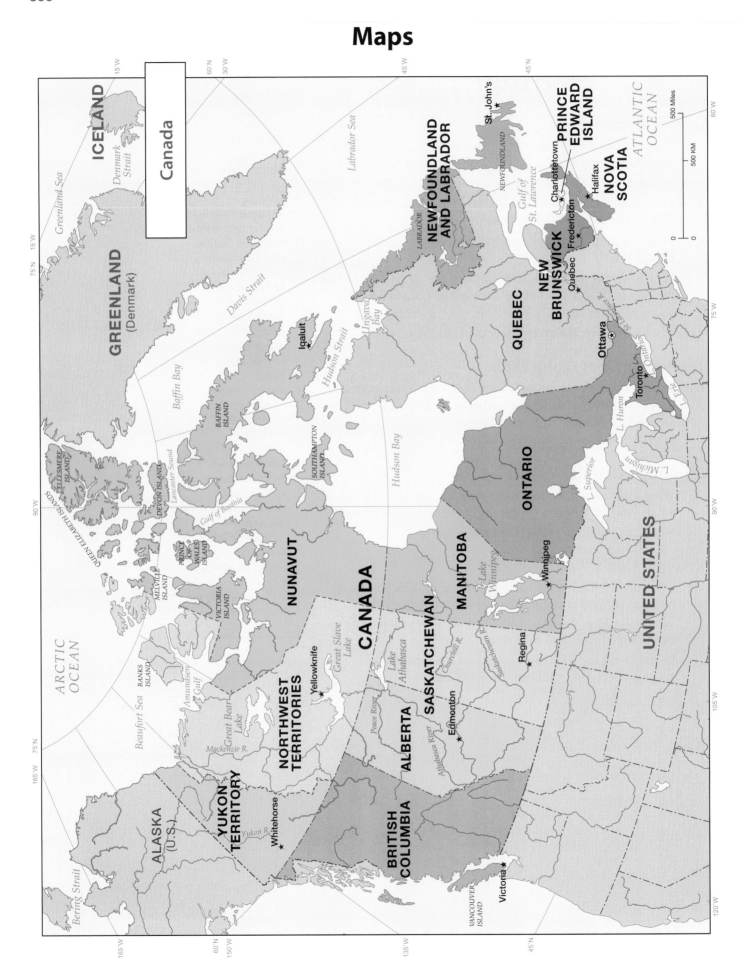

Canada

United States

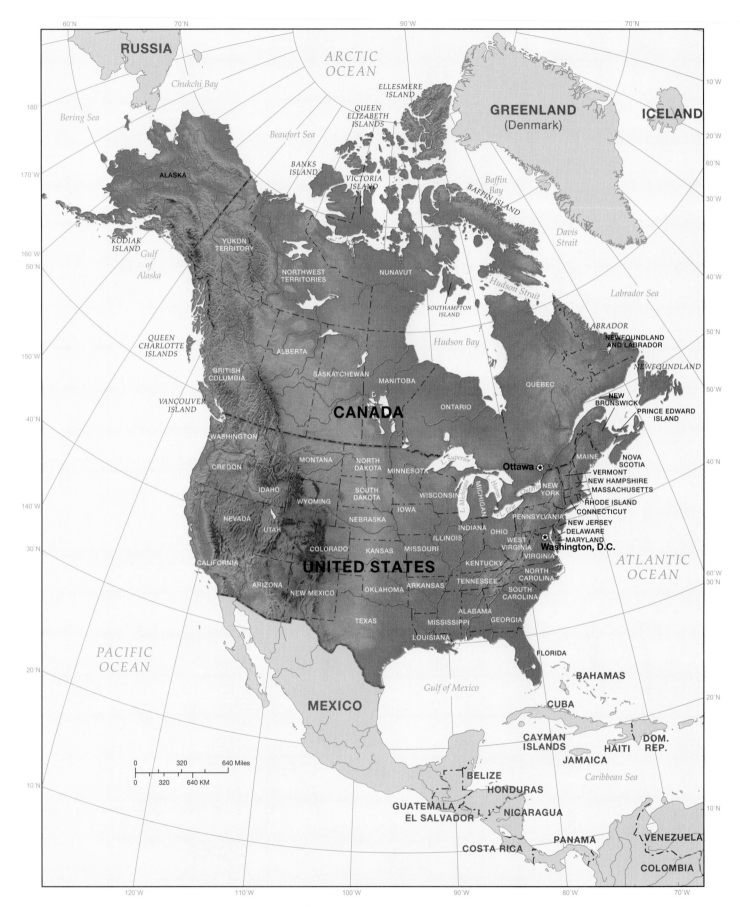

North America

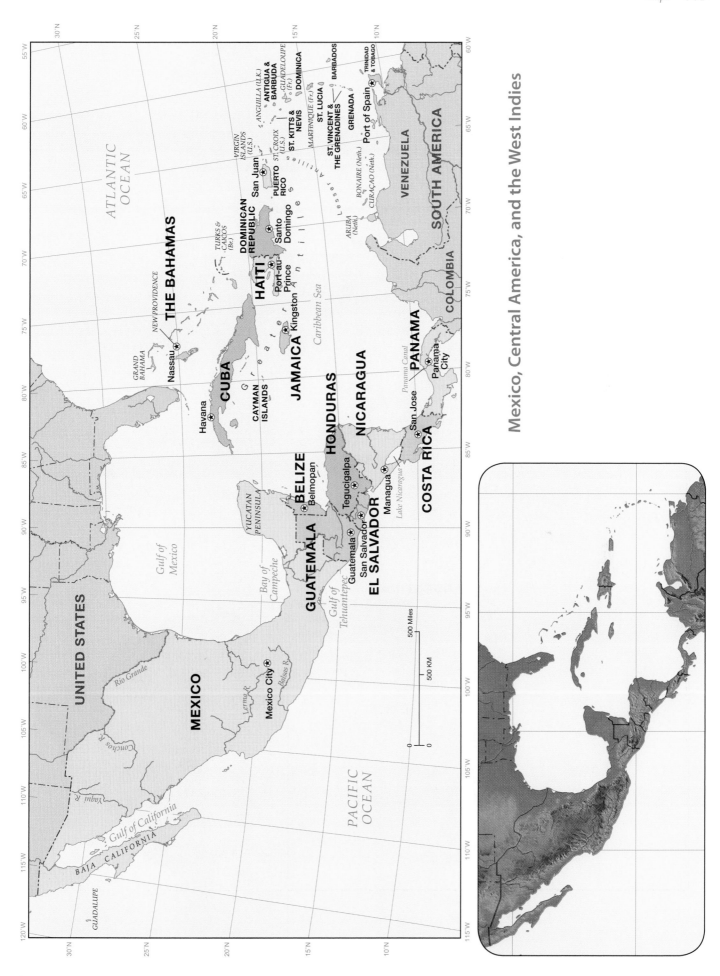

Mexico, Central America, and the West Indies

South America

40°W 30°W 70°N 20°W 10°W 0° 10°E 20°E 30°E 40°E 50°E 70°N 60°E 70°E

GREENLAND

Greenland Sea

40°W

Denmark Strait

Barents Sea

70°E

60°N

ICELAND
Reykjavik

Norwegian Sea

White Sea

60°E

30°W

FAROE
ISLANDS
(Denmark)

*Gulf of
Bothnia*

SWEDEN

FINLAND

RUSSIA

Volga R.

60°N

SHETLAND
ISLANDS

0   500 Miles

0   500 KM

HEBRIDES

*ORKNEY
ISLANDS*

NORWAY

Helsinki

*Gulf of
Finland*

Oslo

Stockholm

Tallinn

ESTONIA

Volga R.

Moscow

50°E

SCOTLAND

North Sea

DENMARK

Riga

LATVIA

NORTHERN
IRELAND
Belfast

Edinburgh

Copenhagen

LITHUANIA
Vilnius

Minsk

50°N

Dublin

U. K.

BELARUS

IRELAND

NETH.
Amsterdam

Berlin

POLAND

Dnieper R.

WALES
Cardiff

The Hague

Warsaw

20°W

London

Brussels

GERMANY

Kiev

Dnieper R.

Don R.

English Channel

BELGIUM

LUX.
Luxembourg

Prague

UKRAINE

Europe

*Bay of
Biscay*

Seine R.

Paris

CZECH REP.

SLOVAKIA
Bratislava

Dniester R.

MOLDOVA

*Sea of
Azov*

Elbe R.

Rhine R.

Danube R.

LIECH.

Vienna

Budapest

Chisinau

Bern

Vaduz

AUSTRIA

HUNGARY

SWITZERLAND

Loire R.

FRANCE

Rhône R.

Ljubljana

SLOVENIA

Zagreb

ROMANIA

Bucharest

Black Sea

40°N

Garonne R.

ANDORRA

Po R.

CROATIA

Belgrade

PORTUGAL

Duero R.

Madrid

MONACO

ITALY

*Adriatic
Sea*

Sarajevo

SERBIA

BOSNIA AND HERZ.

Danube R.

BULGARIA

40°N

Lisbon

Tagus R.

Rome

Pristina

Sofia

40°E

SPAIN

CORSICA

Podgorica

KOSOVO

Skopje

MONTENEGRO

MACEDONIA

SARDINIA

Tirane

*Strait of
Gibraltar*

Gibraltar

MAJORCA

ALBANIA

TURKEY

GREECE

Mediterranean Sea

*Tyrrhenian
Sea*

*Ionian
Sea*

SICILY

Athens

SYRIA

PELOPONNESUS

Aegean Sea

CYPRUS

RHODES

LEBANON

Valletta

CRETE

Mediterranean Sea

MALTA

URAL MTS.

Extent of Europe

Ural R.

CAUCASUS MTS.

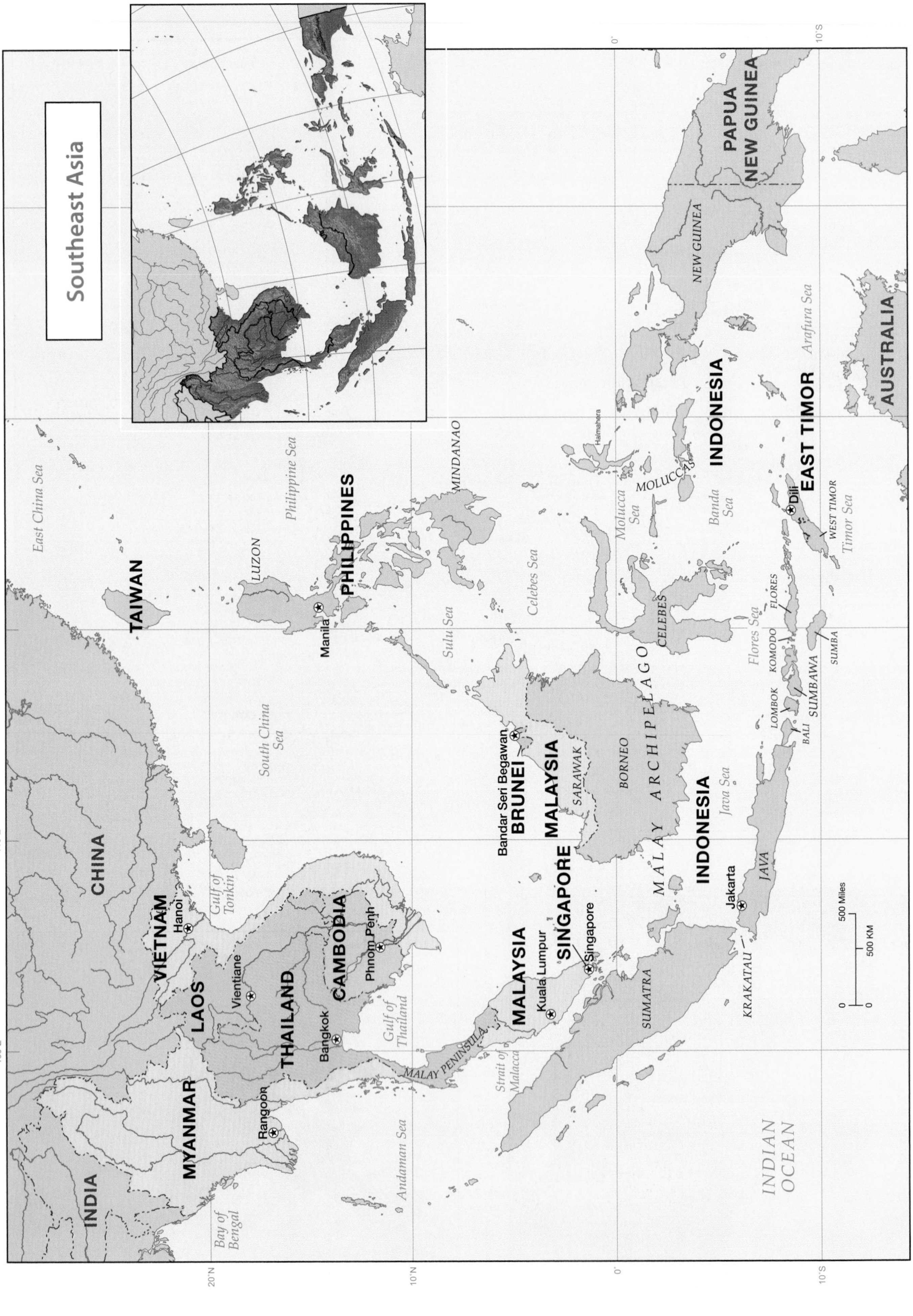

Southeast Asia

INDIA

CHINA

MYANMAR

LAOS

VIETNAM

Hanoi

Vientiane

THAILAND

Bangkok

CAMBODIA

Phnom Penh

Rangoon

TAIWAN

East China Sea

Gulf of
Tonkin

South China
Sea

Bay of
Bengal

Andaman Sea

MALAY PENINSULA

Gulf of
Thailand

Strait of
Malacca

MALAYSIA

Kuala Lumpur

SINGAPORE

Singapore

SUMATRA

INDIAN
OCEAN

KRAKATAU

JAVA

Jakarta

Java Sea

MALAY ARCHIPELAGO

BORNEO

SARAWAK

BRUNEI

Bandar Seri Begawan

MALAYSIA

PHILIPPINES

Manila

LUZON

Philippine Sea

MINDANAO

Sulu Sea

Celebes Sea

CELEBES

CELEBES

Molucca
Sea

MOLUCCAS

Banda
Sea

Halmahera

INDONESIA

INDONESIA

Flores Sea

BALI

LOMBOK

KOMODO

SUMBAWA

FLORES

SUMBA

WEST TIMOR

EAST TIMOR

Dili

Timor Sea

Arafura Sea

NEW GUINEA

PAPUA
NEW GUINEA

AUSTRALIA

500 Miles

500 KM

0

140°E

130°E

120°E

110°E

100°E

140°E

130°E

120°E

110°E

100°E

20°N

10°N

0°

10°S

0°

10°S

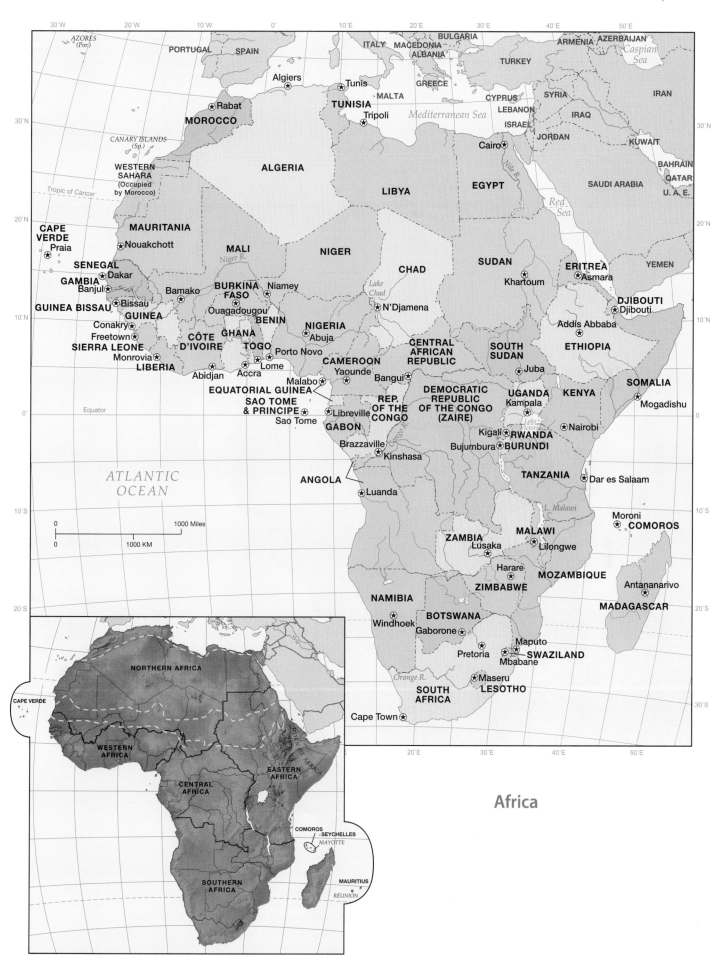

Africa

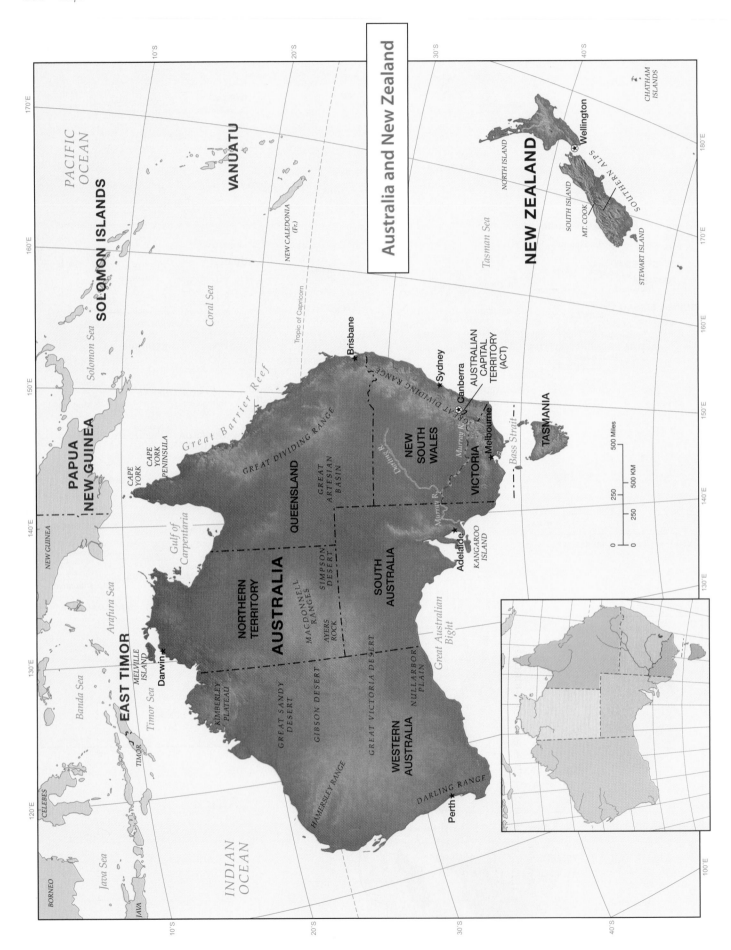

Australia and New Zealand

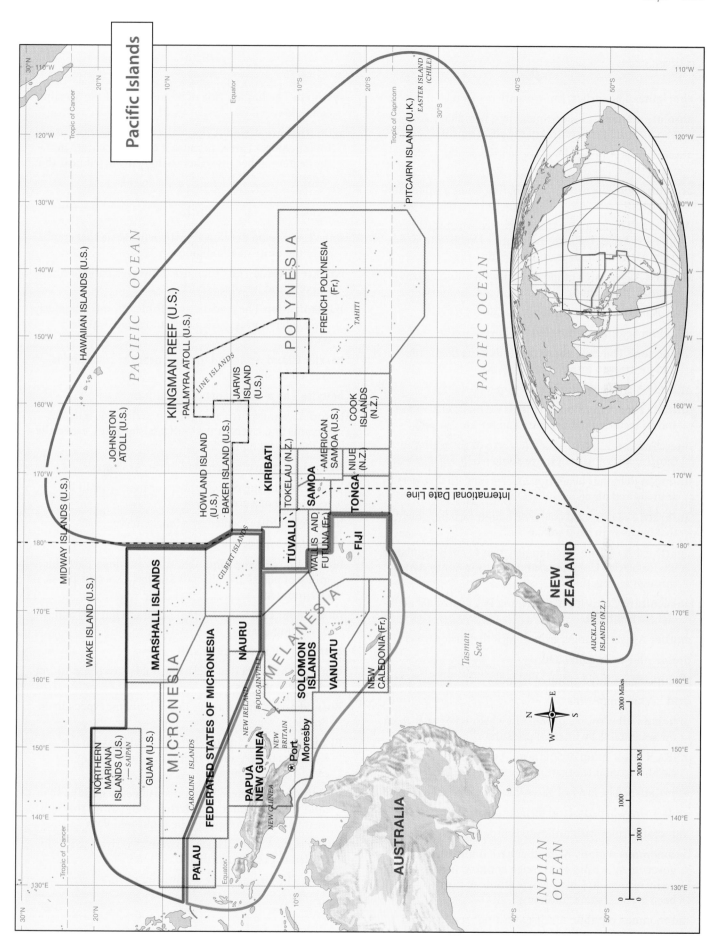

Pacific Islands

Glossary

A

aborigines The earliest known settlers of a region

absolute monarchy Government by a hereditary ruler who has complete control of the government

abyssal plain A broad, level area on the depths of the ocean floor

acculturation The process of adopting foreign values and practices

Afrikaans The language that developed when the Boers of South Africa blended their native Dutch with words from African languages such as Zulu

air mass A large area of moving air with a similar temperature throughout

alloy A mixture of two or more metals

alluvium Sediment deposited by flowing water

alpine zone The zone above the timberline that is too cold for trees to grow

altitude A land's elevation as depicted on a map

altitude zone A division of land based on its elevation and its resulting temperature and terrain

anarchy a condition in which no form of governing authority exists and people are doing whatever they want

animism Religious belief that ascribes spiritual powers to animals and plants

anthracite coal A hard coal with a high carbon content that burns with little smoke

apartheid A rigorous racial policy that severely regulated life for blacks, Coloureds, and Asians in South Africa through segregation

aquaculture Cultivation or farming in a controlled artificial environment

aquifer A layer of underground rock that yields water

arable Able to be cultivated

archipelago A large group of islands

arid Lacking moisture

artesian well A source of water in which water rises from the water table by internal pressure

ASEAN Association of Southeast Asian Nations; a political and economic organization formed in 1967

atmosphere The layer of gases that surrounds the earth

atoll A ring-shaped island formation formed by coral

autocrat A ruler with unlimited authority

autonomous regions Areas that have limited self-government within a sovereign country; used especially of areas in China where ethnic minorities have been granted some autonomy

autonomous republic A self-governing republic; used especially of the countries that were once part of the former Soviet Union

ayatollah The highest title of honor that a Shiite Muslim can hold

azimuthal projection A flat-plane map projection; useful for compact areas because it is most accurate in the center but becomes increasingly distorted near the edges

B

Baha'i A religion developed in ancient Persia that emphasizes the unity of all religions

balance of trade The difference between a nation's total imports and its total exports

Balkanization The tendency of ethnically and religiously diverse territories to break up into small, hostile nations

barrier island An island that lies near the coast and is created by silt deposits

bauxite The principal ore of aluminum

bayou A swampy area along slow-moving, meandering streams and rivers of the Gulf Coastal Plain, especially in the Mississippi Delta

Bedouin A nomadic shepherd of the Arabian desert

bicameral Having two chambers or houses, as in the legislature of a government

bight A large bay formed by a long, curving coast

bilingual Using or knowing two languages

biome A large geographic area that contains a particular group of plants and animals and has a specific physical environment

bituminous coal Soft coal that occurs frequently and is of varying quality

bluff A steep riverbank or cliff

bog A spongy area that looks dry but is covered with wet organic materials

Bosniaks Muslims who live in the Balkans, especially in Bosnia

Brahmins Priests and teachers, who, along with the Ksatriyas (rulers and warriors), occupy the highest caste of Hinduism

Buddhism An Eastern religion founded by Buddha that offers release from the suffering of the world through meditation and following the Eight-fold Path

buffer state A neutral state between two rivals that is intended to prevent conflict

Burma The former name of Myanmar

C

caciques Local "party bosses" in Mexico who rule as small-town dictators, making their money by selling alcohol at pagan religious festivals

Cajuns Residents of Louisiana whose ancestors were French refugees from an area of Maine and Canada known as Acadia

cantons Self-governing districts in Switzerland

capital Money used to build or operate a business or industry

capitalism A free market economy in which anyone may go into business in an attempt to make a profit; most businesses are privately owned instead of government owned.

cargo cult A religion that Melanesians developed when they were exposed to the riches of European traders; they had no idea how the goods were made or where they came from and concluded that they came from the spirit world.

cartography The art of mapmaking

cash crop A crop raised specifically for sale rather than for personal use

cassava A shrubby tropical plant grown for its large, starchy roots

caste A system within Hinduism that assigns people to different classes, each with its own privileges and responsibilities but also limitations, and strictly determines one's social status

cataclysm A violent upheaval or change in the earth's crust, such as a flood

census An official government count of the entire population within a nation's boundaries

civil war A war between factions or regions of a country in which both sides are trying to take over the government

climate The usual temperature, precipitation, and wind conditions of a certain area

climograph Chart that shows the average temperature and the average total precipitation of a particular place during each month

commercial farmer Someone who grows crops for sale and profit rather than merely for personal use

common metals Metals, such as copper, lead, and iron, that are mined in great quantities from the earth's surface and are therefore common

communism The most radical form of socialism in which the government owns everything (in the name of "the people") and no private property or free-market business transactions are allowed

condensation The process whereby water vapor becomes liquid

confluence The point at which two rivers join to form one larger river

Confucianism A Chinese philosophy that teaches harmony through proper treatment of others

conic projection A type of map projection made by placing a cone-shaped piece of paper on an imaginary wire globe and tracing the shadow onto the cone; most accurate where the cone touches the line and good for showing wide regions

conifer A tree that produces its seed in a cone (e.g., a pine tree)

constitutional monarchy (or limited monarchy) A government that includes a hereditary ruler whose powers are strictly limited by law (a constitution)

continent One of the seven primary landmasses of the earth's surface

continental divide A chain of mountains that divides the flow of river systems between oceans

continental drift theory The idea that the continents were once one landmass but at some point drifted apart (see also **plate tectonics theory**)

continental island An island, usually large and high, formed near a continent out of the same landmass

continental shelf The border of a continent that lies underwater and slopes at first gradually and then more abruptly toward the ocean floor

continental slope The gradual decline of the continental shelf toward the ocean bottom

contour lines The lines that separate colors on a relief map and that indicate all points on the map that have the same altitude

convection precipitation Precipitation that occurs when an air mass warms and rises rapidly, then cools to the dew point as it gains altitude

copra The dried flesh of a coconut from which coconut oil is extracted

coral Any of various types of skeletal sea creatures that attach themselves to objects by secreting a glue-like substance and then harden to form reefs

cordillera A chain of mountains

core The central portion of the earth that lies below the mantle

coup A sudden overthrow of a government by a military leader or government official (from coup d'etat)

Creation Mandate The unique calling of God to humankind to exercise dominion over the earth; based on Genesis 1:26

Creole A language that mixes French and African words and is spoken by Haitians; also a person with Spanish ancestry who was born in South America

crude birthrate The number of people born each year per one thousand people in the total population

crude death rate The number of people who die each year per one thousand people in the total population

crust The solid outer part of the earth

culture A people's way of life, including their political, economic, religious, lingual, social, intellectual, and artistic practices and beliefs

culture region A distinct area in which a specific culture thrives

currents, ocean Patterns in the flow of seawater through an area of relatively stationary water around it, similar to prevailing winds

cylindrical projection A type of map projection made by shaping a chart into a cylinder, placing it around a globe that is lit from the inside, and tracing the shadows cast by the light and then unrolling the paper to get a flat map; the most important such projection was done by Mercator.

Cyrillic A modified Greek alphabet used for Slavic languages such as Russian

czar The title of rulers of Russia from 1547 to 1917; also spelled tsar

D

deciduous Plants that shed their leaves before a period of dormancy

deep Ocean depths below 18,000 feet

deforestation The cutting down and clearing of trees; often viewed as a negative activity

demilitarized zone (DMZ) A neutral zone separating hostile countries; used especially in reference to North and South Korea

democracy A form of government whereby the people rule themselves

demography The study of population characteristics

depositional mountains Mountains formed from volcanic deposits

desalination The process of removing salt from water

desert A dry area with little or no vegetation

desertification The changing of arable land into desert

developed country A country that has a wide range of industries that take full advantage of its people's skills

developing country A country whose industries do not take full advantage of its natural or human resources

devolution A passing down and breaking up of central power whereby a central government shifts some responsibilities to local governments

dialect A regional variety of a language

dictatorship Rule by a person or group with the authority of military strength

dikes Strong walls of stone and earth built to restrict or restrain the flow of water

diplomacy The art of negotiating agreements between nations

distortion A problem in mapmaking that occurs when a globe is transferred onto a flat map

division of labor The distribution of a country's workers over various occupations

domestic trade Economic activity between states

drainage basin The area drained by a river system

drift The slowest ocean currents

duchy A country, such as Luxembourg, that is ruled by a duke

durable manufacturing The mass production of goods that are expected to last more than one year

dynasty A family whose members rule over a country for several generations

E

E pluribus unum A motto of the United States, meaning "From many, one"

economic self-sufficiency The ability of one country to produce everything it needs without buying or selling from other countries

economics The study of the process by which people make decisions; includes ways by which people make a living, buy and sell, grow crops, manufacture goods, and provide services

embargo A prohibition on trade

emirate A country ruled by an emir

empire Lands gained outside the national borders of a country

equator The imaginary line that divides the earth into the Northern and Southern Hemispheres

erosion The natural breakdown and removal of materials on the earth's surface

estuary The widening mouth of a river as it approaches the ocean where it has a tendency to form a delta

European Union An organization of twenty-eight countries that seeks to form a single European community that can compete on the world stage economically and politically

evaporation The process whereby liquid water changes into a vapor

exclusive economic zone A region up to two hundred miles offshore from a country in which that country controls fishing and mining and in which it is protected from exploitation by any other country

exosphere The outer half of the thermosphere where particles can escape into outer space

export Any product that one country trades to another country

extended family The nuclear family (parents and children) plus grandparents, uncles, aunts, and cousins

F

fales Framed houses that have a thatched roof and open sides

fall line The area of the eastern United States where the rivers drop from the Piedmont to the Coastal Plain and where many waterfalls occur

family The foundation of society which the Lord instituted in the Garden of Eden, consisting of a man, his wife, and often children

fault A crack in the earth's surface where two pieces of land have moved in different directions

fault mountains Mountains formed by deep cracks in the earth's surface where two pieces of land have moved in different directions

favela A slum district on the outskirts of (or sometimes even within) cities of Brazil

federal districts Political divisions of a large country, like Russia, based on geography

federal republic A representative government that has both individual state governments and a more powerful national government that share power

fjord A long, narrow bay carved by a glacier and filled with seawater

fold A bend in a portion of the earth's crust caused by pressure

fold mountains Evidence of tectonic activity in which unconsolidated sediment is bent upwards

foreign aid Gifts of money, goods, or technology to foreign nations

foreign policy The set of principles that guides a government's international relations

foreign trade Economic activity between nations

forestry Wood products industry, such as lumber operations

free enterprise capitalism An economic system in which private individuals own most of the factors of production, make most of the economic decisions, and compete with other individuals or companies to earn money

free market An economic system in which the law of supply and demand is restricted very little, if at all (see also **free enterprise capitalism**)

free trade An economic concept whereby countries trade with the fewest possible restrictions, such as high tariffs or embargoes, among them

front A line along which two different air masses meet, producing changes in weather

G

gap An opening through a mountain (see also **notch** and **pass**)

gaucho A cowboy of the South American Pampas

geocentric theory A view that states that the sun, stars, and planets revolve around the Earth

geography The detailed study of the earth, especially its surface; a description of humanity's God-given abode—and everything and everyone on it—and how people interact with it and on it in fulfilling their God-given role as stewards of God's creation; from two roots meaning "earth" (geo-) and "written description" (-graphy)

geometric boundary A boundary usually drawn as a straight line to connect specific points or to follow a line of latitude or longitude

geothermal energy Power derived from heated water and steam beneath the earth's surface

ger A collapsible round tent used in Mongolia; called a yurt in Russian

geyser A hot spring that spews water into the air

glacier A large mass of ice, formed from compacted snow, that slowly moves over a land area

glen A narrow valley carved by a glacier

gore One of twelve paper strips that are used to cover a typical globe

grassland A region with plenteous grass but few trees

great circle Any imaginary line that can be drawn around the earth to cut it into equal hemispheres

grid A regular pattern of intersecting vertical and horizontal lines superimposed on a map to assist in locating places; first introduced by Hipparchus

Gross Domestic Product (GDP) The monetary value of all the goods and services produced for sale within a country's borders over the course of a year

groundwater Water that has seeped into the earth's crust and is held below the surface of the earth

Group of 8 (G–8) The group of eight countries that produce more than three-fourths of the world's manufacturing value

growing season The time when most crops are grown, from the last killing frost of spring until the first killing frost of fall

guru Spiritual leader in Hinduism who attracts followers to his own teachings

H

hacienda A vast ranch in Mexico

Hamas An Islamic terrorist group of Palestinians that is dedicated to the destruction of Israel

harbor A sheltered body of deep water next to the shore

heliocentric theory A view that states that the Earth and other planets revolve around the sun

hemisphere Either of the two equal parts of the earth, as divided by the equator or a meridian

Hezbollah An Islamic terrorist group in Lebanon, supported by Syria and Iran, that is dedicated to the destruction of Israel

high island A volcanic island that usually rises above the sea, displaying hills and mountains

highlands The world's most rugged plateaus

high latitudes Zones of the earth between the North Pole and the Arctic Circle in the Northern Hemisphere and between the South Pole and the Antarctic Circle in the Southern Hemisphere

high pressure An atmospheric condition that generally indicates good or improving weather

high sea An area of ocean outside of any country's territorial jurisdiction and free for everyone to use

Hinduism The prevalent religion of India that emphasizes reincarnation, a supreme being with many forms, and the caste system

Holy Land The biblical region of Palestine

human geography The study of humans as they live on the earth and use its resources

humanism The belief that human (rather than religious) thought and values should be the central features of culture and that humans can solve all of their problems on their own

humidity The amount of water vapor in the air

humus A soil ingredient produced by the slow decomposition of leaves and other organic materials

hydroelectricity Renewable energy from moving water

hydrologic cycle A cycle whereby water evaporates from oceans, lakes, and the soil to form clouds that, in turn, precipitate water to the earth; also known as the water cycle

hydrosphere All the water that exists on or around the earth

I

iceberg A large chunk of floating ice that has broken off the edge of a glacier

ice caps Areas in Antarctica and Greenland that have a thick layer of ice that never melts

ice floe A large, flat sheet of floating ice that has formed from seawater

ice shelves Glaciers that flow from West Antarctica out onto the water and into the Ross Sea and Weddell Sea

immigration The movement of foreigners into another country

imperialism The acquiring of an empire

import Any product that one country buys from another country

Indochina The mainland portion of Southeast Asia, including Vietnam, Laos, Cambodia, Thailand, and Myanmar

industrial country A country in which the majority of people work in secondary or tertiary industries rather than primary industries

infant mortality rate The number of infants per one thousand live births that died before their first birthday

infrastructure The basic energy and equipment needs of all industries, such as electricity production, bridges, and roads; divided into three types: utilities, transportation, and communication

initiation rites A multiple-step process that some young men and women undergo (such as in Africa) to mark their transition into adulthood

institutions The formal organizations by which society transmits traditions

insular countries Countries that are isolated or cut off from other countries

intensive farming A form of subsistence farming in fertile areas that allows many individuals to raise crops on a small plot of land

international date line An imaginary line near 180° longitude where time on the east side is one day behind time on the west side

interrupted projection A map in which the areas of landmasses remain fairly accurate and the shapes of continents are less distorted than shapes on a gore map but in which distances and all north-south directions are distorted

ionosphere The inner half of the thermosphere

Islam A religion founded by Muhammad that emphasizes good works; a form of monotheism

Islamic jihad A doctrine of Islam that teaches that true believers are to conduct "holy war" against all "infidels," or non-Muslims

island A landmass surrounded by water

isthmus A land bridge; a narrow link of land that spans an expanse of water between two bodies of land

J

Jainism A religion of India related to both Hinduism and Buddhism; sometimes classified as a heretical version of Hinduism

jet stream Wind patterns that occur where temperate air meets air of more extreme temperature; used by meteorologists in predicting the weather

Juche Worship of the North Korean state as represented by Kim Il Sung; also known as Kimilsungism

Judaism The religion of Israel and the Jews based on the Old Testament law and Jewish tradition

juntas Councils of military and civilian leaders who seize power, often resulting in civil wars

K

karst An area of water-carved limestone formations, such as caverns and rugged peaks

khat An East African shrub with leaves that are chewed as a stimulant or made into a tea

Knesset The legislative branch of the government of Israel

krai A territorial district in Russia

Kremlin The large walled fortress in Moscow that is the center of the government of Russia

L

lake A body of water fully enclosed by land

land bridge A region connecting two larger regions, such as Middle America connecting North America and South America

landform A feature of the land, such as a hill, peninsula, or mesa

landlocked Completely surrounded by land; having no direct access to the sea

land reform An attempt to more fairly distribute land in regions that depend on agriculture for survival

landscape The physical size, characteristics, and features of a country's land

language family A group of languages that share many common characteristics

lapse rate The rate of decrease in temperature with increase in altitude

latitude The distance north or south of the equator measured in degrees

leaching The dissolving of soil minerals by water and their removal downward through the soil

leeward Away from the wind; the direction opposite of that from which the wind is coming

legend A feature, usually on the corner of a map, that explains the symbols representing various features on the map

life expectancy The number of years a person can reasonably be expected to live following birth

lignite Brown coal with high moisture content

lingua franca A common language that is used by people of different nations in business, science, and politics

literacy The ability to read and write

literacy rate The percentage of the adult population of a country who are literate

lithosphere The area of solid matter on the surface of the earth

loch A deep, narrow lake carved by a glacier

lock A section of water with gates on both sides, in which ships enter one gate, the water level is changed to match the other side, and then the ships exit the other gate

loess A very fine silt that has been deposited by the wind

longitude The distance east or west of the prime meridian measured in degrees

lough A freshwater lake in Ireland

low island A coral island that does not stand high above the water

low latitudes A zone that lies between the equator and the Tropic of Cancer in the Northern Hemisphere and between the Equator and the Tropic of Capricorn in the Southern Hemisphere

low pressure An atmospheric condition that generally indicates bad or deteriorating weather

M

madrasah An Islamic religious school

malaria An infectious disease spread by the Anopheles mosquito; common in wet, tropical countries

mandate Authorization for one country to exercise administrative control over a territory

mantle The portion of the earth's interior lying between the crust and the core

manufacturing The process of making finished goods from raw materials

map projection A method of drawing features of the earth's surface on a flat map

maritime Bordering the sea; describes Canada's eastern provinces along the Atlantic Coast

market People or businesses interested in buying a product

marsh A wetland area with standing water, grasses, and small water plants

mass communication Communication intended to reach a large number of people

megalopolis A combination of several metropolitan areas that have grown together; other similar terms include *metropolis* and *megacity*

Mercator Projection A variation of the cylindrical projection in which all lines of latitude and longitude look straight

meridian A line of longitude

mesosphere Middle region in the upper atmosphere extending about sixty miles from the earth

mestizo Latin Americans of mixed European and Indian blood

metal A substance that can conduct electricity and is usually shiny, malleable (can be shaped), and ductile (can be pulled into a wire or hammered thin)

middle latitudes The temperate regions between the Tropic of Cancer and the polar region in the Northern Hemisphere and between the Tropic of Capricorn and the polar region in the Southern Hemisphere

militarized states Countries that have a large number of soldiers and spend a large percentage of their GDP on weapons

minarets Towers around mosques from which criers or loudspeakers call Muslims to prayer

mineral A solid, naturally occurring, inorganic material with a definite chemical composition and crystal structure

mixed economy Attempt to combine elements of capitalism and socialism

monarchy A government with a hereditary ruler, such as a king or a queen

monsoon A seasonal wind caused by the heating and cooling of large landmasses

moor A wasteland on a high, treeless plateau that cannot be cultivated but that often has patches of peat bog or sphagnum moss; often called a *heath* because of the heather that grows on it

Mormonism A religion founded by Joseph Smith that claims to have revelations beyond what is given in the Bible

mosque An Islamic place of worship

mountain range A formation of many mountains together

mulattoes People who have a mixed African and European ancestry

multinational states Governments that rule over many nations

Muslim A follower of Islam

N

NAFTA The North American Free Trade Agreement; between Canada, Mexico, and the United States

nation A group of people with a common heritage, culture, and homeland

national interest A nation's concerns that guide its foreign policy

national parks Areas of natural wonders preserved for the benefit of future generations

nation-state A nation with its own established government and political boundaries

NATO The North Atlantic Treaty Organization; originally formed to counter the threat to Western Europe by the Soviet Union following World War II

natural boundary A boundary drawn along prominent landscape features, such as coastlines, rivers, and mountain ranges

natural increase Method of measuring a country's population; found by subtracting the number of deaths (per one thousand people) per year from the number of births (per one thousand people) per year

natural resource Any useful substance that can be found in the earth

navigable river A river that is deep enough to allow deep-draft boats to move great distances

near abroad The term that Russia applies to the Commonwealth of Independent States, countries that were once part of the Soviet Union

Negev An arid region in the extreme southern portion of Israel that produces—with the help of irrigation—abundant crops and has rich deposits of potash, bromine, and copper

Nippon What the Japanese call their country

nirvana A spiritual state in Buddhism in which one frees himself from desires and worldly things, finds release from suffering, and reaches a state of complete happiness and rest

nomadic herding The wandering of stock and herdsmen from place to place to find new pastures

nondurable manufacturing The mass production of goods that are expected to last for less than one year

nor'easter A severe storm that blows from the northeast; common in the Northeast of the United States

notch An opening through a mountain (see also **gap** and **pass**)

nuclear family Parents and their immediate children

nuclear fuel A method of making electricity by splitting atoms to create enough heat to drive steam turbines

nunatak An isolated mountain that sticks up above an ice sea

O

oasis A watered, fertile area in the desert

oblast A large region or administrative district in Russia; similar to a state or province

ocean basins Regions in the ocean floor typically ranging from thirteen thousand to eighteen thousand feet deep

ocean current A basic path of water flow within an ocean

oceanic island An island that rises from the ocean floor rather than from the edge of a continent

oceanic ridge An undersea mountain range found along the edges of some tectonic plates

oceans Major bodies of water; together contain 97 percent of the earth's water

okrug A large, sparsely populated area of northern Russia

OPEC Organization of Petroleum Exporting Countries; founded in 1960 with the goal of coordinating levels of oil production to sustain a desired price

orographic precipitation Snow and sleet; weather conditions common in cold mountainous regions

Outback What Australians call the vast, sparsely populated interior of their country

ozone A form of oxygen that appears in the upper stratosphere and helps to shield the earth from harmful ultraviolet rays

P

Pacific Rim The countries that touch the Pacific Ocean, especially those of East Asia

panhandle Shape of a region consisting of an extended narrow strip of land

pantheism The view that God is nothing more than the life force throughout the world

parallel A line of latitude

parliamentary government A representative government led by a parliament and a prime minister

pass An opening through a mountain (see also **gap** and **notch**)

per capita GDP The Gross Domestic Product (GDP) of a country divided by the number of people in the country

permafrost Ground that remains permanently frozen even though the top few inches may thaw during a short summer

photic zone Region of the ocean consisting of the upper seven hundred feet and having enough light for photosynthesis

physical geography The study of the earth and its resources

physical maps Common type of maps showing mountains, rivers, lakes, elevation, and other natural features, often using color extensively to indicate bodies of water, various elevations, etc.

physiological density The population of a country divided by the area of available land in the country

Piedmont The region of the eastern United States that lies between the Atlantic Coastal Plain and the Appalachian Mountains

piranha A flesh-eating fish that lives in the Orinoco and Amazon Rivers in South America

plain A broad, level expanse with no visible elevation

plantation economy An economy based on large-scale agricultural operations and employing and housing many workers and producing one product, such as rubber, sugar, or cotton.

plate tectonics theory The view that large sections of the earth's crust move about, producing earthquakes and volcanoes (see also **tectonic activity**)

plateau A large, relatively flat area that is elevated above the surrounding landscape; a tableland

plaza Public square around which a village is built and which is the center of life in the town

PLO Palestine Liberation Organization; an organization of Palestinians who have worked to destroy Israel and to secure a Palestinian homeland

polar regions The areas north of 66½° in the Northern Hemisphere and south of 66½° in the Southern Hemisphere

polder A parcel of land reclaimed from the sea

political boundary A boundary that divides the territory of one country from that of another

political maps Common type of maps indicating state or national boundaries, capitals, and major cities

population density The population of a country divided by its area to reveal the average number of people per square mile or kilometer in the country

prairie A rolling plain with high grasses

precious metals Metals, such as gold, silver, and platinum, that are considered valuable for their beauty, durability, scarcity, and trade value

precipitation Any form of moisture that falls from the atmosphere, such as rain, hail, sleet, or snow

preemptive strike A military attack launched by one country to prevent an attack by another country

prefecture An administrative district

premier A chief administrative official similar to a prime minister

primary industry Work that makes natural resources available for use, such as agriculture, mining, and fishing

prime meridian The meridian passing through Greenwich, England, which is the base line for determining longitude and the reference point for the various time zones around the world

Protestantism Christian churches that follow the broad teachings of the Reformers

Q

Qur'an The holy book of Islam

R

rain forest A dense forest found in tropical or temperate areas with heavy precipitation

rainshadow The area opposite the windward side of a mountain; usually receives little precipitation

Ramadan One month each year when Muslims fast between sunrise and sunset

ranching A method of animal husbandry in which wealthy landowners let their herds and flocks roam freely on vast tracts of land

raw material A material used in making manufactured items

Reconstructionists A liberal branch of Judaism whose adherents. *See* Judaism not as a religion but only as a source of social identity

regional free trade agreements Negotiations among countries with common interests who drop trade restrictions within a region but keep a wall of protective tariffs against outsiders

regional geography A method of studying geography that examines only one region of the world at a time, tying together all of the branches of geography simultaneously

regs Flat desert areas covered with pebbles

reincarnation A belief in a repeated cycle of birth and death; each person supposedly lives one life after another.

relief The different heights and depths of a surface or region

renewable resource An energy source that is unlimited in supply, such as the sun, wind, rivers, and tides

representative democracies A form of elected government in which the people indirectly elect representatives who vote on laws for them

republic A government characterized by a representative system and operated according to a constitution

reservation A portion of land set aside by the federal or state government for American Indians

retail business A business that sells goods to the general public, usually in a small quantity

Ring of Fire A string of volcanoes that encircles the Pacific Ocean

river basin All of the land drained by a river and its tributaries

river system A main river and all of its tributaries

Robinson's projection A kind of cylindrical projection that combines the best elements from the Mercator's and Goode's Interrupted Projections to minimize all distortions on a map

rogue nation A country that ignores the most fundamental principles of international relations and willingly uses chemical weapons, terrorism, or any other means deemed necessary—even against its own people—to get its way or increase its power

Roman Catholicism The form of Christianity that follows the teachings and traditions of the Roman Catholic Church and the pope

rural Of or related to the country, as opposed to things that relate to city (urban) or suburban life

S

savanna The vegetation of tropical areas with a long dry season; has grasses and scattered drought-resistant trees

scale A calibrated (marked) line on a map that indicates distance

sea A partially enclosed arm of the ocean

seamounts Isolated underwater volcanoes

secondary industry A manufacturing industry that produces products from raw materials or from manufactured materials

sediment Particles of sand, silt, and clay produced by the weathering of rock

self-determination The ability of a group of people to determine their own form of government and economy

selva A dense tropical rainforest in the Amazon

separation of powers A system that ensures the independence of a country's legislative, executive, and judicial functions

shah The title of the traditional hereditary monarch of Iran; overthrown in 1979 by a radical Muslim regime

sharia A social and governmental system in which all activities are judged according to the Qur'an and Muslim laws

shatter belt A region that is under continual political pressures and is often fragmented by warring factions and invaded or heavily influenced by surrounding rival countries

Shephelah An area in Israel where, inland from the Plain of Philistia, the land rises into an area of low hills

Shiites The largest minority sect of Islam (about 20 percent of all Muslims)

Shintoism A Japanese religion that promotes the worship of many gods

shrub forests Vegetation in the mild Mediterranean climate, where the dry summers do not provide enough rain for trees to reach great heights; also called woodlands or chaparral

Siam The former name of Thailand

Sikhism An Indian religion founded by Nanak that tries to combine the teachings of Hinduism with Islam

Six-Day War A war in which Israel launched a devastating preemptive strike against the surrounding Arab states, capturing Gaza, the Sinai Peninsula, the West Bank, and the Golan Heights

slash-and-burn agriculture The cutting and burning of a vegetation area to provide fields for temporary use; also called shifting agriculture

socialism An economic system in which the government owns the major industries and promises to make production decisions for the welfare of society; a command economy

society A group of people who share common characteristics, relationships, institutions, and culture

soil The thin layer of the earth's surface where plants grow

solar energy Energy produced from the sun's heat or light

sonar A method of using underwater sound waves, or "echoes," to detect objects or waves

sovereignty A state's unlimited authority to run affairs within its own borders

Soviet bloc The Soviet Union and its Eastern European puppet governments during the period of 1917–1991

Special Economic Zone One of several industrial and trading areas established by the Chinese government to attract foreign trade, investment, and technology

specialized farming The raising of only one crop or one type of stock

sphere of influence A powerful nation's cultural and political leadership over weaker neighbors whom it seeks to influence

station An Australian ranch, especially one for raising sheep

steppe A rolling grassland area, particularly of Central Asia and Eastern Europe

stratosphere Region of the upper atmosphere extending from nine to thirty-five miles above the earth

subcontinent The general term applied to the area of Asia that is bounded by the Himalayas on the north and by the Indian Ocean on the south; bigger than a peninsula but smaller than a continent

subpolar regions Cold sections of the world that are not as severe in the summer, permitting hardy evergreen trees to grow

subregion A smaller area within a larger region

subsistence farming Agriculture that supplies only the basic food and material needs of the farmer and his immediate family

suburb A residential community outside city limits but not in the rural area farther away

Sufi An Islamic mystic

sultanate A Persian Gulf country that is ruled by a sultan

Sun Belt The southern third of the United States from the Carolinas to California

Sunnis The largest sect of Islam (about 80 percent of all Muslims)

survey A count of a small sample that is considered to be representative of the total population

sustainable development The ability to meet present needs without depleting the resources necessary to support future generations

Swahili A language spoken by Bantu tribes living along the eastern coast of Africa from Somalia to Mozambique

swamp A wetland area of standing water in which large trees grow

systematic geography Method of studying the main branches of geography by examining one branch at a time, tying together examples from every region of the world

T

taiga High-latitude evergreen forests, such as those in Canada and Siberia

Taoism A religion of China that promotes the belief in two matched forces called yin and yang

tariff A tax on imports or exports

taro A tropical plant that is widely cultivated in Asia and the Pacific islands for its starchy roots

technology The application of science for practical and industrial purposes

tectonic activity The movement of the earth's crustal plates and the resulting seismic and volcanic activity (see also **plate tectonics theory**)

telecommunications Sending messages through electronic impulses

tell A mound in the Middle East that is formed when successive settlements are built one on top of another

temperate zones The middle latitudes with seasonal changes caused by nearly direct sunlight half of each year

terracing The building of level areas that stair-step along hillsides or mountainsides to reduce erosion and provide areas for efficient cultivation

territorial integrity A country's ability to defend its borders

territorial waters A zone off the coast of a country that it claims and controls as its own sovereign possession

tertiary industry A service industry involving the distribution of goods and services rather than the manufacturing of products or the harvesting of crops or other natural resources

theocrat One who rules by religious or divine authority

thermosphere Region of the upper atmosphere that extends about six hundred miles from earth and consists of the ionosphere and exosphere

Tidewater Coastal region in which the ocean tides flow into and out of rivers' mouths

till plains Flat to gently rolling areas of deep fertile soil left by glaciers

timberline The altitude of a mountain system at and above which trees do not grow

time zones Twenty-four divisions of the world roughly following meridians

topographic map A map that shows the shape and elevation of an area

topography The shape and elevation of the land features of an area

Torah The first five books of the Bible that Orthodox Jews believe and follow; also called the Pentateuch

totalitarian government A government that totally controls the affairs of a country and limits the freedoms of its citizens

township The smallest organizational unit of local government in New England states

trade Buying and selling among countries

trade wars Economic disputes among nations that lead to warfare

trade winds The common easterly winds of tropical regions

transitional zone An area that lies between two other regions and has characteristics of both

treaty A formal agreement between nations

trench A long, steep-sided valley on the ocean floor

tribalism Strong identity with and loyalty to a tribe

tribe A large group of people who share a common ancestor and are usually governed by elders

tributary A river that flows into and feeds another river

tropical rain forest A type of biome in the tropics where many kinds of trees and animals proliferate

tropics The latitude zone lying between the Tropic of Cancer and the Tropic of Capricorn, with warm temperatures caused by direct sunlight

troposphere Region consisting of the lowest nine miles of the atmosphere

truck farming The raising and selling of vegetables and fruits

tsetse fly An African fly that spreads sleeping sickness

tsunami A seismic sea wave caused by an earthquake

tundra Regions of cold climate displaying little vegetation other than mosses, lichens, and similar small plants

typhoon A hurricane that occurs over the waters near eastern Asia

U

unicameral Having one chamber or house, as in the legislature of a government

uniformitarianism The belief that only those forces that are presently acting on the earth have shaped the earth in the past

universal manhood suffrage The right of every adult male to vote

untouchables People at the bottom of the Hindu caste system who are considered outcasts

urban area An area where the population and industry are centralized and developed; city area, as opposed to rural or suburban area

urbanization The movement of people from rural areas to cities and the growth of those cities

utilities Type of infrastructure that governments usually own or oversee and that provides for electricity, gas, water, trash collection, and sewage-disposal services

V

value added The value that manufacturers add to raw materials

vegetation The plants in an area or region

village A small group of dwellings in an isolated area

vital statistics Official records of births, marriages, divorces, and deaths

volcano A depositional mountain built from solidified molten rock coming from deep in the earth

voodoo A pantheistic religion practiced in some Caribbean countries, especially Haiti, that blends West African animism with elements of Roman Catholicism

W

wadi A usually dry streambed in a desert area

wastelands Areas that are barren most of the year because of low amounts of precipitation

watershed An area of land that drains into a certain river or river system

water table The level below which the ground is saturated with water

wattle A wall, roof, or fence that some Australians made by weaving, or "wattling," acacia trees together

weathering The degenerative process that contributes to the breaking up and alteration of rock materials

westerlies Storms that come from the west

wetland An area of stagnant water, such as a swamp, marsh, or bog

wheat belt Fertile grasslands in the American Plains which receive enough rain for growing wheat

wholesale business A business that sells goods in quantity to retail businesses

wind belts The movement of warm and cold air masses, combined with the Coriolis effect, explaining the basic movement of thermal energy around the earth

woodlands Biomes in which shrub forests occur in a mild Mediterranean climate where dry summers do not provide enough rain for trees to reach great heights; also called chaparral

world ocean The whole system of oceans that flow into each other

WTO World Trade Organization; formed in 1995 to regulate trade between member countries

Y

yellow fever An infectious tropical disease transmitted by mosquitoes

Z

Zionist movement A Jewish movement that seeks the growth and development of the nation of Israel

Zoroastrianism A religion founded by Zarathustra during the ancient Persian Empire

Index

Chiapas 194
Chichen Itza 195
chief 493
Chihuahuan Desert 190
Chile 228–30
Chimborazo 222
China
    economy 396–97
    government 396–97
Chittagong 361
chokepoint 436
chott 530
Christianity 356
Chuuk Islands 575
climate 46
climate change 41
coal 67, 68, 158
Coastal Mountains 178, 180
Coastal Plains 446
Coastal Ranges 124, 136
Colca Canyon 224
Cold War 315
Colombia 217
Colorado 176
Colorado Basin 178
Colorado Plateau 177
Colorado River 178
Coloureds 460
Columbia Plateau 175
Columbia River 124
Columbus, Christopher 43
commercial farmers 60
common metals 65
commonwealth 211
Commonwealth of Independent
    States (CIS) 307, 316
Commonwealth of Nations 251
communism 77
Comoros 474
compass rose 21
Concord 156
Confucianism 407
Congo, Republic of 498
Congo Basin 495
Congo River 495
conic projection 20
coniferous forest 50
Connecticut 155–56
Connecticut River 156
constitutional monarchy 100
continental divide. *See* Eastern
    Continental Divide; Western
    Continental Divide
Continental Europe 261. *See
    also* France; Low Countries;
    Germany; Alpine Regions
continental islands 30
continental shelf 590
continents 30
contour lines 23
Contras 203
convection 45
Cook, James 546
Cook Strait 561

Copenhagen 259
Copernicus, Nicolaus 15
copper 65
Copper Canyon 190
copra 566
Coptic Church 537
Copts 537
Cousteau, Jacques 594
cordillera 124
Cordillera Central 217
Cordillera Occidental 217
Cordillera Oriental 217
core (of the earth) 30
Coriolis effect 42
corn belt 173
Cameron, James 594
Coromandel Coast 353
Corsica 263
Cortés, Hernando 192
Cossacks 324
Costa Rica 204
Côte d'Ivoire 510
Cotopaxi 222
coup 192
Cousteau, Jacques 588
Crater Lake 180
Creation 27
Creation Mandate 3
Creole (language) 209
Creoles 167
Crete 284
Crimean Mountains 309
Crimean Peninsula 309
criollos 193
Croatia 299
crude birthrate 94
crude death rate 94
crust, earth's 30
CCS *Housatonic* 593
CSS *Hunley* 593
Cuba 207
cultural convergence 93
Cultural Revolution 396
culture 3, 85
culture region 88
Cumberland Gap 134
Cumberland Plateau 163
Cuquenán Falls 220
Cusco 224
cylindrical projection 19
Cyprus 440–41
Cyrillic language 297
czars 313
Czech Republic 294

D

Dakar 516
Dalai Lama 399
Dalmatia 299
Dama ceremony 524
Damascus 443
Danube River 273, 296
Dardanelles 438
Darfur 488

Dasht-E-Kavir 431
Dasht-E-Lut 431
Daugava River 292
Dayton Peace Accords 299
Dead Sea 36, 453
Dead Sea Scrolls 453
Death Valley 180
Deccan Plateau 352
deciduous forest 51
deep-sea vents 591
Deep South. *See* Lower South
deforestation 242
deformational mountains 39
Delaware 159–60
Delaware River 158
Delhi 351
Delmarva Peninsula 159
demilitarize 119
democracy 100
Democratic People's Republic of
    Korea 404
Democratic Republic of Congo 497
demographics 144, 146
demography 94
Denakil Desert 484
Deng Xiaoping 396
Denmark 259
desalination 424
desert 52
desertification 524
Des Moines 171
Detroit 170
developed countries 79
developing countries 79
Devil's Island 221
devolution 317
dew point 44
Dhaka 361
Dhofar 422
dialect 87
dictatorship 99
Dien Bien Phu 377
Dinaric Alps 297
diplomacy 102
distortion 18
District of Columbia 159
division of labor 79
Djibouti 486
Dnieper River 309
Dniester River 309
Dominica 211
Dominican Republic 209
domino theory 377
Dom Pedro 237
Donets Basin 309
Don River 324
downs 249
Drake Passage 230
Drakensberg Mountains 461
drainage basin 34
drift 170
Driftless Area 171
Drift Prairie 171
Druze 444

Photograph Credits

Cover

(map background) © iStockphoto.com/Media Mates Oy; (map texture) © iStockphoto.com/billnoll; (globe line art) © iStockphoto.com/Shanina; (front cover) stocker1970/shutterstock.com; (back cover) Oscar Garriga Estrada/shutterstock.com

Front Matter

i (map) © iStockphoto.com/Media Mates Oy; i (map texture) © iStockphoto.com/billnoll; i (globe line art) © iStockphoto.com/Shanina; viii Getty Images/iStockphoto/Thinkstock; ix © iStockphoto.com/belinski; x t © iStockphoto.com/Heidi Kristensen; x c © iStockphoto.com/sdominick; x b pancaketom/Bigstock.com; xi t Hemera/Thinkstock; xi c © iStockphoto.com/macbibi; xi b © Dirk Sigmund|Dreamstime.com

Unit Openers

xiv–1 loops7/iStock/Thinkstock; 56–57 Tokle/iStock/Thinkstock; 106–107 RudyBalasko/iStock/Thinkstock; 184–185 Robert Frerck/The Image Bank/Getty Images; 244–245 JoseIgnacio/iStock/Thinkstock; 332–333 GOLF3530/iStock/Thinkstock; 412–413 VUSLimited/iStock/Thinkstock; 456–457 © iStockphoto.com/THEGIFT777; 54–41 © iStockphoto.com/illarionovdv

Chapter One

2, 9 Getty Images/iStockphoto/Thinkstock; 3 "Pieskowa Skała ogród zamkowy" by Jan Jerszyński/Wikimedia Commons/CC-BY-SA 2.5; 4 © iStockphoto.com/Claudia Dewald; 10 "Harmony Day"/DIAC images/Wikimedia Commons/CC 2.0

Chapter Two

12 ExactoStock/SuperStock; 13 © iStockphoto.com/wsfurlan; 15 Getty Images/Photos.com/Thinkstock; 18 © iStockphoto.com/Floortje; 23 pancaketom/Bigstock.com

Chapter Three

26, 37, 38, 39, 40b, 48, 52t Getty Images/iStockphoto/Thinkstock; 27 © iStockphoto.com/Alexey Stiop; 28t © iStockphoto.com/Beau Snyder; 28b Getty Images/Zoonar RF/Thinkstock; 31 © SNEHIT-Fotolia.com; 32t catolla/Bigstock.com; 32b Getty Images/Hemera/Thinkstock;

34 Rodrigo Balela/LatinContent/Getty Images; 35 Getty Images/Comstock Images/Thinkstock; 36t © iStockphoto.com/Alexey Avdeev; 36b © iStockphoto.com/Nisangha; 40t joegeough/Bigstock.com; 40c "Briksdalsbreen"/Wikimedia Commons/Public Domain; 42 ASSOCIATED PRESS; 49t © iStockphoto.com/Steve Geer; 49b © Susan E. Degginger/Alamy; 50 Getty Images/Ron Chapple Studios RF/Thinkstock; 51 © iStockphoto.com/Joseph C. Justice Jr.; 52c © iStockphoto.com/Uwe Halstenbach; 52b © iStockphoto.com/Yenwen Lu; 53 © iStockphoto.com/Yan-chun Tung; 54 Tupungato/Bigstock.com

Chapter Four

58 Schmidt-Luchs/Mauritius/SuperStock; 60t Universal Images Group/SuperStock; 60bl Getty Images/Comstock Images/Thinkstock; 60br © iStockphoto.com/Pakkawit Anantaya; 61 ED JONES/Staff/AFP/Getty Images; 62 Getty Images/iStockphoto/Thinkstock; 63 SONNY TUMBELAKA/Stringer/AFP/Getty Images; 64l © iStockphoto.com/Darin Burt; 64r © PiLensPhoto-Fotolia.com; 64b, 65t, 65c, 68br, 75 Getty Images/iStockphoto/Thinkstock; 65b michal812/Bigstock.com; 66 John Cancalosi/age fotostock/SuperStock; 68t Nigel Hicks/Purestock/SuperStock; 68bl "West Ford Flat Geothermal Cooling Tower"/Rtracey/Public Domain/Wikimedia Commons; 69 © iStockphoto.com/Teun van den Dries; 70 Digital Vision/Thinkstock; 71t © Fotosearch.com; 71c Formlabs and Andy Ryan Photography; 71br devon/Bigstock.com; 72 © iStockphoto.com/Robert Churchill; 73 "Oil tanker Heather Knutsen in Halifax Harbour-Nova Scotia, Canada-20 June 2012"/Dennis Jarvis/Wikimedia Commons/CC-BY-SA 2.0; 74 © iStockphoto.com/John Kirk; 77 Felipe Dupouy/Thinkstock; 81 EvrenKalinbacak/Bigstock.com

Chapter Five

84 © iStockphoto.com/TommL; 88t © iStockphoto.com/Alexander Klemm; 88c Yadid Levy/age fotostock/SuperStock; 88b Photononstop/SuperStock; 89t Ton Koene/age fotostock/SuperStock; 89b © paylessimages-Fotolia.com; 90t © iStockphoto.com/Stan Rohrer; 90bl, 95tl Getty Images/iStockphoto/Thinkstock; 90br almoko/Bigstock.com; 95tr andres/

Bigstock.com; 95bl © iStockphoto.com/Jacom Stephens; 95br Getty Images/Fuse/Thinkstock; 96 © iStockphoto.com/Volodymyr Kyryluk; 97t Christopher Pillitz/The Image Bank/Getty Images; 97b © Galyna Andrushko-Fotolia.com; 99t © Blend Images-Fotolia.com; 99b AFP/Staff/AFP/Getty Images; 100t ALI AL-SAADI/Staff/AFP/Getty Images; 100b Getty Images/Fuse/Thinkstock; 102 The White House/Bill Fitzpatrick; 103 © iStockphoto.com/Samuel Kessler; 104 © iStockphoto.com/Markus Seidel

Chapter Six

108 Robert Harding Picture Library/SuperStock; 111l NOAA; 111r © seb hovaguimian-Fotolia.com; 112 Wallace Ellison; 113b "Swallowtail Lighthouse - Grand Manan Island NB 2009" by Kate Wellington/Wikimedia Commons/CC BY 2.0; 113tl, 113tr Breck P. Kent; 114, 117t, 119, 121b, 123b Getty Images/iStockphoto/Thinkstock; 115 "North America terrain 2003 map"/USGS/Wikimedia Commons/Public Domain; 116 Courtesy of Saint Lawrence Seaway Development Corporation; 117b © iStockphoto.com/Tony Tremblay; 120 paulmckinnon/Bigstock.com; 121t Minden Pictures/SuperStock; 122 maXx images/SuperStock; 123t Design Pics/SuperStock; 124t John E Marriott/All Canada Photos/SuperStock; 124b © msghita-Fotolia.com; 125 © Accent Alaska.com/Alamy; 126l Studebaker National Museum; 126tr, br Library of Congress; 128 The Arms of Canada is the symbol of Her Majesty the Queen in Right of Canada.

Chapter 7

130c, l, 134c, 135, 137, 146, 150 Getty Images/iStockphoto/Thinkstock; 130r prochasson/Bigstock.com; 131t Getty Images/Digital Vision/Thinkstock; 131b Joe Traver/Getty Images News/Getty Images; 132 David McNew/Staff/Getty Images News/Getty Images; 133 © iStockphoto.com/Entropyd; 134t © iStockphoto.com/drnadig; 134b photojohn830/Bigstock.com; 136tl © iStockphoto.com/trait2lumiere; 136tr PhotoDisc; 136b "PanoMacKinley" by Nic McPhee from Morris, MN, USA/Wikimedia Commons/CC-BY-SA 2.0; 138t NOAA/Collection of Dr. Herbert

K; 138b "Sandy Oct 25 2012 0400Z"/NOAA Environmental Visualization Lab/Wikimedia Commons/Public Domain; 140 Bridgeman-Giraudon/Art Resource, NY; 145t Getty Images/Stockbyte/Thinkstock; 145l, r Getty Images/Top Photo Group RF/Thinkstock; 147b © iStockphoto.com/Kativ; 149t "NYSE New York Stock Exchange floor" by Ryan Lawler/Wikimedia Commons; 149b Getty Images/Hemera/Thinkstock

Chapter 8

152, 162b, 163t, 165c, 170t, 171, 172t, 179, 180b Getty Images/iStockphoto/Thinkstock; 155t © iStockphoto.com/kickstand; 155b Fred Hirschmann/Science Faction/SuperStock; 156 © iStockphoto.com/DenisTangneyJr; 158t Mark52/Bigstock.com; 158c © iStockphoto.com/sdominick; 158b pancaketom/Bigstock.com; 159t Sissie Brimberg/National Geographic/Getty Images; 159b Photo courtesy of the Chesapeake Bay Bridge-Tunnel; 162t "Shenandoah River, aerial" by La Citta Vita/Wikimedia Commons/CC-BY-SA 2.0; 163b Stephen Alvarez/National Geographic/Getty Image; 164 © iStockphoto.com/Davel5957; 165t Middleton Place, Charleston, South Carolina; 165b Getty Images/Comstock Images/Thinkstock; 166t actionsports/Bigstock.com; 166b Tom Bean/Stone/Getty Images; 167 William Scott/Bigstock.com; 169t IMS/Bill Watson; 169b © iStockphoto.com/jskiba; 170c Iron Range Resources, Eveleth, Minnesota; 170b © iStockphoto.com/BanksPhotos; 173 Jim Reed/Science Faction/SuperStock; 174t, b Jupiter images/Comstock/Thinkstock; 177t © iStockphoto.com/ventdusud; 177b EricBVD/Bigstock.com; 178t alexeys/Bigstock.com; 178b Andy777/Bigstock.com; 180t © iStockphoto.com/Pgiam; 181 © iStockphoto.com/urbanglimpses; 182t © iStockphoto.com/AlbertoLoyo; 182b Peebles/Mauritius/SuperStock

Chapter 9

186, 192t, 193t, 205, 206 Getty Images/iStockphoto/Thinkstock; 189 "Border Mexico USA"/Sgt. 1st Class Gordon Hyde/Department of Defense/Wikimedia Commons/Public Domain; 190 "Barranca del cobre 2" by Jens Uhlenbrock/Wikimedia Commons/Public Domain; 191t © iStockphoto.com/mbogacz; 191b © iStock